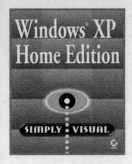

WINDOWS XP HOME EDITION SIMPLY VISUAL

BY FAITHE WEMPEN

ISBN 0-7821-2982-X
448 pages; 8" x 10"
$24.99 US

Take the fundamental first step toward mastering Microsoft Windows XP Home Edition! Learning how to use Windows has never been easier, thanks to the Sybex Simply Visual method of teaching. Now you can use this proven method to master the essentials of Microsoft Windows XP Home Edition. Featuring easy-to-read screens, step-by-step instructions, and to-the-point explanations, this book shows you how to navigate Windows XP Home Edition, manage files and documents, and use its key features and tools. *Windows XP Home Edition Simply Visual* makes learning the fundamentals of Microsoft's newest operating system a walk in the park!

WINDOWS XP HOME AND PROFESSIONAL EDITIONS INSTANT REFERENCE

BY DENISE TYLER

ISBN 0-7821-2986-2
464 pages; 5 7/8" x 8 1/4"
$24.99 US

This book is exactly what you need to ease your transition to the latest version of Windows—and the perfect companion to *Mastering Windows XP Professional* or *Mastering Windows XP Home Edition*. Small enough to carry anywhere but big on content, this guide puts key information at your fingertips, in an easy-to-use glossary format.

WINDOWS XP HOME EDITION COMPLETE

WINDOWS® XP
HOME EDITION
COMPLETE

SYBEX®   SAN FRANCISCO ▸ PARIS ▸ DÜSSELDORF ▸ SOEST ▸ LONDON

Associate Publisher: Joel Fugazzotto

Acquisitions and Developmental Editor: Ellen L. Dendy

Compliation Editor: Faithe Wempen

Revisors: Faithe Wempen, Susan Glinert Stevens, Adrian Kingsley Hughes

Editor: Colleen Wheeler Strand

Production Editor: Mae Lum

Technical Editor: Donald Fuller

Book Designer: Maureen Forys, Happenstance Type-O-Rama

Electronic Publishing Specialist: Maureen Forys, Happenstance Type-O-Rama

Proofreaders: Laurie O'Connell, Nancy Riddiough, David Nash, Yariv Rabinovitch

Indexer: Nancy Guenther

Cover Designer: Design Site

Cover Photographer: Getty Images/Arthur Tilley

Library of Congress Card Number: 2001096119

ISBN: 0-7821-2984-6

Acknowledgments

T his book is the work of many, both inside and outside Sybex including the publishing team members Dick Staron, Joel Fugazzotto, Raquel Baker, and Ellen Dendy, and the editorial/production team of Colleen Strand, Mae Lum, Don Fuller, Maureen Forys, Laurie O'Connell, Nancy Riddiough, David Nash, Yariv Rabinovitch, and Nancy Guenther.

Faithe Wempen deserves particular thanks for making sure all of the material in this book was up-to-date, organized, and flowed together in a cohesive manner. She was assisted by revisers Susan Glinert Stevens and Adrian Kingsley Hughes.

Finally, our thanks to those contributors who agreed to have their work excerpted into Windows XP Home Edition Complete: Robert Cowart, Guy Hart-Davis, John Ross, Faithe Wempen, Mark Henricks, and Denise Tyler.

CONTENTS AT A GLANCE

CONTENTS

Chapter 4   □   Making and Using Shortcuts   85

Chapter 5   □   Running Programs   103

Part II ▸ Customizing, Optimizing, and Troubleshooting Windows XP Home Edition   235

Chapter 9 ▫ Customizing System Settings   237

Chapter 10 ▫ Customizing the Desktop, Taskbar, and Start Menu   255

Part III ▸ Communications and the Internet   343

Chapter 14 ▫ Connecting to the Internet   345

Chapter 15 ▫ Browsing the Web with Internet Explorer 6   365

INTRODUCTION

Windows *XP Home Edition Complete* is a one-of-a-kind computer book—valuable both for the breadth of its content and for its low price. This thousand-page compilation of information from some of Sybex's very best books provides comprehensive coverage of Windows XP Home Edition. This book, unique in the computer book world, was created with several goals in mind:

- ► To offer a thorough guide covering all the important user-level features of Windows XP Home Edition at an affordable price.

- ► To acquaint you with some of our best authors, their writing styles and teaching skills, and the level of expertise they bring to their books—so that you can easily find a match for your interests and needs as you delve deeper into Windows XP Home Edition. *Windows XP Home Edition Complete* is designed to provide you with all the essential information you'll need to get the most from Windows XP Home Edition and your computer. At the same time, *Windows XP Home Edition Complete* will invite you to explore the even greater depths and wider coverage of material in the original books.

If you have read other computer "how-to" books, you have seen that there are many possible approaches to effectively using the technology. The books from which this one was compiled represent a range of teaching approaches used by Sybex and Sybex authors. From the concise, step-by-step coverage of *Windows XP Home Edition Simply Visual* to the wide-ranging, thoroughly detailed *Mastering Windows XP Home Edition* style, you will be able to choose which approach and which level of expertise works best for you. You will also see what these books have in common: a commitment to clarity, accuracy, and practicality.

In these pages, you will find ample evidence of the high quality of Sybex's authors. Unlike publishers who produce "books by committee," Sybex authors are encouraged to write in their individual voices, voices which reflect their own experience with the software at hand and with the evolution of today's personal computers. Nearly every book represented here is the work of a single writer or a pair of close collaborators. Similarly, all of the chapters here are based on the individual experience of the authors, their first-hand testing of pre-release software and their subsequent expertise with the final product.

In adapting the various source materials for inclusion in *Windows XP Home Edition Complete*, the compilation editor preserved these individual voices and perspectives. Chapters were edited to minimize duplication, omit coverage of non-essential information, update technological issues, and cross-reference material so you can easily follow a topic across chapters. Some sections may have been edited for length in order to include as much updated, relevant, and important information as possible.

WHO CAN BENEFIT FROM THIS BOOK?

Windows XP Home Edition Complete is designed to meet the needs of a wide range of computer users working with the newest version of Microsoft's operating system. Windows XP Home Edition is an extraordinarily rich environment, with some elements that everyone uses, as well as features that may be essential to some users but of no interest to others. Therefore, while you could read this book from beginning to end—from upgrade decisions, to installation, through the features, and on to expert tinkering—all of you may not need to read every chapter. The contents and the index will guide you to the subjects you're looking for.

Beginners Even if you have only a little familiarity with computers and their basic terminology, this book will start you working with Windows XP Home Edition. You'll find step-by-step instructions for all the operations involved in running application programs and managing your computer system, along with clear explanations of essential concepts. You'll want to start at the very beginning of this book, Part I, which covers the basics.

Intermediate Users Chances are you already know how to do routine tasks in Windows 9*x*/Me and have a head start when it comes to XP. You know your way around a few productivity applications, use e-mail extensively, browse the Web a little, and maybe have a favorite game or two. You also know that there is always more to learn about working more effectively, and you want to get up to speed on the new Windows XP Home Edition features. Throughout this book, you'll find instructions for just about anything you want to do. Nearly every chapter has nuggets of knowledge from which you can benefit.

Power Users Maybe you're a hardcore multimedia fiend looking to take advantage of Windows XP Home Edition's expanded capabilities, or the unofficial guru of your office, or an Internaut ready to try Web publishing. There's plenty for you here, too, particularly in the chapters from the Mastering books.

This book is for people using Windows XP Home Edition in any environment. You may be a SOHO (small-office/home-office) user, working with a stand-alone computer or a simple peer-to-peer network with no administrators or technical staff to rely on. In that case, you'll find plenty of information about maintaining and troubleshooting your computer. Or your company may have upgraded your desktop PC to Windows XP Home Edition or, even better, replaced your old PC with a brand new Windows XP Home Edition machine, and you simply want to get a leg up, quickly and inexpensively, as your office migrates to the new operating system.

HOW THIS BOOK IS ORGANIZED

Part I: Windows XP Home Edition: The Basics The eight chapters in Part I cover all the essentials—installing the operating system, navigating and setting up the desktop, running programs, and organizing your files. You'll also learn how to work with printers, and much more. Anyone migrating from a previous Windows version (3.1, 95, 98, or Me) will want to start with Chapter 1's summary of the new features.

Part II: Customizing, Optimizing, and Troubleshooting Windows XP Home Edition Now that you've got the basics down, it's time to get Windows XP Home Edition to do things your way. Part II shows you how to customize your setup and keep your computer running smoothly. You'll learn how to tweak system settings to your liking, how to customize the desktop, taskbar and Start menu, and how to troubleshoot problems. Part II also shows you how to use Windows XP's built-in maintenance and monitoring features.

Part III: Communications and the Internet Face it, being online is just plain cool these days. Part III takes you all the way from getting connected to the Internet to browsing the Web with the latest version of Internet Explorer. You'll also learn how to send e-mail with Outlook Express, and how to publish pages on the Web with confidence. Finally, you'll learn how to connect to your own PC via the Internet so you can access important data while you're away, and how to utilize the Remote Assistance feature—a surprising new feature that lets someone in a remote location securely access your PC in order to provide you with help.

Part IV: Networking and Securing Windows XP Home Edition Got more than one PC? Part IV shows you how to get a peer-to-peer network up and running, and how to implement security measures that will keep your valuable data safe and sound from those sneaky hackers and crackers.

Part V: Having Fun with Windows XP Home Edition You've put in a hard day's work, and now it's time to play. Part V shows you how use the exciting multimedia features of Windows XP Home Edition, including playing audio CDs, DVD movies, MP3 music files, Internet Radio stations, and video and sound clips. And if that's not enough, you'll also learn how to make the most of your scanner and digital camera, edit video footage, and combine it with still photos, soundtracks, and narration to make your own movies. This part sums up with a chapter on burning CDs, one of the hottest new tech-trends around.

Appendix: Windows XP Home Edition Instant Reference This handy, comprehensive reference puts key information at your fingertips, in an easy-to-use A-Z format.

A FEW TYPOGRAPHIC CONVENTIONS

When a Windows operation requires a series of choices from menus or dialog boxes, the ➢ symbol is used to guide you through the instructions, like this: "Select Programs ➢ Accessories ➢ System Tools ➢ System Information." The items the ➢ symbol separates may be menu names, toolbar icons, check boxes, or other elements of the Windows interface—any place you can make a selection.

`This typeface` is used to identify Internet URLs and HTML code, and **boldface type** is used whenever you need to type something into a text box.

You'll find these types of special notes throughout the book:

TIP

You'll see a lot of these Tips—quicker and smarter ways to accomplish a task, which the authors have based on many hours spent testing and using Windows XP Home Edition.

NOTE

You'll see Notes, too. They usually represent alternate ways of accomplishing a task or some additional information that needs to be highlighted.

WARNING

In a few places, you'll see a Warning like this one. There are not too many because it's hard to do irrevocable things in Windows XP Home Edition unless you work at it. But when you see a warning, do pay attention to it.

YOU'LL ALSO SEE SIDEBAR BOXES LIKE THIS

These sections provide added explanations of special topics that are referred to in the surrounding discussions, but that you may want to explore separately in greater detail.

FOR MORE INFORMATION

See the Sybex Web site, www.sybex.com, to learn more about all the books contributed to *Windows XP Home Edition Complete*. On the site's Catalog page, you'll find links to any book you're interested in. Also, be sure to check out the Sybex site for late-breaking developments about Windows XP Home Edition itself.

We hope you enjoy this book and find it useful. Happy computing!

PART i

WINDOWS XP HOME EDITION— THE BASICS

Chapter 1

INTRODUCING WINDOWS XP HOME EDITION

This chapter discusses what Windows XP Home Edition is, what it does, and who it's for. It covers in some detail the features and improvements in Windows XP Home, so that you'll know what the operating system offers, and mentions which chapter of the book covers which feature.

The chapter then discusses whether you should upgrade from your current version of Windows. As you might imagine, the answer depends on which version of Windows you're currently running, what you're trying to do with it, and what degrees of success and satisfaction you're experiencing. But for most people who have adequate hardware, Windows XP offers significant improvements over all previous versions of Windows.

Adapted from *Mastering Windows XP Home Edition* by Guy Hart-Davis
ISBN 0-7821-2980-3   1040 pages $39.99

At the end of the chapter, you'll find a discussion of the main ways in which Windows XP Professional differs from Windows XP Home, because you may want to consider Professional rather than Home if you need any of the additional features that Professional offers.

WHAT IS WINDOWS XP HOME EDITION?

In a nutshell, Windows XP Home Edition is the latest version of Windows aimed at the consumer market. Windows XP Home comprises a feature set designed for home users, while its more powerful (and more expensive) sibling Windows XP Professional offers features designed for professional and corporate users.

If you've used Windows before, or if you're currently using Windows, you may wonder what the big deal is. The good news is that Windows XP *is* a big deal, especially if you've had less-than-satisfactory experiences with Windows in the past. Windows XP isn't the be-all and end-all of operating systems, but it's a great improvement on its predecessors.

As you probably know, through the second half of the 1990s and up until 2001, Microsoft offered two main categories of Windows versions for personal computers: the Windows 95 family and the Windows NT family. In the Windows 95 family were Windows 95 itself, naturally enough; Windows 98; Windows 98 Second Edition, which (despite its unassuming name) was a major upgrade to Windows 98; and Windows Millennium Edition, also known as Windows Me. In the Windows NT family were Windows NT versions 3.1, 3.5, 3.51, and 4, each of which came in a Workstation version and a Server version, and then Windows 2000, which came in a Professional version and several Server versions.

The Windows 95 family, widely referred to as Windows 9x in a brave attempt to simplify Microsoft's inconsistent naming, offered impressive compatibility with older hardware (*legacy hardware*, as it's sometimes politely termed) and software (*legacy software*), including full (or full-ish) DOS capabilities for running games and character-based programs. These versions of Windows kept their hardware demands to a reasonable minimum. They were aimed at the consumer market. When things went wrong (which happened regrettably often), they became unstable. And they crashed. Frequently.

Many of those people—both professionals and home users, who couldn't stand or afford to lose their work because of Windows 9x's frequent crashes—migrated to Windows NT instead. (Others tried OS/2 while it lasted, then returned disconsolately to Windows. Others went to Linux, and mostly stayed with it.) NT, which stands for New Technology, had a completely different underpinning of code than Windows 9x. NT was designed for stability, and as a result, it crashed much less frequently than Windows 9x. Unfortunately, though, NT wasn't nearly as compatible as Windows 9x with legacy hardware and software. Most games and much audio and video software wouldn't run on NT, and it was picky about the hardware on which it would run. (Actually, this wasn't unfortunate at all—it was deliberate on Microsoft's part, and probably wise. But the result was far from great for many users.)

So for the last half-dozen years, users have essentially had to decide between stability and compatibility. This led to a lot of unhappy users, some of whom couldn't run the software they wanted, and others who kept losing work or at least having to reboot their computers more than they should have had to.

The Windows 9x line culminated in Windows Me, which tacked some stability and restoration features onto the Windows 9x code base. NT culminated in Windows 2000 Professional, which featured increased compatibility with programs over NT (which wasn't saying all that much), a smooth user interface, and usability enhancements.

Windows 2000 Professional was arguably the most stable operating system that Microsoft had produced until Windows XP came along. (Some old-timers reckoned Windows NT 3.51 was more stable.) But Windows 2000 Professional's stability came at a price: It had no interest in running any games or other demanding software that wouldn't conform to its stringent requirements. And while it was compatible with quite an impressive range of legacy hardware, many items still wouldn't work. Even up-to-date hardware could be problematic, especially if it connected via USB.

Since the late 1990s, Microsoft had been promising to deliver a consumer version of Windows that melded the stability of NT and the compatibility of Windows 9x. In Windows XP Home Edition, that version of Windows is finally here.

What's New in Windows XP Home Edition?

This section outlines the most striking and appealing new features in Windows XP, starting with installation and upgrading, moving through the user interface and visible features, and ending up with the features hidden under the hood.

Some of these new features fall into convenient categories, and this section presents them in categories. Others don't; this section presents these features individually.

Easier Installation and Updating

Windows XP includes several features designed to make it easier to install and keep up to date. These include Dynamic Update and Windows Update; the Files and Settings Transfer Wizard; more Wizards for a variety of tasks; a wider selection of device drivers; simplified installation for multifunction devices; and effective uninstall back to Windows 98 and Windows Me.

Dynamic Update and Windows Update

If you're installing Windows XP, one of the first new features that you'll notice is Dynamic Update, which runs during setup and offers to download the latest patches, packages, and fixes so that they can be installed during the setup process.

Dynamic Update may prove to be a great feature. It goes hand in hand with its terrible twin, Windows Update, which runs periodically after setup and offers to download the latest patches, packages, and fixes and install them so that your copy of Windows is as up to date, secure, and compatible as possible. (You can also run Windows Update manually whenever you want to.)

Files and Settings Transfer Wizard

Making its debut in Windows XP is the Files and Settings Transfer Wizard, a feature that Windows users have been demanding for a good 10 years. The Files and Settings Transfer Wizard provides a way of transferring designated files and settings from one computer to another, or from one installation of Windows to another on the same computer. You'll still need to reinstall all your programs on the new computer or new installation of Windows, but you can transfer your data and a good amount of information about your work environment easily.

If you're migrating from an old computer to a new computer, or if you're installing Windows XP as a dual-boot with an existing version of Windows, you can use the Files and Settings Transfer Wizard to clone your existing Desktop and files and transfer them to the new computer or new version of Windows.

More Wizards to Make Tasks Easier

Windows XP includes a slew of Wizards designed to walk you through complicated processes (and some that aren't so complicated). Perhaps most welcome are the improvements to the Network Setup Wizard (discussed in Chapter 20), which provides effective configuration of simple networks and Internet connection sharing, and the two Hardware Wizards, the Add Hardware Wizard and the Found New Hardware Wizard.

On the less useful front, Windows XP also includes Wizards such as the Desktop Cleanup Wizard, which pops out periodically like the neighborhood dog and tries to persuade you to let it herd the stray icons on your Desktop into a folder where they'll be available but less obtrusive. If you refuse, it wags its tail and goes away for a while.

More Device Drivers

Windows XP comes complete with drivers for a large number of devices, including scanners, digital still cameras, digital video cameras, printers, and so on. So there's a better chance than with another version of Windows (say Windows Me or Windows 2000) that when you plug in a new device, Windows XP will be able to load a driver for it and get it working without any fuss.

You'll probably want to take this improvement with a grain of salt. It's great when Windows XP installs a new device without any effort on your part. But to enjoy the latest features and the best performance from a new device, you may well need to install the driver that comes with the device or (better) download the latest version from the manufacturer's Web site rather than wait for updated drivers to filter through Windows Update.

Simplified Installation for Multifunction Devices

Apart from having more drivers (as described in the previous section), Windows XP makes it easier to install multifunction devices—for example, a multifunction printer/scanner/fax device (the kind that people sometimes call *hydra* machines), a PC Card that combines a network interface card with a modem, or a sound board with extra features.

Previous versions of Windows tended to recognize the component pieces of multifunction devices separately in sequence. If you installed a hydra, Windows would recognize the printer and demand the installation software for it. Once that was done, Windows would recognize the fax and demand the software for *that*. After that, it would recognize the scanner and suggest you might want to install yet more software. Windows XP improves on this social ineptitude by recognizing multifunction devices as such the first time you introduce it to them, and so it demands the installation software only once.

Effective Uninstall Back to Windows 98 and Windows Me

Windows XP Home provides an effective uninstall feature for rolling back the Windows XP installation to your previous installation of Windows 98 or Windows Me. You can't uninstall Windows XP Home and revert to an operating system other than these two. (Windows XP Professional supports upgrading from and uninstalling back to a different set of previous versions of Windows, as you'll see later in this chapter.)

Effective Multiuser Capabilities

Windows XP provides far better multiuser capabilities than Windows 9*x*. You'll notice this at once when you start Windows XP, because by default the Welcome screen that's displayed when Windows starts lists each user who has an account on the computer.

While Windows 9*x* let anybody log on to the computer by creating a new account, Windows XP requires an existing account in order to log on. By default, no account has a password in Windows XP Home, though, so in effect anybody can log on using one of the existing accounts until you require passwords—and you ought to require passwords immediately to protect your data.

Windows 9*x* let you create a profile for each separate user, so that each user could have their own Desktop, Start menu, and set of programs; but it didn't offer any features for preventing one user from seeing another user's files. By contrast, Windows XP takes the approach of NT and Windows 2000, which keep each user's files separate, so that no user can see another user's files unless they have been shared deliberately.

Windows XP goes further than NT and Windows 2000, though, in that it lets multiple users be logged on at the same time, each with programs running. Only one user can be actually *using* the computer, or *active* in Windows XP parlance, at any one time, but the other user sessions continue running in the background (*disconnected*, in Windows XP parlance). When you've finished with the computer for the time being, you can log off Windows, just as you did in previous versions of Windows. Logging off closes all the programs you were using and frees up the memory they took up. But if you stop using the computer only temporarily, you may prefer to *switch user*, which leaves your programs running but lets someone else use the computer in the interim. Further encouraging you to switch user, Windows' default screen saver setting is to display the Welcome screen after 10 minutes of inactivity, performing the equivalent of a Switch User command as it disconnects the user but leaves their session running hidden in the background.

Enhanced User Interface

Windows XP has a completely revamped user interface with a large number of visual enhancements and improved functionality. Some of the visual enhancements improve usability, while others are mere eye candy. But the overall effect is mostly easy to use and mostly looks good—and if you don't like the look, you can restore the "classic" Windows look with minimal effort.

The following sections discuss the main changes to the user interface.

Redesigned Start Menu

Windows XP sports a redesigned Start menu that's supposedly easier and quicker to use. Whether you find it so depends on your experience with the Start menu found in Windows 9*x* and Windows 2000. But don't worry if you like the "classic" Start menu—you can restore it easily enough with a few clicks of the mouse, as discussed in Chapter 10.

The Start menu appears as a panel containing two columns (shown in Figure 1.1). The right-hand column remains the same unless you customize it. The left-hand column starts off with items Microsoft thinks you ought to know about immediately after installation. It then automatically reconfigures itself to show your most used programs. You can pin an item to the Start menu to prevent it from moving and keep it available.

FIGURE 1.1: The redesigned Start menu contains a static column of choices on the right and a variable column of choices on the left.

As you can see in the figure, the current user's name appears in a bar across the top of the Start menu, and the Log Off button and Turn Off Computer button appear at the bottom of the menu.

Redesigned Explorer

Explorer windows use a pair of technologies called WebView and ListView to present context-sensitive lists of tasks you may want to perform or other locations you may want to access. If that sounds a bit vague, that's because WebView and ListView mean that what you see in an Explorer window changes depending on the item that's displayed.

For example, when you select a file (as in Figure 1.2), you see a list of File and Folder Tasks (including links for Rename This File, Move This File, and Delete This File), a list of Other Places (other folders you may want to access from this folder), and a list of Details (which contains information about the file selected and is off the screen in the figure). When you select a folder, Explorer displays a list of File and Folder Tasks (including links for Rename This Folder, Copy This Folder, and Publish This Folder to the Web). When you select your My Network Places folder, you get a Network Tasks list (including links for View Network Connections and Set Up a Home Network). When you select the Recycle Bin... Okay, you get the idea.

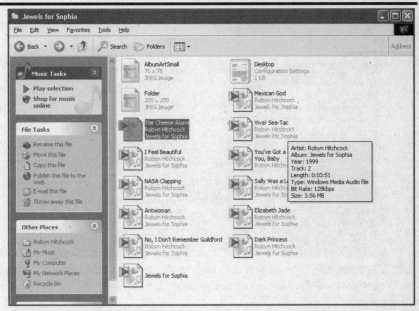

FIGURE 1.2: Explorer windows use the new WebView and ListView technologies to present lists of tasks associated with the selected item.

Context menus (right-click menus) in Explorer are also improved, with more context-sensitive commands added where appropriate. But most of the action takes place in the Tasks list for the selected item. That's because some 80 percent of users apparently weren't using the context menus successfully—an impressive and frightening statistic thrown up by Microsoft's research on Windows users.

Redesigned Control Panel

Windows XP also has a redesigned Control Panel (shown in Figure 1.3) that uses WebView and ListView technology to present Control Panel as categories of items and actions you can take with them. (If you regard Control Panel as an oddly behaved Explorer window, it should come as no surprise after reading the previous section that Control Panel uses WebView and ListView.)

New users will likely find the Category view of Control Panel easy to use. Users comfortable with the regular manifestation of Control Panel in Windows 9x, Windows NT 4, and Windows 2000 will probably prefer to use the Classic view.

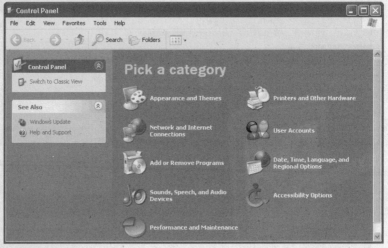

FIGURE 1.3: Control Panel also uses WebView and ListView by default, dividing its bevy of icons into categories. You can use the Classic view to see all the icons at once.

Eye Candy

To complement its highly graphical interface, Windows XP includes a dangerous amount of eye candy. Most people will like at least some of it. Some users will love all of it. And no doubt some people will claim to detest every pixel of it.

The prime example of eye candy is the My Pictures Slideshow screen saver, which lets you set up an automated (or mouse-controlled) slideshow of designated pictures instead of a regular screen saver. This feature seems destined to be widely popular.

Less assured of a rapturous welcome are the staggering amounts of adornment in the interface, such as shadows under the mouse pointer and under menus; the color gradient in the title bar of windows; and the effect of sliding icons, controls, and Taskbar buttons. This overbearing emphasis on graphics places heavy demands on your graphics card and processor, and if your computer's hardware tends to the lukewarm rather than the hot, you may find that the eye candy exacts an unacceptable performance penalty. Microsoft has had the sense to let you set performance options to balance the demands of appearance against your need for performance, so you can turn off the least necessary effects and speed up your computer.

Taskbar Changes and Enhancements

Windows XP includes a number of tweaks to the Taskbar. These seem designed for beginners, so if you're an experienced Windows user, you may find some good and others bad. Fortunately, you can change the Taskbar's behavior back to how it was in previous versions of Windows. You'll find the details in Chapter 10.

Taskbar Locking

By default, the Taskbar is locked in Windows XP Home so that you cannot resize it or move it. Presumably this is intended to help prevent users from dragging their Taskbar to an inaccessible line at the edge of the screen, but it will annoy experienced users who want to be able to resize and move their Taskbar freely. (You can unlock it easily enough.)

Taskbar Scrolling

If you read the previous paragraph, you probably started raising objections: If the Taskbar is a fixed size, the buttons for the running programs must become tiny and useless as soon as you've got 10 or more programs running.

Two other changes come into play here, of which the first is Taskbar scrolling. When the Taskbar is locked, Windows keeps the buttons bigger than a minimum size. To accommodate the buttons, Windows increases the depth of the Taskbar, but displays only its top row. On the displayed portion of the Taskbar, Windows puts scroll buttons so that you can scroll the Taskbar up and down one row of buttons at a time.

Taskbar Button Grouping

The second change that makes Taskbar locking reasonable is Taskbar button grouping.

By default, Windows XP groups related taskbar buttons once you've opened enough windows to more or less fill the taskbar. Whereas other versions of Windows displayed one taskbar button for each program window, Windows XP groups them onto a pop-up menu from a single taskbar button. For example, if you open nine Internet Explorer windows in Windows 98, Windows displays nine Internet Explorer buttons on the taskbar. Having all these buttons can make it easy to find the window you want, but the buttons take up a lot of space (or each button on the taskbar gets shrunk to a tiny size to fit them all in).

In Windows XP, if the program has multiple open windows, the taskbar button displays the number of windows, the title of the current active window or last active window, and a drop-down arrow. To access one of the other open windows, click the taskbar button. Windows displays a list of the windows by title (shown in Figure 1.4). Select the window you want, and Windows displays it.

FIGURE 1.4: Several windows represented by a single taskbar button.

Notification Area

By default, Windows XP Home collapses the notification area (also known as the System Tray) so that only the icons you've used most recently are displayed. To display the other icons in the notification area, click the << button at the left end of the notification area.

Better Audio and Video Features

Windows XP includes a slew of new features and improvements for audio and video. These include a new version of Windows Media Player; better features for grabbing and handling images from digital input devices such as scanners and cameras; and Windows Movie Maker, a modest video-editing program.

Windows Media Player Version 8

Front and center among the improved audio and video features of Windows XP is Windows Media Player version 8, which combines a video and DVD player, a CD player, an Internet radio tuner, and a jukebox for playing and organizing digital-audio files such as Windows Media Audio (WMA) files and MP3 files. Windows Media Player 8 comes with a number of visually interesting *skins* (graphical looks) that you can apply at will. You can even create your own skins if you have the time and talent to invest.

All in all, Windows Media Player 8 is a huge improvement over the 98-pound weakling version of Windows Media Player shipped with all previous versions of Windows except Windows Me. (Me included Windows Media Player 7, which offered many of the features of version 8.) Windows Media Player can even burn audio CDs at the full speed of your CD-R or CD-RW drive.

Windows Media Player is a strong program, but two missing features will disappoint many users:

▶ Windows Media Player has no codec (coder/decoder) for playing back DVDs. If you want to watch DVDs, you'll have to add a codec of your own—and almost certainly pay for the privilege.

▶ Windows Media Player can encode audio to the universally popular MP3 format—but only if you add a third-party encoder. You'll probably have to pay for this too.

Chapter 22 discusses Windows Media Player.

My Music Folder and My Pictures Folder

Like several of its predecessors, Windows XP uses custom folders for music (the My Music folder) and pictures (the My Pictures folder). Again like its predecessors, it tries none too subtly to persuade you to save your music in these folders. But Windows XP goes further, in that it makes these folders much more useful than they were in earlier versions of Windows.

As you'd expect, the My Music folder and the My Pictures folder use WebView and ListView to present customized lists of actions you can take with music files and picture files. Some of these actions tend to the commercial—for example, the Order Prints from the Internet link in the Picture Tasks list, and the Shop for Music Online link in the Music Tasks list. But others are solidly useful—for example, the Play All link in the Music Tasks list, which lets you play all the music in a folder without spelunking into it, or the View As a Slide Show link in the Picture Tasks list, which lets you set a whole folder of pictures running as a slideshow with a single click.

Not surprisingly, the My Music folder works hand in hand (or is it glove?) with Windows Media Player. Windows Media Player is definitely happy for you to keep your music in the My Music folder, though it will let you keep your music elsewhere as well. Better yet, Windows Media Player's features for cataloging music tracks are flexible enough to keep track of music files even when you move them from one folder to another.

The My Pictures folder works closely with Windows Image Acquisition, Image Preview, and Paint (all three of which are discussed in the next section). The folder includes a slideshow applet and a filmstrip view, and it can publish your pictures to the Web.

Better Image Acquisition and Handling

Windows XP provides strong features for capturing images from scanners, still cameras, and video cameras. It also provides better throughput for video streams, though unless you have a duplicate computer running an older version of Windows to use as a benchmark, you could be forgiven for failing to go into raptures over the improvement. Less cynically, the improvement in throughput is unquestionably a good thing, and on decent hardware, Windows XP delivers adequate-to-impressive video performance; but the chances of your confusing your PC with your Dreamcast remain poor.

One of the central tools for image acquisition and handling is the Scanner and Camera Wizard. This Wizard has a variety of duties, including transferring image files from still cameras and digital media (for example, CompactFlash cards and SmartMedia cards) to the computer. Most of its capabilities stay on the useful side of the esoteric. For example, you can scan multiple pages into a single image file, an ability that can come in handy in both home and business settings.

Windows XP provides some basic tools for handling still images. As mentioned in the previous section, the My Pictures folder acts as a default repository for images and provides some basic image-handling abilities, such as rotating an image. The Image Preview feature lets you examine an image (and annotate a fax). And Paint, the basic image-manipulation and drawing package that's been included with Windows since Windows 3.x, has been beefed up as well. Paint can now open—and save—JPEG, GIF, TIFF, and PNG images as well as Windows bitmap (BMP) files, making it about five times as useful as before.

Windows Movie Maker

Windows XP includes Windows Movie Maker, a basic package for capturing video, editing video and audio, and creating video files in the Windows Media format. You won't find yourself making the next *Timecode* or *Traffic* with Windows Movie Maker, but it's good enough for home-video editing. You can also create video slideshows with still images, for those family occasions on rainy weekends or holidays.

Chapter 23 discusses how to get started with Windows Movie Maker.

CD Burning

Windows XP comes with built-in CD-burning capabilities. You can burn CDs from an Explorer window with minimal effort. You can also burn CDs directly from Windows Media Player, which lets you easily create audio CDs that you can play in regular CD players.

Chapter 24 discusses how to burn CDs.

Compressed Folders

Windows XP has built-in support for compressed folders in both the ubiquitous ZIP format and the Microsoft Cabinet (CAB) format. You can create ZIP folders containing one or more files or folders. Better still, you can view the contents of a ZIP or CAB folder seamlessly in Explorer as if it were a regular folder.

Improved Features for Sending Attachments

Windows XP includes improved features for sending files and folders as attachments to e-mail messages. Instead of blindly attaching the files and folders identified by the user, Windows offers to optimize the file size and display size of the pictures so that they transfer faster and fit onto the recipient's screen when they arrive. If the recipient is using Windows XP, they get to choose whether to open the file or files at the original size or at the optimized size.

Because this feature can actually change the files sent, it seems suspect. But if it reduces the number of multimegabyte digital pictures landing on your ISP's mail server, you may well find it a positive feature—even if you choose never to use it yourself.

Chapter 16 discusses how to use Outlook Express for e-mail, including attachments.

Search Companion

Windows XP includes Search Companion, an enhanced search feature for finding information both on your PC and in the wider world. You can use Search Companion to search for files, for computers or people online, or for information in Help and Support Center. Search Companion brokers the search requests that you enter and farms them out to the appropriate search mechanisms.

You can choose between having Search Companion appear in a straightforward and unexceptionable window and having it manifest itself using one of various animated characters reminiscent of the Microsoft Office Assistant.

Chapter 6 discusses how to use Search Companion.

Easy Publishing to the Web

Windows XP makes it easier to publish files or folders to a Web site by using a Web-hosting service. Windows XP includes a feature called Web Digital Authoring and Versioning (WebDAV for short) that lets you save information to the Web from any program rather than having to use the regular Web-publishing protocols.

Chapter 18 discusses how to publish information to the Web.

A Sane Implementation of Autoplay

If you've used Windows 9x, NT 4, or 2000, you'll know all about the Autoplay feature and how it used to drive people crazy. You remember Autoplay—the moment you insert a CD, it starts playing the music from it or installing any software it contains. By default, Autoplay was enabled, so you had to switch it off (or override it by holding down the Shift key while closing the CD tray) to prevent this from occurring.

Windows XP includes a new version of Autoplay that's improved in several ways. First, you can customize it. Second, you can configure it to take different actions depending on what the CD (or other medium) contains. For example, you might want Windows to play your audio CDs automatically when you insert them (okay, you don't—but you *might*), or you might want Windows to display a slideshow automatically when you insert a CD containing nothing but pictures.

What's that about *other medium*? That's the third thing: In Windows XP, Autoplay works for CDs, DVDs, assorted flash cards (including Compact-Flash, Memory Stick, and SmartMedia), PC Cards, Zip and other removable disk drives, and FireWire hot-plug external drives.

More Games

Windows XP includes more games than previous versions of Windows. Some of these are single-player games (for example, Spider Solitaire). Others are multiplayer games that you can play across the Internet via MSN's Zone.com Web site.

Remote Desktop Connection

Windows XP Home includes Remote Desktop Connection, a technology that lets you use your computer to access a remote computer (for example, your computer at the office) that's running Windows XP Professional. Once you've connected to the remote computer, you can control it as if you were sitting at it.

Chapter 19 discusses how to use Remote Desktop Connection.

A More Useful Winkey

A what? *Winkey*, pronounced "win-key" rather than as the diminutive of *wink*, is the Windows key on the keyboard—the key with the Windows logo. Most keyboards have one or two Winkeys, usually located next to the Alt key or keys.

Windows XP includes more functionality for the Winkey. You can still press the Winkey to open or close the Start menu, but you can also use it in a number of key combinations. For example, pressing Winkey+M issues a Minimize All command, and pressing Winkey+Shift+M issues an Undo Minimize All command.   .

Improvements for Portable Computers

Windows XP includes several improvements for portable computers.

First, Windows XP supports processor power control, which lets the computer make use of features in chips such as Intel's SpeedStep, in which the processor runs at full speed when the computer is plugged into the main power supply (or told that it's plugged in) but at a lower speed to save power when it's running on battery power (or told that it is).

Throttling back the processor like this reduces the computer's power usage a bit, improving battery life, but in most portables, the screen consumes far more power than the processor. Windows XP also targets the screen, providing a couple of features designed to reduce power use when the computer is running on battery power. First, Windows XP turns off the display when the user closes the computer's lid, on the basis that the user probably isn't looking at the display. Second, it runs the screen at a dimmer brightness when the computer is running off the battery. The cynical among you will point out that the better-designed portables implement both these functions already in hardware. Still, it shouldn't do any harm to have Windows help out for the manufacturers who design their machines a little less carefully.

Windows XP also includes some other less obvious visual enhancements, such as support for ClearType, a Microsoft text-display technology that improves the look of fonts on LCD screens that have digital interfaces. While these screens aren't strictly confined to portables, that's where the bulk of the market is.

Faxing

Windows XP Home contains a built-in fax client that's more than adequate for most home needs and many home-office needs. You can send faxes from any program that supports printing, and you can specify whether to print out incoming faxes automatically or store them in a folder. You can even configure different fax/modems to take different roles. For example, if you use faxes extensively, you might want to keep separate incoming and outgoing fax lines. You'll need a modem for each of the phone lines involved, but that's about as difficult as it gets.

More Help

Windows XP delivers more Help—and more different types of Help—than any other version of Windows.

If you've searched fruitlessly for information in the past, you'll be aware that Windows' Help files have never exactly delivered the ultimate in user satisfaction. Digging information out of Help often felt so difficult that if you knew Windows well enough to find Help on the right topic, you could probably solve the problem without Help's assistance.

Windows XP takes a new approach to Help. There are Help files on your hard drive still, but they're integrated into a program called Help and Support Center. Help and Support Center not only works with the Help files but also with the Microsoft Knowledge Base (a database of support queries) and other online sources of information. For example, if you run a query within Help and Support Center to find information on hardware, it might return some information from local files, some information from the Microsoft Web site, and some information from hardware manufacturers' Web sites, all packaged into one window so that you can access the information conveniently.

Help and Support Center also provides a gateway to other areas of support, including Microsoft Assisted Support and Microsoft Communities, and to programs that you can use to get help from other users (such as Remote Assistance) and troubleshoot your computer (such as System Configuration Utility and System Restore).

The following sections discuss some of the Help and Support Center features. Chapter 3 discusses how to use Help and Support Center.

Microsoft Assisted Support

Windows XP's Microsoft Assisted Support feature lets you automatically collect information on a problem you're having and submit it to Microsoft electronically. A Microsoft technician then sends a solution, which appears as a pop-up in your System Tray. You can read the response in the Help and Support Center window and apply the wisdom it contains to fix the problem.

Microsoft Assisted Support is designed to bypass the problems inherent with tech support via phone call, namely that it's difficult for the user to tell the Help technician what's wrong with their computer; it's even harder for the technician to get a good idea of what's going wrong without knowing a fair bit of technical information about the computer; and waiting on hold for tech support is nobody's idea of fun, especially if you're paying for a long-distance call as well as for the support.

Support Communities

Instead of contacting a Microsoft technician via Microsoft Assisted Support, you can try to get support from one of the support communities that Microsoft is building online. These comprise the Windows Newsgroups, which are Microsoft-hosted newsgroups dedicated to Windows, and MSN Communities, forums and message boards on MSN for discussing how to use Windows, Microsoft software, and computers in general.

Remote Assistance

Remote Assistance is an ingenious feature by which you can get assistance from a friend or other knowledgeable person remotely by computer.

Here's the brief version of how Remote Assistance works. You send out an invitation file via e-mail, via MSN Messenger instant messaging, or via a file saved to the network (for example, in a business environment) or floppy disk. Your helper receives the invitation and responds to it. Remote Assistance sets up a secure connection between their computer and yours, using a password to verify their identity. Your helper can then view your screen remotely and chat with you (via text chat and voice). If you trust your helper, you can even let them control your computer so that they can take actions directly.

Chapter 19 discusses how to use Remote Assistance.

Help Queries: Errors, Events, and Compatibility

You can use Help queries to search for information on error messages, event messages, and compatibility. Help and Support Center's integrated approach lets you search seamlessly across multiple Web sites (for example, the Microsoft Knowledge Base and the hardware manufacturer's Web site) to find the information you need

Tools Center

Help and Support Center includes a Tools Center that gives you quick access to information about your computer (My Computer Information and Advanced System Information) and its configuration (System Configuration Utility); network diagnostic tools (Network Diagnostics); the System Restore feature; and more. In addition to the tools that Microsoft makes available in the Tools Center, OEMs (original equipment manufacturers) can add tools of their own, so you may also find custom tools provided by your computer manufacturer.

Many of the tools accessible through the Tools Center are also accessible in other ways through the Windows interface. For example, Windows XP includes an improved version of Disk Defragmenter, which you can use to keep your hard disk from becoming fragmented (fragmentation decreases performance). You can run Disk Defragmenter from Tools Center, but you can also run it from the System Tools submenu of the Start menu (Start ➤ All Programs ➤ Accessories ➤ System Tools ➤ Disk Defragmenter). Similarly, you can run Windows Update from inside Help and Support Center. This can be convenient, but it offers no great advantage over running Windows Update from the Start menu.

Fixing a Problem Tool

Help and Support Center includes an area called Fixing a Problem that contains a number of troubleshooters for walking you through the steps of diagnosing and curing various common problems. Fixing a Problem isn't a panacea, but it's a good place to start, and it can save you a call to a guru or even a trip to your local computer shop.

Device Driver Referral Site

Help and Support Center contains a system for referring searches for drivers that don't come with Windows or with the hardware device. When you plug in a new hardware device, and Windows finds that it doesn't have a driver for it and you can't supply a driver, Windows invites you to send information about the hardware to Microsoft. Once you've sent the information, you can take a variety of actions depending on what information is available. For example, you might be able to view a list of compatible devices (if any), search for information on compatible devices or Knowledge Base articles about the hardware, or find a link to the vendor's Web site.

Other Help Improvements

Help and Support Center includes assorted other Help improvements that can save you time. For example, you can print out a whole chapter of Help information at once instead of having to slog through it screen by screen. And you can open multiple Help and Support Center windows at

the same time. This makes it easier to pursue different avenues of explo-
ration for the information you need. When you find useful information,
you can create a favorite for it so that you can access it quickly again
when you need it.

Network Connectivity

Windows XP provides various improvements in network connectivity,
from creating a home or home-office network to joining a computer to
two separate networks. There are also great improvements in Internet
connectivity, discussed in the next section.

Network Setup Wizard

The Network Setup Wizard simplifies the process of creating a network;
sharing printers, Internet connections, and other resources; and configuring protocols and security.

Chapter 20 discusses how to use the Network Setup Wizard to set up a
network.

All-User Remote Access Service

The All-User Remote Access Service lets you create a credential for all
users of the computer so that they can share a connection. For example,
you can make your high-speed Internet connection available to all the
users of the computer without divulging the account password to them.
The name is a bit intimidating, but the process is easy.

Alternative TCP/IP Configuration

Windows XP provides an alternative TCP/IP configuration that allows
you to connect to a network that has a DHCP server and to a network
that doesn't without changing your TCP/IP settings. For example, you
might use a laptop at work (where the network has a DHCP server) and
at home (where your network doesn't).

Network Bridging

Windows XP's network-bridging capability lets you use a computer with
two or more network adapters to join two separate networks. You're perhaps unlikely to have two (or more) networks at home or in a small

office–unless you have a wired network to which you've added a wireless component to provide roaming capabilities for some of the computers.

Internet Connectivity and Web Browsing

Windows XP provides a number of enhanced features for Internet connectivity and Web browsing, from favorites for Internet connections to a new version of Internet Explorer.

Internet Connection Favorites

Windows XP lets you create favorites for your Internet connections. By using favorites, you can switch easily from one Internet connection to another. This is a great time-saver if you use multiple ISPs or (perhaps more likely) travel frequently and need to use different dial-up numbers from different locations.

Internet Connection Sharing and Internet Connection Firewall

Like Windows 98 Second Edition, Windows Me, and Windows 2000, Windows XP includes an Internet Connection Sharing (ICS) feature that lets you share an Internet connection on one computer with one or more networked computers. Windows XP's version of Internet Connection Sharing has some tweaks; for example, you can disconnect the shared Internet connection from another PC if you need to use the phone line that the connection is using. Windows XP includes a Quality of Service Packet Scheduler that works to optimize the utilization of a shared Internet connection.

Internet Connection Sharing is a great convenience, particularly if you have a high-speed connection such as a DSL or a cable modem—but it lays your network open to assault from the Internet. Windows XP goes one better than its predecessors by including a firewall (called *Internet Connection Firewall*) to protect the Internet connection (whether shared or not).

Chapter 21 discusses Internet Connection Firewall.

New Version of Internet Explorer

Windows XP includes Internet Explorer 6, the latest version of Internet Explorer. Even if you feel you've already had it up to here with new versions of Internet Explorer, stifle your impatience, because Internet Explorer 6 offers a number of welcome innovations, including the following:

► You can save images, music, and videos more easily to your computer.

► The new Media bar lets you listen to streaming audio directly in Internet Explorer and (perhaps a less welcome feature) access WindowsMedia.com easily.

► IE 6 provides better handling of cookies and digital certificates for securing information transfer and authenticating content.

► IE 6 can automatically resize an image you've displayed directly. If you've ever used Internet Explorer to open a digital photo, and found it displayed bigger than your screen so that you could see only part of it, you may appreciate this feature. (But you'd be better off opening the photo in Paint in the first place.)

► IE 6 has more integrated functionality for handling different file types. This won't strike you over the head; you'll simply find that more file types open without your being prodded to download and install extra components. For example, IE 6 has built-in support for Macromedia Flash and Shockwave animations, and support for Cascading Style Sheet (CSS) Level 1. The net result is that more animations will play without your needing to add software, and documents formatted with CSS1 style sheets will be displayed as their authors intended. (They may still look horrible, but at least you'll know that they're meant to look that way.)

Chapter 15 discusses how to configure and use Internet Explorer.

MSN Explorer

Windows XP includes MSN Explorer, an Internet client dedicated to MSN. If you don't have an ISP, you may want to use MSN Explorer to connect to the Internet.

.NET Passport Integration

In order to implement many of its Internet services, Windows XP relies heavily on Microsoft's .NET Passport feature. For example, you need to get a .NET Passport in order to use Windows Messenger for instant messaging, to use Hotmail (Microsoft's Web-based e-mail service), to create Web pages on MSN, or to visit a Web site that requires a Passport sign-in (for instance, to download certain files from the Microsoft Web site).

.NET Passport (or, more simply, just *Passport*) is an electronic identifier that's associated with your user account on your PC. (If you use the same Passport with multiple PCs, it can be associated with multiple user accounts.) You can sign up for a Passport by using an existing e-mail account. If you don't have an e-mail account, Microsoft encourages you to base your Passport on a Hotmail account or an MSN account.

Passport enables many cool features—but it also locks you into using Microsoft technologies when you may not want to use them. Worse, it can (or *could*) give Microsoft a way to track some of your actions online. Microsoft protests that it is committed to your online privacy, and does give you the choice of opting out of some of the tracking features, but you don't need to be paranoid to find Passport's possibilities frightening.

You can use Passport Wallet features to (in Microsoft's words) "simplify your online shopping experience"—in other words, spend money faster online and with less effort. You get to decide whether this is a good idea. (Hint: Evaluate Passport Wallet carefully. Don't rush into anything.)

What's Hiding under the Hood

The features mentioned so far catch the eye—some even on a cursory scan of the Windows XP Desktop and interface.

Less glamorous, but more important in the long run, are the enhancements hiding under Windows XP's hood. This section discusses the major enhancements that you probably *won't* see.

Protected Memory Management

Windows XP improves on Windows 9x/Me by offering fully protected memory management. Windows 9x/Me didn't protect the areas of memory used by the operating system. This meant that if a program tried to store information in memory already used by another program or by the operating system, the program could crash not only itself but also the operating system. If you've used any version of Windows 9x for any length of time, you're probably familiar with these crashes. Typically, you see a succession of instances of the Blue Screen of Death with assorted error messages, and eventually have to perform a warm reboot (Ctrl+Alt+Delete) or a hard reboot (by powering the computer down and back up again). In the mean-time, you lose any unsaved work in the programs you're using.

With protected memory management, Windows XP can handle memory errors with more aplomb. When a program tries to access memory that doesn't belong to it, Windows XP can close the program without affecting any other running program. You still lose any unsaved work in the guilty program, but all your other programs continue running.

While Windows XP is dealing with the misbehaving program, you can move the program's window so that it doesn't obstruct your view of any other programs you have open.

System File Protection

Windows XP offers a feature called System File Protection that protects your system files from ill-advised actions on your part.

Windows XP tries to persuade you not to view the contents of folders that you probably shouldn't be messing with, by refusing to show them to you until you demand it show them. You can then delete system files if you want (except for any file that's actively in use, which is locked auto-matically). But the next time that Windows boots, or if it catches the damage you've done before you reboot it, it replaces the files you deleted without notifying you.

This is about all you need to know about System File Protection.

System Restore

Windows XP offers a System Restore feature similar to but more effective than the System Restore feature in Windows Me. System Restore auto-matically creates restore points both periodically and each time you make a change to the system—for example, by installing a program or a driver. You can also create system restore points manually. When one of your changes leads to an unwelcome result, such as your computer failing to boot, you can use System Restore to roll back the change to an earlier point at which the system was working properly.

Chapter 12 discusses how to use System Restore.

Device Driver Rollback

Device drivers have long been the bane of Windows—okay, *one* of the banes of Windows. By installing the wrong driver, or a buggy driver, you could render your computer useless until you reinstalled Windows (or turned in frustration to another operating system).

Windows XP tracks the drivers you install and lets you roll back the installation of the driver—in other words, you can revert to the driver you were using before.

Better yet, Windows XP stores details of the previous driver in what's called the *Last Known Good Configuration*—the configuration used the last time the computer seemed to be running okay. This means that if installing a new driver prevents your computer from booting as normal, you can boot into Safe mode and use the Last Known Good Configuration to restore the previous driver.

NTFS

Where Windows 9x versions used the FAT (File Allocation Table) and VFAT (Virtual File Allocation Table) file systems, Windows XP prefers NTFS, the NT file system. NTFS provides security features (including file-level security) and stability that FAT and VFAT do not.

Compatibility with Windows 9x Programs

Windows XP aims to be able to run all programs that would run on Windows 9x, Windows NT, and Windows 2000. As you'll know if you've struggled to run a Windows 9x program on NT or Windows 2000, this is quite a challenge. NT-based operating systems (including Windows XP) handle memory and hardware access in a different way than Windows 9x operating systems. These differences mean that programs designed for Windows 9x often won't run satisfactorily on NT and Windows 2000.

Being able to run these legacy programs is a big feature of Windows XP—but because Microsoft has implemented this feature very successfully, it remains hidden most of the time. Usually, you can simply install a legacy program and run it without complications. Behind the scenes, Windows XP may be running the program in its Compatibility mode or applying one of its new AppFixes to the program (to prevent it from detecting the wrong operating system and from causing problems such as referencing memory once it's been freed up), but you often won't know about it. You may need to specifically run some programs in Compatibility mode, and you may see Windows Update automatically downloading new information for AppFixes to keep your copy of Windows up to date, but most of the time, your old programs will simply work—which of course is the way it should be.

SHOULD YOU UPGRADE TO WINDOWS XP HOME EDITION?

Whether you should upgrade to Windows XP Home Edition depends on your needs, how well your current version of Windows is fulfilling them, and whether your hardware is up to the test. The decision is wholly yours (of course), but the following sections offer some suggestions, depending on where you're coming from.

Windows 9x

If you're using one of the versions of Windows 9x/Me—Windows 95, Windows 98, Windows 98 Second Edition, or Windows Me—the main attractions of Windows XP Home are much greater stability, the enhanced user interface, and the extra features that Windows XP includes.

Exactly which extra features Windows XP includes depends—obviously enough—on which version of Windows 9x/Me you have. Not surprisingly, later versions of Windows 9x offer more features than earlier versions. For example, the Internet Connection Sharing feature debuted in Windows 98 Second Edition, so ICS might be a reason to upgrade to Windows XP if you have Windows 95 or Windows 98 (first edition), but not if you have Windows 98 Second Edition or Windows Me. (The Internet Connection Firewall feature, however, is new, and is a strong attraction unless you're already using an effective hardware or software firewall.) Likewise, Windows Me includes Windows Media Player 7, a version that greatly improved on the earlier, anemic versions of Windows Media Player but isn't as capable as Windows Media Player 8, the version included in Windows XP. From Windows Me, the new version of Windows Media Player provides only a modest incitement to upgrade, whereas from earlier versions of Windows 9x, it provides much more encouragement—assuming you're interested in multimedia, that is.

Whichever version of Windows you're using, you'll need to make sure that your hardware is up to scratch for Windows XP. Very generally speaking, if your computer is capable of running Windows 98 or Windows Me at a decent clip, it should be able to run Windows XP without much trouble (though you might need to add memory).

You'll find details of Windows XP's hardware requirements in Chapter 2.

Windows 3.1

If you're still using Windows 3.1 and DOS as your main operating system, Windows XP Home Edition represents a considerable upgrade. There are two major considerations in taking this step:

- ▶ Unless you've installed Windows 3.1 on a modern system (as you might have done for backward-compatibility with ancient programs), you'll almost certainly need to get a new PC to run Windows XP. You *could* upgrade an older system, but it'd be a real grandfather's ax of an upgrade: hard drive, processor, RAM, graphics card... (Don't you remember the anecdote? There's this guy in the bar (or wherever) who says "I have my grandfather's ax. My father replaced the handle, and I gave it a new blade. But it still cuts great!" Your upgraded Windows 3.1 computer would be like that ax.)

- ▶ If you will need to continue running DOS programs and 16-bit Windows programs (rather than upgrading to 32-bit programs that provide similar functionality), check to make sure that these programs are compatible with Windows XP before upgrading. As mentioned earlier, Windows XP runs older 32-bit Windows programs quite impressively, but it has problems with some 16-bit programs.

Windows 2000 Professional

If you're currently using Windows 2000 Professional and are happy with it, stick with it for the time being. The "natural" upgrade path from Windows 2000 Professional is to Windows XP Professional Edition, but make this upgrade only after carefully evaluating the benefits that Windows XP Professional will provide. If Windows 2000 Professional is currently fulfilling all your computing needs, stick with it.

SHOULD YOU UPGRADE TO WINDOWS XP PROFESSIONAL EDITION INSTEAD?

So you've decided that Windows XP offers features that you must have—but should you get Windows XP Home Edition or Windows XP Professional

Edition? This section discusses the biggest differences between the two. This isn't an exhaustive breakdown of all the differences—just the ones that will probably affect your decision the most.

Intended Usage

As its name suggests (and is designed to suggest), Windows XP Professional is geared toward use in a professional setting—for example, in an office or in a corporate setting. That doesn't mean you can't use it at home if you want, just that it has features designed for use in office and corporate settings. For example, it's designed to connect to Windows 2000 servers running Active Directory domains, and it has features for being managed remotely by administrators. Professional also has features for using a portable computer as a complement to a desktop computer (rather than instead of a desktop computer) and lets you easily synchronize files between two computers.

By contrast, Windows XP Home is designed for home use. It features more relaxed security settings than Windows XP Professional, comes set up for sharing files and folders easily among users of the same computer, and has no interest in being managed remotely by administrators or anyone else.

Cost

As you'd expect, Windows XP Professional is more expensive than Windows XP Home, though if you need the extra features it offers, it's affordable enough. But you'll certainly want to avoid first buying Windows XP Home and then upgrading to Windows XP Professional.

Hardware Requirements

Windows XP Professional runs adequately on the same hardware as Windows XP Home. While Professional doesn't actually *need* better hardware than Home, it probably *appreciates* better hardware more than Home does, because its extra features (detailed after the next section) need some extra memory and processing power.

Upgrade Paths to Windows XP

You can upgrade to Windows XP Professional from Windows 98, Windows 98 Second Edition, Windows Me, Windows NT 4 Workstation, and

Windows 2000 Professional. You can upgrade to Windows XP Home from only Windows 98, Windows 98 Second Edition, and Windows Me.

Windows XP Professional Features

Professional is essentially a superset of Home: It has all the features that Home has, plus extra features. You can also look at this the other way around, and say that Home is a subset of Professional. In some ways, this might be truer, as Home can be regarded as Professional with a number of features—some very attractive, some less so—taken out.

The following list details the features that Professional has that Home does not have, in descending order of excitement.

Multiple monitor support—for both desktops and laptops
Several versions of Windows have had multiple monitor support for desktops: By installing two or more graphics cards, each hooked up to a monitor, you can spread your Desktop across two or more monitors, giving you far more space to view multiple programs. Windows XP Professional includes multiple monitor support like its predecessors, while Windows XP Home supports only a single monitor. Windows XP Professional also includes a new technology called DualView, which lets you hook up two monitors to a single graphics card that supports two interfaces. Relatively few AGP and PCI graphics cards support two interfaces, though you'll find a number of cards with digital outputs (for LCD panels) that have a regular VGA connector as well. Most of the excitement here is for laptops, most of which have a connector for an external display as well as the internal connector for the built-in screen. Instead of using the external display to display the same image as the built-in screen, you can use DualView to make the external display an extension of your Desktop. This is a wonderful feature for laptop users who crave more screen space.

Personal Web Server and Internet Information Services
Windows XP Professional includes Personal Web Server and Internet Information Services, which let you run a modest-scale Web server on XP.

Fax sharing   As mentioned earlier in the chapter, Windows XP Home has strong fax features for the individual user. Windows XP Professional goes one better by letting you

share a fax/modem with other computers: Your computer can
provide fax services to other computers to which it is networked, or your computer can send a fax via a fax/modem on
another computer. These features can save a great deal of time
and effort, not to mention phone lines.

Backup and Automated System Recovery (ASR)
Windows XP Professional includes a Backup utility and an Automated System Recovery feature that can be activated from boot-
up to restore a damaged system. Windows XP Home doesn't have
these features—though, as mentioned earlier in this chapter,
Windows XP Home does have the System Restore feature for
rolling back the installation of bad drivers and programs.

Offline files   Offline files let you cache (store) copies of files
located on network drives on your local drive so that you can
work with them when your computer is no longer connected to
the network. Windows XP Professional can encrypt the Offline
Files database to help keep the information in the files secure.
Windows XP Home doesn't offer offline files.

Multiprocessor support   Windows XP Professional Edition
offers multiprocessor support, while Home doesn't. You probably won't care about this omission in Home unless you're one
of the (very) few people who have a multiprocessor computer at
home, but in a way it's rather sad, because the multiprocessor
code is all written and available—Microsoft just decided to take
this functionality out of Home, presumably to provide another
point of differentiation with Professional. So if you do have a
multiprocessor machine, and you want to use both processors,
you need Professional rather than Home. (You might also consider Linux, which will love the extra processor and will cost
you less.)

Remote Desktop   Windows XP Professional offers Remote
Desktop technology, while Home doesn't. Remote Desktop is a
little confusing because of the terminology. The Remote Desktop component lets you make a computer available for remote
control. Professional has this capability; Home doesn't. The
Remote Desktop *Connection* component lets you use a computer to access a remote computer that's running Remote Desktop. Both Professional and Home have Remote Desktop

Connection. So you can use a computer running Home to access a computer running Professional, but not the other way around. If you need to be able to connect to your computer remotely via Remote Desktop Connection, you need Professional rather than Home. (Alternatively, you can use NetMeeting's remote features to control a Home computer, or one of the many third-party remote-control packages.)

Ability to upgrade from more versions of Windows   You can upgrade to Windows XP Professional from Windows 98, Windows 98 Second Edition, Windows NT 4 Workstation, and Windows 2000 Professional.

Security features   Windows XP Professional includes a number of security features that Windows XP Home lacks. For example, Windows XP Professional lets you control access at the level of individual files as well as folders, while with Windows XP Home, you can control access only at the folder level. Windows XP Professional supports the Encrypting File System (EFS) for encrypting files on the local disk; Windows XP Home does not support EFS.

Networking features   Windows XP Professional has many networking features that Windows XP Home does not. These include the Simple Network Management Protocol (SNMP), the Client Service for NetWare, Simple TCP/IP Services, and the Multiple Roaming feature. If you need to connect to a NetWare server, or if you need to use roaming profiles, you'll need Windows XP Professional rather than Windows XP Home.

Management features   Windows XP Professional has extensive management features that allow remote administration. Windows XP Home can't log on to an Active Directory domain, so it doesn't have management features associated with domains and remote administration. For example, Windows XP Home doesn't support Group Policy or Microsoft's IntelliMirror feature. Similarly, Windows XP Professional can wake up a laptop via a Card-Bus LAN card, while Windows XP Home cannot.

One other thing—there will be a 64-bit version of Windows XP Professional for the Intel Itanium processor. By contrast, Windows XP Home runs only on 32-bit Pentiums and their equivalents.

WHAT'S NEXT

This chapter has discussed what you need to know about Windows XP Home Edition in order to decide whether to upgrade to it, stay with your current version of Windows, or buy Windows XP Professional Edition instead.

In the next chapter, Robert Cowart discusses how to install Windows XP Home Edition, both as an upgrade and as a clean installation from scratch.

Chapter 2

INSTALLING WINDOWS XP

Chances are good that your computer came installed with Windows XP already, in which case reading this chapter isn't necessary for you. On the other hand, if you are still using an earlier version of Windows, or you have no version of Windows on your computer at all, you'll want to read this chapter.

If at some point after you install Windows you discover that you are missing some of the components discussed in this book, you can install them later from the Windows Control Panel's Add/Remove Programs applet, as explained in Chapter 5, "Installing and Running Programs."

Adapted from *Mastering Windows Me* by Robert Cowart

ISBN 0-7821-2857-2   960 pages $39.99

WHAT'S YOUR SITUATION?

You can upgrade from an existing version of Windows or install Windows XP onto a clean hard disk. You can install it from a Windows XP CD-ROM or from installation files on a network or other hard disk.

If you have a choice, the best way is to use the Windows XP CD-ROM to upgrade your present Windows version, because you'll be able to keep all your present settings and you won't need to reinstall your applications.

Microsoft has done a laudable job of making the Windows XP installation process pretty painless, thanks to the Setup Wizard, which provides a pleasant question-and-answer interface. Therefore, I'll spare you the boredom of walking you through *every* step here on paper. Rather, I'll get you going and discuss some of the decisions you'll have to make along the way.

TIP

Setup requires a 300 MHz processor (233 MHz minimum), 128MB of RAM, and approximately 1.5GB of hard disk space to complete.

WARNING

Microsoft strongly suggests that you back up any important existing data and programs before you upgrade to Windows XP, just to be safe.

UPGRADING FROM AN EARLIER VERSION OF WINDOWS

You can upgrade to Windows XP Home Edition from Windows 95, Windows 98, Windows 2000, or Windows Me. (You can't upgrade from Windows XP Professional.)

Before beginning, make sure you have at least 1.5GB of free hard-disk space on the drive you're going to install Windows XP on. You can use Windows Explorer or the DOS dir command to check this.

When you insert the Windows XP CD-ROM into a computer running an earlier version of Windows, a message appears asking what you want to do.

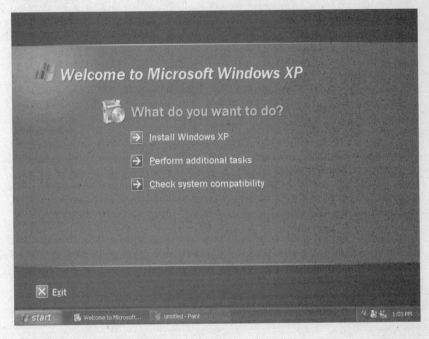

You can click Install Windows XP to start the Setup program right away, or click one of the other options.

Checking for Compatibility

Windows XP is trouble-free when you have hardware that supports it, so before you upgrade to Windows XP you might want to check for compatibility. If you don't run this test and install Windows anyway, it might not install properly, it might install but some devices might not work correctly afterward, or the computer may lock up immediately or intermittently.

To run the compatibility check from the opening screen shown in the preceding section:

1. Click Check System Compatibility.

2. Click Check My System Automatically. The utility will catalog the hardware installed on your PC and compare it to a list to make sure all your hardware is supported.

3. A box appears letting you know the results. Click Finish.

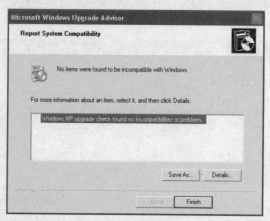

4. Click Back to return to the main menu of choices.

If it found any incompatible items, you will need to remove them or get updated drivers for them before you can successfully install Windows XP.

Starting the Setup Utility

When you are ready to upgrade, do the following:

1. Click Install Windows XP. A Welcome to Windows Setup window appears, with Upgrade preselected as the installation type. Click Next to get started.

2. Next, you'll see a license agreement. If you agree to the terms, click I Accept This Agreement, then click Next.

3. You'll be prompted to enter the Product Key, which is a 25-digit number you should have received with your Windows XP CD. After you enter it, click Next again.

4. Next it asks whether you want to download updated Setup files. If you have an Internet connection available, leave Yes selected. Otherwise click No. Then click Next.

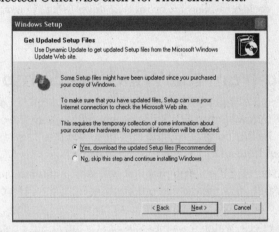

Setup now restarts your PC, and it enters a setup mode designed to copy the needed files quickly and efficiently. It copies files from the CD to your hard disk, and a status bar keeps you abreast of the progress of the file-copying operation. This phase takes several minutes. When it is finished, the PC restarts again, and more file-copying takes place, for about 20 minutes.

INSTALLING WINDOWS XP FROM SCRATCH

You may prefer to install Windows XP "from scratch" if one of the following conditions exists:

▶ You have no version of Windows on the machine.

▶ You already have a previous version of Windows on another hard disk in the same PC, and you want to be able to dual-boot (that is, choose which Windows version you want, each time the computer starts up). To do this, the Windows versions must be on separate hard disks; they cannot share one disk.

TIP

If you have a very large hard disk, and it's partitioned as a single drive, you could break it up into two or more drives using a program like Partition Magic, and then install Windows XP on the new partition.

Booting from the Windows Setup CD-ROM

To install Windows XP on a blank hard disk, you'll boot from the Windows Setup CD. To do so, simply start up the computer with the Windows Setup CD in your drive. You'll see: Press any key to boot from CD.

Do so, and the Setup program will start automatically from the CD. If you don't see a message about booting from the CD, your BIOS will need to be configured to boot from CD.

To check, watch for a message at startup about pressing a certain key to enter Setup. Then do it. The setup program that runs is the BIOS setup—the setup program for your motherboard. Look for a Boot Sequence or similar setting, and make sure it's set to boot from the CD. Then save your changes and exit to reboot.

If your BIOS does not support booting from a CD, you must contact the motherboard manufacturer to obtain the proper procedure for *flashing,* or upgrading your BIOS.

Continuing the Setup Program

When the Windows XP setup program gets underway, a blue Welcome to Setup screen appears, like the one in the following graphic. Press Enter to begin setting up Windows.

Part i

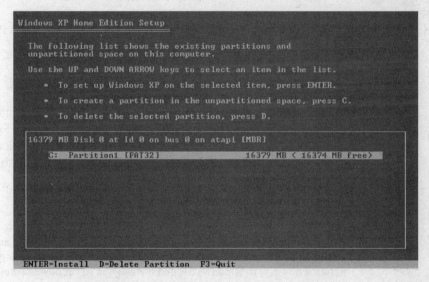

```
Windows XP Home Edition Setup

Welcome to Setup.

This portion of the Setup program prepares Microsoft(R)
Windows(R) XP to run on your computer.

    • To set up Windows XP now, press ENTER.
    • To repair a Windows XP installation using
      Recovery Console, press R.
    • To quit Setup without installing Windows XP, press F3.
```

Then follow these steps:

1. A license agreement appears. Press F8 to accept it.

2. A list of the current disk partitions on your system appears.
   If you have only one hard disk and it has only one partition,
   you'll have just one entry here, as shown below.

```
Windows XP Home Edition Setup

The following list shows the existing partitions and
unpartitioned space on this computer.

Use the UP and DOWN ARROW keys to select an item in the list.

    • To set up Windows XP on the selected item, press ENTER.
    • To create a partition in the unpartitioned space, press C.
    • To delete the selected partition, press D.

┌─────────────────────────────────────────────────────────────┐
│ 16379 MB Disk 0 at Id 0 on bus 0 on atapi [MBR]              │
│     C:  Partition1 [FAT32]               16379 MB ( 16374 MB free) │
│                                                               │
│                                                               │
│                                                               │
│                                                               │
└─────────────────────────────────────────────────────────────┘

ENTER=Install   D=Delete Partition   F3=Quit
```

If, on the other hand, you have multiple partitions, you can
install Windows XP on any of them. If you install it on the
same partition as an existing version of Windows, your
existing version will no longer work, so make sure you
choose a different partition if you plan to dual-boot.

You can also press **D** to delete the current partition and create new partitions for an existing drive if you prefer.

NOTE

Windows XP makes dual-boot setup very easy; it configures everything automatically for you when you install Windows XP on a different drive from an existing operating system.

3. Next it asks what file system you want to use. If placing Windows on an empty partition, choose Format the Partition Using the NTFS File System (Quick). If placing Windows on a partition that contains information you want to keep, choose Leave the Current File System Intact.

WARNING

If you are dual-booting this PC with Windows 9x/Me, you will not be able to access an NTFS partition from within those operating systems.

4. If you chose to format the disk in Step 3, press **F** to format it.

Windows begins copying the needed files to the hard disk. This takes several minutes. Then Windows restarts in a more graphical mode.

5. Follow the prompts to continue the installation. It is very similar to the Upgrade setup described earlier, except it asks for information toward the end of the process—your installation key, name, initials, and so on. Just follow along, filling in the blanks.

NOTE

The first time Windows runs after you install it, you'll be prompted to activate your copy of Windows. You can do it either over the Internet or by telephone. Activation is new to Windows XP, and is designed to cut down on software piracy. It generates a unique numeric code based on the serial number of your copy of Windows and on the hardware installed in your PC, and then registers your copy of Windows to that code. You cannot install the same copy of Windows on a different PC; the hardware will be different and activation will not be allowed. You can use Windows XP for 30 days without activating it, but after 30 days it will not start anymore. If you install new hardware and then reinstall Windows, and you have problems with activation, you can call Microsoft and they will help you.

CONFIGURING WINDOWS AFTER SETUP

When Setup has completed, your computer will restart one more time and then you'll see a blue Welcome to Microsoft Windows screen. Click Next, and work through the prompts it presents you with:

1. When prompted to activate Windows, if you have an Internet connection available now, click Yes. If you don't, click No. (You will be reminded to activate later.) Then click Next.

2. If you chose to activate, you're asked whether you want to register with Microsoft now. (This is optional.) Click Yes or No, and then click Next. You won't see this if you chose No in Step 1.

3. If you chose to register in Step 2, a form appears to fill out. Do so, and click Next. You won't see this if you chose No in Step 2.

4. Continue working through the screens by clicking Next until you get to the final one; then click Finish. The exact screens that appear will depend on your choices in Steps 1-3 and whether you are upgrading or installing from scratch.

If you are installing from scratch, it asks you to enter your name and the names of other people who will be using this computer, and it sets up user accounts for them.

DUAL-BOOTING IN WINDOWS XP

You don't need to do anything special to set up dual-booting in Windows XP—that is, having a choice of which operating system to start. When you install Windows XP on a computer that already has an operating system installed (on a different drive), a menu automatically appears each time you start the computer, asking which operating system you want. After 30 seconds, it starts the default operating system (probably Windows XP) without intervention.

WHAT'S NEXT

Now that Windows is installed and ready to roll on your PC, let's move on. The next chapter, "Exploring the Windows XP Desktop," demystifies the Windows screen, and explains windows, dialog boxes, menus, and the other major features of the interface.

Chapter 3
Exploring the Windows XP Home Edition Desktop

This chapter explains how to start and exit Windows and the purpose of some of the items you see on-screen. You'll also learn how to open the built-in Help and Support system and how to look up information in it.

This chapter also teaches you about the parts of a window and how to open, close, resize, and reposition a window on your screen. You'll also learn how to work with menus and toolbars in a window, and how to make selections in dialog boxes that open as a result of selecting a menu command or clicking a toolbar button.

Adapted from *Windows XP Home Edition Simply Visual* by Faithe Wempen
ISBN 0-7821-2982-X   448 pages $24.99

STARTING WINDOWS

Windows XP Home Edition starts automatically when you turn on your computer—you don't need to do anything special to start it. Windows takes from 1 to 3 minutes to load when you turn on the computer, and while it loads, you see messages and introductory graphics on the screen.

When Windows finishes loading, you see the Windows desktop, which is discussed further in the next section.

If the PC happens to be set up for multiple users, a screen appears before you get to the desktop, asking which user you are. Just click your username to continue, or click Guest if you don't have a username.

LEARNING THE PARTS OF THE SCREEN

If you are brand-new to the Windows operating system, this section will help you get up to speed on basic navigation and terminology.

The *desktop* is the background you see on-screen. When you first install Windows XP, the picture on the background shows a green-meadow landscape, but you can change that picture (as you'll learn in

Chapter 10) or remove the picture entirely, leaving a solid-color background. Everything that happens in Windows starts from the desktop, and most of the other parts of the screen are connected to it.

Start Button and Start Menu

The Start button, in the lower-left corner, is your gateway to the programs you can run and the settings you can adjust. When you click the Start button, a two-column menu opens.

In the left column are frequently used programs, along with an All Programs option. Click All Programs to see a complete list of programs you can run. To run one of the programs on the All Programs list or in the left column, simply click it. You'll learn more about running programs in Chapter 5.

NOTE

If you've used earlier versions of Windows, the Windows XP Start menu might seem strange to you. If you prefer, you can go back to the look and feel of the Classic Start menu. To do so, right-click the Start button and choose Properties. Then click Classic Start Menu and click OK.

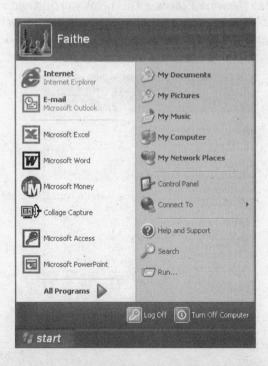

At the top of the right column are shortcuts to various special-purpose folders:

My Documents   This is a storage folder for data files you create in applications, such as Microsoft Word and Microsoft Excel. (Chapter 5 covers working with programs.)

My Pictures   This is a storage folder for photographs you have scanned or transferred from a digital camera. (See Chapter 24.)

My Music   This is a storage folder for music and video clips used in Windows Media Player. (See Chapter 23.)

My Computer   This opens a file management window in which you can browse all the drives on your computer. (See Chapter 6.)

TIP

Earlier versions of Windows included a My Computer icon on the desktop. If you miss that, you can create a My Computer shortcut on the desktop, as explained in Chapter 4.

My Network Places   This helps you find and view files and folders on other computers in your *local area network (LAN)*, if you have one. (See Chapter 20.) This shortcut doesn't appear if you don't have a network.

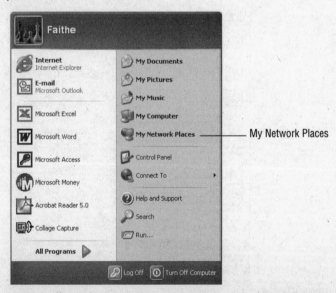

Farther down in the right column is an assortment of useful commands, each of which is covered later in the book:

Control Panel   This enables you to customize how Windows looks and performs. It's covered in Chapters 9 and 10.

Help and Support   This opens the Help and Support Services window, where you can get information about Windows functionality. It's covered later in this chapter.

Search   This helps you locate a file or folder stored on one of your PC's drives. See Chapter 6.

Run   This opens a text box in which you can type a command that you want to run. This is an advanced feature that beginners will seldom use.

At the bottom of the Start menu are buttons for logging off and for turning off, or shutting down, the computer. Shutting down is covered later in this chapter. Logging off is applicable only if you have multiple users set up; see Chapter 11.

Icons

Icons are the small pictures that sit on the desktop. They represent files, folders, or applications to which you might want quick access. Windows XP comes with a Recycle Bin icon on the desktop, and you can add your own favorite items there, too (see Chapter 10).

NOTE

Other programs you install may also add icons to the desktop; for example, if you have Microsoft Office installed, a Microsoft Outlook icon appears on the desktop.

Some icons represent the actual file or folder, such that deleting the icon on the desktop will delete the original item. Other icons are merely *shortcuts*, or pointers, to the original item. Shortcut icons can be distinguished from regular icons by the small, curved arrow in the corner. Deleting a shortcut icon does nothing to the original item.

Taskbar

The taskbar is the horizontal bar at the bottom of the screen. The Start button is at the left end, and a clock is at the right end. In the middle are rectangular bars for any open applications or other windows. (If you don't have anything open, this area will be empty.)

NOTE

In earlier Windows versions, a Quick Launch toolbar appeared by default to the right of the Start button. Right-click the taskbar and choose Toolbars ➢ Quick Launch to use it now.

You can switch between windows by clicking the bar for the window you want to work with. Chapter 5 goes into that in more detail.

The area to the immediate left of the clock is the *system tray*, displaying the icons for any programs that are running in the background.

NOTE

If you see a left-arrow (‹) button there, it means that some of the system tray icons are hidden; you can click that button to display them. When the system tray is open, the button changes to ›.

Using Help and Support

Windows XP doesn't come with a printed manual, but all the information that would have gone into a manual (and more) is available through the Help and Support utility.

To open Help and Support, follow these steps:

1. Click the Start button, then click Help and Support.

2. The Help and Support Center window opens.

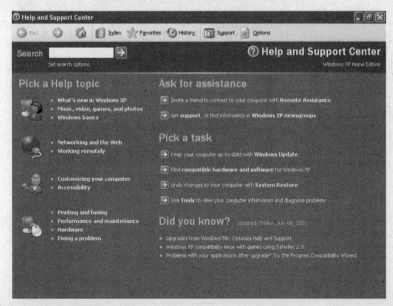

TIP

You can press the F1 key as a shortcut to performing these steps.

There are several ways to locate information in the Help and Support Center window, as the following sections explain.

Browsing Help Topics

From the main Help and Support Center window, you can browse some popular topics much as you might skim a book to look for a subject of interest. Just follow these steps:

1. In the left column, click a topic to browse, such as Windows Basics, for example. This opens a two-pane window.

2. In the left pane, click the subject area you want. A list of help articles appears in the right pane. Click the name of the help article you want to read, such as Start a Program.

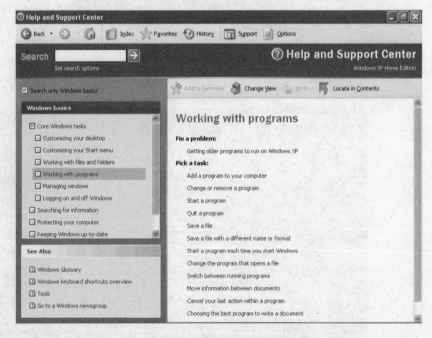

NOTE

When you point to a title, the mouse pointer turns into a hand, just as when you're working with hyperlinks on a Web page. Chapter 15 talks more about Web pages.

3. The article you clicked appears in the right-hand pane.

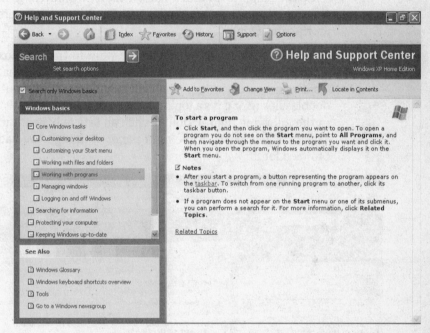

4. (Optional) If you want to return to the preceding screen, click the Back button in the top toolbar.

You can return to the opening screen at any time by clicking the Home button.

NOTE

See "Working with Help Topics" later in this chapter to learn about the features of the help articles themselves, including what the various colors of underlined text signify.

Using the Help Index

If you know the name of the feature you want to learn about, you can look it up in the index. Just as in a book, the index is an alphabetical listing of terms.

1. In the Help and Support Center window, click Index. The left pane displays an index list. (If there was anything in the right pane from a previous activity, it remains there for the time being.)

2. Begin typing the word or phrase you want in the text box above the list. The index list will automatically scroll to that word's portion of the list. When you see the word you want, double-click it; or if it's a topic heading (such as "passwords" in the following figure), double-click an article beneath it. That article appears in the right pane, as though you had browsed for it.

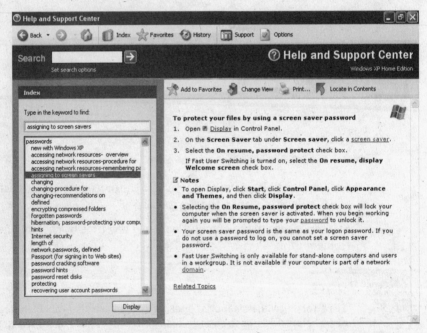

3. Some topics display a Topics Found dialog box when you double-click them, listing multiple topics that feature the

word you chose. If that happens, click the article you want to read (in this case, "Change a User's Password") and then click Display.

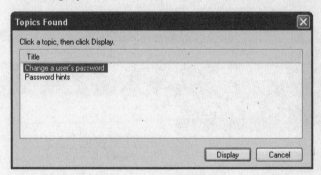

Searching for a Help Topic

If you aren't sure of the official name for what you want to know, try the Search feature. It does a full-text search for a particular word and brings up a list of every topic that contains that word.

For example, suppose you have upgraded from Windows Me, and you miss that little toolbar that used to appear next to the Start button. (It's called the Quick Launch toolbar, by the way, but let's say you don't know that.) You could search for the word *toolbar*, in the hope that something about that missing item will turn up.

NOTE

There is also a search feature in Windows itself that lets you search the complete text of all files on your entire computer. You'll learn about it in Chapter 6.

1. Type a word in the Search text box near the top of the Help and Support Center window and then click the right-arrow button.

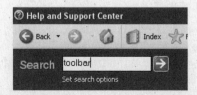

2. In the Search Results pane that appears, click the topic that most closely matches what you want. The article for that topic appears in the right pane, with all instances of the searched-for word highlighted.

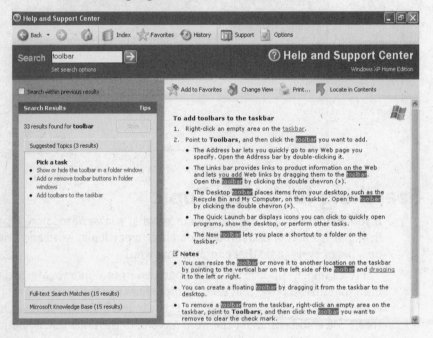

Working with Help Topics

Regardless of how you arrive at a particular help topic, you work with it the same way. The following sections explain what you can do with a help topic after locating it.

Working with Underlined Text

Depending on the article, you might see red-, green-, and/or blue-underlined text in it.

Green-underlined text   Indicates that a definition of the underlined word(s) is available. To see the definition in a pop-up box, click the word. In the figure that follows, the green-underlined word *drag* has been clicked, and, as you can see, its definition has popped up.

- If a program doesn't appear on the **Programs** menu or one of its submenus, you can perform a search for it, create a <u>shortcut</u>, and then

> **drag**
> To move an item on the screen by selecting the item and then pressing and holding down the mouse button while moving the mouse. For example, you can move a window to another location on the screen by dragging its title bar.

Blue-underlined "Related Topics" text   Indicates that there are topics related to the article that you're currently viewing. Click Related Topics to see a list of topics you can jump to. In the following figure, the blue-underlined Related Topics has been clicked. Notice that the underlining goes away when the associated list appears.

Related Topics

> Add a destination to the Send To menu
> Copy a user profile
> Delete a user profile
> Send files and folders to another place quickly
> Switch between a roaming and local user profile

NOTE

Blue-underlined Related Topics text turns red when you move the mouse over it.

Blue-underlined text with an arrow symbol   Indicates a link to a window or feature in Windows itself. These shortcuts appear in some help topics to give you a head start in performing a task. If you were to click Add or Remove Programs in the example below, the Add or Remove Programs dialog box would appear.

1. Open 🖼 <u>Add or Remove Programs</u> in Control Panel.

NOTE

A blue-underlined link to a program feature turns red after you click the link to open that feature. It remains red even after you close the feature's window.

Changing the Help Window View

By default, the Help and Support Center window takes up the whole screen. If you would like a smaller window, click the Change View button. This hides the left pane, leaving only the right one (the one containing the help article).

Printing a Help Topic

We'll get into printing in more detail in Chapter 8, but here's a quick pre-view—enough to get you started printing the information you find in the help system.

1. Display the help topic you want to print, then click the Print button.

2. The Print dialog box opens. Change any of the print settings if needed, then click Print.

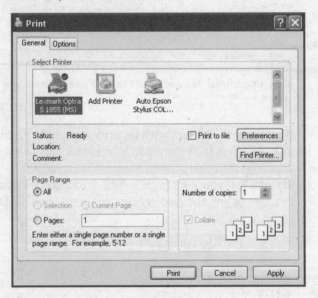

To close the Print dialog box without printing, click Cancel. You'll learn more about dialog boxes later in this chapter.

Browsing Support Options

In Windows XP, Microsoft has changed the name of the help system to Help *and Support,* and there's a reason for that. You can click Support to display a selection of topics that detail how you can get more help if you still have a question or problem after reviewing the help system's offerings.

To check out the support features, follow these steps:

1. Click the Support button.

2. Several categories of support options appear in the left pane. Click the one you want. For example, you might click Get Help from Microsoft. In the following figure, I have clicked that, and it has connected me to a Web page that's now asking for my contact information so that help can be provided.

NOTE

If you choose Ask a Friend to Help, you'll be guided through the Remote Assistance feature, which is covered in detail in Chapter 19.

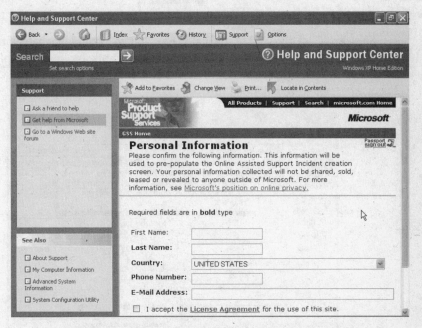

3. Work through the prompts to ask a question, look up information, or whatever you need to do.

Closing the Help System

 When you are finished using the Help and Support Center window, click the red Close button to close it.

NOTE

If you have changed your desktop appearance or scheme, the Close button may not be red. Chapter 10 explains desktop appearance options.

Using What's This?

Besides the formal help system that you've just seen, you can also get informal, on-the-spot help in many dialog boxes. Whenever you see a question mark in the top-right corner of a window, you can do the following:

1. Click the question-mark button. The mouse pointer changes to an arrow with a question mark.

2. Click the part of the dialog box that you would like help with. If help is available for that object, it appears. For example, here the Name box was clicked, and then, as you can see, a help box popped up.

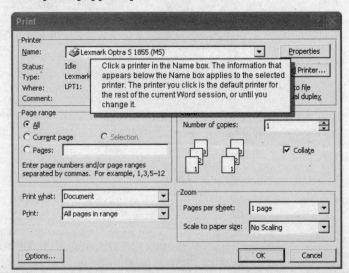

Shutting Down Windows

When you are finished using your PC, you shouldn't just turn off the power, because that could cause later problems in Windows. Instead, you should use the Shut Down command on the Start menu to ensure that Windows shuts down in an orderly way that closes all open files and saves your work in any open programs.

When shutting down, you have two options: Turn Off and Restart. If you are going to be away from the PC, you will probably want to turn it off. If the computer is acting strangely and you want to start fresh, you will want to restart.

Turning Off or Restarting the PC

Follow these steps to turn off or restart the PC:

1. Click the Start button. The Start menu opens.

2. Click Turn Off Computer.

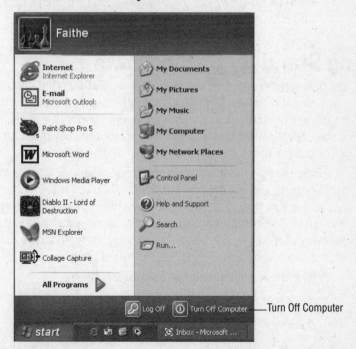

Part i

3. A box appears, asking what you want to do. Click Turn Off or Restart, depending on which you want to do.

The third option, Stand By, puts the PC in a low-power-usage mode but leaves it turned on. See the following section.

If you chose Turn Off, Windows shuts down; and, if your computer will allow it, Windows turns off the computer's power switch. If not, a message appears on-screen instructing you to turn off the power yourself. (Don't forget that the monitor has a separate power switch.) If you chose Restart, the PC resets itself and reloads Windows. (It takes about 1 minute.)

Using Stand By or Hibernate

Some computers have power management features that enable you to put them in a low-power, "sleeping" state when you aren't using them, rather than shut them down entirely. Some people prefer this to shutting down the computer—it helps them save electricity but they don't have to wait for Windows to reload when they return to the computer.

While the computer is in this state, any programs you were using remain open, along with any data files. When you want to start working again, you just press a button and everything springs awake again, just as you left it. The computer still uses a tiny bit of power to maintain its memory of the system's status, but the big energy-burning components shut down, such as the display and the hard disks.

Follow these steps to put the computer to sleep:

1. Click the Start button. The Start menu opens.

2. Click Turn Off Computer.

3. Click Stand By.

Then, when you are ready to wake the computer up, simply press its power button. (Don't hold it down; just press and release.) The computer springs back to life.

WARNING

In earlier versions of Windows, some computers occasionally had trouble waking up from Stand By. The computer would appear to be "dead" because it wouldn't come out of its sleep state. If you experience this, try holding down the computer's power button for 5 seconds to force it to restart. Then contact your PC manufacturer to see if a fix is available.

Hibernate has the same end result as stand by, but works differently. Hibernate uses a small amount of hard-disk space to store the contents of the computer's memory before shutting down completely. Then, when it wakes up from hibernation, it reads that data from the hard disk and rewrites it back to memory, and suddenly you are exactly where you left off.

Because Hibernate stores memory content to the hard disk, the computer doesn't use any power at all while it is hibernating. This is great for laptops because of the limited battery power, but it isn't very useful for desktop PCs because they are always plugged in. Unless you have a laptop, the Hibernate option does not appear by default.

TIP

You can enable or disable Hibernate and set automatic Stand By and Hibernate thresholds using Power Options in Control Panel.

PARTS OF A WINDOW

All windows have some common features, no matter what program you are using or activity you are performing in Microsoft Windows:

Title bar　The colored bar across the top of the window.

Window controls　The three buttons at the right end of the title bar, which you can use to change the size of the window. See the "Minimizing and Maximizing" section later in this chapter.

Menu bar   The row of words directly below the title bar. Each word represents a menu that drops down when you click on it, displaying commands you can issue. See "Working with Menus" later in the chapter.

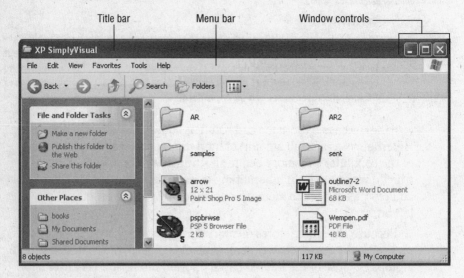

Title bar   Menu bar   Window controls

In addition, some windows have these additional elements:

Toolbars   One or more rows of graphical buttons that provide shortcuts to common activities in the program you are working with.

Status bar   A thin bar at the bottom of the window, in which status messages appear. This bar's exact content changes depending on the program or activity.

Explorer bar   A pane that shows details about the selected file(s) or folder(s) in a *file management window*.

Scroll bar   A bar that appears to the right of (or sometimes below) the window content when there is more content than can fit in the window at once. It enables you to scroll the undisplayed content into view. For details, see "Scrolling a Window's Content" later in this chapter.

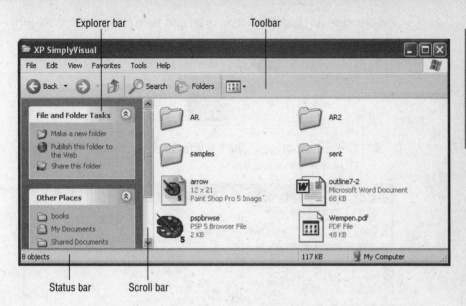

Explorer bar   Toolbar

Status bar   Scroll bar

OPENING AND CLOSING A WINDOW

Nearly every activity in Windows XP causes a window to open. You can open a window containing a program by starting the program from the Start menu, as you will learn in Chapter 5. You can open a file management window by opening My Computer, covered in Chapter 6. In addition, most of the icons on the desktop represent files or utilities you can open in a window by double-clicking them.

Regardless of how you opened the window, you can close it by clicking the Close button (the big red X) in the top-right corner.

NOTE

The Close button may not be red if you're not using the default desktop appearance settings. See Chapter 10 to learn about changes you can make that will cause windows and other on-screen objects to have a different look.

For practice, do the following to open and then close the Recycle Bin window:

1. Double-click the Recycle Bin icon on the desktop.

2. You should now see the Recycle Bin window. Click the Close (X) button to close it.

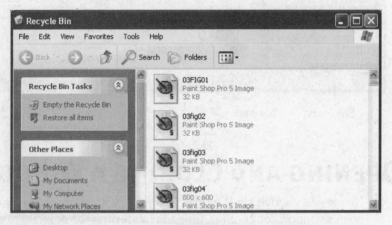

MINIMIZING AND MAXIMIZING

Most windows have two other buttons besides the Close button at the right end of the title bar: Minimize and Maximize. These buttons hide the window and enlarge it to its maximum size, respectively.

Minimizing a Window

Minimizing a window hides it so that it doesn't take up space on-screen, but doesn't close it. If you have many windows open at once, you might want to minimize some of them to reduce the clutter on your Windows desktop.

The minimized window appears in the taskbar at the bottom of the screen, and you can *restore* it by clicking its name there.

To try minimizing a window, do the following:

1. Double-click the Recycle Bin icon to reopen the Recycle Bin window.

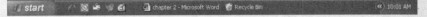

2. Click the Minimize button in the top-right corner of the Recycle Bin window.

3. The Recycle Bin window disappears, but its name still appears in the taskbar. To restore the window, click the name there.

Part i

NOTE

Many beginners get confused about closing versus minimizing. Closing clears the window and its contents from the computer's memory completely. If you were working on a document, for example, and you closed its window, you would need to restart your word processing program and reopen that document if you wanted to make more changes to it. Minimizing hides the window, but the window remains open and its content remains active; you can redisplay it by simply clicking its name in the taskbar.

Maximizing a Window

Maximizing a window enlarges it so that it fills the entire screen. You might want to maximize a window containing a word processing document you are working on, for example, so that you can see more of the document on-screen at once.

When you maximize a window, the Maximize button is replaced with a Restore button. You can use this button to return the window to its normal size when you are finished working with it in maximized form.

NOTE

In the next section, you'll learn how to change the window's nonmaximized size and position. Those settings aren't applicable for a maximized window because it has only one size—full-screen—and only one position.

To maximize and then restore the Recycle Bin window you've been practicing with, for example:

1. Click the Maximize button. The window enlarges to fill the entire screen.

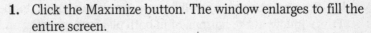

2. Click the Restore button. The window returns to its original size.

MOVING AND RESIZING A WINDOW

A nonmaximized window (that is, one that doesn't fill the entire screen) can be moved and resized to fit your needs. For example, you might want to move a window out of the way so you can access an icon on the desktop, or to make a window larger or smaller to accommodate the content in it.

Moving a Window

To move a window, drag it by its title bar. The title bar functions as a "handle" for repositioning the window anywhere you want it.

Resizing a Window

You can resize a window by dragging the left, right, or bottom border. When you position the mouse pointer over a border, the pointer changes to a double-headed arrow, indicating that you can hold down the mouse button and move the mouse to change the window's size.

If you point to a corner of the window, the pointer changes to a diagonal two-headed arrow, and you can change both the height and the width of the window at the same time by dragging.

SCROLLING A WINDOW'S CONTENT

When a window contains more content than can fit at once in the window at its current size, a scroll bar appears. It can appear to the right of the window, at the bottom, or in both places, depending on the program, the amount of undisplayed content, and the arrangement of the content.

NOTE

Scroll bars appear only when there is extra content that won't fit in the window. Therefore, the scroll bar may appear or disappear when you resize a window.

To scroll through the window's content, drag the scroll box up or down (or to the right or left on a horizontal scroll bar). You can also click the arrows at the ends of the scroll bar to scroll in the indicated direction.

NOTE

The window shown here has two panes, and each pane has its own scroll bar.

If there is a lot of undisplayed content, you might find it helpful to scroll through it one "windowful" at a time. To do so, click below the scroll box to scroll down or click above the scroll box to scroll up.

SWITCHING BETWEEN OPEN WINDOWS

Part of Microsoft Windows's appeal is that you can have many windows open at once, each doing its own thing. Only one window is active at a time, however. In the following illustration, the active window is the Calculator; all other windows are inactive. Notice also that in the taskbar, Calculator appears different from the other window names.

The active window's title bar looks different from that of the other windows. In Windows XP's default appearance theme, the difference is subtle; the title bar is simply a little brighter and more vibrant. In other desktop themes, the difference may be more obvious. See Chapter 10 for more on desktop themes. If any part of the window you want is visible on-screen, you can simply click on any visible portion of it to bring it to the front and make it active. For example, to make the My Computer window active in the preceding illustration, you could click on its title bar or on any other part of it.

If, however, the active window is maximized or sized so that it completely obscures the window you want, you must resort to some other way of making the desired window active. One way is to use the taskbar. For example, if I wanted to make the My Computer window active, I'd click its name on the taskbar.

Another way is to use the "Alt+Tab" method. People who are more comfortable using the keyboard than the mouse often prefer this method:

1. Press and hold down the Alt key.

2. Press and release the Tab key. A box appears with an icon for each open window.

3. While holding down the Alt key, press the Tab key to move the selector from one icon to the next. The window's title appears beneath the selected icon.

4. When the desired window's icon is selected, release the Alt key. That window becomes active.

Working with Menus

Menus are great because they help you avoid having to memorize commands that you want to issue. Back in the olden days of MS-DOS, users needed to memorize commands to type, as well as the optional parameters for each command. In a menu-based environment like Windows XP, you can simply open the menu, peruse your options, and make your selection from the list.

You'll find several kinds of menus in Windows XP. The following sections detail each type.

Drop-Down Menus

Almost every window has a menu bar directly beneath its title bar. Each word on the menu bar is the name of a menu.

To open a menu and select a command, follow these steps:

1. Click the menu name to open its menu.

NOTE

If a command on the menu appears gray or dimmed, that command is not currently available. Usually this is because the command requires you to select something before you issue it.

2. Click the command you want. Depending on which command you choose, any of several things could happen:

NOTE

Notice that each menu name and each command has an underlined letter. This is its selection letter. If you prefer using the keyboard, you can hold down the Alt key and press the selection letter to make your selection.

▶ A command could execute.

▶ A feature could be selected from a group of features. Commands with a round dot next to them are selected from a group. When you make another selection in that group, the original selection becomes deselected.

▶ A dialog box could open, requesting additional information about what you want to do. Most commands that open dialog boxes have an ellipsis (...) next to them. You will learn more about dialog boxes later in the chapter.

▶ A submenu with additional commands could pop out. Commands that open submenus have a right-pointing arrow next to them.

▶ A feature could be turned on or off. Commands with check marks beside them are currently on; each time you select one of these commands, the check mark toggles on or off.

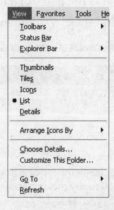

Start Menu

The Start menu is not part of a particular window; it is a Windows XP feature in itself. Clicking the Start button (in the bottom-left corner of the screen) opens the Start menu, from which you can select programs you want to run or activities you want to perform (such as searching for a certain file or changing system settings).

1. Click the Start button. The Start menu opens.

2. If you see what you want on the initial menu, click it. Otherwise, go on to Step 3.

3. Point to All Programs. A menu of the programs installed on the PC appears. Some of the items on the menu represent submenus; others represent the programs themselves. The submenus have right-pointing arrows next to them.

4. Point to a submenu to open it, or click a program to run it. In the example shown, I have selected the Accessories submenu and have also selected Calculator as the program I want to open.

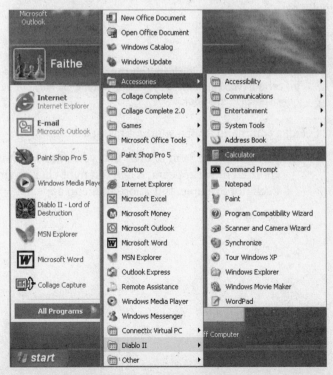

You'll learn more about starting programs in Chapter 5.

Shortcut Menus

For most items in Windows, there are several possible actions. When you double-click (or single-click in some cases), the default action happens. But if you want one of the other actions instead, you must right-click the item to open a shortcut menu.

Which commands you see on the shortcut menu depend on what the mouse pointer was pointing at when you right-clicked—that is, the commands depend on the context. Another name for shortcut menus is *context menus*.

Almost everything in Windows has a shortcut menu associated with it, and the commands on each shortcut menu are appropriate for the specific item. For example, when you right-click a document file, you see commands for renaming, deleting, copying, and so on. In contrast, when you right-click on the taskbar, you see commands for changing settings, arranging windows, and controlling the taskbar's toolbars.

NOTE

Some programs that you install place extra commands on the shortcut menus for certain types of items, so your shortcut menus may not be exactly like the ones shown in this book.

Select a command from a shortcut menu as follows:

1. Right-click the item or area that you want to act upon. The shortcut menu appears. When you right-click on the desktop itself, for example, this shortcut menu appears:

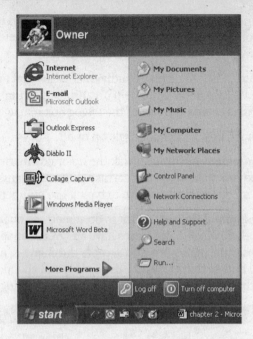

2. Click (with the *left* mouse button) the command you want.

WORKING WITH DIALOG BOXES

Some commands can be executed in a variety of ways, and Windows needs some guidance as to your wishes. Such commands have an ellipsis (...) after their name on the menu and open a dialog box when you select them.

Some dialog boxes are extremely simple, asking a single question and providing only a few *command buttons* for your answer.

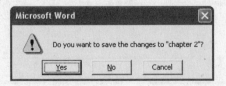

Other dialog boxes have many more settings and many different types of controls with which you may specify your preferences. Here are some of the control types that you might encounter:

Tab   Click to display a individual pages that are full of controls. Tabs are used to help organize large numbers of settings while keeping the size of the dialog box manageable.

Check box   Click to toggle on or off.

Increment buttons   Click the up or down arrows next to a text box to increase or decrease a numeric value incrementally, as an optional alternative to typing the number manually.

Command button   Click to do something apart from this dialog box. Most dialog boxes have an OK command button that closes the dialog box and accepts the changes, as well as a Cancel button that closes the dialog box and abandons the changes. Other command buttons open additional dialog boxes.

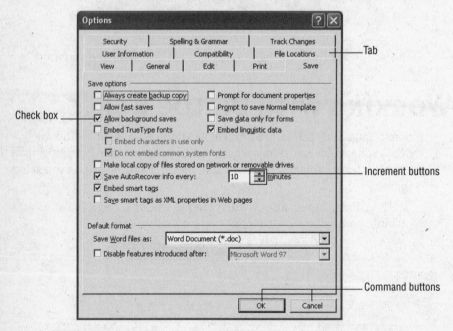

Option button   Click a button to select a single item from a group of options. Like radio buttons on a car, when you make a new selection, the previous selection becomes deselected. (In fact, these button are sometimes called *radio buttons*.)

Text box Type the desired value or setting.

NOTE

Dimmed items in a dialog box are unavailable, as in menus.

Drop-down list Click the down arrow next to the present selection, and then make a new selection from the list that appears.

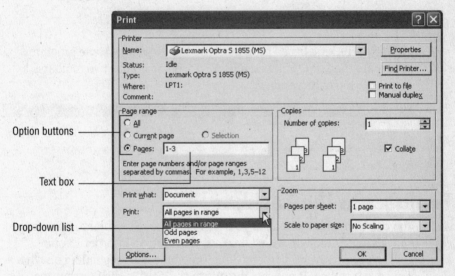

WORKING WITH TOOLBARS

Toolbars are almost as central to the Windows operating system as menus are. You'll find toolbars in Windows XP windows, in application windows, and on the taskbar.

What's the difference between a button and an icon? Recall from earlier in this chapter that an *icon* is a little picture that represents a file, folder, or application. You'll find icons on the desktop and in file management windows, and you double-click them to activate them. You'll see lots of icons in Chapter 6, when you begin working with files and folders. A *button*, in contrast, is a rectangular area on a toolbar that provides a shortcut to a particular command or program feature. Some buttons are graphical (that is, they display a picture); others are text-only. You single-click a button to activate it.

Toolbars in Windows

One of the most common toolbars in Windows XP is the Standard Buttons toolbar. It appears in file management windows, as shown below. You'll learn more about it in Chapter 6.

Many Windows-based programs also have toolbars; some programs have more than one. For example, Microsoft Word has two toolbars across the top of its window:

Toolbars in the Taskbar

You can also have toolbars in your taskbar. The most common one is the Quick Launch toolbar, which displays shortcuts to Internet Explorer, Outlook Express, and perhaps other programs, too, depending on what you have installed. It appears directly to the right of the Start button.

If the Quick Launch toolbar doesn't appear, you can turn it on by doing the following:

1. Right-click the taskbar. A shortcut menu opens.

2. Point to Toolbars. A submenu opens.

3. Click Quick Launch.

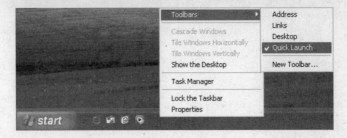

One of the most useful buttons on the Quick Launch toolbar is the Show Desktop button. Clicking it minimizes all open windows, giving you instant access to the desktop. This is handy if you need access to a desktop icon, such as the Recycle Bin, but several open windows are obscuring your view of it.

There are other toolbars available in the taskbar, as you may have noticed from the submenu shown above. None are quite as useful as the Quick Launch toolbar, but you might want to experiment with them on your own:

Address   Provides an Address box into which you can enter the path to a file, folder, or Web page you want to view.

Links   Displays a toolbar based on the Links list from Internet Explorer, providing easy access to some popular Web sites.

Desktop   Displays a toolbar containing the icons on your desktop.

WARNING

If you turn on the display of multiple toolbars in the taskbar, there won't be much room left there for the names of open windows and running programs. I recommend that you use only the Quick Launch toolbar.

WHAT'S NEXT

In this chapter, you got a crash-course in Windows navigation basics, including how to move around in Windows and how to control a window. In the next chapter, you will learn from John Ross how to make and use Windows shortcuts.

Chapter 4
MAKING AND USING SHORTCUTS

In Windows, the term "shortcut" has two distinct meanings. It refers to icons that are pointers to specific programs or data files on your hard disk, and also to key combinations you can press as time-saving alternatives to using menu commands for certain activities. In this chapter, you'll learn about both types of shortcuts.

Adapted from *Windows Me! I Didn't Know You Could Do That...* by John Ross
ISBN: 0-7821-2829-7   272 pages $19.99

DELETE THE SHORTCUTS YOU NEVER USE

Most programs that you install "helpfully" place a shortcut for themselves on the desktop. Over time, this can result in a lot of clutter, as shown in the next figure.

Just because somebody at Microsoft or some other software company decided to place a shortcut on your desktop, that's no reason to keep it there unless you expect to use it. There are probably at least half a dozen icons on your desktop right now that you will never use. They're not useful shortcuts, they're clutter.

Get rid of them.

"But what if I need one of those icons later?" you ask. You can create a new shortcut in 10 seconds. If you don't use it, get rid of it.

Useless shortcuts are like that bottle of cardamom that has been sitting on my spice shelf since 1972. It's just taking up space, and it probably lost its flavor 20 years ago. I should throw it away. If I ever need some cardamom, I'll get a new bottle.

If you use a shortcut everyday, or even every week, it belongs on your desktop. If you use it once a month, it belongs in the Start menu. If you never use it at all, it belongs in the Recycle Bin.

To remove unnecessary icons from your desktop, follow these steps:

1. Take a close look at each icon.

If you don't know what it does, right-click the icon and choose Properties from the pop-up menu. The Shortcut tab contains a description of the target application or data file that opens when you double-click the icon. Click Close when you are finished looking.

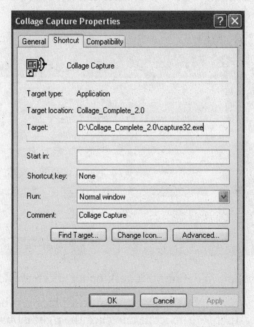

2. If you decide that this icon is a shortcut that you will never use, right-click and choose the Delete option from the pop-up menu.

3. If you decide that you might use this shortcut some day, but you don't need it on the desktop, move it to a Shortcut folder (see the following section) or a submenu in the Start menu. (See Chapter 10 to learn how to add shortcuts to the Start menu.)

If you decide later that you want to restore a deleted shortcut, you can simply recreate it. See "Create New Program Shortcuts" later in this chapter.

CREATE A FOLDER FULL OF SHORTCUTS

If you have a batch of icons on the desktop that are shortcuts to programs you don't use very often, you can create one or more folders on the desktop and move those icons into a new folder.

For example, I like to listen to radio stations from around the world, through the Internet. Rather than keeping the shortcuts on the desktop for all of them, I organize them in a folder, and only that folder appears on the desktop. I can double-click that folder at any time to see its content, as shown below.

To create a folder on your desktop for shortcuts, follow these steps:

1. Move your mouse cursor to a place on the desktop where there are no icons and click the right mouse button.

2. Choose the New option from the pop-up menu and select Folder from the submenu. A folder icon called New Folder will appear on your desktop, with the name selected.

3. Type a name for the folder and press Enter.

4. Double-click the New Folder icon to open the folder.

5. Drag the icons you want to move to the folder from the desktop to the folder window.

6. Close the folder window.

CREATE NEW PROGRAM SHORTCUTS

Now that you have eliminated the icons that you don't want on your desktop, you can also add some new shortcuts that open programs and data files that you do use all the time. For example, if you use a Windows utility such as WordPad a lot, you might want to add a shortcut to that program.

To create a new shortcut to a program, follow these steps:

1. Find the target program in your Start menu, in My Computer, or in a Windows Explorer folder window.

2. Right-drag it to the desktop (that is, drag using the right mouse button).

3. Release the mouse button, and a pop-up menu appears. On it, choose Create Shortcuts Here.

4. If desired, rename the shortcut. To do so, right-click the shortcut icon and choose Rename. Then type a different name and press Enter.

CREATE SHORTCUTS TO TEXT AND DATA FILES

Programs are not the only things that you can use as targets for shortcuts. If you frequently work on a particular text file, spreadsheet, or other data file, you can put a shortcut to that file on the desktop.

You can either create a shortcut to a data file with the right-drag method you learned in the preceding section, or you can create a shortcut in the same folder and then move it to the desktop as explained here:

1. Open the folder that contains the file you want to use as a target for the shortcut.

2. Right-click the icon for the target file and select Create Short-cut from the pop-up menu. The shortcut will appear at the bottom of the window.

3. Drag the shortcut icon to the desktop.

In many cases, you may not want to open the same document, spreadsheet, or other data file every time, but you will want to use a standard format or template. To do this, open the application program that you use to work on that kind of file and create a new, blank document or file using the template or other formatting tools for the standard format. Save the blank document and create a shortcut to it. When you use the formatted file to create a new document or data file, remember to use the Save As command to save it under a new name.

CREATE SHORTCUTS TO WEB SITES

If you look at a Web site several times a day, you may want to create a desktop shortcut that starts your browser and immediately opens that page. The method for creating a shortcut to a Web page is the same in both Microsoft Internet Explorer and Netscape Navigator:

1. Open your browser and jump to the Web page you want to use as the target for your shortcut.

2. After the page loads, move your cursor to a location within the body of the page but not over a link or a picture.

3. Click the right mouse button and choose Create Shortcut from the pop-up menu. In Internet Explorer, you will be asked whether you want a shortcut to the current page to be placed on the desktop; click OK. In Netscape, the short-cut to the current page will appear in your desktop.

TURNING ON/OFF ADDITIONAL SHORTCUTS

By default Windows XP places only one system shortcut on your desktop: the Recycle Bin. Earlier versions of Windows included shortcuts for My Computer, My Network Places (or Network Neighborhood), and others. If you miss those shortcuts and would like them to display on the desktop in Windows XP, do the following:

1. Right-click the desktop and choose Properties. A Display Properties dialog box opens.

2. Click the Desktop tab, and then click the Customize Desktop button. The Desktop Items dialog box opens.

3. On the General tab, mark the check boxes for any additional icons you would like on the desktop.

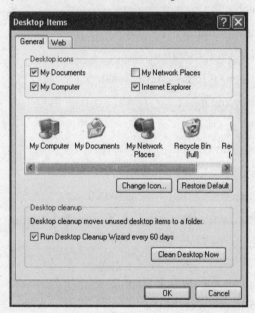

4. Click OK. Your new choices will now be on the desktop.

MOVE AROUND YOUR DESKTOP FROM THE KEYBOARD

Some people like to do as much as they possibly can without lifting their hands from their computer keyboards; others prefer to use the mouse as much as possible.

On the surface, Windows XP seems to have been designed for the mouse people rather than the keyboard folks. All those icons, drop-down and pop-up menus, and other graphic elements of the Windows screen are constructed for pointing and clicking. But there are plenty of alternatives for diehard keyboard loyalists; Windows XP accepts dozens of common and obscure keystroke commands.

For example, Windows XP accepts these keyboard combinations as desktop commands:

Help	F1
Rename the Selected Item	F2
Search for Files or Folders	F3
Refresh the Active Window	F5
Select Another Item	Arrow Keys
Select All Items on the Desktop	Ctrl+A
Copy an Object	Ctrl+C
Cut an Object	Ctrl+X
Paste an Object	Ctrl+V
Undo the Last Command	Ctrl+Z
Open the Currently Selected Object	Enter
Display the Properties of the Selected Item	Alt+Enter
Open the Start Menu	Ctrl+Esc or Windows Key
Open a Right-Click Menu	Shift+F10
Close an Open Menu	Esc
Minimize All Open Windows	Windows+M
Open Windows Explorer	Windows+E
Shift Focus to a Different Open Window	Alt+Tab
Move the Selected Item to the Recycle Bin	Delete
Delete the Currently Selected Item	Shift+Del
Shut Down the Currently Active Window	Alt+F4
Shut Down Windows	Alt+F4
Open the Windows Task Manager	Ctrl+Alt+Del

USE A KEYBOARD IN WINDOWS EXPLORER AND MY COMPUTER

The desktop isn't the only part of Windows XP that accepts keyboard shortcuts. You can use these shortcuts in the My Computer and Windows Explorer windows:

Help	F1
Rename the Currently Selected Icon	F2
Search for Files and Folders	F3 or Ctrl+F or Ctrl+E
Open or Close the Address Menu	F4
Refresh the Current Window	F5 or Ctrl+R
Toggle between the Address Toolbar and Panes	F6 or Tab
Toggle Backward between the Address Toolbar and Panes	Shift+F6 or Shift+Tab
Open a Menu on the Menu Bar	Alt
Open the System Menu	Alt+Spacebar
Close a Menu	Esc
Open or Close the Favorites Bar	Ctrl+I
Open or Close the History Bar	Ctrl+H
Go Back to the Previous Window	Alt+←
Go Forward to the Next Window	Alt+→
Select All	Ctrl+A
Open a Right-Click Menu	Shift+F10
Move Around a Window, Toolbar, or Folder	Arrow Keys
Close the Current Window	Alt+F4 or Ctrl+W
Move Up One Level in the Folder Structure	Backspace
Organize the Favorites List	Ctrl+B
Copy an Object	Ctrl+C
Cut an Object	Ctrl+X

Paste an Object	Ctrl+V
Undo the Last Command	Ctrl+Z
Open or Run the Currently Selected Item	Enter
Place the Current Item in the Recycle Bin	Del
Delete the Current Item	Shift+Del
Expand an Item in a Tree List	←
Collapse an Item in a Tree List	→

USE THE KEYBOARD IN DIALOG BOXES AND MENUS

Most Windows XP dialog boxes and utilities also accept keyboard short-cuts. A handful of keyboard commands are common to most dialog boxes, but others are specific to each one.

The standard keyboard shortcuts in dialog boxes are:

Help	F1
Open or Close a Drop-Down Menu	F4 *or* an Arrow Key
Refresh the Current View	F5
Move to the Next Option	Tab
Move to the Previous Option	Shift+Tab
Move within the Current Option	Arrow Keys
Run or Open the Current Option	Enter
Move Up One Level	Backspace
Move to the Next Tab	Ctrl+PageDown *or* Ctrl+Tab
Move to the Previous Tab	Ctrl+PageUp *or* Ctrl+Shift+Tab
Move to the Next Tab in the Current Row	→
Move to the Previous Tab in the Current Row	←
Close the Dialog Box	Esc

When you press the Alt key while a dialog box is on-screen, underlined letters appear in the names of various controls. That letter, combined with the Alt key, is a keyboard shortcut. For example, in the Properties dialog box for the file Memo.doc shown below, you can move directly to the Value field by holding down the Alt key and pressing the **V** key. To apply your changes, enter Alt+A since A is the underlined letter in the Apply button's name.

Part i

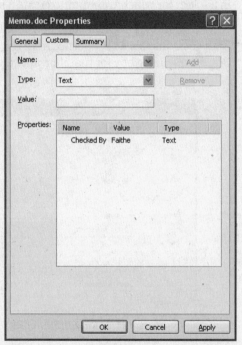

CREATE YOUR OWN KEYBOARD SHORTCUTS

Windows XP comes with a large set of standard keyboard shortcuts, but if you're truly committed to living a mouse-free life, you will also want to add your own custom shortcuts to open the programs, data files, and Web sites that you use most often.

The standard keystroke combination for a custom keyboard shortcut to a Windows program or data file is Ctrl+Alt+a letter, number, or function key. Keyboard shortcuts to DOS programs use either Ctrl or Alt. So you can assign a logical initial letter for each shortcut you create—such as *W* for Word or Web, or *J* for journal—or use the function keys along the top or side of your keyboard.

To assign a custom keyboard shortcut to a program, a data file, or a link to a Web page, follow these steps:

1. Select the shortcut icon in the Start menu, on the desktop, or in a folder for which you want to create a keyboard shortcut.

2. Either right-click the selected icon or menu item, or press Shift+F10, and select Properties from the pop-up menu. The Properties dialog box for that item appears. Select the Shortcut tab.

3. Move to the Shortcut Key field and press the key you want to use (with Ctrl+Alt) as a keyboard shortcut to this item. Windows will fill in the Ctrl and Alt automatically. To remove a shortcut key, go to the Shortcut Key field and press the spacebar.

4. Click the OK button to save your choice and close the dialog box.

WARNING

Once you have defined a keyboard shortcut, no other program can use that combination of keystrokes. If a Windows program uses the same hotkeys for some other purpose, the hotkeys in the program will not work.

The new shortcut will take effect the next time you start the computer.

CREATE HIDDEN SHORTCUTS

The target for a custom keyboard shortcut does not need to appear on the desktop or the Start menu; it can be located in any folder on your system. So you can use keyboard shortcuts to open programs, files, or Web sites that you don't want other people to know about (yes, those programs and files will still be buried down in the file structure somewhere, but they don't have to be out there in plain sight).

Follow these steps to create one or more hidden shortcuts:

1. Open My Computer or Windows Explorer. Move to the folder or subfolder where you want to hide a shortcut.

2. Choose File ➤ New ➤ Folder to create a new folder for hidden shortcuts.

3. Rename the new folder with some obscure or misleading name, such as "Wr5498K" or "Alternate Video Drivers." If you call the folder "Hidden Shortcuts," you will defeat the point of hiding them.

4. Keep the new folder open, and open a new My Computer window to drill down to the file or program for which you want to create a keyboard shortcut.

5. Right-click the target program or file and choose Create Shortcut from the drop-down menu. A new shortcut icon will appear at the bottom of the window that contains the target icon.

6. Drag the new shortcut icon to the hidden shortcuts folder.

7. Right-click the shortcut icon, and select Properties from the drop-down menu. The Properties dialog box for this shortcut will appear.

8. Choose the Shortcut tab, and use the Shortcut Key field to assign a keyboard shortcut.

9. Click the OK button to save your choice and close the dialog box.

Move Your Mouse Cursor Using the Keyboard

Windows XP includes a tool that allows users to bypass the mouse or other pointing device: the MouseKeys program. It moves the cursor around the screen in response to keystrokes. MouseKeys was designed for users who have difficulty manipulating a mouse, but there's no rule that forbids other people from using it.

To turn on MouseKeys, choose Start ➢ Control Panel ➢ Accessibility Options ➢ Accessibility Options. Then click the Mouse tab, and select the Use MouseKeys option.

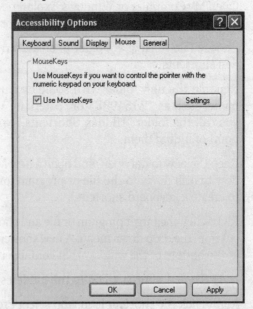

Click the Settings button to open the Settings for MouseKeys dialog box, in which you can adjust the cursor's speed and acceleration, and set other MouseKeys options.

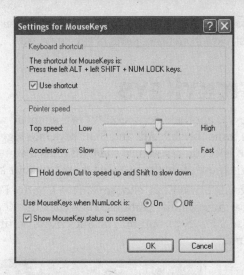

Depending on the setting you chose in the Options dialog box, the NumLock key turns MouseKeys on and off. When MouseKeys is turned on, you will see a mouse icon in the system tray. When it is off, you will see a circle and slash over the system tray icon.

To move the mouse cursor, press one of the keys in the numeric keypad at the extreme right side of the keyboard. Use the arrow keys to move left, right, up, and down, and use the Home, PgUp, PgDn, and End keys to move diagonally. To click, press the **5** key in the middle of the numeric keypad.

MouseKeys also accepts these keystrokes:

Double-Click	+ (plus sign)
Right-Click	– (minus sign)
Click Left and Right	*
Hold Down the Right Mouse Button	Ins
Release the Right Mouse Button	Del

To drag an object, follow these steps:

1. Move the cursor over the object you want to drag.

2. Press the Ins key.

3. Move the cursor to the destination.

4. Press the Del key.

Always use the keys in the numeric keypad; MouseKeys won't recognize keystrokes from other parts of the keyboard.

USE STICKYKEYS

StickyKeys is another "accessibility" tool supplied with Windows XP. This one turns the Ctrl, Alt, and Shift keys into toggle switches that remain in effect until you turn them off. This feature was designed for people who have difficulty pressing more than one key at a time.

To activate StickyKeys, choose Start ➤ Control Panel ➤ Accessibility Options ➤ Accessibility Options. Then click the Keyboard tab and turn on the Use StickyKeys option. The StickyKeys Settings buttons configure the program.

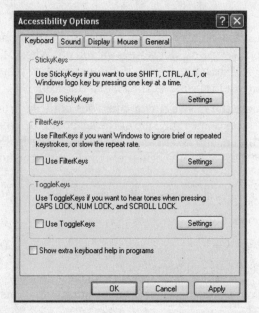

When StickyKeys is active, the Ctrl, Alt, and Shift keys lock on when you press them, and they remain on until you press and release any other key. So you could enter Ctrl+F4 by pressing the Ctrl key and then pressing the F4 key. If you press Ctrl, Alt, or Shift twice, it will be locked down until you press the same key again.

USE AN ON-SCREEN KEYBOARD

It's not exactly a keyboard shortcut, but there's one more keyboard-related program buried in Windows XP that you might want to know about. The On-Screen Keyboard program displays the keyboard layout and accepts mouse-clicks on individual keys as if they were keystrokes on a conventional keyboard.

To run On-Screen Keyboard from the Start menu, select All Programs ➢ Accessories ➢ Accessibility ➢ On-Screen Keyboard. An introductory box appears; click OK to clear it.

To use the On-Screen Keyboard, select and click a key with your mouse to enter the letter, number, or function of that key.

On-Screen Keyboard also echoes the keys you press on the keyboard by changing the color of an on-screen key when you press a physical key. Other than impressing your friends with the flashing buttons as you type (especially if you're a speedy typist), this is not likely to contribute very much to your life, but it might be an entertaining distraction for a cat or a small child who is watching you work.

WHAT'S NEXT

In this chapter, you learned how to make shortcuts for those things you use often. In the next chapter, you'll find out how to install and run programs in Windows with Windows expert Robert Cowart.

Chapter 5
RUNNING PROGRAMS

This chapter is all about running programs in Windows. That's probably why you bought Windows in the first place, right? If you've just upgraded from Windows 9x or Windows Me, you already know a lot about how to use Windows and Windows applications. A few things will be different with Windows XP Home Edition, but you'll probably pick those up quickly.

Adapted from *Mastering Windows Me* by Robert Cowart
ISBN 0-7821-2857-2   960 pages $39.99

Running Programs

As with many of the procedures you'll want to do while in Windows, starting up your programs can be done in myriad ways. Here's the complete list of ways to run programs:

▶ Choose the desired application from the Start button's menu system.

▶ Click a shortcut for a frequently used application in the left column of the top-level Start menu.

▶ Add the application to the Quick Launch toolbar and click it to run.

▶ Open My Computer, navigate your way through the folders until you find the application's icon, and double-click it.

▶ Run Windows Explorer, find the application's icon, and double-click it.

▶ Find the application with the Search command and double-click it.

▶ Locate a document that was created with the application in question and double-click it. This will run the application and load the document into it.

▶ Right-click the desktop or in a folder and choose New. Then choose a document type from the resulting menu. This creates a new document of the type you desire, which, when double-clicked, will run the application.

▶ Open the My Recent Documents list from the Start button and choose a recently edited document. This will open the document in the appropriate application.

NOTE
The My Recent Documents list does not appear by default. To display it, right-click the taskbar and choose Properties. Then on the Start Menu tab, click Customize. Click the Advanced tab, and mark the List My Most Recently Opened Documents check box.

▶ Choose Run from the Start menu and enter the name of the file you want to run.

▶ Enter command names from an MS-DOS window within Windows. In addition to the old-style DOS commands that run DOS programs and batch files, you can run Windows programs right from the DOS prompt. To open an MS-DOS window, choose Start ➢ All Programs ➢ Accessories ➢ Command Prompt.

▶ Double-click a shortcut icon on the Windows desktop. Many programs place shortcut icons on the desktop to make launching them easy, and you can also create your own desktop icons.

In deference to tradition, I'm going to cover the approaches to running applications in the order listed above. That is, application-centric first rather than document-centric. Realize, however, that all the approaches are useful while using Windows, and you will probably want to become proficient in each of them.

Running Programs from the Start Button

When you install a new program, a shortcut to the program is almost always added to the Start button's menu system. When this is the case, you just find your way to the program's shortcut on the menu, choose it, and the program runs.

For example, suppose you want to run Notepad:

1. Click the Start button.

2. Point to All Programs. The following menu appears.

This menu contains two types of items: shortcuts to programs, and folders. Notepad isn't here, so let's continue.

3. Point to Accessories. A submenu swings out, displaying more shortcuts (and more folders too).

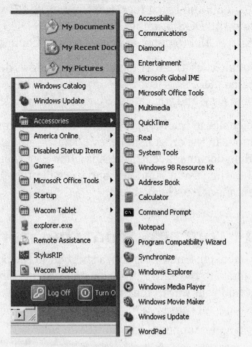

4. Click Notepad. The Notepad program starts.

You've now successfully opened Notepad. It's sitting there with a blank document open, waiting for you to start typing. Chapter 7 covers the ins and outs of using Notepad, so I won't discuss that here. For now, just click the Close button, or choose File ➢ Exit.

As you may have already noticed with this exercise, sometimes locating a program on a menu is a visual hassle. Computers are smart about alphabetizing, so notice that the items in the lists are in order from A to Z. Folders appear first, in order, then programs after that. This ordering is something you'll see throughout Windows. To make things even simpler, you can press the first letter of the item you're looking for, and the highlight will jump to it. If there are multiple items starting with that letter, each key press will advance one in the list. This works fairly reliably unless the pointer is sitting on an item that has opened into a group.

TIP

When you first install a program, its shortcut or submenu appears at the bottom of the menu. When you restart the PC, it usually takes its alphabetical place in the menu.

NOTE

By default a newly installed program appears highlighted in the All Programs list. If you don't want that behavior, right-click the Start button, select Properties, choose Customize. Select the Advanced tab and clear the Highlight Newly Installed programs check box.

New in Windows XP, shortcuts to the programs you run most frequently appear on the top-level Start menu, in the left column. You can click one of these shortcuts as an alternative to locating the program on the Start ➢ All Programs menu.

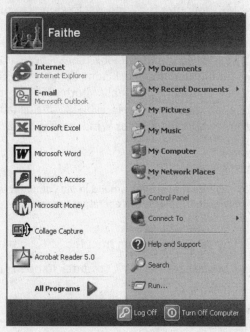

If you accidentally open the wrong menu, press the Esc key. Each press of Esc closes one level of any open list. To close down all open lists, just click anywhere else on the screen, such as on the desktop or another window, and all open Start button lists will go away.

Running Programs from My Computer

There are times when you might want to do a little sleuthing around on your hard disk using a more graphical approach, as opposed to hunting for a name in the Start menu system. The My Computer window lets you do this; it's an entry point to all the drives on your system.

NOTE
You will learn more about My Computer and Windows Explorer in Chapter 6.

To use My Computer (or Windows Explorer) to run a program, you must know in which folder that program resides. This can be tricky to determine. Many programs, however, are in subfolders within the Program Files folder, so you might look there. These program-running techniques, of finding and double-clicking the program file, are useful chiefly for situations in which a program's shortcut is not on the Start menu. When the Start menu method is available, it's usually faster and easier to use than using My Computer or Windows Explorer.

NOTE
You may find that moving around in My Computer is very Mac-like, if you're familiar with the Macintosh operating system.

Here's how to run a program from the My Computer window:

1. Choose Start ➢ My Computer to open the My Computer window.

TIP
The My Computer window and the Windows Explorer window (which you'll learn about later in this chapter) are identical except the Windows Explorer window contains a folder tree to the left of the file listing. You can switch between the two views by clicking the Folders button on the toolbar.

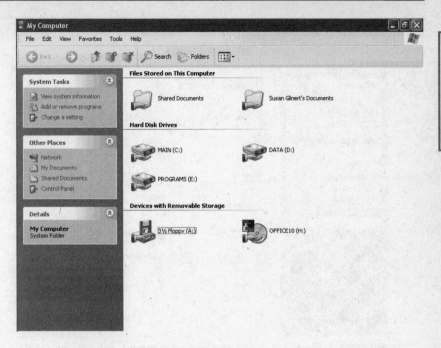

2. Double-click the drive icon to display the drive content. Programs are typically located on drive C:, your hard disk. If you have more than one hard disk, they may be on D:, E:, or some other drive. Figure 5.1 shows the content of drive D:.

NOTE

If you see the message: "These Files are Hidden," select the Show the Contents of this Drive option in the System Tasks menu on the left side of the window.

TIP

Pressing Backspace while in any folder window will move you back one level. While in the D: drive window, for example, pressing Backspace takes you back to the My Computer window. Or, if you're looking at a directory, Backspace will take you up to the root level. The Up button on the toolbar works, too. (It's the one that looks like a folder with an up arrow in it.) The Back button takes you back to the previously viewed folder.

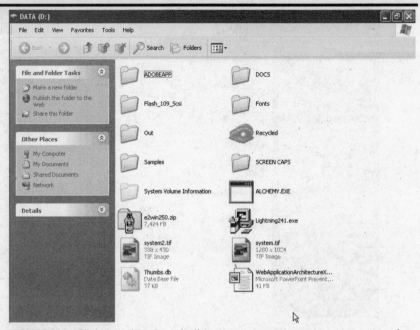

FIGURE 5.1: Clicking a drive icon displays its contents. Here you see a portion of what I have on my D: drive. Folders are listed first. Double-clicking a folder will reveal its contents.

3. Double-click the folder containing the program you want to run. Keep double-clicking folders until you find the file for the program.

4. When you see the program you want to run, click it. For example, in Figure 5.2, I've found AOL.EXE, the file that runs the America Online application.

Be careful not to double-click too slowly (that is, don't pause too long between clicks). If you do, Windows thinks that you want to change the file's name. You'll know this has happened when a little box appears around the name of the file, shown in the graphic below.

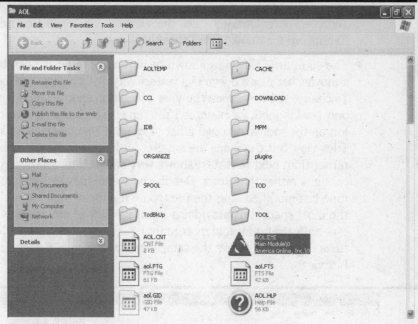

FIGURE 5.2: Run a program by double-clicking its icon.

If you do find yourself in this position, just press Esc to get out of editing mode. To be safe, it's better to click on an item's icon (the picture portion) when you want to run it, open it, move it around, and so forth.

Keep in mind some of the things you should know about running programs this way:

- ▶ Program files usually have an .exe or .com file extension; that's how to determine which file in a particular folder is the one that starts the program. A file extension is a code (usually 3 characters) following a period in the file's name that indicates the file's type.

- ▶ By default, Windows does not show file extensions for file types that it recognizes, so it can be difficult to tell which file to double-click to start the program. Usually, the program file has a unique icon, like the one for AOL in Figure 5.2. You can also turn on the display of file extensions, as in Figure 5.2. To do so, choose Tools ➤ Folder Options. Click the View tab, and clear the Hide Extensions for Known File Types check box.

▶ The standard Tiles view shown in Figures 5.1 and 5.2 can be annoying because it doesn't let you see very many objects at once. To change the view, open the View menu and choose a different one. (List is good, for example.) You can also click the Views button on the toolbar to open a list of views. Icon view is just like Tiles view but the icons are smaller and sit over the filename rather than next to it. List shows very small icons arranged in columns rather than rows. Details shows the file size, date and time last modified, and the file type. Thumbnail view takes up the most space, but provides a small preview of picture files—especially useful for folders containing images, such as My Pictures. Figure 5.3 shows the same window as Figure 5.2, but in List view.

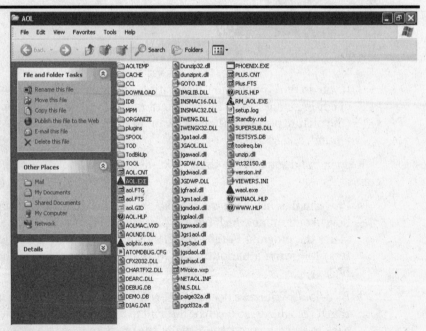

FIGURE 5.3: List view makes each file take up less space in the window so you can browse with less scrolling.

Running Programs from Windows Explorer

Working your way through a lot of folder windows, as you did in the preceding section, can get tedious. You might find it more efficient to work your way through the folder structure using a folder tree, which is what Windows Explorer offers. To switch to Windows Explorer from a My Computer window (like the ones in Figure 5.1 through 5.3), just click the Folders button on the toolbar. You can also open a Windows Explorer window from the Start menu system.

Part i

Here's how to use Windows Explorer to run your programs:

1. If you're already in a My Computer window, click the Folders button on the toolbar. If not, choose Start ➤ All Programs ➤ Accessories ➤ Windows Explorer. Figure 5.4 shows what Windows Explorer looks like.

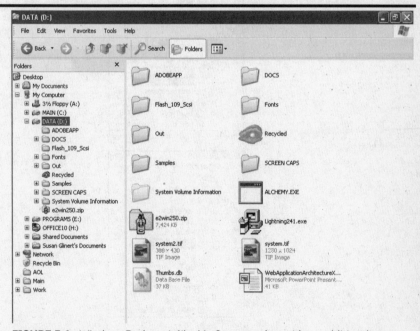

FIGURE 5.4: Windows Explorer is like My Computer but with an additional pane to the left that displays the folder tree.

TIP

Another way to run Explorer is to right-click My Computer, or a drive's icon in the My Computer window, and choose Explore.

2. When the Explorer window comes up, adjust the view as desired. For example, you might choose to maximize the window or to choose a different view (such as Icons or List).

3. The items on the left side are folders. Scroll down to the folder that contains the program you're looking for (folders are listed in alphabetical order). If a folder has a + sign next to it, it has subfolders. Clicking the + sign displays the names of any subfolders.

4. Click the folder containing the program you want to run. When you do this, its contents appear in the right pane.

5. Then double-click the program you want to run. Here, I'm about to run Microsoft Word.

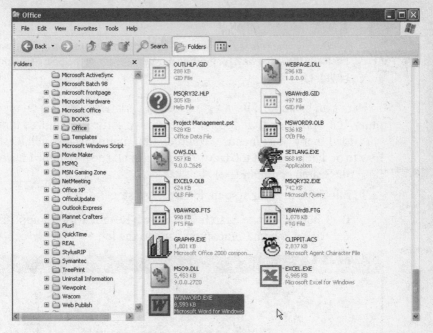

Just as in My Computer, you can change the appearance of listed items by clicking the View button, using the little list next to the View button, or opening the View menu and choosing Thumbnails, Tiles, Icons, List, or Details. It's easier to see which file is a program when the display is set to Tiles (because you can see the icon clearly) or Details (because the third column will list the file type as *application* if the file is a program). See Chapter 6 for more information about file management.

Running Applications from the Search Command

The Search feature in Windows XP helps you find the file if you know the filename of the program you're looking for but don't know where it's located. It can even cut you some slack if you don't know the whole name because you can specify just part of it. When you provide Search with a program (or other file, such as a document) name, it will begin looking through a specific disk or the whole computer (multiple disks) to find the program in question. Once Search accumulates the results, you can double-click the correct program from the resulting list, and it will run. Pretty spiffy.

NOTE

In Windows *9x*, this feature was called Find instead of Search, but it worked basically the same way. For more complete coverage of the Search feature, see Chapter 6.

Here's an example. I have a game called Tyrian somewhere on my computer. It's a program that doesn't have its own setup program, so it never got added to my Start menus. I could do that manually, as you'll learn how to do later, but I'm too lazy to do that for all the programs I have. So I use the Search command.

To find a file on your system, follow these steps:

1. Choose Start ➤ Search. The Search Results window appears with a Search Companion pane to the left.

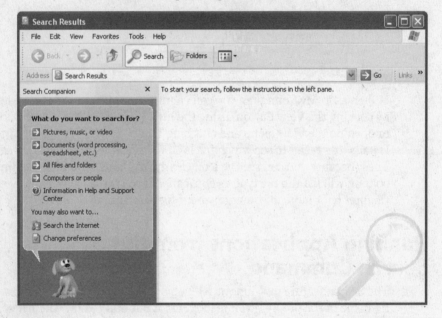

TIP

If you are already in My Computer or Windows Explorer, you can open the Search pane by clicking the Search button on the toolbar.

2. Select the type of file you are looking for from the list. When looking for a program, the best choice is All Files and Folders.

3. Enter the file's name in the All or Part of the File Name text box. If you don't know the exact name, enter as much of it as you do know.

TIP

The Search utility accepts wildcard specifications for filenames. An asterisk stands for any number of characters; a question mark stands for a single character. So, to find all files that begin with W, you would search for W*. Or, to find all files that begin with W and have exactly three letters in the name, you would search for W??.

4. (Optional) If you want to confine the search to a certain drive, select it from the Look In drop-down list.

5. Click Search. After a moment or two a list of files matching your criteria appears.

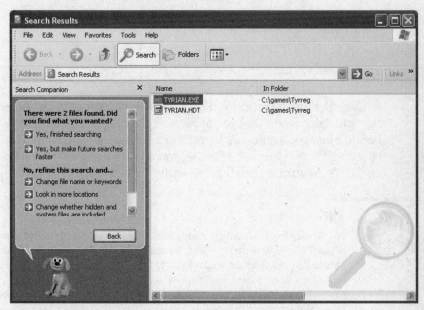

6. Double-click the found application file.

Part i

Starting a Program Using a Data File

As I mentioned earlier in the chapter, some documents will open up when you double-click them—if they are *registered*. Windows has an internal registry (basically just a list) of file extensions that it knows about. Each registered file type is matched with a program that it works with. When you double-click any document, Windows scans the list of registered file types to determine what it should do with the file. For example, clicking a file with a .bmp extension will run Paint and load the file (unless you have installed some other graphics editing program that has usurped the .bmp file extension for itself).

The upshot of this is that you can run an application by double-clicking a document of a known registered type. For example, suppose I want to run Word. All I have to do is spot a Word document somewhere. It's easy to spot one, especially in Tiles view, because all Word documents have Word's telltale identifying icon:

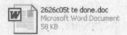

Unregistered documents have a generic-looking icon.

Once the program runs, you may decide you don't want to work with the actual document that you used to get the program going. That's OK, because most programs will let you close the current document (try choosing File ➤ Close) and then let you open a new document (usually via File ➤ New) or an existing one with File ➤ Open.

TIP

Try clicking the Start button and choosing My Recent Documents to see a list of the files you've recently edited. Depending on what's on the list, you may be able to run the program you're looking for without first opening the application. If My Recent Documents is not present in the Windows XP Start menu, right-click the Start button, choose Properties, click the Customize button, select the Advanced tab, and mark the List My Most Recently Opened Documents check box.

Running an Application by Right-Clicking the Desktop

When you don't want to bother finding some favorite program just to create a new document, there's an easier way. How often have you simply wanted to create a To Do list, a shopping list, a brief memo, a little spreadsheet, or what have you? All the time, right? Microsoft figured out that people often work in just this way—they don't think, "Gee, I'll root around for Excel, then I'll run it, and then I'll create a new spreadsheet file, save it, and name it." That's counterintuitive. On the contrary, it's more likely that they think "I need to create a 'Sales for Spring Quarter' Excel spreadsheet."

You can just create a new *empty document* of the correct type on the Desktop and name it. Then, by clicking it, you will be able to run the correct program. Windows takes care of assigning the file the correct extension so that the whole setup works internally. Try an experiment to see what I'm talking about.

1. Minimize open windows so you can see your Desktop area.

TIP

Remember, you can click the Show Desktop button in the Quick Launch toolbar to minimize all the open windows. You can reverse the effect and return all the windows to view by clicking the button again.

2. Right-click anywhere on the Desktop. From the resulting menu, choose New. You'll see a list of possible document types. As an example, Figure 5.5 shows the types in my computer.

3. Click a document type from the list. A new document icon appears on your Desktop, such as the one below, which appeared when I chose Adobe Photoshop Image.

4. The file's name is highlighted and has a box around it. This means you can edit the name. As long as the whole name is highlighted, whatever you type will replace the entire name.

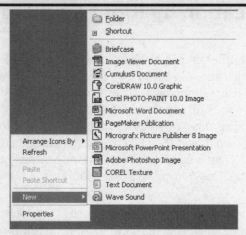

FIGURE 5.5: You can create a variety of new document types by right-clicking the Desktop. This creates a blank document that you then name and run.

NOTE

Do you need to type the extension to indicate the file type? It depends on whether you have set up Windows to show file extensions for known file types or not. If Windows is set to hide file extensions, you need not type one, but if you have turned on file extension display, you must include the file extension in the name you type.

5. Double-click the icon. Its associated program will run. In the case of the Photoshop file, the Photoshop program will run, open the new blank image, and wait for you to add paint to the canvas.

Some programs, such as Paint Shop Pro, for example, open the program and the new file for editing immediately when you create it using the preceding method. Other programs, like Excel, simply create the icon and wait for you to double-click it (Step 6).

Using the Start ➢ My Recent Documents List

As I mentioned earlier, choosing Start ➢ My Recent Documents (Windows XP Start menu) lists the documents you've recently created or edited. It's an easy way to revisit projects you've been working on. This list is maintained by Windows and is *persistent,* which means it'll be there in subsequent Windows sessions, even after you shut down and reboot. Only the last 15 documents are remembered, though, and some of these won't be things you'd think of as documents. Some of them might actually be more like programs or folders. Check it out and see if it contains the right stuff for you. Figure 5.6 shows my list the day I wrote this section.

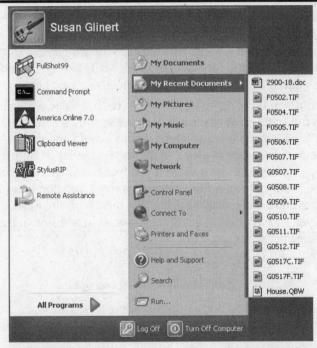

FIGURE 5.6: The My Recent Documents list from the Start button provides a no-brainer path to ongoing work projects, but only the last 15 documents you viewed or edited are shown.

Many Windows programs have a similar feature that lists your most recently edited documents at the bottom of their File menus. Because many of my favorite programs sport this feature, I tend to rely on that more than on the Documents list.

TIP

You can clear off the items in the My Recent Documents list and start fresh if you want to. Right-click the Start button and choose Properties. Click the Customize button, select the Advanced tab, and click the Clear List button.

Running a Program with the Run Command

The Run command on the Start menu enables you to type in the name of a program you want to run, much like you would type a command in at an MS-DOS prompt (for those of you who still remember MS-DOS!). This is useful for quickly starting a Windows utility that doesn't have a shortcut on the Start menu (Sysedit, for example, or Msconfig), or for running an MS-DOS program that requires startup parameters or switches.

It's less common these days than it used to be, but some programs allow you to run them in certain special modes by adding additional commands after the filename when you type it in at a command prompt. For example, suppose you want to play a DOS-based game called Nethack. You can play it in a special cheat mode if you type **Nethack /w** at the DOS prompt, but if you run it from within Windows, you don't have the opportunity to enter any special switches like that. With the Run command, however, you can type in anything you want in addition to the command name before letting it rip.

Follow these steps to use the Run command:

1. Choose Start ➢ Run. The Run dialog box opens.

2. Type the filename and any extra parameters in the Open text box. See Figure 5.7.

3. Click OK.

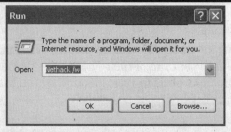

FIGURE 5.7: The Run command offers a way to include extra parameters when running a program.

One snag you might run into is that the Run command can't find the file. This can happen if the folder in which the file is located is not in the *system path*. The path is the group of folders in which the system looks for files. If you see a message that the file was not found when trying the Run command, enter the complete path in the Open box. For example, if my Nethack file is in a folder called Games, I would enter **C:\Games\ Nethack /w.**

Running a Program from Task Manager

In earlier versions of Windows, the Task Manager was used either to see what tasks were currently running or to shut down an errant program. In Windows XP, the Task Manager can also be the starting place to run a program, as well as switch to an application that is already running.

1. Right-click the Taskbar, select Task Manager, and click the New Task button.

2. Type in the name of a program, folder, document, or Internet resource or browse for the item—Windows will then open the appropriate application for you.

Making Programs Run in Startup

Windows XP uses a special folder, called Startup, for holding shortcuts to programs that run every time the operating system loads. Some programs, for example, virus checkers, automatically place a shortcut in Startup without telling you about it. This can be a good thing if you want the application to run automatically, but if you rarely need the program, loading at startup occupies memory that might be better used elsewhere. On the other hand, if you use a program every day and are tired of loading it manually, you can have Windows XP take over this chore. The contents of the Startup folder can be edited just like any other in Windows XP.

Before we add programs to this folder, first check out the current contents of your Startup folder by clicking Start ➤ All Programs ➤ Startup. You may be surprised at what this folder contains and there may be programs in there that you don't want or need. You can delete them easily by right-clicking the name and selecting Delete.

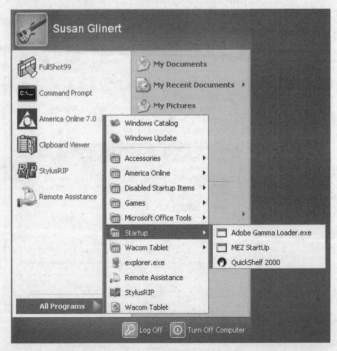

TIP

If you want to keep the shortcut around so you can run the program when you need it, create a folder and call it something like Disabled Startup, then move the shortcut in there.

There are two basic ways to add programs to the Startup folder: direct drag-and-drop or opening the Startup folder and transferring a shortcut to it using copy and paste.

Here's how to do the drag-and-drop maneuver:

1. Locate the icon for the program you want to add in Windows Explorer or My Computer. Highlight it and, *keeping the left mouse button pressed*, drag the icon to the Start button.

2. *Keeping the mouse button pressed*, hold the icon over the Start button until the Start menu opens.

3. Move the mouse pointer over the All Programs button and hold it there until the menu opens. Don't release the mouse button yet.

4. Move the icon over the Startup folder and when it opens, release the mouse button. A shortcut to the program is placed in the folder.

If you don't care much for the strain on your index finger, you can add the shortcut by opening the Startup folder and transferring a shortcut via copy and paste.

1. Choose Start ➢ All Programs.

2. Move the mouse to the Startup folder, right-click, and select Open All Users if you want the program to start for everyone using your machine or Open if you want the program to start only when you yourself log on.

3. If the folder is maximized, reduce it so you will be able to see the second folder you are about to open.

4. Open My Computer or Windows Explorer and navigate to the program you want to add to the Startup folder.

5. Right-click the program icon and select Copy.

6. Switch back to the Startup folder, right-click, and select Paste Shortcut. Don't choose Paste or you will copy the program itself to the Startup folder, not a shortcut.

RUNNING DOS PROGRAMS

These days, you'd be hard-pressed to find a new program that runs under MS-DOS. But 10 years ago, MS-DOS ruled, and almost all programs were DOS- rather than Windows-based. Windows XP has less support for DOS-based programs than earlier versions of Windows did, simply because the DOS system is dying out and there's not much demand anymore for it.

Windows XP will run most MS-DOS–based programs adequately, and there are some tweaks you can perform to make them run a little bit better. But the direct MS-DOS mode support of Windows 9x is gone, as is the ability to write custom configuration files for MS-DOS mode. In the following sections, I'll show you what you can do to make an MS-DOS program run as well as possible under Windows XP.

Techniques for Running DOS Programs

You can run most MS-DOS programs using most of the same techniques that were explained earlier in the chapter:

- ▶ Double-click the program's name in a folder (pretty good method) in Windows Explorer.

- ▶ Enter the program's name at the Run command (an acceptable method, but cumbersome since you will probably need to type the complete path).

- ▶ Choose Start ➢ All Programs ➢ Accessories ➢ Command Prompt and then type in the program's name and click OK. (You might need to use the CD *folder* command to change to a different folder first.)

- ▶ Double-click a document file with an extension that you've manually associated with the DOS program.

I explained the first two of these techniques earlier. The only difference between running Windows programs and DOS programs using those techniques is that DOS programs don't normally have an identifying icon, such as a big "W" for Word. Instead, they tend to have a boring, generic icon that looks like the one below.

Therefore, you have to rely on the icon's name alone. This one is for Image Alchemy, but because the actual program's name on disk is alchemy.exe, that's what you see.

Because the last two approaches in the above list differ from running Windows programs and haven't been covered, let's check those out. Then, I'll tell you a bit about how DOS programs operate in Windows and what you can quickly do to modify their behavior.

First, consider the option of running a DOS program from the good old DOS command prompt.

To run a DOS session, do the following:

1. Choose Start ➢ All Programs ➢ Accessories ➢ Command Prompt and then type in the program's name at the command prompt.

2. The result will be what's called a *DOS box*—a window that operates just like if you were using a computer running DOS. Try typing **dir** and pressing Enter. You'll see a listing of files on the current drive, as shown in Figure 5.8. Note that both short and long filenames are shown in this new version of DOS.

3. Type **exit** and press Enter when you are finished running DOS programs or executing DOS commands. This will close the DOS window and end the session.

NOTE

If no DOS program is actually running, clicking the DOS window's Close button will also end the DOS session. If a DOS program is running, trying this results in a message prompting you to quit the DOS program first.

```
Command Prompt                                              _ □

C:\>dir
 Volume in drive C is MAIN
 Volume Serial Number is 336B-14E2

 Directory of C:\

11/27/1998  02:25 AM    <DIR>          WINDOWS
02/22/1999  03:23 PM    <DIR>          WEBSHARE
12/05/1998  09:46 AM    <DIR>          Temp
08/04/2001  04:09 PM    <DIR>          Program Files
12/04/1998  03:11 PM    <DIR>          Utils
02/23/1999  06:01 PM    <DIR>          NetFax
08/20/2001  06:59 PM               262 .ind
08/04/2001  02:41 AM               758 SCANDISK.LOG
12/04/1998  01:31 PM             4,423 FRUNLOG.TXT
05/06/1998  08:01 PM           129,080 STRTLOGO.OEM
02/16/1999  05:40 PM               109 AUTOEXEC.SYD
02/19/1999  11:16 PM                63 WINDOWSWinHlp32.BMK
05/31/1994  06:22 AM            25,361 MSCDEX.EXE
06/08/1995  01:33 AM            10,515 SJCDAPI.SYS
08/04/2001  08:06 PM                91 Autoexec.bat
09/23/2000  01:56 PM               415 SETUPXLG.TXT
08/24/2000  03:34 PM               147 event.log
08/08/2000  06:26 PM             1,759 nrunonce.log
07/26/2001  11:18 AM               178 Config.sys
01/08/2001  05:02 PM               174 setup.log
07/26/2001  11:18 AM    <DIR>          My Music
08/04/2001  03:52 PM    <DIR>          Documents and Settings
08/07/2001  03:33 PM    <DIR>          FullShot99
              14 File(s)        173,335 bytes
               9 Dir(s)   6,898,925,568 bytes free

C:\>
```

FIGURE 5.8: The DOS box lets you enter any standard DOS commands and see their output. Here you see the end of a DIR listing and the DOS prompt that follows it.

Options While Running a DOS Session

While running a DOS session, there are several simple adjustments you can make that are either cosmetic or actually affect the performance of the program. You can easily do any of the following:

▶ Toggle the DOS session between full screen and windowed.

▶ Adjust the font appearance.

▶ Set the cursor size.

▶ Set the text and background colors.

▶ Resize the DOS box.

▶ Copy and paste from Windows to DOS and vice versa.

Let me briefly discuss each of these options.

First, if the DOS window is taking up the whole screen (all other elements of the Windows interface have disappeared) and you'd like to have the DOS program running in a window so that you can see other programs, press Alt+Enter to switch it to a window. Once windowed, you can return it to full-screen mode, either by clicking the Full Screen button or pressing Alt+Enter again.

To set options for the command prompt window, right-click its title bar and choose Properties and then set the following on the Options tab:

Cursor Size   Lets you choose between a small, medium, and large cursor.

Command History   Determines how many commands typed at the DOS prompt can be stored in memory. Use the Buffer Size spin button to set aside an amount of RAM. The default 50KB is fine for a single DOS window. You can run several concurrent DOS sessions, each of which can have its own history buffer. Set the Number of Buffers spin button to the number of histories you want Windows XP to remember. The Discard Old Duplicates check box tells Windows XP to throw away duplicate commands in the Command History to save memory.

Display Options   Lets you run the DOS box as either a window or in full-screen mode.

Edit Options   Lets you choose QuickEdit and/or Insert Mode. When QuickEdit Mode is checked, dragging the cursor selects text for copying. If Insert mode is checked, you can insert text at the cursor. If left unchecked, typing replaces existing text.

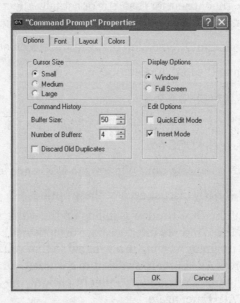

The Font tab includes a list of adjustable fonts you can use in a DOS box, one of the nice features in Windows. Using this list is the easiest way to change the font.

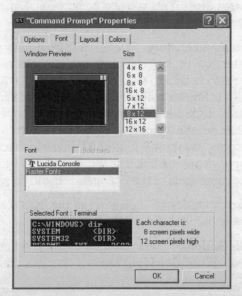

· In this list, fonts are listed organized by the size of the character matrix (in points) that comprises each displayed character. When you select a point size, you'll see the character size in pixels displayed at the bottom right of the dialog box. The larger the matrix, the larger the resulting characters (and consequently the DOS box itself) will be.

In the Layout tab, you can set the size of the window and allot a specific amount of memory to the Screen Buffer. If you deselect the Let System Position Window check box, you may also set the exact location of the window.

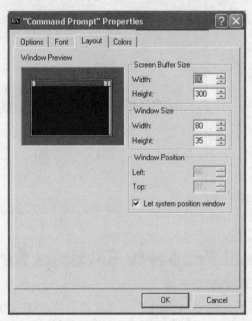

TIP

You can have multiple DOS sessions running at the same time in separate windows. This lets you easily switch between a number of DOS programs that can be running simultaneously.

NOTE

You can copy and paste data from and to DOS applications, using the Windows clipboard. See "Sharing Data between Applications" later in this chapter for details.

Finally, you can use the options in the Colors tab to set the appearance of text and background.

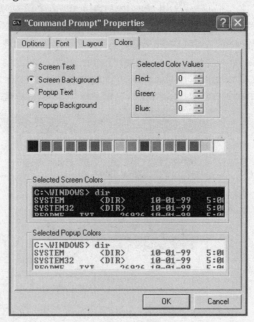

Additional Property Settings for DOS Programs

Though you can run more than one DOS window simultaneously, as mentioned above, DOS programs were designed to run one at a time, and they are usually memory hogs. They often need as much as 560K of free conventional memory, and some may require some additional expanded or extended memory to perform well. Since DOS programs think they don't have to coexist with other programs simultaneously, they are often written specifically to claim all available system resources for themselves unless told otherwise. That's why you might need to adjust the properties for a DOS program to make it run nicely under Windows. This usually involves faking out the DOS program into believing that the system resources it is receiving constitute all that the PC has to offer, when in fact the PC is apportioning out resources to several programs at once.

In most cases, Windows XP does pretty well at faking out DOS programs without your help by using various default settings and its own memory-management strategies. However, even Windows isn't omniscient, and you may occasionally experience the ungracious locking up of a program or see messages about the "system integrity" having been corrupted.

TIP

In reality, what Windows is doing when running DOS programs is giving each of them a simulated PC to work in called a *VDM (Virtual DOS Machine)*.

If a DOS program doesn't run properly under Windows, or if you wish to optimize its performance, you can fine-tune the settings.

Consider the following to fine-tune the DOS environment for running a program:

▶ If the program will run at all under Windows XP without crashing:

1. Run it as explained earlier in the chapter.

2. If it's not in a window, press Alt+Enter to run it in windowed mode.

3. Right-click the title bar and select Properties. Choose settings as described in the previous section.

▶ If the program *won't run without crashing*:

1. Navigate with My Computer or Windows Explorer to the folder containing the DOS program.

2. Find the program's icon and right-click it.

3. Choose File ➢ Properties.

Now you'll see the DOS program's Properties sheet, from which you can alter quite a healthy collection of settings (see Figure 5.9).

NOTE

The Properties dialog box replaces the PIF editor used in earlier versions of Windows.

After you have spent some time looking through the tabs and exploring your options, simply select your settings as necessary. When you're happy with them, click OK to save them. The next time you run the program by double-clicking the shortcut or the program's icon, these settings will go into effect.

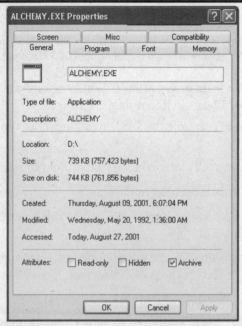

FIGURE 5.9: The Properties box for the program Image Alchemy

What settings should you change? Good question. It's a complex procedure to determine what settings will make a particular MS-DOS program run better. Fortunately, the Windows Help system offers excellent and descriptive information. To read about it, open the Help system (Start ➤ Help) and search for MS-DOS.

Here's a quick rundown of some of the more common fixes:

▶ If the program can't find some of its data files as it runs, enter the program's folder path in the Working text box on the Program tab.

▶ If the program is designed to use specific `autoexec.bat` and `config.sys` files, you can specify them by clicking the Advanced button on the Program tab.

▶ Set the font that the program uses on the Font tab.

▶ Allocate a specific amount and type of memory to the program on the Memory tab.

▶ Choose between full-screen and windowed operation and set video performance on the Screen tab.

▶ Try turning off Fast ROM Emulation on the Screen tab if you are having problems with the program writing text to the screen. Be aware that this slows down the program's performance, however.

▶ Try turning off Dynamic Memory Allocation on the Screen tab if you are having display problems switching back and forth between Windows and this program.

▶ Turn off Allow Screen Saver on the Misc tab if problems occur when the screen saver kicks in when the program is running.

▶ Try different compatibility modes in the Compatibility tab. For example, set the number of colors to 256 or run in 640 × 480 screen resolution.

▶ See the following section for help with compatibility with earlier operating systems.

RUNNING PROGRAMS IN COMPATIBILITY MODE

Most programs will load and run fine in Windows XP, but you may experience problems with some older applications. A few short-sighted programs were written for a specific version of Windows and others—older games, for example—may have specific display or system requirements that you have to tweak to get the program to work properly. Unlike earlier

Part i

versions of Windows where you were on your own when it came to program/operating system harmony, XP has two built-in tools for adjusting application compatibility settings: the Program Compatibility Wizard and the Compatibility Shell Extension.

1. To start the Program Compatibility Wizard, click Start ➤ All Programs ➤ Accessories ➤ Program Compatibility Wizard.

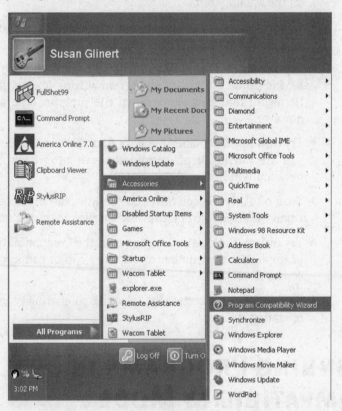

2. Click Next to get past the Welcome screen. The first dialog box gives you options for locating the program to work with. You can choose from a list of programs, have Windows XP use the program on the CD-ROM drive, or you may locate the program manually.

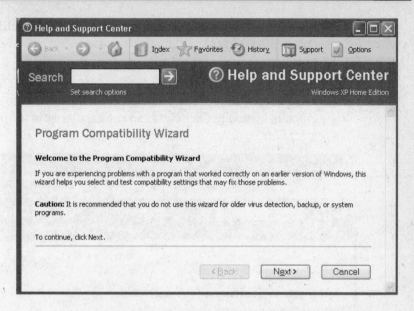

3. If you want Windows XP to search for all executable programs in your system, select the first option and click Next. Select the desired program from the list and click Next.

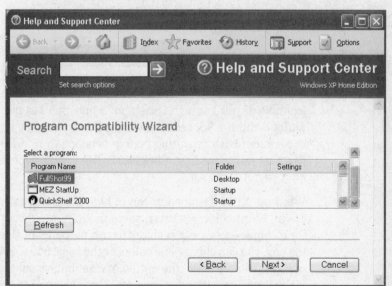

4. If you select the Use the Program in the CD-ROM drive option, the Wizard automatically advances to the next screen.

5. If you want to locate the program by typing in a path and file-name or browsing for the file, select the I Want to Locate the Program Manually. Click Next and enter the name of the program file.

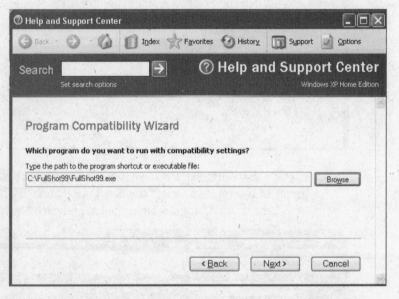

6. Choose which operating system you want to emulate. For example, if you know the program in question ran perfectly under Windows 95, select the first option. You may have to experiment with operating system versions to find the setting that works the best. Click Next. (See first graphic on the next page.)

7. Windows XP is designed to run in high-color mode, that is, 16- or 32-bit color. However, some programs—older games, for example—require 256 colors to run properly. In this dialog box, you can choose 256 colors or the basic 640 × 480 resolution. You also have the option of disabling visual themes if they conflict with your program. Click Next. (See second graphic on the next page.)

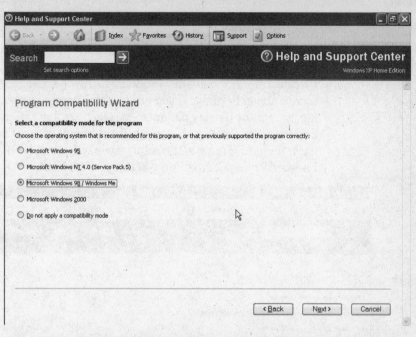

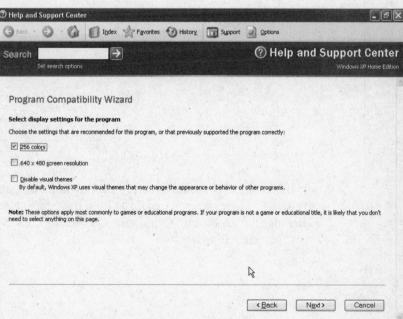

8. You now have a chance to test your settings. When you click Next, Windows runs the program for you. When you close the program, the Wizard asks if the program worked correctly. If so, you can save the compatibility information permanently by selecting Yes, Set this Program to Always Use These Compatibility Settings. If you want to try alternative operating systems or display parameters, select No, Try Different Compatibility Settings. If you just want to quit without saving settings or if none of the settings worked, select No, I am Finished Trying Compatibility Settings. Click Next.

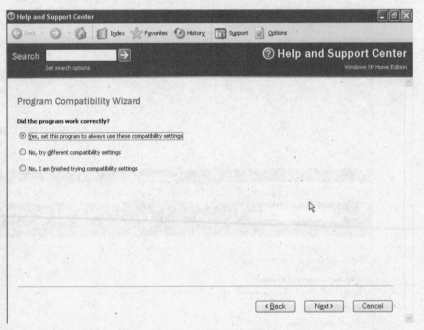

9. At this point, if you want to send your Program Compatibility data to Microsoft, you can do so from the next screen by clicking the Yes button. Otherwise, choose No. click Next, and then click Finish.

Advanced users can use the Program Compatibility shell extension to set compatibility modes directly. Navigate to the program icon using My Computer or Windows Explorer and right-click. Choose Properties and select the Compatibility tab.

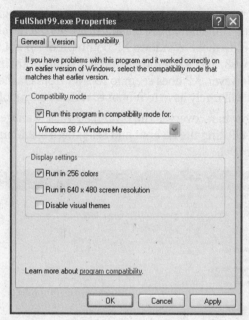

From here, you can choose an operating system to emulate and set display parameters as discussed above. The settings become permanent when you click the Apply or OK button.

NOTE

If a program won't install in Windows XP, try running the Compatibility Wizard on the setup program (almost always named `startup.exe` and usually located on the installation disk). If you are using the Program Compatibility Wizard, selecting the I Want to Use the Program in the CD-ROM Drive option in the second dialog box will most likely find the startup program for you.

Killing Unresponsive Applications

This section is sort of the antithesis of running programs, as it discusses recovering from a program crash. Although the developers at Microsoft tried hard to make Windows XP bomb-proof (or at least more bomb-proof than Me, 98, and 95), I didn't find it any more stable than earlier versions. However, XP does seem to recover from crashes more gracefully, and you will rarely have to reboot to regain control of your machine.

The key to recovery is the revamped Task Manager, which you invoke by right-clicking the taskbar and selecting Task Manager, or by pressing Ctrl+Alt+Del.

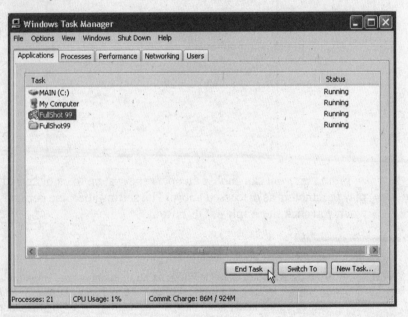

If your program has crashed, bring up the Task Manager, switch to the Applications tab, highlight the errant program, and click the End Task button. Windows XP should close the program and you may continue working.

Sometimes, however, a terminated program leaves parts of itself running. You can check for these bits in the Processes tab.

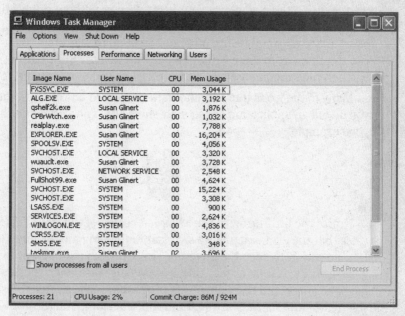

Search the list for filenames that belong to the crashed program, for example, if you were running a program named SurlyWrite, look for filenames like `surlywrite.exe`, `swr.exe`, or `swrite.exe`. Highlight the filename and click the End Process button. Be careful, though. You may accidentally end a process required by Windows in order to function.

USING DESKTOP SHORTCUTS

When it comes to running your programs, Windows has a spiffy feature called *shortcuts*. Shortcuts are alias icons (that is, icons that represent other icons) that you can add almost anywhere, such as in folders or on the desktop, on the Taskbar's Quick Launch toolbar (later for that), or on the Start menu. (As a matter of fact, all the entries on the Start menu are actually shortcuts to the corresponding programs.)

Part i

The neat thing about shortcuts is that since they're really only a link or pointer to the real file or application, you can have as many as you want, putting them wherever your heart desires, without duplicating your files and using up lots of hard disk space. So, for example, you can have shortcuts to all your favorite programs right on the desktop. Then you can run them from there without having to click the Start button, walk through the Program listings, and so forth, as we've been doing.

Many of the icons that are automatically placed on your desktop when you install an application are actually shortcuts. The icon for Outlook is a good example.

Notice the little arrow in the lower-left corner of the icon. This indicates that the icon is actually a shortcut to the program file for Outlook. Double-click it to open the program. This isn't an infallible way to distinguish a shortcut from a "real" file, however, because some shortcuts don't have the arrow, and there are utility programs (such as TweakUI) that will remove the shortcut arrows from shortcut icons. You learned all about shortcuts in Chapter 4, so return there now if you need a reminder about how they work.

SWITCHING BETWEEN APPLICATIONS

Remember, Windows lets you have more than one program open and running at a time. You can also have multiple folders open at any time, and you can leave them open to make getting to their contents easier. Any folders that are open when you shut down the computer will open again when you start up Windows again.

People often think they have to shut down one program before working on another one, but that's neither efficient nor true. When you run each new program or open a folder, the taskbar adds a corresponding button. Clicking a button switches you to that program or folder. For the first several programs, the buttons are large enough to read the names of the programs or folder. As you run more programs, the buttons automatically shrink, so the names may become truncated. You'll learn how to customize and control the taskbar in Chapter 10.

Switching with Alt+Tab

There's another way to switch between programs and folders—the Alt+Tab trick. Press down the Alt key and hold it down. Now, press the Tab key (you know, that key just above the Caps Lock and to the left of the Q). You'll see a box in the center of your screen showing you an icon of each program or folder that's running, like this:

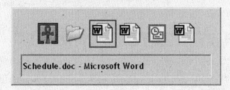

Each press of the Tab key will advance the outline box one notch to the right. The outline box indicates which program you'll be switched to when you release the Alt key. If you want to back up one program (i.e., move the box to the left), you can press Alt+Shift+Tab. Note that the name of the program or folder is displayed at the bottom of the box, which is especially useful when choosing folders, as all folders look the same.

Sharing Data between Applications

One of the greatest features of Windows is the ability to share pieces of information between your programs. You have the ability to mix and match data from a wide assortment of document types, such as text, sound, graphics, spreadsheets, databases, and so forth. This lets you construct complex documents previously requiring physical cutting and pasting and possibly the aid of an art department.

Windows offers three internal vehicles for exchanging data between programs: the Windows Clipboard, Object Linking and Embedding (OLE), and Dynamic Data Exchange (DDE). I'll concentrate on using the Windows Clipboard here because it's the concept you will use most.

NOTE

Many of my examples in this chapter refer to Microsoft products. This isn't necessarily my endorsement of Microsoft products over other competing products! Competition in the software marketplace is a healthy force, ensuring the evolution of software technology, and I highly support it. But, because so many of you are bound to be familiar with the Microsoft product line, I use products such as Word, Excel, Graph, and Access in my examples in hopes of better illustrating the points I'm trying to make here.

Using the Windows Clipboard

Though it's not capable of converting data files between various formats, such as between Excel and Lotus 1-2-3 or Word and WordPerfect, the Windows Clipboard is great for many everyday data-exchange tasks. Just about all Windows programs support the use of the ubiquitous cut, copy, and paste commands, and it's the Clipboard that provides this functionality for you.

The Clipboard makes it possible to move any kind of material, whether text, data cells, graphics, video, audio clips, and OLE objects between documents—and since Windows 95, between folders, the Desktop, Explorer, and other portions of the interface. The actual form of the source data doesn't matter that much, because together, the Clipboard utility and Windows take care of figuring out what's being copied and where it's being pasted, making adjustments when necessary—or at least providing a few manual options for you to adjust. The Clipboard can also work with non-Windows (DOS) programs, albeit with certain limitations that I'll explain later.

How does the Clipboard work? It's simple. The Clipboard is built into Windows and uses a portion of the system's internal resources (RAM and virtual memory) as a temporary holding tank for material you're working with. For example, suppose you have cut some text from one part of a document in preparation for pasting it into another location. Windows stores the text on the Clipboard and waits for you to paste it into its new home.

The last item you copied or cut is stored in this no-man's-land somewhere in the computer until you cut or copy something else, exit Windows, or intentionally clear the Clipboard. As a result, you can paste the Clipboard's contents any number of times.

To place information in the Windows Clipboard, you simply use each application's Edit menu (or the Edit menu's shortcut keys) for copying, cutting, and pasting (see Figure 5.10).

Here are the steps for cutting, copying, or pasting within a Windows program:

1. First, arrange the windows on-screen so you can see the window containing the source information.

2. Select the information you want to copy or cut, such as text, a graphic, a few spreadsheet cells, or whatever. In many programs, simply clicking an object, such as a graphic, will select it. Other programs require you to drag the cursor over objects while pressing the left mouse button.

3. Once the desired area is selected, open the application's Edit menu and choose Copy or Cut, depending on whether you want to copy the material or delete the original with the intention of pasting it into another location.

4. If you want to paste the selection somewhere, first position the cursor at the insertion point in the destination document (which may or may not be in the source document) you're working in. This might mean scrolling up or down the document, switching to another application using the Taskbar, or switching to another document within the *same application* via its Window menu.

5. Open the Edit menu and choose Paste. Whatever material was on the Clipboard will now be dropped into the new location. Normally, this means any preexisting material, such as text, is moved down to make room for the stuff you just pasted.

TIP

There may be some shortcuts for cut, copy, and paste in specific programs, so you should read the manual or help screens supplied with the program. Generally, Ctrl+X, Ctrl+C, and Ctrl+V are shortcuts for cutting, copying, and pasting, respectively.

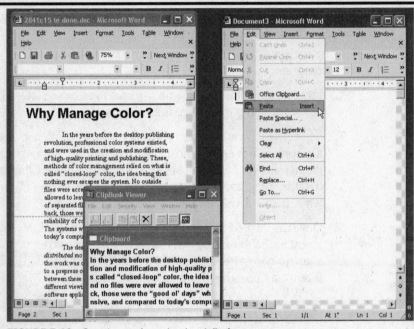

FIGURE 5.10: Copying and pasting in a Windows program

Right-Click Shortcuts for Cut, Copy, and Paste

As mentioned earlier, the cut, copy, and paste scheme is implemented throughout Windows XP, even on the Desktop, in the Explorer, in folder windows, and so forth. This is done using right mouse-button shortcuts. Many applications offer this feature too.

Right-clicking a file in a folder window and choosing Copy puts a pointer to the file on the Clipboard. Right-clicking another location, such as the desktop, and choosing Paste drops the file there. Try clicking the secondary (normally the right) mouse button on icons or on selected text or graphics in applications to see if there is a shortcut menu. Figure 5.11 shows an example of copying some text from a Word document using this shortcut.

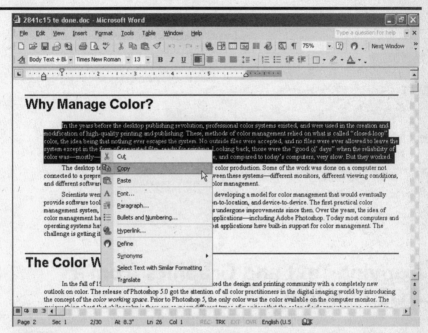

FIGURE 5.11: Shortcuts for cut, copy, and paste are built into much of Windows via the right-click menu. Windows applications are beginning to implement this feature, too, as you see here in Word.

Enhanced Clipboard in Office XP

Microsoft Office 2000 and XP come with an enhanced Clipboard that can store up to 24 different clips at once, rather than only one. When you copy or cut something to the Clipboard in one of those programs, and then copy or cut something else before you paste the original item, the Clipboard toolbar appears, showing each clip as a separate icon. From there, you can select the clip you want to paste. For more information, see the Help system in one of the Office 2000 or XP programs.

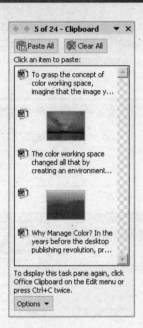

Copying Text and Graphics from a DOS Window

Copying selected graphics from MS-DOS programs is also possible. This is a pretty nifty trick for lifting material out of your favorite DOS program and dropping it into a Windows document. There's only one caveat: The DOS program has to be running in a window, not on the full screen.

When you cut or copy selected material from the DOS box, it gets dumped into the Clipboard as text or graphics, depending on which mode Windows determines the DOS window was emulating. Windows knows whether the application is running in character mode or graphics mode, and it processes the data on the Clipboard accordingly. If text mode is detected, the material is copied as characters that could be dropped into, say, a word-processing document. If the DOS application has set up a graphics mode in the DOS window (because of the application's video requests), you'll get a bit-mapped graphic in the destination document when you paste.

NOTE

As you may know, some fancy DOS programs may look as though they are displaying text when they're really running in graphics mode. For example, Word-Perfect for DOS can run in a graphics mode that displays text attributes such as underline, italics, and bold, rather than as boring block letters displayed in colors that indicate these attributes. When you copy text from such a program and then paste it into another document, you'll be surprised to find you've pasted a graphic, not text. This means you can't edit it like text because it's being treated like a bit-mapped graphic. The solution is to switch the DOS application back to text mode and try again. Refer to your DOS program manual for help.

Because of the Control button options and right-mouse button context menu, the procedure for copying is simple to learn. You can use the Control and context menus almost as if you were using another Windows program. Figure 5.12 illustrates the simple technique. Here are the steps:

1. First, switch to the DOS application and display the material you want to work with.

2. Make sure the application is running in a window, rather than running full screen. If it's not, press Alt+Enter. (Each press of Alt+Enter toggles any DOS window between full and windowed view.)

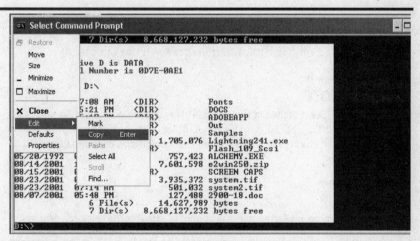

FIGURE 5.12: Copying text from an MS-DOS box is now a simple procedure. Right-click, select Mark, and click and drag across the desired text. Pull down the Control menu and select Edit ➤ Copy.

3. Pull down the Control menu, select Edit, and choose Mark. Or, right-click and choose Mark.

4. Holding the mouse button down, drag the pointer over the desired copy area, dragging from upper left to lower right. As you do so, the color of the selection will change to indicate what you're marking.

```
cx  Command Prompt                                            _ □ ×
:\Documents and Settings\Susan Glinert>d:

D:\>dir
 Volume in drive D is DATA
 Volume Serial Number is 0D7E-0AE1

 Directory of D:\

2/05/1998   07:08 AM    <DIR>          Fonts
02/19/1999  05:21 PM    <DIR>          DOCS
10/21/1999  05:17 PM    <DIR>          ADOBEAPP
02/20/1999  01:39 AM    <DIR>          Out
03/01/1999  11:54 AM    <DIR>          Samples
2/11/2000   10:14 AM        1,705,076 Lightning241.exe
06/26/2001  12:34 PM    <DIR>          Flash_109_Scsi
05/20/1992  01:36 AM          757,423 ALCHEMY.EXE
08/14/2001  12:51 PM        7,601,598 e2win250.zip
08/15/2001  05:49 AM    <DIR>          SCREEN CAPS
08/23/2001  07:13 AM        3,935,372 system.tif
08/23/2001  07:14 AM          501,032 system2.tif
08/07/2001  05:48 PM          127,488 2900-18.doc
               6 File(s)     14,627,989 bytes
               7 Dir(s)   8,667,463,680 bytes free

D:\>
```

5. Release the mouse button. The selected area will stay highlighted.

6. Press Ctrl+C or pull down the Control menu and choose Edit ➢ Copy. The information is now on the Clipboard.

NOTE

Notice that the Cut command (Ctrl+X) doesn't work, because you can't cut from a DOS application in this way. Cutting has to be done using the DOS program's own editing keys, and it won't interact with the Windows Clipboard.

TIP

Typing any letter on the keyboard terminates the selection process.

That's all there is to copying information from an application that's running in the DOS box. Of course, the normal procedure will apply to pasting what was just copied. You just switch to the destination application (which, incidentally, can be a DOS or a Windows program), position the cursor, and choose Edit ➤ Paste to paste in the Clipboard's contents at the cursor position. (For a DOS application as the destination, you'd use the Paste command in the context menu or choose Edit ➤ Paste from the Control menu.)

What's Next

This chapter explained how to run programs, a primary activity for most Windows users. The other important skill that Windows users will need on an everyday basis is file management, so in the next chapter you'll receive a primer on managing files, folders, and disks. This will help you organize your data files, transfer them to other disks for storage, and avoid accidentally deleting important documents.

Chapter 6

MANAGING FILES, FOLDERS, AND DISKS

Files are the basis of almost all computing. Whatever you do—whether it's running a program, typing a memo, or optimizing system performance—you are working with a file. Folders and disks contain and organize those files. This chapter focuses on file, folder, and disk management in Windows XP Home Edition, familiarizing you with concepts and skills you will use over and over in the rest of the book.

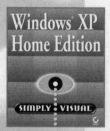

Adapted from *Windows XP Home Edition Simply Visual* by Faithe Wempen

ISBN 0-7821-2982-X   448 pages $24.99

FILE MANAGEMENT OVERVIEW

Files are necessary because computer memory is volatile—that is, whatever it contains is erased when you shut down the PC. In that way, memory is like a worktable that gets cleared off at the end of each workday, and its contents discarded. When you save something as a file, you store it on a disk, where it is safe until you need it again. You can think of a disk as a file cabinet in which you store files for safekeeping.

A computer has at least one hard disk, which is inside the case and cannot be removed easily. In addition, most computers have at least one type of removable drive, such as a floppy-disk drive, a Zip drive, or a CD-ROM drive.

Because a disk can potentially hold hundreds or even thousands of files, folders are used to help keep them organized. If a disk is like a file cabinet, then a folder is like a drawer in the cabinet, or like an expandable cardboard folder within a drawer. (The latter is actually a more apt analogy because computer folders are not fixed in size, but expand or contract to hold whatever you place in them.)

Folders can contain other folders—a folder can be the *parent folder* of one folder and the *child folder* of another. This allows you to create sophisticated file-organization systems. For example, you might have a Projects folder, and within that folder, you could have some word processing files that pertain to all projects in general, plus several child folders for your specific projects. Within each of those individual child folders, you could have more files that pertain generally to that project, plus more child folders for files dealing with certain aspects of the project.

In Windows, all these abstract concepts like file, folder, and disk take on a visual appearance. You can see and work with icons that represent specific files, folders, and drives on your system. You use a program called Windows Explorer to view and manipulate the files, folders, and drives on your system.

NOTE

Windows Explorer is an atypical program in that its name doesn't appear in the title bar. Instead, the name of the folder being browsed appears there.

For example, on the right-hand side of the following figure, the contents of the D: drive appears. Folders are represented by an icon that looks like a paper folder, along with the folder's name. Files are listed with their name, but the icon can vary depending on the type of file. Notice in this figure that the D: drive contains a number of folders, and at the very bottom of the list, there's a single file called Log, with an icon that looks like a notepad.

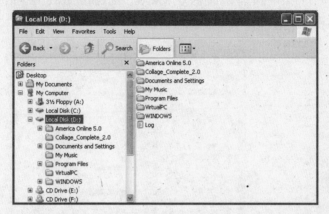

Most files on your hard disk were placed there when Windows or one of your applications was installed, and they don't require any special handling. The primary reason you will want to work with the file system is to manage the data files you create using various applications such as your word processor. You might need to move, copy, or delete those files, check on a file's name, protect a file from changes, or perform some other operation.

The following sections explain how to open a file management window and display the contents of a folder in which a particular file resides. Then the latter part of the chapter explains how to do things to the files themselves.

OPENING A FILE MANAGEMENT WINDOW

There are two main ways to open a file management window, and each results in a slightly different default display, or view:

My Computer   Displays an overview of all the disks on your PC, from which you can begin browsing for a specific disk or folder. It includes a System Tasks pane to the left of the listing instead of a folder list.

NOTE

In earlier versions of Windows, there was a sharp distinction between My Computer and Windows Explorer because only Windows Explorer could contain a folder list. In Windows XP, however, you can switch between the folder list and the System Tasks pane by simply clicking the Folders button on the toolbar.

Windows Explorer Displays the contents of the My Documents folder (on the same disk that Windows is installed on) by default. This display includes the folder list, for easy navigation to some other folder or disk.

Both of these displays are "file management windows" in a generic sense because they help you manage your files. Throughout this book, if the instructions say to start in My Computer or Windows Explorer, you should open that particular window; if the instructions say simply to use a file management window, you may start in either one.

In both displays, when the folder list is turned off, the System Tasks pane appears; it goes away when you turn the folder list back on (by clicking the Folders button on the toolbar). This System Tasks pane contains shortcuts to popular activities such as moving, copying, and deleting, and you'll see it in use later in this chapter.

Opening the My Computer Window

When you want to start looking for a particular folder at a bird's-eye level of your system—with all the available drives to choose from—My Computer is the best place to start. To open My Computer, choose Start ➢ My Computer.

NOTE

In earlier versions of Windows, there was a My Computer icon on the desktop that opened My Computer; it didn't appear on the Start menu. If you miss the convenience of that icon, you can create a shortcut to My Computer on the desktop. See Chapter 4 to learn how to create your own desktop shortcuts.

Opening the Windows Explorer Window

When you start with Windows Explorer, the folder list appears automatically. The contents of the My Documents folder also appears by default. To open Windows Explorer, choose Start ➤ All Programs ➤ Accessories ➤ Windows Explorer.

NOTE

Windows Explorer is a little bit more trouble to open than My Computer, because you have to wade through several menu levels to get to it. However, if you find yourself using Windows Explorer frequently, you can create a shortcut to it on your desktop or in the Quick Launch toolbar, for quicker access. To do so, simply drag-and-drop a shortcut onto the toolbar.

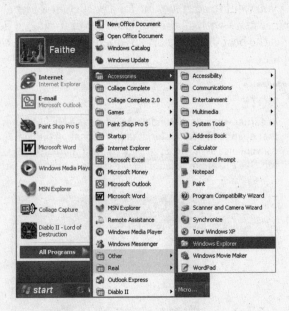

Opening Other File Management Windows

The Start menu also offers shortcuts to several special-purpose folders; you might want to use one of them to jump to a particular folder that you know you need to work with. Each of these shortcuts opens the folder *without* the folder list, although you can easily display it if you want it.

My Documents   Opens the My Documents folder, which most business applications use to store data files.

My Pictures Opens the My Pictures folder, which is a child folder of My Documents and is used primarily to store pictures acquired from scanners and digital cameras (see Chapter 23).

My Music Opens the My Music folder, also a child folder of My Documents. It's used to store music clips for Windows Media Player (Chapter 22), and some other music programs might utilize it as well.

My Network Places Opens the My Network Places folder, which enables you to browse your local area network for access to other computers and shared resources. (More on networking in Chapter 20.) If you don't have a network, you won't see this option on the menu.

NAVIGATING BETWEEN FOLDERS

Once you've opened a file management window (either through My Computer or Windows Explorer), you can choose which drive's or folder's content you want to display. This process of navigating between folders is a very important skill that you'll use over and over as you work with Windows.

Selecting from the Folder List

One of the easiest ways to switch to a different folder is to select it from the folder list (sometimes called a folder tree, because its branches look something like a tree). When you select a folder on the list, its contents appear in the right-hand pane of the file management window.

NOTE
Remember, if the folder list doesn't appear, click the Folders button on the toolbar.

Notice on the folder list that some drives and folders have plus signs next to them. They indicate that there are child folders beneath that don't currently display in the folder list. Click the plus sign to expand the list.

NOTE
Some people don't like to leave the folder list displayed because it takes up so much room on-screen; they prefer to close it and leave that space for the display of the chosen folder's contents. In upcoming sections, you'll learn ways to navigate between folders that don't involve the folder list.

Conversely, a minus sign indicates that all the child folders for that folder currently appear. Click the minus sign to collapse the list and to change the sign back to a plus sign.

Moving Up and Down in the Folder System

Think of the folder list as a branching root system, in which you start off with the disk at the top (the granddaddy parent folder) and then child folders within that disk, and then further child folders within some of the folders, and so on. Moving "up" in the system means moving closer to the top, or toward the *root folder*. Moving "down" means moving into a child folder within the current folder.

You have already seen in the preceding section that you can move freely between folders using the folder list. But if the folder list isn't displayed, you'll need a different method. (You might even prefer the alternative method to the folder-list method.)

Moving to a Child Folder of the Current Folder

To move down into a child folder, display the folder or disk containing the folder you want, and then double-click the icon for that folder. In this example, I'll double-click the Helpnote folder to view its contents.

The folder's contents now appear in the right-hand pane. Notice that the title bar of the screen now displays the name of the folder.

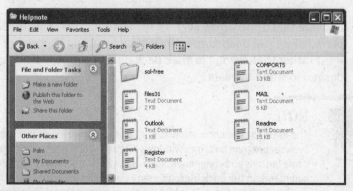

Moving Up One Level to the Parent Folder

 To move back up to the parent folder of the currently displayed one, click the Up One Level button in the toolbar. The contents of the parent folder now appear in the right-hand pane.

Using Back and Forward Buttons

When you display a different disk's or folder's contents, whatever contents were previously displayed in the right-hand pane are replaced by the new display.

NOTE

In some earlier versions of Windows, such as Windows 95, whenever you double-clicked a folder to display its contents, by default it opened in a new window instead of replacing the contents in the existing one. If you want to duplicate this behavior in Windows XP, choose Tools ➢ Folder Options ➢ Open Each Folder in Its Own Window, and click OK. However, if you do this, the steps in the rest of this book may not match what happens on your screen.

If you want to return to the previously displayed contents, click the Back button.

If you want to move ahead again to the display as it was before you clicked Back, click the Forward button.

Notice that each of these buttons has a down-pointing arrow to its right.

Clicking that down arrow opens a list of all the locations that have displayed since you opened the window, and you can choose the one you want rather than having to click Back or Forward repeatedly until your desired location appears.

NOTE

The file management window in Windows is related to Internet Explorer, the Web browser program built into Windows XP, to the point where they share many of the same buttons and commands, such as the Back and Forward buttons. The History command on the Back button's menu opens the Explorer bar with history information displayed in it. This history, however, pertains only to Web pages, not to folders on your local PC—so it won't be important until you get to Chapter 15.

MANIPULATING FILES AND FOLDERS

Now that you know how to display the desired folder, it's time to learn what you can actually *do* with the contents of that folder, and why you might want to do it.

NOTE
When you perform an action on a folder, everything within it (files and child folders) is also affected. For example, if you copy a folder to another disk, everything in that folder gets copied, too.

Selecting Files and Folders

As I mentioned earlier, the primary reason that most people open a file management window is to do something to a data file they've created in some program. For example, you might want to delete a letter you created using your word processor, or to copy it onto a floppy disk.

Before you can act on a file or folder, however, you must *select* it. No matter what the activity, it's always a two-part equation, like a subject-verb sentence: First you select what you want to act on (the subject); then you select the activity (the verb).

To select a single file or folder, simply click it. To deselect it, click somewhere else (away from it). A selected file appears in white letters with a dark background, the opposite of unselected ones. In the following figure, I've selected the "chapter 3" file.

NOTE
In the default Windows XP color scheme, that dark background is blue, but yours might be different depending on the appearance options you've chosen. (See Chapter 10.)

chapter 2   chapter 3

You can select multiple files and/or folders and act on them as a group. For example, if you needed to delete 10 different files in the same folder, you could select them all and then issue the Delete command once. (You can't select multiple files or folders in different locations at once.)

If all the files/folders you want to select are contiguous (that is, listed one right after another), you can select them like this:

NOTE

Is "contiguous" determined by rows, or by columns? It depends on the view. In Icons and Thumbnails views, contiguous runs by rows, from left to right and then down to the next row. In List view, contiguous runs by columns, from top to bottom and then to the next column. In single-column views such as Details and Tiles, it's a nonissue. The figure shown here is in Icons view. To change the view, select one from the View menu.

1. Click the first file or folder you want to select (for example, the AR folder in the next figure).

2. Hold down the Shift key, and click the last file or folder in the group (G0303 in the figure). That file and all the files in between become selected.

3. Release the Shift key. You can now perform the task, and all the selected files or folders will be affected.

If the files are noncontiguous, use this method instead:

1. Click the first file or folder you want.

2. While holding down the Ctrl key, click each additional file you want to select.

3. Release the Ctrl key. Any action you perform now will affect all the selected files or folders.

You can also select files and folders located in a cluster in the window (but not necessarily contiguous in the strict sense) by enclosing them in a "box." To do so, follow these steps:

1. Point to an area above and to the left of the first file you want to include (M0301 in the following figure).

2. Hold down the left mouse button and drag down and to the right, creating a box around your targeted files.

3. Release the mouse button. Any files that fell within the box you drew are selected.

Moving and Copying Files and Folders

Now that you know the various ways to select files and folders, it's time to learn what actions you can take with them. Two very common actions are moving and copying. You might want to copy a file to a floppy disk to share with a friend, for example, or move some infrequently used data files to a secondary hard disk to free up space on your primary disk.

You have a couple of options for moving and copying: You can use the drag-and-drop method with the mouse, or use menu commands. I'll show you both methods in the following sections.

Moving Files and Folders

To move a file using the drag-and-drop technique, do the following:

1. If the folder list doesn't appear, click the Folders button to display it.

2. Display the folder containing the file(s) or folder(s) to be moved.

3. In the folder list, make sure the destination folder's or drive's name is visible (but don't click it to select it). If necessary, click a plus sign to expand the folder list and make the destination visible.

4. Select the file(s) or folder(s) to be moved.

WARNING

Don't move program files or folders—that is, files or folders needed to run particular programs. Most programs will not work anymore if you move their files. Your safest bet is to move only the data files you have created yourself. You can *copy* any files without fear, however.

5. If you are moving from one disk to another, hold down the Shift key. (Otherwise, Windows will copy rather than move.)

NOTE

Windows attempts to guess what you want to do based on the source and destination locations. If you drag from one drive to another, it assumes you want to copy unless you hold down Shift while dragging. If you drag from one folder to another on the same drive, it assumes you want to move unless you hold down Ctrl. If you don't want to remember all that, just get in the habit of always holding down Shift when moving and always holding down Ctrl when copying.

6. Drag the selection to the destination folder or drive on the folder list. For example, in the following figure, I'm dragging the folder named LOD_108 to the A: drive. Then release the Shift key.

NOTE

If there is a plus sign on the mouse pointer as you drag, you are copying rather than moving; press Esc and try again. If there is no plus sign, you are moving.

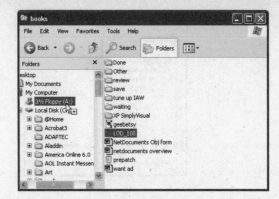

Another way to move a file is to use the Move to Folder command on the Edit menu. This method has the advantage of not requiring the folder list to be visible.

1. Select the file(s) or folder(s) you want to move and then choose Edit ➢ Move to Folder.

2. In the Move Items dialog box, click the plus signs next to drives and folders until the destination location appears, and then select it. (In this example, I want to move the file to the ADAPTEC folder.)

3. Click Move.

NOTE

The Make New Folder button lets you create a new folder on the fly. To use it, be sure to first select the drive or folder that you want as the parent for the new folder. Then click Make New Folder, type a name for the new folder, and click OK. Then click Move to complete the move. You'll learn other ways to create new folders later in this chapter.

Copying Files and Folders

Copying works almost exactly the same as moving, except for a few minor details.

When you copy with drag-and-drop, you must hold down Ctrl as you drag if you are copying within the same drive; otherwise a plain drag-and-drop will move. While copying, the mouse pointer shows a plus sign, like so:

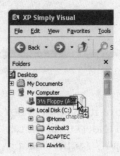

You can also copy using the Copy to Folder command on the Edit menu, which works just like the Move to Folder command you just learned about.

Deleting Files and Folders

You will probably want to delete old data files that you no longer have any use for, to save space on your hard disk and to make it easier to locate the data files you currently need.

Part i

NOTE

When you delete a file or folder, it isn't destroyed immediately; instead, it is moved to the Recycle Bin. You can get it back later by fishing it out of the Recycle Bin, as you'll learn later in this chapter.

To delete one or more files or folders:

1. Select the file(s) and/or folder(s) you want to delete.

2. Press the Delete key.

TIP

To delete the selection permanently without sending it to the Recycle Bin, hold down the Shift key as you press the Delete key in Step 2.

3. In the confirmation box that appears, click Yes.

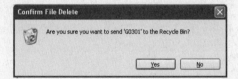

NOTE

As an alternative to deleting old files, you might consider moving them to a floppy disk for archival purposes, or creating a writeable CD containing those files. You'll learn about writeable CDs in Chapter 25.

There are many alternatives to Step 2. Here are some of them:

▶ You can right-click your selection and choose Delete from the shortcut menu that appears.

▶ You can click Throw Away This File from the System Tasks pane.

▶ You can choose File ➢ Delete.

Renaming Files and Folders

Many people, when they start out in computing, give their data files rather generic names, such as Letter1, Memo99, and so on. They don't realize that over time, they will probably write dozens of letters, and it will be difficult to remember which letter is which.

You can rename a file easily in Windows, to give it a better or more descriptive name than the one you originally assigned.

WARNING

Don't rename files or folders needed to run a program, or the program might not work anymore. Rename only data files and folders that you have created yourself.

NOTE

You can rename only individual files and folders; you cannot rename them as a group. The Rename command isn't available when multiple files or folders are selected.

To rename a file or folder:

1. Select the file or folder.
2. Press the F2 key. The name becomes selected.

TIP

Instead of pressing F2 in Step 2, you can select File ➤ Rename, or you can right-click the file and then click Rename from the shortcut menu.

3. Type a new name.
4. Press Enter.

Do you need to type the file extension when renaming? Well, it depends. By default, file extensions are hidden for known file types; so if the file's original name doesn't show a file extension, you don't have to type one when you rename the file. In fact, if you do type one, the file's actual name ends up with two extensions, like MyFile.doc.doc.

However, you can set file extensions to display in file management windows. (To do so, choose Tools ➤ Folder Options in any file management window, and then on the View tab, clear the Hide Extensions for Known File Types check box.) If you rename a file with a displayed extension, you must retype the period and the extension when you type the new name; otherwise, the file will lack an extension, and Windows won't be able to determine its file type.

CREATING NEW FOLDERS

As you saw earlier, you can create new folders on the fly while moving or copying files with the Move to Folder or Copy to Folder command. You can also create new folders at any other time, for any purpose.

For example, suppose you want to organize your documents in the My Documents folder into separate child folders for each member of your family. You could create a folder for each person, and then move that person's document files into that folder.

To create a new folder, follow these steps:

1. Display the folder that should be the parent folder for the new one.

2. Choose File ➤ New ➤ Folder. A new folder appears with the name New Folder. The name is highlighted, and ready to be typed over with a new name.

TIP

Instead of choosing File ➤ New ➤ Folder in Step 2, you can right-click the background of the current folder display and then choose New ➤ Folder from the shortcut menu.

3. Type the name for the new folder and then press Enter.

SEARCHING FOR FILES AND FOLDERS

It's easy to forget in which folder you have stored a particular file, but Windows makes the process of finding lost files painless. Here's what you do:

1. Choose Start ➢ Search.

A Search Results window appears, with a Search Companion pane at the left.

2. Click the category that best represents what you want to search for. These search categories restrict your search to files with certain extensions. If you don't want that restriction, choose All Files and Folders as the category.

The Search Companion pane then changes to show additional controls.

NOTE

Each of the specifications in Steps 3 through 6 is optional; you can use any combination of them to build your search criteria. The more specific your criteria are, the fewer files will be returned. At any point, you can skip to Step 7 to run the search.

3. (Optional) In the Part or All of the File Name text box, type the filename if you know it, or any portion of it that you do know.

    To represent unknown parts of the name, you can use *wildcard* characters. For example, if you know only that it begins with W, you would use W*. Or, if you know it begins with W and contains exactly six letters, you could use W?????.

4. (Optional) If you remember that the filename contains a certain word or phrase, type it in the A Word or Phrase in the File text box.

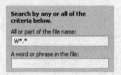

5. (Optional) If you don't want to search all hard drives on your system, open the Look In drop-down list and select a single drive that you want to search, such as the C: drive in this example.

NOTE

You can also click Browse from the Look In drop-down list and pinpoint a specific folder from which to start the search. That way, your search results will reflect only that folder and its subfolders.

6. (Optional) To set any other criteria for the search, click one of the other buttons to display additional controls, and make your selections. Here, for example, I have chosen When Was It Modified? and filled in some date criteria.

7. Click Search to begin the search.

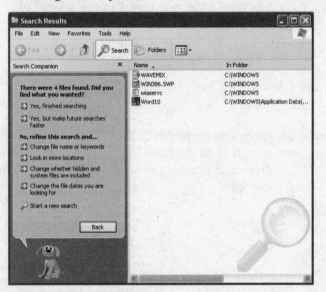

Any files that match all the specifications appear on a list in the right-hand pane.

Working with Search Results

As you can see in the preceding figure, the Search Companion makes it very easy to refine your initial search after you see the results. Just follow the prompts in the Search Companion pane if you need to make changes.

Let's assume for the moment, though, that the file you were searching for *did* appear in the search results. What can you do with it now?

Locate it.   Make a note of the location listed in the In Folder column. Now you know where the file is stored, and you can find it later in Windows Explorer or through whatever program you used to create it.

Open it.   You can double-click the file to open it in the program you used to create it. (You can open a file this way from any file management window, not just from a search.)

Move, copy, rename, or delete it.   The same file management operations that you learned earlier in this chapter can be employed in the Search Results window.

WORKING WITH THE RECYCLE BIN

As I mentioned earlier in the chapter, when discussing deleting, a file is not immediately destroyed when you delete it. Instead, it goes to a folder called Recycle Bin. You can restore a deleted file from the Recycle Bin much as you can fish out a piece of paper from the wastepaper basket next to your desk.

Restoring a Deleted File

The Recycle Bin's icon sits on the desktop, so you can open it and retrieve a deleted file at any time:

1. Double-click the Recycle Bin icon on the desktop.

The Recycle Bin window opens.

2. Select the file you want to restore. (In the following figure, I've selected Introduction.)

3. In the Recycle Bin Tasks pane, click Restore This Item. (Notice the name change here; this pane is usually called System Tasks.)

Part i

NOTE

There are many alternatives to Step 3. You can choose File ➤ Restore, right-click the file and choose Restore from the shortcut menu, or drag the file out of the Recycle Bin window and into some other file management window or onto the desktop.

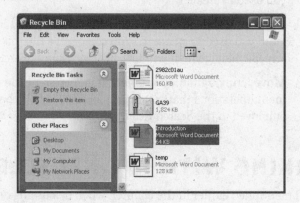

Emptying the Recycle Bin

If you are certain you don't want any of the files in the Recycle Bin, you can empty it to free up the hard-disk space that those files are occupying. If there are only a few small files, the difference might be negligible; but when the Recycle Bin contains many large files and your hard-disk space is running short, emptying the bin is a worthwhile proposition.

NOTE

If you are trying to delete some files to free up hard-disk space for some other purpose, keep in mind that the space is not actually freed until the Recycle Bin is emptied.

You need not open the Recycle Bin window in order to empty the bin; simply do the following:

1. Right-click the Recycle Bin icon on the desktop and then choose Empty Recycle Bin.

2. A confirmation message appears. Click Yes.

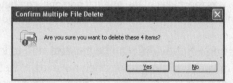

You can also empty the Recycle Bin while its window is open.

1. With no files selected in the Recycle Bin window, click Empty the Recycle Bin in the Recycle Bin Tasks pane.

NOTE

Instead of the clicking in Step 1, you can choose File ➢ Empty Recycle Bin. If you do that, you don't need to worry about making sure no files are selected beforehand.

2. Click Yes to confirm.

FORMATTING DISKS

Formatting a disk creates an organizational structure called a file allocation table, or FAT, that makes it possible for files and folders to be stored on the disk. You can format both hard and floppy disks, but because formatting a disk wipes out any existing content, you will probably never have occasion to format a hard disk.

Many floppy disks sold these days are preformatted, so you may not need to format new floppy disks either. When shopping for floppies, look for disks marked "IBM Formatted." IBM-compatible formatting will work on both MS-DOS and Windows PCs.

NOTE

IBM was the maker of the original personal computer many years ago, and its standard of disk formatting is still the standard today.

Formatting a floppy disk can be a useful skill to know, however, in case you buy unformatted floppies (which are a little cheaper than formatted ones) or you want to reformat a floppy. Since reformatting wipes out all the content on a disk, you can reformat the disk as an alternative to deleting all the disk content using the method you learned earlier in the chapter.

NOTE

Reformatting a disk is not necessarily better than deleting its content manually; it's just an alternative.

To format a floppy disk, do the following:

1. Place the disk to be formatted in your floppy drive.

2. Open the My Computer window.

NOTE

If the items in your My Computer window look different from the ones shown here, switch views from the View menu.

3. Right-click the floppy drive icon and then choose Format from the shortcut menu.

4. You should now see the Format dialog box. Leave the Capacity, File System, and Allocation Unit Size settings at their defaults.

5. If you would like a *volume label* for the disk—an internal label for a disk, which shows up in My Computer next to the drive letter whenever that disk is inserted—enter it in the Volume Label text box, replacing the label that's already there.

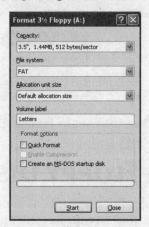

6. (Optional) If you are reformatting an already-formatted disk, you can mark the Quick Format check box to make the formatting happen faster.

NOTE

When you use Quick Format, the disk's FAT is simply rewritten; the disk itself is not checked or prepared in any way. That's why you can use Quick Format only with already-formatted disks.

NOTE

The Create an MS-DOS Startup Disk option enables you to create a bootable floppy that you can use to start your computer if it won't start normally. If you just want a blank, formatted floppy disk, however, you don't want a startup disk.

7. Click Start.

8. A warning message appears. Click OK to begin the formatting.

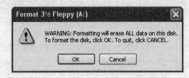

9. Wait for the formatting to finish, and then click OK to accept the confirmation message.

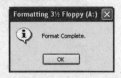

10. Click Close to close the Format dialog box.

COPYING A FLOPPY DISK

If you have a floppy disk that contains important data, you might want to make a copy of it. You can copy its contents to your hard disk and then to another floppy, but going floppy-to-floppy is faster. You can make the copy using a single floppy drive, by swapping the disks out as prompted.

To copy a floppy disk, follow these steps:

1. In My Computer, right-click the floppy drive and then choose Copy Disk.

2. In the Copy Disk dialog box, click Start.

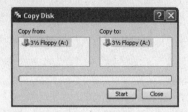

3. Insert the disk to be copied and then click OK. Then wait for the disk to be copied into your computer's memory.

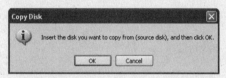

4. When prompted, insert the disk to contain the copy and then click OK.

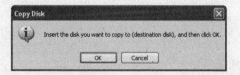

5. When a Copy Completed Successfully message appears, click Close.

WHAT'S NEXT

In this chapter, you learned how to manage files, folders, and disks on your computer. You should now be able to work with files with confidence! In the next chapter, Guy Hart-Davis explains several of the many accessory programs that come with Windows XP Home Edition.

Chapter 7

WINDOWS XP HOME EDITION BUILT-IN APPLICATIONS

This chapter discusses the bundled programs that come with Windows: WordPad, Notepad, Character Map, Paint, Calculator, Windows Picture and Fax Viewer, and Command Prompt. These programs have relatively limited functionality; they're intended to take care of some basic tasks, but not to discourage you from buying fuller programs from either Microsoft or its competitors. Because they're limited, most of these programs are relatively small and easy to use. So as not to waste time belaboring the obvious, this chapter discusses only the most important features of the programs—leaving you to work out the easy stuff on your own.

Adapted from *Mastering Windows XP Home Edition*
by Guy Hart-Davis
ISBN 0-7821-2980-3   1,040 pages $39.99

WORDPAD

WordPad is a lightweight word processing program. It provides rudimentary features including font formatting, bulleted lists, paragraph alignment, margin placement, and support for different sizes of paper. It also lets you insert objects such as graphics and parts of other documents, so in a pinch you can create attractive documents with it. WordPad's Print Preview feature (File ➤ Print Preview) lets you make sure your documents look OK before you commit them to paper. But WordPad has no advanced features; for example, it doesn't offer style formatting, tables, or macros. It also lacks a spelling checker or grammar checker, so you'll need to proof and check your documents visually.

Because of these limitations, if you have Microsoft Word, Corel WordPerfect, Star Office, or another full-fledged word processor, you'll probably have little use for WordPad. But if you don't have another word processor, and if you need to create only simple documents, you may find WordPad useful.

WordPad can open documents in Word format, Windows Write format, Rich Text Format (RTF), and text formats. (Windows Write was WordPad's predecessor for Window 3.*x* versions.) If you have font-formatted documents created in another word processing program, Rich Text Format may prove the best format for getting them into WordPad.

TIP

Because WordPad can open Word documents but doesn't support macros, you can safely use WordPad to view Word documents that may contain dangerous macros or customizations. WordPad doesn't render all Word's formatting faithfully, but you'll be able to see if the document is valuable or merely a vector for macro viruses. (You can also get a free viewer for Word documents that lets you examine their contents without worrying about macros and viruses. Visit the Microsoft Web site, www.microsoft.com.)

Each instance of WordPad can have only one document open at once, but you can run multiple instances of WordPad if you need to have two or more documents open at the same time. Each instance of WordPad typically takes up around 4MB of memory (RAM and virtual memory) plus the size of the document, so if you have 128MB RAM or more, you should be able to have several instances of WordPad open without degrading your computer's performance or impairing its ability to run larger programs at a good speed.

The most complex part of WordPad is the Options dialog box (View ➤ Options), which has six pages: Options, Text, Rich Text, Word, Write, and Embedded:

▶ The Options page (of the Options dialog box—WordPad gets a little recursive here) lets you choose measurement units: Inches, Centimeters, Points, or Picas. (Points and picas are typesetting measurements. A *point* is ¹⁄₇₂-inch, and a *pica* is ⅙-inch, so there are 12 points to the pica.) It also contains the Automatic Word Selection check box, which controls whether WordPad selects the whole of each second and subsequent word when you click and drag to select from one word to the next. If Automatic Word Selection is turned off, WordPad lets you select character by character. (If you've used Word, you're probably familiar with this behavior.)

▶ The Text, Rich Text, Word, Write, and Embedded pages contain options for the different document types that WordPad can handle. For each, you can choose word-wrap settings (No Wrap, Wrap to Window, or Wrap to Ruler) and whether you want to display the toolbar, the Format bar, the ruler, and the status bar.

NOTEPAD

Notepad is a *text editor*, a program designed for working with text files—those files that contain only text (characters): It has no formatting and no graphical objects.

To make life tolerable in the Spartan environment of text files, Notepad lets you select a font for the display of text on-screen (choose Format ➤ Font). It has a word-wrap option (choose Format ➤ Word Wrap) so that lines of text don't reach past the border of the window to the horizon on your right. And you can insert the time and date in a Notepad file by choosing Edit ➤ Time/Date or pressing the F5 key.

TIP

Notepad automatically adds the .txt extension to files you save. To save a file under a different extension, enter the filename and extension in double quotation marks in the File Name text box in the Save As dialog box.

Generally speaking, you shouldn't spend any more time using Notepad than you need to, because Notepad is a very limited program. But it's good for several tasks:

▶ Because Notepad is small and simple, you can keep it running without worrying about it slowing your computer down. Because Notepad takes up little memory, you can run multiple instances of Notepad without slowing your computer down appreciably. This can be useful for taking a variety of notes. Notepad lets you open only a single file at a time, but by opening multiple instances of Notepad, you can open as many files as you need.

▶ Notepad is good for editing configuration files for such Windows programs as still use them. But if you're editing any of the standard Windows configuration files that remain in Windows XP (for example, `autoexec.bat` or `win.ini`), use the System Configuration Editor instead. The System Configuration Editor is essentially Notepad after a couple of doses of steroids and customizations for editing system files. (To run the System Configuration Editor, choose Start ➤ Run or press Winkey+R, enter **sysedit** in the Open text box in the Run dialog box, and click the OK button.)

▶ Apart from working with self-declared text files, Notepad is good for creating and editing other text-only files. For example, it's good for editing playlists for programs such as MP3 players. These are text files, though they use extensions such as M3U and PLS to give them file-type functionality. If you create such a file using Notepad, remember to use double quotation marks around the filename when saving it.

▶ You can use Notepad to open documents other than text files. (Select the All Files item in the Files of Type drop-down list in the Open dialog box.) For example, if Word for Windows crashes, you may end up with a corrupted file that Word itself cannot open. By opening up the file in Notepad, you may be able to save part of the text. You'll see a lot of nonalphanumeric characters that represent things like Word formatting (for example, styles), but you'll also find readable text. Figure 7.1 shows an example of this. If the document has been saved using Word's Fast Save feature, you'll even find deleted parts of the document still in the file—which can be intriguing or embarrassing, depending on whether you wrote the document.

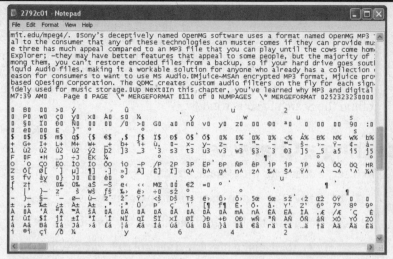

FIGURE 7.1: You can use Notepad to recover text from a corrupted Word document—or to view deleted parts of a fast-saved Word document.

CHARACTER MAP

Character Map is a small utility that lets you insert characters and symbols that don't appear on your keyboard into your documents. Figure 7.2 shows Character Map in its Standard view with the graphical symbols font Webdings displayed.

FIGURE 7.2: Character Map lets you select any character in any font installed on your computer.

Windows hides Character Map on the System Tools menu (Start ➤ All Programs ➤ Accessories ➤ System Tools ➤ Character Map). If you don't find it there but think it's installed on your computer, choose Start ➤ Run (or press Winkey+R) to display the Run dialog box, enter **charmap** in the Open text box, and click the Open button. Failing that, search for `charmap.exe` (it should be in your `\Windows\System32\` folder) and run it from the Search Results window.

Inserting a Character

To insert a character with Character Map:

1. Select the font in the Font drop-down list.

2. Scroll the list box until the character is visible:

    ▶ To display a magnified view of a character, click it. Alternatively, use the arrow keys ($\rightarrow$, $\leftarrow$, $\uparrow$, and $\downarrow$) to select it, and then press the spacebar.

    ▶ Once you've displayed a magnified view, you can use the arrow keys to move the magnifier around the grid of characters.

    ▶ To remove the magnified view, click the magnified character or press the spacebar.

3. Select the character and click the Select button. Character Map copies it into the Characters to Copy text box.

4. Select other characters as necessary, then click the Copy button to copy the character or characters to the Clipboard.

5. Activate the program and paste the characters into it.

NOTE

Some text-based programs cannot accept graphical characters and convert them to the nearest character they support. For example, if you paste a Wingdings telephone character into Notepad, Notepad converts it to a mutated parenthesis. If you paste the same telephone character into WordPad, Word-Pad displays it correctly. Similarly, many e-mail programs strip incoming messages down to text, so it's a waste of time to send the users of such programs messages that contain unusual characters.

Inserting a Character in Advanced View

Character Map's Standard view is fine for inserting many weird and wonderful characters in your documents. But if you want to work with a particular character set, you need to use Advanced view. (Character sets are discussed in the nearby sidebar.) Select the Advanced View check box to display Character Map in Advanced view (shown in Figure 7.3).

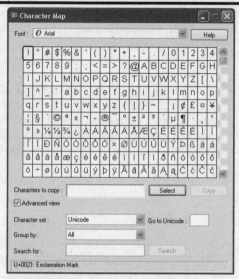

FIGURE 7.3: Select the Advanced View check box to work with a particular character set.

As you can see in the figure, Character Map in Advanced view has several extra controls:

Character Set drop-down list   Use this drop-down list to select the character set you want to work with. The default selection is Unicode.

Group By drop-down list   When necessary, choose a grouping for the character set. Depending on the character sets installed on your computer, you'll see options such as All, Ideographs by Radicals, Japanese Kanji by Hiragana, Japanese Kanji by Radical, Japanese Shift-JIS Subrange, and Unicode Subrange.

Go to Unicode text box   Use this text box to display the Unicode character associated with a character code. Type the code into this text box. When you type the fourth character of the code, Character Map displays the associated Unicode character.

Search For text box and Search button   Use this text box and button to search for a character by its description. For example, to find the inverted question mark character (¿), enter text such as **question inverted** or **inverted question** and click the Search button. Character Map displays all characters that match the criteria.

TIP

If you don't see the character sets you need, they may not be installed on your computer. To install a character set, open Control Panel and click the Date, Time, Language, and Regional Options link. Click the Add Support for Additional Languages link. Windows displays the Regional and Language Options dialog box. Click the Advanced tab to display the Advanced page, then specify the languages to add.

Here's an example of inserting a Japanese kanji using Advanced view:

1. In the Character Set drop-down list, select the Windows: Japanese item.

2. In the Group By drop-down list, select the grouping you want. In the example, this is Japanese Kanji by Hiragana. Character Map opens a window displaying the kanji.

3. In the Japanese Kanji by Hiragana window, select the hiragana (phonetic character) that represents the sound of the kanji character. The main Character Map window (shown in Figure 7.4 with the Japanese Kanji by Hiragana window) displays a scrolling list of kanji that can be pronounced with that sound.

4. Select and copy the character as usual, then paste it into the document.

If you need to enter a particular character frequently in your documents and don't want to have to access Character Map each time, select the character in Character Map and memorize the Alt code displayed in the status bar. (Only some characters have these Alt codes.) To enter the character at the insertion point in a document, make sure that Num Lock is on, then hold down the Alt key and type the code for the character.

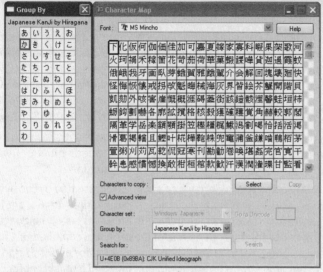

FIGURE 7.4: Using Character Map's Advanced view to select Japanese kanji

EXPERT KNOWLEDGE: ASCII, UNICODE, AND CODE PAGES

Okay, time out: What's ASCII? (It sounds kinda familiar...) What's Unicode? And what are code pages?

Briefly, these are all ways of mapping the binary codes that computers use to store characters to: a) the characters on whichever keyboard you happen to be using, and b) what you see on-screen.

ASCII (American Standard Code for Information Interchange) and Unicode are both standard character-encoding schemes for text-based data. In other words, if you have information that can be represented in characters (such as this paragraph, for example), you can encode it in ASCII or in Unicode so that a computer can store it.

In ASCII, each character is represented by one byte. There are two forms of ASCII: *Standard ASCII* uses a 7-bit binary number combination to represent each character, which gives enough combinations for 128 characters. *Extended ASCII*, which is also known as *high ASCII*, uses an 8-bit number combination for each character, which gives enough combinations for 256 characters.

CONTINUED ➡

Given that the English alphabet uses 26 uppercase letters, 26 lowercase letters, 10 numbers, some punctuation (comma, period, parentheses, and so on), and control characters, standard ASCII's capacity for 128 characters starts to look paltry. Extended ASCII doubles the ante and adds some foreign characters (for example, ú), graphic symbols, and symbol characters to standard ASCII's set.

Extended ASCII works pretty well provided you're satisfied with 256 characters. But even 256 characters is a pathetic number if you want anything beyond the main European languages.

Enter Unicode. In Unicode, each character is represented by two bytes (16 bits), which gives 65,536 character combinations (256 × 256) — enough to cover most of the characters in the world's many languages. As of the year 2000, about 39,000 of those 65,536 combinations had been assigned, with Chinese alone accounting for about 21,000 of them. (Japanese, with its borrowed and mutated kanji, is another of the greedier languages for Unicode combinations.)

When do you have to worry about ASCII and Unicode? Windows XP is pretty savvy about Unicode, so usually you don't have to worry about whether you're using Unicode or ASCII, because Windows XP uses Unicode almost exclusively.

For programs that don't support Unicode, you can use *code pages* to enable the programs to communicate effectively with the user. Briefly, a code page is a table that maps a program's character codes (which are binary) to the keys on the keyboard, the characters on the display, or (preferably) both. Previous versions of Windows used code pages.

If you need to use a program that can't handle Unicode, assign a code page for it as follows:

1. Choose Start ➢ Control Panel. Windows displays Control Panel.

2. Click the Date, Time, Language, and Regional Options link. Windows displays the Date, Time, Language, and Regional Options screen.

3. Click the Regional and Language Options link. Windows displays the Regional and Language Options dialog box.

CONTINUED ➡

4. Click the Advanced tab. Windows displays the Advanced page.

5. In the drop-down list, choose the language in which to display the program.

6. In the Code Page Conversion Tables list box, make sure the check box for the language is selected. If it isn't, select the check box to install the code page conversion table. (You'll need to provide your Windows CD or be connected to a network source of Windows installation files.)

7. If you want to make the code page settings available to your-self and to all new user accounts that you or other Computer Administrator users set up on this computer, select the Apply All Settings to the Current User Account and to the Default User Profile check box.

8. Click the OK button. If you chose to install a code page conver-sion table, Windows prompts you for your CD or installation source.

EXPERT KNOWLEDGE: USING PRIVATE CHARACTER EDITOR TO CREATE YOUR OWN CHARACTERS

Windows XP includes a hidden applet called Private Character Edi-tor that you can use for creating your own characters and logos. To run Private Character Editor, choose Start ➤ Run or press Winkey+R. Windows displays the Run dialog box. Enter **eudcedit** in the Open text box and click the OK button.

PAINT

Paint (Start ➤ All Programs ➤ Accessories ➤ Paint) is a basic illustra-tion program that's been included with almost all known desktop ver-sions of Windows. XP's incarnation of Paint lets you create bitmap files (.bmp, .dib), GIF files, JPEG files (.jpg and JPEG), and TIFF files

(.tif)—enough to make it useful for basic illustration needs, and significantly better than the versions of Paint in most versions of Windows 9x, which could work only with bitmaps.

If you're into creating drawings or paintings on the computer, you'll find that Paint's limitations present more challenges than its capabilities do. Paint's Image menu provides tools for flipping and rotating images, stretching and skewing images, changing their attributes (for example, changing a color file to black and white), and inverting colors—but that's about it. If you want to do serious illustration work, consider a heavy-duty illustration program such as Paint Shop Pro or Adobe Photoshop.

If you're *not* into creating drawings or paintings on the computer, you'll probably find Paint quite useful for some basic graphical tasks such as the following:

Creating background images for your Desktop   If you want to use a digital photo or a scan as a background image for your Desktop, you may need to rotate it from a portrait orientation to a landscape orientation or crop it down to size.

Capturing images directly from a Web camera   You can capture images directly from a Web camera by using the File ➤ From Scanner or Camera command. Chapter 24 discusses how to work with pictures and video.

Cleaning up scanned images   Images you scan can easily pick up dots from specks of dirt on the scanner or from damage to the picture. You can use Paint to edit pictures and remove small defects such as these.

Capturing screens   If you're preparing documentation on how to use software, you may want to capture the screen, or a window. To capture the whole screen to the Clipboard, press the PrintScreen (PrtScn) key. To capture only the active window to the Clipboard, press Alt+PrintScreen. Then choose Edit ➤ Paste to paste the screen or window into Paint, where you can work with it as you would any other graphic.

CALCULATOR

Calculator (Start ➤ All Programs ➤ Accessories ➤ Calculator) seems such a basic program that it barely deserves mention. But there are several things you should know about it:

▶ Calculator displays itself by default in its Standard view, but it also has a Scientific view that's useful if you need to work in hexadecimal, binary, or octal; calculate degrees or radians; or perform similar tasks. To switch Calculator to Scientific view, choose View ≻ Scientific. (To switch Calculator back to Standard view, choose View ≻ Standard.) Figure 7.5 shows Calculator in Scientific view calculating hex. For hex, octal, and binary, you can choose from four display sizes: Byte (8-bit representation), Word (16-bit representation), Dword (32-bit representation), and Qword (64-bit representation).

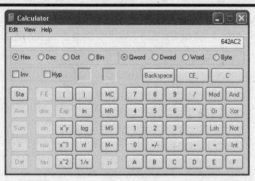

FIGURE 7.5: Calculator offers a Scientific view in addition to its Standard view.

▶ When you switch Calculator from Standard view to Scientific view, or switch it back, it wipes the display. To take the current number from one view to the other view, use the MS button to store it, switch view, and then use the MR button to retrieve it. Binary, octal, or hex numbers get converted to decimal when you move them to Standard view by using this technique.

▶ You can operate Calculator entirely from the keyboard if you want to. Choose Help ≻ Help Topics to open the Help file, then investigate the "Using Keyboard Equivalents of Calculator Functions" topic.

▶ You can use key sequences as functions. For example, the sequence **:p** performs the equivalent of clicking the M+ key. Check the "Using Key Sequences as Functions" topic in the Help file for more information.

▶ If you're working with long numbers, you may want to choose View ≻ Digit Grouping to have Calculator group the digits into threes separated by commas. For example, with digit grouping, 44444444444 appears as 44,444,444,444, making it easier to read.

▶ Press Esc to clear Calculator.

WINDOWS PICTURE AND FAX VIEWER

Windows Picture and Fax Viewer is a sort of stealth program. It's largely subsumed into Windows Explorer, for which it provides the preview functionality (in views such as Thumbnails view), the Filmstrip view in the My Pictures folder, and slideshow views. There's no shortcut for Windows Picture and Fax Viewer on the Start menu, and there's no convenient way to start it other than by opening one of the file types with which it's associated.

Even when Windows Picture and Fax Viewer is running, Windows refuses to acknowledge it as such. The window it runs in is titled Windows Picture and Fax Viewer, but the window is treated as an Explorer window for Taskbar-grouping purposes. This isn't particularly helpful, as it's counterintuitive and means that the Windows Picture and Fax Viewer windows tend to disappear in the welter of Explorer windows that characterizes the busy Desktop. But no doubt it's logical enough. And Task Manager shows you on its Applications page that Windows Picture and Fax Viewer is running, but its Processes page shows only Explorer.

However, when you double-click a picture file in your My Pictures folder (or right-click the file and choose Preview from the context menu), Windows Picture and Fax Viewer springs into action, opening its own window. Figure 7.6 shows an example.

FIGURE 7.6: Windows Picture and Fax Viewer is a stealth program that hides under Explorer's virtual skirts most of the time.

Basic Manipulation of Images

Unlike (almost) all good Windows programs, Windows Picture and Fax Viewer spurns a menu bar in favor of a toolbar. The toolbar icons are marginally intuitive, and Windows Picture and Fax Viewer displays Screen-Tips when you hover the mouse pointer over them—but Windows Picture and Fax Viewer displays a different set of buttons depending on which type of image you have opened. Figure 7.7 shows the basic set of buttons on the Windows Picture and Fax Viewer toolbar with labels.

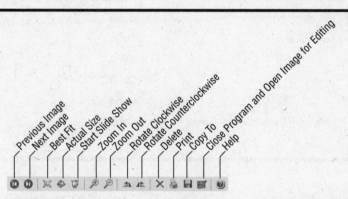

FIGURE 7.7: Windows Picture and Fax Viewer uses a toolbar rather than a menu structure to give you access to its commands.

All these buttons are self-explanatory except for the Actual Size button, which displays the image at 100 percent of its actual size (in other words, not zoomed in or zoomed out at all).

To make Windows Picture and Fax Viewer usable from the keyboard despite its lack of menus, most of these buttons have keyboard equivalents. Table 7.1 lists these keyboard equivalents.

TABLE 7.1: Keyboard Equivalents for Windows Picture and Fax Viewer Toolbar Buttons

BUTTON	KEYBOARD EQUIVALENT
Previous Image	Ctrl+Page Up
Next Image	Ctrl+Page Down
Best Fit	Ctrl+B

Continued on next page

TABLE 7.1:   Keyboard Equivalents for Windows Picture and Fax Viewer Toolbar Buttons *(continued)*

BUTTON	KEYBOARD EQUIVALENT
Actual Size	Ctrl+A
Start Slide Show	F11
Zoom In	+ on numeric keypad
Zoom Out	– on numeric keypad
Rotate Clockwise	Ctrl+K
Rotate Counterclockwise	Ctrl+L
Delete	Delete
Print	Ctrl+P
Copy To	Ctrl+S
Close Program and Open Image for Editing	Ctrl+E
Help	F1

Annotating an Image

Viewing images quickly palls, even if you use the slide show feature, unless of course the images are unusually stimulating. To counter accusations that it's a featherweight, Windows Picture and Fax Viewer also provides features for annotating TIFF images. You might say that this isn't a task you feel compelled to perform with anything approaching frequency, but these features can be especially useful for annotating incoming faxes before printing them out or shunting them along to your colleagues.

To annotate a TIFF, open it by double-clicking it in an Explorer window. The Windows Picture and Fax Viewer window opens, including the image annotation tools on the toolbar. Figure 7.8 shows the extra buttons with labels.

These annotation tools are mostly self-explanatory and easy to use. The one distinction that you need to know is that a text annotation is plain text with no background, while an attached note annotation is a colored rectangular background to which you can add text. A text annotation works well in open space on the document (for example, in one of the margins), while an attached note annotation is good for slapping over part of the document.

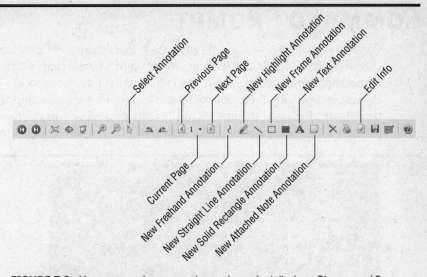

FIGURE 7.8: You can use the annotation tools on the Windows Picture and Fax Viewer toolbar to annotate TIFF files, such as faxes.

Once you've applied an annotation, you can click the Edit Info button with the annotation selected to display the Annotation Properties dialog box, in which you can change the font or color for the annotation.

Continuing its attempt to build a reputation as a maverick Windows program, Windows Picture and Fax Viewer provides some annotation functionality that's available only through the keyboard (as opposed to being available through both keyboard and mouse, as is the case with most functionality in most Windows programs):

▶ Select an annotation and press ← or → to move it 1 pixel to the left or right.

▶ Select an annotation and press ↑ or ↓ to move it 1 pixel up or down.

▶ Select an annotation and press Ctrl+← or Ctrl+→ to move it 10 pixels to the left or right.

▶ Select an annotation and press Ctrl+↑ or Ctrl+↓ to move it 10 pixels up or down.

When you've finished annotating an image, save it and close the Windows Picture and Fax Viewer window.

COMMAND PROMPT

Command Prompt (Start ➢ All Programs ➢ Accessories ➢ Command Prompt) gives you a DOS-like command prompt window that you can use to run character-mode programs or to issue commands. Command Prompt is especially useful for command-line utilities such as ping and tracert, which missed the line when the deity of the GUI was doling out interfaces. Figure 7.9 shows ping running in a Command Prompt window.

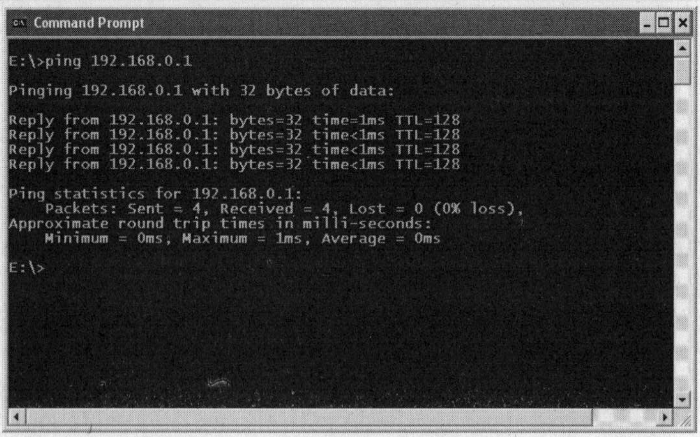

FIGURE 7.9: Running ping in a Command Prompt window

For most purposes, there's no advantage in using Command Prompt to issue commands instead of using the Run dialog box (Start ➢ Run, or Winkey+R) except that in Command Prompt you can see the history of the commands you've issued in this session.

Command Prompt may look as simple as an unadorned DOS prompt— and you can use it as simply as that. But if you use Command Prompt extensively, you'd do well to use its editing capabilities and customize its behavior to suit your needs.

If you *really* want Command Prompt to look like a DOS prompt, try running it full screen instead of in a window. To toggle Command Prompt between a window and full screen, press Alt+Enter. There's also an option setting for this, as you'll see in a moment.

Recalling a Command You've Used

Often, you'll need to reuse a command you've used earlier in the current Command Prompt window, or you'll need to issue a similar command. Command Prompt stores the last few commands you've used (as you'll see in a moment, you can customize the number of commands it stores), so that you can recall them quickly.

To recall a command from the current session, press the ↑ key. The first press displays the previous command, the second the command before that, and so on. If you go too far back in the list, press the ↓ key to go back through the list toward the later commands.

Once you've reached the command you want to use, you can edit it or add to it, or simply press the Enter key to run it.

Selecting, Copying, and Pasting in Command Prompt

Selecting, copying, and pasting in Command Prompt windows are much clumsier than in graphical windows, but they work well enough once you know how to do them.

To use the mouse to select text in Command Prompt, you need to turn on QuickEdit mode. You can turn it on either temporarily (choose Edit ➢ Mark from the title-bar context menu or from the control menu) or permanently (select the QuickEdit Mode check box on the Options page of the Console Windows Properties dialog box or the Command Prompt Properties dialog box).

Once you've turned on QuickEdit, click to place an insertion point, or drag to select a block of text.

To copy, right-click after making a selection. (Alternatively, press Enter, or choose Edit ➢ Copy from the title-bar context menu or from the control menu.) Issuing a Copy command in any of these ways collapses the selection, so that it looks as though the Copy operation has failed, but in fact Windows has copied the selection to the Clipboard, from which you can paste it into another Windows program or back into the Command Prompt window.

You can also copy information from another Windows program and paste it into Command Prompt by placing the insertion point, then choosing Edit ➢ Paste from either the title-bar context menu or the control menu.

Customizing Command Prompt

By default, Command Prompt uses a white system font on a black background—to look as DOS-like as possible, perhaps—but there's no reason to keep it that way if you don't like that look. You can customize Command Prompt easily enough by using its Properties dialog box.

Actually, it's a little more complicated than that. You can customize the settings for the current Command Prompt window, or you can customize the default settings for the Console Window, which affects all Command Prompt windows you open. You can also choose to apply the settings you specify for the current Command Prompt window to the shortcut from which you started Command Prompt, which means that further Command Prompt windows you start from that shortcut will start with those properties. (This is different from changing the default settings for the Console Window—changing the shortcut affects only the Command Prompt windows you start from the shortcut.)

Let's take it from the top.

Customizing the Current Command Prompt Window

To customize the current Command Prompt window, right-click its title bar and choose Properties from the context menu. (Alternatively, open the control menu and choose Properties from it.) Command Prompt displays the Properties dialog box.

Options Page   The Options page of the Command Prompt Properties dialog box (shown in Figure 7.10) contains four group boxes of options:

Cursor Size group box   Choose the Small option button, the Medium option button, or the Large option button as appropriate.

Command History group box   In the Buffer Size text box, you can adjust the number of commands that Command Prompt stores in its buffer. (Storing more commands needs a little more memory, but if your computer can run Windows XP at a tolerable speed, it probably has plenty of memory to store a few extra commands.) In the Number of Buffers text box, you can adjust the number of processes allowed to have distinct history buffers. Select the Discard Old Duplicates check box if you want the buffered list to omit repeated commands. Omitting them reduces the list and can make it more manageable, but it also means that you may not find commands where you expect them in the list. For example, if your third-to-last command was the same as the command 40 commands before, you'll have to go up 42 steps in the list to find it rather than finding it 3 steps up.

Display Options group box   If you want your Command Prompt sessions to be displayed full screen, select the Full Screen option button. Otherwise, leave the Window option button selected, as it is by default.

Edit Options group box   Select the QuickEdit Mode check box if you want to be able to use the mouse for cutting and pasting in Command Prompt. Leave the Insert Mode check box selected (as it is by default) if you like the standard way of inserting text at the cursor, moving along any characters to the right of the cursor instead of typing over them. If you prefer typeover, clear this check box.

Font Page   On the Font page of the Command Prompt Properties dialog box, select the font and font size you want to use for the Command Prompt window.

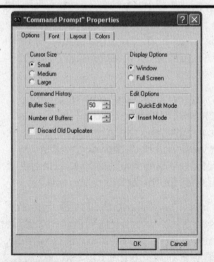

FIGURE 7.10: On the Options page of the Command Prompt Properties dialog box, specify cursor size, command history, display options, and editing options.

Layout Page   On the Layout page of the Command Prompt Properties dialog box (shown in Figure 7.11), specify how the Command Prompt window should look, where it should appear on the screen, and how many commands it should retain:

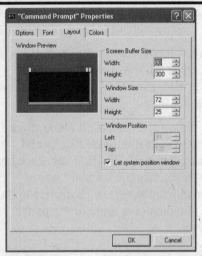

FIGURE 7.11: On the Layout page of the Command Prompt Properties dialog box, specify how you want the Command Prompt window to appear.

Screen Buffer Size group box   In the Width text box, specify the number of characters that you want each line in the buffer to contain. (Note that this is the buffer, not the window.) In the Height text box, specify the number of lines of data that you want to store.

Window Size group box   In the Width text box, specify the number of characters for the width of the window. Usually it's best to set this to the same value as the width of the screen buffer. (You can set it to a smaller value and have the window display scroll bars, but you can't set it to a larger value.) In the Height text box, specify the number of lines for the height of the window.

Window Position group box   By default, the Let System Position Window check box is selected, which lets Windows position the Command Prompt window as it sees fit. You can clear this check box and use the Left text box and the Top text box to specify the position of the left side and the top of the window.

Colors Page   On the Colors page of the Command Prompt Properties dialog box, you can choose colors for the screen text, the screen background, the pop-up text, and the pop-up background. Use the preview boxes to get an idea of the effect you're creating.

When you click the OK button in the Command Prompt Properties dialog box, Windows displays the Apply Properties to Shortcut dialog box asking whether you want to apply the properties you chose to the current window only or to modify the shortcut that you used to open this window. Select the Apply Properties to Current Window Only option button and click the OK button. Windows closes the Apply Properties to Shortcut dialog box and applies your choices.

Customizing All Command Prompt Windows Started from a Particular Shortcut

To change how future Command Prompt windows will be displayed, select the Modify Shortcut That Started This Window option button in the Apply Properties to Shortcut dialog box. Then click the OK button.

Customizing the Console Window Settings

To customize the Console Window settings, right-click the title bar of a Command Prompt window and choose Defaults from the context menu. (Alternatively, choose Defaults from the control menu.) Command Prompt displays the Console Windows Properties dialog box. Choose your customizations and click the OK button to apply them. Note that these customizations don't affect the current Command Prompt window, but they do affect Command Prompt windows that you start by using a shortcut that hasn't been customized or by issuing the **cmd** command.

WHAT'S NEXT

This chapter has discussed some of the programs that come bundled with Windows XP. These programs provide basic functionality for tasks for which you do not have a more sophisticated program (such as a word processing program like Word or a full-featured art program such as Paint Shop Pro). In the next chapter, Robert Cowart introduces printer configuration, explains how to set print options in applications, and how to manage the print queue.

Chapter 8

PRINTERS AND PRINTING

If your printer is of the plug-and-play variety, Windows probably already recognizes it as the default printer. This means you'll be able to print from any Windows program without worrying about anything more than turning on the printer, checking that it has paper, and choosing the File ➢ Print command. If your printer isn't plug-and-play–compatible, wasn't plugged in at the time of installation, or requires its own software to operate, you'll have to manually set up your printer before you can print. This chapter tells you how to do that and how to manage the use of your printer to get your work done.

Adapted from *Mastering Windows Me* by Robert Cowart
ISBN 0-7821-2857-2   960 pages $39.99

WINDOWS PRINTING OVERVIEW

As with Windows 3.1, Windows 9x/Me, and Windows NT/2000, unless you specify otherwise, programs hand off data to Windows XP, which in turn spools the data to a specified printer. Spooling means temporarily putting information on the hard disk that's really headed for the printer. Your document then gets sent out to the printer at the speed at which the printer can receive it. This lets you get back to work with your program sooner. You can even print additional documents, stacking up a load of jobs for the printer to print. This stack is called a queue. Some printers come with their own print software that contains a separate print spooler; if that's the case, Windows hands off the print job to the printer's own software spooler, which in turn feeds it to the printer.

When you print from a Windows program, the built-in Print Manager in Windows receives the data, queues up the jobs, routes them to the correct printer, and, when necessary, issues error or other appropriate messages to print-job originators. You can browse the printer's queue to see where your job(s) is in the print queue relative to other people's print jobs. You may also be permitted to rearrange the print queue, delete print jobs, or pause and resume a print job so that you can reload or otherwise service the printer.

Each printer you've installed appears in the Printers folder, along with an additional icon called Add Printer that lets you set up new printers. Printer icons in the folder appear and behave like any other object: You can delete them at will, create new ones, and set their properties. Deleting a printer icon from the Printers folder removes that printer's driver from your system. Double-clicking a printer in the folder displays its print queue and lets you manipulate the queue. Commands on the menus let you install, configure, connect, disconnect, and remove printers and drivers.

ADDING A NEW PRINTER

If your printer is already installed and seems to be working fine, you probably can skip this section. In fact, if you're interested in nothing more than printing from one of your programs without viewing the queue, printing to a network printer, or making adjustments to your current printer's settings, just skip to "Printing from a Program," later in this chapter. However, if you need to install a new printer, modify or customize your current installation, or add additional printers to your setup, read on.

Before running the Wizard, let's consider when you'd need to add a new printer to Windows XP:

▶ You're connecting a new printer directly to your computer.

▶ Someone has connected a new printer to the network, and you want to use it from your computer.

▶ You want to print files to disk that can later be sent to a particular type of printer.

▶ You want to set up multiple printer configurations (preferences) for a single physical printer so you can switch between them without having to change your printer setup before each print job.

Notice that a great deal of flexibility exists here, especially in the case of the last item. Because of the modularity of Windows XP's internal design, even though you might have only one physical printer, you can create any number of printer definitions for it, each with different characteristics.

TIP

These printer definitions are actually called printers, but you can think of them as printer names, aliases, or named virtual devices.

For example, you might want one definition set up to print on legal-sized paper in landscape orientation while another prints with normal paper in portrait orientation. Each of these two "printers" would actually use the same physical printer to print out on. While you're working with Windows XP's online help and this book, keep this terminology in mind. The word *printer* often doesn't really mean a physical printer. It usually means a *printer setup* that you've created with the Wizard. Typically, it's a collection of settings that points to a physical printer, but it could just as well create a print file instead.

About Printer Drivers

A printer can't just connect to your computer and mysteriously print a fancy page of graphics or even a boring old page of text. You need a *printer driver*. The printer driver (actually a file on your hard disk) translates your text file to commands that tell your printer how to print your file. Because different brands and models of printer use different commands for such things as Move up a line, Print a circle in the middle of the page, Print the letter A, and so on, a specialized printer driver is needed for each type of printer.

NOTE

Because some printers are actually functionally equivalent, a driver for a popular brand and model of printer (for example, an Epson or a Hewlett-Packard) often masquerades under different names for other printers.

When you add a printer, (unless you're installing a plug-and-play–compatible printer, which, luckily, almost all are nowadays), you're asked to choose the brand and model of printer. With plug-and-play printers, if the printer is attached and turned on, Windows queries the printer and the printer responds with its make and model number. As we've already mentioned, virtually all new printers are plug-and-play compatible, but if yours isn't, or you're installing an older printer, you'll have to tell Windows which printer you have so it will install the correct driver.

A good printer driver takes advantage of all your printer's capabilities, such as its built-in fonts and graphics features. A poor printer driver might succeed in printing only draft-quality text, even from a sophisticated printer.

If you're the proud owner of some offbeat brand of printer, you may be alarmed when you can't find your printer listed in the box when you run the Wizard. But don't worry; the printer manufacturer might be able to supply one. The procedure for installing manufacturer-supplied drivers is covered later in this chapter.

TIP

Some printers now come with special software to replace the Windows print queue or to perform special maintenance procedures like cleaning or print head alignment. Check your printer's documentation to ensure it doesn't require a different installation procedure from what is described here.

Running the Add Printer Wizard

Most printers these days are plug-and-play, such that Windows recognizes them automatically when you turn on the PC after plugging in the printer. If Windows has already found your new printer, you don't need to go through the following steps.

However, if Windows needs a little help finding your printer, or if you want to install another driver for the same printer, follow these steps.

TIP

You might want to install two drivers for the same printer if the printer can operate in multiple modes. For example, some laser printers can operate with both a PCL driver (normal laser printing) and a PostScript driver.

1. Open the Printers folder by choosing Start ➤ Control Panel ➤ Printers and Other Hardware.

2. Click Add a Printer. The Add Printer Wizard runs.

3. Click Next in the first dialog box that appears.

4. You're asked whether the printer is *local* or *network*. Because I'm describing how to install a local printer here, choose Local Printer Attached to This Computer, and then click Next.

5. If Windows detects your printer, skip to Step 11. Otherwise continue to Step 6.

6. Click Next at the message that Windows did not find any new printers, and you see a list of ports. You have to tell Windows which port the printer is connected to. (A *port* usually refers to the connector on the computer—but see Table 8.1 for the "file" exception.)

   Most often, the port will be the parallel printer port called LPT1 (Line Printer #1). Unless you know your printer is connected to another port, such as LPT2 or a serial port (such as COM1 or COM2), select LPT1 as in Figure 8.1.

7. Select the port you want to use and click Next.

8. Next you see a list of brands and models. In the left column, scroll the list, find the maker of your printer, and click it. Then, in the right column, choose the model number or name that matches your printer. Be sure to select the exact printer model, not just the correct brand name. Consult your printer's manual if you're in doubt about the model. What you enter here determines which printer driver file is used for this printer's definition. Figure 8.2 shows an example for an HP LaserJet 5P. Click Next when finished.

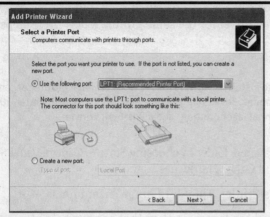

FIGURE 8.1: Choosing the port that the printer is connected to is the second step in setting up a local printer.

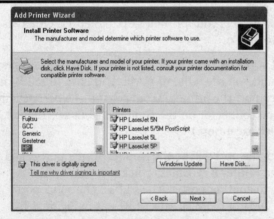

FIGURE 8.2: Choosing the printer make and model. Here I'm choosing a Hewlett-Packard LaserJet 5P.

9. Enter a name for the printer. This name will appear in any printer listing and under its icon.

10. Choose Yes or No to specify whether the printer will be the default printer for Windows programs. Then click Next.

TIP

Remember that you can have only one default printer installed. Adding a new default printer will remove the other printer's default status.

11. If you're on a network, the Wizard asks whether you want to share your printer, and if so, what share name you want to give it. Click the Share Name button and then enter a name, or click Do Not Share This Printer. Then click Next.

TIP

If the printer will be shared on a network with DOS and 16-bit Windows users (such as people running Windows for Workgroups 3.11), you might want to limit the share name to 12 characters because that's the maximum length those users will see when they are browsing for printers. If this is not a problem, it's a good idea to give the printer a meaningful name, such as "Office Printer" or "Kathie's Laser Printer."

12. If you chose to share the printer in Step 11, boxes appear in which you can enter location and comment information about the printer for the benefit of network users. This is optional. Enter text if desired, then click Next.

13. Next, you're asked if you want to print a test page. It's a good idea to do this. Turn on the printer, make sure it has paper in it, and click Finish. If the driver file for your printer is in the computer, you'll be asked if you want to use it or load a new one from the Windows XP CD-ROM. It's usually easier to use the existing driver. If the driver isn't on your hard disk, you'll be instructed to insert the disk containing the driver.

14. The final screen of the wizard shows you the information you have supplied about the printer. This gives you an opportunity to check your settings and go back if there are any mistakes. You can go back to previous screens using the Back button.

15. The test page will be sent to the printer. It should print out in a few seconds, and then you'll be asked if it printed OK. If it didn't print correctly, click No, and you'll be shown some troubleshooting information containing some questions and answers. The most likely fixes for the problem will be described. If the page printed OK, click Yes, and you're done.

Part i

When the printer has been installed, an icon for the printer will show up in the Printers and Faxes category.

TABLE 8.1: Printer Ports

PORT	NOTES
LPT1, LPT2, LPT3	The most common setting is LPT1 because most PC-type printers hook up to the LPT1 parallel port.
COM1, COM2, COM3, COM4	If you know your printer is of the serial variety, it's probably connected to the COM1 port. If COM1 is tied up for use with some other device, such as a modem, use COM2. If you choose a COM port, click Configure Port to check the communications settings in the resulting dialog box. Set the baud rate, data bit, parity, start and stop bits, and flow control to match those of the printer being attached. Refer to the printer's manual to determine what the settings should be.
File	This is for printing to a disk file instead of to the printer. Later, the file can be sent directly to the printer or sent to someone on floppy disk or over a modem. When you print to this printer name, you are prompted to enter a filename. (See "Printing to a Disk File" later in this chapter.)

When You Don't Find Your Printer in the List

When you're adding a local printer, you have to supply the brand name and model of the printer because Windows XP needs to know which driver to load into your Windows XP setup in order to use the printer correctly. (When you are adding a network printer, you aren't asked this question because the printer's host computer already knows what type of printer it is, and the driver is on that computer.)

What if your printer isn't on the list of Windows XP–recognized printers? Many off-brand printers are designed to be compatible with one of the popular printer types, such as the Apple LaserWriters, Hewlett-Packard LaserJets, or the Epson line of printers. Refer to the manual that came with your printer to see whether it's compatible with one of the printers that *is* listed. Some printers require that you set the printer in compatibility mode using switches or software. Again, check the printer's manual for instructions.

Finally, if it looks like there's no mention of compatibility anywhere, contact the manufacturer for their Windows XP–compatible driver. If you're lucky, they'll have one. It's also possible that Microsoft has a new driver for your printer that wasn't available when your copy of Windows was shipped. Check out the Microsoft Web site at `support.microsoft.com/support/printing`.

Part i

TIP

If you are having problems finding a Windows XP driver for your printer, then you might be able to use a Windows 2000 driver for the same printer. Under the hood, Windows XP and Windows 2000 are very similar.

If you have a driver that came on a disk with the printer, or if you have downloaded a driver from the Internet, here's how to use it to set up the printer in Windows XP:

1. Follow the instructions above for running the Add a Printer Wizard.

2. Instead of selecting one of the printers in the Driver list (it isn't in the list, of course), click the Have Disk button. You'll see this box:

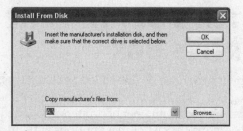

3. The Wizard is asking you to enter the path where the driver is located (typically a floppy disk). Insert the disk (or make sure the files are available somewhere), enter the path, and click OK. Enter the correct source of the driver. Typically, it'll be in the A: drive or your CD-ROM drive (usually D:).

TIP

Windows XP remembers the location from which you installed Windows XP originally. If you installed from a CD-ROM, it's likely that the default location for files is always going to be the CD-ROM drive's logical name (typically some higher letter, such as E: or F:). If you have done some subsequent installs or updates from other drives or directories, those are also remembered by Windows XP and will be listed in the drop-down list box.

TIP

Incidentally, the Wizard is looking for a file with an `.inf` extension. This is the standard file extension for manufacturer-supplied driver information files.

4. Click OK.

5. You might have to choose a driver from a list if multiple options exist.

6. Continue with the Wizard dialog boxes as explained above.

If you choose an *unsigned* driver—that is, a driver that has not been officially certified to work with Windows XP—you'll see a dire-sounding warning on-screen. It's better to use signed drivers, but if all you can find is an unsigned one, go ahead and try it. The worst that can happen is it won't work.

ALTERING THE DETAILS OF A PRINTER'S SETUP—THE PROPERTIES BOX

Each printer driver can be fine-tuned by changing settings in its Properties dialog box. This area is difficult to document because so many variations exist due to the number of printers supported. The following sections describe the gist of these options without going into too much detail about each printer type.

The settings pertaining to a printer are called *properties*. As I discussed earlier, properties abound in Windows XP. Almost every object in Windows XP has properties that you can examine and change at will. When you add a printer, the Wizard makes life easy for you by giving it some default properties that usually work fine and needn't be tampered with. You can change them later, but only if you need to. It may be worth looking at the properties for your printer, especially if the printer's acting up in some way when you try to print from Windows XP.

1. Open the Printers folder (Start ➢ Control Panel, then choose the Printers and other Hardware category, and then the Printers and Faxes category).

2. Right-click the printer's icon and choose Properties. A box such as the one in Figure 8.3 appears.

TIP

You can also press Alt+Enter to open the Properties box. This is true with many Windows XP objects.

3. Notice that there is a place for a comment. This is normally blank after you add a printer. If you share the printer on the network, any text that you add to this box will be seen by other users who are browsing the network for a printer.

4. Click the various tab pages of your printer's Properties box to view or alter the great variety of settings. These buttons are confusing in name, and there's no easy way to remember what's what. But remember that you can get help by first clicking the ? in the upper-right corner and then clicking the setting or button whose function you don't understand.

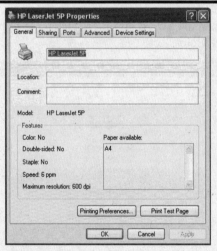

FIGURE 8.3: Each printer has a Properties box such as this, with several tab pages. Options and tabs differ from printer to printer.

DELETING A PRINTER FROM YOUR PRINTERS FOLDER

You might want to decommission a printer after you've added it, for several reasons:

▶ You've connected a new type of printer to your computer and you want to delete the old setup and create a new one with the correct driver for the new printer.

▶ You want to disconnect from a network printer you're through using.

▶ You've created several slightly different setups for the same physical printer, and you want to delete the ones you don't use.

In any of these cases, the trick is the same:

1. Open the Printers folder (Start ➤ Control Panel, then choose the Printers and other Hardware category, and then the Printers and Faxes category).

2. Click once on the icon to select it and press Delete, or right-click it and choose Delete.

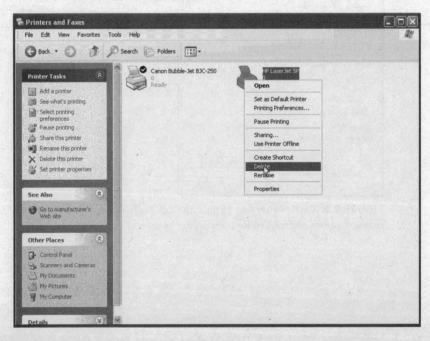

You will see at least one confirmation box before the printer is deleted. To delete the printer, click Yes. You may see another warning if there are print jobs in the queue for the printer.

NOTE

Deleting a printer in one user profile will not affect the printer's availability in other user profiles.

PRINTING DOCUMENTS FROM APPLICATIONS

By now, your printer(s) is (are) added and ready to go. The procedure for printing in Windows XP is simple. Typically, you just open a document, choose File ➢ Print, make a few setting choices such as which pages to print, and click OK. (You might have to set the print area first or make some other setting choices, depending on the program.) If you're already happy with the ways in which you print, you might want to skim over this section. However, there *are* a couple of conveniences you might not know about, such as using drag-and-drop to print or right-clicking a document to print it without opening the program that created it.

About the Default Printer

Unless you choose otherwise, the output from Windows programs is routed to the print queue for printing. If no particular printer has been chosen (perhaps because the program—for example, Notepad—doesn't give you a choice), the default printer is used.

NOTE

The default printer can be set by right-clicking a printer icon and choosing Set as Default Printer.

Exactly how your printed documents look varies somewhat from program to program because not all programs can take full advantage of the capabilities of your printer and printer driver. For example, simple word processing programs like Notepad don't let you change the font, while a full-blown word processing program such as Ami Pro or Word can print out all kinds of fancy graphics, fonts, columns of text, and so forth.

When you print from any program, the file is actually printed to a disk file instead of directly to the printer. The print queue then spools the file to the assigned printer(s), coordinating the flow of data and keeping you informed of the progress. Jobs are queued up and listed in the print queue window, from which their status can be observed; in this window, they can also be rearranged, deleted, and so forth.

Printing from a Program

To print from any program, follow these steps:

1. Check to see that the printer and page settings are correct. Some program's File menus provide a Printer Setup, Page Setup, or other option for this. Note that settings you make from such a box temporarily (sometimes permanently, depending on the program) override settings made from the Printer's Properties dialog box.

2. Select the Print command on the program's File menu and fill in whatever information is asked of you. For example, in WordPad, the Print dialog box looks like that in Figure 8.4.

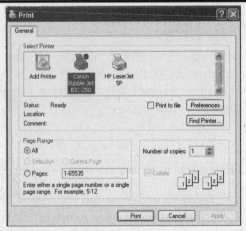

FIGURE 8.4: When you choose Print from a Windows program, you often see a dialog box such as this that allows you to choose some options before printing.

Some programs have rather elaborate dialog boxes for choosing which printer you want to print to, scaling or graphically altering the printout, and even adjusting the properties of the printer. Still, you can normally just make the most obvious settings and get away with it:

- ▶ Choose the correct printer.

- ▶ Choose the correct number of copies.

- ▶ Choose the correct print range (pages, spreadsheet cells, portion of graphic, etc.).

- ▶ For color printers, choose which ink cartridge you have in (black and white or color).

3. Click OK (or otherwise confirm printing). Windows XP intercepts the print data, writes it in a file, and then begins printing it. If an error occurs—a port conflict, the printer is out of paper, or what have you—you'll see a message such as this:

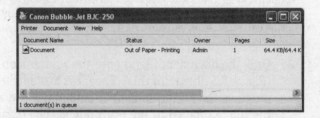

Check the paper supply, and check to see that the printer is turned on and that it's online (there may be a switch on the printer for this). If it's a network printer, make sure it's shared and that the computer it's connected to is booted up.

TIP

When printing commences, a little printer icon will appear in the Taskbar next to the clock. You can double-click this icon to see details of your pending print jobs.

Printing with Drag-and-Drop

You can quickly print Windows program document files by dragging them onto a printer's icon or window. You can drag from the desktop, a folder, the Search window, or the Windows Explorer window. This will only work with documents that have an association with a particular program. To check if a document has an association, right-click it. If the resulting menu has an Open With command on it (not Open, which all files have), it has an association.

To print with drag-and-drop, follow these steps:

1. Arrange things on your screen so you can see the file(s) you want to print as well as either the printer's icon or its window (you open a printer's window by double-clicking its icon).

TIP

You can drag a file into a shortcut of the printer's icon. If you like this way of printing, keep a shortcut of your printer on the Desktop so you can drag documents to it without having to open up the Printers folder. By double-clicking a printer shortcut icon, you can easily check its print queue, too.

2. Drag the document file(s) onto the printer icon or window (Figure 8.5 illustrates this). The file is loaded into the source program, the Print command is automatically executed, and the file is spooled to the print queue. The document isn't actually moved out of its home folder; it just gets printed.

FIGURE 8.5: You can print a document by dragging it to the destination printer's icon or window.

If the document doesn't have an association, you'll see an error message:

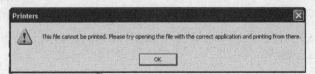

Also, a nice feature of this approach is that you can drag multiple files onto a printer's icon or open window at once. They will all be queued up for printing, one after another, via their source programs. You'll see a message asking for confirmation before printing commences.

TIP

The drag-and-drop method can be used with shortcuts, too. You can drag shortcuts of documents to a printer or even to a shortcut of a printer, and the document will print.

TIP

In addition to using drag-and-drop, you can also right-click many documents and choose Print from the context menu that appears.

WORKING WITH THE PRINT QUEUE

If you print more than a few files at a time, or if you have your printer shared for network use, you'll sometimes want to check on the status of a printer's print jobs. You also might want to see how many jobs need to print before you can turn off your local computer and printer if others are using it. Or you might want to know how many other jobs are ahead of yours.

You can check on these items by opening a printer's window. You'll then see the following columns:

Document Name   Name of the file being printed and possibly the source program.

Status   Whether the job is printing, being deleted, or paused.

Owner   Who sent each print job to the printer.

Progress   How large each job is and how much of the current job has been printed.

Started At   When each print job was sent to the print queue.

Figure 8.6 shows a sample printer with a print queue and related information.

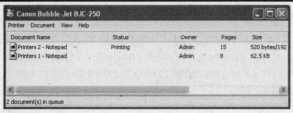

FIGURE 8.6: A printer's window with a print job pending

Complete the following steps to see the queue on a printer:

1. Open the Printers folder.

2. Double-click the printer in question.

3. Adjust the window size, if necessary, so that you can see all the columns.

NOTE

If the print job originated from a DOS program, the document name will not be known. It will appear in the Document Name column as Remote Downlevel Document, meaning that it came from a workstation that doesn't support Microsoft's RPC (Remote Procedure Call) print support. Additional examples of programs that this may happen with are Windows for Workgroups, LAN Manager, Unix, and NetWare.

TIP

If the printer in question is a network printer and the printer is offline for some reason—such as its computer isn't turned on—you'll be forced to work offline. An error message will alert you to this, and the top line of the printer's window will say User Intervention Required—Work Offline. Until the issue is resolved, you won't be able to view the queue for that printer. You can still print to it, however.

Refreshing the Network Queue Information

Often the network cabling connecting workstations and servers is quite busy, so Windows usually doesn't bother to add even more traffic to the network by polling each workstation for printer-queue information. This is done when necessary, such as when a document is deleted from a queue. So, if you want to refresh the window for a printer to get the absolute latest information, just press F5. This immediately updates the queue information.

Deleting a File from the Queue

After sending a file to the queue, you might reconsider printing it, or you might want to rework the file and print it later. If so, you can simply remove the file from the queue.

1. Open the printer's window.

2. Select the file by clicking it in the queue.

TIP

I have found, especially with PostScript laser-type printers or ink-jet printers with large file buffers, that after deleting a file while printing, I'll have to reset the printer to clear its buffer or I will at least have to eject the current page by pressing the page eject button (not all printers have a page-eject button). To reset, you'll typically have to push a button on the printer's front panel or turn the printer off for a few seconds and then back on again.

3. Choose Document ➢ Cancel, press Delete, or right-click and choose Cancel. After clicking Yes in the Are You Sure You Want to Cancel the Selected Print Jobs? dialog box, the document item is removed from the printer's window. If you're trying to delete the job that's printing, you might have some trouble. At the very least, the system might take some time to respond.

Of course, normally you can't delete someone else's print jobs on a remote printer. If you try to, you'll be told that this is beyond your privilege and that you should contact your system administrator. You can, however, kill other people's print jobs if the printer in question is connected to your computer.

Pending print jobs will not be lost when computers are powered down. Any documents in the queue when the system goes down will reappear in the queue when you power up. When you turn on a computer that is the host for a shared printer that has an unfinished print queue, you will be alerted to the number of jobs in the queue and asked whether to delete or print them.

Canceling All Pending Print Jobs on a Given Printer

Sometimes, because of a megalithic meltdown or some other catastrophe, you'll decide to bail out of all the print jobs that are stacked up for a printer. Normally you don't need to do this, even if the printer has gone wacky. You can just pause the queue and continue printing after the problem is solved. But sometimes you'll want to resend everything to another printer and kill the queue on the current one. It's easy:

1. Select the printer's icon or window.

2. Right-click and choose Cancel, or, from the printer's window, choose Printer ➢ Cancel All Documents. All queued jobs for the printer are canceled.

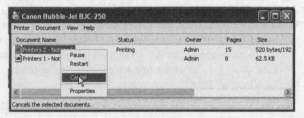

 WARNING

Make sure you really want to cancel the jobs before you do this. This is a good way to make enemies if people on the network were counting on their print jobs being finished any time soon.

Pausing (and Resuming) the Printing Process

If you're the administrator of a printer with a stack of jobs in the print queue, you can pause a single job temporarily or you can pause all jobs on a particular printer at any time. This can be useful when you need to take a minute to add paper, take a phone call, or have a conversation in your office without the noise of the printer in the background. The next two sections explain the techniques for pausing and resuming.

Pausing or Resuming a Specific Print Job

You can pause documents anywhere in the queue. Paused documents are skipped and subsequent documents in the list print ahead of them. You can achieve the same effect by rearranging the queue. When you feel the need to pause or resume a specific print job, follow these steps:

1. Click the document's information line.

2. Choose Document ➤ Pause (or right-click the document and choose Pause Printing, as you see in Figure 8.7). The current print job is temporarily suspended, and the word "Paused" appears in the status area. (The printing might not stop immediately because your printer might have a buffer that holds data in preparation for printing. The printing stops when the buffer is empty. This will result in some wasted paper.)

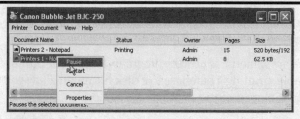

FIGURE 8.7: Pause the printing of a single document with the right-click menu. Other documents will continue to print.

3. To resume printing the document, repeat Steps 1 and 2 to turn off the check mark next to Pause Printing.

Pausing or Resuming All Jobs on a Printer

In similar fashion, you can pause all jobs on a given printer temporarily. You might want to do this for a number of reasons including the following:

▶ To load paper or otherwise adjust the physical printer

▶ To alter printer settings from the printer's Properties dialog box

Follow these steps to pause or resume all jobs for a printer:

1. Deselect any documents in the printer's window; press the spacebar if a document is selected.

2. Choose Printer ➣ Pause Printing. The printer window's title bar changes to say "Paused."

3. To resume all jobs on the printer, choose Printer ➣ Pause Printing again to turn off the check mark next to the command. The "Paused" indicator in the title bar disappears, and printing should resume where the queue left off.

PRINTING TO A DISK FILE

There are times when you may want to print to a disk file rather than to the printer. When you print to a disk file, the codes and data that would normally be sent to the printer are shunted off to a disk file—either locally or on the network. Typically, the resulting file isn't just a copy of the file you were printing; it contains all of the special formatting codes that control your printer.

Why would you want to create a disk file instead of printing directly to the printer? Printing to a file gives you several options not available when you print directly to the printer:

▶ Print files are sometimes used by programs for specific purposes. For example, printing a database to a disk file might allow you to work with it more easily in another application.

▶ You can send the file to another person, either on floppy disk or over the phone lines with a modem and a communications program such as HyperTerminal. That person can then print the file directly to a printer (if it's compatible) with Windows or a utility such as the DOS copy command. The person doesn't need the program that created the file and doesn't have to worry about any of the printing details—formatting, setting up margins, and so forth.

▶ It allows you to print the file later. Maybe your printer isn't hooked up, or there's so much stuff in the queue that you don't want to wait. Later, you can use the DOS copy command or a batch file at the command prompt with a command such as copy *.prn lpt1 /b to copy all files to the desired port. Be sure to use the /b switch. If you don't, the first Ctrl+Z code the computer encounters will terminate the print job because the print files are binary files.

In some programs, printing to a disk file is a choice in the Print dialog box. If it isn't, you should modify the printer's configuration to print to a file rather than to a port. Then, whenever you use that printer, it uses all the usual settings for the driver but sends the data to a file of your choice instead of to the printer port.

To set up a printer to print to a file, follow these steps:

1. In the Printers folder, right-click the printer's icon and choose Properties.

2. Select the Ports tab.

3. Under Print to the Following Port, choose FILE:.

NOTE
For some printers, this setting might be on a different tab than Ports. It might be on a Details tab, for example.

4. Click OK. The printer's icon in the Printers folder will change to indicate that printing is routed to a disk file.

Now, when you print a file from any program and choose this printer as the destination for the printout, you'll be prompted for a filename.

TROUBLESHOOTING PRINTER PROBLEMS

Having some trouble getting the printout you want? Here are some troubleshooting tips:

Printing doesn't work at all.   Here are some tips to try:

- ▶ Check that the printer is on, online, filled with paper, and wired securely.

- ▶ Try printing a test page by opening the Printers folder (from Control Panel), right-clicking the printer, choosing Properties, and clicking Print Test Page. If the page prints, the problem is with your document or application program, not the printer or Windows XP. If the page doesn't print, make sure the Ports or Details tab shows the correct port for the printer (typically LPT1).

▶ Make sure that you have a good-quality bidirectional printer cable and that it's snugly connected both to the printer and to the PC.

Printing looks wrong.   Here are some troubleshooting tips to try:

▶ If a partial page printed, check the page orientation. It may be set to Landscape.

▶ Check the page-layout command in the program you are printing from *and* in the Properties box for your printer. If just the edges of the printout are missing, decrease the margins for your document and try again.

▶ Make sure the paper size you are using matches the document size you are printing.

▶ If you get PostScript error codes instead of normal text and graphics, either you are trying to use a PostScript printer driver with a non-PostScript printer or the printer needs to be set to PostScript mode. Add the printer to your computer again using the Add Printer Wizard.

▶ Make sure that the correct driver is installed for the printer you are using.

▶ Make sure you are not running low on hard disk space. Large print jobs are stored temporarily on the hard disk before being sent to the printer, and you need to have several megabytes of free space on your hard disk for that to happen.

Fonts don't print correctly.   Try the following:

▶ Use TrueType or printer fonts whenever possible. Screen fonts—such as MS Sans Serif or System—aren't good choices. Change the font in the document and try printing again.

▶ If your printer has plug-in font cartridges, you may have the wrong one installed. In the printer's Properties box, click the Fonts tab and ensure that the correct Fonts cartridge is selected. You may have to go to Install Printer Fonts if the cartridge isn't listed.

▶ If TrueType fonts still aren't printing correctly, as a final resort you can try printing them as bitmaps instead of outlines (select this option from the Fonts tab of the Properties box).

Color printing comes out black and white. Check that you have installed the correct print cartridge by looking inside the printer. In the printer's Properties box, check for a possible cartridge-selection option (it might also be available for the program you're using; select File ➤ Printer Setup).

Printing is slow. Here are some tips to try:

▶ Open the Properties box for the printer, click the Details or Ports tab, and check the spool settings. Spooling should be turned on.

▶ If you're waiting a long time for a printout to appear, open the printer's Properties box, click the Details or Ports tab, and click Spool Settings. Try changing the spool setting from EMF to RAW.

What's Next

The next chapter starts a new part of the book, a part that is all about customizing your Windows XP experience. In Chapter 9, Faithe Wempen shows you how to customize Windows system settings so that Windows looks and operates the way you like.

PART II

Customizing, Optimizing, and Troubleshooting Windows XP Home Edition

Chapter 9
CUSTOMIZING SYSTEM SETTINGS

Windows can be customized in almost every conceivable way! If you don't like something about the way it operates, you can probably change it. In this chapter, you will learn how to change the date and time, adjust keyboard and mouse performance, and change audio and system sounds.

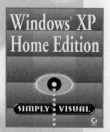

Adapted from *Windows XP Home Edition Simply Visual*
by Faithe Wempen
ISBN 0-7821-2982-X   448 pages $24.99

SETTING THE DATE AND TIME

Have you ever wondered how your computer always seems to know the date and time? It's because of timekeeping circuitry built into the motherboard. There is a small battery on the motherboard that keeps this clock powered even when you turn off the computer.

If you move to a different time zone, or if your computer's clock starts losing time (which can happen if the battery needs changing), you can adjust the date and time setting through Windows.

NOTE

Windows XP comes with a feature that will automatically synchronize the time on your computer with a time server on the Internet once a week. You'll see how to turn it on or off in these steps.

To change the date or time, follow these steps:

1. Double-click the clock on the taskbar.

   The Date and Time Properties dialog box appears.

2. If the date shown on the Date & Time tab is incorrect, click the correct date on the calendar. To see a different month or year, open the Month or Year drop-down list and make another selection.

3. If the time shown is incorrect, enter a new time in the text box below the clock.

4. If you have changed time zones, click the Time Zone tab. Then select your time zone from the drop-down list.

5. To check the time against a time server on the Internet, click the Internet Time tab and then click Update Now. If one server doesn't work, try choosing another one from the list of servers and clicking Update Now again.

NOTE

A time server is an Internet site that's set up to provide the correct date and time to anyone who requests it. It's sort of like those "time and temperature" phone numbers you might have called before.

6. If you don't want to use the time server automatically in the future, clear the Automatically Synchronize with an Internet Time Server check box.

TIP

You might turn off automatic synchronization if your computer isn't connected to the Internet full-time. That way, you can manually use Update Now whenever you happen to be connected instead of worrying about trying to be connected when the next update is scheduled.

7. Click OK.

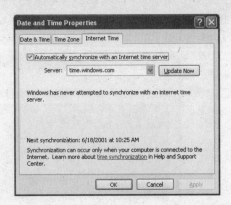

Part iii

CHANGING KEYBOARD PROPERTIES

The keyboard works pretty well right out of the box; you don't need to do anything special to make it work. However, you can make a few fine-tuning adjustments to its performance to make typing more convenient.

Two of the keyboard settings you can adjust have to do with key repeat. You can set the repeat delay (the amount of time before a key starts repeating) and the repeat rate (the speed at which repeating occurs once it starts).

The other keyboard setting is cursor blink rate. When you type in a word processor or other program, the cursor (usually a vertical line) blinks to make it easier for you to locate it. The cursor blink rate controls the speed of the blinking.

Follow these steps to set keyboard properties:

1. Choose Start ➢ Control Panel.

2. In Control Panel, click Printers and Other Hardware.

NOTE

If your Control Panel is in Classic view, you won't see Printers and Other Hardware. Double-click Keyboard and skip to Step 4.

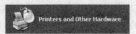

3. In the Printers and Other Hardware window, click Keyboard.

4. In the Keyboard Properties dialog box, click the Speed tab if it isn't already selected.

5. Drag the sliders to adjust repeat delay and repeat rate. To test the settings, click inside the text box and then hold down a key.

6. Drag the Cursor Blink Rate slider to adjust the blink rate.

NOTE

Both the keyboard and the mouse have a Hardware tab in their Properties boxes, but most people won't need to use it. It contains options for installing a different device driver, in case Windows has detected your keyboard or mouse incorrectly (not likely) or in case you have a custom driver that you want to install.

7. Click OK to close the Keyboard Properties box.

8. Close Control Panel.

Part ii

ADJUSTING MOUSE OPERATION

Since you use your mouse for almost all activity in Windows, it's imperative that the mouse operate the way you want it to. Fortunately, almost every aspect of mouse operation is customizable. You can change the range of cursor motion, the size of the cursor, and many other factors.

To explore mouse settings, and possibly make some changes, do the following:

1. Choose Start ➤ Control Panel.

2. Click Printers and Other Hardware.

NOTE
If Control Panel is in Classic view, double-click Mouse instead of following Steps 2 and 3.

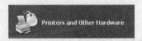

3. In the Printers and Other Hardware window, click Mouse.

4. On the Buttons tab in the Mouse Properties dialog box, adjust any of these settings if desired:

Switch Primary and Secondary Buttons   If you are left-handed and you want to use your strongest finger for the primary mouse button, you might want to switch the button functions.

Double-Click Speed   Drag the slider to adjust the speed at which you must double-click in order for Windows to recognize your intent as a double-click and not two single clicks. Slow it down if you are having trouble double-clicking fast enough; speed it up if you are accidentally double-clicking frequently. Test the new setting by double-clicking the folder to the right of the slider.

ClickLock   This setting turns the mouse button into a toggle, like the Caps Lock key, so that you don't have to hold it down when you want to drag. It's useful for people with limited mobility or dexterity—but irritating for almost everyone else.

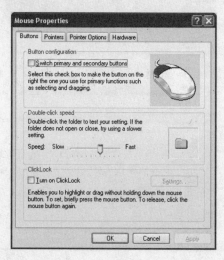

5. Click the Pointers tab; then open the Scheme drop-down list and select a different pointer scheme if desired.

6. To enable or disable the pointer shadow, click the Enable Pointer Shadow check box.

7. (Optional) If you want to customize the chosen pointer scheme, click an individual pointer on the list and then click Browse.

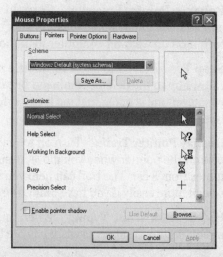

A Browse dialog box opens, showing all the available pointers. Select a different pointer and click Open.

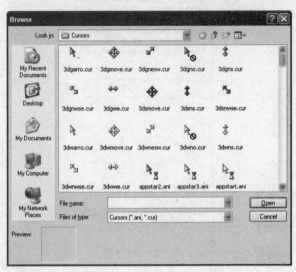

8. Click the Pointer Options tab and then adjust any of these settings as desired:

Pointer Speed Drag the slider to change the mouse sensitivity—that is, the distance that the mouse pointer moves on-screen in relation to the distance that you physically move the mouse.

Enhance Pointer Precision Turn this feature on to enable some minor improvements to pointer movement; turn it off on a slower computer to improve performance.

Snap To Turn on to make the mouse pointer automatically jump to the default command button in a dialog box whenever one is open, making it easier for you to click that button.

Display Pointer Trails Turn on to make a "trail" appear behind the pointer when you move it—similar to exhaust fumes from a car. The trail can help you find the mouse on-screen more easily if you have limited vision.

Hide Pointer While Typing When this is enabled, the mouse pointer disappears when you are typing in a program such as a word processor, to avoid confusion between the mouse pointer and the cursor. When you move the mouse, the cursor pops back into view.

Show Location of Pointer When this is enabled, you can press the Ctrl key to make a radiating circle flash around the pointer. This is good for people with limited vision or those who tend to "lose" the pointer on-screen, but who don't like the pointer trails feature.

9. Click OK to accept your new settings.

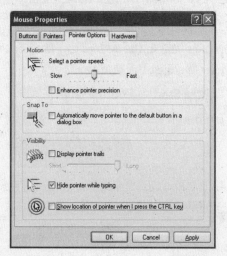

SETTING SOUND AND AUDIO PROPERTIES

Sound and audio properties control how sound comes out of your PC. Most PCs have a sound card, or sound support built into the motherboard. You plug speakers into the sound card or into a built-in speaker jack on the PC, and Windows sends forth sounds and music from the sound card. It's all pretty straightforward, unless you have more than one sound card or some special speaker configuration. In that case, you might need to adjust the sound and audio properties for best performance with your system.

Part ii

TIP

Why might someone have more than one sound card? Primarily so that they can have more than one set of speakers plugged in simultaneously, each doing its own thing. People who use a computer to record their own music might find this especially useful. For example, with two sound cards, you could have external speakers playing an audio CD while an electronic keyboard plugged into another sound card feeds music into some headphones and records only the keyboard track to disk.

Even though you probably won't need to adjust your sound and audio settings, it's a good idea to check them out anyway just for your own education. There are also a few little tweaks and secrets hidden in these properties that everyone can benefit from, such as the ability to show or hide the speaker icon in the system tray for quick volume adjustments.

Here's how to adjust the settings:

1. Choose Start ➢ Control Panel.

2. In Control Panel, click Sounds, Speech, and Audio Devices.

3. In the Sounds, Speech, and Audio Devices window, click Sounds and Audio Devices.

4. On the Volume tab of the Properties dialog box, change any of the following settings as desired:

Device Volume   Drag the slider to adjust the overall system volume.

Mute   Mark this check box to temporarily disable all sounds from the speakers.

Place Volume Icon in the Taskbar   Select or deselect to add or remove a shortcut for adjusting the volume in the system tray (next to the clock).

Double-clicking that icon in the system tray will open the full Play Control dialog box; single-clicking it will open a single Volume slider like this:

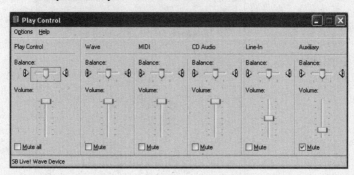

Advanced (in Device Volume Section)   Click this button to open the Play Control dialog box, through which you can adjust the volume for individual devices such as the microphone, speakers, and line in. This is the same dialog box that you get when you double-click the speaker icon in the system tray.

Part ii

Speaker Volume   Click to open a dialog box in which you can adjust the volume for right and left speakers separately.

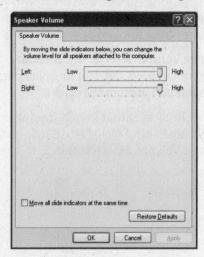

Advanced (in Speaker Settings Section)   Click to open an Advanced Audio Properties dialog box, where you can choose a speaker configuration that takes advantage of any extra speaker features you have, such as a woofer or Surround Sound.

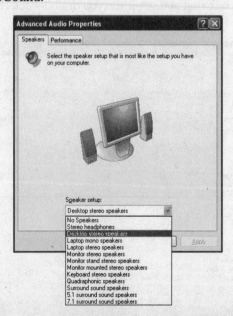

5. Click the Audio tab and then make any changes needed to the following controls:

    Sound Playback   If you have more than one sound card, choose the one you want to use as the default. The Volume and Advanced buttons in this section are the same as those on the Volume tab.

    Sound Recording   If you have more than one sound recording device, select the default one. Normally, this would be the same as your default playback device—your sound card. However, if you have more than one sound card, you might use one for playback and another for recording.

    MIDI Music Playback   Select the default device to use for MIDI music. If you aren't sure, leave it set for the default.

NOTE

MIDI stands for Musical Instrument Digital Interface. It's the interface through which digital instruments like keyboards are attached to your sound card for input.

6. Click OK to close the Sounds and Audio Devices Properties box.

7. Close Control Panel.

NOTE

You will learn in the next section how to select system sounds on the Sounds tab of this dialog box.

ASSIGNING SOUNDS TO EVENTS

You may have noticed that in your day-to-day Windows activities, sounds play at certain times. For example, there's a startup sound, a shutdown sound, a sound when an error occurs, a sound when you receive new e-mail, and so on. You can control these sounds, either by selecting a different sound scheme or by assigning individual sounds to program events.

NOTE

Anything that happens in Windows is technically a program event. This can include a menu opening or closing, a dialog box opening or closing, a program opening or closing, an error occurring, and so on. Another name for this is *system event*.

To change your system sounds, follow these steps:

1. Repeat Steps 1–3 of the preceding procedure to reopen the Sounds and Audio Devices Properties dialog box.

2. Click the Sounds tab; then open the Sound Scheme drop-down list and select a scheme. (Or, to turn off all sounds, choose No Sounds. This removes sound assignments for all system events.)

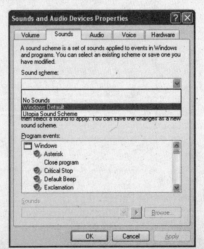

3. If any sound changes have been made since you last selected a scheme, a warning box appears. Click No to decline to save your current settings, or click Yes to save them. (If you choose Yes, enter a name for the new scheme and then click OK.)

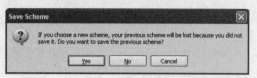

4. To change an individual program event's sound, select the event in the Program Events section and then choose a sound from the Sounds drop-down list.

   Or, to assign a sound that isn't on that list, click Browse, locate and select the sound file, and click OK.

   To preview a sound, click the Play button.

5. Repeat Step 4 for each program event you want to change.

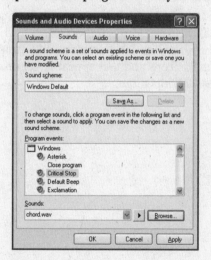

6. (Optional) If you want to save your changes as a new scheme, click Save As. The Save Scheme As dialog box opens.

Part ii

7.   Type a name for the new scheme and then click OK.

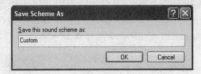

8.   Click OK to close the Sounds and Audio Devices Properties box.

9.   Close Control Panel.

There are many more Windows settings you can change than this chapter has explored. You might want to go through Control Panel on your own, icon-by-icon, and see what's available. For example, if you have a game controller, you can calibrate it using the Game Controllers Properties in Control Panel.

WHAT'S NEXT

In this chapter, you learned about several settings that affect the way Windows behaves. Next up is Robert Cowart, who will tell you how to change the way the Windows desktop looks. You'll learn how to change the colors, make icons and text appear larger or smaller, apply appearance themes, and lots more.

Chapter 10

CUSTOMIZING THE DESKTOP, TASKBAR, AND START MENU

Customizing your desktop and display can make a big difference in the overall usability of your PC. In this chapter, you'll learn how to change the display settings to make your desktop look different and how to add and arrange shortcuts on the desktop, on the taskbar, and on the Start menu in a way that makes sense for your work habits.

Adapted from *Mastering Windows Me* by Robert Cowart
ISBN 0-7821-2857-2   960 pages $39.99

CUSTOMIZING THE DISPLAY

The Display applet packs a wallop under its hood. For starters, it lets you choose colors, backgrounds, and other decorations for prettying up the general look of the Windows screen. It also includes the means for changing your screen driver and resolution.

TIP

The Display properties are accessible either from Control Panel or from the desktop. Right-click an empty area of the desktop and choose Properties.

Here are some of the functional and cosmetic adjustments you can make to your Windows XP display from this applet:

- ▶ Choose an appearance theme for the display.
- ▶ Set the background and wallpaper for the desktop.
- ▶ Set the screen saver and energy conservation.
- ▶ Set the color scheme and fonts for Windows elements.
- ▶ Set the display device driver and adjust resolution, color depth, and font size.
- ▶ Change the icons you want to use for basic stuff on your desktop, such as My Computer and the Recycle Bin.
- ▶ Set color management compatibility so that your monitor and your printer output colors match.

Let's take a look at this dialog box page by page. This dialog box is a fun one to experiment with and will come in handy if you know how to use it.

Choosing a Theme

Themes are sets of color, menu, font, and background choices that you apply as a group. If you upgraded to Windows XP from an earlier Windows version, you might have noticed that the entire windows environment has a different look-and-feel; that's because of the new Windows XP theme.

If you prefer a different theme, you can choose one from the Themes tab in the Display Properties dialog box.

1. Right-click the desktop and choose Properties.

2. Click the Themes tab.

3. Select a theme from the Theme drop-down list. If you want your screen to look more like an earlier version of Windows, for example, choose the Windows Classic theme.

4. Click OK.

You can create your own themes by adjusting the display settings manually, such as choosing different colors or a different wallpaper (covered later in this chapter) and then saving your changes like so:

1. On the Themes tab, click Save As. A Save As dialog box opens.

2. Type a name for the new theme.

3. Click Save.

TIP

Choose More Themes Online to connect to a Microsoft-sponsored Web site where you can download additional themes.

Choosing a Background Image

By default, a picture of a sunny green meadow appears as the background image in Windows XP. The Desktop tab lets you select a different picture to use instead.

Windows XP comes with several images suitable for use as a background image, and you can also use any image you have on disk as well. For example, you could take a digital photo of your children and use that photo as the background image.

The pictures that Windows provides for background use are exactly the right size to fit your display, but other pictures might not be. The Desktop tab's Position setting specifies what should happen when an image is too small to fill the entire screen.

The Centered option places one copy of the image in the center of the screen, and applies a solid color around the edges. Stretch stretches a single copy to fill the screen, distorting the image if needed. Tile places multiple copies of the same image on the desktop to fill the available area. (Tile is a good setting for very small pictures.)

To select a background image, follow these steps:

1. Right-click the desktop and choose Properties, then click the Desktop tab.

2. Choose the file you want to use from the Background list. The pictures on the list are the pictures and Web pages in the C:\Windows folder, plus any other pictures you have added to the list.

   To use a picture that doesn't appear on the list, click Browse, locate it, and click OK to select it.

3. Open the Position drop-down list and choose Center, Tile, or Stretch to position the chosen item.

4. Click OK to close the Display Properties dialog box, or continue making display changes as described in the next sections.

TIP

You can quickly download any image you find on a Web page to your PC and set it as your wallpaper by right-clicking it in your Web browser and choosing Set as Wallpaper. When you do so, the image is saved in the C:\Windows folder, under the name Internet Explorer Wallpaper. However, it is not permanently saved. When you do the same thing to another picture, the older picture is overwritten. To permanently save a picture to your hard disk from a Web page, right-click it and choose Save Picture As.

Customizing Desktop Settings

If you click the Customize Desktop button on the Desktop tab, a Desktop Items dialog box appears. In this dialog box, you can choose which system items (such as My Documents and My Computer) will appear as shortcuts on the desktop and what icon pictures they will have.

In earlier versions of Windows, icons for My Documents, My Computer, My Network Places, and Internet Explorer all appeared by default on the desktop. They do not in Windows XP, but you can use the following procedure to turn on any of them that you miss having around.

From the Desktop tab of the Display Properties dialog box (see the preceding section), do the following:

1. Click the Customize Desktop button. The Desktop Items dialog box opens.

Part ii

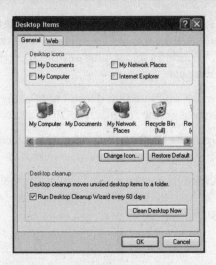

2. Mark or clear the check box(es) to place or remove a short-cut on the desktop for My Computer, My Documents, My Network Places, and/or Internet Explorer.

3. To change an icon, click its picture in the middle section of the dialog box and then click Change Icon. Then select a new icon in the Change Icons dialog box and click OK.

NOTE
To return an icon to its default appearance, click Restore Default.

4. Repeat Step 3 for other icons, if desired; then click OK when you are finished to return to the Display Properties dialog box.

5. Click OK to close the Display Properties dialog box, or leave it open to continue in the next section of this chapter.

You aren't limited to the icons that appear in the Change Icons dialog box by default. You can find icons in several ways:

▸ You can locate an .ico file. This is a little graphic designed specifically to be an icon.

▸ Another source of icons is .exe and .dll files. Most executable files contain one or more embedded icons that you can "borrow" as needed. For example, in the previous graphic, the icons displayed are the ones embedded in Explorer.exe.

▸ You can also download icons from the Internet. Just search for *Icons or .ico.*

Setting the Screen Saver

A screen saver will blank your screen or display a moving image or pattern if you don't use the mouse or keyboard for a predetermined amount of time. Screen savers can prevent a static image from burning the delicate phosphors on the inside surface of the monitor, which can leave a ghost of the image on the screen for all time, no matter what is being displayed. They can also just be fun.

NOTE

The monitors built these days are not as susceptible to burn-in as early models were, so you don't really need to use a screen saver. Most people use them just for the fun of it.

The screen saver options allow you to choose or create an entertaining video ditty that will greet you when you return to work. You also set how much time you have after your last keystroke or mouse skitter before the show begins. And a password can be set to keep prying eyes from toying with your work while you're away.

To select a screen saver and set its options, do the following:

1. If the Display Properties dialog box is not already open, right-click the desktop and choose Properties.

2. Click the Screen Saver tab.

3. Open the Screen Saver drop-down list and choose a screen saver. It appears in the preview window, as in Figure 10.1.

FIGURE 10.1: Setting up a screen saver

Want to see how it will look on your whole screen? Click Preview. Your screen will go black and then begin its antics. The show continues until you hit any key or move your mouse.

4. If you want to change anything about the selected screen saver, click Settings. You'll see a box of settings that apply to that particular screen saver. For example, for the 3D Pipes screen saver, this is the Settings box:

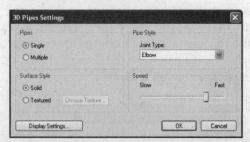

Most of the option boxes have fun sliders and stuff you can play with to get an effect you like. Depending on which screen saver you chose, you'll have a few possible adjustments, such as speed, placement, and details pertinent to the graphic. Play with the settings until you're happy with the results, and then click OK in the Settings box.

5. Back at the Screen Saver page, the next choice you might want to consider is using a password. Click the On Resume, Display Welcome Screen check box if you want protection.

NOTE

Previous versions of Windows enabled you to set a specific screen saver password, but in Windows XP, the screen saver password is the same as your local user logon password, if you have one. If you do not have a password for your user ID, turning on password protection for the screen saver will bring up a password dialog box at which you can simply press Enter to get back to Windows. To set up a password for your user ID, set it up in the Users section of Control Panel, as explained in Chapter 11.

6. In the Wait text box, enter the number of minutes you want your computer to be idle before the screen saver springs into action. Either type in a number or use the increment buttons to change the time.

7. If you want to adjust the power settings that turn your monitor off completely after a certain period of inactivity, click the Power button. Then open the Turn Off Monitor drop-down list and select an amount of time, and then click OK.

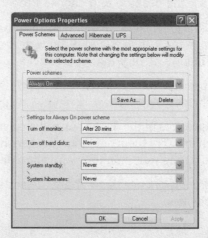

8. When all the settings are correct, click OK to close the dialog box, or click Apply to apply your settings and leave the dialog box open for the next section.

Adjusting the Display Appearance

The Appearance tab of the Display Properties dialog box lets you change the way Windows assigns colors and fonts to various parts of the screen, as well as how the menus and windows are styled.

First, what's this style thing about? Well, Windows XP has a new style of title bars and window borders compared to earlier Windows versions. The new style is called Windows XP; the alternative is called Windows Classic, and it mirrors the earlier Windows versions' style.

You can also choose a color scheme. The available color schemes depend on the style you chose (see above). There are many color scheme choices for Windows Classic style, but only a few for Windows XP style.

In addition to applying a color scheme, you can also customize the colors and properties of individual screen elements. For example, you might start with a certain color scheme but then change the title bar color or font.

Selecting a Style and Color Scheme

Before customizing individual screen elements, first try selecting a style and loading one of the supplied color schemes; you may find one you like:

1. If the Display Properties dialog box is not already open, right-click the desktop and choose Properties. Then click the Appearance tab.

2. Open the Windows and Buttons drop-down list and choose Windows XP or Windows Classic.

3. Open the Color Scheme drop-down list and choose a color scheme.

   The colors in the dialog box will change, showing the scheme. Try them out. Some are garish, others more subtle. Adjusting your monitor may make a difference, too.

4. Click Apply or OK to apply the settings to all Windows activities.

Note that some color schemes not only apply different colors but also apply different fonts for common elements such as title bar text and menu text. In the following section you'll learn how to select any font installed on your system for these elements and others that involve text.

Customizing the Colors and Fonts Used On-Screen

If you don't like the color schemes supplied, you can make up your own. It's most efficient to start with a scheme that's close to what you want and then modify it. Once you like the scheme, you may save it under a new name for later use. Here's how:

1. From the Appearance tab, click the Advanced button. The Advanced Appearance dialog box opens. See Figure 10.2.

FIGURE 10.2: Customize the current scheme here.

2. In the preview area at the top of the dialog box, click the Windows element whose color or other attributes you want to change. Its name should appear in the Item box. You can click menu names, title bars, scroll bars, buttons—anything you see. You can also select a screen element from the Item drop-down list box rather than by clicking the item directly.

3. Click the Color 1 button to open up a series of colors you can choose from.

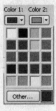

4. Click the color you want. This assigns it to the item.

5. If the Color 2 drop-down list is available, choose from it a second color for the selected item.

Color 2 is available only if the particular screen item you have selected supports two color choices. Window title bars support this, for example. If you choose two colors, one color gradually fades into the other across the item's surface.

TIP

Want more colors? Click the Other button. This pops up another 48 colors to choose from. Click one of the 48 colors (or patterns and intensity levels, if you have a monochrome monitor) to assign it to the chosen element.

6. If the chosen item has an adjustable size (such as Active Window Border, for example), the Size text box is available. Enter a size, or use the up/down increment buttons to change the size.

7. If the chosen item contains text, the Font drop-down list is available, along with a Size and Color control for it. Choose a font, a font size, a font color, and font attributes (Bold and/or Italic). These controls will not be available if you have chosen an item that does not involve text.

8. Repeat the process for each color you want to change. Then click OK.

9. Click OK to close the Display Properties dialog box if you're finished with them, or leave the dialog box open for the next section.

TIP

If you want to save the new color/font combination as a new theme, click the Themes tab and click Save As. Type a name for the new theme and click OK.

Choosing from a Wider Selection of Colors

If you don't like the colors that are available, you can create your own. There are 16 slots at the bottom of the larger color palette for storing colors you set using another fancy dialog box called the Color Refiner. Here's how:

1. When choosing a color, click Other. The Color dialog box opens.

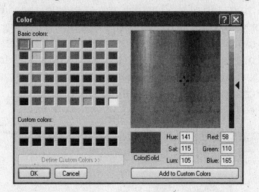

2. Do one of the following:

    ▶ In the Basic Colors area, click a color you want, and then skip to Step 4.

    ▶ Click in the color palette (the rainbow area) to the right, picking a precise color.

    ▶ To adjust the chosen color's intensity (light/dark), click the vertical bar to the right of the color palette.

    ▶ To enter a precise color by HSB number, enter numbers (0 through 255) in the Hue, Saturation, and Lum (Brightness) boxes.

    ▶ To enter a precise color by RGB number, enter numbers (0 through 255) in the Red, Green, and Blue boxes.

Part ii

NOTE

HSB and RGB are two different methods of defining a color. Both have their proponents, so Windows includes both as alternatives for you.

3. If you did anything in Step 2 besides clicking one of the Basic Colors, click the Add to Custom Colors button, moving your new color choice to a rectangle below the Basic Colors area. You can then choose this color again in the future.

4. Click OK. You return to the Advanced Appearance box, with the new color chosen.

Setting Screen Resolution and Color Depth

The Settings tab of the Display applet tweaks the video driver responsible for your video card's ability to display Windows. These settings are a little more substantial than those that adjust whether dialog boxes are mauve or chartreuse, because they load a different driver or bump your video card up or down into a completely different resolution and color depth, changing the amount of information you can see on the screen at once (see Figure 10.3).

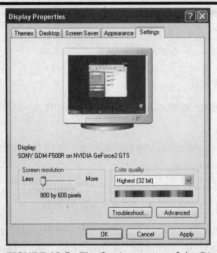

FIGURE 10.3: The Settings page of the Display Properties dialog box controls the video card's device driver.

NOTE

When you change the color depth, you might be asked whether you want to restart your PC. If you don't restart after changing color depth, everything might be okay, or you might see some strange effects on-screen, such as missing or wrong icons. Such problems are not critical, and can be fixed by restarting.

Let's start with the Color Quality setting, which sets the color depth for your screen—the number of unique colors it can display. Open the Color Quality drop-down list, and you're ready to make your selection. Your choices are Medium (16-bit) and Highest (32-bit). Highest is the best setting, generally, but if your system is a bit slow, bumping it down to Medium can sometimes help make the PC run just a bit faster.

The Screen Resolution setting controls your desktop area. Drag the slider to the left or right to adjust it. The higher the resolution you choose, the smaller the icons, windows, text, and everything else will appear on-screen. (The desktop background will expand to fill in the full screen area.) Some jobs—such as working with large spreadsheets, databases, CAD, or typesetting—are much more efficient with more data displayed on the screen. Because higher resolutions require a trade-off in clarity and make on-screen objects smaller, some people prefer a low resolution, such as 800 × 600, where everything appears larger on-screen.

The first time you change to a particular resolution, a confirmation message will appear; click Yes to indicate that the change was successful and your display is still readable. After 15 seconds, if you have not clicked Yes, it reverts to your previous resolution. Windows remembers in the future whether a particular resolution worked with your system, and does not ask again about that resolution.

Changing the Video and Monitor Driver Options

The Advanced button on the Settings tab leads you to a dialog box for your specific video card (shown in Figure 10.4), which allows you to actually change a bunch of nitty-gritty stuff, such as the type of video card and monitor that Windows thinks you have, the refresh rate, and some performance factors. Normally, these settings will be correct already, but if you install a new video card or monitor, you might want to check them.

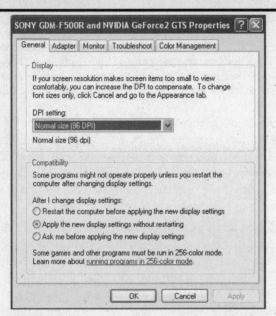

FIGURE 10.4: You can adjust the driver settings for your display here.

The General tab, shown in Figure 10.4, includes a DPI Setting drop-down list. If you want to use a higher screen resolution but find the text too small, you might try switching this setting to Large (120 dpi).

The General tab also has a Compatibility setting, in which you choose what happens when you change the color depth. Some systems are better than others at accepting color depth changes without rebooting, so experiment and then choose the best setting here for your situation.

Adapter Options

On the Adapter tab, you see your current video card listed. If it's wrong, click the Properties button and choose a different video driver.

Monitor Options

Bought a new monitor? Here's the place to tell Windows XP about it. It's important to tell Windows what monitor you have because it uses that information to calculate the optimal refresh rate. If Windows thinks you have a Standard VGA or Standard Plug-and-Play monitor, it's probably not taking advantage of the monitor's best available refresh rate. If the reported monitor is wrong, click Properties, click the Driver tab, click Update Driver, and work through the Wizard to change the driver used for it.

The main thing on the Monitor tab is a Refresh Rate drop-down list. The *refresh rate* is the number of times per second the display is repainted, or refreshed, by the light gun(s) inside the monitor. Higher is better, but your monitor and video card must both support the chosen resolution, or your monitor can be damaged. For best results, set the Refresh Rate to Optimal, allowing Windows to determine the highest available setting that the video card and monitor share. If you do not have an Optimal setting on the list, try a mid-range setting such as 85 Hertz. You can cautiously experiment with higher refresh rates if you know you have a high-quality video card and monitor, but if the screen appears distorted, revert quickly to a lower setting.

Troubleshooting Options

The Troubleshoot tab's main feature is the Hardware Acceleration slider. If speed is your concern (and who isn't concerned with their computer's speed?), make sure the slider is set to Full. This is recommended for most computers. Occasionally, a computer/graphics card combo (the monitor has nothing to do with this) won't be able to take advantage of all the graphics speed-up routines that Windows is capable of for things like moving lots of graphics around the screen quickly (known as *bit blitting*) and such. If you're seeing display anomalies, you might try slowing this setting down a bit, clicking OK, and closing the Display Properties box. Then see if anything improves.

NOTE

Depending on your video card, you might have other tabs in the dialog box, such as Color Management. Consult the documentation for your video card for details.

USING TOOLBARS ON THE TASKBAR

The taskbar, in addition to its other duties, can display a variety of toolbars containing shortcuts for helping you launch programs and work with files. In the following sections, you'll learn something about these toolbars.

Customizing the Quick Launch Toolbar

In Chapter 3, you learned how to display the Quick Launch toolbar on the taskbar. (Right-click a blank area of the taskbar and choose Toolbars ➤ Quick Launch.) This toolbar consists of at least three icons: Internet Explorer, Show desktop, and Windows Media Player. If you have set up your system for e-mail with Outlook Express or Outlook, an icon for that program will also appear there.

You can add your own shortcuts to the Quick Launch toolbar by dragging and dropping them there. For example, here's a shortcut for Microsoft Word being dropped onto the Quick Launch toolbar. Notice that a vertical line appears showing where the new shortcut will be dropped in.

To remove a shortcut from the Quick Launch toolbar, right-click the icon and choose Delete from the shortcut menu; then click Yes to confirm.

TIP

Items on the Quick Launch bar don't have text names, so how do you remember what they do? Folders are especially confusing since they all look identical. Just let the mouse rest over the icon for a moment, and its name will appear. Then click once if you're sure it's the one you want.

Displaying Other Toolbars

Quick Launch is not the only toolbar available for display on the taskbar; there are these others as well:

Address   Adds an address area in which you can type in Web addresses or local resource addresses (for files, folders, or even network resources). This serves the same purpose as the Address bar in a folder window or a Windows Explorer/Internet Explorer window. A window will appear when you enter a resource name and press Enter. Typically, you'll use this for Web page addresses, but you could enter **My Computer** to see your My Computer folder; **command.com** to get a DOS box; **printers** to see the printers folder; or **c:** to see the contents of your hard disk.

Links   Adds a toolbar containing the same quick links that are currently set up in your Internet Explorer's Links bar. Clicking a link brings up or switches you to IE, then connects to the predetermined Web site.

NOTE

If you see a right-pointing arrow at the right end of a toolbar, it means there are more buttons than will fit on the screen at once. Click that arrow to see the others in menu form.

Desktop   Shows shortcut icons for everything on your desktop (My Computer, My Network Places, and so on).

To display or hide one of these toolbars, right-click the taskbar and point to Toolbars; then click the name of the toolbar that you want to display or hide.

Creating Your Own Toolbars

You can also create your own toolbars to display on the taskbar. To do so, you must already have an existing folder from which to create the toolbar; you can't create it out of thin air here. Then the content of that folder appears as a new toolbar. If you want to change what's on the toolbar, change the folder content. For example, you might place shortcuts for some programs or documents in a folder, and then specify that folder for the toolbar.

Why is this better than simply adding the shortcuts to the existing Quick Launch toolbar? Well, it isn't necessarily better. It's simply another way.

Use the following steps to create a toolbar:

1. Right-click the taskbar and choose Toolbars ➤ New Toolbar. A New Toolbar dialog box opens.

2. Select the folder that you want to make into a toolbar.

3. Choose OK.

Of all the toolbars, the Quick Launch and Address are among the best, in my opinion. Also, I find that adding Control Panel (via the New Toolbar option) is useful, since I do lots of system tweaking and access the Control Panel frequently.

Adjusting the Toolbar Position

Each toolbar has its own "thumb tab" at the left, a ridged-looking vertical bar. If you do not see the vertical bar, right-click a blank area of the taskbar and clear the check mark next to Lock the Taskbar. You can move the toolbar around by dragging it by that tab.

You can slide it to the right or left, for example, to change the amount of space allocated for that toolbar on the taskbar. To do so, position the mouse pointer over the vertical bar so that the mouse pointer changes to a double-headed arrow, and then drag.

To move a toolbar onto the taskbar, point the mouse at any blank area of it (but not the vertical bar) and hold down the mouse pointer so that the pointer turns into a four-pointed arrow. Then drag the toolbar where you want it.

You can even drag the toolbar off the taskbar, making it a floating toolbar in its own window.

TIP

When you drag a toolbar back onto the taskbar, you might have some trouble getting it repositioned to the left of the running programs. If so, turn it off (right-click a blank area of the taskbar and choose Toolbars and then the toolbar name) and then turn it back on again.

Controlling Taskbar Size, Positioning, and Options

With all the toolbars turned on, everything is all scrunched up on the taskbar, so nothing is very readable.

Fortunately, you can give the taskbar extra rows, so that each toolbar can have its own line (or even multiple lines). To do so, position the mouse pointer at the upper edge of the taskbar and drag upward. Figure 10.5 shows a really huge taskbar with many different toolbars displayed.

FIGURE 10.5: You can add new rows to the taskbar by dragging its top edge upward.

By default, each toolbar appears in its own column. If you prefer you can drag a toolbar up or down to make them appear in rows, as in Figure 10.6, instead.

FIGURE 10.6: Toolbars can also appear row-by-row instead of in columns by dragging them where you want them.

Part ii

To resize the taskbar back to normal, drag its top border back down where you want it.

The taskbar can also be moved to other sides of the screen if you don't want it at the bottom. To drag it, simply point to any empty area of the taskbar and drag it where you want it. Figure 10.7 shows it on the right side, for example.

FIGURE 10.7: You can drag the taskbar to position it wherever you want it.

You can "auto-hide" the taskbar, too, so that it appears only when you point the mouse pointer at the bottom of the screen (or wherever you have placed the taskbar). This saves space on the screen. Auto-Hide is one of the taskbar's options you can set through the taskbar and Start Menu Properties:

1. Right-click a blank area of the taskbar and choose Properties. The Taskbar and Start Menu Properties dialog box opens, as shown in Figure 10.8.

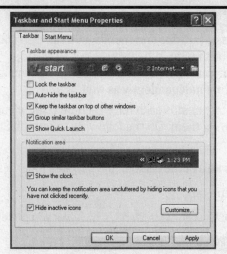

FIGURE 10.8: Choose the basic appearance options for the taskbar and Start menu here.

Part ii

2. Select or deselect any of the check boxes as desired:

Lock the Taskbar Prevents accidental (or intentional) moving or resizing of toolbars on the taskbar, or of the taskbar itself.

Auto-Hide the Taskbar Makes the taskbar disappear until you point to the area on-screen where it should be; then it appears.

Keep the Taskbar on Top of Other Windows Prevents a window from obscuring the taskbar. Leave this on.

Group Similar Taskbar Buttons Enables several open windows to share a single button on the taskbar if they are similar (for example, if they represent documents created in the same program).

Show Quick Launch Shows or hides the Quick Launch toolbar. (This is simply another way of showing/hiding it besides the right-click method you learned earlier.)

3. Choose OK.

Choosing the XP or Classic Start Menu

In addition to the XP or Classic buttons and menus, you can also choose between the XP or Classic Start menu. When you select a Desktop Theme, the corresponding menu is automatically selected, but you can also select a Start menu setting independently as well.

The XP and the Classic Start menus each have their own set of customizations you can perform on them. Do the following to select a Start menu type and customize it:

1. Right-click a blank area of the taskbar and choose Properties.

2. Click the Start Menu tab.

3. Click Start Menu or Classic Start Menu, whichever you prefer.

4. (Optional) Click the Customize button next to the menu type you chose in Step 3 (the other one is unavailable), and change any settings desired in the dialog box that appears. Then click OK to return.

5. Click OK to apply your new settings.

MODIFYING THE START MENU

You can add and remove shortcuts from the Start menu, and move them around so that the shortcuts that you use most often are conveniently located. In the following sections, I'll explain several techniques for this customization.

Adding a Program to the Top-Level Start Menu

The menu that appears when you first click the Start button is the top-level Start menu. There are several areas on this top-level Start menu, and each has a different purpose:

- ▶ The top part of the left column has shortcuts for your default Web and e-mail programs.

- ▶ The bottom part of the left column has temporary shortcuts for the programs you have used most recently or frequently.

- ▶ The top part of the right column has shortcuts to folders that contain data you might want to access, such as My Documents and My Pictures.

- ▶ The bottom part of the right column has shortcuts to some utilities and to Control Panel.

Of these four areas, the only one you can modify manually is the first one—the upper left corner. You can drag shortcuts into that area to give priority placement to a few programs that you use most frequently. For example, in the graphic below, I have placed a shortcut for Microsoft Word there.

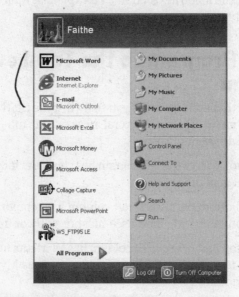

NOTE

If you chose the Classic Start menu, you won't have four areas as shown here; your Start menu will look as it did in earlier Windows versions.

Adding Programs to the All Programs Menu

When you click All Programs, the full menu of installed programs appears, and you can add shortcuts to this menu system too.

As with most activities in Windows, there are several ways to add items to the Start menu. This chapter teaches the simplest method: drag-and-drop.

To add a shortcut to the Start menu from the desktop, simply drag the application, folder, or document's icon onto the Start button—but don't release the mouse button yet. Keep holding it down, and point to All

Programs. That menu opens too. Then drop the shortcut where you want it on the All Programs menu, or point to a submenu, wait for it to open, and then drop it there.

NOTE

As mentioned in Chapter 3, a shortcut is not the application, folder, or document's *real icon*; it's a pointer to that icon. The result is the same either way. Clicking a shortcut has the same effect as clicking the object's original icon. In the case of the Start button's menu, choosing the shortcut item from the menu will run the application, open the folder, or open the document.

Rearranging the All Programs Menu

You can add a shortcut to any of the menus on the All Programs menu, not just on the top-level Start menu. To do so:

1. Point to a shortcut anywhere on the Start menu or its All Programs menu.

2. Drag the shortcut. If you need to open a different submenu, pause the mouse pointer over it with the mouse button held down; the submenu will open momentarily.

3. Keep opening levels of submenus until you see the spot where you want to drop the shortcut.

4. Position the mouse pointer where you want the shortcut to appear; a horizontal line shows the selected position.

5. Release the mouse button, dropping the shortcut there.

Removing an Item from a Menu or Toolbar

There will no doubt be times when you'll want to remove an item from your Start menu, such as when you no longer use a program often enough to warrant its existence on the menu. To remove a shortcut from the Start menu or from a taskbar-based toolbar such as Quick Launch, you can do any of the following:

▶ Drag it off the toolbar or menu and onto the desktop. Then drag it from the desktop into the Recycle Bin. Click Yes to confirm.

▶ Right-click it and choose Delete. Then click Yes to confirm.

Part ii

NOTE

Removing a shortcut from the Start button menu does not remove the actual program from your hard disk. For example, if you remove a shortcut to Word for Windows, the program is still on your computer. It's just the shortcut to it that is being removed. You can always put the shortcut back on the menu.

WHAT'S NEXT

In this chapter you learned how to customize your Windows desktop and Start menu. Stay tuned for the next chapter, in which Windows expert Faithe Wempen explains how to set up your PC for multiple users so that each person in your household can have his or her own settings and preferences.

Chapter 11

SHARING A PC WITH MULTIPLE USERS

I n many households, there is only one computer and several
people who need to use it. Each person has their own ideas
about what constitutes attractive screen colors and important
shortcuts to place on the desktop, but everyone can have separate settings in Windows XP with the User Accounts feature.
Each person simply logs in as him- or herself, and Windows
remembers all the settings and preferences. In this chapter, you
will learn how to create and delete user profiles and how to
switch between users without rebooting.

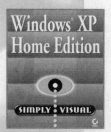

Adapted from *Windows XP Home Edition Simply Visual*
by Faithe Wempen
ISBN 0-7821-2982-X   448 pages $24.99

INTRODUCING USER ACCOUNTS

User accounts allow individual users to have their own settings in Windows. These settings include screen appearance choices, Start menu customizations, Favorites lists in Internet Explorer, and other individual options.

Depending on the way your PC is currently set up, you may or may not be prompted to select a user account when you start up your PC. If only one user is set up, Windows won't ask who you are—it will simply start up.

If there are multiple users, however, Windows will display a Welcome screen, from which you click your name to indicate who you are.

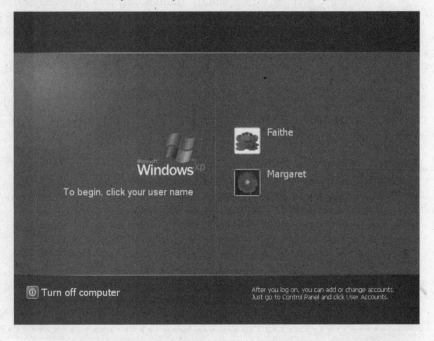

With the Welcome screen shown above, a password is not required to log on as a particular user. In most homes, password security is not needed. However, if you would like each person to enter a password in order to log on, you can set a password for each account. You'll learn how to do that later in the chapter in "Managing Account Passwords."

If you prefer, you can also set up Windows to display the same type of login dialog box used in earlier versions of Windows:

See "Changing the Login Screen" later in this chapter.

NOTE

A user account in Windows XP Home Edition can have one of two statuses: Administrator or Limited. An Administrator account can install and remove programs, read and change existing data files, and make changes to its own and other user accounts. A Limited account can only run programs and change its own user account password. Most adult household members will probably need an Administrator account, but you might want to assign children a Limited account to prevent them from making changes that will cause problems.

When different users are logged in, several parts of Windows are different as well. For example, a different My Documents folder is accessible for each user, and different shortcuts appear on the Start menu. The Favorites and History lists in Internet Explorer are different, and different desktop shortcuts and appearance settings might appear as well.

LOGGING OFF

When you are finished using the computer, you can shut it down as you learned in Chapter 3, or you can simply log off. Logging off closes all your open programs and files and returns to the Welcome screen, so that someone else can log on.

To log off, follow these steps:

1.   Click Start ➤ Log Off.

2.   Depending on how your PC is set up for user accounts, you
     might see a dialog box like this:

Or it might look like this:

Either way, click Log Off. All open programs close, and the Welcome screen returns.

SWITCHING BETWEEN USERS

When you log off, all your programs and files are closed. Windows XP, however, also includes the ability to switch users while leaving the first user's programs and settings active. This enables you to quickly switch to your own settings and perform a few tasks with minimal disturbance to someone else who is also working on the computer.

NOTE

Fast User Switching must be turned on in order for the following procedure to work. See "Changing the Login Screen" later in this chapter if Switch User does not appear as an option for you.

To switch users, do the following:

1. Click Start ➢ Log Off.

2. In the Log Off Windows dialog box, click Switch User.

The Welcome screen returns, with an indicator showing that the previous user still has programs running:

3. Click some other user's name to switch to.

MANAGING USER ACCOUNTS

When you first installed Windows XP, you were probably prompted to enter your name and the names of anyone else who would be using the PC. Windows created user accounts for each of those names at that time. You can set up more accounts any time you like.

Opening the User Accounts Window

Most of the activities in the remainder of this chapter will start from the User Accounts window, so let's open it now.

1. Choose Start ➢ Control Panel.

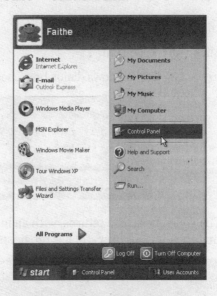

2. In Control Panel, click User Accounts.

The User Accounts window opens. From here, you can create new accounts, delete or change existing ones, and choose between the normal Welcome screen and the more secure "classic" login.

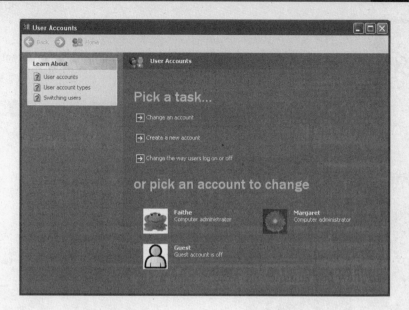

Adding an Account

You can add new accounts at any time, whenever someone in your household would like to use the computer with their own settings. To do so, start at the User Accounts window and then do the following:

1. Click Create a New Account.

2. Type the name of the person for whom you are creating the account, and then click Next.

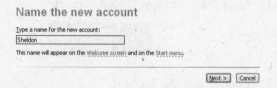

3. Choose the type of account you want: Computer Administrator or Limited. Users with Computer Administrator privileges have free access to change anything about the computer's configuration; those with Limited privileges can only run programs and change their own password.

TIP

Creating Limited accounts for children, teens, and novice users can ensure that they don't delete important files.

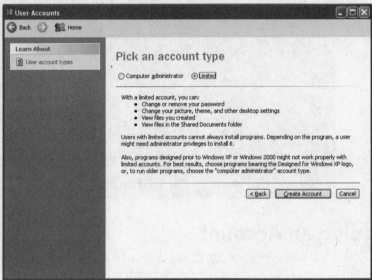

4. Click Create Account. The account is created.

Deleting an Account

If you decide you don't need an account you have set up, you can delete it. To do so, start at the User Accounts window and then do the following:

1. Click the account you want to delete.

2. Click Delete the Account.

3. If you plan to move this user's settings to another computer, choose Keep Files. This will create a folder on the desktop

with that user's name, containing the user's documents and desktop shortcuts. If you won't need that user's documents and settings, click Delete Files.

WARNING

Each user has their own My Documents folder, separate from other users' folders. If you choose Delete Files in Step 3, any documents that were in that user's My Documents folder will be deleted. If you have any doubts about whether to keep any of the files, choose Keep Files. You can then sort through them later and copy anything worth keeping to your own My Documents folder.

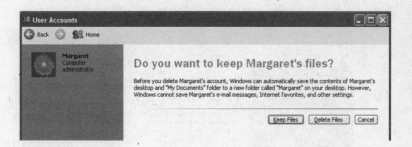

4.   A confirmation message appears. Click Delete Account.

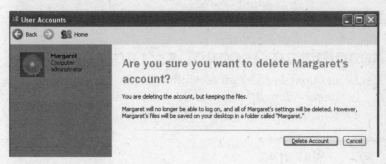

Renaming an Account

You might sometimes need to rename an account. For example, perhaps when you initially set up your user accounts, you included each person's first and last name in the account names. But now you realize that because everyone in your family has the same last name, you would prefer that the account names be first-name only. Or perhaps you want everyone in the whole household to use a single account, so you plan to rename one of the accounts "Everyone" and delete all the others.

Part ii

To rename an account, start at the User Accounts window and then do the following:

1. Click the account you want to change.

2. Click Change My Name.

3. Type the new name and then click Change Name.

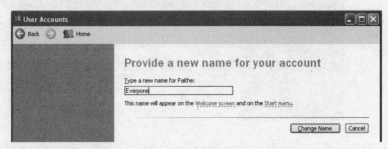

   4. Click Back to return to the User Accounts window.

Changing an Account's Privileges

As mentioned earlier, an account can have one of two privilege sets: Computer Administrator or Limited. To switch between the two for an account, do the following from the User Accounts window:

WARNING

To use this procedure, you must be logged in with a Computer Administrator account (not a Limited account).

1. Click the account you want to change.

2. Click Change the Account Type.

➡ Change the account type

3. Click the account type you want: Computer Administrator or Limited. Then click Change Account Type.

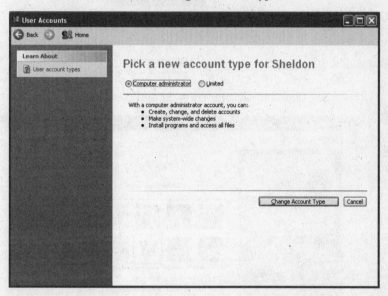

4. Click Back to return to the User Accounts window.

Changing an Account's Picture

When you create a new account, it is assigned a picture at random. You can choose a different picture from the several pictures that come with Windows XP, or you can assign a picture from a file.

TIP
You could take digital photos of each person in your household and then assign those picture files to the user accounts.

To change an account's picture, do the following:

1. From the User Accounts window, click the account you want to change.

2. Click Change the Picture.

3. Click the picture you want and then click Change Picture.

Or, to choose your own picture, click Browse for More Pictures. Then navigate to the picture you want to use, click it, and click Open.

NOTE

If the picture needs to be scanned or acquired from a digital camera, click Get a Picture from a Camera or Scanner and then refer to Chapter 23.

The new picture now appears for the account, replacing the previously used picture.

MANAGING ACCOUNT PASSWORDS

If you don't want everyone to have free access to every account, you must specify a password—that is, enable *password protection*—for each account. Then, every time someone tries to log on or switch accounts, a password prompt will appear.

WARNING

When you turn on password protection for an account, all stored passwords, cookies, and security certificates for that account are wiped out. This might affect your Web surfing. For example, if you automatically log on to a certain Web site because your username and password are stored in Internet Explorer, the next time you visit that site, you might need to reenter that information.

Setting a Password

To set a password for an account, do the following from the User Accounts window:

1. Click the account for which you want to set a password.

2. Click Create a Password.

 Create a password

3. Type the password in the Type a New Password text box, and then again in the Type the New Password Again to Confirm box.

4. (Optional) If you want to provide a password hint, enter it in the Type a Word or Phrase to Use As a Password Hint box.

WARNING

Password hints make it easier for users to remember their passwords, but also make it easier for someone to guess the password, decreasing the security of your system.

5. Click Create Password.

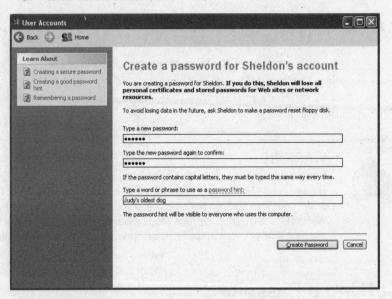

 6. Click Back to return to the User Accounts window.

Now, whenever someone chooses that user account, a password box appears, prompting for the password. You can click the **?** button to get the hint, as shown here.

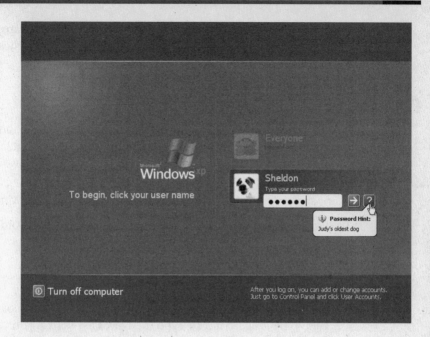

Removing a Password

Removing a password disables the password protection for the account, so that it is once again freely accessible by anyone. To remove a password, do the following from the User Accounts window:

NOTE

Removing the password is not the same as setting the password to be blank; if you do that, Windows will prompt you for a password and you must press Enter without typing anything as your password.

1. Click the account for which you want to remove the password. Notice that password-protected accounts are marked as such on-screen.

2. Click Remove the Password.

➡️ Remove the password

3. Some information appears about losing personal certificates and stored passwords for the account. Read it and then click Remove Password.

Changing a Password

Security experts recommend changing a password occasionally for added security, so that would-be intruders have less time to try to guess it. You might want to change your password every month or so if you are worried about others accessing your sensitive documents.

To change a password, do the following from the User Accounts window:

1. Click the account for which you want to change the password.

2. Click Change the Password.

   ➔ Change the password

3. Enter a new password in the Type a New Password text box; then type it again in the Type the New Password Again to Confirm box.

4. (Optional) Enter a password hint in the Type a Word or Phrase to Use As a Password Hint box.

5. Click Change Password.

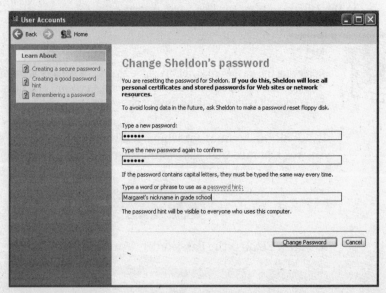

CHANGING THE LOGIN SCREEN

By default, Windows XP Home Edition uses the Welcome screen you've already seen. If you prefer, you can make Windows use a regular Log On to Windows dialog box, as in earlier versions of Windows:

If you haven't assigned a password to the user account, you can leave the Password box empty.

NOTE

If you click the Options button in this Log On to Windows box, a Shut Down button appears, enabling you to shut down the computer rather than logging on.

To set up this type of login box instead of the Welcome screen, do the following from the User Accounts window:

1. Click Change the Way Users Log On or Off.

2. Clear the Use the Welcome Screen check box to use the classic Log On dialog box, or ensure that the check box is marked if you want the Welcome screen.

3. If you are using the Welcome screen, the Use Fast User Switching check box is marked by default. Clear this check box if you don't want *Fast User Switching*.

NOTE

Fast User Switching is a feature that enables another user to log on without the first user logging off. For example, suppose you are working with Excel, and your daughter wants to check her e-mail. She can log on and do so without your having to exit Excel. Then you can switch back to your own user account and resume your work.

4. Click Apply Options.

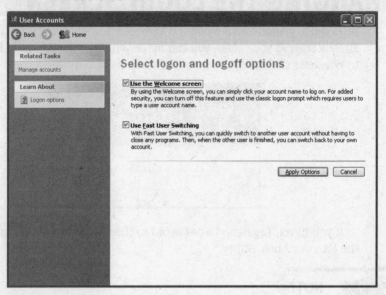

    5. Click Back to return to the User Accounts window.

TURNING THE GUEST ACCOUNT ON

The Guest account allows visitors and other people not specifically authorized to use your computer to have access to it. If you set passwords for all of the "real" user accounts, you might want to enable the Guest account in case someone wants to use the computer but doesn't know any of the passwords.

By default, the Guest account is off. It has Limited privileges, so anyone using it can only run programs; they cannot make changes to system settings that could affect performance or ruin anyone else's documents or programs.

To enable the Guest account, do the following from the User Accounts window:

1. Click the Guest account.

2. Click Turn On the Guest Account.

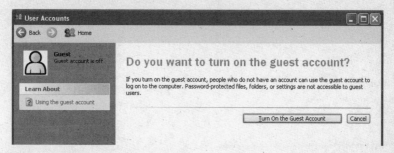

Now the Guest account will appear along with the other accounts on the Welcome screen.

What's Next

In the next chapter, Robert Cowart explains some important utilities for keeping your PC healthy. An ounce of preventive maintenance can often spare you many pounds of trouble down the road! You'll learn about utilities such as Check Disk, Disk Defragmenter, Disk Cleanup, and more.

Part iii

Chapter 12
PC HEALTH FEATURES

There are two sides to PC health: preventive maintenance and troubleshooting. This chapter covers the first part of that equation: everyday maintenance tasks for keeping your PC running smoothly and problem-free. Then in Chapter 13, you'll learn about some more advanced tools for troubleshooting problems as they occur.

Adapted from *Mastering Windows Me*
by Robert Cowart
ISBN 0-4821-2857-2   960 pages $39.99

and

*Windows Me: I Didn' t Know You Could
Do That!* by John Ross
ISBN 0-4821-2829-7   272 pages $19.99

KEEPING YOUR SYSTEM UP-TO-DATE

Windows works best when it has the latest versions of everything, including any patches or updates that prevent or fix problems with Windows XP and Internet Explorer. There are a couple of ways you can get those latest versions. One of them, Windows Update, has been around since Windows 98 and still works beautifully. The other, AutoUpdate, automates the process of checking for, retrieving, and installing the latest updates. Both require Internet connectivity, so start your Internet connection before using either one.

Using Windows Update

Windows Update connects you to a Web page that runs an application to analyze your current system settings. Then it recommends updates you can download.

Follow these steps to use Windows Update:

1. Choose Start ➤ All Programs ➤ Windows Update. A Welcome to Windows Update Web page appears.

2. Click the Scan for Updates hyperlink. See Figure 12.1.

3. Wait for Windows Update to analyze your system. If you see a prompt asking whether it is OK for Windows to do this, click Yes.

4. If recommended updates appear for your system, select or deselect them as desired. Then follow the prompts to install them. If your system is already up-to-date, a message will appear to that effect instead.

NOTE
You should always choose to install any critical updates. The others are optional, depending on your interests. For example, if you don't use MSN Explorer, you probably don't need a new version of it, and if you don't speak Chinese, you probably don't need Web support for Chinese characters.

You can remove or reinstall updates later if needed. Notice the View Installation History hyperlink in Figure 12.1. Click that and a list of already-installed updates will appear.

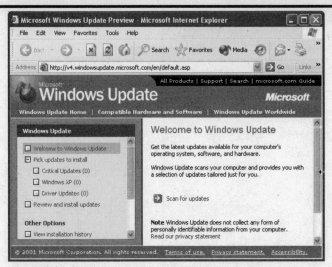

FIGURE 12.1: Windows Update will scan your system and recommend updates.

Some updates can be removed. A Remove hyperlink appears next to updates that fit that description; click it and follow the prompts.

Using AutoUpdate

When you install Windows XP, an AutoUpdate icon appears in your System Tray. At some point, a Microsoft AutoUpdate box pops up, explaining the feature and asking you to agree to its license restrictions. Click Yes to accept it. This happens only once, and by the time you read this, it has probably already come and gone on your PC.

AutoUpdate automates the work of using Windows Update by periodically checking for updates and downloading them to your computer. Then it notifies you that they have arrived, and asks your permission to install them. It's turned on by default, but you can adjust its settings by doing the following:

1. Click the Start button and then right-click My Computer and choose Properties. The System Properties dialog box opens.

2. Click the Automatic Updates tab. (See Figure 12.2.)

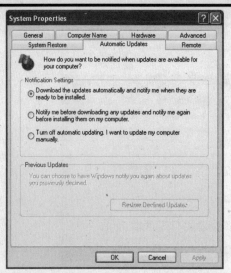

FIGURE 12.2: Configure AutoUpdate here if you want to change the default settings.

3.   Select one of the update options:

Download the Updates Automatically and Notify Me When They Are Ready to Be Installed.   This is the default and the best option for most people.

Notify Me before Downloading Any Updates and Notify Me Again before Installing Them on My Computer.   This is for those who are suspicious about things being downloaded to their PCs but who still want to use AutoUpdate.

Turn off Automatic Updating. I Will Update My Computer Manually.   This setting turns off AutoUpdate completely.

4.   Click OK.

When an update is available, you will see a bubble over your Auto-Update icon (assuming you didn't turn off AutoUpdate completely) in the System Tray announcing it. Click the AutoUpdate icon to open the Microsoft AutoUpdate window. From there, click the Install button and wait for the update to be installed. When it is finished, a message to that effect appears; click OK.

CHECKING FOR ERRORS WITH CHECK DISK

Disk errors can result in all kinds of puzzling, tough-to-troubleshoot problems. Fortunately, there is a solution: Check Disk. It corrects both physical and logical disk errors. Many people run Check Disk every week or so even when there are no obvious problems, just for general prevention of problems.

NOTE
Check Disk was called Scandisk in earlier versions of Windows.

A *physical disk error* is a bad spot on your hard disk. It's usually caused by trauma to the system, such as knocking it off a table. A *logical disk error* is a glitch in the File Allocation Table (FAT), which keeps track of which files are stored in which locations on the disk. Logical errors are usually caused by shutting down your PC improperly (i.e., by turning off the power button instead of using the Start ➤ Shut Down command) or by programs crashing or freezing up. Of the two types, logical errors are much more common.

If you are experiencing lots of error messages in Windows, the first thing you should do is run Check Disk, as shown in the following steps:

1. Choose Start ➤ My Computer.

2. Right-click the drive you want to check, and choose Properties.

3. Click the Tools tab, and then click Check Now.

Part ii

4. (Optional) Mark either or both of the check boxes:

    Automatically fix file system errors   Fixes errors without prompting. Recommended for beginners.

    Scan for and attempt recovery of bad sectors   Performs both a physical and a logical check. If you do not mark this check box, it performs a logical check only. A physical check can take a long time (several hours).

5. Click Start. The testing begins.

6. When testing is complete, a Disk Check Complete box appears. Click OK.

7. Click OK to close the Properties box for the disk.

WARNING

Don't use your computer while Check Disk is running, because if the drive content changes, Check Disk starts over from the beginning. If you have problems with Check Disk restarting a lot and being unable to finish, make sure all other programs are shut down, including programs running in the System Tray.

DEFRAGMENTING A DISK

The storage system on a hard disk is not physically sequential. Files are stored in any available physical area. The *File Allocation Table (FAT)* keeps track of where each piece of each file resides. Then, when Windows calls for a file, it looks up in the FAT the location of the file, or the locations of pieces of the file, and puts the pieces together in memory.

When you initially write a file to disk, it's stored in one contiguous mass; but as you edit the file, the file can become fragmented. For example, suppose you have a hard disk that already has some data on it, and also some empty space. You write a new report, and its file takes up eight contiguous clusters on a disk. You then copy some other data to the disk, so that there is no longer any empty space next to the original eight clusters.

Then you edit your report, adding five clusters' worth of additional text. Where will it be stored? There is no room next to the original file on the disk, so the additional data is stored in some other empty area. Now the file is fragmented.

As you can imagine, it takes longer to open a fragmented file than an unfragmented one, because the disk's read/write head must hop around on the disk, picking up the pieces of the file. That's why defragmenting a drive can improve its performance. Defragmenting a drive rearranges the files stored on it so that each file is stored in a single, contiguous area.

WARNING

Defragmenting takes a long time (an hour or more), so you might want to begin it before you go to bed or go out for the evening and let the program run while you are away.

WARNING

Disable your screensaver and antivirus program before running the Defragmenter to minimize restarts due to conflicts from program access.

To defragment a disk, do the following:

1. Choose Start ➤ All Programs ➤ Accessories ➤ System Tools ➤ Disk Defragmenter.

2. Select the drive you want to defragment. Then do one of the following:

   ▶ Click Analyze (recommended) to check how badly the drive needs to be defragmented. This is the best choice. If the computer does not recommend defragmenting the drive, don't defragment it. Always run Check Disk prior to a defragmentation.

   ▶ Click Defragment to start defragmenting the drive now. Then skip to Step 4.

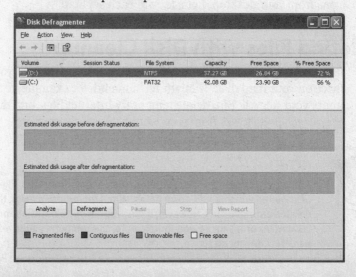

3. If you chose Analyze in Step 2, a dialog box appears momentarily with a recommendation. Do one of the following:

    ▶ Click Defragment if defragmenting is recommended.

    ▶ Click View Report if you are interested in the statistics.

    ▶ Click Close to close the dialog box without defragmenting that drive. You can then return to Step 2 to select another drive.

4. Wait for the drive to be defragmented. It can take hours, depending on the drive size, processor speed, and amount of free space left on the disk. When defragmentation is complete, a message appears; click Close.

WARNING
You can continue to use your computer while it defragments, but usage may cause the defragmenter to restart frequently, increasing the overall time required.

CLEANING OUT UNWANTED FILES

Windows XP has two utilities for cleaning up your system. Disk Cleanup finds and deletes unnecessary files from your hard disk, freeing up overall disk space, and the Desktop Cleanup Wizard eliminates unused shortcut icons from your desktop. Let's look at each separately.

Deleting Files with Disk Cleanup

Disk Cleanup recommends certain files for deletion, to help you free up space on your hard disk. It might recommend, for example, that you empty your Recycle Bin, delete temporary Internet files, and delete some leftover *temporary files* from your word processing program.

NOTE
As a program operates, it sometimes creates temporary files, like scrap pieces of paper on which it jots down notes. When the program exits, these files are deleted automatically. However, if the program terminates abnormally, due to locking up or losing power, for example, the temporary files remain on your hard disk, taking up space.

1. Choose Start ➤ My Computer. Right-click the drive you want to clean up and choose Properties.

2. In the Properties dialog box, click Disk Cleanup.

3. In the Disk Cleanup dialog box, a report appears for the chosen drive, showing what files Windows thinks can be safely deleted. Mark or clear the check box for each category of files that Windows presents.

NOTE

For some categories, a View Files button appears in the Disk Cleanup dialog box. You can click it to see which files will be included in the deletion. Not all categories offer this.

4. After making your selections, click OK.

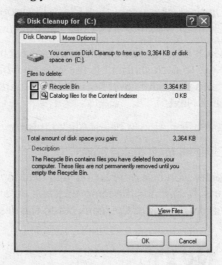

5. A warning box appears. Click Yes to confirm. The files are deleted, and the Disk Cleanup dialog box closes.

Tidying Up with the Desktop Cleanup Wizard

Whereas Disk Cleanup actually frees up space on your drive, the Desktop Cleanup doesn't delete anything. Instead, it takes icons on your desktop

Part ii

that are unused and moves them to a folder, reducing the clutter on your desktop.

NOTE

How did those unused icons get on the desktop in the first place? Well, many programs that you install place icons for themselves there automatically. Also, at some point, you may have accidentally dragged icons from a file management window to the desktop.

Every 60 days, a reminder appears in your system tray prompting you to run Desktop Cleanup. If you see such a reminder, you can click it to run the program. Otherwise, do the following to start Desktop Cleanup:

1. Right-click the desktop and choose Properties.

2. Click the Desktop tab. Then click Customize Desktop.

3. On the General tab, click Clean Desktop Now. The Desktop Cleanup Wizard starts. Click Next to continue.

4. Mark or clear the check boxes for each desktop shortcut. Next to each shortcut is the date on which it was last used; items that have never been used are marked by default. Then click Next.

5. A confirmation appears. Click Finish.

6. Close all open dialog boxes.

A new folder icon now appears on your desktop called Unused Desktop Shortcuts. It contains the removed icons. At any time, you can open this folder and drag one of the icons out to the desktop again.

WHAT'S NEXT

This chapter explained some of the routine preventive maintenance features of Windows XP. You can use them to avoid many common problems. However, if you do experience a problem, the next chapter will likely be of interest to you. In it, you'll learn about troubleshooting an ailing Windows XP computer.

Chapter 13

TROUBLESHOOTING
WINDOWS XP HOME EDITION

For most of us, the internal operation of our computers is no more obvious than most of the other machines in our lives: You press a key on the keyboard or move the mouse across your desk, and something happens on the screen. Or you push the accelerator pedal and your car moves forward. But just as it's useful to have gauges on your car's dashboard that tell you how fast you're moving and how much fuel you have left, it's often helpful to have tools that can display information about how your computer is performing.

This chapter starts out by explaining the System Restore feature and providing some general troubleshooting tips and hints. Then it provides descriptions of diagnostic tools that measure and display many of the features and functions of your computer's hardware and software. Some of these measurements are invaluable when it comes to troubleshooting problems that you might be having with your Windows XP operating system and PC.

Adapted from *Mastering Windows Me*
by Robert Cowart
ISBN 0-4821-2857-2   960 pages $39.99

and

Windows Me: I Didn't Know You Could Do That! by John Ross
ISBN 0-4821-2829-7   272 pages $19.99

Recover from Problems with System Restore

System Restore, which was introduced in Windows Me and continues in Windows XP, provides a functionality that has previously been available only in third-party utility programs such as Go Back. It takes a snapshot of your system configuration (including your Windows settings), a list of which programs have been installed, and so on. You can then restore that configuration in the future if your system starts giving you problems.

For example, suppose you install a new shareware program you've downloaded from the Internet, and suddenly you can't get your e-mail anymore. You then try to uninstall the program, but it doesn't help. You can use System Restore to restore your system to the condition it was in before you installed that program.

Windows takes a daily snapshot automatically and keeps it around for about two weeks. You can also take your own snapshots at any time. For example, if you are not sure what a particular program will do to your system, you might take a snapshot right before installing it.

NOTE

System Restore is completely reversible. If you revert to a previous configuration and decide that it was a mistake to do so, you can go "forward" again to the settings you had before you reverted.

Taking a System Snapshot

To take a system snapshot with System Restore, follow these steps:

1. Choose Start ➢ All Programs ➢ Accessories ➢ System Tools ➢ System Restore. System Restore opens, as shown in Figure 13.1.

2. Choose Create a Restore Point and click Next.

3. Type a description for the restore point and click Next. Use any description that will help you remember why you created the restore point. For example, you might enter something like **Before Installing New Game**.

4. Click OK.

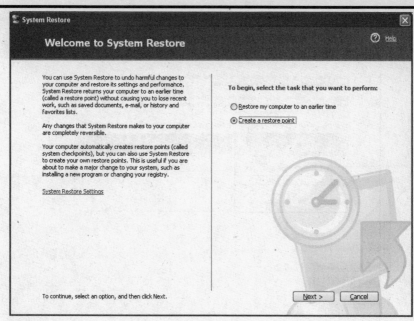

FIGURE 13.1: The opening screen of System Restore

Restoring a Previous Configuration

If you ever need to go back to a previous configuration, here's how to do it:

1. Choose Start ➤ All Programs ➤ Accessories ➤ System Tools ➤ System Restore.

2. Choose Restore My Computer to an Earlier Time, and click Next.

3. Choose the date on the calendar for the snapshot you want to return to. A list of available snapshots for that date appears, as seen in Figure 13.2.

4. Click Next. A confirmation appears; click Next again and another confirmation appears.

5. Click Restore. The system files are modified as needed, and your computer is restarted.

6. After the restart, the System Restore box reappears. Click Close.

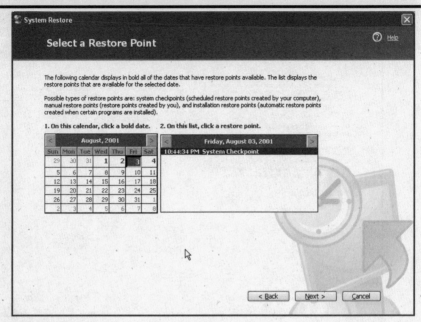

FIGURE 13.2: Select a snapshot to restore.

NOTE

Windows XP comes with another great new feature that safeguards your Windows system: System File Restore. It works automatically behind the scenes. If you install a program that overwrites a file that Windows needs to operate, System File Restore automatically reverses that overwriting, ensuring that Windows does not become corrupted by rogue programs installing their own versions of system files.

TROUBLESHOOTING TIPS

The first thing you should try when experiencing system problems is to check the disk for errors with Check Disk, as described in Chapter 12. From there, depending on the problem, a variety of steps might be appropriate. Here are some additional tips for troubleshooting common Windows XP computer-system maladies.

Windows XP doesn't start up when you turn your computer on. Here are some troubleshooting tips to try:

▶ Remember that booting up can take up to a minute or so. Don't assume there is trouble unless there is absolutely no activity on the screen. Sometimes the only movement you'll see is in the little green bar on the startup screen.

▶ Check that the power is connected, the monitor is on, the brightness isn't turned down, the monitor cable is secure, and there's no floppy disk inserted in Drive A:.

▶ If the problem persists, press the reset switch or turn the computer off, wait a second, and turn it on again. Let it try to boot again. Windows is pretty good at repairing itself. It notes when a startup has been unsuccessful, and will try to boot one way or another. It may take some time, grinding away on the hard disk for a while. If there is a problem with the Registry, the Registry Checker may kick in and fix the problem for you at startup.

▶ Still no go? If you see the Starting Windows message, you're getting somewhere at least. Press the Reset switch on your computer, then press and hold the left Shift key while the computer and Windows attempt to boot. This should boot you into Safe Mode (though it might take the better part of a minute or two). Safe Mode uses the most rudimentary of drivers to boot with, to prevent incompatibilities. While booted up in Safe Mode, your job is to discover which setting (such as screen driver) was wrong. Do this using Control Panel, Device Manager, etc. Sometimes just shutting down from Safe Mode and booting again will result in a proper full boot.

▶ Another means of getting into Safe Mode is to press F8 while Windows is first booting (when you see "Starting Windows" in character mode, before the Windows splash screen appears). This will present a menu of startup options. Choose Safe Mode.

Part ii

▶ If you can't even boot from the hard disk into Safe Mode, insert your Windows XP CD-ROM and turn the computer off and on again. When you see Press Any Key to Boot from CD, do so, and choose to repair the Windows installation.

You are seeing messages about running low on memory. Here are some things to try:

▶ Try closing some programs and/or documents.

▶ Empty the Recycle Bin. Remove any unnecessary programs from the Startup folder.

▶ Use Windows Explorer or My Computer to delete some files. Empty the Recycle Bin again.

▶ Make sure you have at least several (preferably 20 or more) megabytes of free space on your hard disk.

▶ Let Windows manage your virtual memory settings (using Control Panel's System applet).

▶ If you have less than 64MB of RAM in your computer, upgrade to at least 64, preferably 128MB.

You see messages about running out of disk space.   Try the following:

▶ Empty the Recycle Bin.

▶ Delete files you don't need.

▶ Remove whole components of Windows that you never use, perhaps Wallpaper, Exchange, sound schemes, or accessories. (Some of these consume large amounts of space.)

▶ Purchase a higher-capacity hard disk.

▶ Right-click your hard disk's icon (for example, from My Computer), click Properties, and click Disk Cleanup.

The computer seems "stuck."   Try the following tips:

▶ First, press Esc once or twice.

▶ If it's still stuck, use Alt+Tab or the taskbar to switch to another program to see if Windows is really locked up.

(Alt+Tab is the standard keyboard combination for switching from one program to another.)

▶ If the taskbar is in Auto Hide mode and doesn't appear, try Ctrl+Esc to bring up the Start list. (This is the standard keyboard combination for keyboards that don't have a Windows key.)

▶ Use these techniques to get to and save any documents you are working on, then close all programs if possible. If you suspect only one program is having trouble (such as being stuck), press Ctrl+Alt+Del once, then wait. In a few seconds, a list of programs should come up. Select the program that is listed as not responding and click End Task; repeat for each stuck program.

▶ Save your work and restart the computer as soon as possible.

Nothing is solving your problem. You're pulling out your hair.   Here are some troubleshooting tips to try:

▶ On your computer (if possible), try the troubleshooters that are built into Help and Support.

▶ On your computer or another, use Microsoft online Help via a browser and the World Wide Web.

▶ On your computer or another, read the additional Help text files included on the CD.

The following sections explain some Windows utilities that can provide you with information about your computer's operation, to possibly assist you in troubleshooting a puzzling error or problem. In order to use these tools, you must have an understanding of what you're looking for, so they're not terribly useful for the beginner. However, as you progress in your Windows XP skill, you might find them handy.

CONTROL WHAT LOADS AT STARTUP

Sometimes Windows itself is okay, but a program that automatically loads at startup causes a problem.

Part ii

Some programs start automatically because there is a shortcut for them in the Startup folder of the Start menu. To prevent such a program from loading at startup, simply delete that shortcut:

1. Choose Start ≻ All Programs ≻ Startup.

2. Right-click the shortcut and choose Delete.

3. Click Yes to confirm.

Not all programs that load at startup, however, have shortcuts in the Startup folder. Some of them start because of entries in the Registry.

Windows XP, like earlier versions, includes a System Configuration Utility program that you can use to fine-tune Windows startup by disabling certain Registry entries. Because it has tremendous potential for making matters worse rather than better, however, this program is not available on the Start menu; you must start it with the Run command. (Microsoft probably figured anyone who knows enough to start it manually is experienced enough to be able to use it intelligently.)

The filename of the utility is MSCONFIG, so to start it:

1. Choose Start ≻ Run.

2. Type **MSCONFIG**.

3. Click OK.

The utility has six tabs. The one that you should be most interested in is the Startup tab, shown below. On it, you can deselect the check boxes for items that currently load when Windows starts that you want to disable. This can allow you to disable a particular item that consistently produces an error message or locks up Windows, for example.

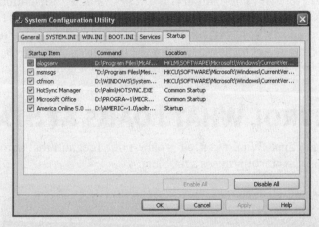

VIEW SYSTEM INFORMATION

The System Information utility supplied with Windows XP supplies as much information about the computer's hardware and software as most users will ever need. Among other things, it displays specific information about the CPU, memory, and other hardware components inside your computer, information about hardware addresses, interrupt requests (IRQs), and memory addresses, and a snapshot of all the programs, drivers, and other software currently running on the system.

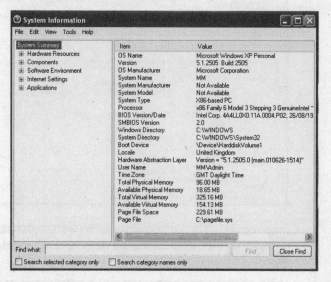

A shortcut to the System Information program is located in the Start ➢ All Programs ➢ Accessories ➢ System Tools menu. You can also open it from Start ➢ Run by typing **MSINFO32**.

The System Information window has two panes. The pane on the left contains a list of information screens available in System Information, organized into a tree structure. To open any of the top-level categories, click the plus sign (+) next to the name of the category. The pane on the right contains specific system information for the category selected in the left pane. To view an information window, click the category name.

System Information includes these major categories:

System Summary   The System Summary shows general information about your computer and about Windows XP, including the manufacturer and type of processor, the name and type of computer, and data about memory usage.

Hardware Resources   The screens in the Hardware Resources category show information about the way your computer relates to internal and external hardware. The Hardware Resources screens include a display of shared and conflicting hardware, devices that use Direct Memory Access (DMA), and lists of interrupt requests (IRQs), I/O addresses, and memory addresses.

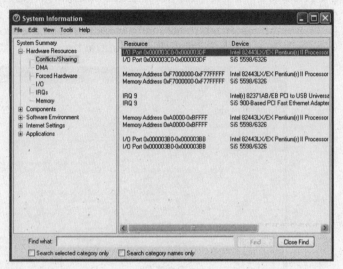

Components   The Components screens show details about the device drivers, multimedia services, and other hardware connected to your system.

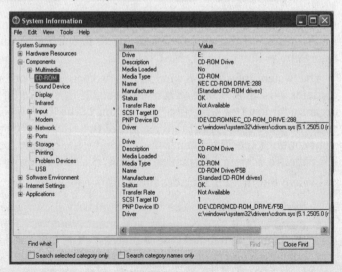

Software Environment The Software Environment screens show information about the software currently loaded in the computer's memory, including active programs, drivers, environment settings, queued print jobs, and so forth.

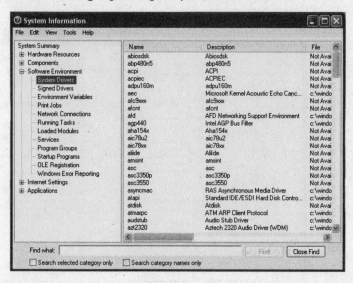

Internet Settings The Internet Settings screen gives you detailed information on the version of Internet Explorer installed, along with security settings and cached files information.

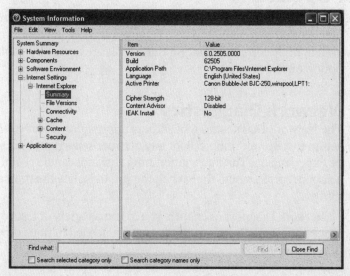

Applications   Many Microsoft application programs, including the ones in the Office family and some from other suppliers, have links to the System Information utility that can allow System Information to display details about current activity in those programs.

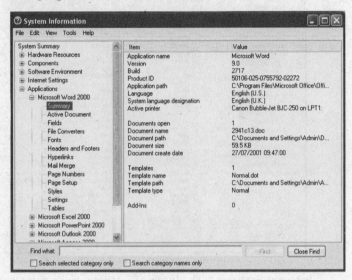

Tool Options

The System Information application also gives you access to a whole host of tools that you can use to help you troubleshoot problems or keep your system in tip-top condition. All these tools are accessible from the Tools option on the menu.

Network Diagnostics

The Network Diagnostics tool gathers information about your computer set-up to help you troubleshoot any network-related problems you might be experiencing. The information from this tool can be useful to you or to a support professional that is helping you to isolate the problem you are having.

Network Diagnostics enables you to run a variety of tests on your system and gathers the relevant information needed to track down network difficulties.

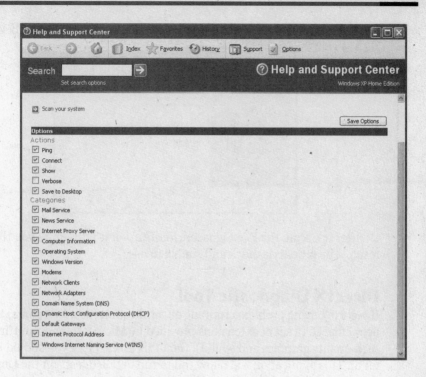

Part iii

File Signature Verification Utility

The File Signature Verification utility is a tool that you can use to make sure that you can spot if any of the critical system files have been changed.

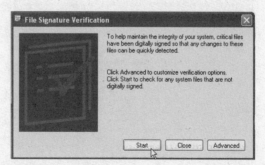

It can spot changed critical files because all the critical files on the system have been digitally signed, so all the utility has to do is compare the files to the digital signatures.

To start the checking process, click Start. The utility will then begin its scan of your system.

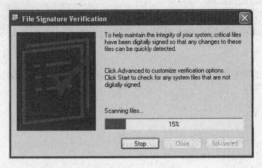

After the scan, the File Signature Verification utility shows you the result. The process is quick and simple to use.

DirectX Diagnostic Tool

If you are having problems running an application (usually a game) that uses DirectX (a set of extensions provided by Microsoft for outputting high-quality graphics and sound), then this is one place you should head off to. This application will allow you to run detailed tests on the DirectX system and verify the version numbers of the files in use.

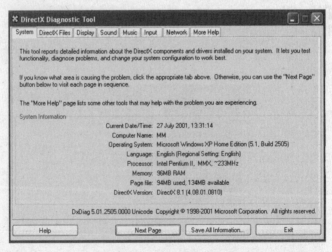

The DirectX Diagnostic Tool is divided up into eight sections:

System   This gives you information about your system, including processor type, memory, and DirectX version.

DirectX Files   This screen gives you a rundown of the DirectX files installed on your system, along with individual version numbers and file dates.

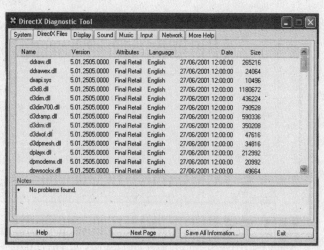

Display   This screen gives you information on your display device and drivers and allows you to run tests on your system to check DirectX compatibility.

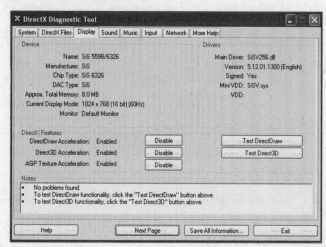

Sound This screen gives you information on your sound device and drivers and allows you to run tests on your system to check DirectX compatibility.

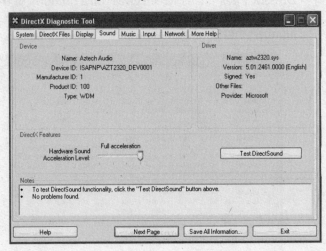

Music This screen gives you information on your MIDI music devices, drivers, and ports, and allows you to run tests on your system to check DirectX compatibility.

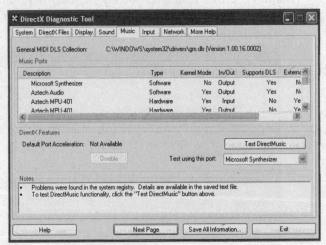

Input   This screen gives you information on your input devices and drivers.

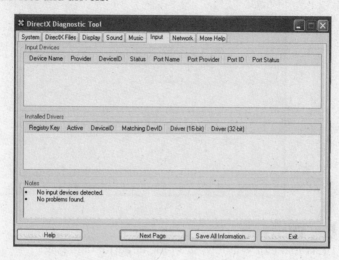

Network   This screen gives you details on the DirectPlay services installed on your system and DirectPlay applications. (DirectPlay allows you to play games over a network or the Internet.)

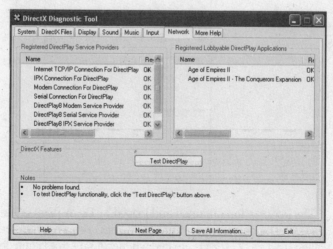

More Help   This screen is where you go if you haven't been able to solve your problems and it allows you to access relevant help files and MSInfo.

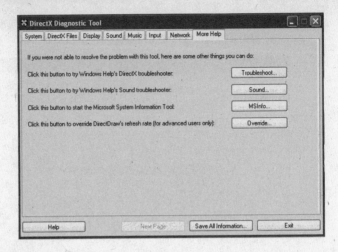

Dr. Watson

Dr. Watson for Windows is a program-error debugger.

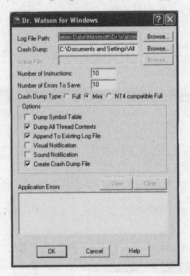

The information obtained and logged by Dr. Watson is the information needed by technical support groups to diagnose a program error. A text file (called Drwtsn32.log) is created whenever an error is detected, and this file can be sent to support personnel to help them diagnose the problem.

You also have the option of creating a crash dump file, which is a binary file that a programmer can load into a debugger. Sometimes support technicians ask for this.

If a program error occurs, Dr. Watson will start automatically.

To start Dr. Watson manually, click Start ➤ Run, and then type **drwtsn32**.

VIEW DEVICE STATUS INFORMATION

The Windows Device Manager is a very valuable tool for finding and fixing problems with device drivers and related hardware and software. To view the Device Manager:

1. Choose Start ➤ Control Panel.

2. Click Performance and Maintenance.

3. Click System.

4. On the Hardware tab, click Device Manager.

TIP

Another way to access Device Manager is by right-clicking the My Computer icon on the Start menu and selecting Properties, then clicking on the Hardware tab and finally on the Device Manager button.

The Device Manager display is a tree structure with a top-level item for each type of device in your system: drives, display adapters, the mouse, the keyboard, and so forth. When you open a top-level category, you will display entries for all of the devices of that type currently installed in your system.

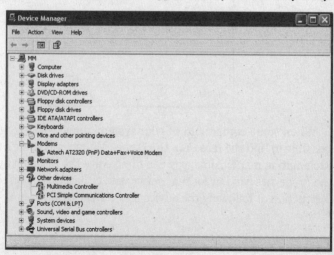

To see more information about a device, double-click the item listing, or select it and click the Properties button. The Driver and Resources tabs in the Properties window provide still more information about the device's driver and associated IRQ.

You can also remove any device from the computer's current hardware profile; this is the same as turning it off without removing the hardware or software. This is not something you will want to do very often, but it can sometimes be a useful troubleshooting technique. If an individual device listing has a red X over the icon, that device has been disabled.

When the Device Manager detects a device with an address or interrupt conflict, or some other problem that keeps the device from operating properly, it displays a yellow exclamation mark (!) over the icon for that device. The Properties window for a device with a problem will contain an explanation and instructions for solving the problem in the Device Status section of the General tab.

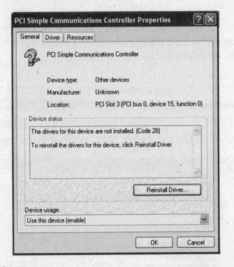

When some component of your system stops working, it's often possible to find the reason in the Device Manager. If there's an X or an exclamation mark visible, you can often solve the problem by opening the Properties window for that device, and either turning off the Disable instruction or following the advice in the Device Status box.

IDENTIFY RUNNING TASKS

Sometimes it's good to be able to find out what tasks are running on your system (especially if you are trying to increase the performance of your system or free up additional resources). Under Windows 98/Me, it was hard to get at this information, but Windows XP (like Windows NT and Windows 2000 before it) makes this really easy.

You identify running tasks using the Windows Task Manager, which you can access in one of two ways:

▶ Right-click on the taskbar and select Task Manager.

▶ Press Ctrl+Alt+Delete and Task Manager will appear.

Task Manager gives you access to a wide variety of information, divided into five categories:

Applications   The Applications tab is the default tab that the Task Manager opens up on. This shows you the applications that are running currently and gives you the ability to end a task, switch to a task, or start a new task.

Processes   The Processes tab gives you a complete listing of the processes running on your PC. Processes are individual components and one application can have more than one process. Windows XP also has many core processes that are part of the operating system itself.

This tab also allows you to end a process by selecting it and clicking the End Process button—be careful doing this, though, as it can cause system problems. If in doubt, don't end processes.

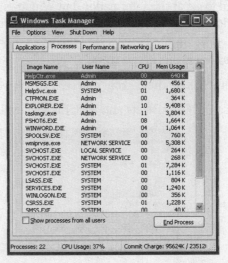

Performance   The Performance tab is a whole mine of information about how well your PC is running. Of all the information it gives you, the most important are the two graphs:

- ▶ CPU Usage
- ▶ PF (Page file or swap file) Usage

These two graphs give you a snapshot of the health of your system; if you feel that things are going slower than usual, take a look at these. If your CPU or PF usage is high, then you might have an unnecessary process or application running that you can get rid of (or it might be time for an upgrade or a new system!). This screen is your window into how your PC is running.

TIP

If you want more detailed information like the kind on the Performance tab, use the Performance utility described in the next section.

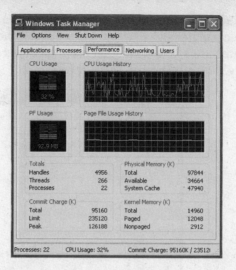

Networking   The Networking screen gives you information on the speed of the network and has a handy graph showing network utilization.

Users   The Users screen shows you the users currently using the computer and allows you to see users who are logged on, switch users, and send other users messages (which will be displayed on-screen when they log back on).

Monitor Performance

Performance is a new tool in Windows XP, but it's very similar to the System Monitor feature in earlier versions of Windows. It shows you a graph of various system statistics, as events are occurring, and is a more sophisticated version of the monitoring tools in the Task Manager.

To start Performance, follow these steps:

1. Choose Start ➢ Control Panel.

2. Click Performance and Maintenance.

3. Click Administrative Tools.

4. Double-click Performance.

By default there are three statistics reported: Pages/Sec, Avg. Disk Queue Length, and % Processor Time. Each is represented by a different color line on the graph, as shown in Figure 13.3.

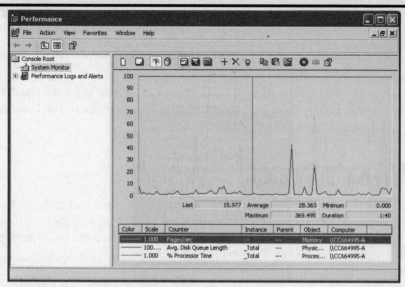

FIGURE 13.3: The System Monitor graphs system usage so that you can watch the effect of opening or closing a specific application.

Use these steps to add another counter to the display:

1. Click the Add Counter button (which looks like a plus sign). The Add Counters dialog box opens.

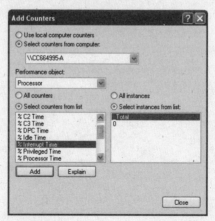

2. Open the Performance Object list and select a category; then select a counter from the Select Counters from List area and click Add.

Part ii

3. Repeat Step 2 to add other counters if desired; then click Close.

To remove a counter, simply select it at the bottom of the Performance window and press the Delete key.

So what do you *do* with this information? If you're an average user, not much. But if you're a programmer or a PC technician, you can use the data to track down problems.

WHAT'S NEXT

In this chapter, you learned about some techniques and tools for troubleshooting system problems in Windows XP. The next chapter shifts gears a bit, and explains how to use Windows XP to connect to the Internet, courtesy of Windows expert Faithe Wempen.

PART iii
COMMUNICATIONS AND THE INTERNET

Chapter 14

CONNECTING TO THE
INTERNET

If you already have an Internet connection up and running, good for you! You can skip this chapter. But if you don't have an Internet account yet, or you have one but it isn't currently set up on your computer, stick around; in this chapter, you'll learn how to get connected.

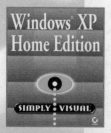

Adapted from *Windows XP Home Edition Simply Visual*
by Faithe Wempen

ISBN 0-7821-2982-X   448 pages $24.99

Understanding Internet Service Providers

The Internet is a vast network of interconnected computers. Most of these computers aren't the ordinary desktop PCs that you have in your home; they're big, powerful servers with permanent connections to the Internet.

Ordinary people like you and me can't afford one of these big computers with full-time Internet connectivity, so we pay a monthly fee to subscribe to a service that owns one of the big computers and leases the use of it. Such companies are called Internet service providers, or ISPs. When you sign up with an ISP, you get a username and password and the right to connect to the server by phone, cable modem, or other method. That connection serves as your on-ramp to the rest of the Internet.

If you have cable Internet access, you don't have a choice of ISPs; you must use the cable company as your provider. With DSL service, you might have a choice, depending on what is available in your area.

You can choose a regular ISP--either national or local—or an online service like America Online (AOL) that also provides Internet access as part of its service. There are literally thousands of ISPs out there, with dozens to choose from in most metropolitan areas.

Through the Internet Connection Wizard in Windows XP, you can view a list of service providers in your area, choose one, and sign up, all in one convenient procedure. Or, if you already have an ISP account, you can set it up to work with your PC.

Signing Up for a New Internet Account

If you don't yet have an Internet account, you can go any of three ways:

▶ You can research all the providers in your area, talk to friends, and make a decision on your own. Then you call the ISP and ask them to send you a startup kit including your username and password. They might also send you a CD with Setup software. If you get a Setup CD, use it to set up your connection; you don't need the rest of this chapter. If you get a username and password from the ISP, set up the connection using the directions under "Setting Up a Connection Manually," later in this chapter.

▶ You can sign up with MSN (Microsoft Network), the Microsoft-owned ISP. This is very easy and painless, and MSN offers good service at an average monthly rate.

▶ You can select a provider from a list of ISPs that Microsoft recommends. Depending on where you live, there might be several to choose from, or there might be none.

Checking the Microsoft Referral Service for ISPs

Before you decide on MSN or a particular local provider, you might want to check out the Microsoft referral service to see what offers are available in your area. Here's how:

1. Open a file management window and navigate to `Program Files\Online Services` on the hard drive on which Windows XP is installed. (It's D: in the following figure, but it's probably C: on your PC.)

NOTE

To open the Online Services folder, start in My Computer and double-click the drive on which Windows is installed. Then double-click the Program Files folder, and then double-click the Online Services folder.

2. Double-click Refer Me to More Internet Service Providers.

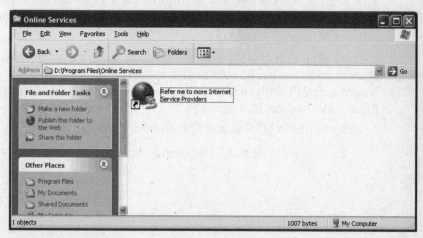

Part iii

3. Wait while the Internet Connection Wizard dials a toll-free number and connects to Microsoft. After a short wait, you will see one of two things.

   ▶ If any providers in your area have signed up for the Microsoft referral service, you will see them listed; click the one you want and then complete the wizard by filling in the blanks provided. (The exact steps depend on the provider chosen.)

   ▶ If there are no providers in your area that are part of the Microsoft referral service, a message will appear to that effect. Click Finish.

Signing Up with MSN as an ISP

The name MSN refers to several separate services, all owned by Microsoft:

▶ MSN is the name of the news service that appears by default when you start Internet Explorer (see Chapter 15). Anyone can browse this Web site at www.msn.com.

▶ There's also a program called MSN Explorer that you can use instead of Internet Explorer to browse Web content. You can access it from within Windows XP by choosing Start ➤ All Programs ➤ MSN Explorer.

▶ MSN is also the name of Microsoft's ISP service. Microsoft recommends that you use MSN Explorer with an MSN ISP account, but it's not required.

The ISP portion of MSN costs about the same per month as most other providers; it has no outstanding pros or cons. However, if you bought a new PC with an MSN rebate, you must sign up for MSN as your ISP in order to claim that rebate.

To sign up with MSN as your ISP, do the following:

1. Choose Start ➤ All Programs ➤ MSN Explorer.

2. A confirmation box appears. If you want to use MSN Explorer for Web browsing and e-mail, click Yes. You probably haven't made up your mind yet, though, so I recommend choosing No. (It'll ask again next time.) Either way, a Welcome screen appears.

3. Click Continue.

4. If prompted for your location, open the Country/Region drop-down list and select your country; then click Continue.

5. Leave the default option selected: "Yes, I would like to sign up for MSN Internet Access and get a new MSN e-mail address." Click Continue.

Part iii

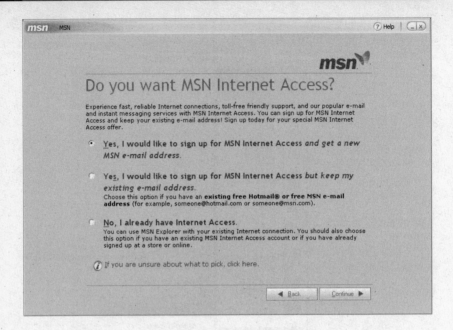

6. Mark any of the dialing options that apply to your situation and then click Continue.

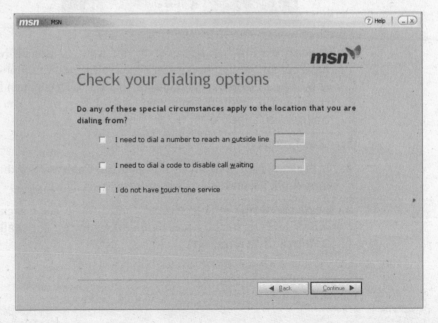

7. Wait while your modem dials a toll-free number and connects to MSN.

8. Complete the remainder of the sign-up process by filling in the blanks provided. In each case, click Continue to move to the next blank.

The remainder of the sign-up process is easy and self-explanatory. After completing it, you will be ready to move on to the next chapter.

SETTING UP A CONNECTION MANUALLY

If you already have an ISP account that connects through a modem, or if you just signed up for one with a service provider other than Microsoft, you must set up the connection yourself. Don't panic—it's not difficult. (If you have cable or DSL service, different directions apply; see your ISP for help. In most cases, an installer comes to your home and sets up the connection for you.)

NOTE

If you signed up with an ISP that provides a Setup disc, insert it in your CD-ROM drive and follow the prompts. You don't need the following steps.

When you sign up with an ISP, you should receive an information sheet containing this information:

Username and password Required to identify yourself when logging on

Phone number(s) to dial Required to connect to the ISP's computer

Incoming and outgoing mail server Required to send and receive e-mail (see Chapter 16)

Newsgroup server Required to read and participate in newsgroups

Part iii

NOTE

A newsgroup is a public forum where people can read and post messages on specific topics. A newsgroup is like a public bulletin board on which anyone can tack up notes and read notes posted there.

Armed with that information, do the following to set up your Internet connection:

1. Choose Start ➢ All Programs ➢ Accessories ➢ Communications ➢ New Connection Wizard.

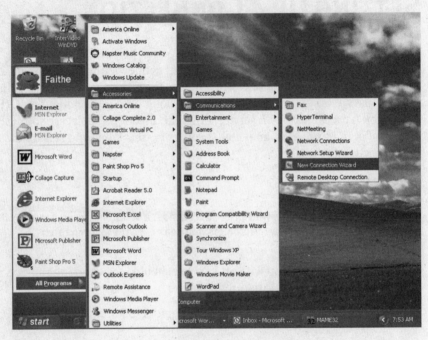

2. At the wizard's Welcome window, click Next.

3. Leave Connect to the Internet selected and click Next.

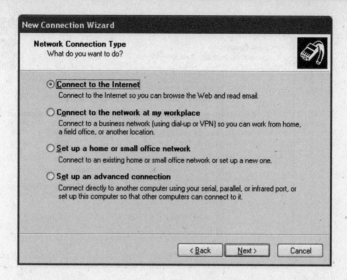

4. Choose Set Up My Connection Manually and then click Next.

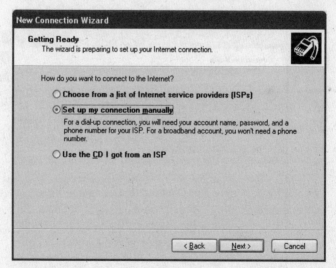

5. Leave Connect Using a Dial-up Modem selected and click Next. (If one of the other options applies better to your situation, choose it instead and then go on your own for the rest of this procedure.)

Part iii

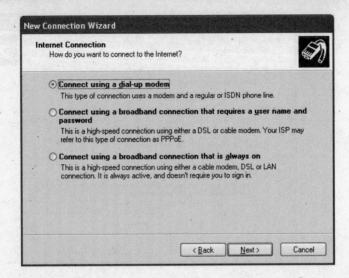

6. Type the ISP's name. This is for your own use; it will be the name for the connection's icon. Then click Next.

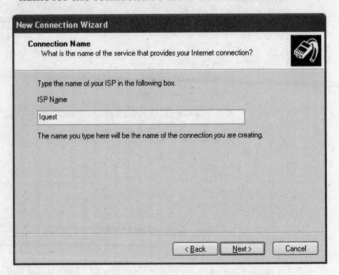

7. Type the ISP's phone number; then click Next.

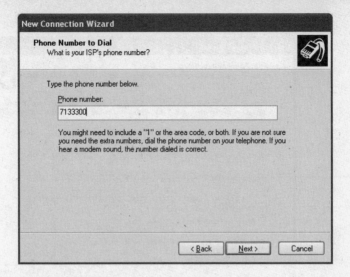

8.   Enter your username and password. Then retype the pass-
     word for confirmation.

9.   All of these check boxes are marked by default; clear any of
     them as needed:

     **Use this account name and password when anyone con-
     nects to the Internet from this computer.**   If you clear this
     check box, only the current user account will have access to
     the connection. Leave this marked unless other people using
     other user accounts have their own Internet accounts.

     Make this the default Internet connection.   If you clear
     this check box, this connection will not be the one that is
     automatically used when an application needs Internet
     access. Leave this marked unless you have more than one
     Internet connection.

     **Turn on *Internet Connection Firewall* for this connec-
     tion.**   In most cases, you should leave this marked, for
     protection against intruders.

NOTE

The Internet Connection Firewall is a feature in Windows XP that provides protection from people on the Internet who might try to use your Internet connection to view and alter the contents of your hard drive.

10. Click Next to continue.

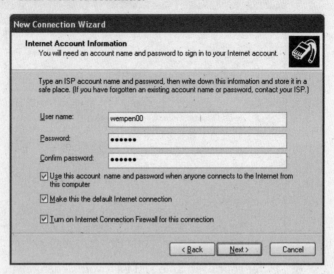

11. Mark the "Add a Shortcut to This Connection to My Desktop" check box if desired. Then click Finish. Your connection is now set up.

TIP
You might want to put a shortcut to the connection in the Quick Launch toolbar for quick access to it.

When you double-click the connection icon, a Connect dialog box opens. Your username and password are already stored, as well as the phone number to dial. Click Dial, and the connection is established.

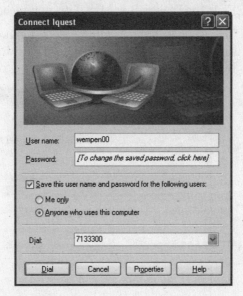

CONFIGURING DIALING RULES

The first time you use your modem or some other device that employs the telephone line, you are prompted to enter your area code and other information about dialing from your current location.

You can change that information at any time, and even set up other dialing locations. For example, on a laptop you might want different dialing locations for each city in which you connect to the Internet. The dialing location information includes the local area code, whether to dial

Part iii

any special numbers to get an outside line, whether to use a credit card or calling card for long-distance calls, and more.

To access the dialing properties, do the following:

1. Choose Start ➢ Control Panel.

2. Click Printers and Other Hardware.

3. Click Phone and Modem Options.

4. Click the Dialing Rules tab if it's not already displayed.

5. To edit an existing location, select it and click Edit (or just double-click it). Or, to create a new location, click the New button.

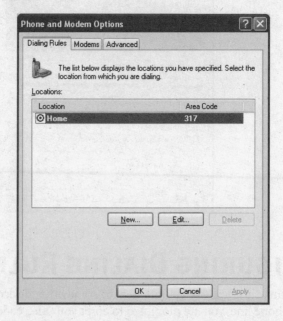

6. In the Edit Location (or New Location) dialog box, enter information about the connection. Give it a name, enter the area code, and specify any dialing rules as needed.

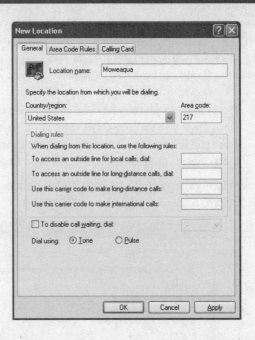

7. If you need to set any area code rules, click the Area Code Rules tab. Then click New, create a new rule in the New Area Code Rule dialog box, and click OK.

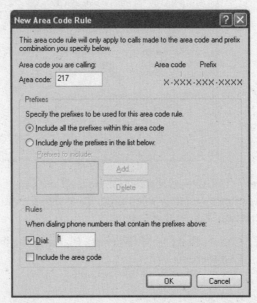

NOTE

An area code rule would be necessary, for example, in a metropolitan area in which local calls can be placed between area codes.

8. If you need to place calls via a calling card when in this location, click the Calling Card tab. Then select the card type from the list and enter the card information. If your brand of card doesn't appear, you can click New to add it.

9. When you are finished with all properties for the location, click OK.

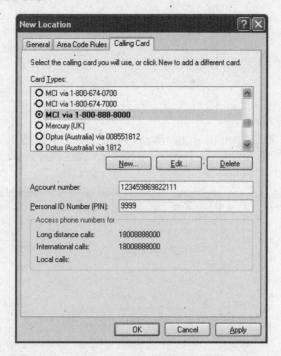

By default, a dial-up connection doesn't use any dialing rules; it simply dials the number exactly as entered. To assign a dialing location to a dial-up connection, follow these steps:

1. Choose Start ➤ My Network Places and click View Network Connections.

2. In the Network Connections window, right-click the dial-up connection and choose Properties.

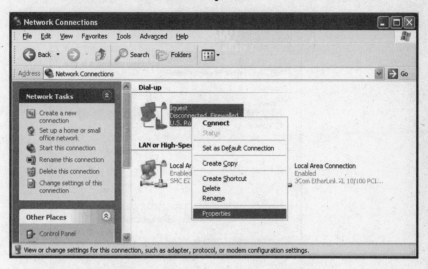

3. On the General tab of the Properties dialog box, mark the Use Dialing Rules check box and then click the Dialing Rules button.

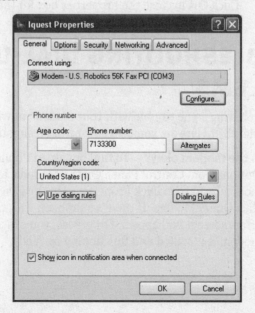

4. The Phone and Modem Options dialog box appears. Select the location to use for this connection and then click OK.

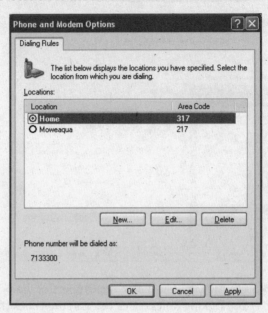

5. Click OK to close the Properties box for the connection.

TROUBLESHOOTING DIAL-UP PROBLEMS

Are you having some trouble with your modem, or with connecting to a particular ISP? Here are some ideas for troubleshooting:

Is the modem okay? To find out, open Phone and Modem Options from Control Panel. On the Modems tab, select your modem, and then click Properties. On the Diagnostics tab, click Query Modem. If there's a problem with the modem, an error message will appear. Otherwise, you can assume that your modem is installed and functioning correctly.

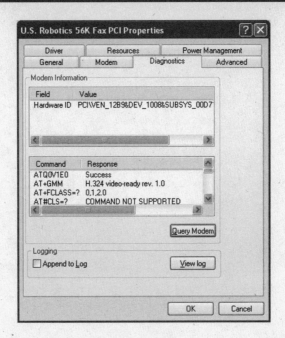

No dial tone?   Make sure the phone cable is connected from the wall to the modem. Try hooking up a phone directly to that line and listening for a dial tone.

Static or line noise?   Make sure the phone line is plugged into the correct jack on the modem. Most modems have two jacks: one for the line and one for a phone. If you get them switched, the modem might still work, but with lots of static.

Frequent disconnects?   Check with your ISP to see if there are any advanced Windows settings you can adjust that can help improve the stability of the connection.

Frequent busy signals?   Check with your ISP to find out if there are any alternate phone numbers you can dial.

WHAT'S NEXT

Now that you are connected to the Internet, you can start using it productively. In the next chapter, Robert Cowart explains how to browse the Web with Internet Explorer. Then in Chapter 16, he continues by explaining how to send and receive e-mail with Outlook Express.

Part iii

Chapter 15

BROWSING THE WEB WITH INTERNET EXPLORER 6

Internet Explorer is your window not only to your own computer and network, but also to the World Wide Web and all you'll find there. Although it's really "just a browser," you'll see in this chapter that Internet Explorer does a lot more than simply display pages from the Web. In fact, you'll find that Internet Explorer is now an integral part of Windows, just as the worldwide network called the Internet is now an integral part of our lives.

Adapted from *Mastering Windows Me* by Robert Cowart

ISBN 0-7821-2857-2   960 pages $39.99

INSIDE INTERNET EXPLORER

You'll find that Internet Explorer has many similarities to other Windows programs you have used, especially those in Microsoft Office (Word, Excel, Access, and so on). The primary difference between Internet Explorer and other programs is that you use it for viewing files, not editing and saving them. Let's begin by seeing how you can start Internet Explorer.

Starting Internet Explorer

Like almost all Windows programs, Internet Explorer can be started in many ways. You can also run more than one copy of the program at a time, which allows you to view the pages from multiple Web sites or different sections of the same page.

To start Internet Explorer at any time, simply choose it from the Windows Start menu. In a standard installation, choose Start and it's at the top, or choose Start ➢ All Programs ➢ Internet Explorer. The program will start and open its *start page*, which is the page Internet Explorer displays first whenever you start it in this way.

NOTE

As with so many other Windows programs, Internet Explorer can be launched in several different ways. Perhaps the easiest is to click the Internet Explorer icon on the Quick Launch toolbar. One change to what you might be used to is that there is no longer an Internet Explorer icon on the desktop that you can use to launch the browser. You can, however, add your own icon if that is how you wish to work.

If the start page is available on a local or networked drive on your computer or if you are already connected to the Internet, Internet Explorer opens that page immediately and displays it.

If you use a modem or Internet Connections Sharing to connect to the Internet, however, and the start page resides there but you're not currently connected, Internet Explorer opens your Dial-Up Networking connector to make the connection to the Internet.

Here are some ways you can start Internet Explorer:

▶ Open an HTML file (one with an `.htm` or `.html` filename extension) in Windows Explorer, and that file will be opened in Internet Explorer (assuming that Internet Explorer is the default browser on your computer).

▶ Open a GIF or JPEG image file, either of which is associated with Internet Explorer, unless you have installed another program that takes those associations.

▶ While in another program, click (activate) a hyperlink that targets an HTML file to open that file in Internet Explorer. For example, while reading an e-mail message you have received in Outlook Express (as shown below), click a hyperlink in the message that targets a Web site, and that site will be opened in Internet Explorer.

> For updates and information about · Outlook Express 6 visit Microsoft on the Web.

NOTE

If you have installed another browser since installing Internet Explorer, Internet Explorer may not be set as your default browser, and that other browser will be called upon to open any Web pages you request. If a message appears that IE is not your default browser, click Yes to set it to be in the future.

To close Internet Explorer, choose File ➢ Close as you would in many other programs. Unlike a word processor or spreadsheet program, when you have been viewing sites on the Web in Internet Explorer, there are normally no files to save before exiting the program.

When you started Internet Explorer, it may have caused Dial-Up Networking to make the Internet connection. In that case, when you later exit Internet Explorer, you should be asked if you want to disconnect from the Internet. You can choose to stay connected if you want to work in other Internet-related programs, but don't forget to disconnect later by double-clicking the Dial-Up Networking icon in the System Tray of the Windows taskbar. Then click the Disconnect button in the dialog box.

The Components of Internet Explorer

Now we'll look at the features and tools that make up Internet Explorer. Figure 15.1 shows Internet Explorer while displaying a Web page. As you can see, the Internet Explorer window contains many of the usual Windows components.

A company or an Internet service provider (ISP) can customize Internet Explorer to make it look and act as though it were its own browser

Part iii

and then distribute it to employees or customers. So if your ISP or your employer gives you a copy of Internet Explorer, it may not look exactly like the one shown in Figure 15.1.

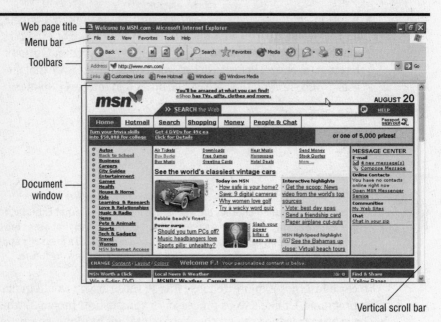

FIGURE 15.1: The Internet Explorer program window contains many components that are common to other windows.

TIP

When you want to show as much of the Web page as possible, try the View ➢ Full Screen command, or press F11 on your keyboard. Internet Explorer will be maximized to occupy the entire screen; it will lose its title bar, status bar, two of its toolbars, and even its menu bar. (You can right-click a toolbar and choose Menu Bar to display it again, or press F11 again to toggle back to the standard view.) You can switch back to the normal view by choosing the Full Screen command again.

The following list gives the parts of Internet Explorer that are labeled in Figure 15.1:

Web page title   At the top of the window is the usual title bar. It displays either the title of the Web page you are viewing or the document's filename if it is not a Web page. On the right side of the title bar are the Minimize, Maximize/Restore, and Close buttons; on the left side is the System menu.

Menu bar Beneath the title is the menu bar, which contains almost all the commands you'll need in Internet Explorer. Keyboard shortcuts are shown next to those commands that have them. For example, you can use the shortcut Ctrl+O instead of choosing the File ≻ Open command. The Internet Explorer logo to the right of the menu bar is animated when the program is accessing data.

Toolbars By default, the toolbars appear beneath the menu bar and contain buttons and other tools that help you navigate the Web or the files and other resources on your computer. The three toolbars are Standard, Links, and Address (refer to Figure 15.1).

Document window Beneath the menu and toolbars is the main document window, which displays a document such as a Web page, an image, or the files on your computer's disk. If Internet Explorer's program window, which encompasses everything you see in Figure 15.1, is smaller than full screen, you can resize it by dragging any of its corners or sides. The paragraphs in a Web page generally adjust their width to the size of the window.

TIP
You cannot display multiple document windows in Internet Explorer. Instead, you can view multiple documents by opening multiple instances of Internet Explorer (choose File ≻ New ≻ Window or Ctrl+N). Each instance of the program is independent of the others.

Scroll bars The horizontal and vertical scroll bars allow you to scroll the document window over other parts of a document that are otherwise too large to be displayed within the window.

Status bar At the bottom of the Internet Explorer window is the status bar. It displays helpful information about the current state of Internet Explorer, so keep an eye on it. For example, when you are selecting a command from the menu bar, a description appears on the status bar. When you point to a hyperlink on the page (either text or an image), the mouse pointer changes to a hand, and the target URL (Uniform Resource Locator) of the hyperlink is displayed on the status bar. When you click a hyperlink to open another page, the status bar indicates what is happening with a progression of messages. Icons that appear on the right side of the status bar give you a status report at a glance. For example, you'll see an icon of a padlock when you have made a secure connection to a Web site.

TIP

You can use the Toolbars and Status Bar commands on the View menu to toggle on or off the display of the toolbars and status bar.

Explorer bar   When you click the Search, Media, Favorites, or History button on the toolbar (or choose one of those commands from the View ➤ Explorer Bar menu), the Explorer bar will appear as a separate pane on the left side of the window. This highly useful feature displays the contents for the button you clicked, such as the Media options shown in Figure 15.2. This allows you to make choices in the Explorer bar on the left, such as clicking a link, and have the results appear in the pane on the right. To close the Explorer bar, repeat the command you used to open it, or choose another Explorer bar.

Some Commands You'll Use Frequently

Here's a short list of the Internet Explorer commands that you might use on a regular basis:

File ➤ Open   Opens an existing file (an HTML file on your hard disk) in the current Internet Explorer window.

File ➤ New ➤ Window   Opens an existing file in a new Internet Explorer window, while leaving the first window open. You can switch between open windows in the usual ways, such as by pressing Alt+Tab.

File ➤ Save As   Lets you save the current document to disk as an HTML file.

File ➤ Properties   Displays the Properties dialog box for the current document.

FIGURE 15.2: The Explorer bar displays hyperlinks you can click to display Web-based content.

Explorer bar

File ➤ Work Offline   Lets you browse without being online, as data is opened from your Internet Explorer cache on your local disk.

TIP

Any data not found in the Internet Explorer cache cannot be viewed when offline.

Edit ➤ Cut/Copy/Paste   Lets you copy or move selected text or images from Internet Explorer to another program.

TIP

Don't forget that you can access some of these commands from the buttons on the Standard toolbar. Also, try right-clicking an object in Internet Explorer—such as selected text, an image, or the page itself—and see what choices are offered on the shortcut menu.

Edit ➢ Find (on this page)   Lets you search for text in the current page, just as you can do in a word processor.

View ➢ Stop   Cancels the downloading of the current page. You can also click the Stop button on the toolbar or press Esc.

View ➢ Refresh   Updates the contents of the current page by downloading it again. You can also use the Refresh button on the toolbar or press F5.

View ➢ Source   Displays the HTML source code for the current page in your default text editor, such as Notepad, which is a great way to see the "inner workings" of a page and learn more about HTML, the Hypertext Markup Language.

Go ➢ Back/Forward   Lets you move between the pages you've already displayed. You can also use the left and right arrow buttons on the toolbar for Back and Forward, respectively.

TIP

The Back and Forward buttons have drop-down lists associated with them. You can go back or forward several pages at a time by choosing a page from one of these lists.

Favorites   Lets you open a site that you have previously saved as a shortcut on the Favorites menu. The Favorites button on the toolbar opens your Favorites list in the Explorer pane; the Favorites menu lets you choose from the list without opening a separate pane.

Favorites ➢ Add to Favorites   Lets you add the current URL to this menu and establish a subscription to the site, if you wish.

Favorites ➢ Organize Favorites   Opens the Favorites folder so you can rename, revise, delete, or otherwise organize its contents.

Tools ➢ Internet Options   Lets you view or change the options for Internet Explorer (the command is called View ➢ Folder Options when you are displaying the contents of your local disk).

Using the Toolbars

The three toolbars in Internet Explorer (Standard, Links, and Address) are quite flexible. You can change the size or position of each one in the trio, or you can choose not to display them at all. In fact, the menu bar is also quite flexible and can be moved below one or more toolbars, or share the same row with them. Here are some common actions you can perform on the toolbars:

- To hide a toolbar, choose View ➤ Toolbars and select one from the menu; to display that toolbar, choose that command again. Or right-click any of the toolbars or the menu bar and select a toolbar from the shortcut menu.

- To show descriptive text below the Standard toolbar buttons and make the buttons larger, choose View ➤ Toolbars ➤ Customize. In the Customize Toolbar dialog box, choose Show Text Labels in the Text Options list box and then click Close. Open the dialog box again to change the display back.

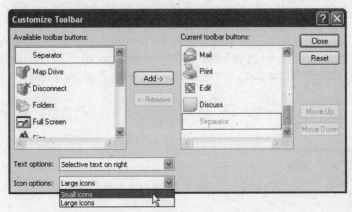

- To change the number of rows that the toolbars use, point to the bottom edge of the bottom toolbar; the mouse pointer will change to a double-headed arrow. You can then drag the edge up to reduce the number of rows or drag it down to expand them.

- To resize a toolbar when two or more share the same row, drag its left edge to the right or left.

Part iii

TIP

If you find that you cannot reposition toolbars, they are probably locked. Choose View ➢ Toolbars ➢ Lock the Toolbars to unlock them.

▸ To move a toolbar, drag it by its left edge. For example, you could drag the Links toolbar onto its own row. (By default it shares a line with the Address toolbar.)

NOTE

Remember that you'll also find these same toolbars when you are browsing the files and folders on your local computer; the Address and Links toolbars are also available on the Windows Taskbar.

Standard Toolbar

The buttons on the Standard toolbar in Internet Explorer (the toolbar just beneath the menu bar in Figures 15.1 and 15.2) are shortcuts for the more commonly used commands on its menus. For example, you can click the Stop button to cancel the downloading of the current page instead of using the View ➢ Stop command, or click the Home button as a shortcut for the View ➢ Go To ➢ Home Page command.

TIP

Point at a button to see its name appear in a ToolTip.

Links Toolbar

Each of the buttons on the Links toolbar is a hyperlink to a URL. (You can also access these links from the Links command on the Favorites menu.) By default, they all target Microsoft Web sites that serve as gateways to a wealth of information on the Web (if you received a customized version of Internet Explorer, these hyperlinks may point to other locations).

All the Links buttons are customizable. To customize, do the following:

▶ To modify a button's target, right-click it, choose Properties from the shortcut menu, and then choose the Internet Shortcut tab.

▶ To change any aspect of a button, including its display text, choose Favorites ➢ Organize Favorites and then open the Links folder, where you'll see the names of all the buttons on the Links toolbar. Rename a button just as you rename any file in Windows, such as by selecting it and pressing F2. Delete a button by selecting its name and pressing Delete.

▶ To add a new Links button, simply drag a hyperlink from a Web page in Internet Explorer onto the Links toolbar. When you release the mouse button, a new button will be created that targets the same file as the hyperlink.

▶ To rearrange the buttons, drag a button to a new location on the Links toolbar.

Once you've tried these buttons and have a feeling for the content on each of the sites, you can revise the buttons or create new ones that point to sites that you want to access with a click.

Address Toolbar

The Address toolbar shows the address of the file currently displayed in Internet Explorer, which might be a URL on the Internet or a location on your local disk. You enter a URL or the path to a file or folder and then press Enter to open that Web site or file.

TIP

When you are entering a URL that you have entered once before, Internet Explorer's AutoComplete feature tries to recognize the URL and displays a list of possible matches in a drop-down menu. You can either click one of the URLs or continue to type a new one. If AutoComplete does not seem to be working, go to Tools ➢ Internet Options, click on the Advanced tab, and make sure that Use Inline AutoComplete is checked.

To revise the URL, click within the Address toolbar and use the normal Windows editing keys. Then press Enter to have Internet Explorer open the specified file. Also, the arrow on the right side of the Address toolbar opens a drop-down list of addresses that you've previously visited via the Address toolbar. They're listed in the order you visited them. Select one from the list and Internet Explorer will open that site.

NOTE

The Radio toolbar, which was present in earlier versions of Windows, is no longer available in IE 6.0. Internet Radio is now accessed via the Media task pane, or through Windows Media Player.

Getting Help

Internet Explorer offers the usual variety of program help, with a few touches of its own. Choose Help ➤ Contents and Index to display its Help window, where you can browse through the topics in the Contents tab, look up a specific word or phrase in the Index tab, or find all references to a word or phrase in the Search tab.

To see if there is a newer version of any of the Internet Explorer software components, find answers to questions or problems, or add new components, choose Help ➤ Online Support, which is an easy way to keep your software current—immediately and online.

If you'd like to improve your Web-browsing skills, click Help ➤ Tip of the Day to view short but informative tips for using Internet Explorer. Users familiar with Netscape Navigator or Communicator can click Help ➤ For Netscape Users to get up to speed on the ins and outs of Internet Explorer.

NOTE

The Microsoft Home Page command is not the same as the Go ➤ Home Page command (or the Home button on the toolbar), which opens your chosen start page.

MOVING BETWEEN PAGES

The feature that perhaps best defines the whole concept of browsing in Internet Explorer is your ability to move from page to page, winding your way through the Web. The most common way to do so is by clicking a hyperlink, but this section will also show you some other ways to jump to another page.

Making the Jump with Hyperlinks

You can click an embedded hyperlink (either a text link or a graphic image link) in a page on the Web or your intranet to open the target file of that link. The target can be anywhere on the Web or your local computer. Clicking a link in a page that's on a server in Seattle might open a page on the same server or on a server in London, Tokyo, Brasilia—or maybe next door.

When you point with your mouse to a text or image link in Internet Explorer, the pointer changes to a small hand. Click here to jump to the link destination. Clicking a hyperlink with your mouse is the usual way to activate a link, but you can activate a link in Internet Explorer in several other ways, such as the following:

► You can press Tab to move to the next hyperlink in the page; you'll see a dotted outline around the currently selected link. Press Enter to activate the selected link.

► Right-click a hyperlink and choose Open from the shortcut menu.

► Choose Open in New Window to open the target in a new Internet Explorer window.

► Choose Save Target As to save the target of the link to disk (you will be prompted for a location). In this case, Internet Explorer will not display the target.

► Choose Print Target to print the target of the link without opening it.

► Choose Add to Favorites to have the URL that the link points to added to your favorites list.

You can use any of these methods to open the target of a hyperlink, whether the link is text, an image, or an image map.

In many cases, the target of a hyperlink will be another Web page that will probably have hyperlinks of its own. Sometimes, however, the target will be another kind of resource, such as an image file or a text file that contains no links of its own. In this instance, you'll have to use the Back button to return to the previous page.

Another type of target uses the *mailto* protocol. For example, many Web pages have a link via e-mail to the Webmaster, the person who created or maintains the site. When you click such a link, your e-mail program, such as Outlook Express, opens a new message with the address of

Part iii

the target already entered in the Recipient field. You can then fill out the subject and body of the message and send it in the usual way.

Other Ways to Move between Pages

Although clicking a hyperlink in Internet Explorer is the usual way to open another resource (a file, such as a Web page or an image), you'll undoubtedly use other means on a regular basis.

Using the Back and Forward Commands

Once you jump to another page during a session with Internet Explorer, you can use the Back and Forward commands to navigate between the pages you've already visited. You can either use those commands on the View ➤ Go To menu or use the Back and Forward buttons on the toolbar.

TIP

Alt+Left Arrow and Alt+Right Arrow are keyboard shortcuts for Back and Forward, respectively.

You can right-click either button or click the down arrow to its right to see a menu of the places that button will take you. The first item on the menu is the site you would visit if you simply clicked the larger button. Select any site from the menu to go directly to that site.

NOTE

The Back and Forward buttons work exactly the same when you are browsing your local or network drive in an Explorer window. As you display various folders, you can use these buttons to open folders that you have already visited. This is a useful shortcut for finding where you were when performing operations such as copy and paste.

Using the Address Bar

As mentioned before, you can also jump to another page by typing its URL in the Address toolbar and pressing Enter. Keep the following in mind when you do:

- ▶ Spelling counts! The bad news is that if you do not type in the address exactly right, Internet Explorer will not be able to open the site and will display an error message to that effect. The good news is that the URL you typed might take you to some new and exciting place on the Web. Good luck!

▶ If you're entering a complete URL including a filename with a trailing filename extension, watch that extension. Some Web sites use the traditional four-letter extension for a Web page, .html. Other sites may have adopted the three-letter extension, .htm. If you are after different content (such as images), remember to use the correct extension.

TIP

One way to take advantage of the Address toolbar is by taking advantage of the Windows Clipboard. For example, you can copy a URL from a word processing document and paste it into the Address toolbar; after that, all you need to do is press Enter to go to that site. Another time Copy and Paste come in handy is when you are using URLs from some e-mail packages. Sometimes when the URL is on more than one line, it is broken up and might not work properly.

Choosing from Your Favorites Menu

In Internet Explorer, you can create a list of your favorite Web sites or other destinations, such as folders on your local disk, by adding each one to the appropriately named Favorites menu. You don't need to remember a site's URL in order to return to that site—simply select it from the Favorites menu.

You'll learn more about adding to and organizing the Favorites menu later in this chapter in "Returning to Your Favorite Pages."

Digging into the History and Cache Folders

Internet Explorer keeps track of both the URLs you visit and the actual files that are downloaded. The paths to the storage folders for this content and how this information is used are described here.

History   Internet Explorer keeps a list of the URLs you visit in its History folder. You can access these URLs in Internet Explorer with the View ➢ Explorer Bar ➢ History command or by clicking the History button on the toolbar. Your past history will be displayed in chronological order in the Explorer bar in the left-hand pane of the Internet Explorer window, where you can select one of the URLs to open in the right-hand pane. Your browsing history is discussed in greater detail later in this chapter in "Using History to See Where You Have Been."

Temporary Internet Files   Internet Explorer saves the files it downloads in a folder on your local drive, which serves as a cache. By default, this folder is C:\Documents and Settings\ *User*\Local Settings\Temporary Internet Files, where *User* is the name of the user who visited the site. When you return to a site, any content that has not changed since the last time you visited that site will be opened directly from the cache on your drive. This saves a lot of time compared to downloading those files again (especially images). You can also open this folder and then open or otherwise use any of the files it contains. Choose Tools ➤ Internet Options, select the General tab, click the Settings button, and then click the View Files button.

NOTE

When multiple users share one computer, each will have their own Temporary Internet Files folders, which will reside within their respective folders in C:\Documents and Settings*User*, where *User* is the logon name of the user.

BROWSING OFFLINE

When you have saved a Web page from the Internet to your local hard disk, you can open that page at any time in Internet Explorer; there's no need to be connected to the Internet to do so. However, think about what happens when you click a link in that page. You opened the page itself from your local hard disk, but more than likely, the target file of that link is still back on the Web and not on your disk. To open that file, Internet Explorer needs access to the Internet.

If you have a full-time Internet connection, you might not even notice that Internet Explorer had to go on the Internet to open that file. If you have a dial-up connection, however, Internet Explorer will first have to make the call and connect to the Internet before opening the file, as shown in Figure 15.3.

FIGURE 15.3: When you are not currently connected to the Internet but click a link that targets a file there, you have the choice of connecting or working offline.

The Dial-Up Networking connector offers three choices:

Connect   Go ahead and connect to the Internet so Internet Explorer can find the targeted file.

Properties   Set the properties for the dial-up connection.

Cancel   Close the dialog box without making a connection.

If you choose Cancel, Internet Explorer will attempt to open and display the specified file from your Temporary Internet Files folder (the cache). Remember that most of the files that are opened while you're browsing the Web are saved in this cache folder, as explained in the previous section, so the requested file might be available offline. If the file isn't found there, however, Internet Explorer displays a dialog box.

As before, you can choose to connect to the Internet to find the file. In that case, the Working Offline icon disappears once you're connected. If you choose to stay offline, the requested file will not be opened because it does not reside locally.

At any time, you can also choose File ➢ Work Offline, which will again display the Working Offline icon on the status bar. Internet Explorer will not attempt to connect to the Internet when you request a file, but will look only in its cache.

NOTE

Sites you've never visited or haven't visited recently can't be accessed while offline, but chances are good that files for those sites you visit frequently are still in your cache.

When you're browsing Web pages from your cache in offline mode, you'll notice that when you point to a link in a page whose target file is *not* available locally in the Internet Explorer cache, the mouse pointer changes to the little hand, as usual, but also displays the international

Part iii

No symbol. This reminds you that you won't be able to open the target of this link while you are offline.

When you want to return to browsing online when needed, choose File ➤ Work Offline again. The next time you request a file that is on the Internet, a connection will be made in the usual way. You can also click the Connect button in the Connect To dialog box (refer back to Figure 15.3) when you have requested a file that is not available locally. The connection will be made, and you will no longer be working in offline mode.

Being able to browse offline without worrying about Internet Explorer trying to make a connection is especially valuable when you have subscribed to various Web sites and have chosen to have their content downloaded automatically.

With offline browsing, you don't need to go out of your way to return to sites to see if they've been updated, or wait at the keyboard while large files are downloaded, perhaps from a site that is busy during the times you normally access it. Instead, you can set up Internet Explorer to check the sites you want at any time of the day or night, notify you that those sites have been updated, and optionally download any new pages. You can then browse those sites offline and let Internet Explorer load the pages and assorted files directly from your Temporary Internet Files folder (the cache). Not only will these sites load almost instantly, but you can also view them while sitting in your beach chair near the breaking waves.

RETURNING TO YOUR FAVORITE PAGES

If you've browsed in Internet Explorer for more than a few hours, you've undoubtedly run into what is perhaps the easiest thing to do on the Web—lose your place and be unable to find your way back to a page that you really, really want to visit. Whatever your reasons for wanting to return to a specific page, the Favorites menu offers the best solution for finding your way back.

The Structure of the Favorites Menu

On the Favorites menu, you can store the names of any sites, folders, or other resources that you might want to return to. To visit one again, simply select it from the Favorites menu. Remember that you'll also find the

Favorites menu on the Windows Start menu, and you can access your Favorites folder from just about any Files dialog box in a Windows program.

This menu is put together in much the same way as your Windows Start menu. For example, the Favorites menu is built from the Favorites folder within your Windows folder, just as the Start menu is built from the Start Menu folder. The items on the Favorites menu are actually shortcuts that reside in the Favorites folder. You can create submenus on the Favorites menu to help you organize items into relevant categories. The submenus are actually folders within the Favorites folder.

Don't forget that you can also display your Favorites menu in the Explorer bar. Choose View ➤ Explorer Bar ➤ Favorites, or click the Favorites button on the toolbar. You'll be able to click a link in your Favorites menu in the Explorer bar and see the target open in the pane on the right.

Adding Items to the Favorites Menu

When you browse to a page or other resource that you just might want to return to, the smart thing to do is add it to your Favorites menu. To do so, choose Favorites ➤ Add to Favorites, or right-click anywhere within the page and choose Add to Favorites. You are then presented with the Add Favorite dialog box, shown in Figure 15.4, in which you can do the following:

▶ Specify the name of the page as it should appear on the menu.

▶ Choose to place the new item in a submenu on the Favorites menu.

▶ Choose to make the page available in offline mode. If you select this option, you can click Customize to decide if pages that are linked to this favorite should also be available offline, to set a schedule for updating the page, and to enter a Web site password if one is required. This feature used to be called Subscriptions in IE4, but the whole concept was far too complicated, so it has been simplified here.

Naming an Item for the Favorites Menu

When you are adding a Web page to the Favorites menu, Internet Explorer by default uses the page's title as its name on the Favorites menu. In Figure 15.4, the page's title is "Welcome to the Microsoft

Corporate Web Site." If you are viewing a file or folder from your local or network drive, the file or folder name will be used as the default name for the Favorites menu.

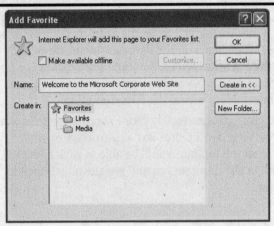

FIGURE 15.4: When you add an item to the Favorites menu, you can specify the name that will appear on the menu as well as the submenu (folder) in which it should appear.

In either case, you are free to revise the name to make it more recognizable when you later want to find it on the menu. For example, in Figure 15.4, you could shorten the name to "Microsoft." Not only is this name quite recognizable, but it will also be alphabetized appropriately on the menu.

Try to keep names short and descriptive. Any menu works best when you can quickly scan it to find the item you want. Additionally, the Favorites menu displays only the first 40 characters or so of any long names.

Choosing a Submenu for the New Item

When you add an item to the Favorites menu, it appears on the top-level menu by default, so that you'll see that item when you first open the menu. However, this is usually *not* the best place to add new items. In the real world, you'll end up with dozens or, more likely, hundreds of items on your Favorites menu. Opening that menu and finding one long list could soon be less than helpful.

You can avoid this by adding a new item within a submenu so that the item appears "farther down" in the nest of menus. Again, this is the same concept and mechanism as your Windows Start menu.

TIP

Keep at least one submenu that serves as a catchall for items that you can't readily categorize. You can call that submenu something like Temp or Misc. Then, when you can't decide in which submenu to place a new item, you don't have to put it on the top-level menu. Put it in the catchall menu instead, where it will be out of the way so that you can deal with it later when you organize your Favorites menu.

In most cases, when you're creating a new item in the Add Favorite dialog box (as shown earlier in Figure 15.4), you'll want to click a subfolder in the list at the bottom of the box. If the list isn't shown, click the Create In button to make it look like the list in Figure 15.4. Select the folder you want for the new item so that the folder icon appears opened. Then click OK.

If a suitable folder does not yet exist in your Favorites folder, click the New Folder button in the Add Favorite dialog box. Enter a name for the new folder and click OK. The new folder is created within the currently selected folder. You can then select the new folder and add the new item to it.

TIP

If you create a new item in the Links folder, that item appears as a new button on the Links toolbar.

Organizing Your Favorites Menu

When you add a new item to the Favorites menu, you can change its name, place it in a submenu off the Favorites menu (a subfolder of the Favorites folder), or create a new submenu (folder) for it.

The Favorites menu isn't static, however. You can change it whenever the need arises. You can make most changes right from the menu simply by right-clicking a menu item to access its shortcut menu. So if you want to delete an item from the Favorites menu, rename it, or change its target, just right-click it.

If you want to make several changes to the menu, you'll probably find it easier to choose Favorites ➤ Organize Favorites. You'll see the Organize Favorites dialog box, as shown in Figure 15.5. Before you read about the changes you can make to the Favorites menu, you should consider the ways you might organize your menu.

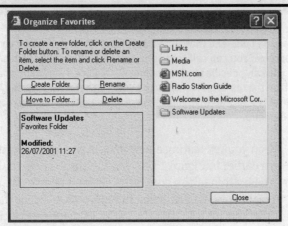

FIGURE 15.5: You can make changes to the files or folders in the Favorites folder with the Organize Favorites dialog box.

You'll want to organize your Favorites menu every bit as well as you do your day-to-day files on your hard disk. Keeping the things you need well organized, whether they are items on the Favorites menu or files on your hard disk, will make your daily routines much more efficient. So what's the best way to organize your Favorites menu? The answer is "Any way you want."

The trick is to create categories (folders) that are relevant to the types of sites you are collecting and the way you would naturally group them. No doubt you'll be creating new subfolders and rearranging the existing ones on a regular basis. In fact, the more you browse the Internet, the more you'll realize how powerful a well-organized Favorites menu can be.

TIP

The menu item named Software Updates in the Organize Favorites dialog box in Figure 15.5 was created so that you can keep on top of the software you have. When you buy new software, you'll probably receive information from the publisher about how to download updates and other useful information from their Web site. If you add those update sites to the Software Updates folder, you will have one central place to check on all of your software quickly and easily.

In the Organize Favorites dialog box, you select items as you always do; you can select multiple items with Shift+Click or Ctrl+Click. You can perform just about any file operation on the selected items, using either the buttons in the dialog box or the commands on the shortcut menu when you right-click a selected item. For example, you can move an item from one menu (folder) to another or delete an item to remove it from the menu. Once you've become familiar with a Web site, you might want to rename its shortcut on your Favorites menu to make it shorter or more recognizable.

SEARCHING THE WEB

One of the most substantially revised aspects of Internet Explorer 6 is its Search feature. Microsoft has incorporated a new Search Companion into Internet Explorer, replacing the Search Assistant feature of earlier versions. It works much like the Search Companion in Windows XP itself, covered in Chapter 6.

The Companion pools the resources of several different search engines, meaning that whether you're looking for a Web site, an old friend's phone number, or even maps, you aren't limited to the resources of a single search engine. Of course, you may not like this feature if your favorite Internet search engine wasn't included in Microsoft's list. If this is the case, you will have to enter the URL for the search engine in the Address bar and access it that way.

Searching in the Explorer Bar

If you want to search for something on the Internet, the simplest way to begin is to click the Search button on the toolbar. This will open the Search Companion in the Explorer bar, as shown in Figure 15.6.

Type a word or phrase you want to search for, and then press Enter or click Search. You should see a list of search results similar to those in Figure 15.7.

NOTE

In the example shown here, I searched for the phrase "Bichon Frise." Obviously, some of the results match what I'm really looking for better than others. See "Performing Effective Keyword Searches" later in this chapter for more information.

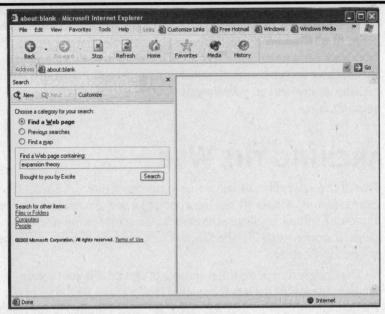

FIGURE 15.6: The Explorer bar opens with the Search Assistant. Type the word, name, or phrase you want to look for.

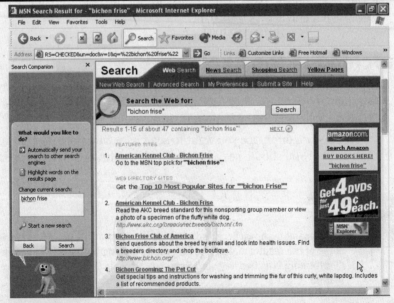

FIGURE 15.7: The Search Companion displays a list of search results. Click one of them to visit the page.

By default, the MSN search engine is used. If you don't like the results produced by the current search engine, click the Automatically Send Your Search to Other Search Engines hyperlink, shown in Figure 15.7. A list of several other search engines appears in the Search pane, as shown next. You can click one of them to try your search at that site.

See "Using Common Search Engines" later in this chapter to learn more about using specific engines.

TIP

When you are done searching, click the Close (X) button at the top of the Explorer bar to make more room on the screen for viewing Web pages, or click the Search button again to toggle it off. Alternatively, you can drag the border of the Explorer bar with the mouse to make it use less space on the screen without closing it.

Customizing the Search Companion

As mentioned earlier, one of the great features of the Search Companion is that it can be customized to work the way you want. For instance, if you want a different search engine to be the first one that appears when you conduct a Web search, you can easily change that here. To do so, follow these steps:

1. Open the Search Companion in IE, and click Change Preferences. The How do you want to use Search Companion? window opens.

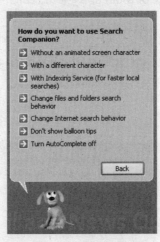

2. Click Change Internet Search Behavior.

3. Choose whether you want to use the Search Companion or Classic Internet Search.

4. Select the Default Search Engine, from the list of engines to choose from.

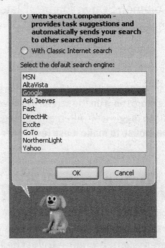

5. Click OK.

Performing Effective Keyword Searches

If you are searching for Web pages, a common method is a keyword search. A *keyword* is simply a word that represents information you want to find. It is generally a noun, but may also be a verb or some other part of speech. When you use a search engine, you are searching a database for documents that have words that match the keyword(s) you've entered.

NOTE

The most common words, such as conjunctions ("and," "but," etc.), pronouns ("I," "he," etc.), and prepositions ("of," "for," "into," etc.) are ignored by search engines.

Typically, you may enter as many keywords as you want. The engine will search for all the words and find any document that contains one or more of those words. In most search engines, multiple keywords are treated as having an implicit Boolean OR operator. For example, if you entered the keywords **Chevy Impala,** the server would return documents that contain the word "Chevy" *or* the word "Impala." It would, therefore, include pages containing mention of "Chevy Impala," some pages containing a mention of "impala" (probably natural wildlife pages, actually, since an impala is an animal), and pages that merely include a mention of "Chevy" (without necessarily including "Chevy Impala"). Note that pages containing both words would be ranked higher and appear first in the resulting list.

NOTE

Most search engines ignore the capitalization of your request.

Notice that for the OR search of the preceding paragraph, you did not have to enter the word "OR." To search only for pages that contain both Chevy *and* Impala, however, you would have to insert the word **AND** between the two words: **Chevy and Impala**.

NOTE

Some search engines infer an "AND" between the words you enter, and find pages that match all the words only. Check the Help information at the search site you're using to find out the syntax for that particular engine.

Even with the AND approach, however, you might still turn up pages that don't mention Chevy Impalas; it's possible you'll turn up pages describing somebody's trip across the country to photograph wild animals (lions, wildebeests, impalas) from the back of their Chevy station wagon. If you wanted to find only pages that contain the words "Chevy" and "Impala" together as a phrase (okay, I admit I should have told you this up front—but, hey, I'm using this example as a teaching tool), then you should put the words together between quotes: **"Chevy Impala"**.

See also the discussion later in this section called "Exact Matches"; there are some variations on this approach from one search engine to another.

Combining Criteria

Many engines let you combine criteria in complex ways. Here's a typical example. Suppose you wanted to find pages about child safety that do *not* discuss adolescents. Proper use of the words AND and NOT will help you: **child and safety not adolescents**.

Wildcards

Most engines will let you enter partial keywords by means of *wildcards*. Here's an example. Suppose you were doing research about a car brand and wanted to see any and all pages about it. You might want listings of any occurrences of "Chevy" or "Chevrolet." You could do two separate searches, one for each. Or to be more expedient, you could use a wildcard in your search: **Chev***.

The * character applied at the end of a partial keyword will match all documents that contain words that start with the partial word.

Exact Matches

Often you'll want to search for an exact match of the words you enter. For example, you might want to find pages that contain the entire phrase "Hubble telescope repair." Typically, you would specify that you want an exact match of this phrase by enclosing it with quotes (') or double quotes ("). Some engines, however, want you to use the + sign between the words instead. Thus, depending on the search engine you're using, you may have to try

'Hubble telescope repair'

or

"Hubble telescope repair"

or

Hubble+telescope+repair

One of these should find pages that contain that exact phrase.

TIP

As a general game plan, when you're doing complex searches, start out with a simple search (it's faster and easier), and then check the first 10 pages or so of those results to see what they contain. In many cases, this will provide you with whatever you need, and you won't have spent your time concocting a complex set of search criteria. Of course, if too many pages are found and only a few of them are meeting your actual needs, you'll have to narrow the search. On the other hand, if no pages result ("no matches found"), you'll have to try again by widening the search.

Using Common Search Engines

Some search engines, such as Go and Yahoo! offer a Browse option as well as a Search option. This means that in addition to being able to search for keywords, you can look through topics by category, such as "business," "entertainment," or "magazines," just to see what is available. This is great if you are interested in seeing what's out there in a general category instead of searching for a specific topic.

This section describes some of the most common search engines on the Web. Some of these search engines are available in the Search Assistant, and some aren't.

AltaVista (www.altavista.com)   Digital Equipment Corporation's AltaVista claims to be the largest search engine, searching 31 million pages on 627,000 servers, and 4 million articles from 14,000 Usenet newsgroups. It is accessed over 30 million times per weekday.

Google (www.google.com)   This model of simplicity has more than 1.3 billion searchable Web pages cataloged. The "I'm Feeling Lucky" button takes you to the site Google thinks is most likely to be the one you're looking for, based on the keywords you enter.

Go (www.go.com)   Combines two powerful search systems, as well as a great news search engine that enables you to search wire services, publications, and more.

Lycos (www.lycos.com)   Searches not only text, but also graphics, sounds, and video!

Yahoo! (www.yahoo.com)   Started by two graduate students at Stanford, Yahoo! is considered the first search engine and still one of the most comprehensive. If you are looking for the address for a Web site, such as the New York Times Web site, this is a good way to find it.

Excite (www.excite.com)   If you can't describe exactly what you're looking for, Excite's unique concept-based navigation technology may help you find it anyway. Excite's Web index is deep, broad, and current: It covers the full text of more than 11.5 million pages and is updated weekly.

Magellan (magellan.excite.com)   A different concept in search engines. This one ranks the results using its own independent system in an effort to help you make more refined searches.

CNET (www.cnet.com)   This search engine lets you search up to eight search engines at one time. This is a pretty unique and powerful approach to searching. If nothing else, you'll probably get lots of results from almost any search! It's also a good site for linking to other engines.

HotBot (www.hotbot.lycos.com)   HotBot is a favorite search engine among many Internet power users, and has been highly rated for its ability to perform powerful and exhaustive Web searches. HotBot now includes a directory system as well.

WebCrawler (www.webcrawler.com)   Offers a speedy Web search engine and a Randomlinks feature to find new and unusual sites. It also features a list of the 25 most visited sites on the Web.

Deja (www.deja.com)   Enables you to search through millions of postings to Usenet newsgroups. Now owned by Google.

BigBook (www.bigbook.com)   National Yellow Pages list that covers nearly every business in the U.S., with detailed maps of their locations.

WhoWhere (www.whowhere.lycos.com)   This is a comprehensive White Pages service for locating people, e-mail addresses, and organizations on the Internet. WhoWhere intuitively handles misspelled or incomplete names, and it lets you search by initials.

WWWomen (www.wwwomen.com)   The premier search directory for women.

Environmental Organization Web Directory (www.webdirectory.com)   The categories in this Web directory cover topics such as animal rights, solar energy, and sustainable development.

CNET'S Shareware Directory (www.shareware.cnet.com) This one makes it simple to find trial and demo versions of software. More than 170,000 files are available for easy searching, browsing, and downloading from shareware and corporate archives on the Internet.

The Electric Library (www.elibrary.com)   This address searches across an extensive database of more than 1,000 full-text newspapers, magazines, and academic journals, images, reference books, literature, and art. (This is a pay-subscription site, but a free trial is offered.)

Homework help (www.bjpinchbeck.com)   This Web site was put together by a nine-year-old boy (with the help of his dad) and provides a comprehensive collection of online information designed to help students with their homework. This excellent reference has won many awards.

TIP

An invaluable spot for comparing computer prices is www.computers.com.

The ability to search the Web for specific sites or files relies on one tiny factor: the existence of searching and indexing sites that you can access to perform the search. These sites are often known as Web spiders, crawlers, or robots, because they endlessly and automatically search the Web and index the content they find.

Search sites literally create huge databases of all the words in all the pages they index, and you can search those databases simply by entering the keywords you want to find. Despite the size of this vast store of information, they can usually return the results to you in a second or two.

This is definitely a Herculean task, because the Web is huge and continues to grow with no end in sight. Plus, a search engine must regularly return to pages it's already indexed because those pages may have changed and will need to be indexed again. Don't forget that many pages are removed from the Web each day, and a search engine must at some point remove those now invalid URLs from its database.

To give you an idea of just how big a job it is to search and index the Web, the popular AltaVista search site at www.altavista.digital.com recently reported that its Web index as of that day covered 31 million pages from 1,158,000 host names on 627,000 servers. AltaVista also had indexed 4 million articles from 14,000 newsgroups. On top of that, this search site is accessed more than 30 million times each day.

Keeping track of what's on the Web is definitely a job for that infinite number of monkeys we've always heard about!

Using History to See Where You Have Been

Internet Explorer remembers where you have been when you roam the Internet. It keeps track of every single Web site you visit, and makes that information available to you should you need it. This is particularly useful when you want to revisit a Web site, but you can't remember the URL and you didn't add it to your Favorites list.

Your browsing history is organized by day and week, so it is helpful to remember approximately when you last visited the site you are trying to find. The files for Internet Explorer's History are on your hard drive. You can access Web pages directly from that folder if you are viewing it using Windows Explorer, but the easier way is to simply view the history in the Explorer bar. To begin, launch Internet Explorer and click the History button on the toolbar.

Your browsing history will open in the Explorer bar, as shown in Figure 15.8. At the top of the list, you will see listings labeled by days of the week and by week. To see the Web sites you visited on a given day, click the day. A list of the Web sites will expand below the day, and each site will have a folder icon next to it.

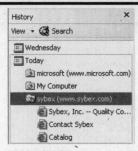

FIGURE 15.8: Your browsing history opens in the Explorer bar.

Each Web site is listed as a folder icon because you probably accessed several pages within the site. Click the site listing to see the pages you visited there, and then click a page listing to link to it. In Figure 15.8 you can see that I visited the Sybex online catalog of books and materials. I could click the page listing in the Explorer pane to redisplay that page.

NOTE

Keep in mind that most Web pages change frequently, even ones you might have visited just yesterday. Accessing pages through the History listing links to the page as it appears now, so don't be surprised if the page's contents have changed since the last time you visited. In fact, there is a chance that the page might not be there at all.

When you are done viewing the History listing, click the Close (X) button on the Explorer bar.

Clearing Your History

Useful though Internet Explorer's History listing may be, there is a chance that it can come back to haunt you as well. Anyone who has access to your computer can open the History and see where you have been on the Web. If you value your privacy, this could be a problem; but fortunately it is possible to clear Internet Explorer's History.

To clear the History, open the Internet Options dialog box by clicking Tools ➤ Internet Options. On the General tab you will find several History options as shown in Figure 15.9. You can quickly and easily remove everything in the History list by clicking Clear History. While you're at it, click Delete Files under the Temporary Internet Files field so that others can't view the pages in offline mode.

FIGURE 15.9: Clear Internet Explorer's History here, or change how long the history is kept.

NOTE

Notice that you can also adjust how long the History is kept. The default setting is 20 days, but if you want to be able to go further back in time than that, you might want to change the setting here.

WARNING

If you click Clear History, keep in mind that when it's gone, it's gone. You won't be able to restore the listing later if you decide you really needed something in the list.

CHECKING IMPORTANT INTERNET EXPLORER OPTIONS

Internet Explorer contains a number of important option settings that you should be aware of. They can be accessed via the Internet Options dialog box. Among other things, the Internet Options dialog box controls many aspects of how Internet Explorer works, and it's worth your while to spend a few minutes going through the tabs to see how you can make the settings work better for you.

You can view Internet Explorer options by clicking Tools ➤ Internet Options from within Internet Explorer. Visit each tab and check the following items:

General   On this tab you can set a new home page if you desire. This is the page that opens first whenever you launch Internet Explorer or when you click the Home Page button on the toolbar. The default home page is the MSN main page, but you might prefer to set this to the home page for your local ISP, a weather or news site, or even your own Web page.

Click Delete Files to clear your disk cache of the Temporary Internet Files that are stored there.

Security   Adjust your Security settings here. For more information, see "Setting Security Levels" later in this chapter.

Privacy   The Privacy tab allows you to configure how cookies are handled based on the new P3P standard (Platform for Privacy Preferences Project—a standard developed by the World Wide Web Consortium). This standard allows the Web site developers to include information on their site stating how your information will be handled.

The Medium setting for this allows for the best compromise of privacy and convenience.

Content   On this tab, you can enable the Content Advisor to control access to objectionable material. Once enabled, the settings are password protected.

Also, if you have certificates to authenticate your identity to certain Web sites, you can view them here.

You can also use this tab to enter personal information about yourself. This might be used to make completing forms on the Internet easier, or to make online shopping more efficient.

Connections   Use this tab to modify settings for your Internet connection. See Chapter 14 for more details.

Part iii

Programs   On this tab, you can specify the default programs you want to use for editing HTML documents, reading e-mail and newsgroups, making Internet calls, and keeping a personal calendar and a list of contacts.

Advanced   Here, you can review various advanced settings for Internet Explorer. Perhaps the most useful settings here can be found under Multimedia, where you can specify whether Web page elements such as sounds, videos, or pictures are displayed automatically.

Setting Security Levels

Personal security is something you should always be concerned about when you are browsing the Internet. Unscrupulous people are out there, and it is possible to get victimized if you are not careful. Potential dangers abound, and range from having your computer infected with a harmful virus to having personal information or files on your computer compromised.

Internet Explorer makes protecting yourself relatively simple, but you need to make some decisions about how secure you want to be. Inevitably, your decision will probably boil down to a compromise between security and convenience, because in general, tighter security settings will make browsing more difficult.

You can adjust your security settings in the Internet Options dialog box. If Internet Explorer is already open, click Tools ➢ Internet Options, and then click the Security tab (Figure 15.10).

Internet Explorer offers the four basic levels of security, as described in the following list:

High   Offers the highest level of protection. Cookies are disabled, which means you won't be able to view many popular sites.

Medium   The most common setting, it provides a reasonable level of protection from the most insidious hazards, but cookies will be enabled. Possibly harmful ActiveX controls won't run.

Medium-Low   Internet Explorer will warn you against using this setting. Many of the protections available in the Medium level are here, but you won't receive prompts before running ActiveX controls and other potentially harmful applets.

Low   Offering almost no protection, this level is not recommended for free roaming of the Internet.

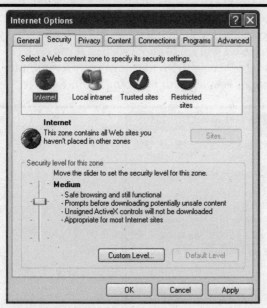

FIGURE 15.10: Set your Internet Explorer security level here.

Of all the levels, Medium generally offers the best compromise of security and convenience. You can also customize security settings, if you
wish, by clicking Custom Level.

The Privacy tab offers its own slider bar to control how much information about your browsing habits will be available to the Webmasters of
the sites you visit. Many Web sites make it a practice to track user activity
using a feature called cookies, for example. *Cookies* are tiny little files
that Web sites can leave on your computer when you visit. They can serve
a variety of purposes, such as acting as a counter for how many times you
visit a certain Web site, or storing your login name and password for a
site. Crafty Webmasters can even use cookies to track the kinds of Web
sites you visit, providing them with potentially valuable marketing information. Drag the slider on the Privacy tab up or down to control the settings for cookies and other identifiers. See Figure 15.11.

Part iii

Cookies have been controversial, to say the least. Many people see them as an invasion of privacy because others can monitor your Web-browsing habits. If you agree, you can disable cookies, but it can make browsing some Web sites very inconvenient. Every time you try to visit a site that uses cookies, a confirmation box will pop up asking your permission. Some Web sites will simply not function if you click No. You'll probably get tired of seeing these warnings every few minutes, but that is the price to pay for keeping your browsing habits a secret.

FIGURE 15.11: Change the privacy setting on the Privacy tab.

TIP

It seems like every day the news media is reporting another security flaw in Internet Explorer or Microsoft Outlook. To ensure that you always have the most recent security patches, choose Tools ➢ Windows Update, click Product Updates, and allow the utility to check your system. If any critical updates are recommended, follow the prompts to download them.

What's Next

This chapter explained Internet Explorer 6 and showed you how to locate the information you want on the Web. In the next chapter, you'll learn how to communicate online using Outlook Express, the popular e-mail program that comes free with Windows XP.

Chapter 16

COMMUNICATING WITH OUTLOOK EXPRESS

O utlook Express is an Internet standards–based e-mail and newsreader you can use to access Internet e-mail and news accounts. In this chapter, we'll look first at how to use Outlook Express Mail. We'll then look at Outlook Express News and conclude by showing you how to customize Outlook Express so that it works the way you want to work with your computer.

To start Outlook Express, choose Start ➢ All Programs ➢ Outlook Express, click the Launch Outlook Express icon on the Quick Launch toolbar (if displayed), or click the Outlook Express shortcut on your desktop if you have one. (To learn how to create shortcuts on the desktop, see Chapter 4.) To go to Outlook Express from within IE, choose Tools ➢ Mail and News.

Adapted from *Mastering Windows Me* by Robert Cowart
ISBN 0-7821-2857-2   960 pages $39.99

A QUICK TOUR OF OUTLOOK EXPRESS

When you first open Outlook Express (OE), you see the window shown in Figure 16.1.

TIP

Before you do anything else, place a check mark next to "When Outlook Express Starts, Go Directly to My Inbox." With this option selected, OE will open to the more useful Inbox instead of the generic Outlook Express screen when you open the programs.

If you click Inbox, Outlook Express opens your Inbox in Preview Pane view, and you may well have a message or two from Microsoft, as Figure 16.2 shows.

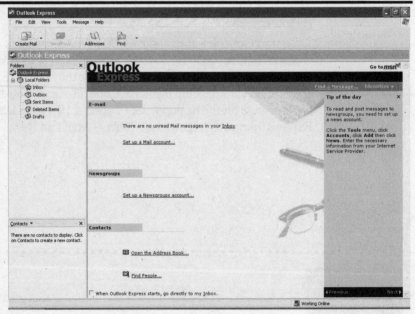

FIGURE 16.1: The Outlook Express window

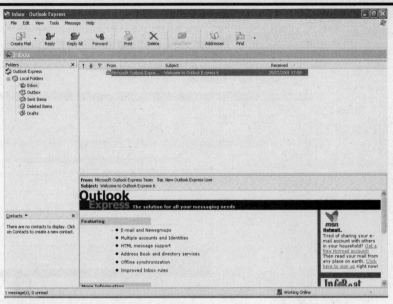

FIGURE 16.2: The Outlook Express Inbox window in Preview Pane view

Figure 16.2 shows all the potential on-screen elements for Outlook Express. As you can see, this view is extremely cluttered, so choose a few elements that you want displayed. For instance, when I use Outlook Express, I normally have only the toolbar, folder bar, folder list, contacts, status bar, and message list displayed. You can customize the layout by clicking View ➣ Layout to open the Window Layout Properties dialog box.

Part iii

As you can see, in the Basic section of this dialog box, you can choose to display the contacts, folder bar, folder list, Outlook bar, status bar, toolbar, and views bar. In Figure 16.3, they are all displayed.

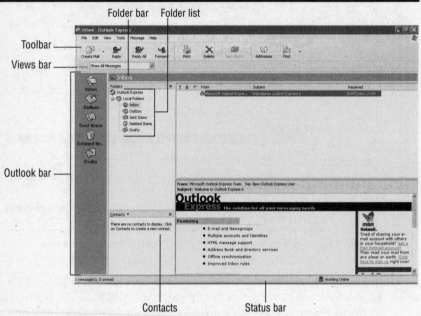

FIGURE 16.3: Outlook Express displaying all components

NOTE
We'll look at the Toolbar section of the Window Layout Properties dialog box later, in the section "Customizing the Toolbar."

You use the options in the Preview Pane section to select how you want to display header information and messages. Check and uncheck these options until the user interface is to your liking and fits the way you like to work when reading messages. You can also adjust the area for the Preview pane and the Message list by dragging the divider between them.

Moving Around

You can move around in Outlook Express in a variety of ways. Perhaps the easiest way is to simply choose a folder from the folder list. You can also click an icon on the Outlook bar, but since it and the folder list are redundant, I don't recommend displaying both. The folder list displays all of the important locations within Outlook Express.

To move to a different location in Outlook Express, simply click the appropriate listing in the folder list. For instance, if you want to review messages you have sent out recently, click the Sent Items folder. If you want to read new messages that you have received, click the Inbox.

NOTE

Unread messages are displayed with boldfaced titles in Outlook Express. Likewise, any folders that contain unread messages will appear bold in the folder list as well.

GETTING CONNECTED

Before you can actually use Outlook Express to send and receive messages or to read and post news articles, you must set up an Internet e-mail account and an Internet news account. Doing so tells Outlook Express how to contact your e-mail and news servers. You can initially set up one account or multiple accounts, and you can always add more as the need arises.

NOTE

See Chapter 14 to learn how to connect to the Internet. The ISP that you use for connection will typically provide at least one e-mail account for your use, as well as a news server. If you don't already have it, get the mail and news server information from your ISP before continuing in this chapter.

Part iii

Setting Up an E-Mail Account

You need the following information to set up an e-mail account in Outlook Express:

▶ Your e-mail address and password. This might or might not be the same as your logon name and password for your Internet connection.

▶ The type of server that will be used for incoming mail (POP, NNTP, or HTML)

▶ The names of the servers for incoming mail and outgoing mail. These names typically have several parts separated by periods, and the last few parts mirror your e-mail address. For example, your e-mail address might be expert@casindy.org, and your mail server might be mail.casindy.org.

NOTE

Some e-mail services use separate mail servers for incoming and outgoing mail. For example, incoming might be pop.casindy.org and outgoing might be smtp.casindy.org. Or there might be a single mail server for both functions.

When you have this information, you can follow the steps below to start setting up your e-mail account with the Internet Connection Wizard.

1. In Outlook Express, choose Tools ➢ Accounts. In the Internet Accounts dialog box, click the Mail tab and click Add ➢ Mail to open the Internet Connection Wizard.

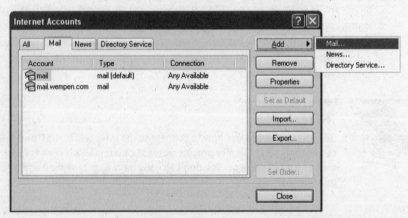

2. In the Display Name text box, enter the name that you want to appear in the From field of outgoing messages, and click Next.

3. In the Internet E-Mail Address text box, enter the e-mail address that your ISP assigned you, and click Next.

4. The Internet Connection Wizard asks you to specify the type of server that will be used for incoming mail and the names of the servers for incoming mail and outgoing mail. Enter this information and click Next.

5. In the Internet Mail Logon dialog box, enter the e-mail address and password that your ISP assigned you. If your ISP requires Secure Password Authentication, click the Log On Using Secure Password Authentication (SPA) button. When you are done, click Next.

6. In the Friendly Name dialog box, enter a name for your e-mail account in the text box, and click Next; then click Finish.

You have now set up an Internet e-mail account and can send and receive messages. By default, the new account is set to use any dial-up connection available. If you want the account to use a specific connection, see "Customizing Mail and News Options" later in this chapter to learn how.

 POP3, IMAP, AND SMTP

POP3 is an abbreviation for Post Office Protocol 3, a popular method used for receiving Internet mail. Many Internet mail applications require a POP3 mailbox in order to receive mail. Your POP mailbox is usually your Inbox. SMTP is an abbreviation for Simple Mail Transfer Protocol, the TCP/IP protocol used for sending Internet e-mail. Your SMTP mailbox is usually your Outbox. IMAP is an abbreviation for Internet Message Access Protocol, the protocol that allows a client to access and manipulate e-mail messages on a server. It does not specify a means of posting mail; that function is handled by SMTP.

Setting Up a News Account

Before you can read newsgroups, you have to connect to a news server. You set up a news server account in much the same way that you set up a mail server account.

Before you set up a news account, you must have already established an account with an ISP and obtained the name of the news server(s) you plan to use. Also, ask your ISP if you need a username and password to log on to the news server. After you do this, you can follow these steps:

1. Start Outlook Express and choose Tools ➢ Accounts.

2. In the Internet Accounts dialog box, select the News tab and then choose Add ➢ News to open the Internet Connection Wizard.

3. In the Display Name field, enter the name that you want to appear when you post an article or send an e-mail message to a newsgroup, and then click Next.

4. In the E-Mail Address field, enter your e-mail address and click Next.

5. Now, in the Internet News Server Name dialog box, enter the name of the news server that you received from your ISP (typically something like news.myisp.com). If you have to log on to this server with an account name and password, check the My News Server Requires Me to Log On check box. Click Next, and then click Finish.

You have now set up an Internet news account, and you can read, subscribe to, and participate in newsgroups.

TIP

If you want to remain anonymous while cruising newsgroups, you can enter a fake name in the Display Name field in the first Internet Connection Wizard dialog box. You can use anything you want, but we suggest that you let the limits of good taste guide you. Remember: If you can use a fake name, so can anybody else. If you want to be even more anonymous, enter a fake e-mail address as well. Some ISPs have policies about this; so check to be sure that entering fake information does not violate these policies.

READING AND PROCESSING MESSAGES

Now that your e-mail account is set up, you are ready to begin sending and receiving messages. If you still have the welcome message from Microsoft in your Inbox and if you still have the Preview pane displayed, you'll see the header information in the upper pane and the message in the lower pane.

NOTE

If you have a different configuration, double-click a message header to read the message. The message will open in its own window.

After reading a message, you can do any of the following:

- ▶ Print it
- ▶ Mark it as read
- ▶ Mark it as unread
- ▶ Move it to another folder in the Outlook Express bar
- ▶ Save it in a folder
- ▶ Forward it to someone else
- ▶ Reply to it
- ▶ Delete it

For some of these tasks, you use the File menu, and for some of them you use the Edit menu. In addition, you can take care of some tasks by simply clicking a toolbar icon.

Receiving Mail

Before we get into all the neat things you can do with your messages, let's look at the many ways in which you can retrieve your e-mail:

- ▶ Choose Tools ➢ Send and Receive ➢ Send and Receive All.
- ▶ Choose Tools ➢ Send and Receive, and click the account you want to retrieve mail from (if you have more than one mail account).

▶ Click the Send/Recv icon on the toolbar, which works the same as choosing Tools ➢ Send and Receive ➢ Send and Receive All.

Received messages are placed in your Inbox or in other folders that you have specified using the Inbox Assistant. You can also choose to display only newly received messages. To do so, choose View ➢ Current View ➢ Hide Read Messages.

You can now begin processing your mail, as described in the following sections.

Printing, Marking, and Moving Messages

Printing, marking, and moving messages are simple, straightforward tasks, so we'll start with them.

Printing Messages

On occasion, you may want a paper copy of an e-mail message that you have sent or received. For example, you might work on a large project that involves some people who aren't using e-mail, or you may want to maintain paper files as a backup. To print a message, open it and place your cursor in the message; then either click the Print tool, choose File ➢ Print, or press Ctrl+P.

Marking Messages

When you first receive a message, a closed envelope icon precedes its header, which is in boldface.

After you read the message, Outlook Express marks it Read by changing the icon to an open envelope and changing the header from bold to lightface type. If, for whatever reason, you want to change a message from Read to Unread, select the message header and choose Edit ➢ Mark As Unread. If you want, you can change it back to Read if you want by selecting it and choosing Edit ➢ Mark As Read. (You might want to do either of these to call attention to a message that you want to review.) To mark all messages as Read, choose Edit ➢ Mark All As Read.

Saving Messages

With Outlook Express, you can save messages in folders you create in Windows Explorer, and you can save messages in Outlook Express folders. You can also save attachments as files.

To save messages in Windows Explorer, follow these steps:

1. Select the header of the message you want to save.

2. Choose File ➤ Save As.

3. In the Save Message As dialog box, select a folder in which to save the message. Outlook Express places the subject line in the File Name box. You can use this name or type another one.

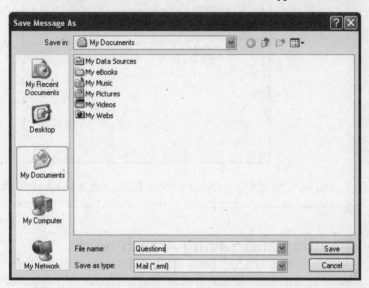

4. You can save the message as e-mail (with the .eml extension) or as HTML (with the .htm or .html extension). Select the file type, then click Save.

Saving Messages in Outlook Express Folders

Although Outlook Express saves messages in the Deleted Items, Inbox, Outbox, and Sent Items folders, you can create your own folders in which to save messages. Once you have created new folders, you can easily move messages from one folder to another by dragging and dropping. You can also right-click messages and choose Move to Folder to open the Move dialog box and select a new location.

To create a new folder in Outlook Express, follow these steps:

1. Choose File ➤ New ➤ Folder.

Part iii

2. In the Create Folder dialog box, type a name for the new folder and click OK.

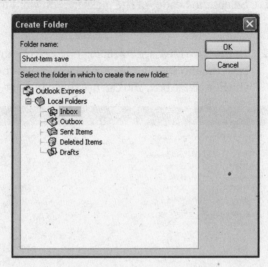

You now have a new folder in your folder list, and you can drag any message from any other folder to it—or from it to any of them.

Reading and Saving Attachments

An attachment is a file that is appended to an e-mail message. You'll know that a message has an attachment if the header is preceded by the paper clip icon. When you open the message, you'll see an attachment icon at the bottom followed by the name of the file and its size.

To read an attachment, simply double-click its icon (if the attachment is a text file). To save an attachment, follow these steps:

1. With the message open, choose File > Save Attachments.

2. Click the filename to open the Save Attachment As dialog box.

3. Select a folder and a filename, and click Save.

NOTE

You have no doubt heard about the phenomenon of e-mail viruses. Many of them propagate themselves via e-mail attachments. The easiest way to protect yourself from this kind of damage is to be *extremely* careful about opening e-mail attachments. If you weren't expecting to receive an attached file, or you are not absolutely sure who the sender is, don't trust it. Delete it without opening it.

Replying to a Message

When a message is selected, you can reply to it in the following ways:

▶ Click the Reply to Sender icon in the toolbar.

▶ Click the Reply to All icon in the toolbar (if the message has carbon copy or blind copy recipients or multiple recipients).

WARNING

If there were blind copy recipients, and you choose Reply to All, those recipients get a copy of your reply too, but you don't get to see who they were. This can be very dangerous if you are replying with sensitive information!

▶ Choose Message ➢ Reply to Sender (Ctrl+R) or Message ➢ Reply to All (Ctrl+Shift+R).

By default, Outlook Express Mail includes in your reply all the text of the message to which you are replying. If you don't want that message included, follow these steps:

1. In the Outlook Express window, choose Tools ➢ Options to open the Options dialog box. (The Options dialog box will be discussed in more depth later.)

2. Select the Send tab, and remove the check mark next to Include Message in Reply.

3. Click Apply, and then click OK.

To include only selected portions of the message in your reply, leave the Include Message in Reply option checked and follow these steps:

1. Click the message header to open the message.

2. Click the Reply to Sender icon. You'll see the message header and the text of the message to which you are replying. The message is now addressed to its original sender.

3. In the body of the message, edit the message so that the portions you want are retained and then enter your response.

4. Click the Send icon on the toolbar to send your reply. (Sending messages will be discussed in more depth later.)

Part iii

Forwarding a Message

Forwarding an e-mail message is much easier than forwarding a letter through the U.S. mail, and it actually works. To forward a message, follow these steps:

1. Open the message.

2. Select Forward in one of the following ways:

   ▶ Click the Forward icon on the toolbar.

   ▶ Choose Message ➢ Forward.

   ▶ Press Ctrl+F.

3. Enter an e-mail address in the To field. (You can also add your own comments to the message, if you choose.)

4. Click Send.

Deleting a Message

You can delete a message in three ways:

▶ Select its header and click the Delete icon on the toolbar.

▶ Select its header and choose Edit ➢ Delete.

▶ Open the message and click the Delete icon.

The message is not yet permanently deleted, however; Outlook Express has simply moved it to the Deleted Items folder. To delete it permanently, follow these steps:

1. Select the Deleted Items folder.

2. Select the message you want to delete.

3. Choose Edit ➢ Delete or click the Delete icon.

NOTE

As you'll see in the "Customizing Mail and News Options" section later in this chapter, you can also specify that all messages in the Deleted Items folder be deleted when you exit Outlook Express Mail.

WARNING

Outlook Express has no Undelete command, so be sure you *really* want to delete a message when you delete it from the Deleted Items folder.

CREATING AND SENDING MESSAGES

By now, you must be champing at the bit to create and send your own messages, so let's do that next. In a later section, you'll explore the many options you have when composing messages. In this section, you'll compose a simple message and send it.

Composing Your Message

You can begin a new message in a couple of ways:

► Choose Message ➢ New Message (Ctrl+N).

► Click the New Mail icon in the toolbar.

When you begin a new message, Outlook Express displays the New Message window, as shown in Figure 16.4.

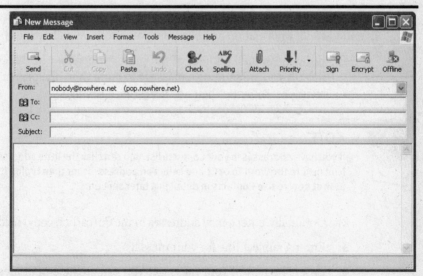

FIGURE 16.4: You have a blank canvas on which to compose your message.

Part iii

Header Information

The header section of the New Message window has four fields:

- ▶ From (available only if you have multiple mail accounts)
- ▶ To
- ▶ Cc
- ▶ Subject

The only field that you must fill in is the To field. All recipients can see the addresses you enter in the Cc, or carbon copy, field.

The From field allows you to choose which e-mail account you want to use to send the message if you have more than one account. (You won't see the From field unless you have more than one mail account configured in OE.) This is a useful feature, especially if you want to specify that a message be sent from your work account or personal account. The e-mail address shown in the From field is the address to which replies will be sent.

If you don't fill in the Subject field, Outlook Express displays a message box asking if you really want to send the message with no subject line. When Outlook Express saves your message in a folder, it uses the subject line as the filename.

Creating Your Message

To enter header information and compose your message, follow these steps:

1. Enter the e-mail address of the primary recipient in the To field. If you are sending a message to more than one primary recipient, separate their addresses with semicolons.

NOTE

If you have addresses in your Contacts list, you can click the little address book icon next to the word To or Cc and select an address rather than typing it. We'll look at how to use Contacts in detail in a later section.

2. Optionally, enter e-mail addresses in the Cc (carbon copy) field.

3. Enter a subject line for your message.

4. Enter the text of your message. You can create e-mail messages in Plain Text or Rich Text (HTML) format. (We'll look at this in detail later.)

You can also set a Priority for your message. By default, the Priority is set to Normal. To set it to High or Low, choose Message ≻ Set Priority, and select from the submenu. You can also use the Priority button on the toolbar.

If you set the priority to High, an exclamation mark precedes the message header in your recipient's mailbox. If you set the priority to Low, a down arrow precedes the message header.

Your message is now complete, and you are ready to send it.

Sending Your Message

You can send your message in several ways:

▶ Click the Send icon on the toolbar in the New Message window.

▶ Choose File ≻ Send Message or File ≻ Send Later.

When you choose File ≻ Send Later, Outlook Express places the message in your Outbox. You can then send it later by clicking the Send and Receive icon on the toolbar in the main Outlook Express window. You might want to do this if you are composing several messages offline, for example.

SPRUCING UP YOUR MESSAGES

Now that we've covered the basics of reading, responding to, creating, and sending messages, let's look at some bells and whistles you can employ.

To see some of the possibilities available to you, compose a new message. Click the New Mail icon to open the New Message window, and then choose Format ≻ Rich Text (HTML). You'll see the screen shown in Figure 16.5. Notice the Formatting toolbar, which contains many of the same tools you see and use in your Windows word processor. You'll also see the Font and Font Size drop-down list boxes that are present in your Windows word processor.

TIP

One tool that you may not see in your word processor is the Insert Horizontal Line tool. Click this tool to insert a horizontal line that spans the width of your message.

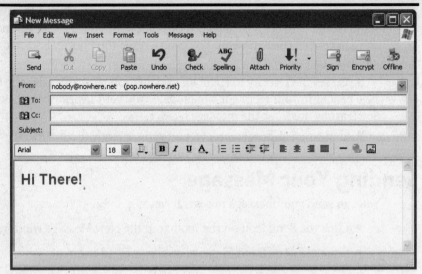

FIGURE 16.5: The New Message screen ready for Rich Text formatting

As you create your message, just pretend that you're using a word processor, and use the formatting tools to apply emphasis to your message.

You can format an e-mail message in the same ways that you format any other document. All the usual design rules apply, including the following:

▶ Don't use too many fonts.

▶ Remember, typing in all capital letters in e-mail is tantamount to shouting.

▶ Don't place a lot of text in italics. It's hard to read on the screen.

▶ Save boldface for what's really important.

NOTE

If you send an HTML message to someone whose mail program does not read HTML, Outlook Express prompts you to send the message as plain text.

Adding a Signature to Your Message

Unless you're new to e-mail, you are probably in the habit of signing your messages in a particular way. If you want, however, you can create a signature that will be automatically added to all messages that you send. To do so, follow these steps:

1. In the main window, choose Tools ➤ Options to open the Options dialog box. Click the Signatures tab to bring it to the front.

2. Click New and type a signature in the Edit Signature box or if you have a signature in an existing file, click the File option and browse for the file.

3. Click to place a check mark next to Add Signatures to All Outgoing Messages. You can also choose whether you want your signature placed in replies.

Adding a Picture to Your Message

Many of the picture-editing features of Microsoft Office 2000 and XP are included with Outlook Express. You can insert pictures, size them, and

Part iii

move them around. Figure 16.6 shows a message that has a picture from Microsoft Office Clip Art inserted into it.

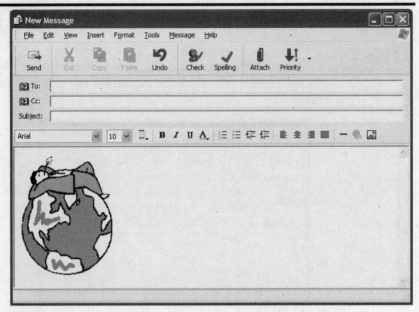

FIGURE 16.6: An e-mail message containing a picture from the Clip Art file

You can insert a picture into a message in two ways:

▶ As a background over which you can type text

▶ As a piece of art

To insert a picture as a background, choose Format ➢ Background ➢ Picture. Outlook Express Mail displays the Background Picture dialog box shown in Figure 16.7. Enter the filename of an image that you want to use as background, and click OK.

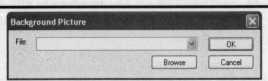

FIGURE 16.7: The Background Picture dialog box

To insert some decorative art in your message, follow these steps:

1. Place the cursor in the body of your message, and click the Insert Picture icon on the Formatting toolbar to open the Picture dialog box.

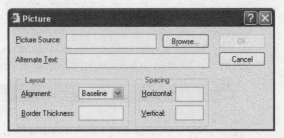

2. If you know the name of the file you want, enter it in the Picture Source box. If you don't know the filename, click Browse and select an image.

3. If you are sending this message to several recipients, some of whom may not be able to view the image, type text to substitute for the image in the Alternate Text box.

4. Specify layout and spacing and click OK.

Adding a Background Color to Your Message

To apply a color to the background of your message, choose Format ➢ Background ➢ Color, and select a color from the drop-down list. The screen in the message body is filled with the color you selected.

Now type something. Can you see it on the screen? If not, you have probably chosen a dark background and your font is also a dark color—most likely black if you haven't changed it from the default.

To make your text visible, you need to choose a light font color. To do so, click the Font Color icon and choose a light color. Now type something else. You should see light-colored letters against a dark background. Impressive for an e-mail message, huh?

ATTACHING FILES TO YOUR MESSAGES

In Outlook Express Mail, sending files along with your messages is painless and simple.

Part iii

To attach a file to a message that you are sending to a recipient who has an Internet e-mail address, follow these steps:

1. In the New Message window, choose Insert ➤ File Attachment. Or, click the Attach icon in the toolbar.

2. In the Insert Attachment dialog box, select the file you want to attach, and click Attach. (You can select multiple files to attach, but be aware that some recipients' e-mail programs might not be able to handle multiple attachments.)

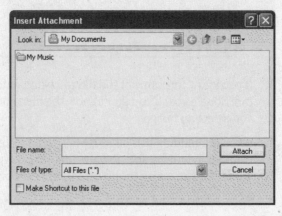

Your message now contains an icon indicating that a file is attached, the name of the file, and its size.

NOTE

As an alternative to the Insert ➤ File Attachment approach, you can drag and drop files from any folder window into the message pane.

TIP

If you accidentally attach the wrong file, select the attachment icon and press Delete.

In addition to attaching a file, you can insert part of a file's text in a message, which is a handy way to avoid retyping something that you already have stored on your computer. To insert only a portion of a text file in your message, follow these steps:

1. In the New Message window, choose Insert ➤ Text From File.

2. In the Insert Text File dialog box, select the file you want, and click Open. A copy of the text file opens in the body of your message.

3. Edit the file so that your message contains only the text you want.

ADDRESSING MESSAGES

Outlook Express uses the Windows Address Book, which is discussed in detail in Chapter 17. However, I'll explain a few basics about using it to address messages in Outlook Express now, for convenience.

If you have the Contacts pane displayed in OE, you can simply double-click on a name to begin a new message to that person. If the Contacts pane doesn't appear, you can click the Address Book button and then double-click a name there to begin a new message.

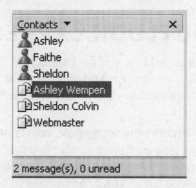

You can also begin the new message first, by clicking Create Mail, and then click the To button to open a dialog box from which you can select recipient names. This list of names comes from the Address Book, so it's simply another way of pulling names from the same source.

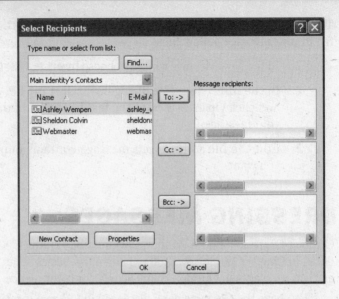

To quickly add someone to your Address Book from whom you have received a message, right-click the message and choose Add Sender to Address Book.

USING OUTLOOK EXPRESS NEWS

If you've subscribed to any of the commercial ISPs, you've no doubt browsed online newspapers and magazines and seen a news flash when you sign on to the service. That's not what we're talking about in this section.

This section concerns *newsgroups,* collections of articles about particular subjects. Newsgroups are similar to e-mail in that you can reply to what someone else has written (the newsgroup term for this is *posted*), and you can send a question or a response either to the whole group or to individuals.

To read newsgroups, you need a *newsreader*, and that is what Outlook Express News is. But before we get into the nuts and bolts of how to use Outlook Express News to read newsgroups, we want to look at the kinds of newsgroups that are available and give you a bit of background about how they work, what they are, and what they are not.

WARNING

If you are new to newsgroups, be aware that they are uncensored. You can find just about anything at any time anywhere. No person has authority over newsgroups as a whole. If you find certain groups, certain articles, or certain people offensive, don't go there. Later in this chapter, you'll see how you can filter out such articles. But remember that anarchy reigns. Forewarned is forearmed.

You can start Outlook Express News in any of the following ways:

▶ From the Outlook Express opening screen, click Read News. (Remember, to get back to the opening screen, click Outlook Express at the top of the folder tree at the left.)

▶ Click News in the Outlook bar.

▶ Choose Tools ➤ Newsgroups.

DOWNLOADING A LIST OF NEWSGROUPS

Before you can access newsgroups, you need to download a list from the ISP's news server. Connect to your ISP and open Outlook Express. In the Outlook bar or folder list, click the icon for your news server to open this dialog box:

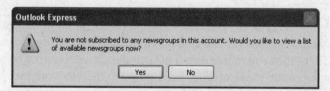

Click Yes to download a list of the newsgroups available on your news server.

Depending on the speed of your connection, this downloading process should take only a few minutes. Watch as the counter increases—you'll be amazed at the number of newsgroups.

TIP

Note that these are the groups carried by your news server; it is not a comprehensive list of all groups on the Internet. Each news server's manager decides which groups to carry and which to omit. If a group you want isn't on the list, you can contact your ISP's news server manager and request it.

Part iii

Once this list is downloaded, your newsgroups dialog box will look similar to this:

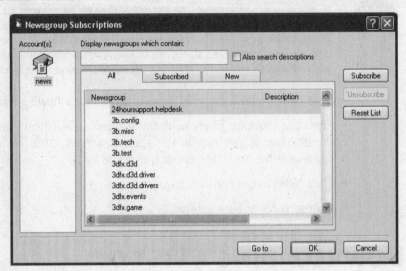

TIP

Only the names of the newsgroups are downloaded to your computer; their content remains on the news server.

Searching for an Interesting Newsgroup

Well, now that you have all this at your disposal, how do you find something that you're interested in? It reminds us of having to go to a department store to select what we're going to wear to work every morning. With so many choices, how can you decide (if money's no object, of course)?

You can select a newsgroup to read in two ways:

▶ You can scroll through the list (this could take some time).

▶ You can enter a term to search on.

Just for the sake of doing it, scroll the list a bit. As you can see, it's in alphabetic order by hierarchical categories. Now let's assume you don't see anything right away that strikes your fancy. Not to worry—you can search for something. To search for a topic, enter the word or words in the Display Newsgroups Which Contain box.

WARNING

Type your entry and then don't do anything! Wait a second, and groups containing what you entered will appear in the Newsgroup area. You don't need to press Enter, click OK, or do anything else. Just wait a nanosecond.

I entered the word **internet**, and Figure 16.8 shows the results.

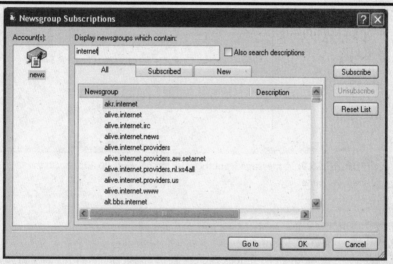

FIGURE 16.8: A list of newsgroups that appeared when I searched on the word "internet"

Reading a Newsgroup

Now you can select a newsgroup to read. To do so, follow these steps:

1. Click the name of the newsgroup.

2. Click Go To.

3. To read a message, click its header. Its content appears in the preview pane below the list of messages.

I chose to read microsoft.public.internet.news.reader .software, and Figure 16.9 shows what I got.

Part iii

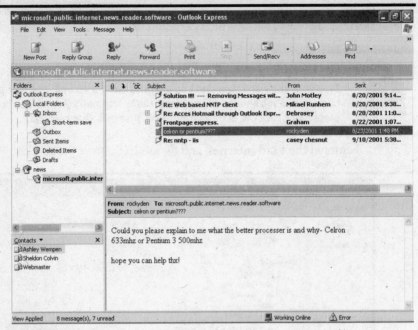

FIGURE 16.9: A message from the selected newsgroup appears in the preview pane.

NOTE

Unfortunately, Outlook Express News doesn't maintain the list that your search found in the Newsgroup dialog box. If you want to select another newsgroup that was in the found group, you have to repeat your search.

Replying and Posting

While you're reading a newsgroup, you can respond to an individual author of a message or you can reply to the entire group. Choose the method most appropriate to the topic and the subject of the newsgroup.

TIP

You'll occasionally see requests for responses be directed toward the individual and not the group; you should honor these requests.

To respond to an individual author, follow these steps:

1. Click the Reply tool button.

2. In the message window, type your message.

3. Click Send.

To reply to the whole group, click the Reply Group tool button. The name of the group will appear in the To field.

To post a new message to a group, click the New Post tool button. To reply both to the author and to the newsgroup, choose Message ➢ Reply To All. You can also use the Message menu to forward articles and to forward articles as attachments.

Subscribing and Unsubscribing to Newsgroups

When you read a newsgroup, it appears as a subfolder in your News folder. When you exit Outlook Express, these folders are deleted from the folder list.

When you *subscribe* to a newsgroup, it also appears as a subfolder in your News folder. When you exit Outlook Express News, however, this folder is retained in the folder list. The next time you access your news server, you can simply click this folder to open the newsgroup.

You can subscribe to newsgroups in the following ways:

▶ In the Newsgroup Subscriptions dialog box, select a group and click Subscribe.

▶ With the newsgroup open, right-click the newsgroup's listing in the folder list and choose Subscribe.

When you no longer want to subscribe to a newsgroup, follow these steps:

1. Click the Newsgroups tool button.

2. In the Newsgroup dialog box, select the Subscribed tab.

3. Select the name of the newsgroup, and click Unsubscribe.

While viewing a newsgroup, you can unsubscribe by right-clicking the newsgroup's listing in the folder list and choosing Unsubscribe.

Part iii

Filtering Out What You Don't Want to Read

As we've mentioned, most newsgroups are not censored in any way. Outlook Express News, however, provides a way that you can be your own censor. You can choose which newsgroups appear on the message list and are downloaded to your computer.

NOTE

Some groups are moderated—that is, someone is in charge of the newsgroup and reads posts and replies. That person applies certain specified criteria, and only those messages that meet these guidelines appear in the newsgroup. When a newsgroup is moderated, you'll see a message to that effect when you open the newsgroup.

Selecting newsgroups and messages that you don't want to appear on your computer is called *filtering*. You might choose to filter groups and messages for any number of reasons, including the following:

▶ To avoid scrolling through messages on topics that don't interest you

▶ To screen out messages that have been around a long time

To filter newsgroups and messages, follow these steps:

1. Choose Tools ➢ Message Rules ➢ News to open the New News Rule dialog box.

2. In Section 1, place a check mark next to each rule you want to use.

3. In Section 2, place a check mark next to the action you want taken.

4. In Section 3, click the blue links as needed to provide more specific information.

5. Click OK when you are done making rules.

How you ultimately use this dialog box will depend on the rules you're making. For instance, if you want to delete any messages that contain objectionable words in the subject line, choose Where the Subject Line Contains Specific Words in Section 1. In Section 2, choose Delete It. In Section 3, click the blue link that says Contains Specific Words, and enter the words you find objectionable.

Viewing, Marking, and Sorting Messages

As is the case with Outlook Express Mail, by default your Preview pane is split horizontally, with header information in the top pane and messages displayed in the bottom pane. To change this format, choose View ➤ Layout to open the Window Layout Properties dialog box. In the Preview Pane section of this dialog box, select the options that correspond to the way you want to display messages.

You can also choose to display only certain messages. Choose View ➤ Current View, and then select an option from the drop-down menu.

You can choose to display the Subject, From, Sent, Size, and Lines fields in headers. Follow these steps:

1. With a newsgroup displayed, choose View ➤ Columns to open the Columns dialog box.

2. Place a check mark next to only the columns you want displayed.

3. When the display is to your liking, click OK.

To return to the default display, click Reset.

NOTE

You can look for messages using the scroll bar, and you can go to certain messages by choosing View ➤ Next and selecting from the drop-down menu. You can then choose the next message or choose the next unread message, thread, or newsgroup. When reading a message, you can click the up and down arrows at the top of the message to go to the previous or next message in the newsgroup.

Part iii

Interpreting the News Icons

When you view a newsgroup, you'll notice that some messages are preceded by a plus sign (+). This means that this message is part of a thread. To view the thread, simply click the plus sign. The message that is part of the thread is displayed. It may also be preceded by a plus sign if it is part of a further, ongoing thread.

When you click a thread to display the further messages, it becomes a minus sign (–). Click the minus sign to once again collapse the thread.

For an explanation of the many, many other news icons, choose Help ➤ Contents and Index, select the Contents tab, select Tips and Tricks, and then click Message List Icons for Outlook Express.

NOTE

A header is the information displayed in the message window. The header may contain information such as the name of the sender, the subject, the newsgroups to which it is posted, and the time and date the message was sent or received.

NOTE

A thread is an original message and any posted replies. If you reply to a message and change the title, however, you start a new thread.

Marking Messages

Although Outlook Express marks messages as you read them and indicates which messages you have not read, you can manually mark messages. As you'll see in the section "Customizing Mail and News Options," you can use the Read tab of the Options dialog box to have Outlook Express automatically mark all messages as read when you exit a newsgroup. You can also mark messages using the Edit menu. For example, to mark a message as read, choose Edit ➤ Mark As Read.

Sorting Messages

By default, Outlook Express displays messages in ascending alphabetic order by subject. For example, in a software engineering newsgroup, a message header about Hungarian notation appears before a header containing "IBM Kasparov vs. Deep Blue."

You can change the order in which messages are displayed. Choose View ➤ Sort By, and then choose an option from the drop-down menu.

To display the most recently sent messages first, select Sent Items in the folder list and then choose View ➤ Sort By ➤ Sent. To display the list so that all messages by any one sender are grouped together, select Inbox in the folder list and then choose View ➤ Sort By ➤ From. (Sorting and grouping headers can make for some interesting reading.)

SETTING KEY MAIL AND NEWS OPTIONS

You can customize many aspects of Outlook Express so that it works the way you like to work. For example, you can place buttons for the tasks you most commonly perform on the toolbar, and you can choose not to display those you rarely need. Also, you can establish all sorts of rules for Outlook Express to follow while you are composing, sending, and receiving messages.

Let's look first at the ways you can customize the toolbar.

Customizing the Toolbar

When you first install Outlook Express, the toolbar in the main window looks like this:

To add or delete buttons or to rearrange them, choose View ➤ Layout to open the Window Layout Properties dialog box, and then click Customize Toolbar.

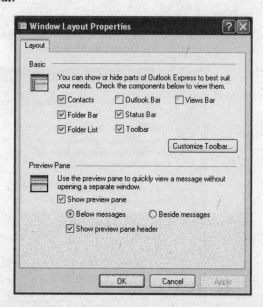

From the Customize Toolbar dialog box, you can add or delete buttons. To add a button, follow these steps:

1. Select the button in the Available Toolbar Buttons list.

2. Click the Add button.

3. Click Close.

4. In the Window Layout Properties dialog box, click Apply, and then click OK.

The button now appears on your toolbar.

TIP

You can return your toolbar to its original format at any time. In the Customize Toolbar dialog box, choose Reset and then Close. Then, in the Window Layout Properties dialog box, click Apply and then click OK.

Customizing Mail and News Options

You can use the Options dialog box to establish your preferences for both Outlook Express Mail and Outlook Express News. Let's start by looking at the General options.

The General Tab

When you choose Tools ≻ Options, Outlook Express displays the Options dialog box with the General tab selected.

Table 16.1 shows the options that you can set up in the General tab.

TABLE 16.1:   The Options in the General Tab of the Options Dialog Box

OPTION	WHAT IT DOES
When Starting, Go Directly to My "Inbox" Folder	Check this item to go immediately to your Inbox when you start Outlook Express.
Notify Me If There Are Any New Newsgroups	Check this option if you want Outlook Express to check for new newsgroups and download their names when you access a news server.
Automatically Display Folders with Unread Messages	Check this option if you want to display only unread messages.
Automatically Log On to Windows Messenger	Mark this if you use Windows Messenger and want to be connected every time you go online.
Play Sound When New Messages Arrive	Of course, this works only when you are connected to your e-mail server. If you don't want to be notified when new mail arrives, uncheck this option. You can customize the sound via Control Panel ➤ Sounds.
Send and Receive Messages at Startup	With this option enabled, Outlook Express will automatically send unsent messages and check for new mail when you start the program.
Check for New Messages Every *x* Minutes	Check this item and then click the spinner-box arrows to select a time interval.
If My Computer Is Not Connected at This Time	If your computer is offline when it becomes time to check for new messages, do you want it to connect or not? Choose an option in the drop-down list here to decide.
Default Messaging Programs	If Outlook Express is not already set as your default mail and/or newsreader, click one of the buttons here to set it.

Part iii

Reading Mail and News

Select the Read tab, and Outlook Express displays this dialog box:

Table 16.2 shows the options in the Read Tab.

TABLE 16.2:   The Options in the Read Tab

OPTION	WHAT IT DOES
Mark Message Read After Displaying for x Second(s)	You can change the number of seconds, and you can uncheck this option to manually mark messages as read.
Automatically Expand Grouped Messages	If you select this option, threads and all replies are displayed when you open a newsgroup.
Automatically Download Message When Viewing in the Preview Pane	If you uncheck this option, select the header and then press the spacebar to display the message body.
Show ToolTips in the Message List for Clipped Items	With this enabled, if you hold the mouse pointer over a clipped item, a ToolTip will appear showing the name of the attachment.

Continued on next page

TABLE 16.2:   The Options in the Read Tab *(continued)*

OPTION	WHAT IT DOES
Get *x* Headers at a Time	Set at 300 by default. You can set this option to a minimum of 50 and a maximum of 1,000. (Would you really want to download 1,000 headers?) If you uncheck this option, all headers in the newsgroup are downloaded, regardless of the number.
Mark All Messages as Read When Exiting a Newsgroup	When you select this option, you choose to read only messages marked as unread when you return to this newsgroup.

You use the Fonts section of the Read tab to change the fonts used when reading messages. When you install Outlook Express, messages you read are formatted in the Western Alphabet using Arial as the proportional font (when you are using the HTML format), using Courier New as the fixed-width font (when you are using the Plain Text format), and a medium font size. To change any of this, click the Fonts button. Outlook Express displays the Fonts dialog box, as shown in Figure 16.10. Click the down arrows to survey your choices.

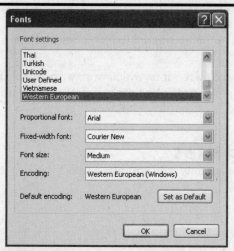

FIGURE 16.10: The Fonts dialog box

Part iii

Mail Receipt

To set preferences for mailing receipts, click the Receipts tab.

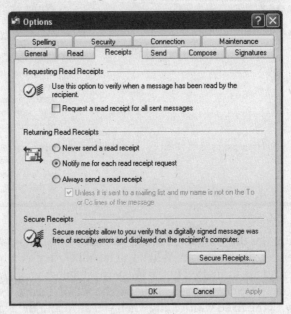

Here you can request a read receipt so that a message returns to you letting you know the recipient has opened your message.

You can also specify how you want to handle requests for read receipts that come from others. Note that because of this capability, you might not always get a receipt when one of your recipients reads a message if they have this setting set to Never Send a Read Receipt.

Finally, you can set up secure receipts, which work with digital signatures to ensure that the intended recipient got the message, and not some interceptor.

Sending Mail and News

To set your preferences for sending mail and news, select the Send tab.

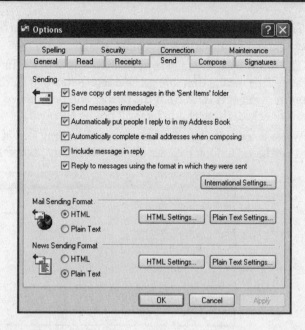

In the upper half of this dialog box, you can choose to include messages in replies and specify when messages in the Outbox should be sent.

In the Mail Sending Format section of the Send tab, you specify whether you want to send mail in HTML or Plain Text format. If you want all messages composed and sent in HTML, check this option and click the HTML Settings button to open the HTML Settings dialog box.

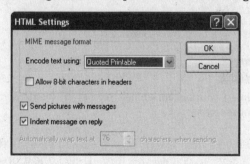

In the Encode Text Using drop-down list box in the MIME Message Format section, you have three choices:

- None
- Quoted Printable
- Base 64

Part iii

These are the available bit and binary formats for encoding your message. Quoted Printable is selected by default.

The Allow 8-Bit Characters in Headers check box is unchecked by default. This means that foreign character sets, high ASCII, or double-byte character sets (DBCS) in the header will be encoded. If this check box is checked, these characters will not be encoded.

When you select Plain Text as your mail sending format and click Plain Text Settings, Outlook Express displays the Plain Text Settings dialog box.

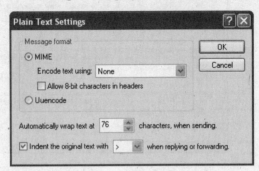

In the Encode Text Using drop-down list in the Message Format section of this dialog box, you have three choices:

▶ None

▶ Quoted Printable

▶ Base 64

None is selected by default.

NOTE

Unless your system administrator or ISP instructs you to do so, don't change these settings.

By default, when you send messages in Plain Text format, lines wrap at 76 characters. To change this format, click the drop-down list arrow and select a greater or lesser number of characters. Also by default, the original text of a message to which you reply is preceded by an angle bracket. To select another character, click the drop-down list arrow.

In the News Sending Format section of the Send tab, you can choose whether to post articles in HTML or Plain Text. Selecting Plain Text is a wise choice if you are posting to a widely read newsgroup. Most newsreaders cannot display articles in HTML. Selecting either HTML or Plain Text and clicking the Settings button opens the Settings dialog box for that selection. In either case, you'll see the same dialog box that opens when you select that option for sending mail.

Table 16.3 lists and explains the other options in the Send tab.

TABLE 16.3:   Additional Options in the Send Tab

OPTION	WHAT IT DOES
Save Copy of Sent Messages in the "Sent Items" Folder	This is handy for verifying that you really sent a message that you intended to send. If it is unchecked, you can still keep a copy by including yourself on the Cc or Bcc line.
Send Messages Immediately	If you check this item, messages are sent when you click the Send button rather than being saved in your Outbox until you send them.
Automatically Put People I Reply to in My Address Book	Check this option if you want the names and e-mail addresses of everybody you reply to in your Address Book.
Automatically Complete E-Mail Addresses When Composing	If you check this option, Outlook Express completes the e-mail address you are typing as soon as it recognizes a series of characters, if this address is in your Address Book.
Include Message in Reply	If you check this option, you can edit the message to which you are replying so that it retains only the pertinent sentences or paragraphs. This device comes in handy when you are responding to a sender's questions.
Reply to Messages Using the Format in Which They Were Sent	To send a message in a different format, uncheck this item.

Part iii

Checking Spelling

If you send and receive lots of e-mail, you're probably used to seeing and, for the most part, ignoring typos. In the early days of e-mail, the only way to check what you were sending was to stop, read it over, and, with minimal editing features available, fix your errors.

This was a time-consuming task associated with a powerful time-saving application, and most people just didn't (don't?) bother. If you're simply communicating with colleagues down the hall or buddies in your bowling league, maybe it doesn't matter. But if you're sending a trip report to your boss or posting a major announcement to a newsgroup, it matters. You want to appear professional, and you certainly don't want to embarrass yourself with a couple of transposed letters.

NOTE

Outlook Express uses the spelling checker that comes with Microsoft Office 95, 97, 2000, or XP programs. If you don't have one of these programs installed, the Spelling command is unavailable.

Using the spelling checker, you can quickly give your messages the once-over before they wend their way to the outside world. Click the Spelling tab to display your options.

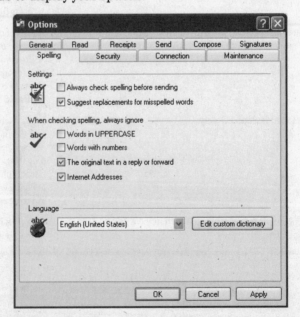

Table 16.4 shows the options available in the Spelling tab.

TABLE 16.4:   The Options in the Spelling Tab

OPTION	WHAT IT DOES
Always Check Spelling before Sending	Check this option if you want Outlook Express to quickly look for typos before a message is sent.
Suggest Replacements for Misspelled Words	With this option checked, Outlook Express checks your spelling as you go along and suggests replacements.
Always Ignore Words in UPPERCASE	When this option is checked, words entirely uppercased are ignored in the spelling check.
Always Ignore Words with Numbers	When this option is checked, words that include numeric characters are ignored in the spelling check.
Always Ignore the Original Text in a Reply or Forward	When this option is checked, only your message is spell-checked, not the message you are forwarding or to which you are replying.
Always Ignore Internet Addresses	If you've ever had your spell checker come to a halt every time it reaches a URL, you'll want to keep this option turned on.

Part iii

By default, your messages are checked against a U.S. English dictionary. If you want to choose British English, click the Language down arrow. To create or change a custom dictionary, click Edit Custom Dictionary.

Enhancing Security

You use the Security tab to establish security zones and to specify how Outlook Express handles digital certificates (also known as digital IDs).

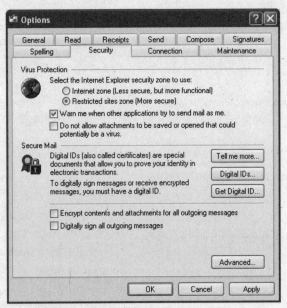

With Internet Explorer, you can assign Web sites to zones that have varying levels of security. If you have a digital certificate, you can add it to all outgoing messages by using the options in the Secure Mail section of this tab.

To obtain a digital ID, click the Get Digital ID button in the Secure Mail section. Or for more information, click the Tell Me More button.

Your Connection Options

As we mentioned early in this chapter, we are assuming a dial-up connection to the Internet. You use the options in the Connection tab to specify how you connect to your ISP when you start Outlook Express.

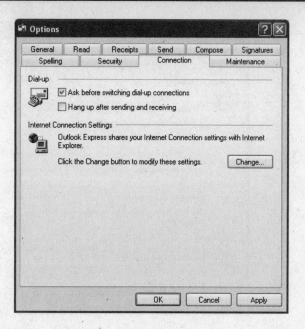

Table 16.5 lists and explains these options.

TABLE 16.5:   The Options in the Connection Tab

OPTION	WHAT IT DOES
Ask before Switching Dial-Up Connections	If you have separate Internet connections for your various accounts, this makes Outlook Express prompt you before it hangs up an existing connection and dials a new one.
Hang Up after Sending and Receiving	When this option is selected, Outlook Express automatically disconnects from your ISP after sending, receiving, or downloading.
Outlook Express Shares Your Internet Connections Settings with Internet Explorer	Clicking the Change button opens the Internet Properties dialog box.

Part iii

The Maintenance Tab

You use the options in the Maintenance tab to determine how your local message files are stored.

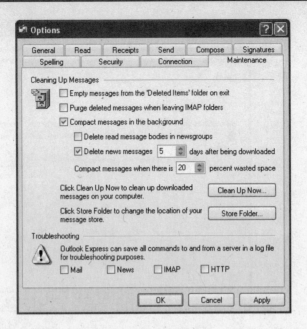

Table 16.6 lists and explains these options.

TABLE 16.6: The Options in the Maintenance Tab

OPTION	WHAT IT DOES
Empty Messages from the "Deleted Items" Folder on Exit	Messages are placed in this folder when you select a message and choose Delete. Check this item if you want the Deleted Items folder emptied when you exit Outlook Express.
Purge Deleted Messages When Leaving IMAP Folders	Deleted messages are purged when you leave folders on the IMAP server.
Compact Messages in the Background	Contains suboptions to help preserve hard-disk space. Set at 20% by default. You can choose a minimum of 5% and a maximum of 100%. This also gives you the opportunity to specify how long to keep the news messages for. The default is 5 days.
Troubleshooting	You can choose to have a log file recorded for the different protocols listed in order to aid in troubleshooting problems. Don't check these options unless you have problems, as they will have an impact on your system resources.

Now let's look at the Clean Up Now button on this tab. When you click this button, Outlook Express News displays the Local File Clean Up dialog box.

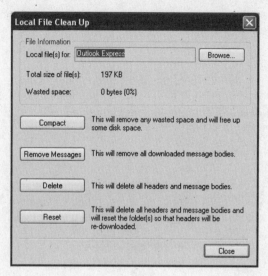

In this dialog box, first specify the files you want, and then click the appropriate buttons to do the following:

- ▶ Compact the files.

- ▶ Remove the message bodies but leave the headers in the files.

- ▶ Remove all messages, headers, and bodies from the files.

- ▶ Reset deletes all headers and message bodies and resets the folders so that headers will be downloaded again.

WHAT'S NEXT

In this chapter you gained a broad overview of e-mail and newsgroup functionality in Windows XP. The next chapter focuses on a specific related feature: Address Book. You can use the Address Book feature within Outlook Express to select recipients for e-mail, and you can also use it independently, as a stand-alone program for managing addresses and other contact information.

Chapter 17

USING ADDRESS BOOK

Windows comes with an address book program, unimagi-
natively named Address Book, for storing contact information: names of people, companies, and organizations; their
phone numbers, addresses, and e-mail addresses; their birth-
days and anniversaries; and even the details of their digital IDs.

Address Book is integrated with Outlook Express, so you can
quickly create e-mail messages to those contacts who are stored
in Address Book. Conversely, you can create new contacts from
the information contained in e-mail addresses.

This chapter discusses the main actions you'll need to perform with Address Book, from adding contacts to your address
book to exporting a list of your contacts for use with another
contact management program.

Adapted from *Mastering Windows XP Home Edition*
by Guy Hart-Davis

ISBN 0-7821-2980-3 · 1024 pages $39.99

STARTING ADDRESS BOOK

You can start Address Book from the Start menu (Start ➢ All Programs ➢ Accessories ➢ Address Book) or in various ways from Outlook Express: Click the Addresses button, choose Tools ➢ Address Book, or press Ctrl+Shift+B. You can also access Address Book via the Select Recipients dialog box that Outlook Express displays when you click the To button or the Cc button from the New Message window.

To make Address Book more quickly accessible from the desktop, copy or move its shortcut from the Accessories submenu. Alternatively, create a new shortcut to the Address Book executable file, WAB.EXE.

When you start Address Book, it displays your main identity. When you first open Address Book, you probably won't have any entries in it. (If you've been using Windows Messenger, you'll find your Messenger contacts in Address Book.) Figure 17.1 shows Address Book with a number of entries already entered in it.

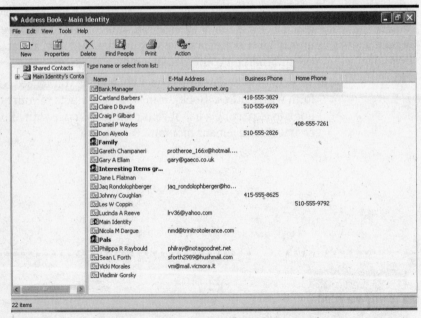

FIGURE 17.1: Address Book with a number of contacts entered

ADDING A CONTACT TO YOUR ADDRESS BOOK

The most conventional way to add a contact to your Address Book is as follows:

1. In the Folders and Groups pane, make sure you have selected your identity's contacts or the Shared Contacts folder as appropriate.

2. Click the New button on the toolbar and choose New Contact from the drop-down menu. (Alternatively, choose File ➤ New Contact or press Ctrl+N.) Address Book displays the Properties dialog box for a new contact, with the Name page foremost (see Figure 17.2).

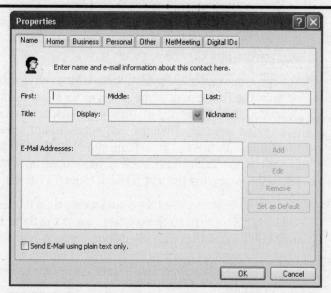

FIGURE 17.2: Use the Properties dialog box to create a new contact.

3. On the Name page, enter the contact's name, title, nickname, and e-mail addresses:

   ▶ Once you've entered the contact's first, middle, and last names, Address Book automatically builds entries for the Display drop-down list. Its default format is First Middle

Last—for example, Randall A Chaucer—but you can choose a different format (Chaucer Randall A or Chaucer, Randall A) in the Display drop-down list. You can also type something completely different—for example, a description such as **Bank Manager**.

▶ You can use the Nickname field in two ways. First, you can use it to hold a nickname associated with the contact but that you don't want to use instead of their actual first name. But even if the contact doesn't have a nickname, you can use this field as a unique identifier within Address Book and Outlook Express. You can type a nickname in the To field or Cc field in a new message in Outlook Express and issue a Check Names command. Outlook Express fills in the corresponding e-mail address. For example, if you entered **Law** as the nickname for your attorney in Address Book, you could enter **Law** as the address in Outlook Express. (If two or more contacts have the same nickname, Outlook Express displays the Check Names dialog box so that you can pick the one you want.)

▶ You can enter multiple e-mail addresses for a contact. By default, the first e-mail address you enter is set as the default address. If you add multiple e-mail addresses and want to use one other than the first as the default, select the address to use as the default and click the Set As Default button. Address Book adds an envelope icon to the left of the listing and the text *(Default E-mail)* to its left.

▶ If you need to send plain-text e-mail rather than formatted or HTML e-mail to the contact, select the Send E-mail Using Plain Text Only check box. If you're not sure whether a contact can receive formatted e-mail, select this check box. That way, the contact will be able to read your message.

4. On the Home page and the Business page, enter home-related information and business-related information for the contact. Almost all the fields and controls on these pages are self-explanatory, but these three deserve comment:

▶ Select the Default check box on either the Home page or the Business page to specify that this is the default

address to use for the contact. Selecting the Default
check box on one page clears it on the other page if it is
selected there.

▶ Clicking the View Map button on either page causes your
browser to look up the address on the Expedia Maps service (maps.expedia.com) and display a map of the area
to you.

▶ The Business page includes a text box for the contact's IP
telephone address, which is useful if you use IP telephony.

5. On the Personal page, enter any personal information known
for the contact:

▶ Address Book creates all contacts as being of "Unspecified"
gender. With luck, you should be able to improve on this.

▶ To add a child, click the Add button. Address Book adds
an entry named New Child and displays an edit box
around it. Type in the appropriate name and press the
Enter key. (If you need to change the child's name afterward, select the child and click the Edit button.)

6. If you have other information about the contact, enter it in
the Notes text box on the Other page. This page also contains the Group Membership text box, which lists any of your
Address Book groups the contact belongs to.

7. If you have conferencing information for the contact, enter it
on the NetMeeting page. This page also contains a Call Now
button that you can click to place a NetMeeting call to the
contact.

8. To import a digital ID for the contact, display the Digital IDs
page, click the Import button, and follow through the import
procedure. You can also export a digital certificate from here,
view its properties, and choose which digital certificate to use
as the default for a contact.

9. Click the OK button to close the Properties dialog box. Your
contact appears in Address Book.

Part iii

EXPERT KNOWLEDGE: CREATING A CONTACT RECORD FROM AN E-MAIL MESSAGE

When you're reading e-mail in Outlook Express, you can add a sender to your Address Book by right-clicking the message in the Inbox and choosing Add Sender to Address Book from the context menu. (Alternatively, select the message and choose Tools ➢ Add Sender to Address Book.) Outlook Express adds the name and e-mail address directly to Address Book. So when you do this, it's usually a good idea to display Address Book and immediately add all the information you know about the contact—before you forget.

From a message window, you can create contacts from the sender, a Cc addressee, or everyone on the addressee list of the message (except any Bcc addressees). Choose Tools ➢ Add to Address Book ➢ Sender; Tools ➢ Add to Address Book ➢ Everyone on To List; or one of the e-mail addresses listed on the Add to Address Book submenu. Alternatively, double-click the From listing, one of the To listings other than yourself, or one of the Cc listings.

Outlook Express displays the Properties dialog box for the contact with a Summary page added and displayed (shown next). At this point, the information is minimal—and in the example, the name consists of the e-mail address. Click the Name page of the dialog box and start improving the information while it's fresh, or just click the Add to Address Book button if you're in a hurry.

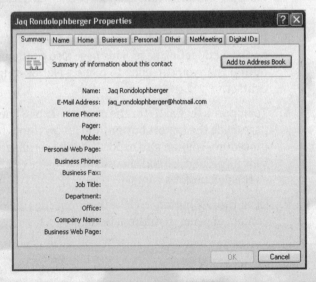

DELETING A CONTACT

To delete a contact, right-click it and choose Delete from the context menu. Address Book displays a dialog box asking you to confirm the deletion. Click the Yes button.

MOVING A CONTACT FROM ONE IDENTITY TO ANOTHER

You can move a contact from one identity to another by dragging it from the list box to the appropriate folder in the Folders and Groups pane. For example, to move a contact from your main identity to the Shared Contacts folder, drag the contact to the Shared Contacts folder and drop it there.

EDITING YOUR PROFILE FOR ADDRESS BOOK

Address Book creates a profile called Main Identity for each user with a user account on the PC. When you start Address Book, it displays the Main Identity profile for the user account under which you logged on to Windows.

Address Book is integrated with the Profile Assistant tool in Internet Explorer. To enable Address Book to provide Internet Explorer with the information it needs for Web sites that request data such as your e-mail address or a digital certificate, you need to create a profile for yourself and associate it with the Main Identity. To do so, follow these steps:

1. Choose Edit ➤ Profile. Address Book displays the Address Book – Choose Profile dialog box (shown in Figure 17.3).

2. Choose whether to use an existing entry for your profile or to create a new entry. If you choose the Select an Existing Entry from the Address Book to Represent Your Profile option button, choose the profile from the list box.

3. Click the OK button. Address Book closes the Address Book – Choose Profile dialog box. If you chose to create a new entry, Address Book displays the Properties dialog box for an

identity named Main Identity. Fill in the information as you would for any other contact (though perhaps with more care), and change the name from Main Identity to your name.

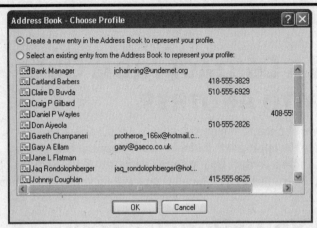

FIGURE 17.3: In the Address Book – Choose Profile dialog box, choose whether to create a new entry for your profile or to use an existing entry.

When Profile Assistant receives a request for information from a Web site, Profile Assistant tells you the URL or IP address of the site requesting the information, the types of information requested, how the site claims it will use the information (invariably for good—*your* good—of course), and whether the connection to the site is secured with SSL. You can choose which information to give the site. If the connection is secure, you can view the certificate for the site to help you decide.

Importing Information into Your Address Book

If you already have information in a data source (for example, in an organizer or in a database), you can import it into Address Book. Address Book can handle formats that include Windows address books, the vCard business-card format, Address Books in Works, Exchange, Microsoft Internet Mail for Windows 3.1, Eudora (Pro and Light), Netscape and Netscape Communicator, and the LDAP Data Interchange Format. If your data is in a different format (for example, a spreadsheet or an organizer), the best way of exporting and importing the information is to use a *comma-separated values* file (CSV file for short)—a file in which the fields are separated by commas.

WARNING

With some data sources, Address Book may fail to preserve divisions between address books—for example, it may lump entries from multiple separate address books into the same category in Address Book. Make sure you keep your data source until you've checked your imported data carefully in case Address Book messes things up and you need to import it all again.

Importing a Windows Address Book

Importing a file in Windows address book (WAB) format is a straightforward process: Choose File ➢ Import ➢ Address Book (WAB), use the Select Address Book to Import From dialog box to identify the file, and click the Open button. Then dismiss the message box telling you that the address book has been imported.

Importing a vCard

Importing a record stored in a vCard business card is equally straightforward. Choose File ➢ Import ➢ Business Card (vCard), use the Import Business Card (vCard) dialog box to select the file, and click the Open button. Address Book displays the Properties dialog box for the contact so that you can check the information is in the right slots and add any other data you want. Then click the OK button. Address Book closes the Properties dialog box and files away the information.

Importing Information Stored in Another Format

Importing address information stored in another format tends to be a more involved process, because you usually need to map the fields in the data source to the fields in Address Book.

EXPERT KNOWLEDGE: EXPORTING YOUR ADDRESS INFORMATION FIELDS IN THE BEST ORDER

If the program from which you're exporting the address information lets you name the fields and specify their order, use this order and these names: First Name, Last Name, Middle Name, Name, Nickname, E-mail Address, Home Street, Home City, Home Postal Code, Home State, Home Country, Home Phone, Home Fax, Mobile Phone, Personal Web Page, Business Street, Business City, Business Postal Code, Business State, Business Country, Business Web Page, Business Phone, Business Fax, Pager, Company, Job Title, Department, Office Location, and Notes. Using this sequence makes the information snap into the fields in Address Book without any remapping.

Here's an example using a comma-separated values (CSV) file:

1. Choose File ➤ Import ➤ Other Address Book. Address Book displays the Address Book Import Tool dialog box (see Figure 17.4).

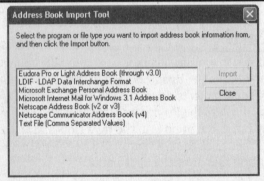

FIGURE 17.4: In the Address Book Import Tool dialog box, select the type of information you want to import and then click the Import button.

2. In the list box, choose the appropriate format. The example uses Text File (Comma Separated Values).

3. Click the Import button. Address Book displays the first CSV Import dialog box, which lets you select the file to import.

4. Either type in the name and path or click the Browse button to display the Open dialog box, specify the location and name as usual, and click the Open button.

5. Click the Next button. Address Book displays the second CSV Import dialog box (see Figure 17.5).

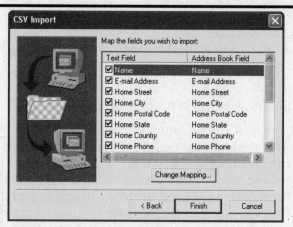

FIGURE 17.5: In the second CSV Import dialog box, check and change the field mapping, and then click the Finish button.

6. Check that each field in the data source (the first column) is *mapped* (matched) to an appropriate field in Address Book (the second column) and that each text field that you want to import has its check box selected:

   ▶ To change the mapping of a field, select it and click the Change Mapping button. Address Book displays the Change Mapping dialog box (see Figure 17.6). In the drop-down list, select the target Address Book field, select the Import This Field check box, and click the OK button.

   ▶ If your data source doesn't have column headings, you'll have to look at it to see which field contains which information. If possible, open it in a spreadsheet program such as Excel, because doing so separates the information into separate columns, making it easier to read. If you don't have a spreadsheet program, open the data source in Notepad and count the commas. (If you have Word, open the data source in Word and convert it to a table.)

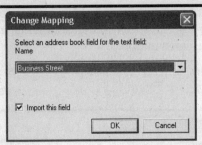

FIGURE 17.6: Use the Change Mapping dialog box to change the mapping of a field as necessary.

7. Click the Finish button to perform the import:

   ▶ If any of the information you're importing does not match the expected field, Address Book displays the Error Importing Contact dialog box, of which Figure 17.7 shows an example. Click the OK button to proceed or the Cancel button to cancel the whole import procedure. Select the Don't Show Me Error Messages Anymore check box if you want to suppress further error messages when proceeding.

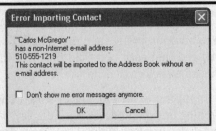

FIGURE 17.7: By default, Address Book displays the Error Importing Contact dialog box to warn you when it encounters data it thinks is unsuitable for a field.

8. When Address Book has finished importing the data, it displays a message box telling you so. Close this dialog box and then click the Close button to close the Address Book Import Tool dialog box.

Double-check the resulting Address Book entries for duplicates and errors before you use them.

EXPORTING INFORMATION FROM YOUR ADDRESS BOOK

As you'd expect, you can also export information from Address Book so that you can import it into an organizer, database, or spreadsheet.

If the recipient program can read the WAB format, use that. Choose File ➤ Export ➤ Address Book (WAB), specify the filename and location in the Select Address Book File to Export To dialog box, and click the Save button. Address Book exports the information and displays a message box telling you that it has done so. Click the OK button to dismiss the message box, and you're done.

To export a single record, save it as a vCard. Choose File ➤ Export ➤ Business Card (vCard), specify the filename and location in the Export As Business Card (vCard) dialog box, and click the Save button.

To export your address book in a format other than WAB, use a CSV file as follows:

1. Choose File ➤ Export ➤ Other Address Book. Address Book displays the Address Book Export Tool dialog box (shown in Figure 17.8).

2. In the list box, select the Text File (Comma Separated Values) entry.

3. Click the Export button. Address Book displays the first CSV Export dialog box.

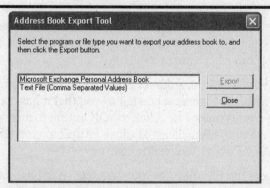

FIGURE 17.8: Choose the Text File (Comma Separated Values) item in the Address Book Export Tool dialog box.

4. In the Save Exported File As text box, enter the name under which to save the exported file. Either type in the name and path or click the Browse button, use the resulting Save As dialog box to specify the location and filename, and click the Save button.

5. Click the Next button. Address Book displays the second CSV Export dialog box (shown in Figure 17.9).

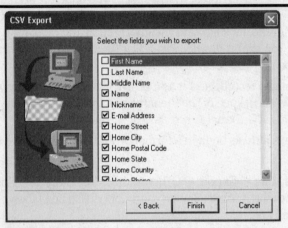

FIGURE 17.9: In the second CSV Export dialog box, select the fields you want to export and then click the Finish button.

6. Select the fields you want to export. By default, the CSV Export dialog box does not select the check boxes for the First Name, Last Name, and Middle Name fields, because it lumps the names together into a single field (called Name), which it selects. If you need to have the individual fields as well, select their check boxes too.

7. Click the Finish button. Address Book exports the address book and displays a message box telling you that it has completed the export procedure. Click the OK button to dismiss the message box, then click the Close button to close the Address Book Export Tool dialog box.

You can now import the CSV file into your organizer, database, or spreadsheet.

ORGANIZING YOUR CONTACTS INTO FOLDERS AND GROUPS

To prevent your contact list from growing to the length of the San Andreas fault, you can divide your contacts up among a number of folders. For example, in a home situation, you might create a folder to contain family members, one for friends, one for local businesses, another for emergency contacts, and so on. You can also create groups to help administer your contacts.

Normally, a folder actually contains a contact, while a group contains only a pointer to a contact. You *can* create contacts that reside only within groups, but usually you'll want to use groups mostly to organize contacts rather than contain them.

Creating a Folder

As you saw earlier in this chapter, Address Book starts you off with a Shared Contacts folder (shared with all the other users of the computer) and a Main Identity's Contacts folder (of which each user has one to her- or himself). Under each of these, you can add as many folders as you need to sort your contacts into logical containers.

To create a new folder, follow these steps:

1. Right-click the folder that will contain it (Shared Contacts or Main Identity's Contacts) in the Folders and Groups pane and choose New ➢ New Folder from the context menu. (Alternatively, select the folder and choose File ➢ New Folder, or press Ctrl+R.) Address Book displays a Properties dialog box.

2. Enter the name for the folder in the Folder Name text box. Address Book displays the folders in alphabetical order. To implement a specific order of your own, add numbering to the beginning of the folder names. To force a single folder to float to the top of the list without numbering, put a space at the beginning of its name.

3. Click the OK button. Address Book creates the folder.

You can then move contacts to the folder by dragging them from their current location and dropping them on the folder.

Deleting a Folder

To delete a folder, right-click it in the Folders and Groups pane and choose Delete from the context menu, then select the Yes button in the confirmation message box.

Deleting a folder deletes all the contacts it contains and is not undoable. Consider backing up Address Book before deleting a folder.

Creating a Group

To create a group, follow these steps:

1. Click the New button on the toolbar and choose Group from the drop-down list (or choose File ➢ New Group or press Ctrl+G). Address Book displays the Properties dialog box for the group with the Group page displayed. Figure 17.10 shows an example.

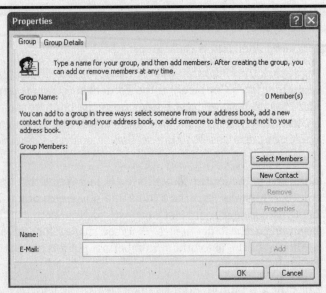

FIGURE 17.10: Use the Properties dialog box for a group to define the group and add contacts to it.

2. Enter the name for the group in the Group Name text box. This is the name that appears in the Folders and Groups pane.

3. Click the Select Members button to display the Select Group Members dialog box.

4. In the left-hand list box, select the contacts to add to the group and then click the Select button to transfer them to the group:

   ▶ Double-click a contact to add it to the Members list box.

   ▶ Use Shift+Click and Ctrl+Click to select multiple contacts at once.

   ▶ To remove a contact from the right-hand list box, right-click the contact and choose Remove from the context menu.

5. Click the OK button. Address Book closes the Select Group Members dialog box. The Group Members list box in the Properties dialog shows the members you added.

TIP

To add a contact to the group but not to Address Book, enter the contact's name and e-mail address in the Name text box and E-mail text box in the Properties dialog box and click the Add button. To add a contact to both the group and Address Book, click the New Contact button and create the contact as usual in the Properties dialog box for the contact.

Part iii

6. If you have details to add for the group (such as an address, phone number, or notes), click the Group Details tab to display the Group Details page, then enter the information there.

7. Click the OK button. Address Book closes the Properties dialog box for the group.

NOTE

You can check which groups a contact belongs to on the Other page of the contact's Properties dialog box.

Removing a Contact from a Group

To remove a contact from a group, select the group in the Folders and Groups pane, then right-click the contact in the list box and choose Delete from the context menu. Address Book displays the confirmation dialog box shown in Figure 17.11 to let you know that you're removing the contact from the group rather than deleting them. Click the Yes button.

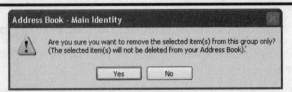

FIGURE 17.11: When you remove a contact from a group, Address Book checks to make sure you understand you're not deleting the contact.

Deleting a Group

To delete a group, select it in the Folders and Groups pane and click the Delete button. Address Book displays the confirmation message box shown in Figure 17.12, reminding you that getting rid of the group does not delete its members. Click the Yes button if you want to proceed.

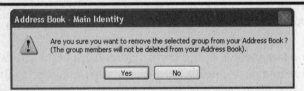

FIGURE 17.12: Address Book double-checks to make sure you want to delete a group.

CHANGING THE FIELDS DISPLAYED

By default, Address Book displays the Name, E-mail Address, Business Phone, and Home Phone columns. You can change any of these fields except the Name field or E-mail Address field by right-clicking its column heading and choosing a different field from the context menu of fields that appears (see Figure 17.13).

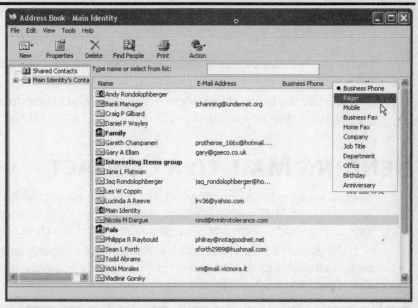

FIGURE 17.13: To change a displayed field, right-click its column heading and choose a replacement from the context menu.

USING VIEWS

Address Book offers four views for scrutinizing your contacts: Details view (the default view), Large Icon view, Small Icon view, and List view. You'll recognize these views from the views in Windows Explorer—they're essentially the same. (Unfortunately—or perhaps otherwise—there's no Thumbnails view, so you can't assign a different picture to each contact.) Details view tends to be the most useful, because it puts the most information on-screen at the same time, but you may want to use Small Icon view or List view occasionally so that you can see a larger number of contacts at once.

To change view, choose View ➤ Large Icon, View ➤ Small Icon, View ➤ List, or View ➤ Details as appropriate.

SORTING YOUR CONTACTS

By default, Address Book sorts your contacts alphabetically by first name. If you're on a first-name basis with them, or have relatively few

Part iii

contacts, this works fine. If not, you'll probably need to sort your contacts into a different order sooner or later.

To sort the contacts by one of the columns displayed, click the column heading once for an ascending sort (alphabetical order) or twice for a descending sort (reverse alphabetical order).

To sort by last name, choose View ➢ Sort By ➢ Last Name. To restore the default first-name sorting, choose View ➢ Sort By ➢ First Name.

SENDING MAIL TO A CONTACT

To send e-mail to a contact, right-click the contact's name and choose Action ➢ Send Mail from the context menu. Address Book activates Outlook Express and starts a new message to the contact you chose.

If the contact has no e-mail address, Address Book displays an exclamation message box alerting you to the problem (see Figure 17.14) and doesn't activate Outlook Express.

FIGURE 17.14: Here's what happens when you try to e-mail a contact who doesn't have an e-mail address in Address Book.

FINDING A FORGOTTEN CONTACT IN ADDRESS BOOK

To access a contact whose name you remember in Address Book, you can type down through the list box until you reach the entry you want. If you can't remember the contact's name but can remember other information about the contact, use the Find feature to locate the contact as follows:

1. Click the Find People button on the toolbar, or choose Edit ➢ Find People, or press Ctrl+F, to display the Find People dialog box (shown in Figure 17.15).

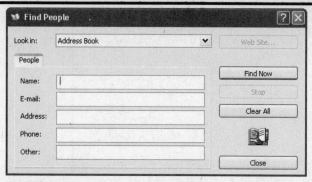

FIGURE 17.15: Use the Find People dialog box to find a contact whose full name you can't remember.

2. In the Look In drop-down list, make sure Address Book is selected if you want to search Address Book. (The alternatives are to search information repositories such as Active Directory and online directory services.)

3. In the Name, E-mail, Address, Phone, and Other text boxes, enter such information as you can remember about the person:

   ▶ The Name, E-mail, Address, and Phone text boxes cause Address Book to search *all* name fields, all e-mail addresses, all address fields, and all phone fields for the contact.

   ▶ Each piece of information doesn't have to be complete: For example, you might enter only part of the last name in the Name text box and only an area code in the Phone text box.

   ▶ The more specific the information you enter, the fewer matches you'll get. If you enter information the contact record doesn't contain, you won't find the contact.

4. Click the Find Now button to perform the search. If it finds matches, the Find People dialog box displays a lower section containing them (see Figure 17.16). If not, it displays a message box saying that it found no matches.

5. Click the Properties button to open the Properties dialog box for the contact. Click the Delete button to delete the contact. Or click the Close button to close the Find People dialog box.

Part iii

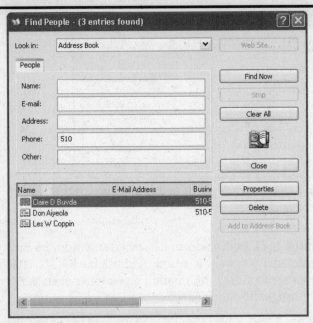

FIGURE 17.16: If it finds matches, the Find People dialog box displays them. You can work directly from the results.

SEARCHING INTERNET DIRECTORIES FOR PEOPLE

If Address Book doesn't have the contact you need, you can search Active Directory or an Internet directory as follows:

1. Click the Find People button on the toolbar, or choose Edit ➢ Find People. Address Book displays the Find People dialog box.

2. In the Look In drop-down list in the Find People dialog box, select one of the directories: Active Directory, Bigfoot Internet Directory Service, VeriSign Internet Directory Service, WhoWhere Internet Directory Service, or one of the other directory services listed. The Find People dialog box reduces the number of fields on its People page to just the Name text box and the E-mail text box but displays an Advanced page as well (shown in Figure 17.17).

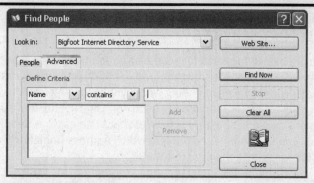

FIGURE 17.17: Use the Advanced page of the Find People dialog box to define criteria when searching for people on directory services.

3. Use the Define Criteria group box on the Advanced page to define criteria for your search:

    ▶ In the first drop-down list, choose Name, E-mail, First Name, Last Name, or Organization as appropriate.

    ▶ In the second drop-down list, choose the appropriate condition: Contains, Is, Starts With, Ends With, or Sounds Like. (The Sounds Like item can give you some peculiar results, but it's worth trying when all else fails.)

    ▶ In the text box, enter the text for the criterion. For example, you might specify **Last Name Starts With Rob** to find people with last names such as Robson, Roberts, or Robertson.

    ▶ Click the Add button to add the criterion to the list box. Then define other criteria as necessary by repeating these steps.

4. Click the Find Now button to execute the search.

NOTE

If the Web Site button is available, you can click it to open an Internet Explorer window showing the directory's Web site, which may offer further search options.

EXPERT KNOWLEDGE: ADDING AND CONFIGURING DIRECTORY SERVICES

If you often need to search for people on directory services, you can add to Address Book's preconfigured list of directory services to increase your chances of finding whom you're looking for. You can also remove directory services that you don't find useful. And if you use more than one directory service to check names when sending e-mail, you can change the order in which Address Book and Outlook Express check the directory services.

To add a directory service, follow these steps:

1. Choose Tools ➤ Accounts. Address Book displays the Directory Service page of the Internet Accounts dialog box.

2. Click the Add button. Address Book starts the Internet Directory Server Name feature of the Internet Connection Wizard.

3. Enter the address of the directory server (for example, ldap .yahoo.com for the Yahoo! directory server) in the Internet Directory (LDAP) Server text box.

4. If you have to log on to your LDAP server before you can use it, select the My LDAP Server Requires Me to Log On check box. When you click the Next button, the Internet Connection Wizard displays the Internet Directory Server Logon panel. Enter your account name and password, and select the Log On Using Secure Password Authentication check box if necessary.

5. Click the Next button. The Internet Connection Wizard displays the Check E-mail Addresses panel. Select the Yes option button if you want to use this directory service to check e-mail addresses. (The No option button is selected by default. This isn't a good idea for conventional e-mail use.)

6. Click the Next button to proceed to the Congratulations panel of the Internet Connection Wizard. Click the Finish button. The Wizard closes itself.

Address Book adds the directory service to the list on the Directory Service page of the Internet Accounts dialog box under a name based on its address. To give the directory service a descriptive name, select the directory service and click the Properties button to display its Properties dialog box (shown below). Enter the descriptive name in the upper text box and click the OK button.

CONTINUED ➡

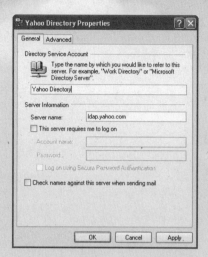

On the General page of the Properties dialog box, you can also change whether you log on to the LDAP server, what your account name and password are, whether you use Secure Password Authentication, and whether Outlook Express checks names against the server when sending e-mail. The Advanced page offers further options, including the maximum number of matches to return from the directory service and whether to use a search base (a grouping) in the directory service.

To change the order in which Outlook Express uses the directory servers when checking names against them, click the Set Order button in the Internet Accounts dialog box. In the resulting Directory Services Order dialog box, use the Move Up button and Move Down button to arrange the accounts into the appropriate order, and then click the OK button.

Part iii

WHAT'S NEXT

This chapter has discussed how to use Address Book for storing and managing contact information. As you've seen, Address Book is limited compared to professional contact management packages, but it provides enough capabilities for most home and home-office use. And the price is right.

Now that you have learned how to get around on the Internet, you might be thinking about publishing your own content there. In the next chapter, Robert Cowart explains Web publishing.

Chapter 18

PUBLISHING ON THE WEB

The Web is a very democratic environment. Unlike newspaper and TV, on the Web everyone can have a voice. All you need to do is create a Web page and upload it to a Web server, and suddenly millions of people all over the world have access to your ideas, opinions, and products/services for sale.

There are entire books written about creating Web sites (that is, collections of Web pages), and I can't hope to make you an expert in a single chapter here. However, I'll review the basic concepts of Web page creation, show you how to create them in Microsoft Word, explain how to use XP's integrated Web publishing feature, and help you choose a Web server on which to publish your pages. I'll also point you toward some resources for making your Web pages more sophisticated when you're ready to take that next step.

Adapted from *Mastering Windows Me* by Robert Cowart
ISBN 0-4821-2857-2   960 pages $39.99

UNDERSTANDING WEB PUBLISHING

One of my favorite things about the World Wide Web is that it was not created by a marketing person; no one with an MBA thought up this business model and then set out to make millions by building a world-wide ad agency. Instead, the Web was created by a group of physicists in Switzerland because they wanted to share their technical diagrams with other scientists. Prior to the Web, most of the information on the Internet was text, and it wasn't even formatted (no fancy fonts, no colored text, not even bold and italics). The creation of the Web in the early 1990s changed all that, making it possible to display images and—later—sound, animation, and video on the Internet. But the Web still suffers from the fact that it was born as a practical solution to a scientific problem—and even its creators could not have predicted its impact.

Today, the Web is the fastest growing part of the Internet and the most dynamic; it's a place where you can create information and make it available to nearly everyone else on the Internet. This brings me to an important distinction that often confuses people. The Web is not the Internet—it's part of the Internet, just as e-mail is part of the Internet. What makes e-mail and the Web so important is that they are the most universally accessible parts of the online world.

Another important thing to understand is that no one "owns" the Internet. It works as a cooperative arrangement among an international group of private and public organizations and individuals. The two organizations that come closest to acting as governing bodies for the Web are the Internet Network Information Center (InterNIC), which manages *domain name* registration, and the World Wide Web Consortium (W3C), which sets HTML standards.

NOTE

The World Wide Web is still in its infancy. Design rules and even the language used to create Web pages are continually changing and evolving. To stay abreast of the latest technical standards, keep an eye on the World Wide Web Consortium at www.w3c.com.

Web Publishing Terminology

Let's start out by reviewing some terms that may or may not be familiar to you from your previous exposure to the Internet. You learned in Chapter 15 about Web pages, Web sites, and hyperlinks. You also learned how you can jump from page to page using hyperlinks or enter Web addresses directly into your Web browsing program. Here are a few more key concepts:

HTML   Stands for *Hypertext Markup Language*. This is the file format for most Web pages. Depending on the program you use to create your Web pages, you may have the choice between saving in HTML format or Web Page format; they are the same thing.

NOTE

There are other, more sophisticated page formats that some Web browsers can display, such as CGI, XML, DHTML, MHT, and XPML. They are primarily for professional Web designers creating sophisticated, interactive Web sites, online stores, and secure database and ordering systems, however. As a beginning Web page artist, you will work with plain-vanilla HTML format.

Web server   A computer that's connected to the Internet full-time and whose job it is to provide access to Web pages stored on it. Your ISP has a Web server, and you probably are allowed a certain amount of free space on it. However, there may be limitations or restrictions, such as no business use or no more than a certain number of visitors per day.

Web host   A company that specializes in renting Web server space. Your ISP might also function as a Web host, but you are free to contract with a Web hosting company separate from your ISP to host your Web site if your hosting needs exceed those provided for free by your ISP.

URL   Stands for *Uniform Resource Locator*. It is the unique address pointing to a particular Web site and usually includes the address of the Web server on which the page is stored. For example, if your ISP's domain name is `Iquest.net` and you're using the free space provided with your account, your Web page's URL might be `www.iquest.net/members/~yourname`.

Domain name   A unique Web address such as `www.something.com`. You can buy the rights to a particular domain name for about $70 for two years. You don't need your own Web server in order to have a domain name; when you contract with a Web hosting company, they will take charge of your domain name and redirect users to your Web site on their server automatically. Using a domain name is optional; it makes more sense for businesses than for individuals.

Other Uses for HTML Documents

As you learned in Chapter 15, HTML is a document format consisting of plain text plus coding that applies formatting to it. This makes it an ideal format for sharing documents across different kinds of computers, such as Macs, PCs, and Unix machines. Increasingly, people are beginning to use HTML as a word processing format when compatibility is important. Most modern word processing programs, for example, Microsoft Word, Corel WordPerfect, and Lotus WordPro, can seamlessly open and save HTML files. Other programs, too—not just word processors—can save in HTML format; so you can create content in programs such as Microsoft PowerPoint or Microsoft Excel and then share that content in HTML format with others who don't have those programs installed on their PCs.

HTML has also become a popular format for sending formatted e-mail messages. Most e-mail programs these days can display HTML coding in an e-mail message; in fact, when you format e-mail in Outlook Express, the formatting is a variation of HTML, called MHT (which stands for mail HTML).

CHOOSING YOUR WEB PAGE CREATION PROGRAM

If you're just starting out with Web page creation (and I'm assuming that's the case in this chapter), you will probably not want to go out and spring for a $500 Web site creation program. Instead, you'll want to ease into the process by creating a few pages with a program that you already have.

There are two types of Web page creation programs: *text editors* and *WYSIWYG (what you see is what you get)*.

You can use any text editor to create an HTML file, including Notepad. Just create a plain text file and save it with an .htm extension. You type the text, enter the coding in angle brackets, and off you go. Unfortunately, you need to be a real programmer in order to do this because it requires knowledge of the HTML language. You have to know precisely where all those codes and brackets go.

More popular and practical for the nonprogrammer is a WYSIWYG program, in which you apply formatting just as you would in a word processor. Then when you save, it converts all that formatting to the needed HTML coding automatically for you.

Do you already have a WYSIWYG Web page creation program? Probably. As I mentioned earlier in the chapter, almost all programs these days have a "Save as HTML" or "Save as Web Page" feature. That means you can use a word processor, a desktop publishing program, or even a spreadsheet or database program to generate Web content.

If you have Microsoft Office, you have Microsoft Word, the leading word processor in the world, which happens to create very nice, amateur-quality Web pages. I'll show you how to use it for Web page creation later in this chapter. Microsoft Publisher also does a good job of creating Web sites.

Some versions of Microsoft Office also come with Microsoft Front-Page, a very powerful tool for creating professional-quality Web sites. If you are fortunate enough to have this program available, you might want to explore its capabilities. There's more to FrontPage than I can tell you about here, but you might like to read *Mastering Microsoft FrontPage 2002 Premium Edition* by Peter Weverka and Molly E. Holzschlag (Sybex, 2001) or *Microsoft FrontPage 2002 Simply Visual* (Sybex, 2001).

NOTE

Windows 98 (the original version, not 98 SE) came with FrontPage Express, a stripped-down version of FrontPage designed for creating simple Web pages. However, Windows Me and Windows XP do not include it.

Some Web professionals turn up their noses at FrontPage, for two reasons. One is that in order to use the Web sites created with FrontPage, the server that hosts them must support FrontPage extensions. This is usually not a big deal, since most Web hosts offer this capability. The other reason is that FrontPage, in its push toward making formatting simple for the non-technical user, internalizes a lot of the formatting and layout functions, thus creating nonstandard HTML that an expert user can't fully control. For example, in a normal HTML document, all the formatting is controlled by text codes in angle brackets such as <b> and <i>. But in FrontPage, formatting is applied through themes (similar to the themes in Windows XP), and the individual formatting of a particular theme is not easily editable. That's why people who are real experts with HTML don't like FrontPage.

When you're ready to move up to the Web site creation tools that professionals use, consider Macromedia Dreamweaver. It creates "pure HTML" files that Web experts prefer and is the top choice of the people who create the sites for large corporations.

CREATING A WEB PAGE IN WORD

Since so many people have Microsoft Word as their word processing program, I'd like to spend a little time looking at it as a Web page creation device, even though it's not, strictly speaking, a part of Windows XP. With Word 2002, you can even create a multipage site, in which all the pages are connected by a navigation bar containing links to each of the other pages.

Starting a New Web Page in Word 2002

Let's begin with something very basic: a simple, one-page Web site in Word. You can start with a blank page, or you can use one of the Web templates supplied with Word that provide preset formatting and placeholder text. In the following steps, just as an example, I'll show you one of the templates.

1. Start Microsoft Word (Start ➢ All Programs ➢ Microsoft Word).

2. Choose File ➢ New. Click the General Templates link in the New From Template section of the New Document panel. Select the Web Pages tab, and then double-click Right-Aligned Column.

A sample Web page appears, ready for your customization, as shown in Figure 18.1.

You can do several different things:

▶ Replace the picture with an image of your own (select it and use the Insert ➢ Picture command, then select one of the import options).

▶ Delete the existing text and type your own.

> ▶ Use the formatting commands and toolbar buttons in Word to add different fonts, boldface and italic, bulleted lists, different text alignments, and so on.

> ▶ Change the sizes of the panes by dragging the gray lines. (The particular layout in our example uses a Word table to organize the text into multiple panes.)

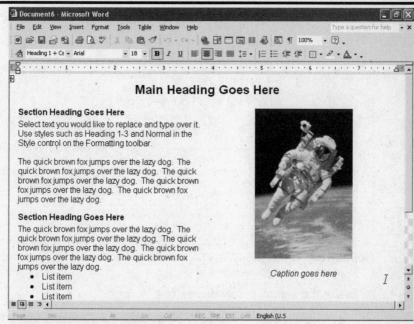

FIGURE 18.1: A Web page template in Word

Creating a Multipage Site

If you want a Web site that contains multiple pages linked together, use the Web Page Wizard instead of one of the other templates when creating your new document in Word. This creates several pages, and adds a navigation bar to link them. Figure 18.2 shows such a site created and ready for your customization.

Navigation Bar for Moving Among Pages

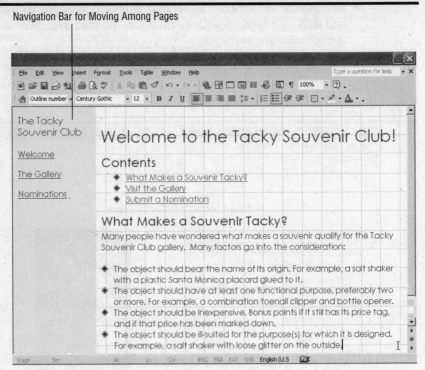

FIGURE 18.2: A multipage Web site created in Word

To use the wizard, follow these steps:

1. In Word, choose File ➢ New. Click the General Templates link in the New from Template section of the New Document pane. Select the Web Pages tab and double-click Web Page Wizard.

2. Click Next to begin.

3. Enter the title for your Web site in the Web Site Title box. This name will appear in the title bar when people use a Web browser to view your site.

4. Confirm the name shown in the Web Site Location box. By default the folder to be created matches the title you entered in Step 3, but you can change it if desired. Then click Next.

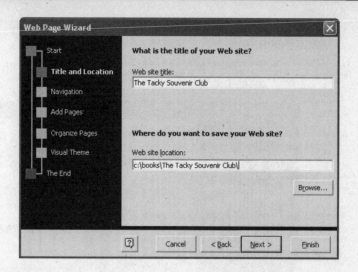

TIP

Make a note of the full path; you will need to know it later when you are ready to transfer the Web site to a server.

5. Choose the type of navigation bar you want for the site, and then click Next.

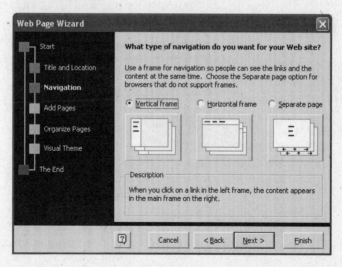

6. If you want more pages in the site than currently appear, add them to the list.

   ▶ To add more blank pages, click Add New Blank Page as many times as needed.

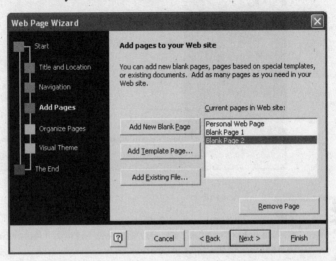

   ▶ To add a template page, click Add Template Page and choose the template you want. The names of the templates appear in a dialog box, and behind it, a preview of the selected template page appears.

   ▶ To add an existing file as a page, click Add Existing File and choose the file you want to use; then click Open.

7. To remove a page from the list, select it and click Remove Page.

8. When you are happy with the number of pages, and the template for each one, click Next.

9. Next, arrange the order of the pages. Click a page, and then click the Move Up or Move Down button to move it on the list.

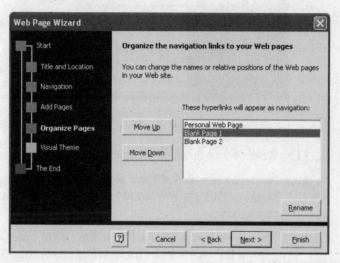

NOTE

Since Web site pages can be viewed in any order, it isn't critical to arrange all pages in a sequential order. However, the order you choose in Step 9 will be the order in which pages appear on the navigation bar; so if you have a preference in that regard, set it here. The top page on the list will be your starting page, or your home page.

10. You will probably want to give each page a more meaningful name than the template name. Click it, and then click Rename. Type a new name in the Rename Hyperlink dialog box, and then click OK.

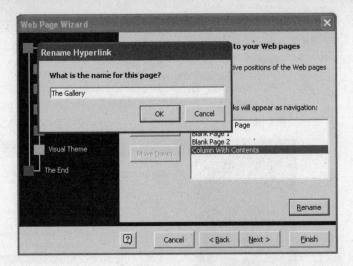

11. When you are finished arranging and naming pages, click Next.

12. Next, you're asked about a visual theme. These are like the Desktop Themes in Windows; they apply a set of formatting to your site.

    Choose No Visual Theme if you don't want one. Or, to apply a theme, click the Browse Themes button. Then select a theme in the dialog box that appears and click OK to return.

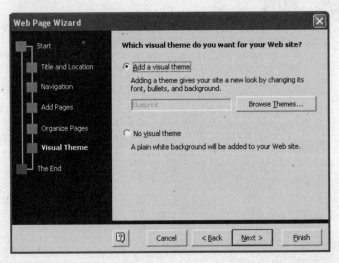

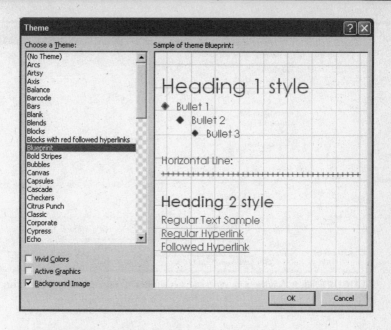

13. Click Next, and then Finish. Your Web site is created in Word.

14. Customize it by adding your own text and formatting. Then see the next section to save your work.

Saving in Web Format

If you create a Web page (or multipage site) using one of Word's Web templates or the Web Page Wizard, you can simply click the Save button on the toolbar or choose File ➢ Save. Word will automatically display the Web-enabled version of the Save As dialog box.

You can also save any existing Word document in Web format by using the File ➢ Save as Web Page command.

From the Save As dialog box, shown in Figure 18.3, you save the same as with any other document, except for one extra feature: the Change Title button. Click it and enter a title if desired (for the title bar). This will already be filled in correctly if you used the Web Page Wizard.

If you need to save with any special options, such as greater backward-compatibility with old Web browsers prior to Internet Explorer 6.0, click the Tools button in the Save As dialog box and choose Web Options from the menu that appears. In that dialog box you can fine-tune the Web format in which your work is saved.

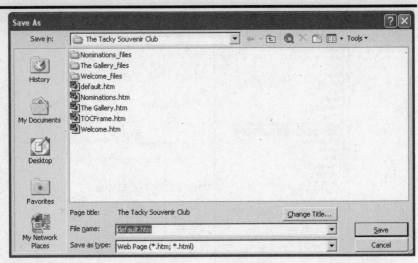

FIGURE 18.3: Saving as a Web page is similar to saving in any other program.

Formatting Text on a Web Page

Formatting text on a Web page is about as easy as formatting text in a word processor. You have similar options, too, such as boldface and italic, indenting, creating lists, and changing size and alignment.

Besides the normal formatting, there are a few formatting capabilities that are especially valuable when working with Web pages in Word. The following sections outline them.

Applying a Visual Theme

You saw earlier when using the Web Page Wizard that you can select a visual theme for formatting your Web page/Web site in Word. But you can also apply these visual themes at any time, to any Web page, even ones that you have created from scratch or by saving existing Word documents in Web format. To do so, choose Format ➤ Theme. The same Theme dialog box appears that you saw earlier. Choose the theme you want and click OK.

Not all of the themes are installed by default when you install Microsoft Word. If you choose a theme that is not yet installed, an Install button will appear instead of a preview of the theme. Have your Word or Office XP CD ready in your drive, and then click Install and follow the prompts to install it.

Applying Web Styles

Most formatting on the Web is based on styles. For example, there's a Heading 1 style, a Heading 2 style, and so on. If you want to make a particular paragraph into a heading, rather than manually apply a certain formatting to it, you can simply apply a Heading style. To do so, follow these steps:

1. Position the insertion point within the paragraph you want to apply a style to.

2. Open the Styles drop-down list on the Formatting toolbar (the left-most list) and choose a style. Or choose Format ➤ Styles and Formatting to open the new Styles and Formatting task pane.

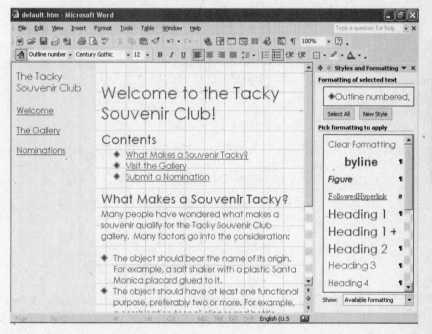

TIP

Only a few styles appear on the list by default. There are many more HTML-based styles you can apply. To see them, hold down the Shift key when you open the Styles drop-down list.

Creating Graphical Bulleted Lists

A popular and attractive trend on Web pages is to use little graphics as bullet characters instead of the traditional round, plain bullets.

To set this up, do the following:

1. Select the paragraphs that you want to make bulleted.

2. Choose Format ➤ Bullets and Numbering.

3. Click the Bulleted tab, select any style, click the Customize button, and click the Picture button. The Picture Bullet dialog box appears.

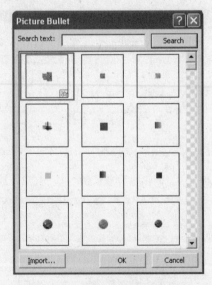

4. Click the graphical bullet you want to use and click OK twice. The bullet is applied to the selected paragraphs.

 For your added convenience, the next time you click the Bullets button on the toolbar, the bullet you just chose will be the default one to appear until you start a new document or choose a different bullet character.

Adding Images to Web Pages

No matter how compelling your text is, the images on your Web page almost always get the most attention. You can add pictures to a Web page the same way you add pictures to a regular word processing document.

1. Place your cursor in the area of your Web page where you want your image to appear.

2. Choose Insert ➤ Picture ➤ From File.

NOTE

You can also insert pictures from the Microsoft Clip Organizer, scanner, or camera. Other types of artwork may also be quickly inserted by choosing Organizational Chart, AutoShapes, WordArt, or Chart.

3. Locate and select the picture you want to use.

4. Click Insert.

To use artwork from Word's extensive Clip Organizer, choose Insert ➤ Picture ➤ Clip Art. The Insert Clip Art task pane appears. Locate and insert the clip you want.

Creating Hyperlinks

The magic of the World Wide Web is the interactive feature known as *links* (sometimes called *hyperlinks*). Links enable a viewer to move from one piece of information (a section of text or an image) to another at the click of a mouse. You can set links to other pages within your Web site or to other Web sites on the Internet.

You can have either text or graphical hyperlinks. Text hyperlinks are underlined; graphical hyperlinks look like any other graphic. But when you hover your mouse pointer over them in a Web browser, the mouse pointer turns to a hand, indicating that clicking the item will take you somewhere else.

Click here for the church's monthly calendar of activities

To insert a hyperlink, follow these steps:

1. Choose Insert ➤ Hyperlink, or click the Insert Hyperlink button on the toolbar. The Insert Hyperlink dialog box appears.

2. The text in the Text to Display box is the text that you highlighted (if any) before selecting the command. If you would like to change it, make your change here.

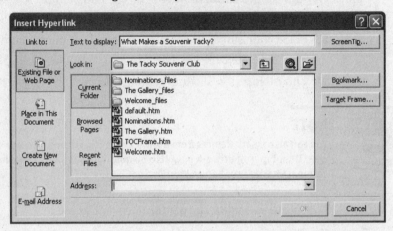

3. Type the desired address in the Address box. This can be the URL of a Web page or the name and path of a locally stored file.

   If you don't know the name or path of the file you want, you can use the following tools to help you enter it:

   ▶ Click a category on the Link To bar to select what type of hyperlink this should be (for example, to an Existing File or Web Page or to a Place in This Document). The other controls in the dialog box change based on your selection here.

   ▶ If you chose Existing File or Web Page, use the Look In drop-down list to navigate to a page on your computer or network.

   ▶ To find a page on the Web, click the small globe icon to the right of the Look In drop-down list. This opens your Web browser, and you can use it to find the page you want. When you've found it, switch back to Word and the URL will be entered automatically.

4. (Optional) If you want certain text to display when the user hovers the mouse pointer over the item, click the ScreenTip button and enter the text for that purpose, then click OK to return.

5. Click OK to create the hyperlink.

Choosing Where to Host Your Pages

As I mentioned at the beginning of the chapter, you'll need a way to put your Web pages online. Unless you work at a big company with its own site or are at a university that provides access to its Web server, you'll probably need a commercial service provider to host your site. The ISP that you use for your Internet connection might provide a limited amount of Web hosting space for free. If you're not sure if your account includes this feature, you should be able to find out by visiting your ISP's Web site or by calling the ISP's technical support or sales office.

However, the free space provided by your ISP might be subject to some limitations. For example, you might not be able to post commercial material there, or you might not be able to use your own domain name if you have one. Therefore, you might find yourself shopping for a Web hosting company in addition to your ISP. There are thousands of companies out there who would like your Web hosting business.

If you just want to post a few personal pages (or even a few dozen), you don't need much server space, so price will probably be the overriding factor in your decision. However, if you want to post an ambitious commercial venture that you expect will draw millions of visits, you'll need to be more particular. (Of course, if you're creating such a site, you are doubtless working with a professional Web designer who will likely have some suggestions as to good Web hosting companies.) The following sections outline some things to look for when choosing a host for your Web page.

Part iii

NOTE

If you want to find a server anywhere in the world, the site called *The Directory* lists more than 10,000 Internet service providers and bulletin board services in 120 countries. Check them out at this URL: www.thedirectory.org.

How Much Do They Charge?

Comparing the pricing among service providers is like comparing long-distance telephone companies. They don't all charge for their services in the same way, so finding out who really has the best deal for you can be difficult. Before you choose a service provider, get a good start on your development plan so you know what kinds of services you'll need. Then look around for the provider that offers the best combination of services for the best price. (Your answers to the other questions in this section will help you understand your options.) You may decide, for example, that 24-hour technical support is worth a little more per month. On the other hand, if you don't plan to sell any products online, you won't want to pay the extra cost for a server that supports secure transactions.

Charges vary dramatically from as little as five dollars per month to hundreds per month. Why should you pay that much? You shouldn't, unless you need tons of space for your site and you are attracting hundreds of thousands of visitors. (If you start getting that kind of attention to your Web site, you should be able to afford to move to a more expensive server, but you probably don't need to start out on one that costs that much. Remember, you can always upgrade later.)

Two basic charges are commonly associated with leasing Web space on a commercial server. The first is based on how much space you want; the second is based on how much traffic you attract (sometimes called *throughput*). The first charge is pretty straightforward. For the base rate of, say, $20 per month, you might get 10MB of space. If you decide later that you need another 5MB, that will probably cost you about $5 more per month. It's a little like renting an office: the more square feet, the more it costs.

NOTE

10 or 20MB of space on a Web server may not sound like much in a world where new computers come with 20 or 30GB hard drives. But on the Web, you want all your files to be as small as possible so they load as quickly as possible for your users; and a site with a few hundred pages and graphics may still be less than 10MB if it's designed efficiently. The one exception to this is if your site features software programs for viewers to download large images, video, or sound files. These types of files are inherently larger and will require more disk space. As a general rule, you should be able to start with minimal server space because you can always add more space later. Just make sure you've made arrangements with your service provider to add more space as you need it.

There are additional charges you may face as well, such as paying more to use your own domain name. You almost undoubtedly have to pay more if you want a Web server that supports secure commerce transactions. Security is a complicated issue on the Web, but mostly it deals with *encryption* (a process of encoding and decoding messages so they are harder to intercept). The more secure the system, the more it usually costs. Getting clear on the kinds of services that are important to you, such as secure transactions, will make sorting through the pricing structures used by different service providers easier.

Do They Provide Technical Support?

Technical support can be crucial. Each server has different features and limitations, and knowing how to use the service can be hard if you can't reach anyone who can explain it. Some service providers have knowledgeable technical support people on call 24 hours a day; others may never answer the phone. A good test is to call several service providers you are considering and see how long it takes them to respond to your initial questions. If you have trouble finding out how to buy their services, you'll probably have even more trouble getting help after they have your money.

Technical support is almost always available by e-mail. It's best if the service provider offers it both ways (that is, phone and e-mail). Some questions (especially as you get more experience) are easily and conveniently handled by e-mail. At other times, you will want a person to talk you through a problem. E-mail is also important if the service provider is not local, because it saves long-distance phone charges. Most service providers also have a FAQ (frequently asked questions) page, a great place to get answers to common questions and find out the common problems users are having.

TIP

Although you should expect your service provider to give you basic assistance, such as helping you understand the specific aspects of its system and how to log on to its server, very few will provide help with HTML development or CGI scripts unless you pay extra. A service provider that employs lots of people to answer your questions may be more expensive than it's worth. Hiring your own consultant to help you sort out how to build your Web site could mean you can choose a cheaper service provider and save money in the long run.

How Reliable Are They?

Your site is up and running. Thousands of people are visiting every day, ordering products, and chatting in the online discussion area. Then, all of a sudden, *crash!* The entire system goes down, and no one can get to your Web site.

This scenario is almost inevitable. Computers crash; systems fail. Don't panic, but keep in mind that some systems crash more frequently than others and some take a lot longer to get up and running again. Ask your service provider about its track record. How often does its system fail? How long does it usually take to get back online? Does the hosting company have technical staff on call 24 hours a day to fix the things that go wrong in the middle of the night? If reliability is important to you, make sure you check out the company's reputation for staying up and running.

Try to ask some of the company's other customers how happy they are. But be aware that running a Web server is a relatively new business, and it's not an easy one. Most service providers suffer growing pains. I've seen this happen with many companies. A new service provider opens up; it gets great equipment, a friendly staff, and a fast connection to the Internet; and it quickly becomes the favorite in town. Then it gets swamped. The service attracts new customers too quickly to keep up with the demand. For a while, the service goes down the tubes: It can't answer all its phone calls, its systems crash too often because it's overloaded, and everyone complains. Then the company catches up, hires more staff, adds phone lines, and gets better equipment, and the service improves dramatically. This is a common scenario. The challenge is to make sure you come in after the company has upgraded and not while it's in the middle of growing pains. Ask around and see how the company is doing, but be sure to check with current customers, not just old ones who may have left before things were improved.

Be sure to talk to more than one customer, especially those you know. Some people will complain about anything. If, for example, the person complains that "it's too slow," ask them to be more specific. Is it that their Web pages take too long to download, or is it that the technical staff are too slow in returning phone calls? Then ask what tests the customer did to determine the cause of the problem. Remember, your goal is to find the best system for *your* needs. Assessing the validity of someone else's complaint can help you determine if you'll have the same problems.

How Many Web Sites Do They Serve, and How Much Traffic Do They Attract?

Viewers on a Web server are like cars on a freeway: The more people on the road, the longer it takes to get home. Service providers put as many as 100 Web sites on one server, sometimes more. But even if the server has only one other Web site, the entire system may slow down if that one site gets heavy traffic.

A Web server may have a fast connection to the Internet, but if the server hosts too many Web sites or if the sites attract a lot of traffic, you may find that it takes longer to download your Web pages, especially at peak times. If the service gets too busy, you may not be able to view your site at all; instead, you'll get an error message stating that the server is too busy and you should try again later. I hate to admit I learned this the hard way. I was in a demo with a client once and couldn't show them one of my Web sites because the service provider was overloaded. Once in a great while, this may be understandable, like the day Princess Diana died; there was so much activity on the Internet that service suffered in most places. But if your site is unavailable on a regular basis, you should definitely consider moving to a better Web hosting company.

On the other side of this issue, be aware that your service provider may charge you much higher rates if your Web site attracts too many viewers and slows down the system. Ask your provider about usage charges, and be prepared to upgrade in a hurry if you expect a large number of users.

A good way to test the speed of a server before you sign on is to visit a few of the Web sites already on the provider's server and compare loading times with other service providers. Note that the size of graphics and other files also affects speed, so try to compare similar HTML pages on each server to make a fair comparison. Most service providers feature a list of their customers, which makes finding sites on their server easy.

What Kind of Backup Systems Do They Have in Place?

Backup systems can be crucial on the Internet. Technical problems are common, and servers go down regularly. Many providers are not established well enough to have an alternate computer, an on-call technical staff, and an emergency power supply. But if you *must* ensure that your Web site is always available, then you must pay for a high-end server with backup systems in place.

Moreover, you should always keep a backup of your own Web site yourself. You can do this simply by keeping a copy of the Web site files on your hard drive (something you may already be doing if that's where you created them). If other people are working on your site, always get copies of their work in case you need it again. You can also create a backup by downloading the new pages and images to your computer, using an FTP program such as WS_FTP.

Do They Provide CGI Scripts and/or Limit the Use of Your Own Scripts?

Many service providers offer common CGI scripts (image maps and basic forms, for example) to all their Web site clients and enable you to use your own scripts to add other functions to your Web site. Other providers may limit your use of scripts or may charge you to test them before they put them on the server. These providers are concerned about security issues and about the fact that a poorly written script can slow down the server and even cause it to crash. If programmers will be working on your site, ask them to check out the service provider to ensure that it accommodates the kind of Web site you want. If you don't have a programmer on staff, you may be especially interested in a service provider that provides the use of common scripts for setting up your own guest book or e-mail forms on your site. Ask the service provider what they have available, or check out their Web site for more information.

NOTE

CGI scripts are special programs that provide greater levels of interactivity than basic HTML. Features such as order forms, guest books, online discussion areas, and shopping systems are made possible by CGI scripts. These scripts are usually written in sophisticated programming languages such as Perl, C, or C++. Writing CGI scripts is much more complicated than creating HTML pages.

How Fast Are the Servers' Connections to the Internet?

The speed of a service provider's connection to the Internet affects how quickly your pages and graphics get to your viewers. The faster the connection, the better the server should perform. For example, a T3 line is faster than a T1 line, but the speed still depends on how many users are being served. Some service providers have more than one connection, allowing them to balance the traffic on their servers.

Do They Provide Security?

A secure server is called secure because the data being transmitted between the client and the server is encrypted. The level of encryption varies, depending on the type of service you use. Some common protocols include Secure Socket Layer (SSL), used by Netscape servers, and Pretty Good Privacy (PGP), used by Mosaic servers. Expect to pay considerably more for your Web space if you want a secure server. The current range is about $60 per month to $1,000 per month, and that only gets you the secure *server* software. If you want password access, for example, you probably have to do your own custom programming (with CGI scripts) to set it up. If you want to offer credit card transactions that will be verified online, you need a processing service such as Cybercash to handle the actual transaction.

Ask your service provider how much support you can expect with a secure server account. Are there trained staff people who can help you set up secure transactions? Do they recommend any consultants? Has the company made any special deals with other vendors who can process online transactions? If your provider has established a relationship with a company such as Cybercash or Checkfree, setting up your Web site may be easier and less expensive. Find out what kinds of support the company offers, whether any discounts come with its service, what exactly the company includes with its monthly rate, and what other costs you should expect to pay to set up the system you want.

Do They Recommend Consultants?

If you need a consultant to help with some or all of the development of your Web site, you may benefit from a service provider that recommends consultants or provides staff members who can help you. Finding a good consultant can be a challenging process and will be easier with a service provider that includes a referral service or staff to help you.

If you are planning to hire a consultant, it's great if you can consider the consultant's recommendations in your decision about where to put your Web site, but be sure you don't choose a service provider just because a consultant recommends it. Some consultants get commissions and other perks from service providers that may taint their judgment about what's best for you. A good consultant will research and recommend two or three service providers that meet your needs and then let you decide which is best for you.

Where Are They Located?

As you look for a server, keep in mind that unlike your dial-up connection—in which there's an advantage to having a local phone number, because it saves you long-distance phone charges—your Web server does not need to be in the same geographic location as you are. You can send files anywhere on the Internet, so your Web site can be almost anywhere. If you are in a small town or an isolated area with limited options, you may want to look beyond your neighborhood to find a better deal.

If you have the opportunity, however, check out the company's office. Visiting a service provider's facility is one of the best ways to assess how reliable that service may be. (It's impossible to determine if someone is running a server from a closet or from a large office just by viewing a Web site online.) Legitimate, reliable service providers should be open to letting you see their offices and equipment.

Publishing Your Web Pages to a Server

There are several ways to place your Web pages on the Web server that you chose in the preceding section. If the program that you use to create the Web pages allows it, you can save directly to the server. If not, you can transfer your pages using an FTP program, or using the Web Publishing Wizard in Windows XP.

Before starting, check with the Web hosting company you are using to find out which method they recommend. You will also need a username and password for access to the Web server, and if you're transferring the pages via FTP, you'll need an FTP address plus a separate FTP username and password.

Saving Directly to the Server

Professional-quality programs like Microsoft FrontPage have a Publish feature that you can use to automatically transfer your pages (and any changes in the future) to the Web server of your choice. Check the program's documentation for the specifics; in FrontPage 2002 the command is File ➢ Publish Web.

In Microsoft Office programs such as Word, PowerPoint, Publisher, and Excel 2002, you can save directly to the server via the Save As dialog box. It allows you to transfer either via the Web or via FTP. The Web method is easier, but because not all servers allow this type of transfer, some of you might be stuck with the FTP method.

As an example, let's look at how to save directly to a Web server in Word 2002.

1. Choose File ➤ Save as Web Page.

2. Open the Save In drop-down list and choose My Network Places.

3. Double-click Add Network Place. The Add Network Place Wizard runs.

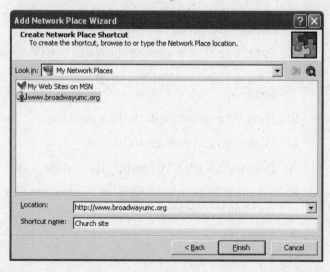

NOTE

If you do not see Add Network Place, try clicking the New Folder button.

4. Select Create a Shortcut to an Existing Network Place if a folder already exists on the Internet or an intranet server. Or select Create a New Network Place if you want to create a new folder on an Internet or intranet server. Then click Next.

5. Enter the URL for the Web site address to which you want to publish. Then click Finish.

Add Network Place Wizard

Create Network Place Shortcut
To create the shortcut, browse to or type the Network Place location.

Look in: My Network Places

My Web Sites on MSN
www.broadwayumc.org

Location: http://www.broadwayumc.org

Shortcut name: Church site

< Back   Finish   Cancel

Part iii

6. If a box appears asking what template you want to use, select one and click Finish.

7. If you have not earlier saved your username and password for this location, an Enter Network Password box appears. Enter your username and password for the Web server, and then click OK.

8. The location shown in the Save As dialog box is now the Web server. Continue saving normally.

In the future, you can skip a lot of this, because the shortcut will have already been set up; perform Steps 1 and 2, and then double-click the existing Network Place.

Saving via FTP within an Application

If the above steps didn't work for you, then perhaps the Web host you are using doesn't support this type of transfer. If that's the case, try the FTP method instead. If you are using a Microsoft Office application or another application that supports direct network access, you can use the following steps:

1. Choose File ➢ Save as Web Page.

2. Open the Save In drop-down list. If your FTP location already appears there, choose it and skip to Step 8. Otherwise, choose Add/Modify FTP Locations.

3. Type the FTP site name in the Name of FTP Site box.

4. Click the User button, and enter your username in the User text box.

5. Enter your password in the Password box.

6. Click Add, and then click OK.

7. Double-click the FTP location you just created.

8. On the FTP server, navigate to the folder where your Web host has instructed you to save files.

9. Click OK.

Using an FTP Program

If you have created your Web pages in a program that doesn't support direct transfer to the Web host, you can use an *FTP program* to transfer them. There are many FTP programs available as shareware, but one of my favorites is WS_FTP. You can download it at www.wsftp.com.

Each program works a little differently, but in WS_FTP, there are two file panes. The one on the left shows your local hard disk, and the one on the right shows the Web server to which you are connected. (You have to connect first, of course, using the FTP username and password provided by your Web hosting company.) Then you click the right-pointing arrow button to transfer the files. Figure 18.4 shows an example.

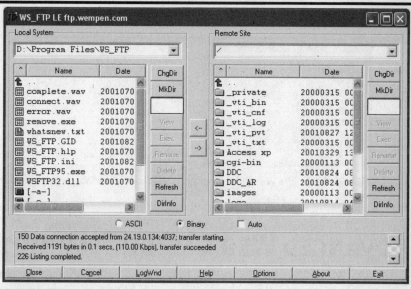

FIGURE 18.4: WS_FTP is a popular FTP program used for transferring Web content to a server.

WARNING

If you transfer via FTP, make sure you get all the associated files, too (graphics, etc.), not just the files with the .htm extensions. Otherwise, your pages will lack their graphical content. Usually all the associated files will be in the same folder as your HTML pages, or perhaps in a subfolder.

Part iii

Using the Web Publishing Wizard

The *Web Publishing Wizard* helps you transfer files or folders to a server. It has evolved from an afterthought buried deep inside the Programs folder to an integral part of My Computer. You'll find the Publish This Folder to the Web command listed under File and Folder tasks once your drive letter is opened. Click this link and the Web Publishing Wizard walks you step-by-step through the file transfer. The Wizard is self-explanatory, so I won't add a belabored explanation here.

If you don't have a service provider for Web hosting already set up, you can publish your files, free of charge, to MSN. Take advantage of the server space to upload Web pages, pictures, movies, and music files and share them with family and friends by choosing the Shared option, or keep your files private with the Personal option.

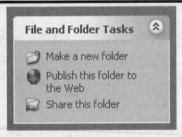

FIGURE 18.5: The Web Publishing Wizard feature is available in every folder.

ADVANCED WEB DESIGN TECHNIQUES

The World Wide Web is evolving to become a more dynamic and entertaining place, thanks to the addition of multimedia to many Web sites. Teaching you how to add multimedia content to your Web site is well beyond the scope of this book. I can, however, give you an overview of the kinds of multimedia features you could add, and direct you to informative Web sites where you can learn more about the technologies that appeal to you.

Animated GIFs

By far the most universally supported animation format is the *animated GIF*. These files are simply a series of GIF images run together to create the illusion of motion. Animated GIFs can be created in programs such as Microsoft's GIF Animator or BoxTop's GIFmation, a more powerful tool that retailed for $29.95 at the time of this writing.

Other technologies offer integrated video and sound as well as interactivity (all great features you can't get from an animated GIF), but these advantages come at a price. The main drawback of many of the following technologies is the requirement that your users have the most up-to-date software—the newest browsers or plug-ins.

Until recently, most nonanimated GIF technologies for animation delivery also required that the entire animation file be downloaded by the Web surfer before it could be viewed, which slowed things down even more. This is now rarely the case. All the technologies described in the following sections transmit frames in playable order, so as soon as the first few frames arrive on your browser, the animation begins to play. This is referred to in the industry as *streaming technology*.

All streaming technologies aren't necessarily identical, however. Animated GIFs, for instance, begin to play as soon as the first frame arrives. Technologies geared toward the delivery of more movie-like presentation (frame rates in excess of 12fps and nonlooping animations in excess of a few seconds) tend to hold the first frames in a buffer until enough frames have arrived to allow the entire movie to play smoothly. That means you can still notice a delay when the animations first load; still, they start playing much sooner than if the entire file had to be downloaded.

Multimedia Technologies for the Web

The following sections provide brief descriptions of the most popular technologies for delivering multimedia Web content.

Macromedia Shockwave for Director

Shockwave enables you to put Director files on a Web page. This is a big deal because Director is the most popular program around for creating CD-ROM multimedia titles, which means the program already has a large following and many people know how to use it. It also means you can create complex multimedia files, using animation, sound, video, and lots of interactive functionality.

Shockwave has proven to be one of the most popular plug-ins on the Web (more than 200 million people have downloaded it). The problem is bandwidth. Most files created for CD-ROMs are huge by Web standards, and consumers are spoiled by the quality and speed of CD-ROMs. Because of the bandwidth limitations on the Web, developers who create with Shockwave for Director are still limited to very simple projects.

To learn more about Shockwave, visit Macromedia's Web site: www .macromedia.com.

Macromedia Flash

Flash has won acclaim because it creates animations that download really fast. It also produces scalable, interactive animations with synchronized sound. All that, and you still get smaller file sizes than with any other animation technology on the Web. Flash files are dramatically faster to download because Flash images are vector-based. The term *vector-based* means the images are made up of coded instructions to draw specific geometric shapes, filled with specific colors. This takes far less space than the data needed for a *raster* image, such as those used by animated GIFs or JPEGs. As a result, Flash files can be significantly smaller than other types of images and animation files. An animated GIF that is 200K and takes about a minute to download on a 56K modem might be only 20K when recreated as a Flash animation.

The same problem that keeps many of these other technologies from reaching the masses hampers Flash as well: the need for a plug-in for viewing them. But Flash has a better chance than most of overcoming this obstacle because on one hand it creates files well-suited to the bandwidth-strapped Web, and on the other it's part of the Macromedia Shockwave suite, which is already one of the most popular plug-ins on the Web.

You can find out more about Flash at Macromedia's Web site: www.macromedia.com.

Apple QuickTime

QuickTime is a cross-platform format that enables you to create digital, real-time video content with synchronized sound for the Web. Because QuickTime content can include almost all types of popular multimedia formats (still images, sound, 3D virtual reality, and QuickTime VR), it's one of the most versatile delivery platforms for the Web. QuickTime content can now also be interactive. The latest version enables you to set links within a QuickTime file that can take users to a different segment of the movie or to a different Web address.

To learn more about QuickTime, visit www.apple.com/quicktime.

Java

Unless you've been hiding under a virtual rock, you know Java is not coffee on the Web. What makes Java special is that programs created in it can be run on any computer system. Usually, if you create a program in another programming language, such as C or C++ (from which Java was derived), you have to create one version for the Macintosh, another for the PC, and a third for the Unix operating system. But Java, created by Sun Microsystems, is a platform-independent programming language that can be used to create almost any kind of program, even something as complex as a word processing or spreadsheet program, and it will work on any type of computer. Java applets can be embedded in Web pages, used to generate entire Web pages, or run as stand-alone applications.

To learn more about Java, visit www.sun.com.

JavaScript

JavaScript is a subset of Java that was created by Netscape. JavaScript can be embedded into HTML pages to create basic animations and other interactive features. You won't get the complex functionality of Java, but JavaScript is a lot easier to create and can be used to deliver animated and interactive content over the Web without requiring plug-ins. Unlike Java, JavaScript doesn't produce stand-alone programs. JavaScript is often used in combination with other multimedia features, such as images or sound files, to add greater levels of interactivity.

For more on JavaScript, check out the JavaScript Guide at http://developer.netscape.com/docs/manuals/js/core/jsguide15/contents.html.

Dynamic HTML and Cascading Style Sheets

Essentially, Dynamic HTML (DHTML) is HTML with a kick. That kick comes from the power of adding scripting languages (usually JavaScript). Adding the power of a scripting language makes it possible to dynamically change the attributes of elements on a page without involving the server, which means features can change quickly because they don't require entire page reloads to take effect.

DHTML and its subsets—features such as Cascading Style Sheets (CSS), Layers, and Filters—will provide great design power on the Web in the future. Unfortunately, today these features are supported only by the latest browsers and even then, don't display the same way on, say, Netscape Navigator as they do on Internet Explorer. As a result, this is a great technology to watch but not one that makes much sense to use today.

A great place to learn more about DHTML is at www.projectcool.com. You can also find information about DHTML at www.dhtml-zone.com.

WHAT'S NEXT

Windows XP Home Edition offers unprecedented support for connecting to other computers via the Internet. Not only can you surf the Web, and publish your own content to it, but you can establish remote connections with individual PCs or servers in remote locations. In the next chapter, Guy Hart-Davis explains Windows' remote connection features.

Chapter 19

REMOTE DESKTOP CONNECTION AND REMOTE ASSISTANCE

This chapter discusses two of the remote-connection technologies built into Windows XP Home Edition: Remote Desktop Connection and Remote Assistance.

Remote Desktop Connection lets you connect to a remote computer over the Internet and work at it as if you were sitting in front of it locally. This might come in handy if you needed to connect to your work computer from home, for example. To take advantage of this feature, you must have Windows XP Professional installed on the PC to which you want to remotely connect.

Adapted from *Mastering Windows XP Home Edition* by Guy Hart-Davis

ISBN 0-7821-2980-3   1024 pages $39.99

Remote Assistance provides a secure way to get help from a friend or other helper at a distance (or to give them help). You invite the helper to connect remotely to your computer, which lets them view your screen and see what the problem is. You decide whether to chat with them (via text or voice) and implement their suggestions—which keeps you secure—or to let them control your computer remotely and take the actions they deem necessary (which is not secure). It works with all versions of Windows XP.

Using Remote Desktop Connection

This section discusses what Remote Desktop Connection is, what it does, and how to use it.

What Is Remote Desktop Connection For?

Remote Desktop Connection lets you connect via a dial-up connection, via a local area network connection, or across the Internet, and take control of somebody's computer (or your own).

Remote Desktop Connection is designed to let you access and control one computer (say, your work computer) from another computer (say, your home computer or your laptop). It's great for catching up with the office when you're at home, or for grabbing the files that you forgot to load on your laptop before you dived into the taxi for the airport.

You can also use Remote Desktop Connection for other purposes, such as helping a friend or family member find their way out of a computing problem from a distance. It's not really designed for this, though, and you'd do better to use Windows XP's Remote Assistance feature, which is designed for precisely that. Similarly, Remote Desktop Connection is not good for collaboration, because only one user can be working with the computer at a time. For collaboration, visit the next chapter, which discusses the NetMeeting collaboration package.

Remote Desktop Connection Terminology and Basics

Remote Desktop Connection terminology is a little confusing. Here are the terms:

▶ The *home computer* is the computer on which you're working. The home computer needs to have Remote Desktop Connection installed. Remote Desktop Connection is installed by default in Windows XP Home Edition.

▶ The *remote computer* is the computer that you're accessing from the home computer. The remote computer needs to have Remote Desktop installed. Remote Desktop is separate from Remote Desktop Connection and is included in Windows XP Professional and the (forthcoming, at this writing) versions of Windows XP Server. Remote Desktop is not included in Windows XP Home Edition.

So the typical scenario is for the home computer to be running Windows XP Home and the remote computer to be running Windows XP Professional. You can also access one Windows XP Professional computer from another Windows XP Professional computer.

NOTE

You can access more than one remote computer at a time from the same home computer. Unless you have impressive bandwidth, though, this results in slow sessions.

In order for you to be able to connect to another computer via Remote Desktop Connection, any active session (whether local or connected via another Remote Desktop Connection) on that computer needs to be disconnected. You get a warning about this, but the other user doesn't. If you choose to proceed, the remote computer displays the Welcome screen while your Remote Desktop Connection session is going on. There's no easy way for anyone looking at that computer to tell that you're remotely connected to it.

Part iii

If a user comes back and starts using the remote computer while your Remote Desktop Connection session is going on, your session will be terminated—with warning on their side, this time, but not on yours. Frankly, this could be more elegant.

In lay terms, Remote Desktop Connection works as follows:

▶ Keystrokes and mouse clicks are transmitted from the home computer to the remote computer via the display protocol. The remote computer registers these keystrokes and clicks as if they came from the keyboard attached to it.

▶ Programs run on the remote computer as usual. (Programs aren't run across the wire—that would be desperately slow.)

▶ Screen display information is passed to the home computer, again via the display protocol. This information appears on the display as if it came from the video adapter (only rather more slowly, and usually in a window).

Sound can be passed to the home computer as well, so that you can hear what's happening at the remote computer. Transferring sound like this enhances the impression of controlling the remote computer, but sound takes so much bandwidth that transferring it isn't a good idea on slow connections. The default Remote Desktop Connection setting is to transfer sound, but you may well want to switch it off.

Setting the Remote Computer to Accept Incoming Connections

The first step in getting Remote Desktop Connection to work is to set the remote computer to accept incoming connections. Remember that this is the computer that's remote from you and that's running Windows XP Professional (or Server).

To set your remote computer to accept incoming connections, take these steps:

1. Display the System Properties dialog box in whichever way you find easiest. For example, press Winkey+Break. Or click the Start button to display the Start menu, right-click the My Computer link, and choose Properties from the context menu.

2. Click the Remote tab. Windows displays the Remote page (shown in Figure 19.1).

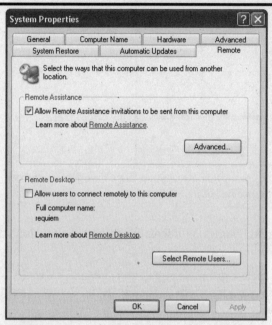

FIGURE 19.1: On the Remote page of the System Properties dialog box for the remote computer, select the Allow Users to Connect Remotely to This Computer check box to tell your computer to accept incoming calls.

3. To allow users to connect to your computer, select the Allow Users to Connect Remotely to This Computer check box.

4. To specify which users may connect via Remote Desktop Connection, click the Select Remote Users button. Windows displays the Remote Desktop Users dialog box (shown in Figure 19.2). The list box shows any users currently allowed to connect to the computer. Below the list box is a note indicating that you (identified by your username) already have access—as you should have.

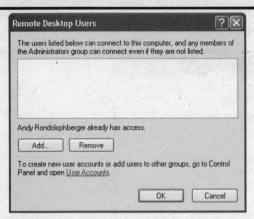

FIGURE 19.2: You can use the Remote Desktop Users dialog box to restrict Remote Desktop use to specified users.

5. Click the Add button. Windows displays the Select Users dialog box.

6. Select a user or group as usual, and then click the OK button. Windows adds them to the list in the Remote Desktop Users dialog box.

7. Add further users or groups as necessary.

8. To remove a user or a group, select them in the list box and click the Remove button.

9. Click the OK button. Windows closes the Remote Desktop Users dialog box.

10. Click the OK button in the System Properties dialog box. Windows closes the dialog box and applies your changes.

The remote computer is all set. Leave it up and running and return to the home computer.

NOTE

There's one other thing that you might need to do on the remote computer—but it's something that you'll almost certainly have done already: Apply a password to any user account that will be used to access the computer via Remote Desktop Connection. See Chapter 11 for information about password-protecting a user account.

Choosing Settings for Remote Desktop Connection

Next, choose settings for Remote Desktop Connection on the home computer. Remote Desktop Connection has a modestly large number of settings, but many of them are set-and-forget. Even better, you can save sets of settings so that you can quickly apply them for accessing different remote computers (or the same remote computer under different circumstances, such as when the cable modem is working and when it's flaked out on you).

To choose settings for Remote Desktop Connection, follow these steps:

1. Choose Start ➤ All Programs ➤ Accessories ➤ Communications ➤ Remote Desktop Connection. Windows starts Remote Desktop Connection and displays the Remote Desktop Connection window in its reduced state (shown in Figure 19.3).

FIGURE 19.3: The Remote Desktop Connection window appears first in its reduced state.

2. Click the Options button. Windows displays the rest of the Remote Desktop Connection window.

3. The General page of the Remote Desktop Connection window (shown in Figure 19.4) offers these options:

    Computer drop-down list Enter the name or the IP address of the computer to which you want to connect; or select it from the drop-down list; or click the Browse for More item from the drop-down list to display the Browse for Computers dialog box, then select the computer in that.

    User Name text box Enter the username under which you want to connect to the remote computer. Windows enters your username by default.

FIGURE 19.4: The General page of the expanded Remote Desktop Connection window

Password text box   If you want to store your password (for the remote computer) for the connection, enter it in this text box and select the Save My Password check box. If you don't enter your password here, you get to enter it when logging on to the remote computer.

Domain text box   If the remote computer is part of a domain, enter the domain name here. If the computer is part of a workgroup, you can leave this text box blank.

Save My Password check box   Select this check box if you want to save your password with the rest of the Remote Desktop Connection information. This can save you time and effort, but it compromises your security a bit.

Connection Settings group box   Once you've chosen settings for a connection, you can save the connection information by clicking the Save As button and specifying a name for the connection in the Save As dialog box that Windows displays. Remote Desktop Connection connections are saved as files of the file type Remote Desktop File, which by default is linked to the RDP extension, in the \My Documents\ Remote Desktops\ folder. You can open saved connections by clicking the Open button and using the resulting Open dialog box.

NOTE

You'll see a file named DEFAULT.RDP in the \My Documents\Remote Desktops\ folder. Windows automatically saves your latest Remote Desktop Connection configuration under this name when you click the Connect button. But by explicitly saving your settings under a name of your choice, you can easily maintain different configurations for different Remote Desktop Connection settings.

4. The Display page of the Remote Desktop Connection window (shown in Figure 19.5) offers three display options:

Remote Desktop Size group box Drag the slider to specify the screen size you want to use for the remote desktop. The default setting is Full Screen, but you may want to use a smaller size so that you can more easily access your desktop on the home computer. When you display the remote desktop full screen, it takes over the whole of the local desktop, so that you can't see your local desktop. (To get to your local desktop, you use the connection bar, discussed in a moment or two.)

Colors group box In the drop-down list, select the color depth to use for the connection. Choose a low color depth (for example, 256 colors) if you're connecting over a low-speed connection. This choice will be overridden by the display setting on the remote computer if you ask for more colors than the remote computer is using.

Display the Connection Bar when in Full Screen Mode check box Leave this check box selected (as it is by default) if you want Windows to display the connection bar when the remote desktop is displayed full screen. The connection bar provides Minimize, Restore/Maximize, and Close buttons for the remote desktop. (When the remote desktop is displayed in a window, that window has the control buttons, so the connection bar isn't necessary.)

FIGURE 19.5: Choose display settings on the Display page of the Remote Desktop Connection window.

5. The Local Resources page of the Remote Desktop Connection window (shown in Figure 19.6) offers the following options:

Remote Computer Sound group box   In the drop-down list, specify what you want Windows to do with sounds that would normally be generated at the remote desktop. The default setting is Bring to This Computer, which transfers the sounds to the home computer and plays them there. This setting helps sustain the illusion that you're working directly on the remote desktop, but it's heavy on bandwidth, so don't use it over low-speed connections. Instead, choose the Do Not Play setting or the Leave at Remote Computer setting. The Leave at Remote Computer setting plays the sounds at the remote computer and is best reserved for occasions when you need to frighten somebody remotely or pretend to be in your office.

Keyboard group box In the drop-down list, specify how you want Windows to handle Windows key combinations that you press (for example, Alt+Tab or Ctrl+Alt+Delete). Select the On the Local Computer item, the On the Remote Computer item, or the In Full Screen Mode Only item (the default) as suits your needs.

Local Devices group box Leave the Disk Drives check box, the Printers check box, and the Serial Ports check box selected (as they are by default) if you want these devices on your home computer to be available from the remote computer. This means that you can save documents from the remote computer to local drives, print them on your local printer, or transfer them via devices attached to serial ports (for example, a PDA). Local disk drives appear in the Other category in Explorer windows, named *Driveletter on COMPUTERNAME*. Local printers appear with *from COMPUTERNAME* in parentheses after them.

FIGURE 19.6: On the Local Resources page of the Remote Desktop Connection window, specify how Windows should handle sound, keyboard shortcuts, and devices on the home computer.

6. The Programs page of the Remote Desktop Connection window (shown in Figure 19.7) lets you specify that Windows run a designated program when you connect via Remote Desktop Connection. Select the Start the Following Program on Connection check box, then enter the program path and name in the Program Path and File Name text box. If you need to specify the folder in which the program should start, enter that in the Start in the Following Folder text box.

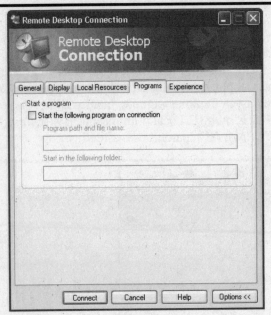

FIGURE 19.7: If you need to have a program run on the remote desktop when you connect, specify it on the Programs page of the Remote Desktop Connection window.

7. The Experience page of the Remote Desktop Connection window (shown in Figure 19.8) contains the following options:

Choose Your Connection Speed to Optimize Performance drop-down list In this drop-down list, select one of the four listed speeds to apply a preselected set of settings to the five check boxes on this page. The choices in the drop-down list are Modem (28.8Kbps), Modem (56Kbps), Broadband (128Kbps–1.5Mbps), LAN (10Mbps or Higher), and Custom.

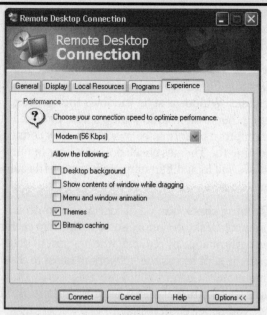

FIGURE 19.8: On the Experience page of the Remote Desktop Connection window, you can customize which graphical information Remote Desktop Connection transmits, in order to balance performance against looks.

Desktop Background check box   This check box controls whether Remote Desktop Connection transmits the desktop background. Because desktop backgrounds are graphical, transmitting them is sensible only at LAN speeds. (If you clear this check box, Remote Desktop Connection uses a blank desktop background.)

Show Contents of Window while Dragging check box This check box controls whether Remote Desktop Connection transmits the contents of a window while you're dragging it, or only the window frame. Don't use this option over a modem connection, because the performance penalty outweighs any benefit you may derive from it.

Menu and Window Animation check box   This check box controls whether Remote Desktop Connection transmits menu and window animations (for example, zooming

Part iii

a window you're maximizing or minimizing). Don't use this option over a modem connection—it's a waste of bandwidth.

Themes check box   This check box controls whether Remote Desktop Connection transmits theme information or uses "classic" Windows–style windows and controls. Transmitting theme information takes a little bandwidth, so you can improve performance over a very slow connection by clearing the Themes check box. But bear in mind that Windows will look different enough to unsettle some inexperienced users.

Bitmap Caching check box   This check box controls whether Remote Desktop Connection uses bitmap caching to improve performance by reducing the amount of data that needs to be sent across the network in order to display the screen remotely. Caching could prove a security threat, so you *might* want to turn it off for security reasons. But in most cases, you're better off using it.

8. If you want to save the settings you've chosen under a particular name so that you can reload them at will, click the Save As button on the General page of the Remote Desktop Connection window.

Connecting via Remote Desktop Connection

Once you've chosen settings as outlined in the previous section, you're ready to connect. If you're connecting via the Internet (rather than a local network) and you have a dial-up connection, make sure it's up and running.

Click the Connect button in the Remote Desktop Connection window. Windows attempts to establish a connection to the computer you specified.

If Windows is able to connect to the computer, and you didn't specify your username or password in the Remote Desktop Connection window, it displays the Log On to Windows dialog box (shown in Figure 19.9). Enter your username and password and click the OK button to log in. Windows then displays the remote desktop. (If you chose to provide your password on the General page of the Remote Desktop Connection window, you shouldn't need to enter it again.)

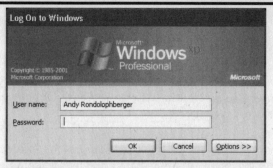

FIGURE 19.9: Windows displays the Log On to Windows dialog box for the remote computer.

If you left a user session active on the computer, Remote Desktop Connection drops you straight into it—likewise if you left a user session disconnected and no other user session is active. But if another user *is* active on the remote computer when you submit a successful logon and password, Windows displays the Logon Message dialog box shown in Figure 19.10 to warn you that logging on will disconnect the user's session. Click the Yes button if you want to proceed. Click the No button to withdraw stealthily.

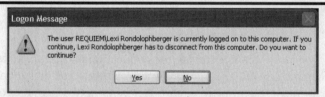

FIGURE 19.10: Windows displays the Logon Message dialog box when you're about to bump a user off the remote computer by logging on.

If you click the Yes button, the active user gets a Request for Connection dialog box such as that shown in Figure 19.11, which tells them that you (it specifies your name) are trying to connect to the computer, warns them that they'll be disconnected if you do connect, and asks if they want to allow the connection.

The active user then gets to click the Yes button or the No button as appropriate to their needs and inclinations. If Windows doesn't get an answer within 30 seconds or so, it figures they're not there, disconnects their session, and lets you in.

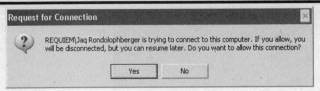

FIGURE 19.11: Windows displays the Request for Connection dialog box to tell the active user of your incoming session.

If the active user clicks the Yes button in the Request for Connection dialog box, Windows logs them off immediately and logs you on. But if the active user clicks the No button, you get a Logon Message dialog box such as that shown in Figure 19.12 telling you that they didn't allow you to connect. Windows displays this Logon Message dialog box for a few seconds, and then closes it automatically, returning you to the Remote Desktop Connection window.

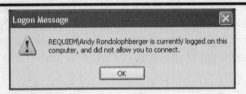

FIGURE 19.12: Windows displays this Logon Message dialog box when the active user decides not to let you interrupt their session on the computer.

If Windows is unable to establish the connection with the remote computer, it displays one of its Remote Desktop Disconnected dialog boxes to make you aware of the problem. Figure 19.13 shows two examples of the Remote Desktop Disconnected dialog box.

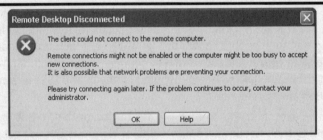

FIGURE 19.13: If Windows is unable to connect, you'll see a Remote Desktop Disconnected dialog box.

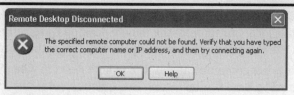

FIGURE 19.13: (continued)

The first example of the Remote Desktop Disconnected dialog box tells you that the client couldn't connect to the remote computer and suggests that you try again later. The second example tells you that the remote computer couldn't be found and suggests checking that the computer name or IP address are correct. This should indeed be your first move—but if that doesn't work, that's about all you can do. If the remote computer has been shut down (or has crashed); or if its network or Internet connection has gone south; or if someone has reconfigured the computer not to accept Remote Desktop Connection connections, or has revoked your permission to connect—if any of these has happened, you're straight out of luck, and no amount of retyping the computer name or IP address will make an iota of difference.

Working via Remote Desktop Connection

Once you've reached the remote desktop, you can work more or less as if you were sitting at the computer. The few differences worth mentioning are discussed briefly in this section.

Using Cut, Copy, and Paste between the Local and Remote Computers

You can use Cut, Copy, and Paste commands to transfer information between the local computer and the remote computer. For example, you could copy some text from a program on the local computer and paste it into a program on the remote computer.

Copying from Remote Drives to Local Drives

You can copy from remote drives to local drives by working in Explorer. The drives on your local computer appear in Explorer windows on the remote computer marked as *Driveletter on COMPUTERNAME*. The drives on the remote computer appear as regular drives. You can copy and move files from one drive to another as you would with local drives.

Part iii

Printing to a Local Printer

You can print to a local printer from the remote desktop by selecting the local printer in the Print dialog box just as you would any other printer.

Printer settings are communicated to the remote desktop when you access it. If you add a local printer during the remote session, the remote desktop won't be able to see it. To make the printer show up on the remote desktop, log off the remote session and log back on.

Returning to Your Local Desktop

If you chose to display the connection bar, it hovers briefly at the top of the screen, then slides upward to vanish like a docked toolbar with its Auto-Hide property enabled. To pin the connection bar in position, click the pin icon at its left end. (To unpin it, click the pin icon again.) To display the connection bar when it has hidden itself, move the mouse pointer to the top edge of the screen, just as you would do to display a docked toolbar hidden there.

The connection bar provides a Minimize button, a Restore/Maximize button, and a Close button. Use the Minimize button and the Restore button to reduce the remote desktop from full screen to an icon or a partial screen so that you can access your local desktop. Maximize the remote desktop window to return to full-screen mode when you want to work with it again. Use the Close button as discussed in the next section to disconnect your remote session.

Disconnecting the Remote Session

You can disconnect the remote session in either of the two following ways:

▶ On the remote desktop, choose Start ➤ Disconnect. Windows displays the Disconnect Windows dialog box (shown in Figure 19.14). Click the Disconnect button.

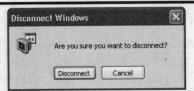

FIGURE 19.14: You can disconnect the remote session by issuing a Start ➤ Disconnect command and clicking the Disconnect button in the Disconnect Windows dialog box.

▸ Click the Close button on the connection bar (if the remote desktop is displayed full screen) or on the Remote Desktop window (if the remote desktop is not displayed full screen). Windows displays the Disconnect Windows Session dialog box (shown in Figure 19.15). Click the OK button.

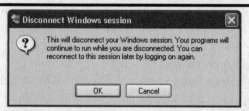

FIGURE 19.15: The Disconnect Windows Session dialog box appears when you click the Close button on the connection bar. Click the OK button to end your remote session while leaving the programs running.

Windows disconnects the remote session but leaves the programs running for the time being. You can then log on again and pick up where you left off.

Logging Off the Remote Session

To log off and end your user session, click the Start button on the remote desktop and choose Log Off from the Start menu. Windows displays the Log Off Windows dialog box (shown in Figure 19.16). Click the Log Off button.

FIGURE 19.16: To log off from the remote computer, choose Start ➢ Log Off and click the Log Off button in the Log Off Windows dialog box.

When someone else bumps you off the remote desktop (by logging on locally or remotely), Windows displays the Remote Desktop Disconnected dialog box shown in Figure 19.17, telling you that the remote session "was ended by means of an administration tool."

FIGURE 19.17: This Remote Desktop Disconnected dialog box appears when you log off and when someone logs you off the remote computer.

If the network connection between the home computer and the remote computer is broken, the home computer displays a Remote Desktop Disconnected dialog box such as that shown in Figure 19.18.

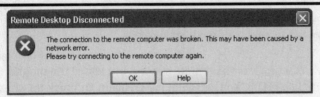

FIGURE 19.18: This Remote Desktop Disconnected dialog box indicates that the network connection between the home computer and the remote computer was broken.

USING REMOTE ASSISTANCE

Remote Desktop Connection is great for accessing your desktop from a distance. But what if you need someone to access your home computer remotely in order to help you fix a problem?

Remote Assistance lets you permit a designated helper to connect to your computer, see what's going on, and help you out of trouble. The helper—a friend or an administrator; whomever you choose—can control the computer directly if you give them permission, or you can simply chat with them and apply yourself such of their advice as you deem fit.

To use Remote Assistance, both your computer and your helper's must be running Windows XP. You send an invitation via e-mail or via Windows Messenger, or save it as a file (for example, to a network location designated for Remote Assistance request files, or on a floppy or CD that you then pop in the snail mail). When your helper responds, you decide whether to accept their help.

Each of the three methods of requesting Remote Assistance has its advantages and disadvantages. An e-mail invitation lets you include details of the Windows problem with which you need help—but you don't know when the recipient will check their e-mail. A Messenger invitation will be received immediately (because you can't send an invitation to someone who isn't online), but you can't include details of the problem. A file invitation, like an e-mail invitation, lets you include details of the problem, but you have no idea of when you'll receive a response to it (if ever).

On the other end of the wire, you can offer help via Remote Assistance. All you need is for someone to send you an invitation.

Security Considerations

Like all remote-control technologies, Remote Assistance has serious security implications that you need to consider before using it.

If you give another person control of your computer, they can take actions almost as freely as if they were seated in front of the computer. You can watch these actions, and you can take back control of the computer at any time, but you may already be too late: It takes less than a second to delete a key file, and little longer to plant a virus or other form of malware.

Even if you *don't* give your helper control, and simply chat, keep your wits about you when deciding which of their suggestions to implement. Malicious or ill-informed suggestions can do plenty of damage if you apply them without thinking. Never take any actions that could compromise your security or destroy your data. Above all, treat any incoming files with the greatest of suspicion and virus-check them using an up-to-date anti-virus program before using them.

One particular problem is that you can't tell that the person at the other computer is who they claim to be. For this reason alone, always protect your Remote Assistance connections with a strong password known only to the person from whom you're requesting help. That way, if someone else is at their computer or has identity-jacked them, they won't be able to respond to the Remote Assistance invitation you send.

Enabling Remote Assistance

Remote Assistance is enabled by default. To find out if Remote Assistance is enabled on your computer, take the following steps:

1. Display the System Properties dialog box (for example, by pressing Winkey+Break or clicking the System link on the Performance and Maintenance screen of Control Panel).

Part iii

2. Click the Remote tab. Windows displays the Remote page (shown in Figure 19.19).

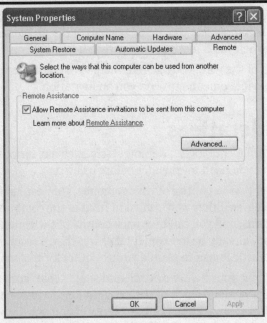

FIGURE 19.19: You can turn Remote Assistance on and off on the Remote page of the System Properties dialog box.

3. Check the status of the Allow Remote Assistance Invitations to Be Sent from This Computer check box. If this check box isn't selected, select it.

4. Click the OK button. Windows closes the System Properties dialog box.

Setting Limits for Remote Assistance

To set limits for Remote Assistance, take the following steps:

1. Click the Advanced button in the Remote Assistance group box on the Remote page of the System Properties dialog box. Windows displays the Remote Assistance Settings dialog box (shown in Figure 19.20).

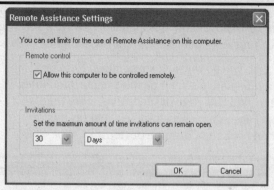

FIGURE 19.20: Set limits for Remote Assistance in the Remote Assistance Settings dialog box.

2. In the Remote Control group box, clear the Allow This Computer to Be Controlled Remotely check box if you don't want your helpers to be able to control the computer. (This check box is selected by default.) Even when this check box is selected, you need to approve each request for control of the PC manually.

3. In the Invitations group box, use the two drop-down lists to specify an expiration limit for Remote Assistance invitations that your computer sends out. The default setting is 30 days; you might want to shorten this period considerably for security.

4. Click the OK button. Windows closes the Remote Assistance Settings dialog box, returning you to the System Properties dialog box.

5. Click the OK button. Windows closes the System Properties dialog box.

You're now ready to start sending out invitations for Remote Assistance.

Sending a Remote Assistance Invitation via E-mail

To send a Remote Assistance invitation as an e-mail message via your existing e-mail account, follow these steps:

1. Choose Start > All Programs > Remote Assistance. Windows opens a Help and Support Center window to the Remote Assistance topic.

Part iii

2. Click the Invite Someone to Help You link. Help and Support Center displays the Remote Assistance – Pick How You Want to Contact Your Assistant screen (shown in Figure 19.21).

The first time you go through these steps, Help and Support Center displays a screen bearing Important Notes. If you want to skip this page in the future, leave the Don't Show This Page Again check box selected (as it is by default) and click the Continue button.

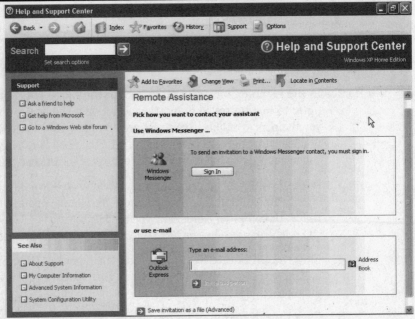

FIGURE 19.21: On the Remote Assistance – Pick How You Want to Contact Your Assistant screen of Help and Support Center, specify which type of Remote Assistance invitation to send.

3. In the Or Use E-mail area, enter your putative assistant's e-mail address in the Type an E-mail Address text box. Either type in the address or click the Address Book button and use Address Book to specify the address.

4. Click the Invite This Person link. Help and Support Center displays the Provide Contact Information screen (shown in Figure 19.22).

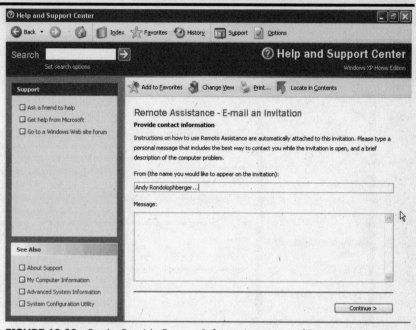

FIGURE 19.22: On the Provide Contact Information screen of Remote Assistance, check your name and enter a message detailing the problem you're having.

5. Change the name in the From text box if you want.

6. In the Message text box, enter a description of the problem and any blandishments necessary to get the help you want.

7. Click the Continue button. Help and Support Center displays the Set the Invitation to Expire screen (shown in Figure 19.23).

8. In the Set the Invitation to Expire area, specify the time limit for the recipient to accept the invitation. Choose a number in the first drop-down list and a time period—Minutes, Hours, or Days—in the second drop-down list.

9. To set a password, make sure the Require the Recipient to Use a Password check box is selected, then enter the password in the Type Password text box and the Confirm Password text box.

Part iii

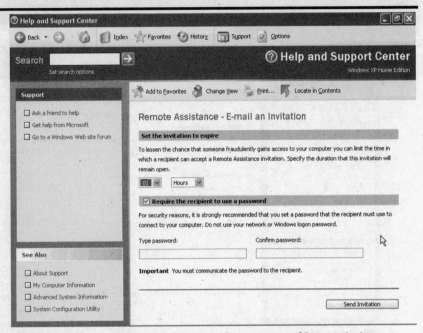

FIGURE 19.23: On the Set the Invitation to Expire screen of Remote Assistance, set the expiration period for the invitation and enter a password.

10. Click the Send Invitation button. Help and Support Center creates a file named rcBuddy.MsRcIncident containing the invitation and sends it via your default e-mail client with a message explaining how to use it. Help and Support Center then displays a screen telling you that the invitation has been sent successfully.

   ▶ If Help and Support Center can't send the file—for example, if your ISP's mail server is down—it invites you to save the file and send it manually.

   ▶ If you've set Outlook Express to warn you if other programs attempt to send mail in your name, Outlook Express will display an Outlook Express dialog box such as that shown in Figure 19.24, warning you that a program (Help and Support Center) is trying to send a message. Click the Send button.

FIGURE 19.24: Outlook Express may warn you that Help and Support Center is trying to send a message on your behalf.

Sending an Invitation via Windows Messenger

To send an invitation via your existing Messenger account, follow these steps:

1. Start Messenger as usual, or activate it from the notification area.

2. Choose Tools ➤ Ask for Remote Assistance and choose either a contact name or the Other item from the submenu.

    ▶ If you choose Other, Messenger displays the Send an Invitation dialog box. Enter the person's e-mail address in the text box and click the OK button.

    ▶ You can also send an invitation to an existing contact by right-clicking them in the Online list and choosing Ask for Remote Assistance from the context menu.

3. Messenger opens an Instant Message window with the specified user and displays a note saying that you've invited the user to start Remote Assistance.

    ▶ To cancel the invitation, click the Cancel link in the Instant Message window, or press Alt+Q.

4. Wait for a response, then proceed as described in "Receiving Remote Assistance," later in this chapter.

Part iii

Saving an Invitation As a File

Saving an invitation as a file works in essentially the same way as sending an invitation as an e-mail message does, except that instead of specifying an e-mail address, you click the Save Invitation As a File link, create the invitation, and then specify a filename and location in the Save File dialog box. For example, your company might designate a network folder as a drop-box for Remote Assistance requests. Administrators would then examine the contents of the folder and respond to the requests accordingly. Alternatively, you could save the file to a floppy disk or other mobile medium and mail it to a helper.

Viewing the Status of Your Invitations

To view the status of the Remote Assistance invitations you've sent (or saved), display the Remote Assistance screen in Help and Support Center.

Click the View Invitation Status link. Windows displays the Remote Assistance – View or Change Your Invitation screen. Figure 19.25 shows an example.

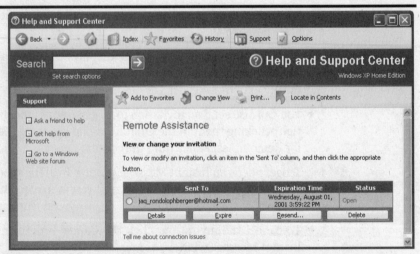

FIGURE 19.25: On the View or Change Your Invitation screen, you can view the Remote Assistance invitations you've sent, "expire" them, resend them, or delete them.

From here, you can view the details of an invitation by clicking the Details button, kill off an open invitation by clicking the Expire button, resend an invitation by clicking the Resend button, or delete an invitation by clicking the Delete button.

Receiving Remote Assistance

The following sections describe what happens when you receive a response to your Remote Assistance request.

E-mail Invitation

When a helper responds to an e-mail invitation, Windows displays a Remote Assistance dialog box such as that shown in Figure 19.26, telling you that the person has accepted the invitation and asking if you want to let them view your screen and chat with you. Click the Yes button to start the Remote Assistance session.

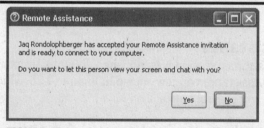

FIGURE 19.26: Remote Assistance dialog box indicating an accepted invitation

NOTE

If you don't take any action for a few minutes, Windows assumes you're not in the market for Remote Assistance and times out the connection.

Windows Messenger Invitation

When an invitee responds to a Messenger request for Remote Assistance, Windows displays a Remote Assistance window such as that shown in Figure 19.27.

Part iii

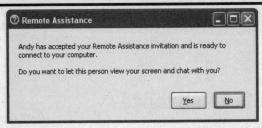

FIGURE 19.27: You'll see a Remote Assistance window such as this when an invitee responds to a Messenger request for Remote Assistance.

File Invitation

When a helper responds to a Remote Assistance request saved in a file, Windows displays a Remote Assistance window telling you that the person has accepted the invitation and asking if you want to let them view your screen and chat with you. Click the Yes button to start the Remote Assistance session.

Receiving Assistance

Once the Remote Assistance session is established, Remote Assistance displays the Remote Assistance window shown in Figure 19.28, which provides a chat pane and control buttons.

Chatting with Your Helper   You can chat both via text and by using voice (if both computers are set up for audio):

▶ Type a message in the Message Entry text box and press the Enter key or click the Send button to send it.

▶ To start voice transmission, click the Start Talking button. Your helper then sees a dialog box asking if they want to use a voice connection. If they click the Yes button, Remote Assistance establishes the voice connection. Talk as usual, and then click the Stop Talking button when you want to stop using the voice connection.

NOTE

The first time you use the talk feature, Remote Assistance runs the Audio and Video Tuning Wizard if you haven't run it before.

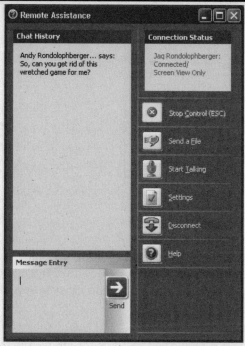

FIGURE 19.28: During a Remote Assistance session, this Remote Assistance window provides a chat pane and control buttons.

▶ To choose voice settings, click the Settings button. Windows displays a Remote Assistance Settings dialog box. Choose the Standard Quality option button or the High Quality option button as appropriate. Alternatively, click the Audio Tuning Wizard button (if it's available) to run the Audio and Video Tuning Wizard to optimize your speaker and microphone settings. Close the Remote Assistance Settings dialog box when you've finished.

Giving Your Helper Control of Your Computer If your helper requests control of your computer, Windows displays the Remote Assistance dialog box shown in Figure 19.29. Click the Yes button or the No button as appropriate.

You can regain control by pressing the Esc key, by pressing Alt+C, or by clicking the Stop Control button.

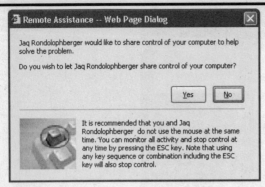

FIGURE 19.29: When your helper requests control of the computer, decide whether you trust them.

Disconnecting Your Helper   To disconnect your helper, click the Disconnect button. Remote Assistance closes the connection and restores your desktop to its full complement of colors (if you chose to optimize performance for your helper).

When your helper disconnects themselves, Windows displays a Remote Assistance dialog box telling you so. Click the OK button to close this dialog box, then close the Help and Support Center window.

Responding to a Remote Assistance Invitation

This section discusses how to respond to a Remote Assistance invitation that someone sends you. As you'd expect, the specifics vary depending on whether it's an e-mail invitation, a Messenger invitation, or a file invitation.

E-mail Invitation

When someone sends you a Remote Assistance invitation via e-mail, you receive an e-mail message with the Subject line "YOU HAVE RECEIVED A REMOTE ASSISTANCE INVITATION FROM *USERNAME.*" The message comes with explanatory text augmenting whatever message text the requester entered, and an attached file with a name such as rcBuddy.MsRcIncident.

Open the file by double-clicking it. Alternatively, in Outlook Express, click the Attachment icon, select the file from the drop-down menu, select the Open It button in the Open Attachment Warning dialog box, and click the OK button. Windows displays a Help and Support Center window such as that shown in Figure 19.30, giving the details of the Remote Assistance invitation: who it's from, and when it expires.

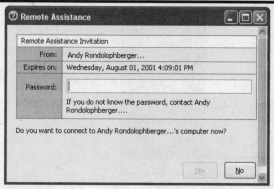

FIGURE 19.30: Double-click the file you receive to open the Remote Assistance invitation.

Enter the password (if the window is displaying a Password text box) and click the Yes button to start the help session. Windows tries to contact the remote computer.

Windows Messenger Invitation

When someone sends you a Remote Assistance invitation via Messenger, you see a Conversation window such as that shown in Figure 19.31. Click the Accept link (or press Alt+T) to accept it or click the Decline link (or press Alt+D) to decline it.

If the user chose to specify a password, you'll need to enter it in a Help and Support Center window after the user accepts the incoming Remote Assistance connection.

File Invitation

If you find a file invitation waiting for you, or receive one on a physical medium, double-click the file to open it. The rest of the procedure is the same as for an e-mail invitation, discussed in the section before last.

Part iii

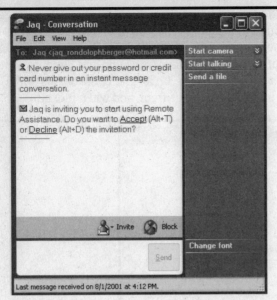

FIGURE 19.31: Receiving a Remote Assistance invitation in Messenger

Providing Remote Assistance

If Windows is able to contact the remote computer, and if the user accepts the Remote Assistance connection, Windows displays the Remote Assistance window (shown in Figure 19.32). As you can see, this features a chat pane, a view pane that shows the user's desktop, and assorted command buttons.

Chatting with the User To chat with the user via text, click the Show Chat button to display the chat pane if it's not currently displayed. Type a message in the Message Entry text box and press the Enter key or click the Send button to send it.

To hide the chat pane so that you can see more of the remote screen, click the Hide button.

To chat via voice, click the Start Talking button. Remote Assistance displays a dialog box asking the person at the other end whether they want to use voice. If they click the Yes button, Remote Assistance activates the audio hardware. Click the Stop Talking button to stop using voice to chat.

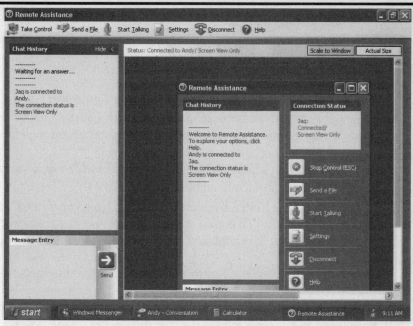

FIGURE 19.32: When you're supplying the assistance in a Remote Assistance session, you can view their screen and chat with the user.

Scaling the Display   You can scale the remote display to fit the area available on your screen by clicking the Scale to Window button, and restore it to its actual size by clicking the Actual Size button. Depending on the resolution you and the remote user have set, scaling the display may make the fonts illegible, but viewing the whole screen at once may make it easier for you to see what's happening on the computer than being able to see only a partial screen and having to scroll to see its outer reaches.

Taking Control of the Remote Computer   To request control of the remote computer, click the Take Control button. Windows displays a Remote Assistance dialog box on the remote screen asking the user if they want to give you control. If they click the Yes button, you get a Remote Assistance dialog box telling you so. When you dismiss this dialog box, you have control of the computer and can take any action with it as if you were working directly on it. To release control, click the Release Control button or press the Esc key.

WARNING

Avoid pressing the Esc key when taking keyboard actions on the remote computer. Even combinations that use the Esc key will release control.

Transferring Files to and from the Remote Computer   To transfer a file to the remote computer, click the Send a File button. Windows displays a Remote Assistance dialog box. Use the Browse button to locate the file, and then click the Send File button to send it. The remote user then gets to decide whether to keep the file and in which folder to save it. (If you have control of the computer, you can make these decisions.)

To transfer a file from the remote computer to your computer, have the user click the Send a File button in their Remote Assistance window. Alternatively, if you have control of the computer, you can do this yourself.

Disconnecting from the Remote Computer   To disconnect from the remote computer, click the Disconnect button. Then close the Remote Assistance window manually. Unless you expect you'll need to reconnect to the remote computer to help the user further during the time remaining before the Remote Assistance invitation expires, delete the invitation file before you forget.

If the person you're helping disconnects the connection, Windows displays a Remote Assistance dialog box telling you so.

What's Next

This chapter has discussed how to use Remote Desktop Connection to connect your computer to a remote computer running Windows XP Professional (or Server) and work on it as if you were sitting at it. It has also discussed how to use the Remote Assistance feature to request, receive, and provide assistance from a distance.

In the next chapter, Robert Cowart explains how to build your own peer-to-peer network in your home or small office using Windows XP Home Edition. You do not need a dedicated server or any special software to connect several computers for file and printer sharing; it's easy and requires only minimal networking hardware.

PART iV
NETWORKING AND SECURING WINDOWS XP HOME EDITION

Chapter 20

BUILDING A PEER-TO-PEER NETWORK

I n addition to local area networks (LANs) in the workplace, small networks are becoming increasingly popular in the home. Affordable PCs have been around long enough that many homes are already on their second or third computer, and it stands to reason that many people want to connect those multiple boxes together to share resources. Hardware producers, such as Diamond Multimedia, 3Com, and a host of others, are rushing to sell packages designed specifically to make home networking easy.

Windows XP Home Edition has all the features necessary to make it the perfect network citizen. Right out of the box—with no additional software required—your PC with Windows XP is capable of connecting to 32 Windows XP Home Edition/9x/Me workstations. And setup is easy, because Windows XP comes with a Network Setup Wizard to automate the process of installing and configuring the network drivers—all this means that you don't have to get your hands dirty configuring anything!

Adapted from *Mastering Windows Me* by Robert Cowart
ISBN 0-7821-2857-2   960 pages $39.99

Because the networking features are truly integrated parts of Windows XP Home Edition, you can access drives and printers located on the network from any Windows application—always in the same way, regardless of the computer you are connected to.

In this chapter, I'll introduce you to some networking basic concepts, and then I'll walk you through setting up a simple peer-to-peer network of Windows XP Home Edition workstations. You'll learn how to obtain and install networking hardware, and then you'll learn how to use the Network Setup Wizard to install the needed drivers and protocols and set up your files and printers for sharing and security.

WINDOWS XP NETWORK OVERVIEW

Windows XP Home Edition is positioned to be an operating system for homes and very small offices (under a dozen PCs or so). Microsoft strongly encourages users who connect to large corporate networks to move to Windows XP Professional, which has much more robust and flexible networking capabilities. If you need to connect to a domain, you'll need Windows XP Professional instead. Windows XP Home also lacks some of the network protocol support needed for more specialized networks, such as Microsoft 32-bit DLC, NetBEUI, and Fast Infrared. If you need that support, Windows XP Professional is the operating system for you. However, that said, Windows XP Home Edition is still a very capable network-aware operating system. You can use it to connect to Windows NT, Windows 2000, Windows XP Professional, Novell NetWare, or Banyan network servers, and you can also use it to create serverless peer-to-peer networks among Windows XP Home Edition PCs.

Additionally, Windows XP Home Edition can act as either a Dial-Up Networking client or as a host so that you can use regular phone lines to extend the reach of your network. This allows you to dial into your office network while you are on the road (or at home, or anywhere) and still have the same resources available as if you were sitting right at your desk.

Client/Server versus Peer-to-Peer Networks

There are dozens of types of networks out there, but they can all be broken down into two large categories: those with servers (client/server networks) and those without (peer-to-peer networks).

A *server* is a PC that's dedicated to the task of running the network; nobody uses it as a workstation. Most large corporate networks employ at least one server. A server takes the network processing workload off the client PCs so that they are completely free to go about the daily business of their owners (running applications, managing files, and so on).

In a home or small office, however, there might not be an extra PC to spare to function as a server, or there might not be money in the budget for the software that runs the server (such as Windows 2000 Server). In that case, a peer-to-peer network is the best choice.

Peer-to-peer refers to the fact that each station on the network treats each other as an equal or a peer. There is no special station set aside to provide only file and print services to all the other stations. Instead, any printer, CD-ROM drive, hard drive, or even floppy drive located on any one station can (if you wish) share access with all the other stations on the network. When you share a resource, such as a disk drive or printer, the computer that shares the resource becomes the server, and the computer that accesses the shared resource becomes the client. In a peer-to-peer network, both peers can share resources and access shared resources equally. In effect, your computer can be both a server and a client at the same time. Figure 20.1 illustrates a peer-to-peer network arrangement.

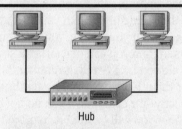

Hub

FIGURE 20.1: A typical peer-to-peer network topology: Notice that no particular station is designated as a stand-alone server.

Of course, there are security features as well, which will allow you to grant or remove access to shared resources on your computer. But first let's get the network up and running.

Most Windows XP Home Edition users contemplating setting up a network will want a peer-to-peer network rather than one that employs a server. Why? Because Windows XP Home Edition is marketed primarily at the home and small-office person, and such users typically have very modest networking needs. Those who need large corporate networks

Part iv

with servers will probably gravitate toward Windows 2000 Server to run the server and Windows 2000/XP Professional for the individual PCs (the *clients*) on the network.

However, Windows XP Home Edition PCs are perfectly capable of hooking into existing client/server networks (as long as the client/server setup doesn't involve connecting to a domain). They can also function as clients on networks in which the server is running Windows XP Professional, NT, Windows 2000 Server, Banyan Vines, or Novell NetWare. (Remember, if you need domain support, you need Windows XP Professional.)

The process of setting up to connect to a server-based network is essentially the same as that to connect to a peer-to-peer network (see "Running the Network Setup Wizard" later in this chapter).

If you need to set up a peer-to-peer network, the remainder of this chapter can help you with that.

Understanding Protocols

A *protocol* is a set of rules and conventions for accomplishing a specific task. In the case of computer networking, a protocol defines the manner in which two computers communicate with each other. As an analogy, consider the protocol you use to place a phone call. Before you dial, you first make sure no one else is using the phone line. Next, you pick up the phone and listen for a dial tone. If you are at your office, you might have to dial 9 and again wait for a dial tone. Then you can dial either a seven-digit number for a local call or a 1 followed by a ten-digit number for a long-distance call. You then wait for the other person to answer. But if you do not follow this protocol correctly—for example, if you do not dial a 9 for an outside line when at the office—you will be unable to place your phone call.

In the world of computers, a protocol works exactly the same way. If a client does not structure and send a request in the exact manner in which the server expects it—and we all know how particular computers can be—it will never establish the connection.

When you first activate the networking component on your computer, Windows XP Home Edition installs the TCP/IP protocol by default. Besides this one, Windows XP Home Edition allows you to install several other protocols that—depending on the design of your network and type of applications you run—might provide better performance or other advantages, such as NetBEUI. (In Windows 98, NetBEUI was installed by default, as a matter of fact.) On a small peer-to-peer network, NetBEUI is great, because it's a very efficient protocol. It can't be used on larger networks, however, because it's not routable (that is, it can't be used on a network that contains routers, which are a type of connector box for connecting subnetworks).

Windows XP Home Edition gives you a choice of several transport protocols. These protocols fall into two broad groups. First, open-systems protocols such as NetBEUI and TCP/IP allow you to connect to several vendors' networks. With them you can communicate over a Windows XP Home Edition peer-to-peer network or over another vendor's network. The second type of transport protocols are the proprietary protocols used to support specific vendors' networks such as Banyan Vines and DEC Pathworks.

Here are a few basics about the open-systems protocols that come with Windows XP Home Edition:

- ▶ TCP/IP is the default protocol for Windows peer-to-peer networks. It's also often used over wide-area networks, for Internet Connection Sharing, and for communicating with computers running some flavor of the Unix operating system.

- ▶ IPX/SPX is the protocol used to connect to Novell NetWare file servers prior to version 5. Microsoft's implementation is called NWLink.

- ▶ IPX/SPX with NetBIOS adds support for the NetBIOS application programming interface (API) to the standard IPX/SPX protocol. Microsoft's implementation is NWLink IPX/SPX/NetBIOS Compatible Transport Protocol.

Don't worry if all those specs make your head swim. For most people using Windows XP Home Edition, all this talk about various protocols is merely academic. If you're building a peer-to-peer network, the Network Setup Wizard will automatically install appropriate protocols for you (TCP/IP and perhaps IPX/SPX), and it will configure your PC to use them.

BUYING YOUR NETWORK HARDWARE

When you go shopping for home networking equipment at your local computer store, you might be surprised at the variety of schemes available. There are wireless networking kits, networking cards that use your home telephone wires instead of network cables, and more. Don't let the plethora of options available intimidate you. All of these networking schemes work more or less the same within Windows. The main differences involve the type of cabling used, and if you buy a kit, it'll automatically come with the right cable type.

Regardless of the network type, each computer in the network needs a *network interface card (NIC)*. Typically, this is an ISA or PCI card that fits into a slot in the motherboard, but on a laptop PC, it could be a PCMCIA (PC Card) device. The network cable plugs into that card. The traditional type of network card is *Ethernet*. There are various flavors of it, including 10Base2, 10BaseT, and 100BaseT (listed here from slowest and cheapest to fastest and most expensive). Of these, 100BaseT is the fastest, but 10BaseT is more economical and probably more than fast enough for the average home network. If you can get a decent price on a NIC that supports both, all the better.

Typically, the other end of the network cable plugs into a *hub*. The hub is like a town square—all the cables from all the networked PCs plug into it, and all the traffic passes through it on its way to its destination. With some wireless home networking kits, there might not be a hub, so be sure to read the directions that come with your hardware.

NOTE

The hardware I'm describing here is for a simple peer-to-peer network; networking hardware can get much more complex as you move into the server-based type.

Assuming you have not bought a networking kit for some special type, such as wireless or telephone-line networking, here's a shopping list of networking equipment you will need:

- ► One 10BaseT NIC for each station you want on the network.

- ► One Ethernet (RJ-45) twisted-pair cable for each workstation to be connected. Cable-length requirements will be based on the distance between the computer and the hub, usually somewhere between 6 and 50 feet, up to 328 feet at the maximum.

- ► A hub. This is a must if you plan to network three or more computers. Two computers can be networked without a hub, but you need to purchase a special cable (called a *crossover cable*) made specifically for that purpose.

TIP

Look in your local computer store for an Ethernet network starter kit. The kit should include everything you need, aside from the computer, to get your network up and running: two software-configurable network cards, about 25 feet of cable, a hub, and complete instructions. You can purchase additional add-on kits that include another network card and more cable, or you can simply buy more network cards and cable separately. If you are buying a kit for a wireless network, the hardware in the kit will probably differ from what is listed here.

Figure 20.2 shows what a typical NIC looks like. The card in Figure 20.2 has two kinds of connectors: RJ-45 and BNC. The RJ-45 connector is the important one for a simple peer-to-peer network of the type we're constructing in this chapter; you don't need the BNC connector. (The BNC connector is used for a different kind of network cabling system than the one you'll want for your small peer-to-peer network.) Simple RJ-45 10Base-T network cards cost around $35 at the time of this writing.

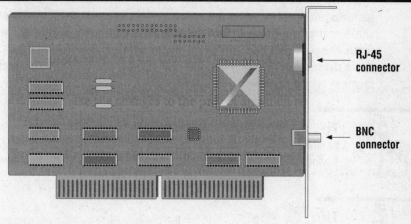

FIGURE 20.2: This is a typical Network combo-card, sporting both RJ-45 and BNC thin coax connectors.

As for the hub, there are very inexpensive models that accept four or five RJ-45 connections. If your network will consist of four or fewer computers, such a hub is your best choice. An 8- or 16-port hub is only a little bit more expensive. (In general, plan on spending around $10 per port.)

There's nothing special you need to know about buying the cables, except to look for RJ-45 on the packaging and to make sure that the cables are long enough (with some to spare) to reach from Point A to Point B.

Part iv

Installing Your Network Hardware

In this section, I'll describe how to install and connect the basic hardware elements of your peer-to-peer network—the NIC and the cables.

Installing the Network Interface Card (NIC)

All modern network cards you buy in stores today are plug-and-play and jumperless (or have a jumperless operation option at least). Windows will assign resources to the card automatically. *Jumpers* are little black blocks that fit down over pins on the circuit board to change a configuration setting. Back before plug-and-play was popular, most circuit boards included jumpers for setting the desired interrupt request (IRQ) and memory address to use.

In the unlucky event that you are working with a network card that still requires jumpers to configure it, you have a little work to do. First, open the card's manual to where it shows how to set the jumpers or switches to configure the card's settings. For now, don't make any changes, but do write down the current IRQ number, direct memory access (DMA) channel, and memory address because you will need these to configure the driver.

TIP

Before the advent of plug-and-play, adding network cards was a nightmare of having to set jumpers and settings manually—now it is pretty much automatic.

TIP

If you have an older network card that is complex to set up you might be better off binning the card and buying a new one as the prices nowadays are very competitive indeed!

Next, physically install the card. Follow these steps to do so:

1. Make sure the PC's power is turned off—unplug it to be really safe—and remove the PC's case. If you have questions about how to remove your computer case, refer to your owner's manual for a complete description.

WARNING

Don't forget to unplug your PC from the AC outlet before opening up the cover. This ensures you have the PC's power turned off, plus it reduces the chance of electric shock. Having come this far, I don't want to lose you. Also, before you install the network card, be sure to ground yourself—by touching the metal case of the computer or by using a grounding strip—to eliminate the possibility of static electricity zapping your network card. Keep the network card in the anti-static bag until you need it, and when you're taking it out of the bag, don't grab it by the circuit board!

2. Remove the screw that holds the thin metal slot cover behind the connector you intend to use for your card. Don't drop the screw into the machine! If you do, you must get it out one way or another, such as by turning the machine over.

TIP

Sometimes the little slot cover isn't held in by a screw but will need to be snapped off—take care when you do this as the edges can be really sharp and can give you a nasty cut. Also, be careful not to damage other components while doing this!

3. Insert the card gently but firmly until it is completely seated in the slot. You may have to wiggle the card a bit (from front to back) to ensure it seats firmly into the connector.

4. Store the metal slot cover somewhere for future use (unless it's a snap-off type, in which case it's useless) and screw the card in securely (this can be a hassle sometimes because the screw may not line up with the hole very well).

WARNING

After installing your network card, it is imperative that you take the time to put the screw back in the bracket and tighten the card down securely. If you don't, once you have the network cable attached to the card, a little tug on the cable could easily uproot the NIC, damaging it and your computer's motherboard (if the power is on). This is not fun. So take the extra time to put the screw back in.

If the PC in question is a laptop computer or a desktop that accepts PCMCIA cards, your chores are much easier. Simply plug the card into an available PCMCIA slot. Your computer (and Windows XP Home Edition)

Part iv

can even be running while you do this. (You might want to verify this first, however, by reading the manual or asking the salesperson since there are a few early PCMCIA cards that should only be inserted when the unit is off. And, of course, it won't hurt to insert the card before turning on the laptop.) If the card is in the next time Windows XP Home Edition starts up, the appropriate driver will be loaded immediately. But the ability to insert the PCMCIA card *while* Windows is running is plug-and-play at its finest. If all goes well, network drivers appropriate to your card will get automatically loaded when you insert the card and unloaded when you remove it. The first time you plug the card in, however, you may be prompted to insert the Windows XP Home Edition CD-ROM to load the correct network card driver.

NOTE

Some network cards may come with updated Windows XP Home Edition drivers included on a disk. Read the documentation that came with your card (or call the manufacturer) to determine whether this is the case, and if it is, insert this driver disk into your drive when you are prompted to do so.

Repeat the above process with each PC you intend to network. When finished, place each PC's cover back on, but do not put all the screws back into the case yet—anyone who's done this before will tell you that screwing the case back on before making sure everything works is the best way to ensure that things will *not* work. Unfortunately, even with plug-and-play network cards, you may still end up having to get back inside your PC to reconfigure that Sound Blaster or some other card that happens to be using a needed IRQ or DMA channel and is not itself plug-and-play compatible. (In my experience, sound cards and modems are the most frequent culprits.)

Setting Up the Hub

A hub has its own power supply, which you plug into an electrical outlet. When you do so, a light on the hub should illuminate, indicating that it is ready for use. (Check the documentation for more info.) Now you're ready to install the cables.

Installing the Cables

Connect the cables to the back of each network card. The connectors work in a similar manner to telephone cables. Connect the other end of each cable to the hub. If you are networking two computers and have decided to forego a hub, you will probably have just one cable that strings from one network card to the other. Remember, a hubless 10BaseT network requires a crossover cable, or else the computers won't recognize each other.

With a network card installed in each of your stations and each card connected to the hub, you are now ready to install and configure your Windows XP software for networking. If all goes well, the hard part of your job is already complete.

Setting Up the NIC in Windows

If you've just finished installing the NIC in the PC, turn the PC on and let Windows start up. One of three things will happen:

- ▶ Windows will automatically detect the network card and automatically install the needed driver for it.

- ▶ Windows will detect the network card and prompt you for a driver disk. In this case, you'll insert the disk that came with the NIC and follow the prompts.

- ▶ Windows will not immediately detect the network card. Use the Add New Hardware Wizard in the Control Panel to manually set it up.

If you are not sure whether Windows has set up your network card correctly, you can check it in Control Panel. Choose Start ➢ Control Panel ➢ Network and Internet Connections, and then click on Network Connections to open the Network Connections dialog box, as shown in Figure 20.3. If your network card is listed, you're ready to go on to the next step.

Running the Network Setup Wizard

In earlier versions of Windows (9x), you had to manually configure a network card and install the needed protocols and clients through the Network applet in Control Panel. You can still do it that way, but the Network Setup Wizard in Windows XP Home Edition makes it much easier to do the same thing. The Network Setup Wizard can also automatically install the needed protocol to share an Internet connection across your network with multiple PCs.

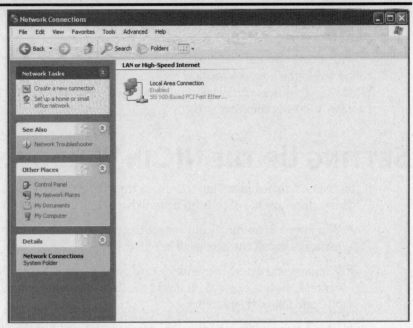

FIGURE 20.3: The Network Connections dialog box

Follow these steps to set up networking on your PC:

1. Choose Start ➢ All Programs ➢ Accessories ➢ Communications ➢ Network Setup Wizard. At the introductory screen, click Next.

2. The next screen gives you the opportunity to review a handy checklist for setting up a network; after doing so, click Next

3. The next screen wants to find out how the computer will connect to the Internet. You have the option to use Internet Connection Sharing—that is, connect to the Internet via the modem on another computer on the network or allow other users to connect to the Internet via your computer. Click Next when you are done. See Figure 20.4.

4. Enter a descriptive name for the computer and also a name for the computer in the Computer Name box. This will be the computer's name on the network, the name by which other computers will know it (see Figure 20.5).

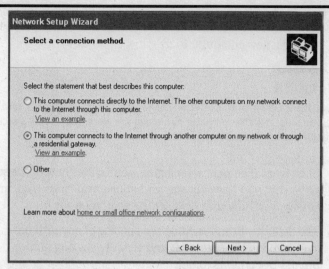

FIGURE 20.4: Internet Connection Sharing options

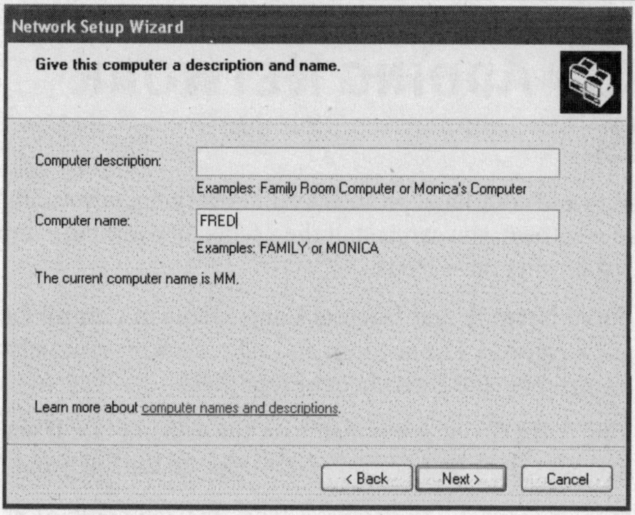

FIGURE 20.5: Specify a name and a workgroup.

5. Next, you need either to accept the default workgroup name, or enter a different workgroup name.

It is better if all the computers on your home network use the same workgroup name for them to communicate, so accept the default name unless you already have a network set up with a different workgroup name and you are merely adding a new computer to it.

WARNING

If you have a cable or DSL Internet connection through a network card in your PC, you must use the computer name and the workgroup name specified by your ISP; otherwise your Internet connection might not work.

6. Click Next. The next screen gives you an overview of the settings that you have chosen and allows you to go back and change anything that isn't set the way you want it.

    The default settings include the sharing of any printers connected to the computer and also the sharing of the Shared Documents folder.

7. Click Next. All of the settings will be automatically set up for you.

MANUALLY ADDING NETWORK DRIVERS

If you need to add additional protocols for networking, or you simply prefer to go on your own, you can install the needed networking components yourself by following these steps:

1. From Network and Internet Connections in Control Panel, click Network Connections and right-click on your network connection and then choose Properties.

2. Check the list of components on the General tab. If you do not see Client for Microsoft Networks, do the following:

    a. Click Install, then click Client, then click Add. A list of Microsoft-provided clients appears.

    b. Click Client for Microsoft Networks, and then click OK.

    c. If prompted to insert the Windows XP disk, do so and click OK.

3. You need at least one protocol. The most common one is TCP/IP. If it's not already there, or if you need to add another protocol, do the following:

   a. Click Install, then Protocol, then Add. The Select Network Protocol dialog box opens.

   b. Click the protocol to install, and click OK.

   c. If you are prompted to insert the Windows XP CD, do so and click OK.

NETWORKING WITH WINDOWS NT/ 2000/XP PROFESSIONAL

Microsoft's modular approach to networking in its operating systems has made internetworking Windows XP Home Edition with Windows NT, Windows 2000, Windows XP Professional and quite simple. This section discusses some of the unique features of an NT/2000/XP Professional network, and describes how to make your Windows XP machines fit in.

NOTE

If you have a simple home network only, and aren't a part of a large, corporate Windows NT/2000 client/server network, you can skip this section altogether.

Workgroups

As you saw when you went through the Network Setup Wizard earlier in the chapter, each PC is a member of a particular workgroup. On a simple peer-to-peer network for home networking, typically, there is only one workgroup, but larger networks running on Windows NT/2000/XP Professional might have many different workgroups. Usually, PCs are assigned to one workgroup or another according to job function, department, or physical proximity—whatever makes the most sense in a given situation. Subdividing the full group of network users into workgroups keeps things simple for the average user, and makes it easier for them to locate the PCs belonging to people with whom they work most closely. And where security is needed, passwords can be assigned within the workgroup on a per-resource or per-user basis (a single password can even be used by a group of users).

Small networks—say, those with a total of 50 or fewer workstations—might find that the workgroup approach is a sufficient and easy enough means for subdividing and organizing the network resources and users, assuming they're subdivided into multiple workgroups. But with very large networks, workgroups are not adequate because there's no way to oversee all the different workgroups. Managing the centralized networking resources on larger networks requires being able to access and configure user accounts and other network resources in a way that transcends the boundaries of individual workgroups.

Domains

For ease of organizing and managing large networks, Microsoft came up with the idea of *domains*. Domains are similar to workgroups but provide the ability to group all users in a single user *database*. This database resides on the Windows NT/2000 Server *domain controller* (and, optionally, in NT 4.0, on *backup domain controllers*). When you log on to a domain from the Windows XP Professional logon dialog box, you are authenticated as a specific user with specific access rights. These access rights are the basis for your ability to use shared resources on the network, such as a shared directory or printer.

For more specific information on NT Server, take a look at *Windows NT Server 4.0: No Experience Required* (Sybex, 1997).

Protocols Required

To allow your Windows XP Home Edition stations to communicate with an NT/2000/XP Professional server, you must make sure they are using one of the protocols used by the server. In most cases, this will probably be either TCP/IP or IPX/SPX. Again, you just need to make sure the Windows XP PCs are talking the same language as your other computers.

Adding a Windows XP Home Edition PC to an NT/2000/XP Professional Network

The Network Setup Wizard can set up a Windows XP Home Edition PC to operate as part of a workgroup the same way that it sets up for a smaller network. Go ahead and run it, as described earlier in the chapter.

This will set up your printers to be shared, if desired, as well as your Shared Documents folder. If you want to share additional folders, or entire drives, or set security restrictions for the sharing, see "Sharing Resources on the Network" later in this chapter.

If you are using NT Workstation, simply make sure you have the same workgroup name specified on the NT workstation as you do for each Windows XP Home Edition station that will be part of this workgroup.

After performing these steps, you should be able to open My Network Places on any Windows XP station in the workgroup and see an icon for the NT or Professional workstation. Also, when using My Network Places, you should now see your Windows XP stations appear as additional workstations in the workgroup.

WORKING WITH NETWORK RESOURCES

Start up Windows XP Home Edition on each of your PCs. You should now see the My Network Places icon on each Desktop. Double-click the icon, and you should see four icons under Network Tasks on the left-hand pane:

Add Network Place   A wizard that walks you through the process of creating a shortcut to a certain computer, drive, or folder on the network.

View Network Connections   Shows you all the active network connections. This is the same screen as the one accessed through Control Panel.

Set up a Home or Small Office Network   Reruns the Network Setup Wizard that you used in the preceding section to set up your network; you can use it to make changes to the network configuration. Here you can also create a disk that will allow you to migrate your network settings to other computers on your network.

View Network Computers   This allows you to browse all the computers connected to the network that belong to your workgroup.

Browsing the Entire Network

Let's start by looking at all the workgroups on your network. Browsing with My Network Places is like working with My Computer, except that it shows your whole network instead of the drives on your local PC.

NOTE
Each PC on your network should appear in Entire Network. If any are missing, or worse, if you do not *have* a My Network Places icon on your Desktop, you'll have to do some troubleshooting. The most common problem, aside from missing protocol(s) and incorrectly configured network cards, will be that one or more of your stations are not set to the same workgroup as all the others.

TIP
Another possible problem might be that you have chosen to hide the Desktop icons—right-click on the desktop and select Arrange Icons By and then check Show Desktop Icons.

In My Network Places, select View Workgroup Computers. For a home-based network, there will be only one workgroup.

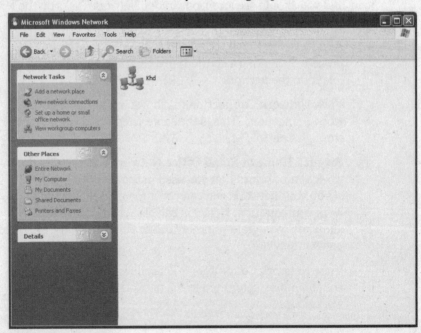

Double-click the workgroup (in the case of multiple workgroups), and a list of computers on that network that have shared resources appears. Any computers that do not have any shared drives, folders, files, or printers will not appear.

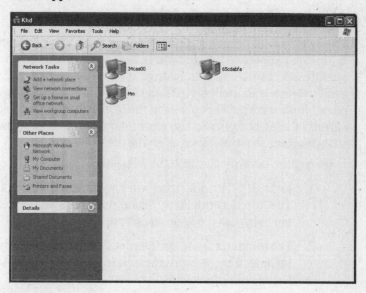

Double-click the computer you want to browse, and a list of shared drives, folders, and printers appears.

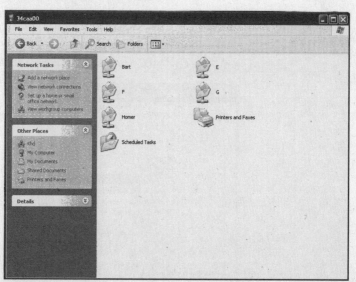

From there, double-click a printer icon to see the printer or double-click a drive icon to browse the shared files there, just as you would when browsing a local drive.

Creating a Network Place

The level-by-level browsing you saw in the preceding section works great if you don't know exactly what you're looking for. However, if you frequently need to access a certain drive or folder on a remote PC, you might want to create a shortcut for it. Such shortcuts are known as *network places*. You create network places in the My Network Places folder (no surprise there), but you can also create shortcuts to them anywhere else that you place shortcuts, such as on the desktop.

To create a network place, do the following:

1. In the My Network Places window, click Add Network Place. The Add Network Place Wizard runs. Click on the Next button to bypass the Welcome screen.

2. The computer scans the Internet. In the Where Do You Want to Create This Network Place? screen, select Choose Another Network Location and click Next.

3. Enter the IP address of a computer or click the Browse button. A Browse for Folder dialog box opens.

4. Click the plus signs to expand the tree to locate the drive or folder to which you want a shortcut and select it. (If you pick a computer and that computer does not have anything available to share, the OK button will not be active.)

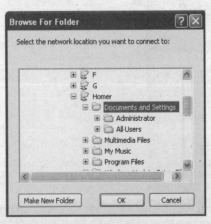

5. Click OK. The network path to that resource appears in the text box.

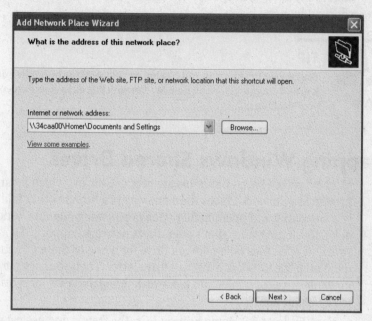

Add Network Place Wizard

What is the address of this network place?

Type the address of the Web site, FTP site, or network location that this shortcut will open.

Internet or network address:

\\34caa00\Homer\Documents and Settings   [Browse...]

View some examples.

[< Back] [Next >] [Cancel]

NOTE

Network paths are always preceded by two slashes: \\. The full network path to a resource includes the computer name, a slash, the drive name, and if it's a path to a folder, another slash and the folder name. It's not necessary to include the workgroup name unless it's in a different workgroup than the computer creating the shortcut. By the way, this naming convention is called UNC (Universal Naming Convention).

6. Click Next.

7. Type a descriptive name for the network place. This text will appear under its icon.

8. Click Next. Then enter a name for the Network Place. Click Next. A screen is now displayed telling you what the shortcut is pointing to. You also have the option to have the link opened as soon as it is created. The new Network Place shortcut appears in the My Network Places window after you click Finish.

Part iv

From then on, whenever you want to use this network resource, you can simply open the My Network Places window and double-click the shortcut icon.

TIP

You can put the shortcut you created on your desktop by holding down the Ctrl key and dragging the icon from My Network Places to wherever you want it on your desktop.

Mapping Windows Shared Drives

Most Windows-based programs are *network-aware*, which means you can browse My Network Places the same way you browse other folders when you are saving and opening files. However, some programs, especially older 16-bit programs, don't offer direct network support. If you want to save and open files on a network drive from one of these programs, you must map the network drive to a drive letter. Then your system sees the network drive (or a folder on a network drive) as a new local drive letter in My Computer.

For Windows XP Home Edition PCs, the fastest and easiest way to map a network drive is to locate the drive or folder in My Network Places, click Tools in the menu and select Map Network Drive. The Map Network Drive dialog box appears.

Choose the Browse button and select the shared folder you want to connect to. Select the drive letter you want to use, choose whether to reconnect this mapping automatically when you start the PC, and then click OK. The drive or folder's contents appear in a folder window for browsing. You can work with it or close it if you don't have to do anything with it right away. Notice before you close it, however, that its title bar now indicates its new drive letter assignment.

NOTE

Note that the Reconnect on Logon option is enabled by default; this is probably what you want. With this option on, whenever the PC in question is booted up, it will automatically log in the remote drive and map it to the desired logical drive.

Using Shared Printers

To use a shared printer on the network, you must set up that printer on your own PC as a network printer (create an icon for it). After that, you can print to the network printer as easily as you print to any local one, simply by choosing it from the Printer list in the Print dialog box of the program from which you are printing.

To set up to print to a network printer, follow these steps:

1. Choose Start ➤ Control Panel and select the Printers and Other Hardware category.

2. Click Add a Printer.

3. Click Next to begin.

4. Click the option to add a network printer, and then click Next.

5. You now have three options:

   ▶ Browse for a printer.

   ▶ Connect to a printer on the network.

   ▶ Connect to a printer on the Internet or on a home or office network.

6. Click Browse for a Printer and click Next. Expand the Computer tree and click on the printer. Click Next. After you choose the printer, you can then choose to make it the default printer.

7. Click Next.

8. A screen now appears that shows you the options you have chosen and gives you the opportunity to change any of them.

9. Click Finish. The files needed for shared use of the printer are copied from the printer's network location to your own hard disk, and the printer is made available.

Printers that you share on the network have a slightly different icon in the Printers folder than the local printers. This window shows both local and network printers installed.

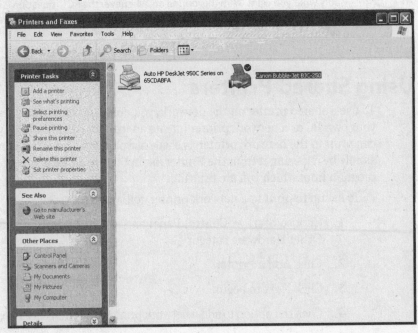

SHARING RESOURCES ON THE NETWORK

Being connected to the network and sharing other PCs and printers does not necessarily mean that your own drives and printers are shared. When you went through the Network Setup Wizard, you shared your Shared Documents folder as well as your connected printer. But there are more sharing options than those simple default ones, as you'll see in this section.

Sharing Drives and Folders

To share a drive or folder, do the following:

1. Right-click it and choose Sharing and Security. There are two kinds of sharing and security on Windows XP—sharing and security amongst the various users of the same PC and network sharing and security.

2. Click the Share this Folder option button (if this button does not appear, you will need to select the Enable File Sharing button first). The rest of the dialog box's controls become available (see Figure 20.6).

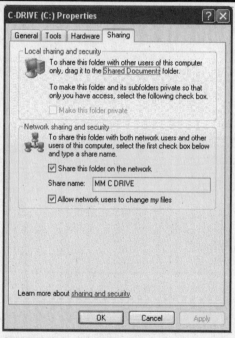

FIGURE 20.6: Set up sharing for a particular drive or folder on your PC.

3. Enter a more meaningful name in the Share Name box. For example, if you are sharing a drive that contains backup files, you might call it Backup.

4. Choose whether you want others to be able to change your files. Not selecting this makes them read-only.

5. Click OK. If the Share Name is longer than 12 characters, you will see a warning that older clients will not be able to access this share. If there are no older clients on your network, don't worry about it and click Yes or alternatively, you can change the share name to less than 12 characters (up to 8 is preferred). The item is now shared, and its icon appears with a little hand under it to indicate that fact.

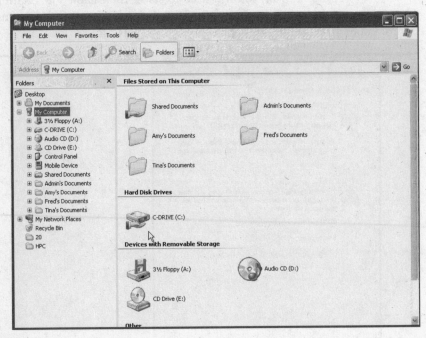

Sharing Printers

Sharing another printer works just like sharing a drive or folder. Right-click it and choose Sharing. Then choose the Share this Printer option button and fill in the other fields as desired, just as you did in the preceding set of steps. The printer icon will change to have the hand underneath it, just as a shared drive or folder had.

WHAT'S NEXT

In this chapter you learned how to configure a basic home network to share files and printers among PCs. The next chapter continues the discussion by explaining how to keep your networked computers safe from viruses, hackers, and other lurking dangers on the Internet and other networks.

Chapter 21

SECURITY: KEEPING YOUR PC, NETWORK, AND FAMILY SAFE

The networked world of computers is a big place, growing by leaps and bounds. And, as you'll find in any large community that is experiencing explosive growth, a lot of the well-intentioned people joining the community are not well protected against a less-well-intentioned minority who are abusing it. These digital hooligans make life difficult for the rest of us by a variety of means, including:

► Releasing disruptive programs, such as computer viruses, into the networked community.

► Trying and often succeeding at penetrating the digital defenses erected by network operators, and then stealing or damaging information or misusing resources.

► Placing offensive material, including pornography, where it can be accessed by children and others for whom it is inappropriate, offensive, or both.

Adapted from *Mastering Home Networks*
by Mark Henricks
ISBN 0-7821-2630-8   544 pages $29.99

To use the analogy of the Internet as frontier boomtown, the local sheriff is overwhelmed by the growth of the community and the lack of familiarity with those who could compromise that community's peace of mind. The result is that, like in the Wild West, all networkers are on their own to a considerable extent. In other words, it's up to you to protect yourself against the viruses, hackers, and offensive material you may encounter via the Internet. The good news is that you don't have to tack on a gold star and unholster your trusty six-shooter to take action. With adequate antivirus software, solid security against hackers, and filters to keep out offensive material, you can keep your network and your household quite safe on the digital frontier.

VIRUSES

If you haven't heard about one or more of the well-publicized computer virus scares by now, you are almost certainly very new to computing (and you never watch television or read newspapers, either). But even if you have heard about the Melissa Word macro virus or another of the infamous computer bugs out there, you may not be quite sure what a virus is. The simple answer is that a virus is a piece of computer code that is hidden in another host program. When the host program is executed or activated, the virus code attaches itself to other programs, which then copies the virus to still other programs. This self-replicating action is intended, and is part of the design of the software.

In addition to copying itself, a virus usually contains a payload. This innocuous-sounding term refers to the malicious side effects of the virus. They may range from harmless messages to data corruption or destruction.

NOTE

A program need not damage, delete, or corrupt files to be considered a virus. Some definitions would even classify ordinarily benign utilities, such as the DOS Diskcopy program, as viruses. However, since these programs aren't specifically intended to copy themselves, they're not viruses that you need to be concerned about.

Viruses can be highly destructive. A virus can destroy small or large chunks of data by copying over files or by replacing sections within a word processing document. In a worst case, a virus could issue a command to, say, reformat your hard drive, erasing all information on the drive. More subtle changes can be just as troublesome, however. A virus may, for instance, make random, hard-to-detect changes in numbers in a spreadsheet document. Viruses have been found that will post messages in your name—perhaps including personal documents from your hard drive—to unsavory Internet newsgroups. It's hard to put a monetary value on that kind of damage.

Many viruses are more irritating than purely destructive. They may, for instance, cause prank messages to pop up on your screen, send blank e-mails to everyone in your address book, or force you to repeatedly click a meaningless dialog box. Even the ones without any significant payload can be seriously disruptive, however. Floods of virus-generated e-mail can overload servers and cause networks to crash.

NOTE

Although having your hard drive reformatted can be truly distressing, the good news is that this is not likely to occur because of a virus. The reason is, a virus that reformats the hard disk will also tend to erase itself. That means it can't spread to other machines, including yours.

Basically, to get a virus, you have to boot your PC from an infected disk or other medium, execute an infected program, or open an infected file. Beyond that, viruses can enter your computer in several ways, including the following:

Floppy disks   Formerly, downloading data from floppy disks was the biggest way for viruses to get on your computer. Today, viruses are mostly spread through network connections.

Electronic mail   Today, the largest number of viruses are disseminated as attachments to electronic mail. E-mail is now the most effective, fastest way for viruses to spread themselves.

Infected files   Downloading files from the Internet represents another likely source of infection, although files from reputable freeware and shareware sites are usually scanned for viruses. You can also encounter infected files over a network.

Infected CD-ROMs   Like the floppies of yore, CD-ROMs can just as effectively spread viruses.

Malicious applets   Acquired when you view Web sites, these applets are created to spread disease.

Commercial software   Even new software in its shrink wrap has been known to ship to customers containing viruses.

Part iv

It used to be said that you could not get a virus by receiving and reading electronic mail. However, viruses have evolved to the point where some can infect computers when electronic mail is merely previewed. Even more worrisome are viruses embedded in the programs used to display World Wide Web pages. These can be downloaded to your machine merely by accessing a malicious Web page.

Not all destructive programs are technically viruses. Some, such as worms and Trojan Horse programs, can do plenty of damage, however. The classification of viruses is a difficult art and gets highly technical very quickly. But, without attempting to be either comprehensive or extremely detailed, here are the different types of viruses and virus-like programs you could encounter:

Boot sector viruses   Infect the data your computer uses to start up.

File viruses   Attach themselves to executable program files, such as .com and .exe programs.

Macro viruses   Infect documents created by word processors, spreadsheets, and databases, including Word, Excel, PowerPoint, and Access files used by Microsoft Office.

Applet viruses   Are buried in Java applets and ActiveX controls. They can be downloaded when users view Web pages containing the controls.

E-mail viruses   Are viruses that spread themselves by infecting e-mail messages and e-mail programs.

Polymorphic viruses   Are complex viruses that can alter their appearance and escape detection.

Encrypted viruses   Use encryption and other techniques to evade detection.

Stealth viruses   Try to avoid detection and removal by the modifications they make to files or boot records.

Worms   Are programs that can spread working copies of themselves to other computer systems, usually through a network. Unlike viruses, worms don't necessarily attach themselves to a host program.

Trojan horses   Can be any program that purposefully does something, usually undocumented, that users don't want it to do. Hoax viruses, as the name suggests, aren't viruses at all. They are just rumors of viruses. In some ways, these are the most popular and easily spread viruses out there, because they travel not by network connection, but by word of mouth. You can check for information about hoax viruses at virus information centers such as the Virus Bulletin home page at www.virusbtn.com.

Protecting against Viruses

Viruses can be a little unsettling. The idea that a piece of computer code that you can't see can enter your computer and destroy data is not particularly comforting. Add in the fact that there are already many thousands of distinct viruses in the wild (the lingo for viruses that have been released into the general computing world) and that many more come out all the time, and it may seem as if you are practically helpless before an onslaught of destructive code. However, it's not inevitable that you'll be harmed by a virus. By employing effective steps to protect your network, you can greatly increase the odds that your household won't get infected. And if a virus does somehow creep in, you can ensure that the resulting problems are short-lived and minor.

NOTE

The first computer virus was reportedly created in the 1980s by a Pakistani programmer who was trying to keep people from pirating software. Today, there are more than 50,000 viruses of a bewildering variety of types, created by thousands of programmers all over the world, most for far less reputable reasons.

Your first line of defense against viruses is to simply be careful. The primary rules are:

▶ Don't accept e-mail from unknown parties, especially if files are attached. Delete them without opening them.

NOTE

If you use Microsoft Outlook or Outlook Express, you should also be careful about previewing electronic mail messages. Some viruses have been found that will infect a user's machine if the preview feature in Outlook is used, even if the mail is not opened.

▶ Don't open e-mail from anybody, especially if files are attached, unless you are sure that the file was sent to you by someone who checked it for viruses first. This also applies to files that come in on floppies.

▶ Avoid Internet viruses by downloading only from safe sites, where all files are scanned by virus-detection software before they are posted for downloading. Safe sites are also called *well-known* sites, such as www.microsoft.com, www.tucows.com, and www.download.com, to mention just a few.

▶ Make sure that you're using the latest update to your antivirus software, and buy new versions when they become available. Updates are critical with antivirus software because viruses change constantly as their creators try to come up with ways to beat antivirus defenses. Antivirus software companies post regular updates on their Web sites, and most send e-mail bulletins or allow you to manually or even automatically update to software owners. Updates help antivirus programs recognize the signatures of new viruses.

▶ Make sure that everyone who uses your network knows that they have to keep their antivirus software active, running and up-to-date.

WARNING

It's important to load antivirus software on all computers on your home network, not just a few. A single unprotected PC can infect the whole household through shared network files and the swapping of floppies.

▶ Authorize only one person—yourself—to issue virus alerts on the network. This will reduce downtime and confusion caused by the common virus hoaxes.

Being careful will only take you so far, however. If you want true peace of mind, you need to use antivirus software. This is utility software that recognizes the signs of infection by a particular virus—called its *signature*—and alerts you if there's a problem. Antivirus software can usually remove the virus from your system as well, although in the case of a very new or very stubborn virus, it may not work.

WARNING

Your chances of getting infected with a virus may be higher than you think, and the pain may be greater. The International Computer Security Association in Carlisle, Pennsylvania, says over 99% of the medium-sized and larger organizations it surveyed had at least one computer virus experience. The annual infection rate is 406 of every 1,000 machines. That's very high—and a virus infection can be quite costly. The average infection of a corporate computer costs over $8,000, mostly for downtime and re-entering lost data. And damages from a virus infection can get worse—much worse. If you negligently forward a virus to someone else and cause their computer to be infected, you could be held legally liable for any damages that are caused.

Antivirus Software

Antivirus programs are utilities designed to sniff out, identify, report, and, when possible, destroy computer viruses on your machine. It's important to realize that not all viruses can be removed by antivirus software. Often, you will need to delete the infected files or programs and replace them with backups. This is, incidentally, why you need backups, even though you may be using antivirus software.

Antivirus software works by scanning files and memory for patterns characteristic of known viruses. Since virus-writers know how antivirus software works, they try to foil the virus-catchers by encrypting their malicious code, changing its appearance on-the-fly, and even intercepting internal system messages so that their presence won't be revealed. Staying on top of evolving viruses requires a significant research and development effort by the virus software companies, which is why, as a general rule, the shareware and freeware virus programs do not afford anything like the same level of protection as commercial programs. You may use a freeware word processor, e-mail program, and even an operating system without missing the commercial programs, but virus software is a different story.

NOTE

Viruses can do a lot of damage, but there are limits to their destructive potency. A virus is just a software program—it doesn't have a physical being like a real germ does. It can't destroy your computer's mechanical or electronic components, such as its disk drives, network cards, and so forth. Whatever happens to your data, you'll still have a computer to rebuild it on.

Selecting Antivirus Software

Most new computers today come bundled with antivirus software. If your new PC does, be sure to update it at the vendor's Web site before considering yourself protected. If you don't have any antivirus software, you have a lot of choices. There are many commercial publishers of antivirus software. Antivirus software is a complex product, but most products do basically the same thing: identify and remove viruses. You want a vendor that stands behind the product with vigorous research into new virus threats, frequent updates, and always-ready technical support. As far as product features, make sure that the software automatically scans floppy disks inserted into your PC, as well as downloaded files.

Here, arranged in alphabetical order, are several products that have gotten good reviews, along with Web sites where you can go to learn more:

Aladdin eSafe Protect Desktop 3.0 (www.ealaddin.com) From Aladdin Knowledge Systems, includes a desktop Internet firewall to stop hackers.

Command AntiVirus from Command Software Systems (www.commandcom.com)   Uses the well-regarded F-PROT Professional virus detection system.

F-Secure Anti-Virus (www.datafellows.com)   From Finnish company F-Secure, it runs on a wide variety of computers and operating systems.

McAfee VirusScan 5.1 (www.mcafee.com)   Is the latest from long-time antivirus leader Network Associates.

Norton AntiVirus 2001 (www.symantec.com)   From Symantec, is the best-selling virus software.

Panda Antivirus Platinum 6.23 (www.pandasoftware.com) From Panda Software, it is both powerful and exceptionally easy to use.

Sophos AntiVirus (www.sophos.com)   Is produced by UK-based Sophos Software, which offers a free downloadable trial version.

WARNING

No antivirus program is foolproof. Virus programmers are constantly working to find ways to beat antivirus software, and, especially in the case of very new viruses, they often succeed, at least for a time. Antivirus software programmers also make mistakes, and release buggy, ineffective products. Finally, antivirus software can be inconvenient; it has to be used to work at all.

Using Antivirus Software

The key to succeeding with antivirus software is less about buying the right kind and more about properly using whatever you do purchase. The main key is to keep it turned on. Antivirus software can be inconvenient to use. It often creates conflicts and must be turned off—temporarily—when installing other programs. Some antivirus programs give false alerts in the presence of certain types of code. Others are simply clunky to use, with unhandy user interfaces. The main thing to remember, however, is that if it's not turned on, it's not protecting you.

WARNING

Always make good backups. This is your first line of defense. Antivirus software is only your second line of defense.

Updating Antivirus Software

Of all the things you can do with antivirus software, updating it is the most important. You should regularly—say, once a month—go to the vendor's Web site and download and install the latest update. This is true even for the latest version of antivirus software that you have just brought home from the store or received in the mail. New viruses can emerge in far less time than it takes to shrink-wrap and distribute a CD-ROM of antivirus software. You need to have the latest update in order to have maximum protection.

What to Do if You Think You're Infected

Someday, you may have a sneaking suspicion that turns into a high probability and finally a certainty: A virus has infected your computer. Now what do you do?

1. Stop working immediately and completely. If you're on a network and think other machines on the network may have been infected, make sure no one is using those machines. Especially be sure that no one is sending e-mails or copying files that could be infected.

2. Using another machine if possible, download the latest antivirus update for your antivirus software from your software vendor's Web site, and update your software's database of virus signatures.

Part iv

3. Run the antivirus program and follow its instructions for removing the virus. This may involve deleting any files the antivirus program identifies as infected.

TIP

You can check for computer viruses even if you don't have any antivirus software installed on your computer, the stores aren't open, and you don't have the inclination to buy downloadable software. Here's how: Using the machine you suspect of being infected, go to an online virus-checking site such as www.mcafee.com and follow the instructions. Online checks let you scan for and delete harmful viruses instantly. You don't have to purchase, load, or upgrade any software—although there may be a charge for subscribing to the service long-term. You just log on after completing a form and signing up for a trial offer, and start the check. When it's done, take a look at your user report to see if any viruses have been detected.

4. See if you can determine the source of the infection. This may require some elementary detective work. For instance, if several documents you received as an e-mail attachment turn out to have been infected, the oldest document was probably the source.

5. Alert the apparent source of the infection. Do this diplomatically; viruses can be hard to detect and whoever gave it to you probably doesn't know that they are infected.

6. Finally, as with any socially transmitted disease, alert anyone you may have infected.

Reporting A New Virus

What if your computer is acting oddly, you scan for a virus, and nothing is found? In that case, chances are good that you have an ordinary system or software conflict that is causing a problem. On the other hand, it's just possible you have a virus that is so new that it hasn't been registered by the virus-detecting databases. Here's what to do if you think you've got an undetectable virus:

1. Try to make sure it's not something else by scanning your hard drive for errors, reviewing your configuration, and checking that your system is set up properly.

2. Obtain an e-mail address of a software virus lab—ideally, one provided by your antivirus software maker—to which you can send any suspicious files.

3. If you get the suspicious effect when you work on a particular document, such as a Word file, send that document to the virus lab. Failing that, send another recently used document of the same type.

4. If it is a particular program that produces the odd results when you run it, or if the virus-like effect takes place when you boot the system, try to send the program file. In the worst case, if your hard disk has been erased or reformatted, check other hard drives on the network, or perhaps floppy disks for files and programs that you may have used since the infection occurred.

If you have additional questions—or even if you don't—a call to the technical support line of your antivirus software company is a good idea.

Protecting against Hackers

Once you're connected to the Internet, especially if you're using an always-on Internet connection such as a DSL line or cable modem, you become vulnerable to hackers. Hackers, of course, are computer vandals who gain unauthorized access to computer systems and networks, and there wreak mayhem by stealing or damaging information or misusing network resources. Hacking is a crime on the rise. According to Kessler & Associates, an investigative consulting company, theft of proprietary information by hackers and other unauthorized people doubled from 1997 to 1999. Misuse of network resources is another popular goal of hackers. They may, for instance, break into a mail server and use it as a place to exchange stolen commercial software.

The term *hacker* originally applied to programmers who created their software in assembly language. Assembly is the programming language just above the binary coded instructions that computers actually read. Assembly programming requires detailed knowledge of a computer's hardware architecture, and is generally the domain of only the most expert programmers. Therefore, hacker started out as a term of respect, if not admiration.

Among programmers, the people who break into computers are known as *crackers* or *computer crackers*. Over time the public has come to associate

Part iv

the term with people who break into computer systems. And these are the people most of us know as hackers. Although they have been benignly described as people who enjoy circumventing the limitations of systems, the hacker label is generally not used as a term of respect, especially with regard to computer security. Keep in mind, however, that while many crackers are hackers, not all people who refer to themselves as hackers are out to attack computers.

The typical computer cracker is a 16-to-25-year-old male who gets interested in breaking into computers and networks to improve his cracking skill, or to preempt network resources for his own purposes. E-mail surveys of newsgroup users who claim to be hackers show that they tend to have a lot of spare time on their hands, which explains why they can be quite persistent in their attacks. Very few hackers go so far as to pick a target in advance. Hackers are generally opportunists, running scanners to examine many thousands of network hosts for weaknesses. Interestingly, after spotting a vulnerable computer and invading it using the weakness he has identified, the hacker will often fix other vulnerabilities to prevent other hackers from gaining access to the host.

Like computer viruses, hackers pose an unfamiliar threat to most home networkers. You're probably wondering: How can you protect yourself from these Internet-borne criminals? What risk do they really pose? There aren't perfect answers to either of these questions. But there are things you can do to help you rest more easily.

TIP
You can find a wide array of anti-hacker information at AntiOnline, an electronic publication for security professionals at www.antionline.com.

Hack Attacks

The first thing to understand about hack attacks is that they come in several varieties. These are among the most common:

> ▶ Attempts to gain passwords or otherwise impersonate authentic users so they can gain access to network resources. This can be done using software that tricks the computers or by social engineering, which is the use of clever e-mail messages to try to trick people into revealing their passwords.

▸ Attempts to harm the network by overloading it with meaningless messages. Examples include pointless requests for network connections and repeated diagnostic messages such as pings. Because these attacks make the network unusable, they're termed *denial of service* attacks.

▸ Attempts to exploit weaknesses in the security of specific programs, such as operating systems, mail programs, and applications software. Many programs have built-in methods for allowing technicians to bypass security protections. When hackers discover these back doors, it can spell trouble.

Within these broad parameters, there are many different ways for a hacker to attack a network, and hackers are constantly thinking up new ones. Any attempt to describe how hackers attack networks would be outdated almost as soon as it was expressed. At this writing, however, here are some of the more popular and enduring types of attacks:

Back Orifice   A set of programs that can let hackers access and control computers running Windows 95/98 and NT.

Changemac   A program designed to make a hacker appear to be an authenticated user.

Deceit.C   A program that attempts to foil an otherwise secure network by tricking users into disclosing their passwords.

Network Scanners   A type of program that scans networks looking for unprotected servers that can be easily hacked.

Password Sniffers   Programs that are designed to snag passwords as they go by on the network.

Ping of Death   A malicious use of a tool, normally used to test networks, that can stall or crash a computer or an entire network by tying up the system with pointless tasks.

Smurfs   Attacks that can overwhelm a network by sending and requesting hordes of echoed data packets.

Syn Flood   A program that floods network ports with so many bogus requests for connections that they can no longer communicate.

Winhack Gold   A hacker program for Windows that scans blocks of network addresses, looking for shared files that anyone can access.

Part iv

What can you do about these hack attacks? One approach to network security is to arm yourself with the same Net-cracking tools as hackers, and try to compromise your own network. You can download many popular attack programs off of the Internet and use them to check for vulnerabilities. The idea is to find your own weaknesses before someone else does it for you. Learn more, and find some of the programs for downloading at www.rootshell.com.

WARNING

Before you obtain and use hackers' tools, be aware that these tools must be handled carefully or you could damage your own network. If you damage someone else's network, even accidentally, you could find yourself in violation of the law.

One of the basic techniques for protecting networks from Internet-borne hackers is to make sure that you do not have unnecessary services set up on your computer. The more open your network, the easier it is for hackers to gain access to it. Of utmost importance: Make sure you don't have Microsoft File and Printer Sharing set up to work with a TCP/IP connection. Finding open shares of this sort is the primary objective of many hacker-scanning programs. Fortunately, it's not too hard to close this hole, even if you wish to retain the ability to share files and printers with other machines on your network.

WARNING

Unbinding TCP/IP file and printer sharing will mean that while you can share with other machines on the network, you can no longer share files and printers from a remote location, such as your workplace. If you need to do this, you should use a firewall, such as the personal firewall software. At the very least, you should use long passwords composed of random characters and change them frequently, since your passwords will be your only line of defense against any hacker whose scanner sniffs out your shared files.

The same protocol that makes Windows networking so easy also makes it less secure. To smooth the configuration of Windows networking, Microsoft has elected to have adapters and services bound to each other by default. Because this mass binding is done automatically, it means you don't have to configure each adapter separately. That speeds the process of preparing your computer for the network. Unfortunately, this also creates some serious security problems.

There are two ways you can help to protect yourself from the possibility of attack due to unnecessary protocols and services. Use the Network Setup Wizard to set up your home network and to use a firewall to defend your system against unauthorized attack from outside your network.

TIP

The most useful source for security-related tips on how to protect yourself from hackers by eliminating unneeded services, bindings, and protocols is Steve Gibson's Shields Up page at www.grc.com.

Removing your open invitation to hackers by not having a poorly set up system will make your network more secure. But nothing is perfect. Hackers are ingenious, and good security involves more than closing the door. To be really safe, make sure you use your locks, in the form of password protection.

Problems with Passwords

If you've read *Arabian Nights* or seen Walt Disney's animated *Aladdin* movie, you are aware that knowing a secret word or phrase like "Open Sesame!" can unlock otherwise impenetrable barriers. There are lots of other instances in which words or names are invested with near-magical powers. In some primitive cultures, for instance, each individual has a personal name that no one else may know. If it were to get out, anyone who knew it would have special powers over that person. In the networking world, knowing your password could similarly give someone special powers over you.

You may suspect that your password, or someone else's on the network, has been compromised if any of the following things occur:

▶ Files mysteriously appear or disappear in your personal directories.

▶ You receive e-mail messages that refer to a message you did not send.

▶ You are unable to log on to the network, despite being sure that you are typing in your username and password properly. In this case, a hacker may have stolen your password and then changed it, so you can no longer access the system.

Effective use of passwords is a primary line of defense against hackers. Ideally, if you require a user to provide an authentic password to gain entrance to your network, then nobody but authentic users will be on your network. Unfortunately, it doesn't always work that way. Here are some of the common problems with passwords:

▶ Hackers can easily guess many passwords, especially those made up of words from the dictionary (there are literally hundreds of dictionary files available on the Web purely to do this) and birth dates.

NOTE

Don't stop your quest for security just by eliminating dictionary words from your password list. Also screen out names of fictional characters and proper names of family and friends. One Internet service provider used a program to automatically check users' passwords against the contents of their personal Web pages. It found that people frequently wanted to use the names of relatives or pets as passwords. While these words might not be found in any dictionary, they could still be seen by anyone surfing their Web page.

▶ Passwords that are too short can be guessed by hackers using powerful and speedy password-guessing programs, even if they consist of random characters.

▶ Careless distribution of passwords, in insecure media such as non-encrypted electronic mail, can place them in hackers' hands.

▶ Hackers can capture passwords from network traffic by using password sniffer software.

▶ Beware also of social engineering by hackers, such as sending you e-mail purporting to be from a system administrator or other supposedly benign individual and requesting your password.

WARNING

Cybercafes, where you can check your e-mail and surf the Internet while downing a cup of good coffee and a scone, are a great invention, to be sure. But if a hacker has installed a keystroke logging program on the machine, it could be acting as a funnel—collecting passwords for users' e-mail boxes, personal Web sites, and network logons—and saving them for the hacker to use to break into your accounts. Keystroke monitoring programs can be silent, invisible, and very hard to detect. Ask the proprietor of a cybercafe what security measures have been taken to prevent keystroke logging before using a public PC for anything more sensitive than figuring out what movie to see after you've had your coffee.

Password File Security

Things nowadays are a lot better than they were. While Windows 95 and Windows 98 may require passwords for you to log on to your network, the truth is, these operating systems are not secure. The reason is that you can get around the password protection by simply hitting the Escape key when presented with the password dialog box, then searching for the password file, deleting it, and rebooting the computer. This will allow anyone to create his or her own user and have full access to your computer.

WARNING

Even more worrisome, hackers have written and distributed over the Internet programs that can decode the encrypted Windows password files and automatically send them out in an e-mail message. While Microsoft periodically releases patches that, to varying degrees, repair these weaknesses, new ones continue to crop up from time to time.

Windows XP also has much better password security than the versions of Windows that have descended to us from DOS. Unless you're using Windows XP (or Windows 2000 or Windows NT—or perhaps Linux, which has even better security) it's important to remember that your Windows password protection is not truly watertight.

NOTE

For more on security issues with Windows, see Microsoft's site on security at www.microsoft.com/security.

But even with all these improvements to Windows XP, you still cannot afford to become complacent. You have to make sure that the passwords you use are up to the job!

Using Passwords Effectively

Getting a good password can take a little thought. Here are some tips to getting a good password:

1. Use a mix of uppercase and lowercase and numbers (and other keyboard characters). Consider these two passwords:

    password

    PaS5w0RD

The second one is much more complex, and hence, harder to guess.

2. Take something you remember and something you can write down and combine the two in an unusual way (using the rule above). So, you might remember the license plate of your first car (XYZ321) and write down and keep (preferably away from your PC) a phrase, sentence, or name (e.g., XP is Great!) and combine them (XYZ321XPisGr8!).

3. Don't get too carried away with passwords though—if you make them too complex, you'll get irritated using them and eventually you (or someone else) will disable them. Keep password length realistic!

Things You Should Never Do With A Password

Never is a long time, but here are things that, at the very least, you should try to never do with your password:

1. Never give your password to anyone else. This simple rule will help you control your password better than almost anything.

2. Never e-mail your password, even if it's in a letter to yourself. E-mail is insecure, and may expose your password to prying eyes.

3. Never write down your password where anyone else could find it. This especially includes a yellow sticky note on the side of your computer monitor.

4. Never use the same password twice. Instead, choose something completely different from your previous password.

There are exceptions to these rules. If the password is the one you use to log on to your Square Dancer's Joke of the Week newsletter subscription, it's probably okay to use something you've used before. But when it comes to the security of your network, don't do anything foolish.

Using Firewalls

A fireplace is one location where you definitely want to maintain separation between two areas. To keep your house from catching fire every time you want to snuggle down in front of a cheery blaze, builders use fireproof walls separating the area where combustion occurs from the area where the people are. Similarly, computer networks are protected from intruders by systems called *firewalls*. In a networking sense, a firewall is a system of hardware and software or, sometimes, software alone, that is designed to keep unauthorized users from accessing a network. They work by requiring all the messages going to or from your network to pass through the firewall. The firewall checks each message against specified security criteria, and blocks any that don't measure up. Figure 21.1 shows a dedicated PC acting as a secure server.

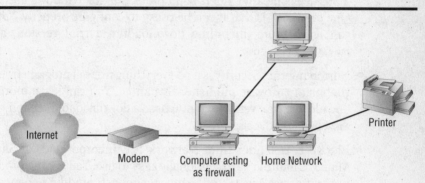

FIGURE 21.1: A firewall sits between you and the Internet, filtering incoming and outgoing messages to make sure they are from authenticated users.

Want to see if your computer is vulnerable to hackers? You can by checking it against Port Probe, a free Web-based service from Gibson Research Corporation. Learn more by going to www.grc.com and clicking the Shields Up! button.

Most firewalls are regular PCs that are loaded with firewall software or have certain security features of their operating systems running.

One nice feature of Windows XP is that is comes complete with a built-in firewall. You can activate the Internet Connection Firewall by clicking on Start ➣ Control Panel ➣ Network and Internet Connections and then click on Network Connections, right-click on the connection and choose Properties, and then select the Advanced tab. Check the box to activate the firewall. You can then, if you want, alter the settings of the firewall by clicking on the Settings button.

TIP

Alter settings only if you know what you are doing—otherwise, it is best to leave them as they are.

The firewall that ships with Windows XP Home Edition is a rudimentary one. It offers you a satisfactory level of protection but you may want something better (clearer interface, greater control, attack information, and so on). In that case you will want to choose a firewall from a third-party vendor.

Here are some firewall programs suitable for home networks:

▶ ConSeal Private Desktop from Signal9 in Ontario, Canada (now a McAfee company), offers solid protection for Windows users. One drawback is that it can be tricky to configure properly. You can learn more, including downloading a trial version, at www.signal9.com.

▶ Norton Internet Security is a do-everything firewall program from the major software publisher Symantec. You can learn more, download a trial version, or purchase a downloadable version at www.symantec.com.

▶ BlackICE Defender from Network ICE Incorporated, of San Mateo, California, is exceptionally easy to use. You get the product and a year's worth of technical support, product enhancements, upgrades, bug fixes, patches, and security updates. You can learn more at www.networkice.com.

TIP

At the time of writing, Windows XP had not been released so no company was advertising a commercial product for XP—however, rest assured that by the time you read this, most, if not all, of the vendors listed above will have products designed for XP!

One effective way to protect your network is to use a simple hardware firewall that will not allow any network traffic to occur while you're connected to the outside world. This approach prevents anyone coming in on a modem connection from accessing your LAN by basically disabling your network connection while a modem session is in progress. The network connection is automatically re-established when you are finished using the modem. The Mini Firewall from Computer Peripheral Systems Incorporated, of Tucker, Georgia, accomplishes this task by using mechanical relays that are difficult for computer hackers to overcome. Although it may be inconvenient to be unable to use the modem and network at the same time, the price—$85—is low compared to other firewall solutions. You can learn more at www.cpscom.com/gprod/firewall.htm.

PRIVACY

Your essential data is not the only thing at risk via your Internet connection. Most people have quite a few personal details of information that, while it may not actually be *harmful* to let it leak out, it *would* be uncomfortable, inconvenient, or embarrassing. After you've used your computer for a while, you're liable to have all sorts of information in it, in the form of financial transactions, appointment schedules, personal letters, and copies of e-mail messages. Once you hook your computer up to a network, this information becomes vulnerable just the same as any other data on a network computer.

Think you don't have any secrets? These potentially troublesome details may include the following:

▶ The information that an Internet user is a child or other vulnerable person.

▶ The results of medical tests that, if known, might result in discrimination or other harm against you.

▶ Your buying patterns as a consumer, which could help businesses target you for potentially unwelcome advertising.

▶ Your financial information, which could be used to identify you as a promising victim for criminals.

▶ Your peace of mind, which could be disturbed by privacy developments beyond anything we've currently run across. Who could have guessed that someday we would all commonly use a form of mail (electronic mail) in which the letters could be freely read by any number of strangers?

Clearly, there's more here to worry about than some *unsolicited commercial e-mail,* or *UCE.* The first thing to do to address these worries is to make sure your network is secure from hackers, as described in the previous section in this chapter. But since a major source of information leakage is from data you voluntarily or unknowingly supply to seemingly reputable organizations, such as the businesses you buy from online, it's also important to look at some other solutions.

The first thing to do is to make sure you do business only with reputable online firms that have publicly posted privacy policies. Be suspicious if a firm doesn't have a description of what it intends to do with the information that it gathers anywhere on its Web site. And you might be amazed at the amount of information a Web site can gather based on a simple transaction. Web site activity logs gather information about the pages you have viewed, the purchases you have made, how you are paying for them, and more. Marketers are willing to pay good money for such details because they help them identify promising prospects. Some people, such as opt-in electronic newsletter publishers, operate their sites primarily to gather and sell marketing fodder. If a Web site operator doesn't explicitly say they won't sell your information, assume they will. And, if privacy is important to you, be prepared to patronize another merchant.

You should also pay attention to what the privacy policy says. A good one will:

▶ State what information about you is being collected.

▶ Explain how that personal data is being collected.

▶ Describe the purpose of the collection.

▶ Say what use that information will be put to.

▶ Disclose which other organizations that personal data will be shared with.

▶ Explain where the personal data is stored and how it is being protected.

▶ Describe any standards that the information-gathering effort adheres to.

▶ Offer you the opportunity to review that information.

▶ Give you the chance to opt out of any information-gathering that is going on.

It's important to check policies even if you're not aware of volunteering any information. The simple act of viewing a Web site—without even making a purchase—can reveal an astonishing amount of information about you, from your name to your e-mail address and even the name of the city and neighborhood where you live. To see an example of this, point your browser to www.anonymizer.com and try out the free privacy analysis of your Web browser. You may be surprised by the amount of information about yourself and your household you are giving away just by using the Web.

What can you do to protect privacy, other than check for good policies? The source for some of this information is the Internet address of your computer or the proxy through which your Internet traffic may go. There's not much you can do to conceal that. However, you can conceal a number of the more personal details, such as the username you are using on a Windows computer, by employing the unbinding procedures described in the previous section in this chapter, "Protecting against Hackers."

Protecting Electronic Mail

One of the problems with electronic mail sent through the Internet is that it is vulnerable to being intercepted and read by other people. While you, personally, can't change the technology underlying the Internet, you can encrypt or encode your e-mail messages so that they can't be read by anyone except the person they are intended for.

Pretty Good Privacy, or PGP, is the world's most popular e-mail encryption software. It was written in 1991 by a programmer named Phil Zimmermann. PGP works by letting you send encrypted or scrambled messages that can only be descrambled by a person who has the appropriate key. A key, in this case, is a string of characters that can allow the possessor and only the possessor to read your message. So, if your e-mail was intercepted in transmission, or a nosy administrator tries to take a peek, it will appear to them as nothing more than a bunch of junk. To make the use of keys more convenient, people can use public key registration sites.

PGP is an effective code-making program. It's so effective, in fact, that the US government bans the use of some of its encoding possibilities. Thus, there are US-approved versions of PGP (as well as other privacy encryption programs) and others for sale to users outside the U.S. You can learn more about PGP from the Web site of the distributor of the U.S. versions, PGP Security Inc., at www.pgp.com.

USING PARENTAL CONTROLS

If you can't make your computer work, find a kid. That wisecrack—which many an adult frustrated with a PC problem has probably heard before—carries more than a little truth. Today's children are growing up with the Internet, computers, and computer networks, and they are likely to far outstrip their parents in their abilities to use these powerful technologies. But a kid's mastery of networks is more than a matter of opportunity. The

Internet and networked computers are highly appealing to children. Children can use networks to do a variety of things:

- ▶ Find out what's happening in places as close as the downstairs game room and as far away as the other side of the world.
- ▶ Study distant or vanishing cultures that they might otherwise never get the opportunity to experience.
- ▶ Complete homework research assignments efficiently and effectively.
- ▶ Find new peers to associate with through chat rooms and child-centered Web portals.
- ▶ Make friends.
- ▶ Stay up on news and information of special interest to children, from sites devoted to popular television cartoons to samples of the latest song from a currently popular musical group.
- ▶ Play games of many varieties.
- ▶ Stay in touch with friends and family members by e-mail.

Clearly, network computers can be powerful forces for helping children learn and experience the world in many new and positive ways.

However, the news is not all good. There are also a lot of things on the Internet that few parents or anyone else setting up a home network would want children exposed to. These include the following:

- ▶ Pornographic Web sites with explicit sexual content.
- ▶ Chat rooms populated by adults frankly discussing material inappropriate for children.
- ▶ Sexual criminals who may cruise the Net searching for children to befriend.

 WARNING

You don't have to use the Internet for long before you are likely to stumble across highly offensive material. For instance, when searching for "fun sites for young children" you may be directed to Web pages catering to pedophiles. A search for "Bond"—as in James Bond—may produce sites devoted to bondage. Simply clicking on a harmless-looking link in an innocuous e-mail message purporting to be from an acquaintance suggesting you "Take a look at this!" may lead the unguarded surfer into a maze of X-rated sites. These sites can even directly, and without warning, download pornographic images to a hard drive. And the sites often refuse to go away, no matter how many times you click the Back button on your browser or try to close a window.

▶ Offensive e-mail messages.

▶ Marketing campaigns targeted toward minor children.

Harm might not only come to your children who use the Internet, but harm to your network can also come from your children who use the Internet. On a purely practical level, when a relatively naive juvenile is using a networked computer to access the Internet, your network may be more at risk of becoming infected with a virus.

NOTE

You could conceivably go overboard in limiting children's use of computers. It's one thing to watch and control a child's use of the network and the Internet, and quite another to choke it off altogether. Before you take too draconian a stance, keep in mind that technology skills are crucial to children's future success, that most new jobs being created in today's economy require technology skills, and that people who use computers on the job tend to earn more than workers who don't.

Software to Limit Web Access

Networked computers raise issues about protecting children, but they also provide some answers, notably in the form of software to restrict or monitor young people's access to potentially objectionable Web sites, chat rooms, newsgroups, and other online communities. There are six basic approaches to using technology to improve the appropriateness of children's use of the Web:

Suggest   There are many Web sites, books, directories, guides, and pamphlets that offer lists of sources of child-suitable content. One example is the Internet Kids & Family Yellow Pages, at www.netmom.com/ikyp.

Search   You can use Internet search engines to find content suitable for children. Many engines let you filter your queries to show only those matches that are appropriate for children. AltaVista, at www.altavista.com, has a Family Filter feature that you can set and control with the use of a password.

Inform   You can encourage your children to use Web site ratings, reviews, and other tools to steer them toward appropriate content.

Monitor   Some programs save a log file of surfing activities. Cyber Snoop logs all Internet activity while a child is online. You can inspect the log file later to see what the child has been up to.

Warn Rating services such as Cyber Sitter, www.cybersitter .com, can give children advance warning about pages and sites they should avoid. Many adult-oriented sites also show a warning about their content on the first page. This approach helps kids decide on their own whether to view possibly objectionable content.

NOTE

The Recreational Software Advisory Council rating service, upon which Internet Explorer bases its ratings, is an independent, nonprofit organization that rates sites by the level of sex, nudity, violence, and offensive language in computer games and sites.

Block Technology can simply keep children from getting to the stuff you think they shouldn't see. The Internet Explorer browser filter, for instance, can screen out content based on a set of criteria chosen by the parent. You can also block out all chat rooms, e-mail, newsgroups, and other content from the Web.

By mixing and matching these methods, you can find the most suitable means for protecting your children. Which methods you choose will depend largely on the age, maturity, and inquisitiveness of your children.

Software for Web Blocking

There are a number of programs you can use to block out Net content. Two of the more popular are Net Nanny and SurfWatch.

Here are capsule reviews of each:

Net Nanny

Net Nanny is an easy-to-use but powerful Internet content filtering and blocking program. It lets a parent set up a customizable screening list. You can build upon the preset list of Web sites, words and phrases, and other criteria it provides.

As is appropriate for software of this type, Net Nanny allows for extensive customization. You can:

▶ Block any words, phrases, Web sites including HTML code, *Internet Relay Chat* (IRC) rooms, newsgroups, and personal information per values you select.

▶ Limit access to only sites you place on a list of acceptable sites.

▶ Monitor transmission of personal information, including children's names, ages, addresses, phone numbers, credit card numbers, and Social Security numbers.

▶ Select several actions when a surfing violation occurs, ranging from simply logging the violation to issuing a warning and refusing to access the site. You can learn more, as well as download a trial version, at www.netnanny.com.

SurfWatch

SurfWatch employs a team of professional Net surfers to rate Web sites and update filters for the sites it considers objectionable. Its software lets you use this constantly refreshed database to block unsuitable content.

SurfWatch uses a basic setup starting with five categories of potentially objectionable content. You select any or all of the categories with a mouse click. You can also add your own filtering based on custom words you create.

Additional features of SurfWatch include letting you:

▶ Block access to a list of more than 100,000 Internet sites with content in categories including pornography, violence, hate speech, gambling, and use of illegal drugs, alcohol, and tobacco.

TIP

It seems that youngsters aren't the only ones who need monitoring. The version of SurfWatch for servers running Windows NT also has Productivity filtering for 15 categories of Internet content that may not be bad for you, but can be for your work. They include astrology and mysticism, entertainment, games, general news, glamour and intimate apparel, hobbies, investments, job search, motor vehicles, personals and dating, real estate, shopping, sports, travel, and Usenet news.

▶ Create custom filters of your choice.

▶ Update filters daily from the SurfWatch database.

NOTE

While SurfWatch has a number of powerful features, it does not provide tools for logging Web activity, reflecting the company's stance that monitoring is not an appropriate tool.

Part iv

- Block access to chat sites and Internet Relay Chat servers.
- Restrict access only to sites approved by the Yahooligans! Rating service.

You can learn more, as well as download trial versions, at www.surfwatch.com.

WARNING

It's important to remember that no filtering system is perfect. SurfWatch estimates that filtering will block no more than 95% of the objectionable content that may be out there.

Controlling Online Time

Since technology creates the problem of protecting children on the Internet, it's only fair that technology should provide some of the solution. But protecting children isn't all a matter of technology. There are also a number of personal practices that you can implement to make sure that children using the Internet over your home network will have the kind of experience you want them to have. To ensure this, you should also:

- Make clear rules about how your children can use the network and the Internet. These should include hours of use, places that can be visited, and activities that can be performed.
- Place children's networked computers where they can be seen, such as in a family room or kitchen.

TIP

There's no hard and fast rule about how much time your child should spend in front of a computer screen, using your local network or the Internet. However, many experts suggest combining computer use with television viewing to create a "screen time" figure of hours or minutes per day that you are comfortable with.

- Make the Internet a family affair. Spend time surfing with your child to monitor their behavior and set standards in person.
- Know and use high-quality family-oriented Web sites, such as Yahoo's www.yahooligans.com.

TIP

You can learn more about aspects of managing children's use of the Internet and networked computers from America Links Up at www.americalinksup.org.

▶ Insist on knowing the e-mail passwords your child uses, and monitor the e-mail they send and receive.

TIP

With a home network, you can check kid's e-mail from another computer on the network if passwords and sharing privileges are set up to allow you access to the child's computer.

▶ Look closely for unsolicited e-mail that may be from persons who intend to harm or exploit your child.

▶ Instruct your child never to meet alone with an acquaintance made online.

▶ Tell your children not to release certain personal information online. This includes phone numbers, addresses, ages, school names, and financial information.

▶ Be a friend, not a foe, so that your children know they can come to you with any questions, problems, or concerns.

TIP

Another reason not to place too much trust in technological solutions to parental concerns is that computers aren't just in the home anymore. Most schools and public libraries have both computers and, increasingly, Internet access. You can't be on hand to oversee your child in these venues. And free speech issues make it difficult for libraries to restrict the use of their computers to access anything a user cares to. So you should probably view home networks as an opportunity to teach good computer use practices, so children will be more likely to demonstrate good judgment when no one is around to watch.

WHAT'S NEXT

Viruses. Hackers. Thieves. Pornographers. Marketers. It's a rough cyberspace out there. Fortunately, you can protect yourself—and your children—with antivirus software, passwords, firewalls, encrypted codes, and Web blocking. In the next chapter, Robert Cowart returns with a look at XP's version of the Windows Media Player.

Part iv

PART V

Having Fun with Windows XP Home Edition

Chapter 22

USING THE WINDOWS MEDIA PLAYER

If you've used Media Player in Windows 9x, you probably can't believe that I'm devoting an entire chapter to it in this book. The earlier Media Player was a very simple program, not particularly feature rich or attractive.

However, the version of Media Player introduced in Windows Me, and refined in Windows XP, is a new and exciting program. The only thing that stayed the same was the name. It's a full-featured multimedia player, capable of playing audio CDs, DVD movies, MP3 music files, Internet Radio stations, and video and sound clips stored in a variety of formats.

Adapted from *Mastering Windows Me* by Robert Cowart
ISBN 0-7821-2857-2   960 pages $39.99

STARTING MEDIA PLAYER

There are a number of ways of starting Media Player. When you insert an audio CD or DVD disc in your computer, it opens automatically and starts playing the CD (unless some other player is associated with those file types). You can also start it in any of these ways:

- ▶ Choose Start ➤ All Programs ➤ Accessories ➤ Entertainment ➤ Windows Media Player.

- ▶ Double-click a sound or video clip in a file management window.

- ▶ Click the Media Player icon in the Quick Launch toolbar, if displayed.

- ▶ Double-click the Media Player icon on the desktop, if there is a shortcut for it there.

Windows Media Player has several pages, each represented by a button along the left side of the window. The Media Guide page, shown in Figure 22.1, appears by default if you started Media Player without specifying a clip to open or inserting an audio CD. The Media Guide content changes every day, so yours will look different from the one shown here.

FIGURE 22.1: Windows Media Player opens to the Media Guide page by default.

USING THE MEDIA GUIDE

You might have heard in the news about the illegal distribution of music clips on the Internet. What you might not have heard, however, is that there is, thankfully, a lot of perfectly legal music and video clips available, including many by big-name artists as well as struggling independent bands.

The Media Guide in Windows Media Player is by no means a comprehensive way of finding clips, but it does include some great features. One is an ever-changing list of featured clips from popular artists. When you click one of those video clip links, Windows Media Player switches to the Now Playing tab and displays the clip.

Take a look at the controls at the bottom of the window in Figure 22.1. There's a Stop button (which is replaced by a Play button when stopped), a Pause button, a Fast-Forward button, and all the other controls you would expect on a cassette tape player, a VCR, or some other real-life media player with which you're familiar. As you'll see in this chapter, that metaphor carries over into all portions of the program.

NOTE

Sometimes when you choose to view a clip, a separate Internet Explorer window pops open with some advertising in it. Close it by clicking its Close (X) button.

As shown in Figure 22.1, the Media Guide page has a navigation bar at the left (but to the right of the main navigation bar for Media Player itself). By default it starts with the Home screen shown in Figure 22.1, but you can click any of the other words on the navigation bar to see similar offerings in specific categories like Music, Radio, or Movies. The Media Guide also includes a very useful Explore Music feature for browsing a large library of clips available for free download.

For example, suppose I'm looking for freebies by Bonnie Raitt. I would click Videos/Downloads in the Media Gallery's navigation bar, and then in the Explore Music area, enter her name in the Find Artist box and click Go.

Find Artist [Go]

Eventually I'd arrive at a bio of the artist and some hyperlinks to free videos I can download, as shown in Figure 22.2.

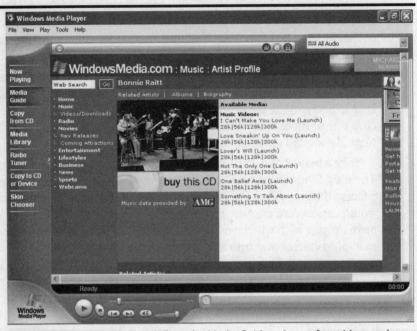

FIGURE 22.2: Use Web Search from the Media Guide to locate free videos and music clips from your favorite artists.

LISTENING TO INTERNET RADIO

Never heard of Internet radio? It's still a fairly well-kept secret, but you can listen to hundreds of radio stations all over the world in static-free glory through the Internet. (A fast Internet connection helps, of course, but is not essential.) Windows Media Player has a whole section devoted to Internet radio stations.

Internet Radio in Media Player

Let's jump right in; here's how to tune in an Internet radio station:

1. Click the Radio Tuner button in Media Player to bring up a searchable list of radio stations.

2. You can now either choose one of the radio stations in the featured list or go looking for a radio station that's not listed.

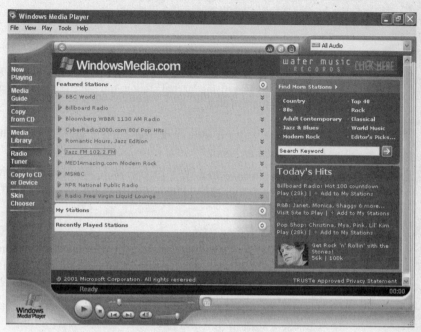

3. Click on a station to see more details about it.

4. When you find a station you want to try, double-click it. It starts playing.

On a slow Internet connection, such as a regular modem, it may take several minutes before the station begins to play. There might also be some pauses or choppiness in the play on a slow connection. (Cable, satellite, and DSL Internet users should not experience these problems.) A station takes a long time to load, because Internet radio is a streaming audio format. The music is transmitted to your PC just in time for it to be played in Media Player. On a slow PC, the least little delay can result in a choppy playback, so Media Player creates a *buffer*, a storage area for several seconds of incoming data. That way, if there is a delay in transmission, the music continues to play out of the buffer while your PC catches up, and there is no interruption in the broadcast. The slower your Internet connection, the longer it takes to fill the buffer initially.

NOTE
When you double-click a station to play it, a Web page may appear in a separate window with advertising for that station. You can close this window; the station will continue to play.

To choose another station, simply double-click it, and choose a different filter from the list as needed.

Internet radio is considered a WAV broadcast in Windows, so you adjust its volume by changing the Wave setting in your Volume control.

Setting Radio Presets

Just as on a car radio, you can create presets for your favorite stations. Media Player comes with a list of presets called Featured, which you can see in the left pane. You can't edit this list, but you can create your own list of favorite stations by doing the following:

1. Choose a station that you like.

2. Click the downward pointing arrows to the left of the station name to expand the information about the station.

3. Click the Add to My Stations button to make a copy of that station into the My Stations list.

Then to tune to a station on your list, just double-click it. To stop the station from playing entirely (for example, if the phone rings and you need silence while you take the call), click the Stop button at the bottom of the screen.

PLAYING AUDIO CDs

When you insert an audio CD in your CD-ROM drive, Media Player launches itself and begins playing the CD.

Occasionally you might run into an audio CD that contains some bonus material accessible by a computer. If that's the case, the computer program on the disc will run automatically when you insert the CD, instead of Media Player playing the CD. Close whatever program starts running, and open Media Player manually to play the CD.

As the CD plays, you can change to any other tab in the Media Player. It will continue to play. The tab that you will want to use most frequently during CD play is the Now Playing tab. You can use the Now Playing tab when playing any format (Internet radio, CDs, digital audio clips, DVD, etc.), but I think it's the most fun with CDs.

Part V

NOTE

If you are used to the old player, one thing that you may have noticed as missing is the CD Audio button on the left hand side. Where's it gone? Well, don't worry—you can still play CDs just as you did before. All that's happened is that the button has been renamed to Copy from CD. Windows Media Player now has the ability not only to play a CD but also to rip (copy) track. Now Microsoft makes no distinction between playing a track and copying it. The ability to copy tracks to your hard drive was there in previous versions, but this version also adds the ability to burn these tracks onto a new CD (if you have a CD-R or CD-RW drive installed).

Working with the Now Playing Controls

The Now Playing tab lists the CD tracks to the right, with a visualization in the center (see Figure 22.3). Visualizations are patterns, colors, or other moving images that react to the music. You can click the right and left arrow buttons under the current visualization to change it, or choose Tools ➤ Download Visualizations to get more from the Microsoft Web site.

The player controls work the same as on a regular CD player or cassette deck. You can pause, stop, fast-forward, rewind, and so on.

Play Stop   Seek

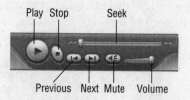

Previous Next Mute Volume

To adjust the volume, drag the Volume slider to the left or right. The Seek slider controls your position within the song being played. You can drag it to jump to a specific spot in the track.

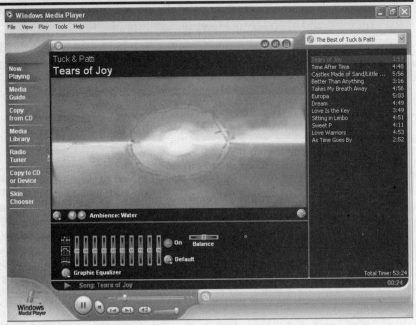

FIGURE 22.3: Use the controls on the Now Playing tab to control the CD play.

TIP
There are equivalent commands on the Play menu for each of the player controls.

Here are some other activities you can do from the Now Playing tab:

▶ Display or hide the Equalizer and Settings pane by clicking the Equalizer and Settings button near the top of the screen. When the Equalizer and Settings pane is displayed, click its View button to change what appears there.

▶ Double-click a track on the Playlist to jump to that track.

▶ Change the visualization by clicking the right and left arrow buttons under it.

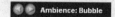

▶ Choose View ➤ Visualizations and then choose one from the submenus.

▶ Click the Shuffle button to play the tracks in random order.

▶ Resize any of the panes by dragging the divider line between two panes.

▶ Turn on/off any of the panes with the buttons in the top-right area of the player or with the commands on the View ➤ Now Playing Tools submenu.

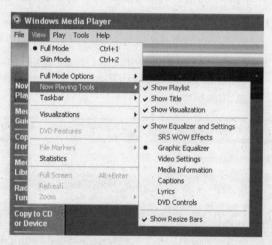

Copying CD Tracks to Your Hard Disk and Portable Device

If you have a lot of audio CDs that you like to play in your PC, you'll appreciate this feature. Windows Media Player enables you to easily copy selected tracks from a CD to your hard disk so that you can play them without the CD having to be present. That way you can create your own custom playlists, alternating songs from several CDs. (Each track takes up several megabytes of space, however, so make sure you have a large hard disk with plenty of free space.)

Media Player copies each track to your hard disk in WMA (Windows Media Audio) format rather than the more popular MP3 format. That shouldn't be a problem as long as you use Media Player rather than some other player to listen to the tracks.

NOTE

You can buy portable devices that play digital audio clips, but the most popular format accepted by these devices is MP3. Some portable media players support WMA format, too, however, and others allow you to record by hooking them into your sound card or USB port, so the original format of the clip is not an issue. See the documentation for your device to find the best way of transferring CD audio tracks to your portable digital music player.

To copy tracks to your hard disk from a CD, follow these steps:

1. On the Copy from CD tab, select all the tracks you want to copy. Remove the check mark next to any you don't want.

2. Click the Copy Music button. The Copy Status column shows the copy progress, as in Figure 22.4, and the button changes to Stop Copy.

FIGURE 22.4: Some tracks being copied to disk

When the tracks have been copied, they appear on the Media Library tab, discussed in the next section. And when you view them on the CD Audio tab, the Copy Status column shows Copied to Library. It's legal to copy your own CDs for your own use like this; it becomes illegal when you distribute them to other people.

ORGANIZING CLIPS IN THE MEDIA LIBRARY

On the Media Library tab, you can manage all of the various types of music that are stored on your hard disk. This could include MP3 files, WMA files, WAV files, and files in any of several other formats, too.

The Media Library tab has a folder tree, as in Windows Explorer.

Notice that there are five major sections: Audio, Video, My Playlists, Radio Tuner Presets, and Deleted Items. Of these, Audio is the one you will likely use most often. It contains the following sections within it:

All Audio   Shows a list of every audio clip. You can sort the list by clicking a column heading (such as Name or Artist).

Album   Shows separate subfolders for each album from which the songs came. (For those of you born after LPs, an "album" is the same as a "CD.")

Artist   Shows separate subfolders for each artist.

Genre   Shows separate subfolders for each genre (Rock, Country, etc.).

NOTE

How does Windows Media Player know what album a track comes from, or what its artist name and/or genre is? Well, when you copy from CD, as you learned earlier in the chapter, it records that information automatically. You can also right-click the track on the list and choose Edit to edit its information, including its Album setting.

To play a clip, simply double-click it, the same as usual. To remove a clip from the Media Library, right-click it and choose Delete from Library. This doesn't delete the file from your hard disk; it simply removes it from Windows Media Player's listing.

Adding Tracks to Your Media Library

You might have audio files on your hard disk already, independently of Media Player. For example, perhaps you downloaded them from a music Web site like www.mp3.com. To include your existing music clips in the Media Library, do the following:

1.   Choose File ≻ Add to Media Library ≻ Add File. An Open dialog box appears.

2.   Locate and select the file you want to add from your hard disk.

3.   Click Open. The song is added to your library.

Editing a Clip's Information

Depending on the source of a clip, it might not contain full information, such as artist name or genre, or the information might be incorrect. For example, the tracks shown in the preceding figure combined the artist and song name in the filename; that's a common quirk you'll find in downloaded clips from services such as Napster.

You can edit a clip's information to provide the details if you know them. Follow these steps to do so:

1. Right-click the clip and choose Edit. The Name field becomes editable.

2. Type over the current name, or click to move the insertion point into it and edit it.

3. Press Tab to move to the next column (Artist), and type the artist name.

4. Press Tab and continue to the next column, completing all the columns as desired.

5. Click away from the clip to take it out of editing mode.

Automatically Adding Many Tracks at Once

You're probably thinking that adding all your clips to the Media Library is going to be a big chore, right? Wrong. Media Player has a feature that searches your hard disk and automatically adds all the clips it finds.

WARNING

Some games come with sound clips for various sound effects in the game, and these will also be added to the Media Library if you go the automatic route described below. You can avoid this by limiting the search to certain folders on your hard disk (the ones where you know your music clips are) or by excluding certain file formats from the search—such as WAV, which is the format that many game sound effect files are in. And you can always remove a clip from the library later if you don't want it there.

To search your hard disk for clips to add, do the following:

1. Choose Tools ➤ Search for Media Files. The Search for Media Files dialog box opens.

2. The Search On drop-down box gives you the opportunity to search all hard drives for media or you can select a hard drive to be searched.

3. If you don't want to search the entire drive, click the Browse button next to Look In, select the folder in which you want to start, and then click OK.

This will search the chosen folder and any subfolders within it, ignoring the rest of the drive.

4. (Optional) Click on the Advanced button. Here you can specify the search to ignore files above or below a certain size and omit Windows supplied media in the system folders.

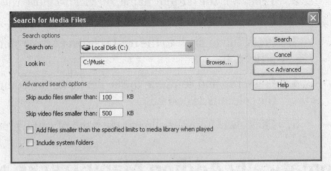

5. When you have selected the search options you want, click Search. The search begins.

6. When a message that the search is complete appears, click Close. Then click Close again to close the Search box. The new clips now appear in your Media Library.

Organizing Clips into Playlists

The full list of your clips can become a bit difficult to manage as you add more and more clips from your CDs and from other sources. That's where custom Playlists come in handy. You can create playlists that contain your favorite tracks for various occasions, like "Mellow Music" or "Party Mix," and then load and play those playlists quickly whenever you want them.

To create a playlist, complete the following steps:

1. In Media Library, click the New Playlist button in the toolbar.

2. Enter the name for the new playlist and click OK.

Now the new playlist appears in the folder tree. Scroll down near the bottom of the folder tree and find My Playlists. Click the plus sign to expand it if needed, and you'll find your new playlist there.

3. Browse the Media Library and select a file that you want to copy to your playlist.

4. Scroll the folder tree pane so that your playlist is visible, then drag the track from the Media Library and drop it onto the playlist.

5. Repeat Steps 3 and 4 to add other tracks to your playlist.

TIP

Here's another way to add a track to a playlist: Select the track and then click the Add to Playlist button on the toolbar. A menu opens containing all your playlists; click the one you want to add it to. Pretty easy, eh?

To add the currently playing track to the displayed playlist, click the Add button above the listing (looks like a plus sign) and on the menu that appears, choose Add Currently Playing Track.

To move a track around in the playlist, simply drag it up or down on the list or right-click it and choose Move Up or Move Down. There are also Move Up and Move Down arrow buttons above the track listing.

To remove a track from the playlist, select it and press Delete or right-click it and choose Delete from Playlist. There's also a Delete button above the track listing; clicking it opens a menu of deletion options.

WORKING WITH PORTABLE AUDIO PLAYERS

If you have a portable MP3 player, you can use Windows Media Player to transfer songs directly to it. (Of course, you can also use the software that comes with the MP3 player if you prefer.)

NOTE

An MP3 player is specifically designed to store MP3 digital audio files; it's different from a mini-disc player. If you have a portable mini-disc player, you might be able to hook it up to your PC and record songs by playing them on your PC and capturing the output on the mini-disc with an audio cable, but that's not the same thing as the direct transfer I'm talking about here. Consult the instructions that came with your mini-disc player for details.

Some MP3 players also play music in other formats, such as WMF (Windows Media File). When Windows Media Player copies songs from audio CDs, as you learned to do earlier in this chapter, it saves them in WMF format, not MP3. So if your MP3 player does not play WMF files directly, you will need to use a separate program for conversion. (You can probably find shareware available on the Internet that does this.)

But for the moment, let's assume that you have MP3s on your hard disk to transfer and a compatible MP3 player hooked up to your PC. Here's how to make the transfer:

1. On the Media Library tab, select the folder containing the song(s) you want to transfer.

2. Click the Copy to CD or Device tab. The songs in the chosen folder appear in the left pane (the Music to Copy section).

3. Ensure that your MP3 player is hooked up and turned on.

4. Remove the check marks next to the files that you do not want to copy.

5. Click the Copy Music button. The chosen tracks are copied to your MP3 player.

CHANGING THE APPEARANCE OF WINDOWS MEDIA PLAYER

So far in this chapter, you've seen the default Media Player in all the figures, but you can radically change its appearance through the use of a feature called *skins*. When you apply a skin to the player, it works the same as always but the controls look different. Figure 22.5 shows an example of a different skin.

Part v

FIGURE 22.5: Skins can make Media Player look different, but it still works the same.

To select a different skin, display the Skin Chooser tab on the main menu. Pick a skin, and then click Apply Skin.

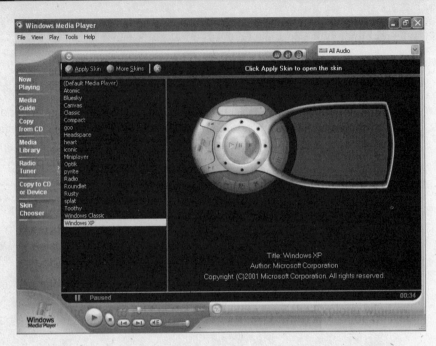

You can get more skins from the Microsoft Web site by clicking the More Skins button. This opens Internet Explorer and displays a page from which you can choose other skins.

What's Next

In this chapter we looked at multimedia audio and video primarily from an application-centric perspective. In the next chapter, "Using Image Acquisition and Movie Maker," you'll learn how to use Windows XP's features for controlling scanners and digital cameras and how to create your own digital slide shows and movies with Windows Movie Maker.

Chapter 23

USING IMAGE ACQUISITION AND MOVIE MAKER

P laying around with graphics can be great fun in Windows. You can download pictures from the Internet, take pictures with a digital camera, scan photos with a scanner, and receive pictures as e-mail attachments from friends and relatives. And the developers of Windows XP Home Edition obviously knew how much home users like to do this because they've included several great new tools and capabilities in Windows XP Home Edition to make it easier.

In this chapter, I'll show you how to make the most of your scanner and digital camera in Windows XP Home Edition by using its built-in Scanner and Digital Camera Wizard. I'll also take you through the Windows Movie Maker, a great new utility that enables you to edit video footage and combine it with still photos, soundtracks, and narration to make your own movies.

Adapted from *Mastering Windows Me* by Robert Cowart
ISBN 0-7821-2857-2   960 pages $39.99

Working with Scanners and Digital Cameras

In earlier versions of Windows, to run a scanner or to copy pictures from a digital camera, you needed to use the software that came with the device. Windows XP Home Edition has changed that, however, by providing direct access to many of the most popular scanner and camera models.

WARNING

Not all scanners and cameras work directly with Windows XP Home Edition. To find out if yours does, go to www.Microsoft.com/hcl. If your device isn't on the list, you can still use it, but you'll need to use the software supplied with the device; you won't be able to use Windows' direct controls that are described in the rest of this section.

If you upgrade to Windows XP Home Edition from Windows 9x/Me and you already had a scanner or camera installed with its own software, that software will still be there, and you can continue to use it normally in most cases. But if your scanner or camera is supported, you can also remove the software that came with the device and rely on Windows XP's built-in support. It's strictly a matter of preference. However, most scanners come with software that starts automatically at startup and stays running all the time. Removing that program from the mix can potentially free up some system resources; it's a good thing to do if you have an older computer without a lot of memory.

For some devices, you must go ahead and install the driver software that comes with the device in order for it to work to its best capability. For example, I bought a digital video camera that connected to my USB (Universal Serial Bus) port. When I hooked up the camera to the computer, Windows XP recognized it immediately and it worked. But the image quality was very bad. So I installed the software that came with it, and the image quality got much better.

Because Windows XP handles scanners and cameras differently than previous versions of Windows, you might find that your old scanner or camera driver doesn't work quite right. If that's the case, either you can fall back on Windows' built-in support or you can visit the device manufacturer's Web site to see whether an update or patch is available free for downloading.

Testing and Configuring Your Scanner or Camera

First things first: Does Windows XP recognize your scanner or camera? To find out, make sure your camera or scanner is connected to your PC and turned on, and then do the following:

NOTE

Some cameras have a mode switch that determines how they are operating. For example, you might see VCR/OFF/CAMERA or CAPTURE/DOWNLOAD. Make sure that the device is set to Camera (or Download), or Windows won't be able to recognize and use it. Check the camera's documentation if you aren't sure which setting to use.

1. Choose Start ➤ Control Panel, then choose the Printers and Other Hardware category.

2. Click Scanners and Cameras. A list of currently installed scanners and cameras appears.

3. If yours appears on the list, right-click it and select Properties to view its properties.

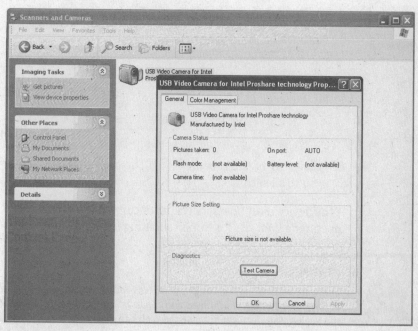

If your scanner or camera doesn't appear on the list, try installing it yourself now by clicking Add an Imaging Device and following the prompts.

4. If the General tab is not on top, click it to make it so.

5. Click the Test button. The exact name of the button varies. Depending on the device, it might be labeled Test Scanner or Camera, or just Test Camera, or just Test Scanner. The test takes only a moment, and a box appears telling you whether your device passed.

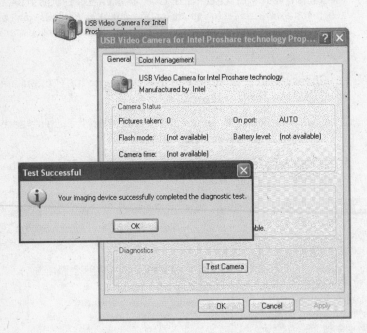

6. Click OK in the results box. If the device passed the test, you're all set.

If the device didn't pass, check its documentation and its manufacturer's Web site for troubleshooting help.

WARNING

There are all kinds of little quirky problems with specific models of computers and specific models of scanners and cameras. Check not only the Web site for the device manufacturer but also the Web site of your PC's manufacturer.

7. Click the other tabs to see what other settings are available. The settings (and tabs) depend on the device model and type.

    For example, some scanners that have quick scanning buttons on their front allow you to customize the buttons on the Events tab, so you can define what program receives the scan when you press each button. Other scanners and cameras don't allow any such customization here.

8. When you are finished, click OK to close the Properties box.

You're ready to use your scanner or camera! See the following sections for details.

Scanning a Picture

If you have a Windows XP–compatible scanner, you can use the following steps to scan a picture using the Scanner and Camera Wizard. For all other scanners, you must use the scanning software that came with the device, and the steps will be a little different.

NOTE

Some scanners might appear to work with Windows XP (that is, they might show up in the Scanners and Cameras window in the preceding section's test), but they won't work when you actually try to scan something with the following procedure. If that's the case, fall back to using the scanner's own software.

1. Place the picture on the scanner bed and close the lid.

2. Choose Start ➤ All Programs ➤ Accessories ➤ Scanner and Camera Wizard.

3. If you have more than one scanner or camera, a box appears asking you to choose which one you want. Click it and click OK.

4. The Scanner and Camera Wizard opens. Click Next to begin.

5. In the Region Selection box, click Preview. A preview of the scanned image appears.

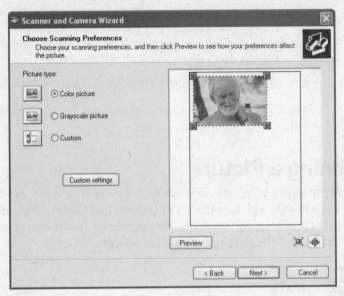

> **NOTE**
>
> If needed, adjust the original on the scanner bed and click the Preview button to preview the picture again.

6. Choose an option button for the image type you want: Color Picture, Grayscale Picture, or Custom.

7. (Optional) To crop the preview so that only a portion of the image gets scanned, drag the red squares in the corners until only the portion you want to keep is enclosed.

8. (Optional) To fine-tune the scan, click the Custom Settings button. Then make fine-tuning selections in the Advanced Properties tab and click OK to return.

Some of the fine-tuning you can do includes changing the scan resolution (higher is better, but results in a larger image file) and adjusting the brightness and contrast.

9. Click Next to move on. The Picture Name and Destination options appear.

10. Enter a name for the picture in the Type a Name for This Group of Pictures box.

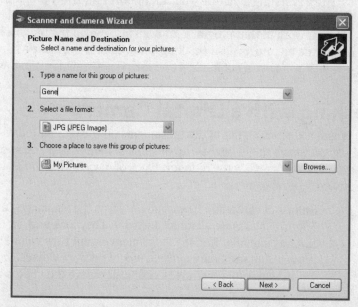

11. Choose a file format for the picture, or leave the default format JPG (JPEG) chosen.

TIP

Different programs accept different picture file formats. JPG is a good choice because many programs accept it, including most Web sites, and because it's a compact format that doesn't take up much disk space.

12. Choose a destination folder for the picture, or leave the default My Pictures selected.

TIP

The My Pictures folder is inside your My Documents folder.

13. Click Next. The scanner scans the picture (for real this time, not just a preview, so it may take a little longer), and Windows saves it to a file as you indicated.

14. Click Next and then Finish to display the scanned picture in a My Pictures window.

After scanning a picture, you can import it into any program that accepts pictures, such as Microsoft Word, FrontPage, or Excel, to dress up your work in that program. You can also e-mail the file to a friend to share the picture, print it (making your scanner work like a copier!), or fax it (if you have a fax modem and faxing software for Windows).

Working with a Digital Camera

There are several types of digital cameras on the market today. The term *digital camera* might conjure up one image in my mind and another in yours, so let's review the different types of devices that are all loosely called "digital cameras":

Snapshot cameras   These are similar to the regular go-anywhere 35mm cameras we all know and love. They look and act the same as a regular film-loaded camera except they record the images digitally. Some of them record on floppy disks, and others on removable cartridges. Still others save the images in the camera itself. When the camera gets full, you hook it up to the PC to transfer the images to your hard disk.

Simple video cameras   These remain attached to your PC at all times. Usually they are small (a few inches high, wide, and deep). One brand is shaped like a ball. You can use them for video teleconferencing or for recording video footage near your computer. Since they are always connected to the PC, they have no image storage mechanism in themselves; you always save directly to the hard disk from them.

Handheld, go-anywhere digital video cameras   These look and act like regular camcorders, except they record digitally rather than on a tape. You can hook them up to your PC to transfer the video footage to your hard disk. They can also take still snapshots.

NOTE

Many digital video cameras require an IEEE 1394 port (a FireWire port) in your computer to connect to. You can buy an interface card for your PC that provides such a connection for about $50. FireWire is similar to (and a competitor of) USB; it is a high-speed interface port for connecting to external devices.

The Scanner and Camera Wizard enables you to

▶ Transfer stored images from the camera to your hard disk.

▶ Take new, still snapshots using an attached video camera.

The Scanner and Camera Wizard works only with still images, not motion video clips. If you need to transfer video footage from a video camera to a file on your hard disk, or if you want to capture new motion video footage using an attached camera, see the "Using Windows Movie Maker" section later in this chapter.

Transferring Stored Images from a Digital Camera

If your camera is directly supported in Windows XP, you can use the following procedure to transfer stored images from it.

1.   Hook up the camera to the PC if it's not already connected.

2. If the camera requires you to do anything special to it to place it in transfer mode, do so. For example, some camera models require you to flip a switch or turn a dial.

3. Choose Start ➢ All Programs ➢ Accessories ➢ Scanner and Camera Wizard.

4. If you have more than one scanner or camera, a box appears asking which you want to use. Select your camera and click OK.

5. The Scanner and Camera Wizard runs. Click Next to begin. The pictures currently stored on the camera appear in thumbnail (miniature) view.

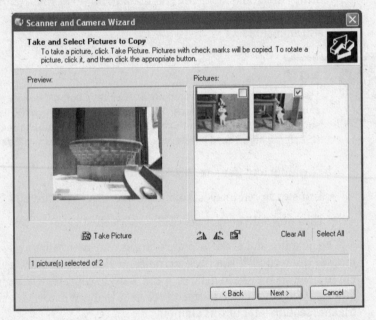

6. Delete any of the pictures that you want to remove from the camera without saving. To delete one, click it and then press Delete on the keyboard.

TIP

To rotate a picture, click it and then click the Rotate button.

7. Select the pictures that you want to transfer to your hard disk. Selected pictures appear with a check mark in the top right corner. Click the Select All button to choose them all, or hold down the Ctrl key as you click each one you want.

8. Click Next to move to the Picture Name and Destination controls.

9. Enter a name for the pictures in the Type a Name for This Group of Pictures box.

   The name you enter will be used as a prefix for each picture you are saving. Windows will tack on a number to the end of the name so that each picture has a unique name. For example, if you leave the default name here of "Family," the first picture will be Family 001, the second one Family 002, and so on.

10. Choose a destination folder for the picture, or leave the default My Pictures selected.

NOTE

The My Pictures folder is inside your My Documents folder.

11. (Optional) If you want to remove the pictures from the camera after saving them to your PC, mark the Delete Pictures from My Device after Copying Them check box.

12. Click Next twice, and then click Finish.

The pictures are saved to your hard disk, and the folder in which you saved them appears. By default the My Pictures window appears in Film-strip view, shown in Figure 23.1. You can select another view from the View menu, the same as in any other window.

In the Explorer pane to the right of the pictures, you'll find shortcuts for common activities pertaining to graphics. For example, you can print a picture, view your pictures as a slide show, order prints from the Internet, or copy a picture to CD.

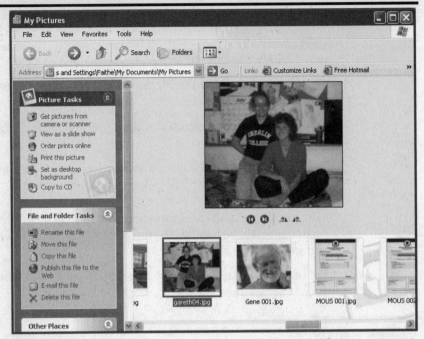

FIGURE 23.1: The My Pictures folder contains pictures acquired from your scanner and digital camera. Here they are shown in Filmstrip view.

Taking Snapshots with a Video Camera

If you have a video-type camera that doesn't store pictures, you can still use it with Windows, but you'll do so through the Explore Camera feature instead.

NOTE
To transfer stored motion video footage from your camera, use Windows Movie Maker, described later in this chapter.

1. Double-click the camera's icon in My Computer to access the camera without going through the wizard.

2. To take a still photo with the camera, click the Take a New Picture hyperlink in Camera Tasks. The picture appears below the preview pane. See Figure 23.2.

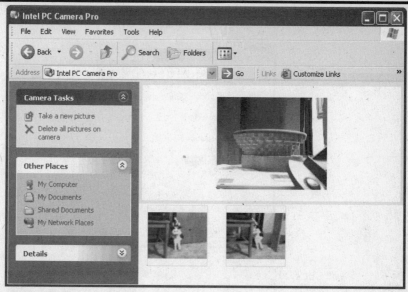

FIGURE 23.2: You can take pictures with a video camera by going through My Computer rather than the Scanner and Camera Wizard.

3. To take more still photos, move the camera and click Take Picture again. Repeat as much as you like.

Now you can use the full Scanner and Camera Wizard to save the still pictures you've taken with your video camera. It'll work the same as if you had a real digital camera.

Transferring Images from a File Management Window

If you don't want to bother with the wizard to transfer the camera's still pictures to your hard disk, you can do the following instead:

1. If you are not already there, double-click the camera's icon in My Computer to open its contents in a file management window.

2. Select the picture(s) you want to transfer and click Copy This File. The Copy Items dialog box opens.

3. Select the destination for the picture (for example, My Pictures within the My Documents folder).

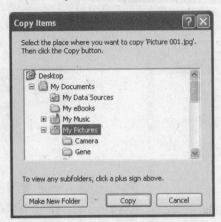

4. Click OK.

USING WINDOWS MOVIE MAKER

Windows Movie Maker helps you organize multimedia clips—that is, pictures, videos, soundtracks, voice narrations, and so on—into "movies" that you can play on your computer monitor, store on your hard disk, and e-mail to friends and family.

Windows Movie Maker also provides a means for transferring video footage from your video camera to your PC. If you have a digital video camera, all you need is a FireWire connection to plug the camera into. As I mentioned earlier in the chapter, FireWire (or IEEE 1394) is a competitor to USB. It's simply a different kind of interface port. Most PCs don't come with this type of port, but you can buy an add-on circuit card that includes one for about $50.

You can also transfer video footage from a regular, or analog, video camera, but you'll need a special analog-to-digital video converter unit. There are several popular models at around $100 to $200; one is called Dazzle. They usually come with their own software, which you might prefer to Windows Movie Maker.

If you don't have a video camera at all, don't fret. You can use Windows Movie Maker with still photos, too. You can, for example, combine a series of still photographs into an automated slide show, complete with soundtrack.

The music for your movie soundtrack can come from a music clip stored on your hard disk. You can copy one from a CD-ROM, or use a clip (such as an MP3 file) that you have downloaded from a Web site.

If you have a sound card and a microphone to plug into it, you can record voice narration for your movie. This is different from a soundtrack, and plays "on top of" the soundtrack at the same time.

An Overview of Movie Making

First, let's look at the big picture. Here's how to create a movie with Windows Movie Maker:

1. Import the content for the show into Windows Movie Maker collections. These collections are not movie-specific; they can be drawn from over and over.

2. Start a new movie, and arrange the video clips and/or still photos in the order in which you want them.

3. Add a soundtrack if desired.

4. Record voice narration if desired.

5. Preview your movie and then save it to your hard disk.

In the following sections, I'll show you how to accomplish each of these steps. But first, you'll need to start Windows Movie Maker. To do so, choose Start ➢ All Programs ➢ Accessories ➢ Windows Movie Maker. Figure 23.3 shows the Windows Movie Maker screen when you first start the program.

Creating Collections

To start off, you'll create at least one collection, and import your content. This gives you some raw material to draw from when assembling the movie.

You can save all your content in the same collection, or you can create different collections for each type of content or for content on particular subjects. Collections are a lot like folders in Windows Explorer.

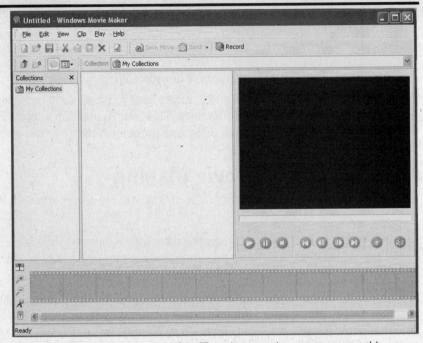

FIGURE 23.3: Windows Movie Maker. There is no movie content open at this point, and no collections.

To create a new collection, follow these steps:

1. Click the collection into which you want to place the new one. (By default this is the top-level collection, called My Collections.)

2. Choose File ➢ New ➢ Collection, or click the New Collection button on the toolbar.

3. Type a name for the new collection.

4. Press Enter.

Now, whenever you are recording or importing content in the following sections, simply make sure the desired collection is selected before you record or import.

Recording New Content

You can record new content for your show right from within Windows Movie Maker. The recording process depends on what input devices you have.

Transferring Footage from a Digital Video Camera

If you have a digital video camera, it probably has two modes: Camera and VCR. In Camera mode, it works as described in the next section, "Recording from a Desktop Video Camera." However, in VCR mode, it plays back the already-recorded footage. You can use this mode to save the footage to your hard disk for use in your Movie Maker projects or for any other purpose.

NOTE

If you have a regular (analog) video camera that records onto tape, you'll need some sort of interface device to connect it to your PC. Depending on the model, it might work directly with Movie Maker, or it might require you to use the software that comes with the interface to first save the video to your hard disk. If that's the case, see "Importing Existing Content from Disk" later in the chapter.

Here's how to transfer some video footage from your digital video camera:

1. Start Movie Maker and select the collection into which you want to place the recording.

2. Connect the camera to your PC and turn it on. Make sure it is set to VCR mode.

   Choose File ➤ Record or click the Record button on the toolbar.

3. To transfer starting at the beginning of the tape, leave the default setting marked and click OK.

The tape rewinds if needed and then starts playing, and Movie Maker starts capturing the video.

4. When you want to stop recording, press the Stop button on the camera (not in Windows). A Save Windows Media File dialog box appears.

5. Enter a name for the video clip in the File Name box. Windows automatically saves in Windows Media Video (WMV) format.

6. Click Save. The clip is saved to your hard disk and placed in the collection that you chose in Step 1.

When you select a video file on your hard disk, a preview of the first frame appears in the preview pane. Notice also that Movie Maker placed the clip in its own subcollection beneath the collection I selected in Step 1.

Recording from a Desktop Video Camera

In addition to transferring saved video, you can also use your digital video camera to capture new footage while connected to your PC. If you have a camera that stays connected to your PC full-time, this is your only option unless you want to use the recording software that came with the camera. (The Scanner and Camera Wizard you learned about earlier in this chapter is for still snapshots only.)

To record "live" from a digital video camera, follow these steps:

1. Ensure that your video camera is connected to your PC and that your PC recognizes it. (See "Testing and Configuring Your Scanner or Camera" earlier in this chapter.) If you're working with a digital video camera that has multiple modes such as Camera and VCR, set it to Camera.

2. In Windows Movie Maker, make sure the collection is selected in which you want to place the clip.

3. Choose File ➤ Record, or click the Record button on the toolbar. The Record dialog box appears. Notice the device listed in the Video Device section.

4. If you have more than one video camera attached, and you want to choose one that's different from the one that appears, click the Change Device button. In the Change Device dialog box, open the Video drop-down list and choose the camera you want. Then click OK.

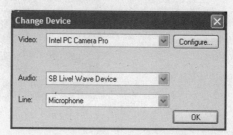

NOTE

Depending on the camera, you might also be able to choose an Audio Device and/or a Microphone from the dialog box above.

5. In the Record dialog box, change any of the following options as desired:

   ▶ Set a Record Time Limit if you want to limit the size of the clip being recorded. (Clips take up a lot of space on your hard disk.)

   ▶ Choose Create Clips if you want the video feed broken into separate clips every time it detects a different frame (such as when you turn the camera on, or turn off the Pause feature). Otherwise, the entire video feed will be stored in a single clip.

   ▶ Choose a quality setting. The default is Medium Quality; higher quality will record more frames per second but will take up more storage space on your drive and will take longer to transmit when you e-mail the movie to someone later.

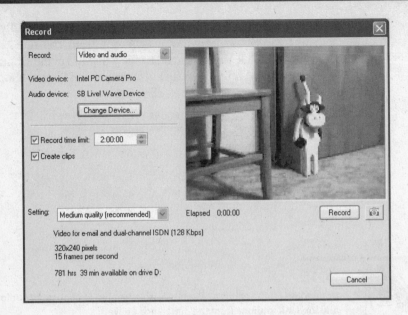

6. When you are ready to record video, click the Record button.

7. When you are finished recording, click the Stop button (in Windows, not on the camera). The Save Windows Media File dialog box appears, in which you can name your clip. (Or, if you're saving a still photo, it's the Save Photo dialog box.)

8. Enter the name you want to use for the clip, and click Save.

NOTE

Video clips are saved in the WMV format; still clips are saved in the JPG format.

The clip now appears in the chosen collection.

More About Clip Splitting

If you chose Create Clips in Step 5 of the preceding procedure, Movie Maker may have broken up your video footage into more than one clip, with each one appearing as a separate item in the collection. Movie Maker does this if it detects a new frame (that is, a jump in the action, such as where you paused the recording and then restarted it.)

The fact that a clip is split is not a problem because when you assemble the movie, you can place each clip adjacent to one another so that it appears to be one long video piece. Splitting merely adds flexibility to the movie-assembly process.

You can also manually split a video clip into one or more separate clips. To do so, play the clip by double-clicking it, and at the desired split point, click the Split button (the rightmost button in the toolbar beneath the video preview pane).

Recording Sound Clips

Recording a sound clip is just like recording a video clip, except you use only your microphone. To do this, you must either have a built-in microphone on your PC (which is often the case with laptops) or a microphone attached to the Mic port on your sound card.

Follow these steps to record a sound clip with your microphone:

1. Select the collection in which the new clip should be placed.

2. Choose File ➢ Record, or click the Record button on the toolbar. The Record dialog box opens.

3. Open the Record drop-down list and choose Audio Only.

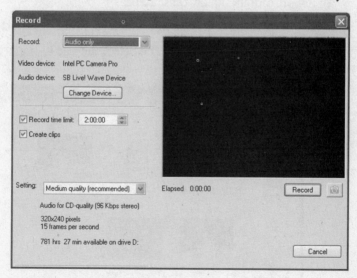

4. If your sound card name doesn't appear next to Audio Device, click the Change Device button, select it, and click OK to return.

5. Set the record quality or any other desired options, as described in Step 5 of the preceding set of steps.

6. Click the Record button, and begin speaking or making noise into the microphone.

7. Click the Stop button when finished. The Save Windows Media File dialog box opens.

8. Enter the name to use. The file will be saved in WMA format.

9. Click Save. The clip is created and placed in the collection.

Importing Existing Content from Disk

If the content that you want to use in your movie is already on your hard disk, you can import it into a collection in Movie Maker. (You must do so if you want to include the content in a movie, because movies draw their content only from collections.)

Importing existing content is the same regardless of the content's format. Media Player accepts content in a wide variety of formats, including all popular digital movie formats such as MPG (MPEG), WMV, and AVI. It also accepts many sound and graphic file formats.

To import content, follow these steps:

1. Display the collection into which you want to import.

2. Choose File ➤ Import. The Select the File to Import dialog box appears.

3. Locate and select the file you want to import. By default, clips you record are in the My Videos folder, within My Documents.

TIP

To narrow down the list of files, you might want to choose a file type from the Files of Type drop-down list. By default, all importable files are shown.

4. Click Open to import the file.

If you find that you have accidentally imported the file into the wrong collection, you can easily drag it to another collection, just as you do when managing files in Windows Explorer.

Building a Project

Now that you've imported or recorded the content for your movie, you're ready to start assembling it in a project, which you'll save in Movie Maker.

Is a project the same as a movie? Well, yes and no. The project is the work-in-progress, and the movie is the finished item. After the project is exactly the way you want it, you publish it as a movie, creating a read-only copy that you can never edit again. If you want to make changes to it, you must make the changes to the project and then republish the movie.

You can assemble a project in any order, but I like to start with the visual images (video clips and still photos) and then add the soundtrack. Finally, as the last step, I add the voice narration.

Starting a New Project

You can start a new project at any time by doing the following:

1. Choose File ➤ New Project, or click the New Project button on the toolbar.

2. If prompted to save your changes to the existing project, click Yes or No and save (or not), as appropriate.

You can then assemble your project on the timeline at the bottom of the program window, as described in the remainder of this chapter.

Adding a Clip to the Project

You build your project by dragging clips from your various collections into the timeline at the bottom of the screen.

There are two views of the project: Storyboard and Timeline. Storyboard is useful for assembling the visual elements in the right order, while Timeline lets you add audio clips and match up your audio soundtrack with the video clips.

To switch between Storyboard and Timeline views, you can use the View menu or click the buttons to the left of the project area:

▶ Storyboard

▶ Timeline

NOTE

You can add audio clips only to Timeline view. If you attempt to drop an audio clip on the Storyboard, a message will appear, telling you that Movie Maker is switching to Timeline view automatically. Click OK to go on.

Here's a project-in-progress in Storyboard view. Notice that only the pictures and video clips appear.

The same project viewed in Timeline view shows that an audio soundtrack is also included.

To remove a clip from the project, click it on the Timeline or Storyboard and press the Delete key. To move it around on the project, drag it to the left or right.

Part v

Setting Trim Points for a Video Clip

If you want to use only a portion of a video clip, you have a couple of options. You can split the clip and then use only one of the split portions, or you can trim the clip. Trimming is active only for the current project; splitting, however, splits the clip in the collection, so it will continue to be split if you use it later in another project.

To set the trim points for a clip, do the following:

1. Add the video clip to the project, either on the Storyboard or on the Timeline.

2. Make sure the clip is selected (again, on the Storyboard or Timeline).

3. Click the Play button beneath the video preview pane, and when the clip reaches the part where you want it to begin, choose Clip ➤ Set Start Trim Point, or press Ctrl+Shift+←.

4. Allow the clip to continue playing, and when it reaches the part where you want it to end, choose Clip ➤ Set End Trim Point, or press Ctrl+Shift+→.

Everything between the two trim points will appear in the movie; everything else will not.

Changing the Duration of a Still Image

When you import a photo, it is assigned a default duration of five seconds to appear on-screen during the movie. You can change the default duration by choosing View ➤ Options and entering a different value in the Default Imported Photo Duration box, shown in Figure 23.4.

NOTE

The photo's default duration is always the setting that was in effect when it was imported. So, for example, if you import a photo when the Default Imported Photo Duration is set to 5 seconds, and you later change that setting to 10 seconds, all photos you imported prior to the change will continue to have 5-second durations.

You can also change a still picture's duration on the Timeline, for each individual usage of it by completing the following steps:

1. View the project in Timeline view.

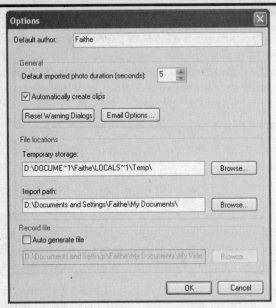

FIGURE 23.4: Change the default duration for imported stills here.

2. Click the Zoom In button to expand the Timeline so you can see each item more clearly.

3. Click the picture for which you want to change the duration. Trim handles appear above it.

NOTE
If you don't see trim handles above the picture, as shown above, click the Zoom In button again to zoom in some more.

4. Drag the ending trim handle (the one on the right) to the left to make the picture appear for fewer seconds, or to the right to make it appear for more seconds.

If the picture was not on the end of the Timeline, and you increased its duration, the picture to its right might now be partially obscured. Select that picture, and then drag its beginning trim handle (the one on its left)

so that the two pictures do not overlap anymore. Continue working your way toward the left until all items are the desired duration.

Creating Transitions

In the preceding section, you saw that it's possible to overlap two objects on the Timeline. When you overlap objects, you create a transition effect between them, so that one fades into the other. It's a pretty neat effect, and certainly looks better than simply replacing one image with the next.

To create a transition effect, simply make the clips overlap slightly. You already saw how to adjust the clip's trim in previous sections.

NOTE

Windows Movie Maker doesn't allow you to choose between different transition effects. If that feature is important to you and you're working only with still images, try a program like PowerPoint for assembling your presentation.

Adding a Soundtrack

To add a soundtrack, drag a sound clip onto the workspace. (That sound clip must already be in a collection, so import it into a collection if needed beforehand.) If you're not already in Timeline view, the view switches for you automatically and a box informs you that it's happening.

You can trim the soundtrack the same as any other object. Select it, and then either drag its trim handles or trim it by playing it and setting start and end trim points as you learned to do for videos earlier in the chapter.

Setting Audio Levels

If the video track has its own audio in addition to the audio tracks you are adding, the two can easily conflict with each another unattractively. You can fix this problem by adjusting the project so that one or the other is dominant. To do so, just follow these steps:

1. Choose Edit ➤ Audio Levels, or click the Adjust Audio Level button to the left of the project area.

2. Drag the slider to control the relative volume levels of the two tracks.

3. Click the Close (X) button on the dialog box to close it.

FIGURE 23.5: Change the default audio level.

Recording Narration

After you've finalized the durations of each clip, you're ready to record your narration. You won't want to record it earlier, because if the durations of the clips change, the narration will be off. To record narration, do the following:

1. Prepare your microphone and ensure that it's working.

2. Choose File ➤ Record Narration, or click the Record Narration button to the left of the Timeline. The Record Narration Track dialog box appears.

3. Set any of the following options:

   ▶ If the device and line are not correct as shown, click the Change button and select the correct ones. The device should be your sound card, and the line should be the line into which your microphone is plugged (probably Mic Volume).

   ▶ If you want to mute the video soundtrack while the narration is speaking, mark the Mute Video Soundtrack check box. Otherwise, the two will play on top of each another.

  ▸ Adjust the recording level using the Record Level slider if desired. Use the meter next to the slider as a guide.

4. When you are ready, click Record. Your presentation begins showing itself in the preview pane.

5. Speak into the microphone, narrating as you go along.

6. When you are finished, click Stop. The Save Narration Track Sound File dialog box appears.

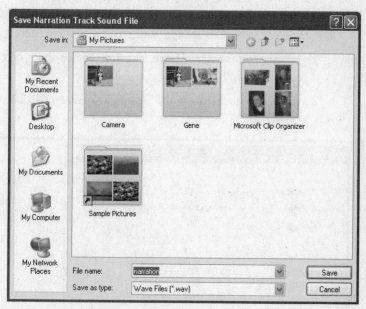

7. Enter a name for the narration track, and click Save. (The track is saved in WAV format.)

If you had a soundtrack, you might find that the narration has forced the soundtrack to move over on the Timeline. To have the two of them play simultaneously, drag them so that they overlap.

Previewing the Movie

Before you publish the movie, you'll want to preview it to make sure everything is as you wish it to be. To preview the movie in the Preview pane, click the Play button while the first frame of the project is selected in the workspace.

To view it full-screen, click the Full Screen button beneath the preview pane, or choose Play ➤ Full Screen.

Creating Your Movie

Before you create your movie, save your project. Remember, you can't make changes to a published movie, so if you want to change it, you'll need to make changes to the project and then republish the movie. To save your project, choose File ➤ Save Project, or click the Save Project button on the toolbar; save as you would any other data file in a program.

Then you're ready to make a movie! To do so, follow these steps:

1. Choose File ➤ Save Movie. The Save Movie dialog box opens, as shown in Figure 23.6.

2. Choose a quality from the Setting drop-down list. The default is Medium.

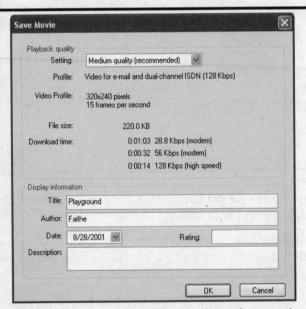

FIGURE 23.6: Set the options for the movie to be created.

TIP

If you'll be distributing the movie via the Internet, set the quality at Medium or lower to keep the file size small. If you'll be distributing the movie on a CD or playing it on your own PC, and you have plenty of disk space, use a higher quality. You can check the file size just above the Download Time area of the dialog box.

3. Enter any information desired in the Display Information area. All of this information is optional.

4. Click OK. The Save As dialog box appears.

5. Enter a name for your movie in the File Name box.

6. Click Save. Your movie is saved, and a message appears asking whether you want to watch it now.

7. Click Yes to watch the movie or No to return to Movie Maker.

NOTE

Movie Maker is not a terribly sophisticated program, and there are a lot of "better" video editing programs on the market today that do more sophisticated things, particularly with transitions. If you buy a digital video camera, or a FireWire port for your PC, it might come with its own video editing software that has more features. For example, when I was shopping for a FireWire port card, I ended up buying Studio DV from Pinnacle Systems for the same price as I would have paid for a card alone. It included a three-port FireWire port card plus some very good editing software.

Once you've created your movie, you can distribute it on disk or by e-mail to others. The format in which it is saved (WMV) is compatible with Windows Media Player, including older versions of Media Player that came with Windows 9x or Me, so any other Windows user should be able to view your movie on-screen with no additional software required.

What's Next

The next chapter covers Windows XP's new and enhanced capabilities for recording CDs. You'll find out how to make both audio and data CDs, as well as how to copy a CD and how to get the best recording performance while avoiding write errors.

Chapter 24

BURNING CDs

From being an exotic, expensive, and erratically performing technological marvel in the mid-1990s, the recordable CD has progressed to being the most convenient and most cost-effective backup and file-transfer medium for the early 2000s. Recordable CDs now hold up to 700MB of data and can be burned in as little as four minutes. So it should perhaps come as no surprise that Windows XP improves on previous versions of Windows by offering CD-writing capability built into the operating system. This chapter discusses how to use those features, how to choose a CD rewriter drive if you don't have one, and how to choose recordable CD media.

This chapter starts by discussing the basics of CD recording. It then covers how to configure a recordable CD drive, how to burn CDs by dragging items to your desktop, how to burn CDs directly from Explorer, and how to burn CDs from Windows Media Player.

Adapted from *Mastering Windows XP Home Edition*
by Guy Hart-Davis
ISBN 0-7821-2980-3   1024 pages $39.99

Choosing a CD Recorder/Rewriter

To record CDs, you need to have a CD recorder or a CD rewriter. If you have one, you're all set to record CDs. You also need media—blank recordable CDs or rewritable CDs. The next section discusses those.

Because of its value for backup and file transfer, a CD rewriter is almost indispensable nowadays. Many new PCs—including some high-end laptops—have built-in CD rewriters. If your PC doesn't have a CD rewriter and you want to get one, this sidebar explains what you need to know.

You'll notice that this sidebar discusses CD rewriters rather than CD recorders. That's because CD rewriters have become so ubiquitous and come down so far in price that they've essentially replaced plain old CD recorders. (If you missed CD recorders: The difference between CD recorders and CD rewriters is that CD recorders could write only once to any given disc, whereas CD rewriters can write either once or multiple times to the same disc. If you'd like the acronyms, CD-R discs are *Write Once, Read Multiple* media—*WORM* for short—while CD-RW discs are *Write And Read Multiple* or *WARM* media.)

Speed

CD rewriter speed is measured by the same rating system as regular old read-only CD drives: 1X, 2X, 4X, and so on. Each X represents 150Kbps (the nominal read rate of the first CD drives), so a 4X drive chugs through 600Kbps, an 8X drive handles 1200Kbps (1.2Mbps), a 12X drive manages 1800Kbps (1.8Mbps), a 16X drive burns 2400Kbps (2.4Mbps), a 20X drive blazes through 3000Kbps (3Mbps), and a 24X drive incinerates 3600Kbps (3.6Mbps).

CD rewriter speed keeps on improving. At this writing, 24X drives are just beginning to appear. These can burn a full CD in 4 minutes (other constraints, such as the speed of your system, permitting). 16X drives are more reasonably priced; they can burn a full CD in 5 minutes. 12X drives are starting to look like old technology, though in 2000 they were state-of-the-art; they can burn a full CD in around 6 minutes. 8X drives take about 9 minutes; 6X drives take about 12 minutes; and 4X drives take about 18 minutes.

Those speeds are for the initial writing to the CD. On high-speed drives, the rewriting speeds are typically considerably slower than the writing speeds. For example, a drive might write at 24X but rewrite at 12X, and a 12X drive might rewrite at only 4X. By contrast, slower drives (for example, 4X) may rewrite at the same speed as they write.

CD rewriter speeds are given with the write speed first, the rewrite speed second, and the read speed third. For example, a $24 \times 12 \times 40$ drive is one that writes at 24X, rewrites at 12X, and reads at 40X.

As you can see, the higher speed ratings don't translate as directly into a speed gain as the lower speeds do. That's because, no matter how fast the drive is able to burn the CD, there's some overhead in creating the file system on the CD and wrapping up the writing process. So until prices on 24X (or faster) and 16X drives come down, there's little advantage in buying them over 12X drives.

CD rewriters almost invariably read data at a faster rate than they write it. Some CD recorders now read up to 32X, making them almost as fast as a dedicated CD drive. Even so, unless you're out of drive bays or ports, look to add a CD recorder to your computer rather than replace your existing CD drive with a CD recorder. That way, you'll be able to duplicate a CD (assuming that you have the right to do so) or install *Quake* at the same time as listening to music.

Internal or External?

Generally speaking, an internal drive will cost you less than an external drive, but you'll need to have a drive bay free in your computer. An external drive will usually cost more, will occupy space on your desk, and will need its own power supply. In addition, most external drives are much noisier than internal drives because they contain their own fans. But if your main computer is a notebook, or if you want to be able to move the drive from computer to computer without undue effort, you'll need an external drive.

EIDE drives are all internal. SCSI drives can be internal or external. Because the parallel port, the USB ports, and any FireWire ports are external connections, almost all of these drives are external only. (You can find internal FireWire CD-R drives if you look hard enough.)

EIDE, SCSI, Parallel Port, USB, or FireWire?

If you have a SCSI card in your computer, you'll probably want to get a SCSI CD recorder, because it will typically perform better *and* put much less burden on the processor than an EIDE CD recorder will. SCSI drives are usually more expensive than EIDE drives of the same speed, but if your computer's already got SCSI, the extra cost is probably worth it. If you need to copy CDs, bear in mind that most SCSI CD recorders will copy CDs directly only from other SCSI drives, not from EIDE drives. If you have a SCSI CD recorder and an EIDE CD drive, you'll need to copy the CD to the hard disk and then burn it to CD from there.

If you don't have SCSI and want an internal drive, or if your CD player is EIDE and you want to do a lot of CD-to-CD duplicating, choose EIDE. Before you buy, make sure that you have an EIDE connector available on your computer. If it's already chock-full of drives (most modern machines can take four EIDE devices), you won't be able to add another without sacrificing an existing one.

If you're looking at an external non-SCSI drive, your current choices are a parallel-port drive, a USB drive, or a FireWire drive. Parallel-port drives perform so slowly—2X at best—that they're barely worth using. USB drives using the USB 1.0 standard are only a bit better—they're limited to 4X speeds by the limitations of USB. (USB 2.0 drives, when they arrive, will be much faster.) FireWire drives offer full speed and great convenience, but if your computer doesn't have a FireWire card, you'll need to add one. (You can get FireWire PCI cards for $100 or so and FireWire PC cards for a few dollars more.)

RECORDABLE CDs AND REWRITABLE CDs

If you've looked at CD-R or CD-RW discs, you'll know that most of them look very different from prerecorded audio or data CDs (*pressed* CDs). Depending on their make and type, CD-R and CD-RW discs may have a gold, green, or bluish coating on their data side. Typically, this is a polycarbonate substrate over a reflective layer of 24-carat gold or a silver-colored alloy.

Information is transferred to CD-R and CD-RW discs by a different process than for pressed CDs. While pressed CDs are pressed in a mold from a master CD, CD recorders and CD rewriters use a laser to burn the information onto the CD-R or CD-RW media. Pressed CDs use physically raised areas called *lands* and lowered areas called *pits* to store the encoded data. Recordable CDs have a dye layer in which the laser burns marks that have the same reflective properties as the lands and pits. To be pedantic, the laser doesn't actually *burn* anything, but it heats the dye layer to produce the marks. But because the term is not only evocative but also distinguishes from the CD-recording that music artists do, it has stuck: CD recorders and rewriters are widely referred to as *CD burners*, and people speak of *burning a CD*.

Not only do CD-R and CD-RW discs look different than pressed CDs, they're also less robust. You can damage them more easily with extreme heat and moderate cold, by scratching or gouging them, or by leaving them in direct sunlight. The data is actually stored closer to the label side of the CD than to the business side, so if you're compelled to scratch one side of the CD, go for the business side over the label side.

CDs on which you can record data come in two basic types:

CD-R discs   CD-R discs, usually referred to as *recordable CDs*, are CDs that you can record data to only once. Once you finish recording data, you cannot change the information on the disc. Regular CD-R discs hold 650MB, the same amount as a standard audio CD. (650MB holds 74 minutes of uncompressed audio.) Extended-capacity CD-R discs hold 700MB, a small increase that's worth having if you don't have to pay extra for it. 700MB holds 80 minutes of uncompressed audio.

CD-RW discs   CD-RW discs, usually referred to as *rewritable CDs*, are CDs that you can record data to multiple times. You can record data to the CD in multiple recording sessions until it is full. You can then erase all the data from the CD and use it again. CD-RW discs specify a theoretical safe maximum number of times that you can reuse them, but if you like your data, you'd be wise not to push them that far. CD-RW discs hold 650MB.

CD-RW discs are more expensive than CD-R discs.

To simplify (or perhaps complicate) the terminology, Windows uses the term *writable CD* to refer to recordable and rewritable discs. This isn't a standard term, but it now seems destined to become one.

When buying CD-R and CD-RW discs, you need to balance economy with quality. Beware of cheapo discs, because they may give you skips and errors—or even lose your precious music or data. If you can, buy a few discs for testing before you buy a quantity that you'll regret if they're not up to snuff.

One way to save some money is to buy CD-R and CD-RW discs without jewel cases. This makes for a good discount, as the jewel cases are relatively expensive to manufacture and bulky to package (and easy to break, as you no doubt know from personal experience). The discs are typically sold on a spindle, which makes for handy storage until you use them—after which you'll have to find safe storage for them on your own. (One possibility is a CD wallet, which can be especially handy if you need to take your CDs with you when you travel. If you buy one, make sure it has soft pockets that won't scratch the CDs as you insert them, and sweep out travel grit frequently.)

For the faster drives, you may need to buy CD-R or CD-RW media designed for use in faster drives. For example, at this writing most 24X drives request (or perhaps require) discs rated at 24X, suggesting that regular (and less expensive) discs will have too many errors to use. Your mileage will vary depending on your discs and your drive, but it's worth testing less expensive discs to see how they perform in a fast drive. If the drive ends up burning at 20X instead of 24X, you lose all of 30 seconds. Unless you're holding your breath for the duration of the burning, you're unlikely to notice the difference.

Audio CDs and Data CDs

Broadly speaking, CDs divide into two categories:

Audio CDs   Audio CDs contain uncompressed audio in pulse code modulation (PCM) format. (PCM files are essentially WAV files with different header information at the beginning of the file.) They can be read by both audio CD players and CD-ROM drives. Audio CDs don't have names, though pressed audio CDs are identified by an ID number linked to the artist and the work.

Data CDs   Data CDs can contain any file type. They can be read by CD-ROM drives but not by audio CD players. Data CDs can have names up to 16 characters long.

WARNING

Because CD-RW discs use a different technology than regular CD-ROMs, they're not as compatible with all CD-ROM drives. If you want to share a CD with someone else, a CD-R disc is a better bet than a CD-RW disc. Likewise, only the most recent audio players can play CD-RW discs, whereas most audio players can play only pressed audio CDs and audio CD-R discs.

CONFIGURING A RECORDABLE CD DRIVE

Before you try to burn a CD, it's a good idea to check the settings that Windows has chosen for your CD recorder or CD rewriter. You may want to tweak the configuration or change the drive used for holding temporary files when burning a CD on the desktop.

To configure a recordable CD drive, follow these steps:

1. Choose Start ➢ My Computer. Windows opens an Explorer window showing My Computer.

2. Right-click the CD drive and choose Properties from the context menu. Windows displays the Properties dialog box for the drive.

3. Click the Recording tab. Windows displays the Recording page (shown in Figure 24.1).

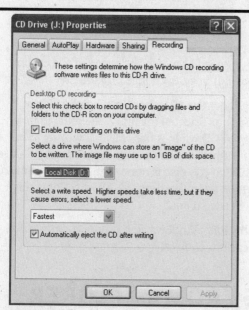

FIGURE 24.1: Check the configuration of your drive on the Recording page of its Properties dialog box.

4. Choose settings that meet your needs:

Enable CD Recording on This Drive check box Select this check box to use this drive for recording. Windows lets you use only one drive at a time for recording. This check box is selected by default on the first recordable CD drive on your system and cleared by default on subsequent recordable CD drives.

Select a Drive drop-down list In this drop-down list, select the drive on which Windows should store an *image* of the CD (temporary files containing the data to be written to the CD) when creating the CD. Windows commandeers up to 1GB of space on the drive for a high-capacity CD, so make sure the disc you choose has more than that amount available. (For a standard CD, Windows needs around 700MB of space.)

Select a Write Speed drop-down list In this drop-down list, you can specify the speed that Windows should use when recording a CD. The default setting is Fastest—the highest speed your drive supports. If Fastest doesn't give good results, try the next lower rate. Windows automatically adjusts this speed to match the speed of the current disc, so you may not need to change it manually.

Automatically Eject the CD after Writing check box Leave this check box selected (as it is by default) to have Windows eject the CD when it has finished writing to it. When you're burning CD-R discs, this ejection can be a useful visual signal that the disc is done, but you may want to disable this option when burning CD-RW discs or when using a laptop in a tight space.

5. Click the OK button. Windows closes the Properties dialog box and applies your choices.

Burning CDs from Explorer

Burning CDs from Explorer is an easy three-step process:

1. Copy the files to the storage area.

2. Check the files in the storage area to make sure that they're the right files and that there aren't too many of them.

3. Write the files to CD.

The following sections discuss these steps.

Copying the Files to the Storage Area

The first step in burning files (or folders) to CD is to copy them to the storage area. You can do so in several ways, of which these three are usually the easiest:

- ▶ Select the files in an Explorer window or in a common dialog box. Then right-click in the selection and choose Send To ➤ CD Drive from the context menu. (Alternatively, choose File ➤ Send To ➤ CD Drive.) This technique is the most convenient when you're working in Explorer or in a common dialog box.

- ▶ Drag the files and drop them on the CD drive in an Explorer window or on a shortcut to the CD drive. For example, you could keep a shortcut to the CD drive on your desktop so that you could quickly drag files and folders to it. This technique is good for copying to CD files or folders that you keep on your desktop.

- ▶ Open an Explorer window to the storage area, then drag files to it and drop them there. This technique is mostly useful for adding files when you're checking the contents of the storage area. When you insert a blank CD in your CD drive, Windows displays a CD Drive dialog box offering to open a folder to the writable CD folder.

When you take one of these actions, Windows copies the files to the storage area and displays a notification-area pop-up telling you that you have files waiting to be written to the CD.

Either click the pop-up or (if it has disappeared) open a My Computer window and double-click the icon for the CD drive. Windows opens an Explorer window showing the storage area, which appears as a list called Files Ready to Be Written to the CD. (For a CD-RW that already contains files, the storage area also contains a list of Files Currently on the CD.) Figure 24.2 shows an example of the storage area. As you can see in the figure, Windows displays a downward-pointing arrow on the icon for each file or folder to indicate that it's a temporary file destined to be burned to CD and then disposed of.

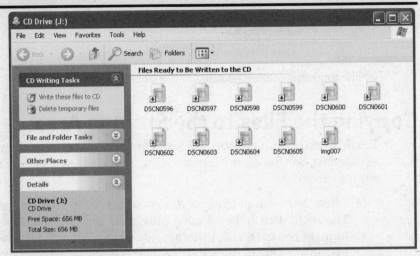

FIGURE 24.2: The storage area holds the copies of files to be burned to the CD. The downward-pointing arrow on each file icon and folder icon indicates that the item is temporary and will be deleted after being burned to CD.

While Windows copies the files, the CD drive will appear to be busy, but it won't actually be writing any information to CD yet.

Checking the Files in the Storage Area

Once you've copied to the storage area all the files that you want to burn to the CD, activate the window that Explorer opened to the storage area and check that the files are all there, that you don't want to remove any of them, and that there aren't too many to fit on the CD. (If you closed the window showing the storage area, you can display the storage area again by opening an Explorer window to My Computer and double-clicking the icon for the CD drive.)

NOTE

By default, the storage area is located in the \Local Settings\Application Data\Microsoft\CD Burning\ folder under the folder for your account in the \Documents and Settings\ folder.

To check the size of files in the storage area, select them all (for example, by choosing Edit ➤ Select All), then right-click and choose Properties from the context menu. Windows displays the Properties dialog box for the files. Check the Size readout on the General page.

Writing the Files to CD

Once you've looked at the files in the storage area and are satisfied all is well, start the process of writing the files to CD. Take the following steps:

1. Click the Write These Files to CD link in the CD Writing Tasks list. Windows starts the CD Writing Wizard, which displays its first page (shown in Figure 24.3).

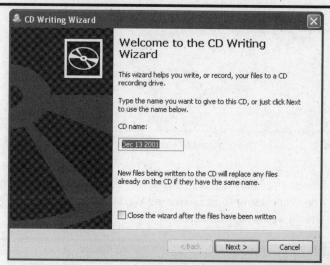

FIGURE 24.3: On the first page of the CD Writing Wizard, specify the name for the CD and choose whether the Wizard should close itself when the CD is finished.

2. Enter the name for the CD in the CD Name text box. CD names can be up to 16 characters long.

3. If you want the Wizard to close itself when the CD is finished, select the Close the Wizard after the Files Have Been Written check box. If you select this check box, you won't have the option of creating another CD containing the same files, because the Wizard automatically clears the storage area.

4. Click the Next button. The CD Writing Wizard displays the page shown in Figure 24.4 as it burns the CD. The burning goes through three stages: Adding Data to the CD Image, Writing the Data Files to the CD, and Performing Final Steps to Make the CD Ready to Use.

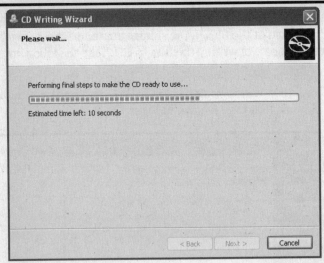

FIGURE 24.4: The CD Writing Wizard shows you its progress in burning the CD.

5. When the Wizard has finished burning the CD, it displays the Completing the CD Writing Wizard page (shown in Figure 24.5) and ejects the CD.

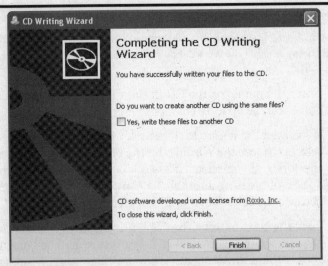

FIGURE 24.5: The CD Writing Wizard displays the Completing the CD Writing Wizard page when it has finished creating the CD.

6. If you want to create another CD containing the same files, select the Yes, Write These Files to Another CD check box.

7. Click the Finish button. The Wizard closes itself and deletes the files from the storage area unless you selected the Yes, Write These Files to Another CD check box.

When Things Go Wrong Writing the CD...

If you try to write more files to a CD than will fit on it, the CD Writing Wizard displays the Cannot Complete the CD Writing Wizard page (shown in Figure 24.6). You can remove some files from the storage area, then select the Retry Writing the Files to CD Now option button, and click the Finish button if you want to try to fix the problem while the CD is open, but in most cases you'll do best to leave the Close the Wizard without Writing the Files option button selected and click the Finish button, then return to the storage area, fix the problem, and restart the writing process.

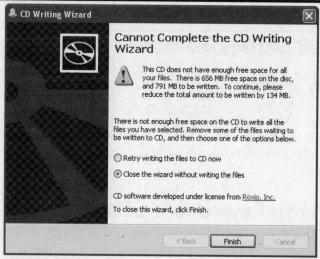

FIGURE 24.6: The CD Writing Wizard displays its Cannot Complete the CD Writing Wizard page to warn you that the files won't fit on the CD.

The CD Writing Wizard may also warn you that there was an error in the recording process, and the disc may no longer be usable. This is the other reason why people like the term *burning* for recording CDs—when things go wrong, you get burned and the disc is toast. In this case, you'll probably want to try writing the files to another CD.

When you've finished creating the CD, test it immediately by opening an Explorer window to its contents and opening some of them. Make sure all is well with the CD before archiving it or sending it on its way.

NOTE

If the CD you create won't read or play properly, it may have suffered recording errors. Try reducing the burning speed by using the Select a Recording Speed drop-down list on the Recording page of the Properties dialog box for the drive.

Clearing the Storage Area

If you end up deciding not to create the CD after all, clear the storage area by deleting the files in it. To do so, click the Delete Temporary Files link in the CD Writing Tasks list. Windows displays the Confirm Delete dialog box (shown in Figure 24.7) to make sure you know the files haven't yet been written to CD. Click the Yes button. Windows deletes the files and removes the Files to Add to the CD heading from the Explorer window.

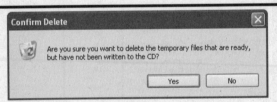

FIGURE 24.7: Windows displays the Confirm Delete dialog box to make sure you want to delete all the files from the storage area.

Working with Rewritable CDs

You record the first set of information to rewritable CDs (CD-RW discs) by using the same procedure as for recordable CDs (CD-R discs). But you can then add further files to them and erase all files from them. The following sections discuss how to take these actions.

Adding Further Files to a Rewritable CD

You can add further files to a rewritable CD by following the same procedure as for initially burning files to it. As mentioned earlier in the chapter, the storage area for a rewritable CD displays a Files Currently on the

CD list for a CD-RW that already contains files or folders. Figure 24.8 shows an example of the storage area for a rewritable CD with some more files queued for adding to the CD.

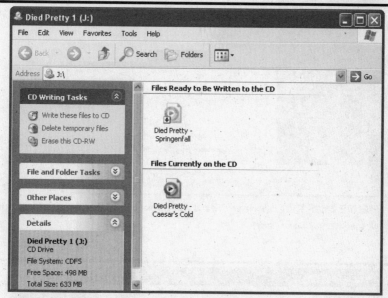

FIGURE 24.8: The storage area for a rewritable CD displays a Files Currently on the CD list.

Erasing All Files from a Rewritable CD

You can erase all the files off a rewritable CD so that all its space is free again. To do so, take the following steps:

1. Open an Explorer window to the CD drive.

2. Click the Erase This CD-RW link in the CD Writing Tasks list. Windows starts the CD Writing Wizard, which displays another Welcome to the CD Writing Wizard page (shown in Figure 24.9).

3. If you want the Wizard to close itself after erasing the files, select the Close the Wizard when Erase Completes check box.

4. Click the Next button. The Wizard displays the Erasing the CD page (shown in Figure 24.10) while it erases the files.

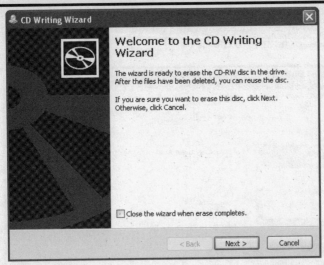

FIGURE 24.9: The CD Writing Wizard walks you through the process of erasing all the files from a CD-RW.

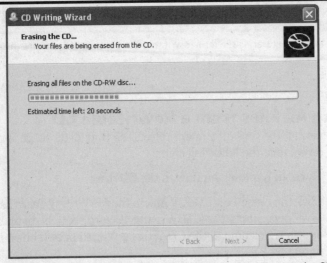

FIGURE 24.10: The CD Writing Wizard displays the Erasing the CD page while it erases the files on the CD-RW.

Part v

5. When the Wizard has finished erasing the files on the CD-RW, it displays another Completing the CD Writing Wizard page (shown in Figure 24.11).

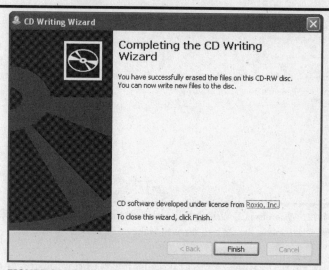

FIGURE 24.11: The Wizard displays this Completing the CD Writing Wizard page when it has finished erasing the files on the CD-RW.

6. Click the Finish button. The Wizard closes itself.

Creating an Audio CD from Explorer

To create an audio CD, you use Windows Media Player, which includes features for creating PCM files from other audio file formats. But you can start the process from Explorer by copying only audio files to the storage area. When you then start the CD Writing Wizard, it displays the Welcome to the CD Writing Wizard page as usual for you to name the CD, but after that it displays the Do You Want to Make an Audio CD? page (shown in Figure 24.12).

To create an audio CD, select the Make an Audio CD option button and click the Next button. The CD Writing Wizard launches or activates Windows Media Player, passes the information across to it, and then closes itself. Create the CD as described in the next section.

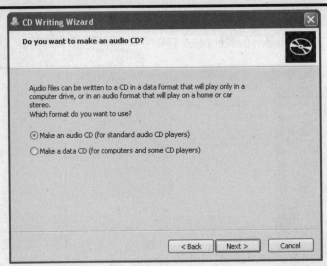

FIGURE 24.12: When the CD Writing Wizard learns that all the files for the CD are audio files, it displays the Do You Want to Make an Audio CD? page.

To create a data CD, select the Make a Data CD option button and click the Next button. The CD Burning Wizard then continues its usual course.

NOTE

If Windows decides that the contents of the current folder displayed in an Explorer window are predominantly music, it displays the Music Tasks list. You can then select a file or folder and click the Copy to Audio CD link. Doing so opens Windows Media Player with the tracks loaded ready for copying to an audio CD.

BURNING CDs FROM WINDOWS MEDIA PLAYER

Windows Media Player includes a feature for burning audio CDs directly from playlists. You can use MP3, WAV, and WMA files to create CDs up to 74 minutes long. (Windows Media Player can't create 80-minute audio CDs.)

TIP

If you want to include tracks in other formats on CDs you burn, convert them to WAV format first. Many sound programs can convert audio files. Sound Recorder, which comes with Windows XP, can convert a wide range of formats.

Burning a CD from Windows Media Player is even easier than burning a CD from Explorer. That's because the only choice you have to make is which tracks you want to include on the CD: You don't have to name the CD (because it's an audio CD), and you don't have to specify whether it's a data CD or an audio CD (for the same reason).

The only other thing you have to worry about is this: if the tracks have digital licenses, whether the licenses allow the tracks to be copied to CD. If they don't, Windows Media Player will warn you of the problem.

To burn a CD from Windows Media Player, take the following steps:

1. Open the playlist you want to burn to CD, or create a new playlist containing the tracks.

2. Check the number of minutes shown: It must be 74 or fewer, otherwise the burning will grind to a halt when the disc is full. Remove tracks if necessary. (Or add more if you have space left.)

3. Choose File ➢ Copy ➢ Copy to Audio CD. Windows Media Player displays the Copy to CD or Device page and inspects the tracks to make sure that there aren't any license problems. Figure 24.13 shows the Copy to CD or Device page with a playlist queued for writing to CD.

4. Click the Copy Music button. Windows begins the copying process, which consists of these three steps:

    Converting Writing out the audio files to uncompressed WAV files. While Windows Media Player converts the tracks, it displays *Converting* and a percentage readout next to the track it's working on.

    Copying to CD Copying the WAV files to the CD. Windows Media Player displays *Copying to CD* and a percentage readout next to each track in turn as it copies the track to the CD.

    Closing the disc When all of the WAV files have been written to the CD, Windows Media Player closes the disc.

Part v

FIGURE 24.13: Windows Media Player ready to write a playlist to CD

5. When Windows Media Player has closed the disc, it ejects the CD. Check the CD manually to make sure that it works (for example, put it back in the drive and try playing it), then label it.

NOTE
You can also launch Windows Media Player and get it ready to burn CDs by selecting music files, right-clicking, and choosing Copy to Audio CD from the context menu. (Alternatively, choose File ➢ Copy to Audio CD.)

COPYING A CD

You can make a copy of a CD by using the same techniques as for copying any other files: Copy the files to the storage area, and then write them to CD. Remember that copying CDs of copyrighted works involves copyright issues.

If you have a CD drive (or DVD drive) other than your CD-R or CD-RW drive, you can simply open an Explorer window to My Computer, then drag the icon for the CD and drop it on the icon for the CD-RW drive. Windows copies the files to the storage area. Click the Write to CD link to start the CD Writing Wizard.

IF WINDOWS' CD-WRITING CAPABILITIES AREN'T ENOUGH

Windows offers what might be termed strong but basic features for burning CDs, letting you burn data CDs easily from Explorer and audio CDs even more easily from Windows Media Player. But if you need more advanced CD-burning features (or more bells and whistles), you'll need to buy third-party CD software.

One package you might consider is Easy CD Creator from Roxio, Inc. (You might also consider Easy CD Creator Deluxe, which comes with not only bells and whistles but also gongs such as features for designing CD labels.) Why consider Easy CD Creator in particular? Well, for one thing, you're using Roxio technology already—the CD-burning functionality in Windows is licensed from Roxio. For another, Roxio is a company spun off in 2001 from Adaptec, Inc., a company that has long been one of the major names in CD burning.

WHAT'S NEXT

This chapter has discussed how to burn CDs from Explorer and from Windows Media Player. It has also provided advice on choosing recordable CD media and CD rewriter drives. The final section of this book contains a Quick Reference to some of the most common Windows XP commands and features.

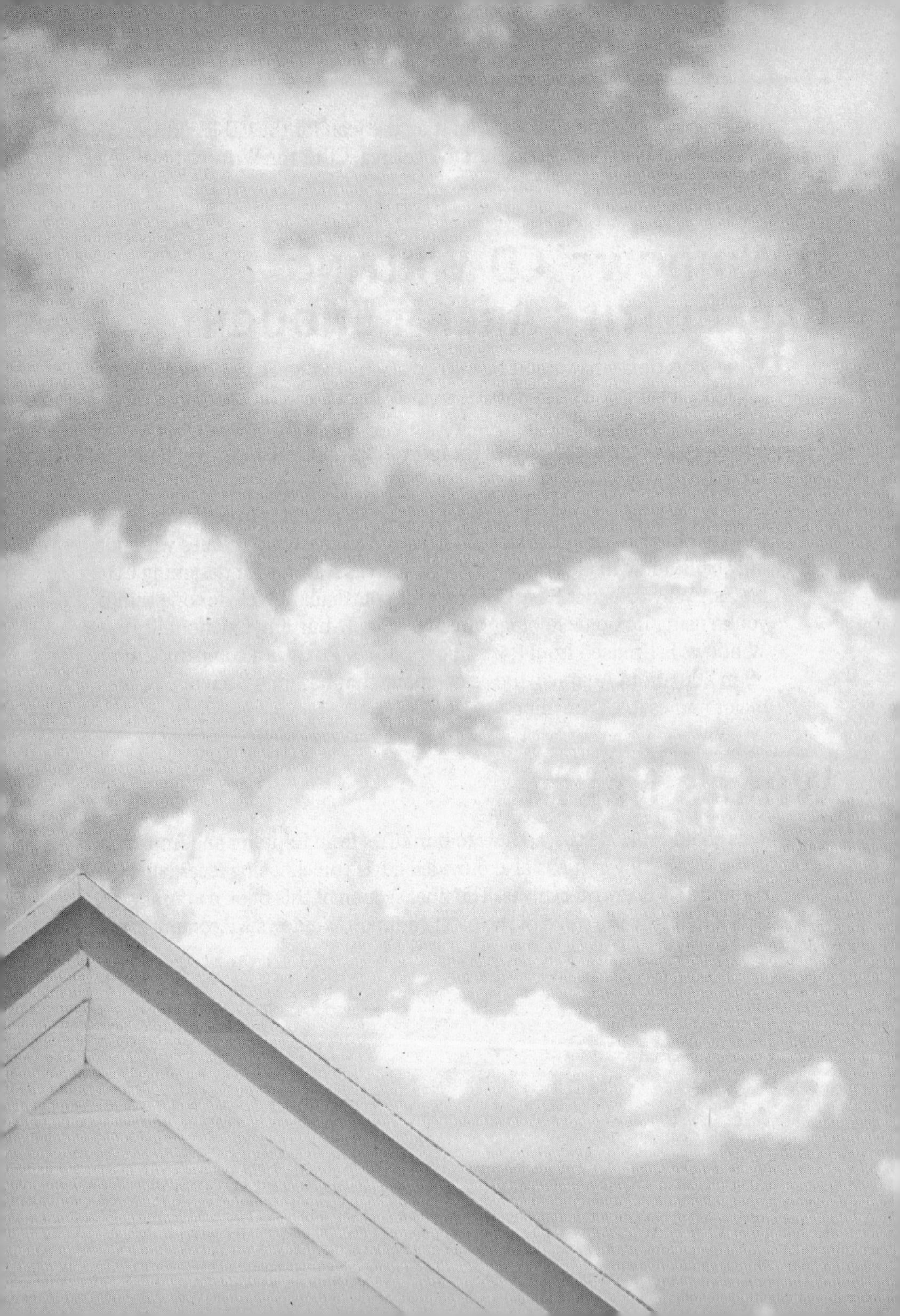

Appendix

WINDOWS XP HOME EDITION
INSTANT REFERENCE

Adapted from *Windows XP Home and Professional Editions Instant Reference* by Denise Tyler

ISBN 0-7821-2986-2   464 pages $24.99

ACCESSIBILITY

 ▸ Program group that helps adjust the computer to users' needs. Choose Start ➢ All Programs (or Start ➢ Programs from the Classic Start menu) ➢ Accessories ➢ Accessibility to access the Accessibility Wizard, Magnifier, Narrator, On-Screen Keyboard, and Utility Manager. For more information on these tools, see their respective main topics and the following subsections.

Accessibility Options

Configures settings that make using the computer easier for users who have physical disabilities, such as hearing and vision impairments, as well as users who have difficulty using the keyboard and mouse.

Choose Start ➢ Control Panel (or Start ➢ Settings ➢ Control Panel from the Classic Start menu) and click Accessibility Options to open the Accessibility Options window.

Accessibility Options Window

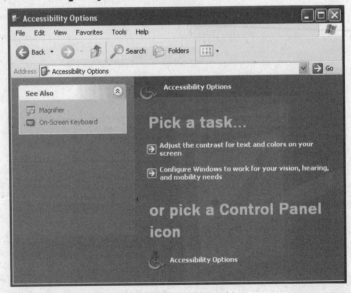

The Accessibility Options window consists of three main areas, which provide the following options:

See Also   Contains links to two accessibility features that you can customize to suit your needs. Use Magnifier to enlarge areas of your screen while you move your mouse. On-Screen Keyboard lets you use a mouse or other pointing device to enter text into dialog boxes or other software programs.

Pick a Task   Click "Adjust the contrast for text and colors on your screen" to open the Accessibility Options dialog box to the Display tab. Select "Configure Windows to work for your vision, hearing, and mobility needs" to open the Accessibility Wizard. Further information on this dialog box and wizard appear in the following sections.

Pick a Control Panel Icon   Click the Accessibility Options icon to open the Accessibility Options dialog box, described next.

Accessibility Options Dialog Box

The Accessibility Options dialog box contains five tabs: Keyboard, Sound, Display, Mouse, and General. Select the appropriate check box to turn on a feature, and click the Settings button to adjust the default settings.

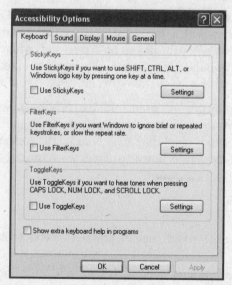

TIP

You can use keyboard shortcuts to turn many of the Accessibility Options on and off. The shortcuts are turned on by default; to turn them off, click the appropriate Settings button and deselect the Use Shortcut check box.

Keyboard tab   Contains the StickyKeys, FilterKeys, and ToggleKeys options, which are useful for those who have trouble using the keyboard. You can also specify that programs display additional keyboard-related help. The StickyKeys feature keeps the Shift, Ctrl, Alt, or Windows logo key activated until you press another key in a keyboard shortcut (such as Ctrl+A or Alt+F). A tone also sounds when you press a key. FilterKeys either repeats or ignores short keystrokes and slows down the repeat rate. ToggleKeys sounds a tone when you press the Caps Lock, Num Lock, or Scroll Lock key.

TIP

If you have shortcuts enabled, press the Shift key five times to toggle Sticky-Keys on. Hold down the Right Shift key for eight seconds to toggle FilterKeys on. Hold down the Num Lock key for five seconds to toggle ToggleKeys on.

Sound tab   Contains the SoundSentry and ShowSounds options, which are useful for those with hearing impairments. SoundSentry flashes an on-screen alert when the system generates a sound. ShowSounds displays text or icons to represent speech or sounds that programs use.

Display tab   Contains the High Contrast option, which is useful for those with vision impairments. High Contrast displays fonts and colors that make reading the screen easier. The Cursor Options section also allows you to adjust the blink rate and width of the cursor.

TIP

To toggle on High Contrast, press Left Alt+Left Shift+Print Screen.

Mouse tab   Contains the MouseKeys option, which allows you to control the mouse with the numeric keypad.

TIP

To toggle on MouseKeys, press Left Alt+Left Shift+Num Lock. For a complete explanation of the MouseKeys feature, search the Help and Support Center index for the keyword *MouseKeys*.

General tab   Contains options for Automatic Reset, Notification, SerialKey Devices, and Administrative Options. Automatic Reset turns off accessibility options after the computer is idle for a specified period. Notification displays warning messages or sounds when you turn features on and off using shortcut keys. SerialKey Devices enables support for a serial input device other than keyboard or mouse. Administrative Options applies default settings for new users and for the logon Desktop.

Accessibility Wizard

Accessibility Wizard   Helps you configure accessibility options to make Windows XP and your computer easier to use if you have difficulties with your vision, hearing, or mobility. To start the Accessibility Wizard, choose Start ➢ All Programs (or Start ➢ Programs from the Classic Start menu) ➢ Accessories ➢ Accessibility ➢ Accessibility Wizard.

Once you have launched the wizard, make the choices and settings indicated in each screen and click Next to continue. You'll be able to:

- ▶ Select the smallest text size that you are able to read.

- ▶ Enable or disable options that allow you to read text more easily (such as changing the interface font size), switch screen resolution, or use personalized menus.

- ▶ Indicate types of features that are difficult for you to use.

- ▶ Adjust the size of scroll bars and window borders if needed.

- ▶ Change the size of icons (normal, large, or extra large).

- ▶ Choose from several color schemes that alter the contrast of text and colors on the screen.

- ▶ Change the size and color of the mouse pointer.

- ▶ Change the cursor blink rate and width.

▶ Display visual warnings when system events occur.

▶ Display captions for speech and sounds.

▶ Use StickyKeys, which makes it easier to use multiple keystroke combinations.

▶ Use BounceKeys, which ignores repeated keystrokes.

▶ Use ToggleKeys, which plays a sound when you press the Caps Lock, Num Lock, or Scroll Lock.

▶ Show extra keyboard help when applicable and available.

▶ Use MouseKeys to control the mouse pointer through the numeric keypad.

▶ Select a right- or left-handed mouse and adjust the mouse pointer speed.

▶ Turn off StickyKeys, FilterKeys, ToggleKeys, and High Contrast features when the idle time exceeds a specified period.

▶ Configure all these settings as the default for new user accounts or for the current user only.

On the Completing the Accessibility Wizard screen, review your choices. If you want to make changes, use the Back button to return to a choice and change it. Finally, click Finish. Windows XP applies the changes when you exit the wizard.

See also   Magnifier, Narrator, On-Screen Keyboard, Utility Manager

ACCESSORIES

▶ Predefined program group that includes many programs to help configure and maintain your Windows XP computer and network or Internet communications. It also provides access to Windows XP multimedia features, games, and other helpful programs that allow you to create documents, work with images, and explore and synchronize Internet content. To access the Accessories group, choose Start ➢ All Programs (or Start ➢ Programs from the Classic Start menu) ➢ Accessories.

The programs and program groups available in Accessories depend on the choices you made during the Windows XP installation and may include additional items if you installed other programs. If you install Windows XP with the default configuration, the Accessories group includes the following:

Programs	Program Groups
Address Book	Accessibility
Calculator	Communications
Command Prompt	Entertainment
Notepad	System Tools
Paint	
Program Compatibility Wizard	
Scanner and Camera Wizard	
Synchronize	
Tour Windows XP	
Windows Explorer	
Windows Movie Maker	
WordPad	

TIP

For more information on these items, see their respective main topics.

ADD NEW HARDWARE

Add Hardware   Starts the Add Hardware Wizard, which helps you add, remove, and troubleshoot hardware on your system, such as network cards, modems, disk drives, and CD-ROM drives.

NOTE

You can search the Windows XP Help and Support Center index for the Add Hardware topic and open the Add Hardware Wizard through a link in the Details pane.

The wizard guides you through the steps to add new device drivers to a Windows XP computer after you physically install the associated hardware. You can also prepare Windows XP before you physically remove or unplug hardware from the computer, or troubleshoot a device that is experiencing problems. The Add Hardware Wizard automatically makes the necessary changes, including changing the Registry and configuration files and installing, loading, removing, and unloading drivers.

NOTE

You must have administrative privileges to add, remove, or troubleshoot hardware with the Add Hardware Wizard.

TIP

The Add Hardware Wizard installs device drivers for Plug and Play, non–Plug and Play, SCSI, and USB devices.

Before you start the Add Hardware Wizard, power off your computer, and install the hardware device or plug it into the appropriate port. Turn your computer back on. If Windows XP detects a Plug and Play device for which it has drivers, it automatically installs the drivers and no further action is required.

If Windows XP does not detect your hardware, follow these steps:

1. To open the Add Hardware Wizard, choose Start ➢ Control Panel (or Start ➢ Settings ➢ Control Panel from the Classic Start menu) ➢ Printers and Other Hardware. From the See Also tasks in the left pane of the window, click the Add Hardware link. Click Next to continue.

2. The Add Hardware Wizard asks whether you have connected the hardware. If you choose No and click Next, the wizard provides an option to turn off the computer when you click Finish, so that you can install the hardware. Click Yes if you have connected the hardware, then click Next to continue.

3. Windows XP searches the hardware that is installed on your computer and displays a list of items that it detected. Select Add a New Hardware Device, and click Next.

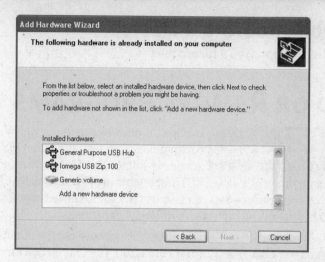

4. The wizard asks whether you want to search for and install the new hardware, or select it manually from a list. Even though the wizard did not detect the hardware the first time, it may find it if you search for it now. If you know the manufacturer and model of the hardware you want to install, choose to select it manually from a list. Click Next.

NOTE

If you allow Windows XP to detect the new hardware, be patient. Searching for the different categories of hardware devices may take some time.

5. The remainder of the process varies greatly, depending on the method you selected and the type of hardware you install. Follow the on-screen instructions or the instructions that were furnished with your hardware.

6. After Windows XP configures the settings for your hardware, a screen informs you that the installation is complete. Click Finish to close the wizard.

See also   Help and Support Center, System, System Information

Removing/Unplugging Hardware

See   Device Manager (Action Menu)

Troubleshooting a Device

See   Hardware Troubleshooter

ADD OR REMOVE PROGRAMS

 Installs or removes programs and Windows XP components from your computer. Examples of programs are Microsoft Word or Microsoft FrontPage; examples of Windows XP components are Administrative Tools or networking options. You can also use Add or Remove Programs to install other operating systems on different partitions.

To open Add or Remove Programs, choose Start ➤ Control Panel (or Start ➤ Settings ➤ Control Panel from the Classic Start menu) and click the Add or Remove Programs icon. The left pane of the following window contains three buttons that allow you to change or remove programs, add new programs, or add or remove Windows XP components (described in the following sections). The information in the right pane changes based on the option you choose.

Change or Remove Programs

Changes or removes programs installed on your Windows XP computer. The Currently Installed Programs box displays a list of programs that are currently installed on your computer.

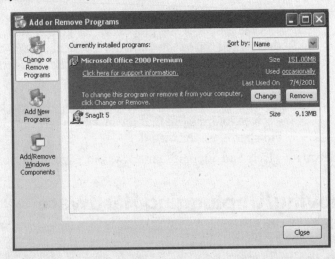

When you select a program in the list, you may see some or all of the following additional information and options:

Size   The amount of space the program takes up on your hard drive.

Used   How often you have used the program in the last 30 days (possible values are Rarely, Occasionally, or Frequently).

Last Used On   The date that you last used the program.

Change, Remove   To change or remove a program, select a program from the list and click the appropriate button. The steps that follow vary, depending on the program you selected. A wizard may guide you through the steps to change, reinstall, or remove the program. Windows XP may prompt you to confirm the removal of program files, program groups, and registration and configuration file entries, or to verify that you want to remove the program before changes are made.

WARNING

After you click the Change or Remove button, Windows XP may remove some programs immediately without showing any warning messages.

Add New Programs

Adds new programs or program updates to your Windows XP computer. Click the Add New Programs icon in the left pane to display two options that allow you to install a new program from CD or floppy disk, or to add new features, drivers, or updates from the Microsoft Web site.

CD or Floppy   To add a new program from CD or floppy disk, click the CD or Floppy button. A wizard guides you through the individual steps that are required to install the program.

From Microsoft   You can use the Windows Update feature to add Windows XP system updates, new features, and device drivers. After you establish an Internet connection, click the Windows Update button to display the Microsoft Windows Update home page, which allows you to download product updates or to view support information.

TIP

In the Classic Start menu, you can also choose Start ➤ Windows Update to access Windows Update.

From Your Network If you're connected to a network, any programs that have been published in the Active Directory and to which you've been given access will appear in the Add Programs from Your Network list box at the bottom of the screen. A network administrator may have placed programs into different categories; select different categories (if available) in the Category drop-down list to find the application you're looking for.

Add/Remove Windows Components

Add/Remove Windows Components

Allows you to add or remove options from your Windows XP installation. When you click the Add/Remove Windows Components icon, the Windows Components Wizard appears.

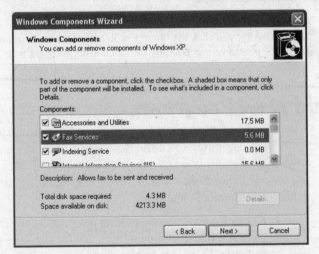

This wizard helps you install, configure, and remove Windows XP components. Follow these steps:

1. In the Components list, select a component to display its description. Clear the check mark to remove a program, or check a component to add it to your Windows XP installation. When you check a component, the bottom of the dialog box

also displays the total disk space required to add the program and the amount of free space on your hard drive.

2. Some Windows components have subcomponents that you can add or remove. To see the list of subcomponents, click the Details button after you select a component from the list. All subcomponents are selected by default. Check or uncheck subcomponents you want to include or remove.

3. Each subcomponent includes a description and disk space information, and may include additional subcomponent levels. After you make your subcomponent selections, click OK until you return to the Windows Components screen. Then click Next to continue.

4. The wizard makes component configuration changes and installs or removes the components you selected. The wizard may prompt you to insert your Windows XP CD, or prompt you to provide an alternate path to Windows XP files. Follow the prompts to complete the changes.

5. When the installation is complete, click Finish to exit the wizard.

TIP

You must configure some Windows XP components before you can use them. In these cases, the wizard displays two choices: choose Configure to configure components, or Components to add or remove components.

See also   Windows Update

ADDRESS BOOK

See   Chapter 17

See also   Outlook Express, Internet Explorer, Search

ADMINISTRATIVE TOOLS

▸ Administrative Tools   ▸ Collection of MMC tools you can use to administer every aspect of your Windows XP computer configuration. The list of available tools depends on whether your computer is a Windows XP Home or Professional computer and which services are installed on the computer.

To access Administrative Tools, choose Start ➤ Control Panel (or Start ➤ Settings ➤ Control Panel from the Classic Start menu) ➤ Performance and Maintenance, then click the Administrative Tools icon.

Common Administrative Tools for Windows XP Home include Component Services, Computer Management, Data Sources (ODBC), Event Viewer, Performance, Services, and Server Extensions Administrator.

See also   Computer Management

APPEARANCE AND THEMES

See   Chapter 10

See also   Accessibility, Display, Folder Options, Fonts, Mouse, Taskbar and Start Menu

AUTOMATIC UPDATES

See   Windows Update (Receiving Update Notification)

AUTOPLAY

Windows XP feature that automatically starts programs or displays media files when you insert removable storage media into the appropriate drive. To configure options for AutoPlay, choose Start ➤ My Computer, right-click a removable storage device (such as a CD-ROM drive or digital camera), and choose Properties. Select the AutoPlay tab. For each media type, click the radio button that describes how you want Windows XP to work when that device is activated: take an action (that you choose in the list box), prompt you for an action, or do nothing.

BROWSE

Browse... Used to find files and directories on the computer or in the network. This button appears in many dialog boxes where you need to provide the name and path of a file or folder or specify an Internet or intranet address.

Click Browse to open the Browse dialog box. The left side of the dialog box displays shortcuts to various locations on the computer or network where you can look for the files you want. Click one of these shortcuts or enter a folder in the Look In field. The contents of the selected folder appear in the window below. Double-click folders in the window to move further down the directory structure.

Use the Files of Type drop-down list to specify the type of files you want to display in the Browse window, or choose to see all files of all types.

Select a file to display it in the File Name field, then click Open. You return to the dialog box from where you were browsing, and the name and path to the file appear in the appropriate field.

See also   My Computer, My Documents, My Network Places

CALCULATOR

See   Chapter 7

CAPTURING IMAGES

Windows XP allows you to capture screen images to the Clipboard, which you can then paste into a document. To capture and paste an image, follow these steps:

1. To capture the entire screen, press the Shift+Print Screen key (often abbreviated as PrtSc). To capture an active window, press Alt+Print Screen.

NOTE
Note that you won't see anything happen on the screen when you capture a screen or window with Print Screen.

2. Place the cursor where you want to insert the image in your document.

3. Press Ctrl+V or choose Edit ➤ Paste. Windows pastes the image into your document.

CD Writing Wizard

See   Chapter 24

Character Map

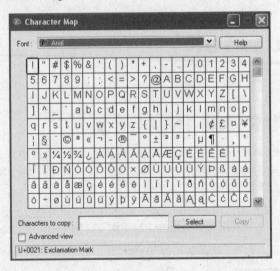

Character Map Allows you to display and copy characters for any installed font or characters you created with the Private Character Editor. Character Map displays Unicode (default), DOS, and Windows character sets. To access Character Map, choose Start ➤ All Programs (or Start ➤ Programs in the Classic Start menu) ➤ Accessories ➤ System Tools ➤ Character Map.

To display character sets for a font, select a font from the Font drop-down list. Click a character to enlarge it. The status bar at the bottom of the Character Map dialog box displays the name and Unicode value (hexadecimal equivalent) for the character. You may also see a keyboard shortcut for the character if one is available.

TIP

The phrase *(Private Characters)* appears after the font name in the drop-down list for fonts that are linked to characters created with the Private Character Editor.

Character Map allows you to copy characters to the Windows XP Clipboard and then paste them into other programs. Click a character and then click Select, or double-click a character, to place it in the Characters to Copy text box. Then click Copy to copy all selected characters to the Windows XP Clipboard.

TIP

You can also select a character in the character set and then drag and drop it into an application that supports drag-and-drop.

Select Advanced View to display additional Character Map–related options. You can select the character set you want to display, group the Unicode character set by Unicode subrange, search for a specific character, or go directly to a character in the Unicode set.

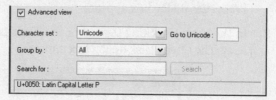

TIP

You cannot resize the Character Map window. If the window does not fit on your screen, you may have to move the window to see certain portions of it.

Instead of displaying all characters in a Unicode character set, you can display only the characters that are part of a selected subrange. This makes it easier for you to find a specific character. To group characters by

Unicode subrange, select Unicode Subrange from the Group By drop-down list, then select a subrange in the following dialog box.

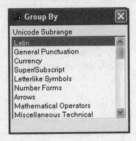

To search for a character, enter all or part of its name in the Search For text box and click Search. Or, select Unicode from the Character Set drop-down list and enter a Unicode value in the Go to Unicode text box. In either case, Character Map takes you directly to the desired character.

See also   Fonts

CHECKING DRIVES FOR ERRORS

To check a floppy or hard disk for any file system and physical errors on the disk, follow these steps:

1. In Explorer, right-click a drive and select Properties. The Properties dialog box appears.

2. In the Error-Checking section of the Tools tab, click Check Now. The Check Disk dialog box appears.

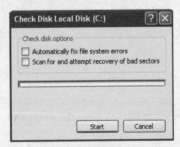

3. Check or uncheck options to automatically fix file system errors or to scan for and attempt recovery of bad sectors, then click Start.

4. After Windows XP scans your disk, the Checking Disk dialog box notifies you that the check is complete. Click OK to close the dialog box, and click OK again to close the Properties dialog box.

See also   Explorer

CLIPBOARD

Temporary holding place for data. When you use the Cut or Copy command in programs running on a Windows XP computer, the selected data is placed into the Clipboard. Use the Paste command to retrieve the contents of the Clipboard. To view the contents of the Clipboard, use the ClipBook Viewer.

WARNING

The Clipboard stores only one item at any time. When you cut or copy a new item, it replaces the contents currently on the Clipboard. You can use ClipBook Viewer to save Clipboard contents into your local ClipBook.

ClipBook Viewer

ClipBook Viewer allows you to view and save the contents of the Windows XP Clipboard. To open ClipBook Viewer, choose Start ➤ Run, then type **clipbrd** and click OK. ClipBook Viewer has two windows: the Local ClipBook and the Clipboard. Maximize or resize the Clipboard to view its contents.

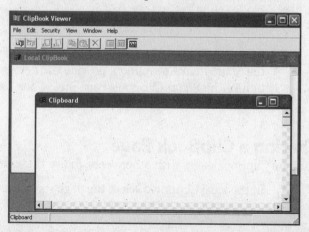

You can save the contents of the Clipboard either to a file or to the local ClipBook.

Saving the Clipboard Contents to a File

To save the contents of the Clipboard to a file (with a .CLP extension), open ClipBook Viewer and click somewhere in the Clipboard window to activate it. Choose File ➢ Save As, browse to the folder where you want to save the file, enter a name for the file, and click Save.

Saving the Clipboard Contents in the Local ClipBook

When you save the Clipboard contents to your local ClipBook, you can share ClipBook pages with other users. You can also set up permissions and auditing for each ClipBook page (for remote user access after you share a page) and take ownership of a page, via the options on the Security menu.

After you place pages in your local ClipBook, you can display them using the Table of Contents view (the default), Thumbnail view, or Full Page view (which displays the contents of the selected page). Access the views either from the View menu or by clicking a toolbar button.

To save the contents of the Clipboard to a page in the local ClipBook, perform the following steps:

1. Click inside the ClipBook window to activate it.

2. Choose Edit ➢ Paste. The Paste dialog box appears.

3. Enter a name for the ClipBook page you're creating. Select Share Item Now if you want to share the page.

4. Click OK. The page is added to the ClipBook. If you selected the Share Item Now option, provide the necessary information in the Share ClipBook Page dialog box (see following section).

Sharing a ClipBook Page

To share ClipBook pages with other users, follow these steps:

1. In the local ClipBook, select the page you want to share.

2. Choose File ➤ Share or click the Share button on the toolbar. The Share ClipBook Page dialog box appears.

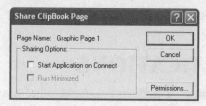

3. Select Start Application on Connect to automatically open the application that was used to create the contents of the page when another user accesses the page. Choose Run Minimized to run the application in a minimized window.

4. Click Permissions to configure the users and groups that are allowed to access the page, and the type of access they should have. Click OK to return to the Share ClipBook Page dialog box.

5. Click OK to share the page. A hand appears at the bottom of the page's icon to indicate that the page is shared.

To stop sharing a page, select the page in the local ClipBook and choose File ➤ Stop Sharing, or click the Stop Sharing button on the toolbar.

Accessing Pages in Another User's ClipBook

To access pages in another user's shared ClipBook, choose File ➤ Connect or click the Connect button on the toolbar. In the Select Computer dialog box, browse to and select the computer to which you want to connect, then click OK. A list of all shared ClipBook pages appears; double-click the ClipBook page you want to open.

To disconnect from the remote computer, choose File ➤ Disconnect, or click the Disconnect button on the toolbar.

Close

 Closes the currently open window or application. You'll find this button in the top-right corner of any open window, next to either the Restore Down or Maximize button.

See also   Maximize and Minimize, Restore Down

COMMAND PROMPT

See   Chapter 7

COMMUNICATIONS

 Communications Predefined program group from which you access the following communication-related program groups: Network Setup Wizard, New Connection Wizard, NetMeeting, Network Connections, Phone Dialer, and Remote Desktop Connection. These items are described in detail throughout this book, each under its own main topic. Choose Start ➤ All Programs (or Start ➤ Programs in the Classic Start menu) ➤ Accessories ➤ Communications to access the Communications program group.

COMPRESSING DRIVES, FOLDERS, AND FILES

You can compress NTFS-formatted drives, and individual folders and files on NTFS drives, to save on disk space. If you copy or add a file into a compressed drive or folder, it is automatically compressed. If you move a file off of an NTFS drive, the file remains in its original compressed or decompressed state.

WARNING
Before you compress a drive, run Scandisk to make sure the drive is free of errors. You should also back up your data before you compress files, in case corruption occurs. Performance may suffer if you compress files that you frequently access.

To compress an NTFS drive, open the Explorer window, right-click the drive, and select Properties. On the General tab of the Properties dialog box, check Compress Drive to Save Disk Space, and click OK. In the confirmation dialog box, specify whether you want only files and folders at the root of the drive to compress or you want subfolders and files compressed as well. Click OK.

To compress an individual file or folder on an NTFS drive, right-click the item in Explorer and select Properties. On the General tab, click Advanced, then check Compress Contents to Save Disk Space, and click OK. Click OK again to close the Properties dialog box. If a folder contains subfolders, Windows XP prompts you to confirm the change and to specify whether you want the changes to apply to any subfolders and files as well. Click OK.

TIP

To display compressed files and folders in a different color, select the View tab in the Folder Options dialog box. Check "Display compressed files and folders with alternate color."

See also Explorer, Folder Options

COMPUTER MANAGEMENT

MMC snap-in that allows you to manage various aspects of your computer. To access Computer Management, choose Start ➢ Control Panel (or Start ➢ Settings ➢ Control Panel in the Classic Start menu) ➢ Performance and Maintenance, click Administrative Tools, and then double-click Computer Management.

Categories appear in this console tree under Computer Management (Local) including System Tools. Each of these contains other items you use to manage your local computer by default that depend on the options you select during Windows XP installation. To manage remote computers, select Computer Management (Local) in the console tree and choose Action ➢ Connect to Another Computer. Select a computer from the list and click OK.

CONTROL PANEL

Allows you to configure and personalize settings for many Windows XP functions and features. Control Panel items are described in individual main topics throughout this book.

To access Control Panel, choose Start ≻ Control Panel (or Start ≻ Settings ≻ Control Panel in the Classic Start menu). You can also access Control Panel through My Computer and Windows Explorer.

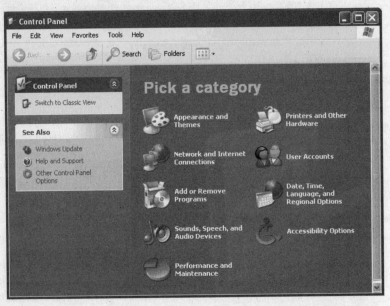

See also   Accessibility, Add or Remove Programs, Appearance and Themes, Date/Time, Network and Internet Connections, Performance and Maintenance, Printers and Other Hardware, Regional and Language Options, Sounds and Audio Devices, User Accounts

COPY DISK

Copy Disk... Copies the contents of a floppy disk to another. The two disks must be of the same type; for example, you can copy one 3½-inch high-density disk to another 3½-inch high-density disk. To copy a floppy disk, insert the source disk into your floppy disk drive. From Windows Explorer, right-click the source drive and choose Copy Disk. Select the source and destination (these are the same if you only have one floppy drive) and click Start.

WARNING

Make sure that you do not have data you want to keep on the target disk. The Copy Disk command overwrites its contents with the contents from the source disk.

See also   Explorer

COPYING FILES AND FOLDERS

Copy   You can copy files and folders to another location, leaving the original items intact in their original locations, using Windows Explorer. To do so, first select one or more files or folders from the right pane of the Explorer window. Hold down the Shift key to select contiguous items, or the Ctrl key to select separated items. Then perform *one* of the following:

➤ Choose Edit ➢ Copy (or Ctrl+C). Select the destination folder, then choose Edit ➢ Paste (or Ctrl+V).

➤ Right-click the selected item or items and choose Copy from the shortcut menu that appears. Then right-click the destination folder and choose Paste.

➤ If both the source and destination folders are visible, you can use drag-and-drop. Hold down the Ctrl key, then left-click and drag the selected item(s) to the destination folder. (If you don't hold down the Ctrl key, Explorer *moves* the selection to the destination instead of copying it.)

See also   Explorer, Moving Files and Folders

CREATING NEW FOLDERS

Windows Explorer allows you to create new folders so that you can organize the files on your computer. To do so, select the drive or folder in which you want to create the new folder. Choose File ➢ New ➢ Folder, or right-click the drive or folder and choose New ➢ Folder from the shortcut menu that appears. A new folder appears beneath the drive or folder you selected. Replace the name New Folder with a descriptive name of your choice. Then press Enter to assign the name.

See also   Explorer

CREATING SHORTCUTS

▣ Shortcut   Shortcuts let you access programs, files, folders, printers, computers, or Internet addresses without having to go to their permanent locations. Windows XP allows you to create shortcuts in many ways.

To create a shortcut in Windows Explorer, select an item and then use *one* of the following methods:

- ▶ Choose File ➢ New ➢ Shortcut, or right-click the item and choose New ➢ Shortcut from the menu that appears. Explorer places the new shortcut in the same folder. Drag the shortcut to a new location (such as another folder, the Desktop, or the taskbar).

- ▶ Press the Ctrl+Shift keys while you left-click and drag the shortcut to a new location.

You can instead right-click the Desktop and choose New ➢ Shortcut. The Create Shortcut Wizard then guides you through the process of creating a new shortcut.

TIP

For information on how to add a shortcut to the Start menu, see the main topic "Taskbar and Start Menu."

TIP

You can also access items through My Computer, My Network Places, and My Documents. They all open Windows Explorer to a different, specific place in the Windows XP file system structure.

After you create a shortcut, you can right-click it and choose Properties to get details about the shortcut (such as file type, size, creation and modification dates) and configure characteristics such as name, attributes (Read-Only, Hidden, Archive, etc.), target, window type, and (on NTFS drives) permissions.

DATE/TIME

See   Chapter 9

See also   Regional and Language Options, Taskbar

DESKTOP

The Windows XP workspace that allows you to organize your folders, files, and shortcuts to frequently used programs. When Windows XP first opens, you see the Desktop, which by default displays a shortcut to the Recycle Bin. The Start button and the taskbar appear at the bottom of the screen.

As you install new programs or make changes to your environment, Windows XP adds new icons to the Desktop and taskbar and may remove others. When you open a program, its user interface appears in front of the Desktop so that you can use the program.

The Display Properties dialog box allows you to specify the appearance of your Desktop, as well as other settings. To open the Display Properties dialog box, right-click an empty space on your Desktop and choose Properties. For further information on this dialog box, see the main topic "Display."

See also Control Panel, Display

DEVICE MANAGER

 MMC snap-in that displays a list of all hardware installed in the computer and provides information about this hardware. Use Device Manager to verify that your hardware is working properly after you install new hardware. You can also use Device Manager to enable, disable, configure, and check the status of devices and to view and update device drivers.

TIP
You must log on as a computer administrator to make certain changes to devices in Device Manager.

To access Device Manager, choose Start ➢ Control Panel (or Start ➢ Settings ➢ Control Panel in the Classic Start menu) ➢ Performance and Maintenance. Next, click the System control panel icon to open the System Properties dialog box. Select the Hardware tab, and click the Device Manager button.

Device Manager lists the hardware on your computer in several different classes (for example, Display Adapters or System Devices). To view the devices in each class, click the plus sign at the left of the class name. Each device appears in the list with an icon, followed by the name of the class or device.

NOTE
If the device icon contains a yellow question mark, the device is unknown. Unknown devices are typically non–Plug and Play devices for which you must install drivers that came with your hardware.

NOTE
If the device icon contains a yellow exclamation point, a hardware or software problem exists for the device. Double-click the problem device to open the Properties dialog box. Click the Troubleshoot button in the General tab to open the Hardware Troubleshooter.

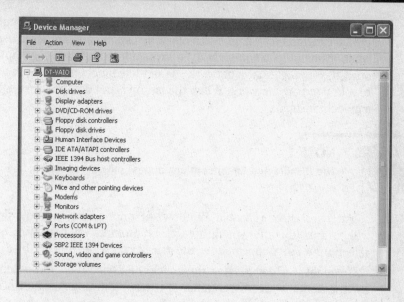

As with all MMC consoles and snap-ins, Device Manager has Action and View menus that contain options specific to the currently active MMC snap-in.

Action Menu

Action   Select a device in Device Manager, and then use commands in the Action menu to perform device-related actions. Commands unique to this menu include Update Driver, Disable (which toggles to Enable), Uninstall, and Scan for Hardware Changes.

TIP

An alternative method for accessing the options available under Action is to select a device and right-click. If you select a device class, only the Scan for Hardware Changes and Properties options are available. If you select the workstation itself, the Disable option won't be available.

Disable and Enable

Disable   Temporarily disables a Plug and Play device. When you disable a device, you do not have to physically remove it from the computer to avoid having Windows XP load drivers for the device.

Use this feature to set up different hardware profiles—for example, one profile to attach your laptop to a docking station and another to use when your laptop is not docked. To explain further, when your laptop is docked, you might use a network adapter to connect to the Internet and to your company network. When the laptop is not docked, you might use a modem instead.

NOTE
The Disable and Enable options appear only if you have administrative privileges.

After you choose Disable, Windows XP informs you that your device will not function after you disable it, and prompts you to confirm your selection. A red X appears over the device icon when it is disabled.

To enable the device later, right-click the device and choose Enable, or use the Action $\succ$ Enable command. The red X disappears, indicating that the device is enabled again.

Uninstall

Uninstall   Allows you to remove a device driver from your Windows XP computer. After you uninstall a device driver, you need to physically remove the hardware device from your computer; otherwise, Windows XP will reinstall the drivers the next time you start up.

When you uninstall a device driver, Windows XP asks you to confirm your action. Click OK to uninstall the device from Device Manager. Then, turn your computer off and physically remove the device.

If you later need to reinstall the device and the device driver, install the hardware in your computer according to the manufacturer's recommendations. Windows XP automatically installs device drivers for Plug and Play devices when you restart your computer. Use the Add New Hardware Wizard to install non–Plug and Play devices.

NOTE
The Uninstall option is available only when you log on as a computer administrator.

TIP

Another way to uninstall a Plug and Play device is to shut down the computer (necessary for most devices), physically remove the device, and then start Windows again. Windows XP automatically removes the device.

Scan for Hardware Changes

Scan for hardware changes   Allows you to manually scan your computer to see whether hardware changes have occurred, such as a device being removed from or added to the computer.

If Windows XP detects changes in your hardware, it takes appropriate action. Windows XP may remove or add devices to the list, and may display messages about the changes it makes. For example, when you remove or unplug a device before you disable the service, Windows XP displays the Unsafe Removal of Device dialog box.

WARNING

You should always disable a device before you remove it from the computer; otherwise, serious problems may result. Many devices also require that you power off the computer before you remove the device. Consult your hardware documentation for more information.

Print

Print   Allows you to print a hard copy of your system summary, information on a selected class or device, or all devices and a system summary. Select the items you want to print (choose Computer from the Device Driver list to print all items), and select report options from the Report Type section of the Print dialog box. Then click Print to print the report to your printer.

Properties

Properties   Allows you to view and change properties of the selected device. To display the Properties dialog box, highlight a device in Device Manager and choose Action ➤ Properties, or right-click the device and choose Properties from the menu that appears. The tabs and settings that appear in the Properties dialog box vary depending on the device you select. The most common tabs are General, Driver, and Resources.

TIP

You can also click the Properties button in the Device Manager toolbar to display properties for a device.

General tab   Displays general information about the device, such as device type, manufacturer, location of the device, and the device status. If the device status indicates that the device is not working properly, click the Troubleshoot button to open the appropriate Windows XP Troubleshooter. Use options in the Device Usage drop-down list to enable or disable the device.

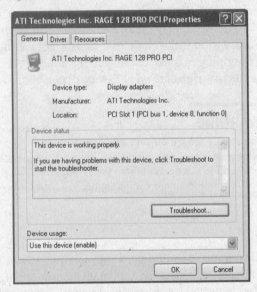

Driver tab   Displays information about the device driver used for the selected device. Information may include driver provider, date, and version, and digital signer. Four buttons appear in the Driver tab:

Driver Details   Opens a dialog box that displays the paths to the driver files that are installed for the device. The information that you see in the Driver tab is repeated in the lower portion of the Driver File Details dialog box.

Update Driver   Opens the Hardware Update Wizard, which allows you to install software for your device. You can install software automatically or select devices from a list or specific location.

Roll Back Driver   Allows you to revert to a previous version of a device driver when you experience trouble with your computer after you change a device driver. If no previous driver files are backed up for the device, Windows XP asks whether you want to launch the Troubleshooter. If one or more previous versions of the driver exist on your system, follow the prompts to select the version of the driver that you want to revert to.

Uninstall   Allows you to uninstall the device driver. Windows XP asks you to confirm the removal.

Resources tab   Displays information about the system resources the device is using. Device information includes the I/O (input/output) port address range, IRQ (interrupt request), DMA (Direct Memory Access) channel, and memory address range. Windows XP automatically assigns resources for Plug and Play devices. For non–Plug and Play devices, you may have to manually configure resource settings.

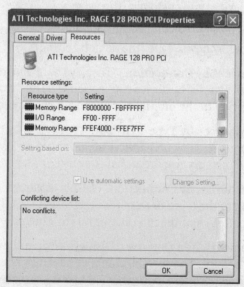

If a conflict exists, the Conflicting Device List displays the device with which your current device conflicts. You will need to select different settings to resolve the conflict. To select different settings, deselect the Use Automatic Settings check box. Then, select a different hardware configuration from the Setting Based On drop-down list, until you locate a setting that does not conflict with other devices or drivers. Alternatively, deselect the Use Automatic Settings check box and select a resource from the Resource Settings list. Then, click the Change Setting button to manually change a resource setting. You cannot change some resource settings.

WARNING

Change resource settings only if you are very comfortable with device hardware settings. Otherwise, the device or other devices may no longer function properly after you make a change.

View Menu

View

The View menu in Device Manager allows you to display devices and resources by using various sorting methods. It also allows you to display hidden devices and customize the view.

Devices by Type Displays hardware devices in alphabetical order by device type (the default setting).

Devices by Connection Displays hardware devices in alphabetical order by device connection. The devices are listed in relation to the interface or bus to which they connect.

Resources by Type Displays the devices by the type of resources they use. Devices are arranged by DMA, I/O, IRQ, and memory resources that they use.

Resources by Connection Displays the devices in a combination of the types of resources they use (DMA, I/O, IRQ, or memory) and the interface or bus to which they connect.

Show Hidden Devices Displays devices that are not visible by default. They can include items such as non–Plug and Play drivers, printers, and other (unknown) devices.

Customize Opens the Customize View dialog box, which allows you to show or hide items in Device Manager. Check or uncheck options to show or hide the console tree, standard menus (Action and View), standard toolbar, status bar, description bar, and taskpad navigation tabs. You can also show or hide Device Manager menus and toolbars.

Additional Toolbar Buttons

In addition to the Action and View menus, the Device Manager MMC snap-in toolbar contains some of the buttons commonly found on MMC consoles, such as Back, Forward, Up One Level, Show/Hide Console Tree/Favorites, and Help. It can also contain various buttons depending on whether you selected the workstation, a device class, or a device, and whether a device is disabled or enabled; these are self-explanatory, except that the Update Driver button opens the Hardware Update Wizard, which allows you to update the driver for the selected device.

See also   Add New Hardware, Administrative Tools, Computer Management, System (Hardware tab)

DISK CLEANUP

See   Chapter 12

See also   Add or Remove Programs, Recycle Bin, Windows - Components

DISK DEFRAGMENTER

See   Chapter 12

See also   Computer Management

DISK MANAGEMENT

🖳 Disk Management   MMC snap-in for Windows XP Home that allows you to manage disks and volumes in a graphical environment. To access Disk Management, choose Start ➤ Control Panel (or Start ➤ Settings ➤ Control Panel in the Classic Start menu) ➤ Performance and Maintenance ➤ Administrative Tools, and double-click Computer Management. Expand the Storage category to display the Disk Management snap-in.

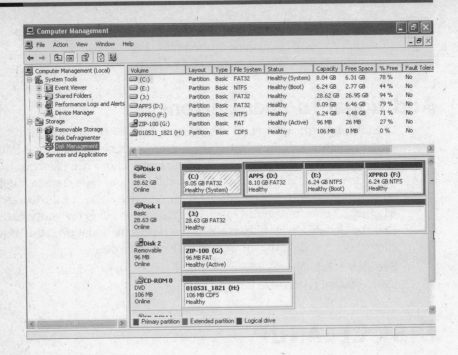

TIP

You must log on as a computer administrator or be a member of the Administrators group to use Disk Management.

Use Disk Management to change drive letters and paths, format disks, create or delete partitions, upgrade basic disks to dynamic disks, and eject removable media (such as Zip disks, Jaz disks, CDs, and DVDs). You can also create and work with simple, spanned, striped, mirrored, and RAID-5 volumes for both basic and dynamic disks.

WARNING

If you upgrade a basic disk to a dynamic disk, you cannot access the disk with any operating system other than Windows XP.

By default, the Disk Management Details pane displays a top and bottom window. The top window displays the volume list, and the bottom window displays a graphical view of your disks. Use commands in the View menu to customize the display to your liking.

Basic Disks

Basic disks are hard disks that contain primary and extended partitions, and logical drives, as well as mirrored volumes, striped volumes, spanned volumes, and RAID-5 volumes. Basic disks can contain a maximum of four primary partitions per disk, or three primary partitions and one extended partition (which can contain multiple volumes or logical drives). Windows XP and earlier versions (including Windows 3.1, 95, 98, Me, NT 4, and DOS) can access basic disks.

Action Menu

The Action menu for a basic disk includes many unique items, on the menu or its All Tasks submenu. The options available depend on which item you've selected in the Details pane and whether you have selected the Disk List or the Volume List.

Refresh   Updates the disk and volume views.

Rescan Disks   Rescans all available disks.

Eject   Ejects removable media from the drive.

All Tasks ➢ Open   Opens the drive in Windows Explorer without an Explorer Bar view selected.

All Tasks ➢ Explore   Opens the drive in Windows Explorer with the Explorer Bar Folders view selected.

All Tasks ➢ Mark Partition as Active   Marks the currently selected partition as active.

All Tasks ➢ Change Drive Letter and Paths   Allows you to change the drive letter and path of a volume.

All Tasks ➢ Format   Allows you to format the drive. You can choose a volume label, file system (NTFS or FAT32), and allocation unit size.

All Tasks ➢ Delete Partition   Deletes the selected partition.

All Tasks ➢ Properties   Opens the drive's properties.

All Tasks ➢ Delete Logical Drive   Deletes the selected logical drive.

Creating Partitions

To create a partition or logical drive using unallocated space, right-click unallocated space in the Graphical view and choose Create Partition, then follow the wizard's instructions.

View Menu

The View menu contains the following unique options when working with basic disks:

Top, Bottom Each contains a submenu that allows you to select what to display in the top or bottom window of the Details pane. Choices include Disk List, Volume List, and Graphical View.

Settings Allows you to configure the color and pattern for each of the disk regions in the Graphical view, such as primary partition, free space, and simple volume. Also allows you to configure the proportion for how disks and disk regions display in the Graphical view.

All Drive Paths Displays all drive paths.

Dynamic Disks

Disk Management allows you to create dynamic disks (hard disks that contain dynamic volumes). There are five types of dynamic volumes: simple, spanned, mirrored, striped, and RAID-5.

NOTE

Only Windows XP and Windows 2000 can access dynamic disks. You can create an unlimited number of volumes on a dynamic disk. However, you cannot create partitions or logical drives on a dynamic disk.

Simple A volume that is made up of disk space from a single physical disk. You can extend the amount of space at any time unless the disk is mirrored.

Spanned   A volume that consists of disk space on more than one physical disk. You can extend the amount of space at any time unless the disk is mirrored.

Mirrored   A volume that is an exact duplicate of a simple or spanned volume. The same drive letter is used for both copies of the volume. Mirrored volumes are available only on computers running Windows XP Server.

Striped   You need at least two dynamic disks, with a maximum of 32 disks, to create a striped volume. Striped volumes are not fault tolerant, and you cannot extend or mirror them.

RAID-5   RAID-5 volumes provide fault tolerance. If you use three 10 GB disks to create a RAID-5 volume, the RAID-5 volume has a 20 GB capacity, and the remaining 10 GB is used for parity. You need at least three dynamic disks, with a maximum of 32 disks, to create a RAID-5 volume. RAID-5 volumes are available only on computers running Windows XP Server. You cannot extend or mirror RAID-5 volumes.

NOTE

You cannot create dynamic disks on portable computers, removable disks, or detachable disks that connect to your computer through USB, FireWire, or shared SCSI interfaces.

Creating a Dynamic Disk

In order to create a dynamic disk, you must format one or more existing drives to create unallocated space on each drive that you want to convert to a dynamic disk. After you format the disk, you can use the New Volume Wizard to step you through the process of creating dynamic disks.

WARNING

You must be logged on as a computer administrator or member of an administrator group to format and create dynamic disks. If your computer is on a network, verify that your network policy settings allow you to complete this procedure.

WARNING

Perform these steps only if you are certain that Windows XP is the only operating system that will access any file stored on or copied from the dynamic drive. DOS and Windows versions earlier than Windows 2000 cannot access dynamic drives. For example, if you copy a file from the dynamic drive to a floppy disk, a Windows 98 or Me computer will not be able to read the file on the floppy disk because it was originally stored on a Windows XP dynamic drive.

To create a dynamic disk, follow these steps:

1. From the Computer Management window, right-click the volume that you want to format and choose Format from the shortcut menu. The Format dialog box appears.

WARNING

Do not select the system or boot volume.

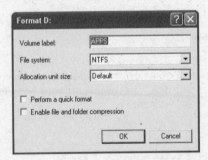

2. Enter a volume label, select a file system (FAT32 or NTFS), and choose an allocation unit size (default, or values between 512 and 64K). Check the Quick Format option only if the disk has been previously formatted and you are certain that the disk is not damaged. Check the Enable File and Folder Compression option if you want to create a compressed NTFS volume.

3. Click OK to format the volume.

4. After you format the volumes necessary to create your dynamic disk (as discussed in Dynamic Disks above), return to the Computer Management window. Right-click the unallocated space on the volume you want to use for your

dynamic disk, and choose New Volume from the shortcut menu to open the New Volume Wizard.

5. Click Next to continue. The wizard asks what type of dynamic volume you want to create.

6. Select the dynamic volume type (simple, spanned, mirrored, striped, or RAID-5), and follow the remaining prompts in the Wizard to complete the process.

DISK SPACE

Windows Explorer allows you to see how much disk space a file uses. From any Explorer window, select a folder in the Folders pane, then select one or more files from the right pane. The status bar displays the amount of space that the file or files use (choose View ➢ Status Bar to display the status bar if it is not visible).

To determine the amount of disk space a folder uses, select a folder in the Folders pane. Choose File ➢ Properties, or right-click and choose Properties from the shortcut menu, to open the Properties dialog box. The General tab displays the total size of the folder (including all sub-folders and files contained within it), the size it consumes on the disk, and the number of files and folders that are included in the folder.

See also Explorer

DISPLAY

See Chapter 10

See also Power Options

DRAG-AND-DROP

Functionality you can use to copy, move, and delete files and folders in many application programs and on the Desktop. To drag and drop a selection, place the mouse pointer over any item (or items). Press and hold the left mouse button while you move the mouse to drag the selection to another folder or drive, to your Desktop, or other destination. Place the pointer over the destination to highlight it, and then release the left mouse button.

The result of the drag-and-drop items can differ, as outlined below:

▶ If you drag a file or folder to a folder on the same disk, Windows moves the item. To copy the item instead, press the Ctrl key while you drag and drop the selection.

▶ If you drag a file or folder to a folder on a different disk, Windows copies the item. To move the item instead, press the Shift key while you drag and drop the selection.

▶ If you drag a file or folder to the Recycle Bin, Windows deletes the item (this is not permanent until you empty the Recycle Bin).

▶ If you drag a file to a printer shortcut on the Desktop, Windows prints the file.

See also   Explorer

ENTERTAINMENT

Entertainment   Program group that provides access to the Sound Recorder, Volume Control, and Windows Media Player. These items are discussed in detail under their own respective main topics in this book. Access the Entertainment program group by choosing Start ➢ All Programs (or Start ➢ Programs in the Classic Start menu) ➢ Accessories ➢ Entertainment.

EXPLORER

See   Chapter 6

See also   Folder Options, Help and Support Center, Internet Explorer, Map Network Drive, My Computer, My Documents, My Network Places, Recycle Bin, Search, Synchronize

FAST USER SWITCHING

☑ **Use Fast User Switching**   Keeps programs running when a user logs off the computer to allow another user to log on. When the original user logs back on to the computer, the Desktop appears exactly as he or she left it.

To enable or disable Fast User Switching, choose Start ➤ Control Panel (or Start ➤ Settings ➤ Control Panel in the Classic Start menu) ➤ User Accounts, then choose Change the Way Users Log On or Off. Check or uncheck the Use Fast User Switching option.

NOTE

You cannot disable Fast User Switching when multiple users are logged on to the computer. Also, only a computer administrator can enable or disable this feature.

See also   User Accounts

FILE AND SETTINGS TRANSFER WIZARD

Files and Settings Transfer Wizard   Allows you to transfer files and settings from your old computer to your new one. In order to transfer the files, you need to run the File and Settings Transfer Wizard on the old computer *and* the new computer. To begin the wizard, choose Start ➤ All Programs (or Start ➤ Programs in the Classic Start menu) ➤ Accessories ➤ System Tools ➤ File and Settings Transfer Wizard.

The wizard guides you through the process of transferring Internet Explorer and Outlook Express information, Desktop and display settings, dial-up connections, and other files from your old computer to your new one. After you select the items that you want to transfer, you can save the files to floppy disk or to another folder on your hard disk. Run the wizard on your new computer to retrieve the files. You may also be prompted to insert your Windows XP CD during the process.

FILE SIGNATURE VERIFICATION UTILITY

To maintain system integrity and detect changes to system files, system files are digitally signed by the software manufacturer to ensure authenticity. The File Signature Verification utility allows you to check for critical system files that should be digitally signed but aren't. To start the utility, choose Start ➢ Run, then type **sigverif** in the Run dialog box. The File Signature Verification dialog box appears.

Click the Advanced button to configure verification options such as receiving notification when system files are not signed, narrowing your search to certain file types or locations, or saving results to a log file. When you are done setting these options, click OK to return to the File Signature Verification dialog box.

Click Start to begin the file signature verification process. A progress bar appears in the dialog box while the utility scans your files. Wait for the process to finish, then do one of the following:

▶ If you receive a message that tells you all files are digitally signed, click OK to return to the File Signature Verification dialog box, then click Close to exit the dialog box.

▶ If some files are not digitally signed, the Signature Verification Results dialog box displays the names of those files. The status bar displays the numbers of files found, signed files, unsigned files, and files not scanned. Make note of the files that are not signed, and click Close.

NOTE
After you create a log, you can return to the Logging tab in the Advanced File Signature Verification Settings dialog box at any time, and click View Log to view a complete log of the files that were reported as signed, unsigned, and not scanned.

FOLDERS

 Folders are part of the Windows XP file system structure. You use folders to organize files on your computer. Folders can contain files and subfolders.

To view a folder, open Windows Explorer. Use the Folders tree in the left pane to find the folder. Select a folder name to display its contents in the main pane. You can also double-click a folder in the main pane or on your Desktop to view its contents.

Right-click a folder name and select Properties to open the Properties dialog box, which can have any or all of the following tabs:

General   Displays the folder's name, type, location, size, content count, and creation or modification date. You can choose to apply the Read-Only and Hidden attributes (and the Archive attribute if formatted with FAT). If the drive is formatted with NTFS, click Advanced to configure additional attributes such as archiving, indexing, compression, and encryption attributes.

Sharing   Allows you to share a folder with other users on the network. For more information, see the main topic "Sharing."

Customize   Allows you to use the display options of the current folder as a template for other folders. You can configure the folder to store documents, pictures, photo albums, or music files. You can also choose a picture that reminds you of the contents that are stored in the folder, and select a custom folder icon to use for all folders.

See also   Explorer, Shared Folders, Sharing

FOLDER OPTIONS

Folder Options   Controls the appearance and use of files and folders and configures file associations. Any settings you make determine how folders are displayed and used in Windows Explorer, My Documents, My Network Places, My Computer, and Control Panel.

To open the Folder Options dialog box, choose Start ➢ Control Panel (or Start ➢ Settings ➢ Control Panel in the Classic Start menu) ➢ Appearance and Themes ➢ Folder Options. The Folder Options dialog box contains four tabs—General, View, File Types, and Offline Files.

TIP

You can also access Folder Options from the Tools menu of any Windows Explorer window.

General Tab

Controls how folders appear and work. The tab is divided into three sections:

Tasks   Allows you to display common tasks in folders (default), or to use Windows classic folders.

Browse Folders   Allows you to open a new folder in the same window (default) or in its own window.

Click Items as Follows   Allows you to open items with a single click or a double click (default). You can also choose to underline icon titles as configured in your Web browser, or only when you point at them.

TIP

If single-clicking is specified, move the mouse pointer over an item to select it.

You can return to default values by clicking Restore Defaults.

View Tab

Controls the appearance and advanced settings for folders. Click the Apply to All Folders button to apply the View tab settings from the current folder to all other folders. This button is available only when you access the Folder Options dialog box from the Tools menu of Windows Explorer. You can reset the view of all folders to the default setting (Large Icons) by clicking Reset All Folders.

In the Advanced Settings list box, select check boxes for the settings you want to apply, such as displaying the full path in the title bar, hiding file extensions for known file types, and showing hidden files and folders.

File Types Tab

Controls which file types are associated with which file extension (.XXX), and the default application used to open a file type. The Registered File Types list displays all registered file types and their extensions. The following buttons are available on the File Types tab:

New   Allows you to create a new file extension. Click the Advanced button to associate a new or existing file type with the new extension. You can also enter an existing file extension and then change the file type associated with the extension.

Delete   Allows you to delete an existing file extension and associated file type.

Change   Allows you to change the default application that Windows uses to open files of the selected extension and file type.

Advanced   Allows you to change the selected file type's associated icon and actions. Any configured actions appear in the File menu and shortcut menu for the item. You can configure a new action by clicking New and then specifying the action as well as the application that is supposed to perform that action. You can also edit or remove existing actions, and you can specify whether you want files to open immediately after they have finished downloading. Finally, you can choose to always show file extensions and to enable browsing in the same window.

Offline Files Tab

Used to configure whether files on the network are available when you are not connected to the network. On this tab, you can choose to: enable or disable offline files, synchronize files when you log on or before you log off, display reminders at regular intervals when you are working offline, encrypt these files to secure data, and adjust the amount of space to store offline files.

The following three buttons appear on the Offline Files tab:

Delete Files   Allows you to delete temporary offline files or all offline files.

View Files   Displays files that are in the Offline Files folder.

Advanced   Allows you to choose events that occur when you lose connection to the network. You can request notification and continue to work offline, or you can choose to never allow the computer to go offline. You can also configure exceptions for specific computers.

See also   Explorer, Internet Explorer, Make Available Offline, Synchronize

Fonts

Folder used to view and manage the fonts (type styles) that are used by Windows XP and Windows applications. To open the Fonts folder in an Explorer window, choose Start ➢ Control Panel (or Start ➢ Settings ➢ Control Panel in the Classic Start menu) ➢ Appearance and Themes.

From the See Also list in the left pane, click Fonts to open the Fonts window. All fonts that are currently installed appear in this window.

Windows XP supports TrueType fonts, Open Type fonts (an extension of TrueType), Type 1 fonts (by Adobe Systems), vector fonts, and raster fonts. The icon in the Fonts folder displays an indicator for each font type. For example, Open Type fonts show an *O* in the font icon; TrueType fonts show two *T*s, and Type 1 fonts display an *A* (for Adobe).

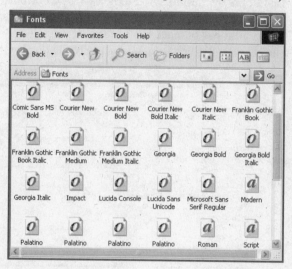

Viewing Font Examples

Double-click a font icon to open a window that contains examples of the font in different sizes. You'll also see information such as font type, typeface name, file size, version, and copyright information. Click Print to print the font example.

If you have many fonts installed on your system, it can get difficult to keep track of what fonts you have available and what they look like. The View menu of the Fonts folder includes two options that make it easier to keep track of your fonts:

List Fonts by Similarity   Produces a drop-down list where you choose a font that you are familiar with. Fonts are then listed by name, arranged by similarity to the font you selected. You can also click the Similarity button on the toolbar to display this view.

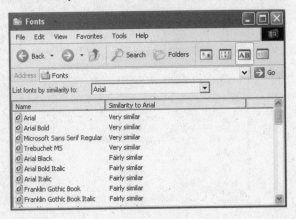

Hide Variations (Bold, Italic, Etc.)   Lists only main fonts and does not show the variations of the font (such as bold or italic). This reduces the number of items in the list and makes it easier to find or choose a font you're looking for.

Adding New Fonts

You can add new fonts to your computer at any time by following these steps:

1. Choose File ➢ Install New Font.

2. Browse for the location of the new fonts.

3. Select one or more fonts from the List of Fonts list box, and check or uncheck the option to copy the fonts to your Fonts folder.

4. Click OK. Windows installs the fonts and returns you to the Fonts folder.

See also   Explorer

FORGOTTEN PASSWORD WIZARD

Allows you to create a *password reset disk*. You can use this disk to log in to your account if you forget your password.

NOTE

The proper time to create a password reset disk is *while you remember what your password is*. Consider creating this disk the first time you log on to your new account. The Forgotten Password Wizard prompts you to enter the *current* password while you create the password reset disk for the account.

To open the Forgotten Password Wizard, use one of the following methods:

▶ If you are logged on as a Computer Administrator, choose Start ➤ Control Panel ➤ User Accounts. From the Pick a Task section, click Change an Account, then select an account to change. In the Related Tasks list in the left pane, choose Prevent a Forgotten Password.

▶ If you are logged on as a Limited user, choose Start ➤ Control Panel ➤ User Accounts. From the Pick a Task section, click Create a Password Reset Disk, then click the Create Disk button.

If you do not remember your password when you log on, you can use the password reset disk to log on to your computer:

▶ In a domain environment, you can press Ctrl+Alt+Del at the Welcome screen and attempt to enter a password. The Logon Failed dialog box appears. Click Reset, and insert your password reset disk into your floppy drive. Follow the instructions to create a new password.

▶ In a workgroup environment, click your username on the Welcome screen, then attempt to enter a password. The Did You Forget Your Password dialog box displays an option to use your password reset disk. Click the option and insert your password reset disk into your floppy drive. Follow the instructions to create a new password.

NOTE

After you use the password reset disk to create a new password, you will need to create a new password reset disk with your new password.

See also   User Accounts

FORMAT

Format... Allows you to format a disk for first-time use, or completely erase the disk's contents. Formatting is required in order for Windows to be able to save information to and read information from any disk device, including hard disks and floppy disks.

NOTE
To format a floppy disk, first insert the disk into the floppy disk drive.

WARNING
Make sure the disk you are formatting is either blank or a disk whose contents you don't need anymore. Formatting a used disk erases all of the contents of the disk.

To format a disk, perform the following steps:

1. Open My Computer or Windows Explorer and select the disk that you want to format.

2. Choose File ➤ Format, or right-click the disk and choose Format. The Format dialog box appears. Choose settings from the drop-down lists as needed.

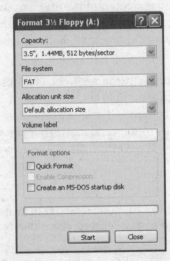

TIP

You cannot format a floppy disk with the NTFS file system.

3. Choose whether you want to perform a quick format. Do this only if you know that the disk does not have any bad sectors. A quick format takes less time because Windows XP does not scan the disk for bad sectors.

TIP

You cannot quick-format a blank, non-formatted disk.

4. If you're formatting a hard disk with NTFS, specify whether you want to enable compression.

5. To make the disk bootable, check Create an MS-DOS Start-up Disk.

6. Click Start to begin formatting. A dialog box asks you to confirm your action. Click OK to continue.

7. When the format is complete, click OK, then click Close.

See also   Explorer, My Computer, NTFS

FTP

Acronym for File Transfer Protocol, a common method for transferring files to or from a remote host (a computer on an IP network). It supports many file types, including ASCII, binary, and EBCDIC. You can also use FTP to display directory lists and file lists.

In Windows XP, FTP is a text-based program that you run from the Windows XP command prompt. To run it, choose Start ➢ Run, enter **ftp** and click OK. A Command Prompt window opens to an FTP prompt (ftp>).

You can type **?** or **help** at the ftp> prompt to display all available FTP commands. You can also type **help** followed by the name of a command to see an explanation of what the command does.

Many of the commands are used for troubleshooting purposes and to navigate the local or remote directory structure. The following commands are most commonly used for file transfer purposes:

open   Opens a connection to the remote computer. You can then enter the IP address of the computer to which you want to connect to establish the connection. You can often use **anonymous** as the username and your e-mail address as the password.

TIP

When anonymous FTP access is allowed, you don't have to use a valid e-mail address; as long as you're following e-mail address format, you'll be allowed access to the remote computer. However, it's considered good Internet etiquette to provide your actual address.

ascii   Establishes the file transfer type as ASCII.

binary   Establishes the file transfer type as binary.

put   Transfers a file you specify from your computer to the remote host.

get   Transfers a file you specify from the remote host to your computer.

quit   Closes the connection to the remote host and ends the FTP session (the **bye** command does the same). You return to the Windows XP Desktop.

GAME CONTROLLERS

Game Controllers   Installs, removes, and configures game controllers, such as game pads, joysticks, flight yokes, and steering wheel/accelerator pedal controllers. To open the Game Controllers dialog box, choose Start ➢ Control Panel (or Start ➢ Settings ➢ Control Panel in the Classic Start menu). Click Printers and Other Hardware, and then click the Game Controllers control panel icon. The dialog box contains the following options:

▶ Click Add to open the Add Game Controller dialog box, which allows you to install standard or custom game controllers.

▶ To remove a game controller, highlight it in the list of installed game controllers, then click Remove.

▶ To test and calibrate an installed game controller, select it from the list and click Properties. Use options in the Text tab to verify that your controller is installed properly. If the test is unsuccessful, click the Settings tab, then click Calibrate to perform a calibration with the Game Device Calibration Wizard.

▶ To configure support for older programs, click the Advanced button. Select your preferred device from the list and choose OK to return to the Game Controllers dialog box.

▶ Click Troubleshoot to open the Games and Multimedia Troubleshooter. Follow the instructions in the troubleshooter to remedy the problem.

GAMES

🎮 Games   Program group that contains ten games. You can play FreeCell, Hearts, Minesweeper, Pinball, Solitaire, and Spider Solitaire on your local computer. Five additional games—Internet Backgammon, Internet Checkers, Internet Hearts, Internet Reversi, and Internet Spades—require an active Internet connection and allow you to play with other users over the Internet. To access the Games program group, choose Start ➤ All Programs (or Start ➤ Programs in the Classic Start menu) ➤ Games. Choose Help from the game menu to learn how to play the game.

HARDWARE

See   Add New Hardware, Device Manager

HARDWARE TROUBLESHOOTER

Special help topic that assists you with diagnosing problems with hard disks, CD and DVD drives, network adapters, input devices, games controllers, USB devices, display adapters, modems, sound cards, and hardware conflicts.

TIP

The Add Hardware Wizard also helps you troubleshoot problems that you may be having with your hardware.

When you are configuring or inspecting hardware devices and associated drivers, various dialog boxes associated with the hardware or device driver display a Troubleshoot button. When you click this button, Windows XP opens the Hardware Troubleshooter in the Help and Support Center window.

To open the Hardware Troubleshooter at any time, choose Start ➢ Control Panel (or Start ➢ Settings ➢ Control Panel from the Classic Start menu), and then click Printers and Other Hardware. From the list of troubleshooters in the left pane, click Hardware.

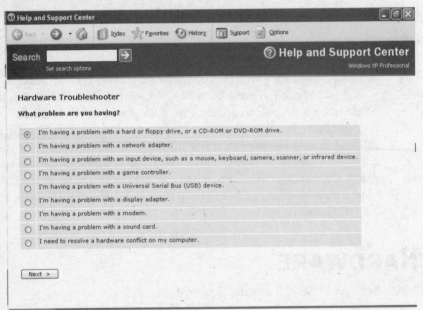

The first screen of the Hardware Troubleshooter asks what type of problem you are having. Select the option that is most appropriate and click Next to step through additional questions that pertain to the hardware item you are troubleshooting.

On each subsequent screen, choose the response that most closely matches the problem you are having and then click:

Next to continue with the diagnosis

Skip to pass by a step and try something else

Back to review a previous step

Start Over to begin an entirely new troubleshooting session

If you can't find the solution in the Hardware Troubleshooter, you can use the options in the Support screen for additional help.

See also   Add New Hardware

HELP AND SUPPORT CENTER

See   Chapter 3

See also   My Computer, Network Diagnostics, Offer Remote Assistance, Remote Assistance, System Configuration Utility, System Information, System Restore, Windows Update

IMAGE PREVIEW

See   Chapter 23

See also   Paint

INTERNET CONNECTION FIREWALL

New feature of Windows XP that provides Internet firewall protection while you are connected to the Internet through your online service provider or home network connection.

The Network Setup Wizard automatically configures and enables Internet Connection Firewall for you if you choose to use it. To run the wizard, choose Start ➢ All Programs (or Start ➢ Programs in the Classic Start menu) ➢ Accessories ➢ Communications ➢ Network Setup Wizard.

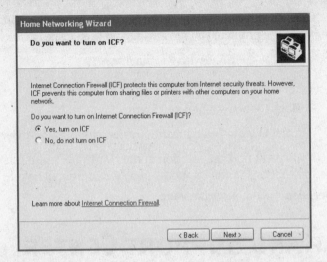

You can also enable or disable Internet Connection Firewall through Network Connections. To enable or disable the firewall for a dial-up, LAN, or network connection, choose Start ≻ Control Panel (or Start ≻ Settings ≻ Control Panel in the Classic Start menu) ≻ Network and Internet Connections ≻ Network Connections. Right-click the icon for the connection that you want to protect. Choose Properties to open the Properties dialog box, and click the Advanced tab. Check or uncheck the option "Protect my computer and network by limiting or preventing access to this computer from the Internet."

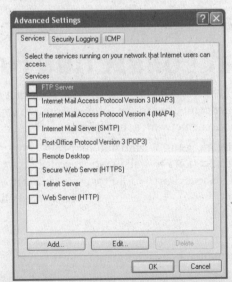

Optionally, click the Settings button in the Advanced tab of the Properties dialog box to configure additional settings for your home network. Use the Services tab to select or deselect Internet services that other computers on your network can access.

The Security Logging and ICMP tabs appear in the Advanced Settings dialog box when you enable Internet Connection Firewall. Use the Security Logging tab to specify whether you want to log dropped packets and successful connections, and to configure a log file name, path, and size. Use the ICMP tab to share error and status information with other computers on the network.

NOTE

If you are using Internet Connection Sharing to provide Internet access to multiple computers on your home network, you should enable the Internet Firewall Connection on the shared Internet connection. You can enable Internet Connection Firewall on any Windows XP computer that has an Internet connection.

WARNING

If you are using virtual private networking, you should disable Internet Connection Firewall.

See also   Internet Connection Sharing, Network Setup Wizard

INTERNET CONNECTION SHARING

Allows you to share a single Internet connection with several computers that are connected on a home network. To share a connection, you must enable Internet Connection Sharing (ICS) on your host computer, which requires two connections. The first connection, typically a network adapter, connects to the other computers on your network (each of which have their own network adapters). The second connection in your host computer is a modem (56K, ISDN, DSL, or cable) that connects the host computer to the Internet. The other computers on the home network use the connection on the host computer for the Internet and e-mail.

The Network Setup Wizard detects your networking hardware and automatically provides all of the network settings you need to share your Internet connection with other computers. You must run the wizard on each one, beginning with the host—the computer that provides the physical connection to your Internet service provider, through your modem. To run the wizard, log on to Windows XP as a computer administrator. Choose Start ➢ All Programs (or Start ➢ Programs in the Classic Start menu) ➢ Accessories ➢ Communications ➢ Network Setup Wizard.

First, run the Network Setup Wizard on your host computer. When the wizard asks how the computer connects to the Internet, choose "This computer connects directly to the Internet. The other computers in my home network connect to the Internet through this computer." By choosing this option, the Network Setup Wizard automatically enables Internet Connection Sharing on that computer.

To configure ICS on your client computers, run the Network Setup Wizard on each of them. When the wizard asks how the computer connects to the Internet, choose "This computer connects to the Internet through another computer in my home network."

After you install and enable ICS, verify that all of your computers can communicate with each other on the network, and verify that they each have Internet access. Then, you can browse the Internet and send and retrieve e-mail as though you were directly connected to an Internet service provider.

See also   Network Setup Wizard

INTERNET EXPLORER

See   Chapter 15

See also   Explorer, Internet Properties, Network and Internet Connections, New Connection Wizard

INTERNET PROPERTIES

Allows you to configure Internet settings and display options for your Windows XP computer. Among other things, Internet Properties allows you to:

▶ Configure your home page

▶ Manage temporary files

▶ Configure Web content colors, fonts, and languages

- ▶ Set up security

- ▶ Specify which applications to use for e-mail and Internet news-groups

Choose Start ➢ Control Panel (or Start ➢ Settings ➢ Control Panel from the Classic Start menu) ➢ Network and Internet Connections. Next, click Internet Options to open the Internet Properties dialog box. This dialog box has seven tabs: General, Security, Privacy, Content, Connections, Programs, and Advanced.

TIP

You can also access the Internet Options dialog box (which displays the same options as the Internet Properties dialog box) by choosing Tools ➢ Internet Options in Internet Explorer.

General Tab

The General tab allows you to configure your Internet home page and specify how you want to handle temporary Internet files and files in the History folder.

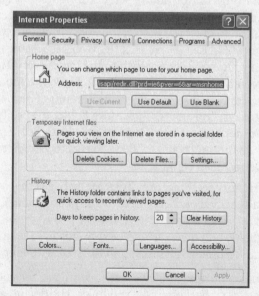

The Home Page section allows you to choose the page that IE displays when you first open it or when you click the Home button in the IE toolbar. Navigate to a Web page and click the Use Current button to change your home page to a specific URL. Click the Use Default button to use the address www.msn.com. Click the Use Blank button to display a blank page as your home page. You can also manually enter a URL in the Address text box.

Some Web sites use *cookies* to save information about the preferences you use when you visit the site; Internet Explorer stores these on your hard disk. IE also stores the content of visited Web pages in a *cache* on your hard drive. The next time you visit a page, IE uses the cached content and only downloads any new content that appears on the page, accessing the entire page more quickly. The options in the Temporary Internet Files section allow you to manage how all these temporary files are stored.

The Delete Cookies button allows you to delete Web page cookies that are stored on your hard drive. (For more on cookies, see the following section "Security Settings Dialog Box.") To delete the files in your cache, click the Delete Files button. Check or uncheck the option in the Delete Files dialog box to also delete your offline content, then click OK.

The Settings button allows you to configure how IE handles new versions of files, and to specify the size of your Internet cache. Click the Settings button to open the Settings dialog box, where you can check how often you would like IE to check the Web page against the version that is stored in your cache (Every Visit to the Page, Every Time You Start Internet Explorer, Automatically, or Never). Move the Amount of Disk Space to Use slider to adjust the maximum amount of disk space that your Internet cache consumes. Click Move Folder to specify a new location for your Internet cache. Click View Files to view a list of pages and images that reside in your cache, or View Objects to view ActiveX or Java controls that reside in your cache.

The History section stores links to the pages that you have viewed within a specified period of time (20 days by default). To adjust the number of days, enter a new value in the Days to Keep Pages in History field, or use the up and down arrows next to this field to increase or decrease the value. To remove all links from the History folder, click Clear History.

Colors button   Allows you to configure the colors for Web page text, backgrounds, and links. The default selection is Use Windows Colors.

TIP

To change the Windows colors, right-click the Desktop and choose Properties, then select the Appearance tab and make your changes.

Fonts button   Allows you to configure the language script and fonts for Web content that does not specify that a certain font be used.

Languages button   Allows you to configure the languages that IE uses for multilingual Web pages. In order to view multilingual content, you must use Regional and Language Options to add the appropriate language character set to your computer.

Accessibility button   Allows you to configure accessibility options for Web pages you view. You can ignore the colors, font styles, and font sizes that appear on the pages and display them as configured in your options. You can also create and specify a style sheet that defines the default settings for font color, style, and size, as well as heading and text background.

NOTE

The style sheets that you specify in the Accessibility dialog box must be written using Cascading Style Sheet rules and saved with a CSS extension.

Security Tab

Use the options in the Security tab to assign Web sites and pages to one of four Internet content zones: Internet, Local Intranet, Trusted Sites, and Restricted Sites. To add or remove sites in a particular zone other than Internet, click a zone's icon, then click the Sites button to open the zone's dialog box.

Internet   IE places all Web sites into this zone unless you specify another zone for the site. The default security level is Medium.

Local Intranet   Use this zone for pages and files on your company intranet. The default security level is Medium-Low.

Trusted Sites   Use this zone for Web sites and pages that you know to be safe and that will not upload harmful content to your computer. The default security level for trusted sites is Low.

Restricted Sites   Use this zone for Web sites and pages that you access but do not completely trust because you suspect that the sites may send potentially harmful content to your computer. The default security level is High.

Security Settings Dialog Box

Use the Security Settings dialog box to customize the security level for any Internet content zone. To open the Security Settings dialog box, open the Security tab in the Internet Properties dialog box. Select the zone that you want to customize (Internet, Local Intranet, Trusted Sites, or Restricted Sites). Then click the Custom Level button to display the Security Settings dialog box.

TIP

Click the Default Level button in the Security tab to return the selected security zone to its default security settings.

TIP

Some sites use cookies to save information in relation to the preferences you use when you visit the site. For example, an online bookstore might keep track of the books that you order so that it can provide additional recommendations for you; or you might frequent message boards on an online community, and a cookie keeps track of the date that you last visited so that you only see new messages when you return. Cookies are used in many ways, and IE stores these cookies on your hard disk unless you disable or delete them.

IE provides several security level settings, each of which offers a different set of options for handling dynamic content such as Java applets, ActiveX controls, and cookies. You can select from the following security levels:

High The most secure setting. Some features may be disabled; cookies are disabled. This setting reduces functionality of Web pages that depend on these features to work properly.

Medium Displays a warning before you download ActiveX controls or Java applets, and does not download ActiveX controls that are not signed.

Medium-Low Does not display a warning before you download ActiveX controls or Java applets. Does not download ActiveX controls that are not signed.

Low Provides the least amount of security. Downloads most dynamic content without prompting. May display a few warning prompts. Do not use this setting unless you trust the Web site.

Choose one of the above security settings for the zone that you want to configure. If you want to customize the settings, select a radio button to select new security levels for ActiveX controls and plug-ins, cookies, downloads, Java, miscellaneous files, scripting, and user authentication. Click the Reset button to return to the default security level settings.

Privacy Tab

The Privacy tab allows you to set the privacy level for the selected Internet content zone. Move the Privacy slider up to increase your privacy or down to decrease it. As you move the slider, a description of the privacy level appears at the right of the slider. To override cookie handling for individual Web sites, click the Edit button. The Per Site Privacy Actions dialog box allows you to allow or block cookies from specific Web page addresses. After you specify the addresses, click OK to return to the Internet Properties dialog box.

Content Tab

The Content tab allows you to restrict access to certain sites, manage certificates, and manage and configure personal information. Three different areas are available on the Content tab: Content Advisor, Certificates, and Personal Information.

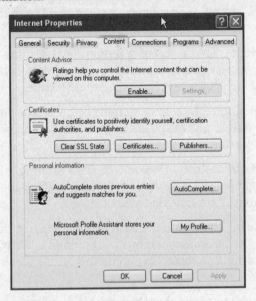

Content Advisor Section

The Content Advisor allows you to control the content that you view on your computer. To turn the Content Advisor on, click Enable to open the Content Advisor dialog box. You use four tabs to configure the settings for the content advisor: Ratings, Approved Sites, General, and Advanced.

TIP

The Content Advisor is very useful for restricting Internet access for children.

Ratings tab   Allows you to select a rating level defined by the Internet Content Rating Association (ICRA, formerly known as RSACi). This rating system identifies Web sites based on the language, nudity, sex, or violence they contain. The default level for all categories is Level 0 (Inoffensive Slang) and prevents the download of anything with a higher rating, providing that the owner of the Web site has labeled the site with an ICRA rating. Increase the level to allow IE to download stronger content.

NOTE

To obtain more information on this rating system, or to learn how to apply ratings to your own Web site, click the More Info button to navigate to the ICRA Web page (`http://rsac.org/ratingsv01.html`).

Approved Sites tab Allows you to specify Web addresses that users can always or never view, regardless of their rating.

General tab Allows you to specify whether users can see sites that are not rated by RSACi/ICRA. By default, users must enter a password, set by the computer administrator, in order to view content that is not rated. To assign or change the password, click the Create Password button. Enter the old password for verification (leave this field blank when you assign the password for the first time), then enter the new password twice (the second entry confirms the first entry). Enter a password hint, then click Apply to set the password permanently.

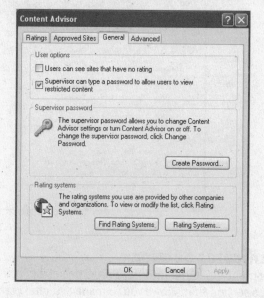

NOTE

Once you set the password, the Content Advisor is enabled, and you need to enter the password to make any other changes in the Content Advisor. After you enable the Content Advisor, the Content tab displays a Disable button in the Content Advisor section. Click Disable and enter your password to disable this feature.

Use the Rating Systems section to add and remove additional ratings systems for your Web pages. When you click Find Rating Systems, Internet Explorer browses to the Internet, where you can select additional rating systems for your Web pages.

Advanced tab   Allows you to choose a ratings bureau that sends Internet ratings to your rating systems, and allows you to view, import, or remove PICSRules files that determine whether a specific site should be viewed by the user.

Accessing a Restricted Page   When the Content Advisor is enabled, a dialog box appears when you try to access pages that are configured for restricted access, including pages that are not rated. The dialog box informs you that you are not allowed to see the site. If you know the password for the Content Advisor, you can check the appropriate radio button to choose how you want to handle the site, and enter the Content Advisor password to make the change.

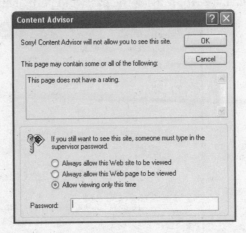

Certificates Section

The Content tab of the Internet Properties dialog box also contains a Certificates section that allows you to manage digital certificates used by applications and certain security services. Certificates enable secure communication, authentication, and data integrity over the Internet or other insecure networks.

Click Clear SSL State to clear the Secure Sockets Layer cache.

Click Certificates to open the Certificate Manager, where you can import, export, remove, and configure your own (personal) certificates, certificates for other people, certificates for immediate certification authorities, and certificates for trusted root certification authorities.

Click Publishers to view or configure software publishers and credential issuers you've specified as trusted. You can remove publishers and issuers from the list, configure certificate purposes and export format, and display certificates by purpose.

TIP

You must have administrative privileges to manage certificates.

Personal Information Section

Click the AutoComplete button (on the Internet Properties dialog box Content tab) to open the AutoComplete Settings dialog box, where you can specify in what situations Windows XP should try to match items you've previously typed so that you don't have to type the same information over and over.

If you specify AutoComplete for usernames and passwords, you can also choose to be prompted to save passwords. You can also choose to remove some AutoComplete entries by clicking Clear Forms and Clear Passwords. To remove Web address AutoComplete entries, you'll have to clear the History folder on the General tab of Internet Properties.

WARNING

Saving passwords poses a potential security risk if you leave your computer unattended without logging out of Windows XP. Anyone could walk up to your computer and access password-protected sites for which you saved the password.

Click the My Profile button on the Content tab to set up a profile that you can send to Web sites that request personal information. Clicking My Profile opens the Address Book–Choose Profile dialog box, where you can either choose an existing profile from your Address Book or create a new entry in the Main Identity Properties dialog box, which adds your profile to your Address Book.

Connections Tab

Use this tab of the Internet Properties dialog box to configure Internet dial-up and LAN connections. You can create new dial-up connections, edit and remove existing ones, and configure LAN connection settings.

Connecting to the Internet

You can start the New Connection Wizard to configure a connection by clicking Setup. This wizard is explained in detail under its own main topic.

Configuring Dial-up Connections

You can configure your existing dial-up and VPN connections by selecting a connection in the Dial-up and Virtual Private Network Settings list and clicking Settings. You can also add a new connection by clicking Add and following the prompts in the New Connection Wizard (see the main topic "New Connection Wizard"), or you can remove a connection by selecting it in the list and clicking Remove.

You can also specify what action Internet Explorer should take if you are trying to access Internet resources and a connection to the Internet is not yet established. The default selection is to never dial a connection. Alternatively, you can choose to dial your default dial-up connection, either always or only when a network connection is not available. If you choose to dial a connection, you can change your default connection setting by selecting a different connection in the Dial-up and Virtual Private Network Settings list and clicking Set Default.

Configuring LAN Connection Settings

If you are connecting to the Internet over a LAN, you can click LAN Settings and choose to automatically detect your proxy server settings, specify an address for an automatic configuration script, or specify a physical address and port for your company's proxy server. If you do this, you can also specify to bypass the proxy server if you are accessing local addresses. Click Advanced to specify addresses for individual proxy servers (such as HTTP, FTP, and Gopher).

Programs Tab

Use this tab of the Internet Properties dialog box to identify which programs you want to use for various Internet services. The types of programs from which you can choose depend on the service; examples are Outlook Express for e-mail and Microsoft NetMeeting for Internet calls. You can specify an application for each of the services shown.

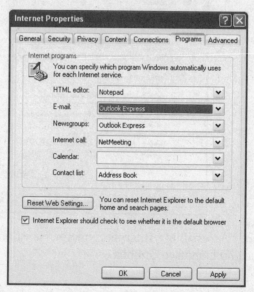

If you've installed another browser and your default settings for home and search pages have been changed, you can click Reset Web Settings to make Internet Explorer settings the default settings again.

If you have multiple browsers installed on your computer but want to retain IE as your default browser, select the "Internet Explorer should check to see whether it is the default" check box. IE then checks every time it starts up; if it determines that another browser has been set as the default, a prompt will ask whether you want to make IE the default browser again.

Advanced Tab

The Advanced tab in the Internet Properties dialog box allows you to configure advanced Internet settings, in categories such as accessibility, browsing, HTTP 1.1, Microsoft Virtual Machine, multimedia, printing, searching, and security. If you have made changes on the Advanced tab and want to return to the Windows XP defaults, simply click Restore Defaults.

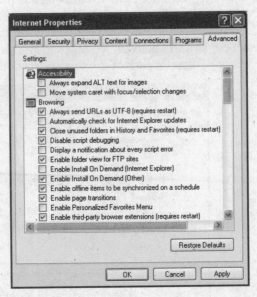

See also   Accessibility, Internet Explorer, New Connection Wizard, Regional and Language Options

KEYBOARD

Keyboard   Lets you configure your keyboard's settings, such as character repeat settings, cursor blink rate, and hardware-related settings. Choose Start ➢ Control Panel (or Start ➢ Settings ➢ Control Panel in the Classic Start menu) ➢ Printers and Other Hardware.

Next, click the Keyboard control panel icon to open the Keyboard Properties dialog box. This dialog box contains two tabs: Speed and Hardware.

Speed Tab

Use this tab to configure character repeat and cursor blink rate options.

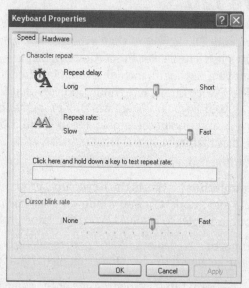

Repeat Delay Controls the amount of time from the instant you press a key to the instant the character associated with that key starts to repeat. Move the slider toward Long to increase the delay or toward Short to decrease it.

Repeat Rate Controls the amount of time between each repetition of a character when you press and hold a corresponding key. Move the slider toward Slow to increase the rate or toward Fast to decrease it.

Test Repeat Rate To test your Repeat Delay and Repeat Rate settings, click in the test box under the Repeat Rate slider. Then press and hold down a key.

Cursor Blink Rate Controls the speed at which the cursor blinks. Observe the blinking cursor at the left of the slider while you adjust the settings. Move the slider toward None to blink the cursor at a slower rate or toward Fast to blink it faster.

The adjustments that you make in the Speed tab take effect immediately in the Keyboard Properties dialog box while you test your new settings. To apply the changes permanently so that they will work in all your Windows applications, click Apply or OK.

Hardware Tab

Use this tab to view, configure, and troubleshoot the hardware settings of your keyboard. The keyboard that is installed on your system appears in the Devices list. The Device Properties area displays additional information about your keyboard, including manufacturer, location, and device status. The Device Status line should indicate that the device is working properly. If your keyboard is not working properly, the Device Status line displays a description of the problem, a problem code, and a suggested solution, if available.

Two buttons appear in the Hardware tab:

Troubleshoot   Starts the Keyboard Troubleshooter in the Help and Support Center window. Follow the prompts in the troubleshooter to resolve keyboard-related problems.

Properties   Displays the Properties dialog box that is unique to the keyboard that you have installed. It has two tabs:

General tab   Displays some of the same information about the device that you saw in the Hardware tab in the Keyboard Properties dialog box.

Driver tab   Displays information regarding the keyboard driver, including the driver provider, driver date, driver version, and the digital signer. Click Driver Details to open the Driver File Details dialog box, which displays information about the drivers installed for the keyboard. Click Update Driver to install a new keyboard driver using the Hardware Update Wizard. If the keyboard fails after you update the driver, click Roll Back Driver to revert back to the previously installed driver. Click Uninstall to uninstall your keyboard driver completely.

TIP
You can also access your keyboard properties through Device Manager. Choose Start ➢ Control Panel ➢ Performance and Maintenance. Next, click the System icon to open the System Properties dialog box. Click the Hardware tab, then click the Device Manager button. Expand the Keyboards list, and click your keyboard device to display its properties.

See also   Device Manager, Regional and Language Options, System

Log On/Log Off

Logs the current user on or off the computer. Each user in Windows XP has a user profile (either a local profile, or a roaming profile that is configured on a network) that contains such items as Desktop preferences, password, synchronization options, and accessibility options. When a user logs on, this profile is used to ensure that the environment is restored to the way the user previously configured it. Logging off enables you to stop working as the current user and then begin working as another user without having to shut down the computer.

When you start Windows XP, a logon screen displays icons for all accounts that are configured on the local computer. Click an icon to log on to a user account. Windows XP prompts you to enter a username and password if the user account is password protected. Click OK to log on.

TIP
You may have to click Options to see all fields available in the Log On to Windows dialog box.

To log off the computer, choose Start ➢ Log Off to display the Log Off dialog box. Then click Log Off again.

See also   System

Magnifier

Magnifier Enlarges certain areas of the screen so that users with vision problems can read them more easily. Choose Start ➢ All Programs (or Start ➢ Programs in the Classic Start menu) ➢ Accessories ➢ Accessibility ➢ Magnifier. Read the message about the limitations of

Magnifier, then select the Do Not Show This Message Again option to disable the message if desired. Click OK to access the Magnifier window (at the top of the screen by default) and the Magnifier dialog box.

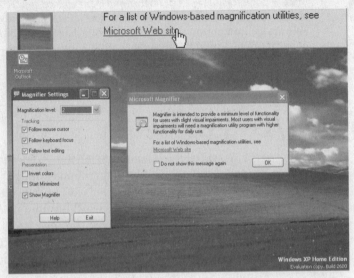

Move the mouse pointer to any area in the Desktop to display an enlarged view of the area in the Magnifier window. To change the size of the Magnifier window, drag its bottom edge downward. Drag the Magnifier window itself to turn it into a floating window.

The Magnifier dialog box allows you to change how Magnifier is set up (changes to the Magnifier window take place immediately). The following options are available:

Magnification Level   Adjust the amount of magnification from 1 (no magnification) to 9.

Tracking   Select Follow Mouse Cursor to magnify the screen area beneath the mouse pointer. Select Follow Keyboard Focus to magnify areas while you navigate with keyboard keys, such as the Tab or arrow keys. Select Follow Text Editing to magnify text around the insertion point while you type.

Presentation   Select Invert Colors to reverse colors in the Magnifier window. Choose Start Minimized to minimize the Magnifier dialog box when Magnifier starts. Choose Show Magnifier to display the Magnifier window when the Magnifier dialog box is open.

4. To permanently map the drive, select Reconnect at Logon. Leave this option unchecked to map the drive for this Windows XP session only. To connect as a different user, click "Connect using a different user name;" enter the username and password and click OK. To connect to a Web folder or FTP site, click "Sign up for online storage or connect to a network server." Follow the prompts in the Add Network Place Wizard.

5. Click Finish to map the drive. Windows XP adds the mapped drive to My Computer. You can also see it in any Explorer window or in the Open, Save, and Save As dialog boxes in any Windows XP application.

NOTE

To disconnect a mapped drive, open Explorer. Choose Tools ➤ Disconnect Network Drive (or right-click My Computer or My Network Places and select Disconnect Network Drive). In the next dialog box, select the drive you want to disconnect and click OK.

MAXIMIZE AND MINIMIZE

 Allows you to change the display of a Windows XP application window. Click the Minimize button to hide the application window and place it on the taskbar. Click the taskbar icon to bring the application window back to its original size. Click the Maximize button to display the application window filling the full screen.

MOUSE

See   Chapter 9

See also   Device Manager, Help and Support Center, System

MOVING FILES AND FOLDERS

Windows XP allows you to move files and folders in a variety of ways. You can use the Edit menu in Windows Explorer windows, drag and drop, or use the shortcut menu that appears when you right-click a file or folder.

To turn off Magnifier, click Exit in the Magnifier dialog box click Magnifier in the taskbar and select Close.

See also   Accessibility, Display

MAKE AVAILABLE OFFLINE

See   Offline Files

MAP NETWORK DRIVE

Map Network Drive... If you're connected to a network, you can assig letter to a share on the network (either on another workstation server). This is called *mapping* a drive. When you assign a drive can easily access specific shares from within Explorer windows cations—for example, those shares that you need to access frequ

To map a network drive, perform these steps:

1. Open an Explorer window (by opening Windows Ex My Computer, My Network Places, or My Computer).

2. Choose Tools ➢ Map Network Drive, or right-click My puter or My Network Places and choose Map Network The Map Network Drive dialog box appears.

3. Use the Drive drop-down list to assign a drive letter. the path to the folder in the Folder text box, or click B to locate the folder.

When you move a file or folder, Windows removes it from the original location and places it in the new location.

To move files and folders in Explorer, select the items you want to move. Choose Edit ➢ Cut (or type Ctrl+X, or right-click the selection and choose Cut). Then select the destination folder and choose Edit ➢ Paste (or type Ctrl+V, or right-click the destination folder and choose Paste).

You can also drag and drop files between folders to move them:

1. Display both the source and destination folders in the Explorer Folders pane or on the Desktop.

2. Select the items you want to move from the source folder.

3. Perform one of the following:

    ▶ Left-click and drag the selection to a destination folder on the same drive.

    ▶ Right-click and drag the selection to a destination folder on a different drive. When you release the mouse button, choose Move from the pop-up menu.

See also   Copying Files and Folders, Explorer

MSN EXPLORER

MSN Explorer   Allows you to log in to your MSN user account, where you can browse and shop on the Internet, communicate with friends, manage finances, and listen to music in one integrated interface. To start MSN Explorer, choose Start ➢ All Programs (or Start ➢ Programs in the Classic Start menu) ➢ MSN Explorer.

NOTE

A hotmail.com or msn.com e-mail address is required to use MSN Explorer.

The first time you start MSN Explorer, a dialog box asks whether you would like to use it to get on the Internet and check e-mail. To disable this dialog box, check Don't Show Me This Message Again. If you don't yet have an account set up on MSN, MSN Explorer guides you through simple setup options. After you complete the setup, you can log in to MSN Explorer.

NOTE

After you configure your MSN account name and password, you must enter the password each time you open MSN Explorer.

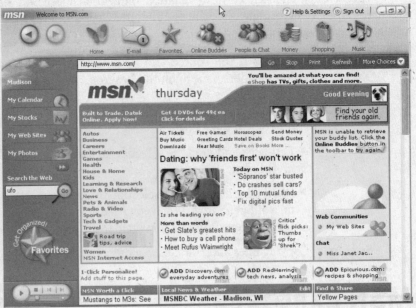

MY COMPUTER

 Allows you to view and navigate the contents of your computer, such as drives, folders, and files. To open My Computer, choose Start ➢ My Computer.

NOTE

You can also choose My Computer from the Folders pane in Explorer to display My Computer contents in the right pane of Explorer.

The right pane in My Computer displays the top-level contents of your computer. Large icons appear by default, but you can change views in this window the same way you can in any Explorer window. These contents include shared and personal documents on this computer, hard disk drives, and removable storage drives. Single-click a drive or folder to display details about the selected item in the left pane.

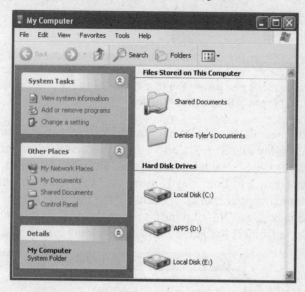

To view the contents of a drive or folder in My Computer, double-click the item. The right pane changes to display the contents of the item, and the left pane displays helpful information, related tasks, and links to other places. Click the Back, Forward, and Up One Level buttons in the toolbar to navigate to previous or higher-level locations.

The left pane of the My Computer window also displays links to system tasks and other places. System tasks allow you to view information in the System Properties dialog box, add or remove programs, or change a setting in a selected Control Panel category. Links to other places include My Network Places, My Documents, Shared Documents, and Control Panel.

See also   Control Panel, Explorer, My Documents, My Network Places, Shared Folders

My Documents

My Documents Default folder where Windows XP stores documents created in such applications as WordPad and Paint. My Documents allows any user that is logged on to the computer to organize and quickly access his or her own personal documents.

To open the My Documents folder, choose Start ➢ My Documents, or navigate to it using the Folders pane or Address bar in any Explorer window.

TIP

To change the location of the My Documents folder, right-click the My Documents shortcut on the Start menu and choose Properties. On the Target tab, enter a new path in the Target text box and click OK, or click Move and then browse to the new target folder.

By default, the My Documents folder contains folders such as My Music, My Pictures, My eBooks, My Received Files, and My Videos. Single-click any folder to display details in the left pane. Windows XP may create additional My Documents subfolders automatically as you work with applications; for example, the Fax Cover Page Editor creates a Fax subfolder. The left pane also allows you to create new folders, publish selected folders to the Web, and share folders over the network.

See also   Desktop, Explorer, My Computer, My Music, My Network Places, My Pictures, Shared Folders

MY MUSIC

My Music   Default folder (within the My Documents folder) that stores music files that you copy from a CD or download from the Internet.

The right pane in the My Music folder displays large icons for each music folder in your music library. If you have ripped songs from a CD, a small picture of the CD cover appears on the folder. The left pane displays a list of music tasks that change, depending on the selections you make in the main pane. When no folder is selected, click Play All to play all songs from the My Music folder in Windows Media Player.

When you select a folder from the main pane, details about it appear in the left pane. Additional options appear in the Music Tasks list, depending on the type of folder you select. Choose Play Selection to play all music in a selected folder. Choose Copy to Audio CD to burn the contents of a selected folder to CD.

MY NETWORK PLACES

My Network Places   Allows you to view and navigate network resources, such as network shares and other computers. To open My Network Places, choose Start ➤ My Network Places. The My Network Places folder displays two panes. The right pane displays large icons for folders that are shared on your network. Select a folder to display details in the left pane, which also includes links to other locations on your computer and to network tasks that allow you to configure additional network options:

- ▶ Add a Network Place opens a wizard. Follow the instructions to configure online storage space, shortcuts to a Web site, an FTP site, or other network location.

- ▶ View Network Connections opens the Network Connections folder, where you can view and configure your connections.

- ▶ Set Up a Home or Small Office Network opens a wizard that sets up your computer for networking.

- ▶ View Workgroup Computers allows you to access other computers in your network workgroup.

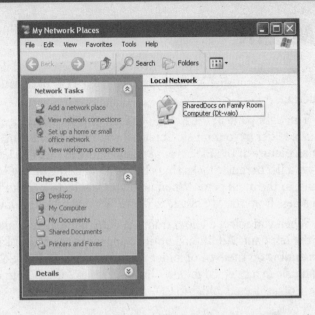

You can also access My Network Places by selecting it from the Folders list or Address drop-down list of any Explorer window. When you display My Network Places in the Folders pane of Explorer, you can navigate all network resources using the Entire Network icon. Select Entire Network to display a hierarchical list of all computers on your network. You can access shared files on the network or print to network printers or faxes.

See also   Explorer, Network Connections

MY PICTURES

 Default folder (in the My Documents folder) that allows you to store, view, and print image files that you create with image programs or obtain from a scanner or camera. To open the My Picture folder, choose Start ➤ My Pictures.

The main pane of the My Pictures folder displays large thumbnails of the files and folders that appear in My Pictures. Select a thumbnail to display file or folder properties in the left pane, which also contains a list of picture tasks. Click Get Pictures from Camera or Scanner to obtain photos from these devices. Click View as a Slide Show to display all pictures as a full-screen slide show; to end the slide show, press the Esc key. Click Order Prints Online to open the Online Print Ordering Wizard. Click Print Pictures to open the Photo Printing Wizard. Click Copy All Items to CD to add selected pictures to the files ready to be written to the CD.

See also CD Writing Wizard, Explorer, My Documents, Online Print Ordering, Photo Printing Wizard

MY RECENT DOCUMENTS

Start menu option that provides a list of shortcuts to the 15 most recently accessed documents so that you can quickly access them again when necessary. The list remains after you shut down and restart Windows XP. To use the My Recent Documents list, choose Start ➤ My Recent Documents, and click any item in the list to open the document in the appropriate application.

NOTE

The submenu also contains a shortcut to My Documents and My Pictures, which are default folders that Windows XP uses to save documents or images from many Windows XP applications.

See also   Start Menu, Taskbar and Start Menu

NAMING A DISK

You can add a label (name) to a floppy or hard disk. To name a disk, perform the following steps:

1. From Windows Explorer, right-click the disk that you want to name, and choose Properties. The Disk Properties dialog box opens to the General tab.

2. Enter a name for the disk in the text box at the top of the dialog box.

3. Click OK to save your changes.

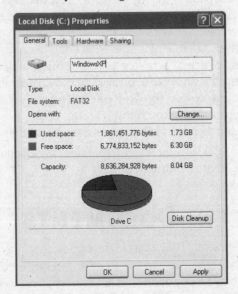

NARRATOR

📖 Narrator   Aids users with vision impairments by "narrating" (reading aloud) on-screen text, menus, buttons, and dialog boxes. A sound card and speakers, or other audio output device, is required to use this feature.

To open Narrator, choose Start ➣ All Programs (or Start ➣ Programs in the Classic Start menu) ➣ Accessories ➣ Accessibility ➣ Narrator. Windows XP displays a message that explains the limited functionality of Narrator. Check Do Not Show This Message Again to disable this dialog box, then click OK to display the Narrator dialog box.

Four options appear in the Narrator dialog box; place a check mark next to the ones you want to activate. The Voice button allows you to adjust the speed, volume, and pitch for the selected voice.

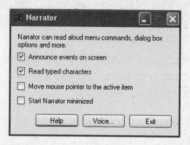

See also   Accessibility

.NET PASSPORT WIZARD

➡ Set up my account to use a .NET Passport   Helps you set up your account to use a .NET Passport, which gives you personalized access to Passport-enabled services by using your e-mail address. You store your name and password in a single sign-in profile that encrypts your personal information. The information that you store is safe on public and shared computers.

For each of the following actions, first go to Start ➣ Control Panel (or Start ➣ Settings ➣ Control Panel in the Classic Start menu) ➣ User Accounts. Then:

▶ To start the .NET Passport Wizard on a domain computer, locate the .NET Passport section in the Advanced tab, then click .NET Passport Wizard.

▶ If you have a computer administrator account on a domain computer, click your account name, then choose Set Up My Account to Use a .NET Passport.

▶ If you have a limited account on a domain computer, click Set Up My Account to Use a .NET Passport.

NetMeeting

 NetMeeting Allows you to use voice and video to communicate with other people over the Internet. To run NetMeeting, your computer must have speakers or headphones, a microphone, and a video camera installed.

NetMeeting enables you to engage in real-time chats, work together in shared applications, send files, and create drawings together on a shared whiteboard. Voice, video, and images display on the screen while you participate in online conferences.

The first time you run NetMeeting, a wizard helps you configure NetMeeting and tune your audio settings. Subsequently, you will be brought directly to Microsoft NetMeeting.

NOTE

To install NetMeeting in Windows XP, open the Help and Support Center topic "What's new in other areas of Windows XP Home." Expand the NetMeeting subtopic to select "Using NetMeeting." Finally, click the "Open NetMeeting" link to start the Microsoft NetMeeting Wizard.

NOTE

When you complete the wizard, check the option to display a shortcut to NetMeeting on your desktop. Click this connection to start NetMeeting at any time.

The Microsoft NetMeeting Wizard helps you configure NetMeeting the first time you use it. At each screen, enter the requested information or choose settings, then click Next to move on. You'll be prompted to enter:

▶ Personal information about yourself that you want to use with NetMeeting

▶ The directory server you want to use, and whether to log on automatically

TIP

The directory servers you log on to are called Internet Locator Servers, or ILS servers. Use your browser and favorite search engine to find available ILS servers.

▶ The speed/type of connection you use to connect to the Internet

▶ Sound settings (the wizard tests both the volume to use with your headphones or speakers and the recording level to use with your microphone)

When you have completed the wizard, click Finish to start Microsoft NetMeeting. If you are connected to the Internet, NetMeeting automatically tries to log on to the directory server you specified.

WARNING

If you are not connected to the Internet, NetMeeting displays a warning that the directory server can't be found. Connect to the Internet, then choose Call ➢ Log On to *Directory Server Name* to log on to the directory server.

TIP

To run the Audio Tuning Wizard again, choose Tools ➢ Audio Tuning Wizard in NetMeeting. Many of these settings can also be adjusted later in the Tools ➢ Options dialog box.

NetMeeting Window

After you configure NetMeeting, click the NetMeeting shortcut on your desktop to use NetMeeting at any time. NetMeeting logs you on to the default directory server or the directory server you specify under Tools ➢ Options. After you log on, other NetMeeting users around the world can see the personal information you specified and place a call to you.

TIP

You must connect to the Internet before you log on to a directory server.

The Microsoft NetMeeting window includes menus, buttons, the video area (which displays video images of other users or of yourself), the data area (which displays the names of participants in a call or meeting), and the status bar.

Most of the NetMeeting buttons perform functions equivalent to the commands on the NetMeeting menus. Find Someone allows you to search the current directory, other directories, the Speed Dial list, the history list, or Windows Address Book for a user's address. (See "Finding a User" later in this topic.) The Adjust Audio Volume/View Participant List button displays either the names of participants in the current call or meeting, or sliders that adjust the microphone and speaker volume.

The left side of the status bar tells you whether you are currently in a call. The right side of the status bar displays two icons: the first indicates whether you are in a call, and the second indicates the server to which you are connected. Hover the mouse over the server icon to see the name of the server that you are logged on to.

NetMeeting Menus

Four NetMeeting menus allow you to work with and configure NetMeeting: Call, View, Tools, and Help.

Call Menu

New Call Opens the Place a Call dialog box. Enter information about the user you want to call or select a previous contact from the To drop-down list. From the Using drop-down list, choose how you want to locate the user (Automatic, Network, or Directory). Optionally, check the Require Security for This Call (Data Only) option to establish a secure connection with your contact. Click the Call button to place the call.

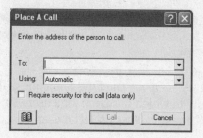

TIP

Alternatively, you can enter the user's address in the Address bar in the Net-Meeting window and then click the New Call button.

After you place the call, the user receives a notification message that you are calling. The user can either accept or ignore the incoming call. To establish the call, the user must click Accept. After a call is established, the names of the participants appear in the data area of the NetMeeting window.

Host Meeting When you host a meeting, others can join. Before the meeting, contact the participants to inform them when the meeting will take place. At the specified time, choose Call ➢ Host Meeting to open a dialog box where you establish a meeting password, enable or disable a secure meeting, and specify the users who can participate.

To remove a user from a meeting you are hosting, right-click the user's name in the data list of the main NetMeeting window, and choose Remove from Meeting.

Meeting Properties   Displays the name of the meeting, whether you can place incoming and outgoing calls, and whether you can start Sharing, Whiteboard, Chat, and File Transfer.

Log On to *Directory Server Name*   Logs on to the specified server. After you log on, this option changes to Log Off from *Directory Server Name*.

NOTE

To change the directory server, choose Tools ➢ Options to open the Options dialog box. In the General tab, enter the name of the directory server that you want to use.

Directory   Opens the Find Someone dialog box. Select a directory in which to search for a user. Enter a username in the Type Name text box or select a user from the list of users.

NOTE

You must have an active MSN Messenger Service account to use the Directory. If Windows XP does not detect an active MSN Messenger Service account, it helps you create one automatically.

Do Not Disturb   Check this option to prevent NetMeeting from notifying you when other calls come in. To resume incoming call notifications, choose Call ➢ Do Not Disturb again to clear the check mark.

TIP

When you have Do Not Disturb active, callers have the option to send you e-mail when they try to call you.

Automatically Accept Calls   Enable this option to automatically accept all incoming calls. To turn off this feature, select Automatically Accept Calls again to clear the check mark.

Create Speed Dial   Opens a dialog box where you can manually create a Speed Dial entry. Enter the user's address in the Address field. Use the Call Using drop-down to select how you want to place the call. Check or uncheck options to add the entry to your Speed Dial list or to save a shortcut on your Desktop.

Hang Up   Ends the current call or meeting.

View Menu

Status Bar   Shows or hides the status bar.

Dial Pad   Displays a telephone-style dial pad in place of the video display in the NetMeeting window. Use the dial pad to place calls to an automated telephone system. To revert back to the video display, choose View ➤ Dial Pad to clear the check mark.

Picture-in-Picture   Displays the video image you send to others in a small window within the video window.

My Video (New Window)   Displays the video image you send to others in a separate window.

Compact   Shows or hides the data area of the NetMeeting window; displays only the video area when the Compact option is checked.

Data Only   Shows or hides the video area of the NetMeeting window; displays only the data area when the Data Only option is checked.

Always on Top   Displays the NetMeeting window on top of other open windows.

Tools Menu

Video   Allows you to send or receive video, and to specify the size of the video window (100, 200, 300, or 400 percent).

Audio Tuning Wizard   Starts the Audio Tuning Wizard, which allows you to configure your audio settings, such as playback and recording volume.

Sharing   Allows you to share an application with other people in the meeting.

Chat   Opens a window that allows you to send and receive messages during a call or meeting. The top area of the dialog box displays the conversation (messages that you send and receive from other participants). Enter text in the Message text box. Select a recipient from the Send To drop-down list. Then click the Send button.

Whiteboard (1.0–2.x)   Displays the Whiteboard on the screen of each user who participates in the call or meeting. The Whiteboard functions similarly to a physical whiteboard; for example, users can jot down meeting notes or agendas, or sketch ideas. You can save the Whiteboard contents as a White-board (.WHT) file.

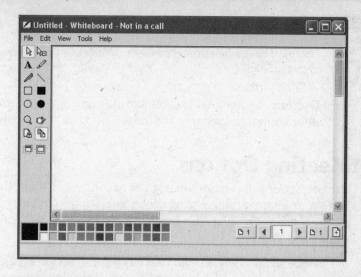

File Transfer   Allows you to send and receive files from other NetMeeting users during a call or meeting. Also allows you to open file folders, including the Received Files folder (which stores files you received from other users).

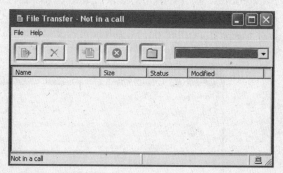

Remote Desktop Sharing   Allows you or another user to connect to your Desktop through another computer that is running NetMeeting. The remote computer can access files, run programs, and download files from your Desktop. The first time you choose this command, a wizard helps you configure your computer to listen for incoming Remote Desktop Sharing calls when NetMeeting is not running. After you configure settings with the wizard, this command opens the Remote Desktop Sharing Settings dialog box.

TIP

You must have administrator privileges to access a computer using Remote Desktop Sharing.

Options Allows you to configure directory options, general information, and security and video settings for NetMeeting.

NetMeeting Options

Use the NetMeeting Options dialog box to configure NetMeeting to best serve your Internet conferencing needs. To open the Options dialog box, choose Tools ➢ Options. The dialog box has four tabs: General, Security, Audio, and Video.

General tab Allows you to specify general, network bandwidth, and advanced calling settings, including the data you entered in the NetMeeting Wizard (personal information that other Net-Meeting users can view, default directory, connection type and speed). Additional options allow you to run NetMeeting in the background when Windows starts, and to display the NetMeeting icon on the taskbar. The Advanced Calling button opens a dialog box where you can choose a gatekeeper to place calls, and a gate-way to call telephones and videoconferencing systems.

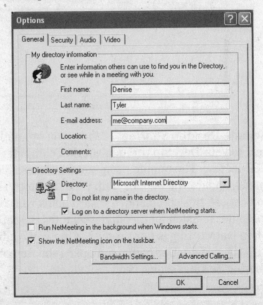

Security tab   Configure whether you want incoming and/or outgoing calls to be secure and whether to use a certificate.

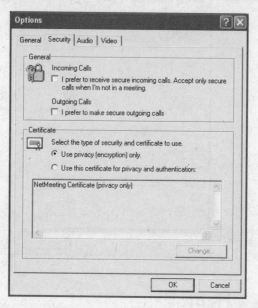

Audio tab   You can choose to enable full duplex audio and auto-gain control, automatically adjust the volume of your microphone while you are in a call, and enable DirectSound for better audio performance. Click the Tuning Wizard button to open the Audio Tuning Wizard; click the Advanced button to configure audio compression settings. Choose whether you want the silence detection sensitivity adjusted automatically or manually with a slider (this feature helps compensate for background noise in your room).

Video tab   Check or uncheck options to automatically send and/or receive video; choose an image size; and adjust the video quality. Use the Video Camera Properties drop-down list to select which video capture device you want to use. Click the Source button to configure video card settings (provided by the manufacturer). If the Source button is grayed out or missing, the Format button may be available, which serves the same function as the Source button.

TIP

The Source button may be available only if you're viewing an image in the Video window.

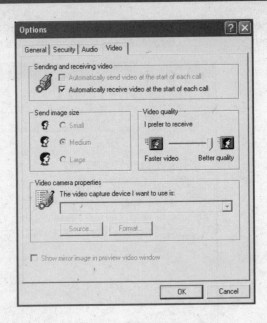

Finding a User

If you want to place a call but don't know the user's directory address, choose Call ➢ Directory, or click the Find Someone in a Directory button to open the Find Someone dialog box.

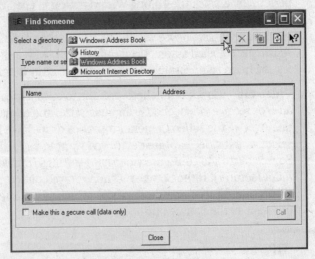

Choosing a Directory

Use the Select a Directory combo box to select or enter the name of a directory, or to select an entry from your Speed Dial or History view, or from the Windows address book. All entries from the selected source appear in the list box below. If you choose a directory other than the one you are currently logged on to, it displays the users that are logged on to that directory but does not log you on.

After you make a selection in the combo box, either select a user from the list, or enter a username in the Type Name or Select from List text box to select the closest match.

User Information

Information about each logged-on user appears in a list. An audio or video icon appears if the user has audio or video capabilities. The list also displays the user's last name, first name, e-mail address, location, and comments. A computer icon appears at the left of each person's e-mail address. If the user is in a call, the monitor in the icon is blue and a red star appears in the top-left corner of the icon. If the user is not in a call, the icon is grayed out.

Click a column header to sort the user list by that information; click the column again to sort the list in the reverse order. Drag a column header left or right to rearrange the order of the columns.

Available Actions

Right-click any user listed in the directory to choose from several actions, such as:

- ▶ Make a call to the user
- ▶ Access the user's properties
- ▶ Add the user to your Speed Dial list
- ▶ Add the user to the Address Book
- ▶ Refresh the directory list (or stop NetMeeting from refreshing the directory)

Sharing an Application

To share an application with other people in the call or meeting, choose Tools ➤ Sharing. The Sharing dialog box allows you to select an application or document to share with the other participants from a list of items on your computer. Select the item you want to share, and click the Share button. When you share an item, meeting participants can see the information you enter in an application, but they cannot make any changes themselves.

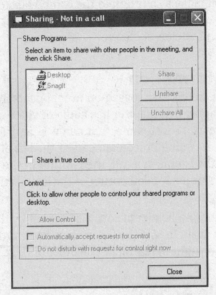

To stop sharing an item, select it in the list and click Unshare. Click Unshare All to stop all sharing. Place a check mark in the Share in True Color check box to share the application in true color (using up to 16 million colors).

WARNING

Microsoft recommends that you don't check the Share in True Color option, as it makes application sharing very slow, especially over dial-up connections.

NOTE

In order for others to view the item you share, they must have the associated application installed on their computer (for example, if you are sharing a Word document, they must have Word installed). The shared document must appear in an active window that appears on top of all other windows on their Desktop.

TIP

Remote users can choose a command from the shared application's View menu to display the shared item in a full screen.

Enabling Control by Other Users

The Sharing dialog box displays options that allow other users to make changes in your shared application. To enable these options, click the Allow Control button. When you enable user control, you can automatically accept requests for control or can temporarily disallow requests for control (the "Do not disturb me with requests for control right now" option).

After you enable user control, the Allow Control button toggles to a Prevent Control button. Click Prevent Control to prevent others from making changes to your application.

Requesting Control

To request control of a document, a user must choose Request Control from the Control menu of the shared application window. If you configured NetMeeting to automatically accept all requests, control of the document switches to the user that made the request. If you didn't select that option, NetMeeting informs you that a remote user would like to take control of the shared program. Click Accept to honor (or Reject to deny) the request. The user must then choose Control ➢ Release Control to turn control back over to the person who is sharing the application.

To grant control directly to a user without a request, right-click the user's name in the data area of the main NetMeeting window, and choose Grant Control. This option is available only if you've shared at least one application.

See also   Address Book, Paint

NETWORK AND INTERNET CONNECTIONS

Windows XP Control Panel group that provides access to utilities that configure (or create) your network connections and set Internet properties. Includes links to Network Connections, Internet Options, Phone and

Modem Options, My Network Places, and Printers and Other Hardware. There are also links to troubleshooters for home networking, Internet Explorer, and network diagnostics. For further information on these topics, refer to individual topics listed below.

See also Internet Explorer, Internet Properties, My Network Places, Network Connections, Network Diagnostics, Network Setup Wizard, Phone and Modem Options, Printers and Other Hardware

NETWORK CONNECTIONS

See Chapter 20

See also Administrative Tools, Device Manager, New Connection Wizard, System, System Information

NETWORK DIAGNOSTICS

Subset of Windows XP Help and Support Center. Network Diagnostics scans your system to gather information about your network hardware, software, and connections. Choose Start ➤ Help and Support to open the Help and Support Center window. From the Pick a Task area, click Tools, and then choose Network Diagnostics from the Tools section in the left pane.

See also Help and Support Center

NETWORK IDENTIFICATION WIZARD

See System (Network Identification tab)

NETWORK PASSWORDS

Allows you to maintain the list of passwords that are stored on your system to log in to Web sites. If you are logged on as a Limited user or Guest, choose Start ➤ Control Panel (or Start ➤ Settings ➤ Control Panel in the Classic Start menu) ➤ User Accounts to access the User Accounts window. Choose Change an Account, select the account you want to alter, then choose Manage My Network Passwords from the Related Tasks section.

NETWORK SETUP WIZARD

Network Setup Wizard Helps you connect multiple home computers. The screens in the wizard help you configure your Internet connection settings, bridge network adapters together to create a home network, and set up a firewall that prevents unauthorized users from gaining access to your files and folders.

NOTE

Before you use the Network Setup Wizard, you must first install and configure your network communication devices (network cards, modems, cables, and device drivers). If you are going to use Internet Connection Sharing (ICS) to share a single Internet connection with more than one computer on your network, run the Network Setup Wizard on the ICS host computer first (the computer that connects directly to the Internet). Then, run the wizard on the other computers that will use the same Internet connection.

To use the Network Setup Wizard, choose Start ➢ All Programs ➢ Accessories ➢ Communications ➢ Network Setup Wizard. The introductory screen appears. Choose Next to continue through each step of the wizard, based on the responses you choose in each screen.

See also   Internet Connection Firewall, Internet Connection Sharing

NEW CONNECTION WIZARD

New Connection Wizard Guides you through the process of setting up either a dial-up or LAN connection to the Internet and setting up Internet e-mail. To start the wizard, use one of the following methods:

▶ Choose Start ➢ All Programs (or Start ➢ Programs in the Classic Start menu) ➢ Accessories ➢ Communications ➢ New Connection Wizard.

▶ Choose Start ➢ Control Panel (or Start ➢ Settings ➢ Control Panel from the Classic Start menu) ➢ Network and Internet Connections. Next, click the Internet Options control panel icon to open the Internet Properties dialog box. Select the Connections tab, and click Setup.

When the New Connection Wizard starts, click Next to display the Network Connection Type screen. This screen gives you four options:

▶ Choose Connect to the Internet to set up an Internet connection. You can choose from a list of Internet service providers (ISPs), set up a connection manually, or use the CD that you received from an ISP.

▶ Choose Connect to the Network at My Workplace to use a dial-up or VPN connection to connect to your business network.

▶ Choose Set Up a Home or Small Office Network to open the Network Setup Wizard. This wizard helps you configure the computer to run on a network.

▶ Choose Set Up an Advanced Connection to connect directly to another computer using a serial, parallel, or infrared port, or to allow other computers to connect to your computer.

NOTE

If you already have an account set up with an ISP and you use different computers frequently, it might be a good idea to store a record of this account and connection information. Then, you can use the New Connection Wizard and the information to quickly set up an Internet connection on a new computer.

Setting Up a Dial-up Internet Connection

The following steps describe how to use the New Connection Wizard to configure a new dial-up connection on your computer, using a modem that connects to an existing ISP. Follow these steps:

1. Choose Start ➢ All Programs (or Start ➢ Programs in the Classic Start menu) ➢ Accessories ➢ Communications ➢ New Connection Wizard.

2. Click Next to display the Network Connection Type screen.

3. Choose Connect to the Internet. Click Next to continue.

4. Choose Set up My Connection Manually. Click Next to continue.

5. Choose Connect using a Dial-Up Modem. Click Next to continue.

6. The Connection Name screen appears. Enter a name for your ISP connection. Click Next.

7. Enter the phone number of your ISP. Click Next.

8. The Internet Account Information screen appears. Enter your username and password, and confirm the password. Check or uncheck options to use this account name and password when anyone connects to the Internet, to make this the default Internet connection, and to turn on Internet Connection Firewall.

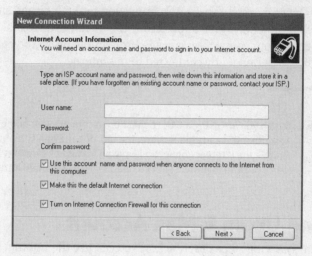

9. The wizard displays a summary of your choices and displays an option to add a shortcut to the connection on your desktop. Click Finish to exit the wizard. If you choose the option to display the shortcut on your desktop, click the connection to connect to your ISP.

Setting Up a LAN Internet Connection

You use a LAN Internet connection to configure your computer to connect to the Internet through your home or office network, or to connect to the Internet with a cable or DSL modem. To set up this type of connection, follow these steps:

1. Choose Start ➣ All Programs (or Start ➣ Programs in the Classic Start menu) ➣ Accessories ➣ Communications ➣ New Connection Wizard.

2. Click Next to display the Network Connection Type screen.

3. Choose Connect to the Internet. Click Next to continue.

4. Choose Set up My Connection Manually. Click Next to continue.

5. Choose Connect Using a Broadband Connection That is Always On. Click Next to continue through the remaining steps in the wizard.

Once you establish a LAN connection to the Internet, simply open a Web browser or e-mail application. You do not need to dial in to an ISP because your connection is made through the proxy server on the LAN, which is permanently connected to the Internet.

TIP

When you are using a LAN connection to connect your home computer or network to a DSL or cable modem, the use of a firewall is highly recommended. Enable the Internet Connection Firewall feature of Windows XP, or use a third-party firewall to protect your computers from unwanted intruders.

Setting Up an E-Mail Account

The following steps describe how you can use the Internet Connection Wizard to connect to an e-mail account with the wizard:

1. Open Outlook Express (for example, double-click the Outlook Express icon on your Desktop).

2. Choose Tools ➢ Accounts to open the Internet Accounts dialog box.

3. Click the Add button, and choose Mail from the submenu. The wizard appears.

4. In the Your Name screen, enter the name that you want to use when you send an e-mail message or post a message to a newsgroup. Click Next.

5. In the Internet E-mail Address screen, enter your e-mail address. Click Next.

6. In the E-mail Server Names screen, choose the mail server type (POP3, IMAP, or HTTP) that your e-mail account uses. Then, enter the addresses for your incoming mail (for example: mail.myisp.com) and outgoing mail (for example: smtp.myisp.com). Click Next to continue.

7. In the Internet Mail Logon screen, enter the account name and password that you use to log in to your e-mail account.

8. If you want Outlook Express to automatically remember your password, check the Remember Password option. Uncheck this option if you want to enter your password each time you connect to your e-mail account.

9. If your ISP requires that you use Secure Password Authentication, check the Log On Using Secure Password Authentication check box.

10. Click Next to continue. The wizard informs you that your information is complete. Click Finish to complete your account setup.

TIP

To modify your e-mail account settings at any time, open Outlook Express and choose the Tools ➣ Accounts command to open the Internet Accounts dialog box. Click the Mail tab, select the account you want to change, and click the Properties button. For further information, see the main topic "Outlook Express."

Connecting to the Internet with a Modem

The Connect dialog box appears when you choose to connect to the Internet for browsing, or when you choose to send or retrieve e-mail. If you have more than one dial-up connection set up, use the Connect To drop-down list to select the connection you want to dial.

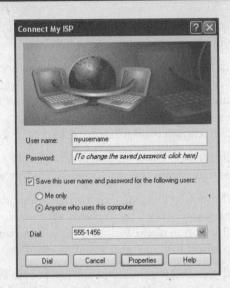

Verify that the username and password are correct for the account you selected. Check the "Save this user name and password for the following users" option to store the password so that you do not have to enter it each time you connect to your account. You can save the information for yourself or for anyone who uses the computer. The Connect dialog box also has the following buttons:

Dial   Connects to your ISP. The modem dials your ISP, and the bottom of the dialog box displays messages that tell you that you are connected to the remote computer and your password is being verified.

Properties   Opens the Properties dialog box to the General tab. For more information, refer to the main topic "Internet Properties."

TIP

While you are connected, an icon with two overlapping (connected) computers appears in the notification area of the taskbar. Double-click this icon to obtain information about the connection, such as how long you've been connected, the speed of the connection, how many bytes have been sent and received, the server type used, and the client and server's IP addresses.

Closing a Modem Connection

After you connect to the Internet for browsing, you can disconnect in one of these ways:

- ▶ When you close Internet Explorer, the Auto Disconnect dialog box appears. Choose Disconnect Now.

- ▶ Right-click or double-click the Connection icon in the notification area of the taskbar, and choose Disconnect.

See also   Internet Explorer, Internet Properties, Network and Internet Connections, Outlook Express

NOTEPAD

See   Chapter 7
See also   WordPad

NTFS

File system for Windows XP computers. NTFS has many advantages over older file systems, such as FAT and FAT32. You can format a disk partition with the NTFS file system during the Windows XP operating system installation, or you can convert an older file system (FAT or FAT32) to NTFS during or after the Windows XP operating system installation using convert.exe.

TIP

For more information on how to convert a file system using convert.exe, choose Start ➢ All Programs (or Start ➢ Programs in the Classic Start menu) ➢ Accessories ➢ Command Prompt, then type **help convert** at the C:\> command prompt.

Features that are available only if you're using NTFS include:

- ▶ Active Directory

- ▶ File encryption

- ▶ Permissions set on files

- ▶ Remote Storage
- ▶ Disk Quotas

See also   Command Prompt

OFFER REMOTE ASSISTANCE

Subset of Windows XP Help and Support Center. Choose Start ≻ Help and Support to open the Help and Support Center window. From the Pick a Task area, click Tools and choose Offer Remote Assistance from the Tools section in the left pane.

See also   Help and Support Center

OFFLINE FILES

✔ Make available offline   Allows you to use network or shared files or folders when you're not connected to the network. From Windows Explorer, right-click a file or folder and choose Make Available Offline.

TIP

To display this menu option in Windows Explorer, choose Tools ≻ Folder Options, and check Enable Offline Files on the Offline Files tab.

WARNING

You cannot make files available offline when Fast User Switching is enabled. To disable this feature, see the main topic "Fast User Switching."

The *first* time you choose the Make Available Offline command, the Offline Files Wizard appears. Complete it as follows:

1. In the Welcome screen, click Next.

2. If you don't want files to synchronize automatically when you log on and off the computer, uncheck the Automatically Synchronize option. Click Next.

3. Check Enable Reminders to receive a periodic message that reminds you that you're working offline. It is also strongly recommended that you check the option "Create a shortcut to the Offline Files folder on my Desktop."

4. Click Finish. The wizard synchronizes the file or folder to the Offline Files folder and you return to Windows Explorer.

Thereafter, whenever you choose the Make Available Offline command, Windows Explorer automatically synchronizes the selected file or folder to the Offline Files folder. Two opposite-facing arrows appear in the bottom-left portion of the icon for an offline file or folder.

TIP

To remove a file from the Offline Files folder, right-click the file and select Make Available Offline. This removes the check mark on the menu item.

When you are offline, you can access your offline files or folders as though you are connected to the network. Click the computer icon in the notification area of the taskbar to see your current offline file status. If you have reminders set up, a pop-up message periodically tells you that you're working offline. Choose Folder Options from Control Panel to further configure reminders.

Offline Files Folder

Offline files are also accessible through the Offline Files folder. Double-click the shortcut on your Desktop (if you created one) to open the Offline Files folder. This folder displays the names of all offline files, the synchronization status, availability, and the access rights you have to each file. If you delete a file from the Offline Files folder, the network version of the file remains.

TIP

You can also browse to offline files or folders with Windows Explorer or My Network Places. The left side of Explorer displays a message that tells you when a folder is offline.

To work on a file offline, select it from the Offline Files folder. Open it and make any changes you need. Synchronization occurs automatically when you connect to the network (unless you change default settings in Synchronization or in the Offline Files Wizard).

To synchronize manually, open the Offline Files folder. Choose View ➢ Details if necessary. The Synchronization column indicates local files that have been modified. To synchronize files, close any offline files that are opened. To synchronize all files, choose Tools ➢ Synchronize, then click Synchronize. To synchronize an individual file, select the file and choose File ➢ Synchronize, or right-click the file and choose Synchronize.

See also   Folder Options, Synchronize

ONLINE PRINT ORDERING

Allows you to order prints of your photos from the Internet. Depending on the vendor you select, you can also print your photos on gift items such as poster-size prints, mugs, mouse pads, sweatshirts, and T-shirts. You must have an Internet connection to use this feature.

To use the Online Print Ordering Wizard, follow these steps:

1. Choose Start ➢ My Pictures. Windows XP opens your My Pictures folder.

2. Select the picture or pictures that you want to order.

3. From the Picture Tasks section in the left pane, choose Order Prints Online. The Online Print Ordering Wizard appears. Click Next to continue.

4. The first screen displays your picture selections. Check pictures to order prints, or clear the check box to remove the picture from your order. You can also use the Select All or Clear All buttons to add or remove all pictures. Click Next to continue.

5. Select the Internet printing company that you would like to print your photos. Highlight a selection in the list, and click Next.

6. The wizard downloads a catalog of product and ordering options from the company you select. The options you see in this screen may vary from vendor to vendor. You can optionally set up a user account and password that allows you to track your orders.

7. Select items that you want to add to your shopping cart, and enter quantities for each item.

8. When you are ready to process your order, click the Check Out button in the company product catalog. You will be prompted to enter payment and shipping information.

9. Continue with the prompts in the wizard until your order is complete.

See also   My Pictures, Scanners and Cameras

ON-SCREEN KEYBOARD

On-Screen Keyboard   Designed for users who have difficulty using a standard keyboard. Users can control On-Screen Keyboard with the mouse or with a switch input device. To display On-Screen Keyboard, choose Start ➤ All Programs ➤ Accessories ➤ Accessibility ➤ On-Screen Keyboard.

Alternatively, you can use the Windows Logo Key + U shortcut to open the Utility Manager. Select the On-Screen Keyboard from the list of utilities and click Start. The Utility Manager also allows you to start the utility automatically when you log on, when you lock your desktop, or when the Utility Manager starts.

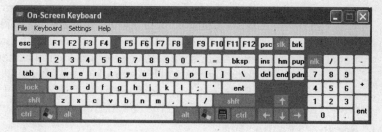

NOTE

The program in which you want to enter text must be active when you're using On-Screen Keyboard.

The Keyboard menu allows you to choose the type of keyboard you want to display. Your choices are Enhanced Keyboard (with a numeric keypad) or Standard Keyboard, Regular or Block Layout, and 101 (U.S. Standard), 102 (Universal), or 106 (additional Japanese characters) keys.

The Settings menu allows you to configure the behavior of On-Screen Keyboard. Choose Always on Top to always display the keyboard on top of other windows. Choose Use Click Sound to play a clicking sound when you press a key on the On-Screen Keyboard. Choose Typing Mode to configure options for typing with a mouse or joystick.

The Typing Mode dialog box lets you set up different typing modes; for example, you can specify that either clicking a key or hovering over a key selects that key. Alternatively, you can choose Joystick or Key to Select and then set up a scan interval to activate scanning of the keyboard. During the scan, each key on On-Screen Keyboard is highlighted and you can select keys by using a dedicated key on the physical keyboard or an external switching device. To specify a key or device, click Advanced and select "Serial, Parallel, or Game Port;" or select Keyboard Key and choose the key you want to use from the drop-down list.

Back on the Settings menu, you can also change the font used for the keys on the keyboard, perhaps making it larger so it's easier to read.

See also   Utility Manager

OTHER CONTROL PANEL OPTIONS

Other Control Panel Options Section of Windows XP Control Panel that stores additional Control Panel options that are installed by other Windows software. Items that you may find in this section include additional Desktop themes and user interface selectors, digital camera settings, live updates for software, and links to additional media players. To view other Control Panel options, choose Start ➢ Control Panel. Select Other Control Panel Options from the See Also section in the left pane.

See also   Control Panel

OUTLOOK EXPRESS

See   Chapter 16

See also   Address Book, Internet Explorer, Network and Internet Connections, New Connection Wizard

PAINT

See Chapter 7

See also Image Preview

PERFORMANCE AND MAINTENANCE

 Control Panel category that provides access to administrative tools, scheduled tasks, system configurations, and power options. Also displays tasks that allow you to free up space on your hard drive, rearrange your hard disk so that programs start more quickly, change performance settings, and restore your system.

See also Administrative Tools, Disk Cleanup, Disk Defragmenter, Power Options, Scheduled Tasks, System, System Restore

PERSONALIZED MENUS

Windows XP feature that displays Start Menu programs and documents that you most frequently and most recently accessed. You can disable this feature to display all menu items, or change the number of items that appear in the menus.

TIP

To access programs that do not appear in personalized menus, choose Start ➢ All Programs, and click the down arrow at the bottom of the menu to display additional programs.

To change personalized start menu options, follow these steps:

1. Right-click the Start button and choose Properties. The Taskbar and Start Menu Properties dialog box opens to the Start Menu tab.

2. Click the Customize button to open the Customize Start Menu dialog box.

3. Use the General tab to specify the number of frequently used programs that appear in the start menu. You can enter any number between and including 0 through 9. Click the Clear List button to remove existing programs from the list.

4. Use the Advanced tab to enable or disable the Show Most Recently Used Documents feature. Click the Clear List button to remove existing documents from the list.

See also   Taskbar and Start Menu

PHONE AND MODEM OPTIONS

See   Chapter 14

See also   Device Manager, System

PHOTO PRINTING WIZARD

Allows you to print photos and images from your My Pictures folder. To open the Photo Printing Wizard, choose Start ➤ My Pictures. Open the folder that contains the pictures you want to print. Then, choose Print Pictures from the Printer Tasks pane on the left side of the screen.

The Photo Printing Wizard prompts you to select a printer and paper size. Next, you select the type of pictures that you want to print. Most standard photo sizes are available, ranging from 8×10 to contact sheets, and you can also print a full-size image. After you complete the steps in the wizard, your printer prints the photo or image.

PORTABLE DEVICE

See   Windows Media Player

POWER OPTIONS

Power Options   Provides settings that reduce the amount of power that your computer consumes. Conserving energy is becoming ever more important, both from an environmental and a cost-savings perspective. Power Options help you conserve valuable resources, such as the electricity you use to run your desktop computer or the batteries on your laptop computer. In the latter case, Power Options can extend the amount of time you use your laptop while you run it on battery power. The options you configure depend on your hardware and system configuration.

To open the Power Options Properties dialog box, choose Start ➢ Control Panel (or Start ➢ Settings ➢ Control Panel in the Classic Start menu) ➢ Performance and Maintenance ➢ Power Options. The tabs you see depend on the power management features that your hardware supports. Common tabs include Power Schemes, Advanced, Hibernate, and UPS. If your computer supports advanced power management (which helps reduce battery power consumption and provides battery status information), the Power Options Properties dialog box also displays an APM tab.

Power Schemes Tab

Power schemes are preset collections of power-usage settings. Windows XP includes several default power schemes and allows you to create your own custom power schemes. The options you see depend on your hardware and system configuration.

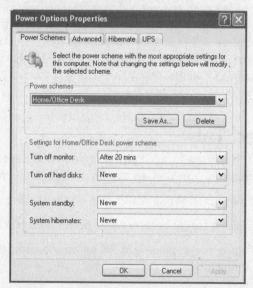

You can specify the amount of idle time that elapses (from never to after five hours) before Windows XP applies power-saving features to your computer hardware. Possible power scheme settings include:

▶ Placing the system on standby (where it uses less power)

▶ Placing the system into hibernation

▶ Turning off the monitor or hard disks (controlled separately)

▶ Settings for AC and battery power on laptops

WARNING

When a computer enters standby mode, Windows XP does not save your open files to disk. If you lose power while you are in standby mode, you may lose unsaved data. Be sure to save your data before you leave your computer idle for an extended period.

TIP

If your hardware supports standby, you can also choose Start ➢ Turn Off Computer and then select Standby to manually place the computer on standby.

To apply a power scheme, select a scheme from the Power Schemes drop-down list, and click either the Apply or OK button. To create a new power scheme, select an existing scheme from the Power Schemes list. Modify the settings for the scheme and click the Save As button. To delete a power scheme, select an existing power scheme and click the Delete button.

Advanced Tab

This tab contains advanced power options that depend on your hardware and system configuration. Examples of the options you see are:

▶ Display or remove a power icon on the taskbar

▶ Display a laptop battery usage power meter on the taskbar

▶ Prompt for a password when the computer comes out of standby mode

You may also be able to configure Windows XP to place your computer on standby when you press the power button on a desktop computer or close the lid on a laptop computer.

Hibernate Tab

This tab is available when your hardware supports hibernation. When your computer enters hibernation mode, Windows XP stores all data from memory onto your hard disk and shuts down the computer. When you bring the computer out of hibernation, Windows XP retrieves the data from the hard disk, opens the necessary programs automatically, and restores your environment to its pre-hibernation state.

Options in the Hibernation tab allow you to enable or disable the hibernation feature. Select the Enable Hibernate Support check box and click the OK or Apply button. Then, choose Start ➢ Turn Off Computer to display the Turn Off Computer dialog box. Choose Hibernate to place the computer into hibernation.

The Hibernate tab also displays the amount of disk space required to enter hibernation and the amount of free disk space on your hard disk.

UPS Tab

This tab lets you configure settings for an uninterruptible power supply (UPS). The Status area displays your UPS power source, estimated run-time and capacity, and battery condition. The Details section displays the manufacturer and model of the UPS.

To select your UPS, click the Select button and choose the manufacturer and model of your UPS and the port to which the UPS is connected. Click Finish to add the information to the UPS tab.

To configure UPS settings (such as notifications and alarms), click the Configure button. You can also specify the actions you want Windows to take in case of power failure (such as shutdown), and turn off the UPS after the computer completes the actions.

PRINTERS AND FAXES

See Chapter 8

PRINTERS AND OTHER HARDWARE

Control Panel category that provides access to information and configuration dialog boxes for printers, faxes, scanners, cameras, game controllers, mice, and keyboards. To open the Printers and Other Hardware category, choose Start ➢ Control Panel (or Start ➢ Settings ➢ Control Panel in the Classic Start menu) and click the Printers and Other Hardware icon.

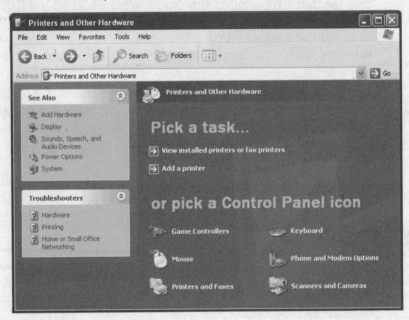

See also   Game Controllers, Keyboard, Mouse, Printers and Faxes, Scanners and Cameras

PROGRAM COMPATIBILITY WIZARD

Program Compatibility Wizard   Helps you select and test compatibility settings to fix programs that worked correctly on an earlier version of Windows but do not run correctly on Windows XP.

To start the Program Compatibility Wizard, choose Start ➢ All Programs (or Start ➢ Programs in the Classic Start menu) ➢ Accessories ➢ Program Compatibility Wizard. The wizard opens in the Help and Support Center. Click Next to step through the wizard.

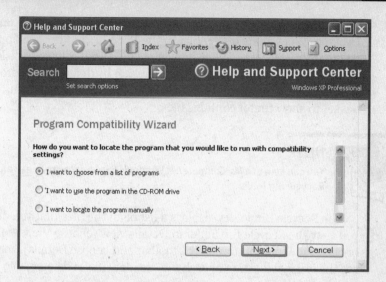

The wizard helps you test programs that are installed on your system or on a CD. During the process, you select items such as the operating system that the program was designed for and the display settings for the software. After you make your selections, the wizard tests the application and asks you whether it started correctly. If so, you can set the program to always use the compatibility settings that you selected in the wizard; otherwise, you can try different compatibility settings or exit the wizard.

RECYCLE BIN

 Folder that stores files and folders you deleted from your hard disk until you permanently remove them. It allows you to quickly restore files that you may have deleted in error.

WARNING

The Recycle Bin does not store files that are deleted from floppy disks, removable disks (such as a Zip or Jaz disks), or from network drives. Use caution when you delete files from these types of drives, as they are permanently deleted.

NOTE

The Recycle Bin is not a substitute for a tape backup system. It is limited in size and only holds the files you most recently deleted.

To open the Recycle Bin, double-click the wastebasket icon on the Desktop. When there are no files in the Recycle Bin, the icon appears as an empty wastebasket. When you delete files from your hard disk (using the Delete key, or through pop-up menus, or by dragging and dropping files to the Recycle Bin), the Recycle Bin icon appears as a full wastebasket to show that it contains files.

NOTE

You can also use My Computer or Windows Explorer to browse to and open the Recycle Bin folder.

The Recycle Bin folder displays a list of all the files that you deleted. If you view the Recycle Bin folder in Details view (choose View ➤ Details, or click the Views button on the toolbar and choose Details), you can also see the original location of each file, the date it was deleted, and the type and size of the file.

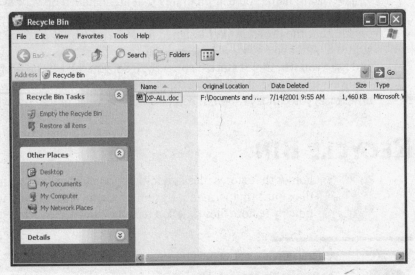

The left pane of the Recycle Bin folder displays two tasks. The first task allows you to empty the recycle bin. The second task allows you restore one or more files to their original location.

Emptying the Recycle Bin

Files that are in the Recycle Bin still take up space on your hard disk. To reclaim that space, you have to delete some files from the Recycle Bin or completely empty the Recycle Bin. As a general rule, you should empty the Recycle Bin once a week. Various methods are available:

▶ To remove all files when the Recycle Bin window is open, choose the Empty the Recycle Bin icon from the left pane. Alternatively, you can choose File ➤ Empty Recycle Bin from the Recycle Bin menu.

▶ To delete one or more selected files when the Recycle Bin window is open, select the file or files you want to delete. Choose File ➤ Delete, or right-click the selection and choose Delete.

TIP

You can also empty the Recycle Bin from your Desktop. Right-click the Recycle Bin icon and choose Empty Recycle Bin from the shortcut menu.

Restoring a File

When you restore a file, you remove it from the Recycle Bin and move it back to its original location on your hard drive. To restore one or more files, select them in the Recycle Bin. Choose File ➤ Restore, or right-click the selection and choose Restore from the shortcut menu.

TIP

You can also restore files using the Restore command in the left pane of the Recycle Bin. This command changes, depending on how many files you select from the Recycle Bin window. With no files selected, click Restore All Items. With one file selected, click Restore This Item. With multiple or all files selected, click Restore the Selected Items.

Changing the Size of the Recycle Bin

Each fixed drive or partition on your computer has its own Recycle Bin. By default, each Recycle Bin is allocated 10 percent of the total space available on its respective hard disk or partition. If you are logged on as a Computer Administrator, you can change the default settings. From your Desktop, right-click the Recycle Bin icon and choose Properties. The Recycle Bin Properties dialog box opens to the Global tab. This tab offers two different methods of managing the Recycle Bin:

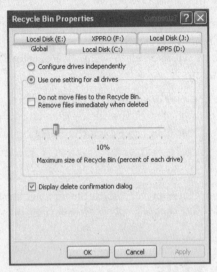

► If you have one or more drives on your system and want to use the same settings on each drive, select the Use One Setting for All Drives radio button. (This is the default option.) Move the Maximum Size of Recycle Bin slider toward the left to decrease the percentage or toward the right to increase the percentage. If you do not want to use the Recycle Bin at all, select the Do Not Move Files to the Recycle Bin check box.

WARNING

When you choose the Do Not Move Files to the Recycle Bin option, any files you delete are removed from your system immediately. You don't have a second chance to retrieve them. Use this option with care.

► If your drives or partitions are sized differently, you can config-ure the space allocated for the Recycle Bin for each drive sepa-rately. To apply different settings to each drive on your system, select the Configure Drives Independently radio button. Click the tab that is associated with the drive you want to configure. Adjust the Maximum Size of Recycle Bin slider accordingly, or check the Do Not Move Files to the Recycle Bin box for the selected drive or partition. Repeat these steps for each drive or partition on your system.

If you want to display a confirmation dialog box before files are removed from the Recycle Bin, select the Display Delete Confirmation Dialog check box. This option is checked by default.

WARNING

Be careful not to make your Recycle Bin too small. If you delete a file that is larger than the Recycle Bin's storage capacity, the file is permanently deleted.

See also   Disk Cleanup

REGIONAL AND LANGUAGE OPTIONS

Regional and Language Options   Enables you to customize the display of fractional or large numbers, currencies, dates, and times as used in your geographical location. Windows XP also supports the use of multiple languages. You can view or change the languages and methods available to enter text, and allow non-Unicode programs to display menus and dialog boxes in your native language.

To display the Regional and Language Options dialog box, choose Start ➢ Control Panel (or Start ➢ Settings ➢ Control Panel in the Classic Start menu) ➢ Date, Time, Language, and Regional Options. Next, select the Regional and Language Options control panel icon. The Regional and Language Options dialog box opens, containing three tabs: Regional Options, Languages, and Advanced.

Regional Options Tab

Select your geographical region here and choose how to format numbers, currencies, times, and short or long dates. You can also select a region for local information such as news and weather.

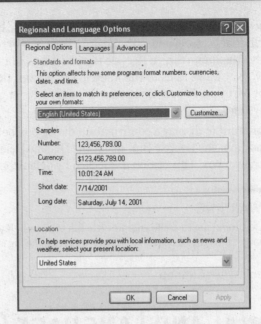

In the Standards and Formats area is a drop-down list where you choose the geographical region that you want to use. By default, this field displays the language option that you selected during Windows XP installation. When you choose another option from the drop-down list, the Samples fields display noneditable examples to show how numbers, currency, time, short date, and long date are formatted in that region. The Location drop-down, at the bottom of the tab, allows you to select a region for local information such as news and weather.

Customizing Regional Options

To customize your regional options, click the Customize button in the Regional Options tab. This opens the Customize Regional Options dialog box, which features four tabs: Numbers, Currency, Time, and Date.

Numbers tab Adjust the display of decimal symbols, the number of decimal digits, the digit grouping symbol, digit grouping, the negative sign symbol, negative number format, display of leading zeros, list separators, and the measurement system. As you enter or select new values for each field, the Sample area displays examples for positive and negative numbers.

Currency tab Adjust the display of the currency symbol, the positive and negative currency formats, the decimal symbol, the number of digits after the decimal, and the digit grouping and digit grouping symbol options. As you enter or select new values for each field, the Sample area displays examples for positive and negative currency values.

Time tab   Adjust the display of times on the clock that appears in the notification area of your taskbar and in related dialog boxes. These times appear in hours (*h*, *hh*, *H*, or *HH*), minutes (*mm*), and seconds (*ss*). Use *h* or *hh* to display time in 12-hour format, and *tt* to display A.M. or P.M. Use *H* or *HH* to display time in 24-hour format. This dialog box also allows you to enter or select symbols for the time separator, as well as for the A.M. and P.M. symbols. As you enter or select new values for each field, the Sample area displays an example of your customized time values.

Date tab   Adjust the display of dates in dialog boxes and in documents that you create with applications such as Microsoft Word. When you enter a two-digit number for a year (such as 02 for 2002) in any dialog box or application that recognizes dates, Windows XP automatically interprets any value starting at 1930 and ending with the value you specify in the ending year field of the Calendar area. In the Short Date area, you can customize the format and separator used to display short dates; the Short Date Sample box displays an example of your customized short date format. In the Long Date area, you can specify how long dates are displayed and see a sample of your customized format.

Languages Tab

Allows you to view or change the languages and methods you use to enter text. The Supplemental Language Support section contains two options:

▶ Select the Install Files for Complex Script and Right-to-Left languages check box if you want to install Arabic, Armenian, Georgian, Hebrew, Indic, Thai, and Vietnamese language files on your computer. These additional files use approximately 10 MB of disk space.

▶ Select the Install Files for East Asian languages check box to install additional files for Chinese, Japanese, and Korean language files. These files use approximately 230 MB of disk space.

To configure language services, click the Details button to open the Text Services and Input Languages dialog box.

Text Services and Input Languages Dialog Box

The drop-down list in the Default Input Language area allows you to specify the default language that you use to enter text. This language is used when you start up or log on to your computer.

The Installed Services area displays all language and text services that are installed and loaded into memory when you start your computer. The text services you can select for each language installed on your computer include keyboard layouts, input method editors, and handwriting and speech recognition options. Use this area to add, remove, or check properties for additional language services.

To install additional language services, follow these steps:

1. From the Text Services and Input Languages dialog box, click Add. The Add Input Language dialog box appears.

2. Use the Input Language drop-down box to select the input language that you want to add.

3. The Keyboard Layout/IME field displays a keyboard layout to correspond with the selection you made in Step 2. You can choose another keyboard layout if you desire.

4. Click OK to return to the Text Services dialog box. The new service appears in the Installed Services list.

NOTE

Language services require computer memory and can affect performance.

NOTE

When you install a new language service, Windows XP may prompt you to insert your Windows XP CD to install additional files, and to reboot your computer in order for settings to take effect.

To remove an installed language service, highlight the service you want to remove, and click Remove.

The Preferences area at the bottom of the Text Services and Input Languages dialog box allows you to specify options for the language bar. If you have speech recognition, handwriting recognition, or an input method editor installed as a text service, a Language Bar button is available; it opens a dialog box that allows you to change the look and behavior of the language bar.

Click the Key Settings button to open the Advanced Key Settings dialog box. This dialog box allows you to configure the hot key settings that you use to switch between your installed language services and to turn off the Caps Lock function. The default hot key to switch languages is Left Alt+Shift.

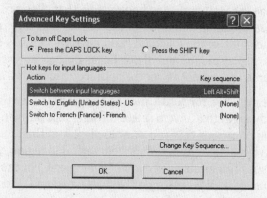

Creating a Document Using Multiple Languages

When you have more than one language service installed on your system, you can create documents that use multiple languages. The following example demonstrates how you can create a multilanguage document in WordPad:

1. Choose Start ➢ All Programs (or Start ➢ Programs in the Classic Start menu) ➢ Accessories ➢ WordPad to open WordPad.

2. Enter text to begin your document in your default language.

3. To switch to another language service, press Left Alt+Shift.

4. Enter the text that you want to display in the alternate language.

5. To return to your original language, or to switch to another language, press Left Alt+Shift again. Select the language you want to use, and enter more text.

NOTE

If you distribute your multilanguage document to others, those who read your document must have the same language services installed in order to read it properly.

Advanced Tab

Unicode is a standard encoding scheme that allows computers to display text-based data in almost all of the written languages of the world. The Advanced tab in the Regional and Language Options dialog box allows you to display menus and dialog boxes in their native language within programs that do not support the Unicode standard.

Language for Non-Unicode Programs   Use the drop-down menu in this area to select the language of the non-Unicode applications that you want to display in their native language. If a language option differs from region to region, you can also specify a localized version of a language. For example, if you are using an older program that was written for French Canadian users, click French (Canada).

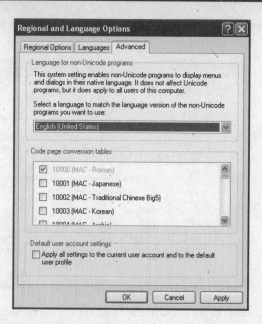

Code Page Conversion Tables These tables allow Windows XP to interpret letters and other characters that a program uses and to display them correctly on your screen. The list displays the available tables, with check marks to the left of tables that are installed. Computer Administrators can install or uninstall code page tables. Click to place a check mark next to additional tables that you want to install, or clear a check mark to remove an installed table.

Default User Account Settings Select the check box in this area to apply the settings in the Regional and Language Options dialog box to your own user account and to all new user accounts that are created on this computer.

See also Keyboard

REGISTRY

Database that holds all information about your system, such as defaults and properties for folders, files, users, preferences, applications, protocols, devices, and any other resources. Information about program installation and changes are saved in the Registry when you install new applications or hardware, or when you make any changes to your system using Control Panel.

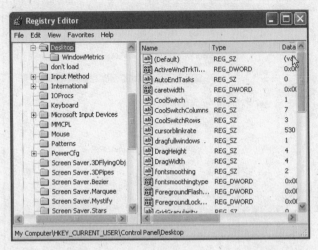

Advanced users can use the Registry Editor to manually edit the Registry. To open the Registry Editor, choose Start ➤ Run, then type **regedit** and click OK.

WARNING

You can cause serious problems with your Windows XP installation, such as the system not functioning properly or not functioning at all, if the Registry changes you make are not correct. Do not make any manual changes to the Registry unless you are *very* familiar with how the Registry database works.

REMOTE ASSISTANCE

See   Chapter 19

See also   Help and Support Center, Windows Messenger

REMOTE DESKTOP CONNECTION

See   Chapter 19

See also   NetMeeting, Windows Messenger

RESTORE DOWN

 Button that appears at the top-right corner of opened windows. Click the Restore Down button to return a window to its original size after you maximize it with the Maximize button.

See also   Close, Maximize and Minimize

RUN

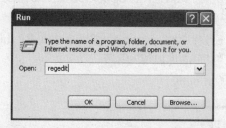 Used to open programs, folders, documents, and Internet resources. Most frequently used to run installation programs. To use this function, follow these steps:

1. Choose Start ➤ Run. The Run dialog box appears.

2. In the Open text box, enter the full path and name of the resource you want to open, or use the Browse button to locate the resource on your hard drive. You can also use the drop-down list to select a resource that you previously opened.

3. Click OK to open the resource.

RUN AS

Used to run a program or MMC tool as a user other than the one currently logged on (for example, as an administrative user). Follow these steps to access the Run As dialog box:

1. In Windows Explorer, select a program you want to run as another user.

2. Hold down the Shift key and right-click.

3. From the shortcut menu, select Run As.

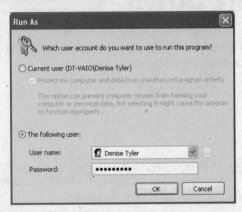

4. In the Run As dialog box, select the The Following User radio button.

5. Enter the username and password for the user that you want to run the program as.

6. Click OK.

NOTE

By default, the Run As dialog box runs the selected program as the current user and displays the name of the user that is currently logged on to the computer. When you run a program as the Current User, you can choose to run the program with or without virus protection. If virus protection causes a program to function improperly, uncheck the "Protect my computer and data from unauthorized program activity" option.

SAFELY REMOVE HARDWARE

 Option that appears in the notification area of the Windows XP taskbar if you have installed removable storage media such as Zip disks, Jaz disks, FireWire drives, compact flash card readers, or SmartCard readers. The Safely Remove Hardware feature allows you to safely dismount your storage device before you unplug the drive.

To safely remove a drive, click the Safely Remove Hardware button in the notification area of the taskbar. A list of removable drives that are installed on your computer appears. Select the device you want to remove. A notification box then tells you that you can safely unplug the device.

To view properties of a removable storage device, right-click the Safely Remove Hardware button in the notification area of the taskbar; or, right-click the Safely Remove Hardware button to display the dialog box shown here. Click the Properties button to view the properties of the selected device, or to troubleshoot the device and update its drivers.

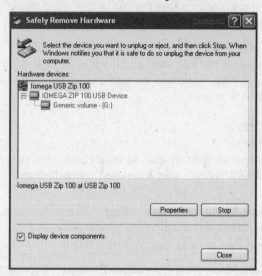

SAFE MODE

Startup option that allows you to troubleshoot system problems when you cannot properly start Windows XP. Safe mode starts Windows XP with a minimal set of drivers so that you can correct installation problems or check driver versions. To access the Safe Mode startup options on the Windows XP Advanced Options menu, follow these steps:

1. If you are currently in Windows, choose Start ➢ Turn Off Computer. Select Restart from the dialog box.

NOTE

If you are unable to start Windows, restart your computer using the Ctrl+Alt+Del keys on your keyboard.

2. Press F8 when your system reboots, and before the Windows XP startup screen appears. The Windows Advanced Options menu appears and displays the options listed below.

3. Use the Up and Down arrow keys to highlight your choice, and press Enter to select it. NumLock must be off in order for the arrow keys to work.

The menu options that appear in the Windows Advanced Options menu are as follows:

Safe Mode   Starts Windows XP but bypasses the startup files (such as the Registry) and loads only basic device drivers (standard VGA, keyboard, mouse, and other basic drivers required to start Windows).

TIP

If you can't start Windows XP in Safe mode, you might need to repair your Windows XP system using Automated System Recovery.

Safe Mode with Networking   Starts Windows XP but bypasses the startup files. Loads network (NIC card) drivers in addition to basic device drivers.

Safe Mode with Command Prompt   Bypasses the startup files and, after logging on, displays the DOS command prompt.

Enable Boot Logging   Starts Windows XP and creates a log file of all of the services and drivers that load during startup. The file, called ntbtlog.txt, is saved in your Windows installation folder.

Enable VGA Mode   Starts Windows XP with the standard VGA driver. You can use this mode to troubleshoot problems you might be having after installing a different video driver.

Last Known Good Configuration   Starts Windows XP using the Registry information that was saved the last time you successfully shut down Windows XP.

Directory Services Restore Mode (Windows Domain Controllers Only)   Restores the Active Directory and the SYSVOL folder on a Windows XP domain controller.

Debugging Mode   Starts Windows XP and sends debugging data to another computer via a serial connection.

Start Windows Normally   Lets you proceed with a normal boot.

Reboot   Exits the Windows Advanced Options menu and reboots your computer.

Return to OS Choices Menu   On a computer where multiple operating systems are installed, returns to the Please Select Operating System to Start screen and allows you to start the selected operating system in the mode you selected.

SCANNERS AND CAMERAS

See   Chapter 23

SCHEDULED TASKS

Add Scheduled Task   Windows XP allows you to schedule tasks, so that you can run programs and scripts or use documents at a certain time, date, or interval. Scheduled Tasks allows you to create, view, and configure tasks as needed.

To open the Scheduled Tasks folder, choose Start ➢ Control Panel (or Start ➢ Settings ➢ Control Panel in the Classic Start menu) and click the Performance and Maintenance control panel icon. Then click the Scheduled Tasks icon. You can also choose Start ➢ All Programs (or Start ➢ Programs in the Classic Start menu) ➢ Accessories ➢ System Tools ➢ Scheduled Tasks.

TIP
Make sure your system time settings are accurate if you want to set up scheduled tasks.

Scheduled Tasks Folder

The Scheduled Tasks folder displays the tasks that you schedule with several details, including task schedule, next and last run times, status, last result, and creator of the task. The Add Scheduled Task icon allows you to manually add additional tasks with the Scheduled Task Wizard.

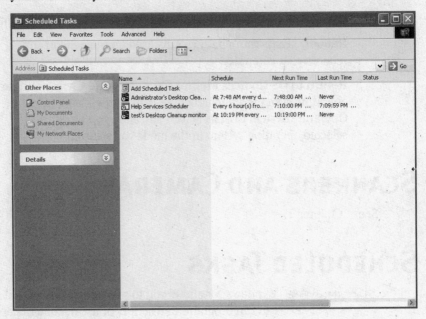

Run and End Task

Right-click any task to display a submenu of options. Two of these options are specific to scheduled tasks. To run the scheduled task immediately, choose Run. To stop a task that is currently running (as shown in the Status column), choose End Task.

TIP

End Task is handy when you want to use the computer and a scheduled task is currently running. End the task and then restart it later, using Run Task. It may take several minutes for the task to actually stop.

Properties

To view or edit properties for a task, double-click a task in the list. You can also right-click any task and choose Properties from the menu that appears. The Properties dialog box has three tabs: Task, Schedule, and Settings.

Task Tab   Use this tab to specify information about the task. The Run field displays the location of the file currently associated with the task. To change the path, simply enter a new path or use the Browse button to locate another application, folder, or file. Use the Start In field to specify the directory that contains the file, or the location of any other files that are required to run the task (which may be located in the same folder, or in a different location). Use the Comments field to enter any comment about the task, such as a description of what the task does.

TIP

To specify command-line parameters for a program, enter them in the Run field after you enter the path to the task's associated file. If spaces appear in any portion of the path to the task's associated file, enclose the path inside double quotation marks.

By default, the creator of the task runs a scheduled task. You can also run a task as a different user: Use the Run As field to specify the user you would like to run the task. The syntax is *computername_or_domainname\ username*. Next, click the Set Password button to specify the user's password.

Use the Enabled option (at the bottom of the Task tab) to enable or disable the scheduled task.

Schedule Tab   The Schedule tab allows you to change the task's schedule—for example, you can change the task to run daily instead of weekly, or change the times the task runs. Choose an option from the Schedule Task drop-down list. With the exception of the At System Startup or At Logon options, the area below the list changes to display scheduling options for the type of schedule you selected (such as days of the month for a Monthly task). As you make your choices, the top section of the tab updates the scheduling information.

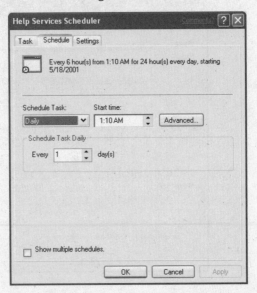

Check the Show Multiple Schedules box to configure more than one schedule for the same task. The top area of the tab now displays a drop-down list of all the schedules you configured for the task. Click New to create additional schedules for the task.

NOTE

Once you create multiple schedules, they always appear; you cannot disable the display of multiple schedules unless there is only one schedule.

To configure advanced scheduling options (such as start and end dates and additional repeat options), click the Advanced button in the Schedule tab to open the Advanced Schedule Options dialog box. Select a start date for the task. To specify an end date, check the End Date box and

choose a date from the drop-down calendar. Use the Until section to specify when you want the Repeat functions to end or how long you want
them to last. Click OK to save your advanced settings.

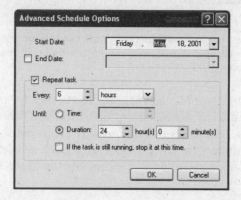

Settings Tab   Use the Settings tab to configure special circumstances
for the task. Use the Scheduled Task Completed section to specify how to
handle the task after it runs. You can delete the task if it is not scheduled
to run again, or stop the task if it runs over a certain amount of time.

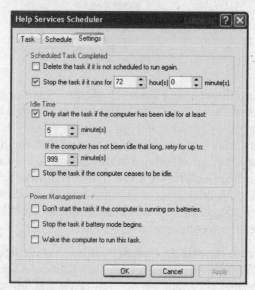

Use the Idle Time section to specify how to handle the task if your
computer is in idle mode. You can start the task if the computer has been
idle for at least a specified amount of time, and specify a time limit within

which Windows retries to start the task. You can also end the task when your computer ceases to be idle.

NOTE

Idle-time configuration can come in handy if you want tasks to run but you still want to be able to use your computer without the task tying up your computer's resources.

Use the Power Management section to specify how to handle the task while your computer is running on batteries, or when your computer wakes up from power management. You can choose not to run the task if your computer is in battery mode, stop the task when your computer goes into battery mode, or wake the computer up to run the task.

Advanced Menu

The Advanced menu is unique to the Scheduled Tasks folder. This menu contains the following five options (the first four are only available for users with administrative privileges):

Stop/Start Using Task Scheduler   Stops or starts the task scheduler service (choose this option to toggle between using the task scheduler and not using it). When you stop the service, any tasks that are scheduled to run won't run until the next time they are scheduled to run, providing the task scheduler has been restarted. Choose Start Using Task Scheduler to start the scheduler again after it has been stopped. When you stop the task scheduler, the Pause/Continue Task Scheduler and AT Service Account menu options are disabled.

Pause/Continue Task Scheduler   Available only if the task scheduler is running. Pause Task Scheduler temporarily pauses the task scheduler service; any tasks that are scheduled to run won't run until the next time they are scheduled to run, providing the task scheduler has been continued. Choose Continue Task Scheduler to resume the operation of the task scheduler after you pause it.

Notify Me of Missed Tasks   Choose this option to receive notification from Windows XP if a task did not run. Click this option to place a check mark next to the option, indicating that it's active. Click the option again to turn off notification.

AT Service Account   Lets you specify which account can run or list scheduled tasks using the command-line AT command.

TIP

For more detailed information about the AT command, search the Help system's index for the words **AT COMMAND**.

View Log   View a log of messages relating to scheduled events and the status of the task scheduler. The log file includes success as well as error messages, and messages regarding starting, stopping, pausing, and continuing the task scheduler service.

Add Scheduled Task

Add Scheduled Task   Starts the Scheduled Task Wizard, which guides you through the process of creating scheduled tasks. To create a scheduled task, follow these steps:

1. In the Scheduled Tasks folder, double-click Add Scheduled Task. The Scheduled Task Wizard appears.

2. Click Next. The wizard displays a list of applications. Select an application from the list, or click the Browse button to locate another application on your local or network computer.

3. Click Next. Enter a name for your task, and then click the radio button that corresponds with how often you want the task to run. Your choices are daily, weekly, monthly, one time only, when your computer starts, or when you log on. Skip to Step 5 if you choose either of the last two options.

TIP

A scheduled task icon has a visual indicator to denote that it is a scheduled task. You may find it easier to distinguish scheduled tasks from actual programs if you use a name that is different than the program you are scheduling—for example, name a scheduled disk cleanup something like My Scheduled Disk Cleanup.

4. Click Next. The options that appear in the next dialog box depend on your choice in Step 3. In this screen, you can specify such items as the time to run the task, or on which days (or weeks, or months) you want to run the task.

5. Click Next to enter your username and password.

6. Click Next. The wizard informs you that your task is scheduled and confirms when it will run. Click Finish to complete the steps in the wizard.

NOTE

The screen in Step 6 provides an option to open an Advanced Properties dialog box after you click the Finish button. You can also double-click any task in the list to open the Properties dialog box, where you can view or modify the settings and schedules of your task. You can also limit the amount of time that a task runs, set idle times, and configure power management options.

See also   Help and Support Center

SCREEN SAVER

See   Display

SEARCH

See   Chapter 6
See also   Help and Support Center

SEND TO

Send To   ▸ Lets you send a file or folder directly to a compressed folder, your Desktop (as a shortcut), a mail recipient, a floppy, Zip, or CD disk, your My Documents folder, or to publish to the Internet.

To send an item to a destination using Send To, perform these steps:

1. In any Explorer window, right-click a file or folder and choose Send To from the menu that appears.

2. Select the destination:

    ▸ Choose Compressed (Zipped) Folder to create a ZIP file that contains the item(s) you selected.

    ▸ Choose Desktop (Create Shortcut) to create a shortcut on your desktop that opens the selected item.

    ▸ Choose Mail Recipient to send the file to a contact from your Address Book, or to the e-mail address you enter.

    ▸ Choose 3-½ Floppy to copy the selection to a floppy disk.

    ▸ Choose My Documents to send the document to your My Documents folder.

    ▸ Choose CD-Drive to write the selected file(s) to CD.

See also   Address Book, Compressing Drives, Desktop, Explorer, Folders, My Documents, Web Publishing Wizard

SETTINGS

Settings   ▸ The Settings option on the Start menu is only available when you use the Classic Start menu. The Settings option gives you access to many Windows XP configuration tools, such as Control Panel, Network Connections, Printers and Faxes, and Taskbar and Start Menu. Choose Start ➢ Settings and make your choice from the submenu.

TIP

To choose the Classic-style Start menu, right-click the Start button and choose Properties. The Taskbar and Start Menu Properties dialog box opens to the Start Menu tab. Select Classic Start Menu and choose OK.

See also   Control Panel, Network and Internet Connections, Printers and Other Hardware, Taskbar and Start Menu

SHARED FOLDERS

 Shared Folders   MMC snap-in that lets you view and manage shares on the computer you're using, remote connections to that computer, and files in use by remote users.

TIP

To use Shared Folders, you must be a member of the Administrators, Power Users, or Server Operators group, and your computer must be on a network.

To access Shared Folders, choose Start ➢ Control Panel (or Start ➢ Settings ➢ Control Panel in the Classic Start menu) ➢ Performance and Maintenance, click Administrative Tools, and double-click Computer Management. From the System Tools category in the console tree, select Shared Folders.

Shared Folders Nodes

Shared Folders contains three nodes: Shares, Sessions, and Open Files.

Shares   Lets you view, stop sharing, and configure properties (such as permissions and security) for existing shares. You can also create new shares. Some default shares for Windows XP are ADMIN$, C$, IPC$, print$, and SharedDocs. Detail columns for each share include the name and path of the share, its type, the number of client (user) connections, and any comments attached to the share.

Sessions   Lets you see which users are currently connected to the computer, disconnect a single session, or disconnect all sessions. Detail columns for each session include User, Computer,

Type, Open Files, Connected Time (the time elapsed since the user connected), Idle Time (the time elapsed since the user performed an action), and Guest (whether the user is connected as Guest).

Open Files Lets you see which files are currently open by remote users on shared folders. Here you can also close a single file or all files. Detail columns for each open file include Open File, Accessed By, Type, Number of Locks, and Open Mode (the permission granted when the file was opened).

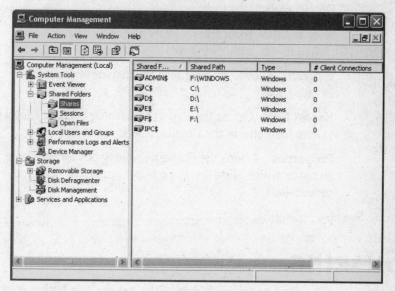

Action Menu

Action   The Action menu in Shared Folders contains many familiar items and some unique ones. The items available depend on whether you're selecting a node in the console tree or an item in the Details pane, and also on the node or item you've selected.

All Tasks ➤ Send Console Message Opens the Send Console Message dialog box, where you can create and send a message to one or more individuals. Available with Shares selected in the console tree.

Disconnect All Sessions   Lets you disconnect all currently open sessions by remote users. Available with Sessions selected in the console tree.

Close Session   Closes the open session that is selected in the Details pane.

Disconnect All Open Files   Closes all files open in shared folders. Available with Open Files selected in the console tree.

Close Open File   Closes the open file that is selected in the Details pane.

New Window from Here   Displays the Share node and shared files in a new window.

Refresh   Allows you to refresh the display of items in the Details pane.

Export List   Opens the Export List dialog box and allows you to save the items in the Details pane as a text file.

Properties   Opens the Properties dialog box for the shared resource, which allows you to set user limits, caching, and share permissions.

See also   Sharing

SHARING

Sharing...   Lets you share folders, disks, printers, and other resources on your computer with other users on a network. When you share a folder or disk, you can specify which users have access to the resource and configure the permissions for them. Sharing settings are configured on the Sharing tab of the resource's property sheet. Users can see and access your shared resources through My Network Places.

Sharing a Folder or Disk

To share a folder or disk with users of the network, perform the following steps:

1. In any Explorer window, right-click the folder or disk you want to share and select Sharing and Security. The Properties dialog box opens to the Sharing tab.

TIP

Alternatively, you can right-click the folder or disk, select Properties, and then select the Sharing tab.

2. Select Share This Folder and enter a name for the share.

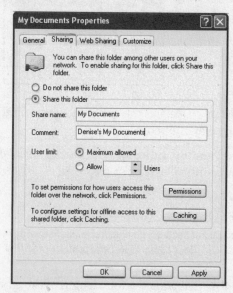

3. Check or uncheck the option to allow network users to change the files.

4. Click OK to apply your selections.

See also   Explorer

SOUND RECORDER

 Sound Recorder   Lets you record, edit, play, and mix audio files from audio input devices installed in your computer. Examples of audio input devices are a microphone (using a sound card) and a CD player.

Choose Start ➤ All Programs (or Start ➤ Programs in the Classic Start menu) ➤ Accessories ➤ Entertainment ➤ Sound Recorder to open the Sound Recorder dialog box.

Sound Recorder Display

The Sound Recorder display provides information about the sound track you're recording or playing back. Several buttons allow you to control recording and playback of the sounds you record.

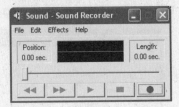

Position   Displays the current location on the sound track during play and recording.

Sound quality indicator   Provides a visual display of the sound during playback or recording.

TIP

If you do not see a green line in the sound quality indicator, this indicates that the sound file is compressed and can't be modified.

Length   Displays the total length of the currently opened audio file.

Position slider   Displays the relative position in the audio file while you record or play it. The slider moves toward the right to indicate the current position, relative to the entire length of the audio file. You can move the slider to change the position.

NOTE

When you record a new track, the entire length of the new track is set to a default of 60 seconds, and the position of the slider is relative to that length while you record.

Seek to Start   Click to position the slider at the beginning of the audio file.

Seek to End   Click to position the slider at the end of the audio file.

Play   Click to play the audio file, beginning at the current position of the slider.

Stop   Click to stop playback or recording of the audio file.

Record   Click to start recording an audio file.

Menus

The commands in the File, Edit, and Effects menus of the Sound Recorder dialog box allow you to create, edit, and add effects to your audio files.

File

Commands in the File menu allow you to open, save, and view properties of audio files. The options are as follows:

New   Creates or records a new audio file. The Sound Recorder prompts you to save changes to your current file before it creates a new one.

Open   Provides a dialog box where you can choose an existing audio file to open.

Save   Saves the current audio file to your My Documents folder, or to the location from which the file was originally opened. The Save command overwrites any previous version of the file that is saved to your hard drive. To keep the original version of the file, use the Save As command to save a new version of the file to a different filename or folder.

Save As   Provides a dialog box where you can save the current audio file to a new folder or using a different filename. If you want to change the format of the audio file, click the Change button to open the Sound Selection dialog box (described later in this section).

Revert   Undoes all changes to the file since you last saved it. This reverts back to the file as you originally opened it. Click Yes to confirm the changes, or No to cancel.

Properties   Provides a dialog box for the sound file that displays copyright information, file length, file size, and audio format. The Properties dialog box also allows you to convert your audio file to a different file playback or recording format. Choose the format you want to display (All formats, Playback formats, or Recording formats) from the drop-down menu in the Format Conversion area. Then click the Convert Now button to open the Sound Selection dialog box, described later in this section.

Edit

Commands in the Edit menu allow you to copy, paste, mix, and delete portions of the current audio file. You can also view the properties of the audio file.

Copy   Places a copy of the current audio file into your Clipboard.

TIP

To combine or mix two audio files using the Clipboard, open the first audio file in the Sound Recorder and copy it to your Clipboard. Then open the second file, and position the slider at the point at which you want to add the first file. Use the Paste Insert or Paste Mix command to paste the file from the Clipboard into the current file. Save the new file under a new name to keep the original file untouched.

Paste Insert   Inserts the contents of the clipboard at the current slider position. The size of the original file expands to make room for the clipboard contents.

Paste Mix   Mixes the contents of the current file with the contents that you have in your clipboard, starting at the current slider position. Files are mixed at equal volume.

Insert File   Provides a dialog box where you can choose a file to insert at the current slider position. The size of the current file expands to make room for the file you insert.

Mix with File   Provides a dialog box where you can choose a file to mix with the currently opened file, beginning at the current slider position. Files are mixed at equal volumes.

TIP

To combine or mix two audio files that are saved to your hard disk, open the first file in the Sound Recorder. Then use the Insert File or Mix with File command to add or mix the second file. Save the combined version under a new filename to keep the two original files untouched.

Delete Before Current Position   Deletes the area between
the beginning of the audio file and the current slider position.

Delete After Current Position   Deletes the area between the
current slider position and the end of the audio file.

Audio Properties   Opens the Audio Properties dialog box to
the Audio Devices tab, where you specify the audio devices that
Sound Recorder should use for playback and recording. This
tab also lets you specify volume and advanced settings. More
information about the Audio Devices tab is available under
"Sounds and Audio Devices."

Effects

The Effects menu allows you to increase or decrease volume or speed of
the audio file, or add additional effects such as echo or reverse. Options
include Increase Volume (by 25%), Decrease Volume, Increase Speed (by
100%), Decrease Speed, Add Echo, and Reverse. When you increase or
decrease volume or speed or add an echo, Sound Recorder applies the
change to the entire audio file. The Reverse command physically reverses
the file so that it plays backward from end to beginning.

See also   Sounds and Audio Devices, Volume Control

Sound Selection Dialog Box

The Sound Selection dialog box allows you to change the format of your
current audio file. To open the Sound Selection dialog box from the
Sound Recorder, choose File ➢ Save As and click the Change button.

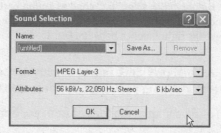

After you choose an audio format in the Sound Selection dialog box,
click OK to return to the Save As dialog box and save your file in the new
audio format.

The following options in the Sound Selection dialog box allow you to create custom presets that you can use to convert your audio files:

Name   Allows you to select a *preset* audio format from a drop-down list. When you select a preset, the Format and Attributes drop-down lists display the settings that apply to each preset. Three presets appear by default: CD Quality (PCM, 44.100 kHz, 16 Bit, Stereo, 172 kb/sec), Radio Quality (PCM, 22.050 kHz, 8 Bit, Mono, 21 kb/sec), and Telephone Quality (PCM, 11.025 kHz, 8 Bit, Mono, 10 kb/sec). These default formats are not compressed.

Format   Allows you to select a custom audio format for a preset. The PCM option creates an audio file that is not compressed; all other options create a compressed audio file. Common choices for compressed audio include MPEG Layer 3 (which creates MP3 audio files), Windows Media Audio V1, and Windows Media Audio V2.

Attributes   Allows you to select a custom target download rate for your audio file. Choose the speed, quality (frequency in Hz), and number of channels (mono or stereo) that is appropriate for your target audience and mode of delivery.

TIP

You can immediately cut the size of an audio file in half by choosing mono instead of stereo. When you compress sound files, they become smaller in size, making them easier to download from the Internet. However, this also reduces the quality of the sound file when compared to its original uncompressed version. Higher "kBit/s" or "Hz" choices sound better but take much longer to download. You will need to experiment with the settings for each sound file to achieve the right balance between file size and sound quality.

Save As   Allows you to save your custom settings as a preset. To create a custom preset, follow these steps:

1. Select an audio format from the Format drop-down list.

2. Select the desired target rate for download speed (kBit/s), quality (Hz), and number of channels (stereo or mono) from the Attributes list.

3. Click the Save As button, and assign a name to your custom preset.

Remove To remove a preset from the Name list, highlight the preset you want to delete and click Remove.

SOUNDS AND AUDIO DEVICES

Lets you assign specific sounds to Windows XP system events, such as receiving e-mail or exiting Windows, and for sound and multimedia device configuration.

Choose Start ➢ Control Panel (or Start ➢ Settings ➢ Control Panel in the Classic Start menu) ➢ Sounds, Speech and Audio Devices, then click Sounds and Audio Devices to open the Sounds and Audio Device Properties dialog box. This dialog box contains five tabs: Volume, Sounds, Audio, Voice, and Hardware.

Volume Tab

The top of the Volume tab displays the name of your WAVE audio device. Move the Device Volume slider to adjust speaker volume. Check the Mute box to turn off the sound completely while remembering the previous volume setting. You can also check an option to display a volume icon in your taskbar's notification area. Click the Advanced button to open the Volume Control dialog box (see the main topic "Volume Control").

Click the Speaker Volume button to open a dialog box where you can individually adjust the balance and volume for stereo or surround-sound speakers. To move all sliders at the same time, check Move All Slide Indicators at the Same Time. Click the Restore Defaults button to revert to the original default settings.

To choose advanced speaker settings, click the Advanced button in the Volume tab. This opens the Advanced Audio Properties dialog box, which consists of two tabs: Speakers and Performance. In the Speakers tab, select your speaker setup from the setup types in the Speaker Setup drop-down list. The settings in the Performance tab allow you to control how Windows XP handles audio acceleration and sample rate conversions. If you are experiencing problems with audio playback, adjust the Hardware Acceleration and Sample Rate Conversion Quality sliders as necessary to improve performance.

TIP

When you move the sliders for hardware acceleration and sample rate conversion quality, the description underneath each slider displays information about the current setting and under which circumstances you should use it.

NOTE

The Advanced buttons in the Audio tab and Voice tab (discussed in following sections) also open the Advanced Audio Properties dialog box.

Sounds Tab

Use the Sounds tab of the Sounds and Audio Device Properties dialog box to assign individual sounds to Windows XP events, such as when Windows XP starts or when you receive an incoming fax. Choose a sound scheme from the Sound Scheme drop-down list. You will be prompted to save any changes you made to your previous scheme if you have not already done so.

NOTE

Sound schemes do not assign a sound to every possible event. After you select a scheme, you may still need to assign specific sounds to additional events.

Use the Program Events list to customize your sound scheme, or to add sounds for events that have no assignment. Highlight the event to which you want to assign a sound, then choose a sound from the Sounds drop-down list at the bottom of the tab. Optionally, use the Browse button to select or preview a sound from your Media folder or another folder on your computer.

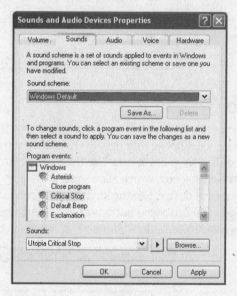

Audio Tab

Use the Audio tab to choose the default devices that Windows XP uses to play or record sound or to play MIDI music. Each audio device has a Volume button that opens the Volume Control dialog box, which allows you to adjust volume and speaker balance for each device, or to control bass and treble settings, if available; see the main topic "Volume Control" for additional information. The Advanced buttons open the Advanced Audio Properties dialog box, discussed under "Volume Tab" earlier in this main topic.

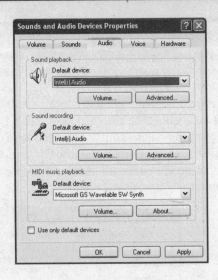

Voice Tab

Use the Voice tab to select and configure the device that you use to play back and record voice. Choose your default devices from the Voice Playback and Voice Recording drop-down lists. Use the Volume buttons to open the Volume Control dialog box, which allows you to adjust playback and recording volumes for each device. See the main topic "Volume Control" for additional information. The Advanced buttons open the Advanced Audio Properties dialog box, discussed under "Volume Tab" earlier in this main topic.

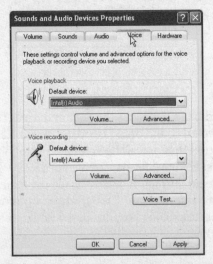

Click the Test Hardware button to open the Sound Hardware Test Wizard, which tests your sound hardware to ensure that you can play sounds and capture your voice properly. Follow the instructions in the wizard to test your sound hardware. You will be prompted to speak into a microphone to test and adjust recording settings and to adjust volumes for playback.

Hardware Tab

Use the Hardware tab of the Sounds and Audio Device Properties dialog box to configure hardware settings for your sound and multimedia devices and drivers (including CD-ROM drives).

To troubleshoot problems with a device, select an item from the Devices list. Then click the Troubleshoot button to open the Help and Support Center troubleshooter. Follow the prompts in the troubleshooter to resolve the problem.

To view or adjust settings for a device, select an item from the Devices list. Then click the Properties button to open a properties dialog box for the device. This dialog box displays several tabs, depending on the device you select. Typical information in these tabs includes device type, manufacturer, device status, and driver information.

TIP

You can also view and edit device properties through the **Device Manager.** Choose Start ➤ Control Panel (or Start ➤ Settings ➤ Control Panel in the Classic Start menu), and click Performance and Maintenance. Click the System control panel icon to open the System Properties dialog box. Select the Hardware tab, and click the Device Manager button to open the Windows XP Device Manager. Expand the appropriate device heading to right-click a device, and choose Properties.

See also   Accessibility, Sound Recorder, System, Volume Control

START MENU

See   Chapter 5

See also   Taskbar, Taskbar and Start Menu

SYNCHRONIZE

Synchronize   Allows you to update the content of Web pages that you have selected to view offline. The Synchronize feature compares versions on your hard disk to versions on the Internet, and updates your local version accordingly.

Choose Start ➤ All Programs (or Start ➤ Programs in the Classic Start menu) ➤ Accessories ➤ Synchronize to open the Items to Synchronize dialog box. This dialog box displays any files or Web pages that are available for offline viewing. Check the items that you want to synchronize, and uncheck those that you do not. The Items to Synchronize dialog box contains four buttons:

Properties   Opens the Properties dialog box for the selected item. The Schedule tab in the Properties dialog box allows you to synchronize the item automatically, or based on a schedule that you configure. The Download tab allows you to specify what content to download when you synchronize the item, or to notify you by e-mail when the online item changes.

Synchronize   Synchronizes the selected items.

Setup   Opens the Synchronization Settings dialog box. Use the Logon/Logoff tab to specify the items you want to synchronize automatically when you log on or off the computer. Use the On Idle tab to specify the items you want to synchronize when the computer is idle. Use the Scheduled tab to configure a schedule for synchronizing items (using the Scheduled Synchronization Wizard).

Close   Closes the dialog box.

See also   Offline Files

SYSTEM

System   Controls system properties, including network identification configuration, hardware device configuration (including hardware profile configuration), user profile configuration, and advanced properties, including performance, environment variable, and system startup and recovery configuration.

Choose Start ➤ Control Panel (or Start ➤ Settings ➤ Control Panel in the Classic Start menu), then choose Performance and Maintenance.

Then, click the System control panel icon to open the System Properties dialog box. This dialog box contains seven tabs: General, Computer Name, Hardware, Advanced, System Restore, Automatic Updates, and Remote; these are described in the following subsections.

TIP

Alternatively, you can right-click My Computer and choose Properties to access the System Properties dialog box.

General Tab

The General tab provides information about your system, such as the version of the operating system you are running, to whom the operating system is registered, and information about the physical computer.

Computer Name Tab

Use this tab to view and configure the full name of your computer and the workgroup or domain to which it belongs. Each computer in a network must have a unique name by which you and other users can identify it. If the computer is a member of a domain and you've specified a DNS domain name for the computer, then the DNS domain name becomes part of the full name.

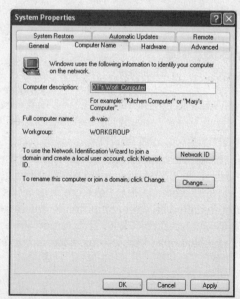

Click the Network ID button to open the Network Identification Wizard, which helps you join a domain and create a local user account.

To assign a new name for your computer, click the Change button to open the Computer Name Changes dialog box. Enter a new name for your computer and click OK to apply it.

Hardware Tab

Use this tab to configure the hardware on your computer. This tab gives you access to the Add Hardware Wizard, Driver Signing options, Device Manager, and Hardware Profiles.

Add Hardware Wizard

| Add New Hardware Wizard | Click the Add Hardware Wizard button to start the Add Hardware Wizard. This wizard allows you to add new hardware to a Windows XP computer after you have installed it on your machine. It also prepares removable hardware so that you can safely remove or unplug it from your computer, and allows you to troubleshoot devices that are not operating correctly.

The wizard automatically makes required changes to your Registry and configuration files. It also installs, loads, removes, or unloads drivers as necessary. For further information about the wizard, see the main topic "Add New Hardware."

Driver Signing

| Driver Signing | Click the Driver Signing button to open the Driver Signing Options dialog box, where you can configure how you want to handle file signatures that ensure the integrity of a file. This allows you to prevent the installation of files that may adversely affect the operation of your system.

Choose the verification level that you want to use from the File Signature Verification section. You can ignore the file signatures completely, receive a warning when a file is not signed, or block unsigned files so that they are not installed on your computer. If you are logged on as an administrator, you can also check Make This Action the System Default to use this setting for each user that logs in to the computer.

Device Manager

Device Manager Click the Device Manager button to open the Windows XP Device Manager, which lists all hardware installed in the computer. Device Manager also enables you to configure the properties of hardware devices, check the status of installed devices, view and update device drivers, and disable and uninstall devices. Device Manager is explained in detail under "Device Manager."

Hardware Profiles

Hardware Profiles Hardware profiles allow you to select the drivers that Windows XP loads at system startup in the event that you frequently change your hardware configurations. For example, you may use a modem to connect to the office and to the Internet while you are on the road with a laptop computer. Then, when you return to the office, you may attach your laptop to a docking station that connects to the network and the Internet through a network adapter. To handle these different hardware configuration needs, Windows XP allows you to set up multiple hardware profiles. At system startup, you can then choose which profile to use.

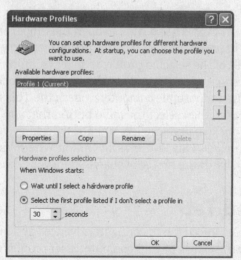

NOTE

If the computer is a laptop, the default profile will be called either Docked Profile or Undocked Profile.

To configure a hardware profile, click the Hardware Profiles button to open the Hardware Profiles dialog box. By default, this dialog box displays your original hardware profile as Original Configuration. Where there are multiple profiles, use the up and down arrows to move the highlighted selection to a new location in the list. The hardware profile that is currently being used appears at the top of the list, with (Current) appended to the hardware profile name.

NOTE

By default, when you add new hardware, the settings are saved in the Original Configuration hardware profile.

Click Copy to create a duplicate of the current profile under a new name. Click Rename to assign a new name to the selected profile. Click Delete to remove the selected profile from the list.

NOTE

You must be logged on as a computer administrator to copy hardware profiles.

Click the Properties button to open the Properties dialog box for the selected hardware profile. Use this dialog box to view and configure the properties of the selected profile; it displays information such as the manufacturer's dock ID and serial number of a docking station. To specify settings for portable computers, check the This Is a Portable Computer option, then select the radio button that applies to your docking station (docked, undocked, or unknown docking state). Check the Always Include This Profile as an Option When Windows Starts option to make the hardware profile available when your computer starts.

Advanced Tab

Use the Advanced tab to configure advanced system settings that relate to the performance of your computer, user profiles on the computer, or startup and recovery options. This tab presents three Settings buttons (one each for Performance, User Profiles, and Startup and Recovery) plus buttons for Environment Variables and Error Reporting.

Performance Settings

To control how your computer uses resources for visual effects, processor scheduling, memory usage, and virtual memory, click the Settings button in the Performance section. This opens the Performance Options dialog box, which consists of two tabs: Visual Effects and Advanced.

Visual Effects Tab   Use the Visual Effects tab in the Performance Options dialog box to configure how your computer handles various graphical elements. You can let Windows choose the settings that are best for your computer, or select from additional options. Choose Adjust for Best Appearance to select all of the features in the features list (such as animated windows, gradients in dialog boxes, menus that fade in and out, and other graphic options). Choose Adjust for Best Performance to disable all of the options. Choose Custom to check or uncheck options manually.

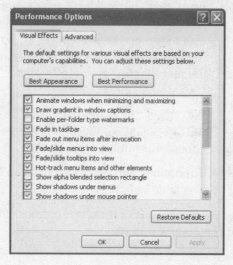

Advanced Tab   Use the Advanced tab in the Performance Options dialog box to choose how you want your computer to utilize its processor, physical memory, and virtual memory.

    Processor Scheduling   This choice controls how your computer optimizes processor usage for the applications you run. Choose the Programs radio button to optimize processor usage for applications that are running in the foreground. Choose the Background Services radio button to optimize your processor usage so that all applications receive equal amounts of processor resources.

Memory Usage   This choice controls how your computer optimizes memory usage for the applications you run. Choose the Programs radio button to use all physical memory for applications before using the system cache. Choose System Cache to balance memory usage between physical memory and system cache.

Virtual Memory   The Virtual Memory section displays the current size of the virtual memory paging files on your hard drives. To change the size of the paging file, click the Change button to open the Virtual Memory dialog box. Select a drive from the Drive list, and perform one of the following operations:

- ▶ To customize settings for the paging file on the selected drive, click the Custom Size radio button. Enter new values (in MB) for the Initial Size and Maximum Size boxes. Size recommendations appear at the bottom of the dialog box, along with the minimum allowed and the amount that is currently allocated.

- ▶ To have Windows XP manage the size of your paging files, check the System Managed Size radio button. Initial Size and Maximum Size fields are disabled when you choose this option.

- ▶ To eliminate the use of paging files, check the No Paging File radio button.

After you choose one of the above options, click the Set button to apply the new settings.

TIP

The Initial Size is the size of the paging file when Windows XP starts. The Maximum Size is the maximum size that you want to allow for the paging file. As a general rule, the Initial Size should be 1.5 times the amount of RAM that is installed in your computer.

NOTE

When you reduce the size of the Initial or Maximum paging files, Windows XP prompts you to restart your computer. You do not have to restart the computer when you increase the size of the paging files.

User Profiles Settings

To view or edit user profiles that are stored on the computer, click the Settings button in the User Profiles section of the Advanced tab in the System Properties dialog box. This opens the User Profiles dialog box, which displays a list of user profiles that are set up on the computer. If you are logged on as a computer administrator, use the buttons to edit the items in the list.

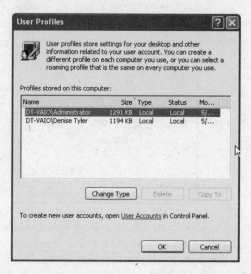

- ▶ To change the user account type, highlight the user account that you want to change, and click the Change Type button. In the Change Profile Type dialog box, choose Roaming Profile or Local Profile. Then click OK to apply the change.

- ▶ To delete a user account from the computer, highlight the user account that you want to delete, and click the Delete button.

- ▶ To create a copy of a user account, highlight the account you want to copy, and click the Copy To button. The Copy To dialog box allows you to choose a directory in which to copy the file, and to configure which users or groups are permitted to use the profile.

Startup and Recovery Settings

To view or edit startup and recovery settings, click the Settings button in the Startup and Recovery section of the Advanced tab in the System

Properties dialog box. This opens the Startup and Recovery dialog box, which consists of two sections: System Startup and System Failure.

If you have more than one operating system installed on the computer, a list of operating systems appears when you first start your computer. Settings in the System Startup section of the dialog box allow you to configure options for this list. Use the Default Operating System drop-down list to select which operating system you want your computer to start automatically if no alternate selection is made. You can also specify how long to display the list of operating systems and recovery options before starting the default operating system if no selection is made. Click the Edit button to open the Boot.ini file in Notepad.

WARNING

Do not make any changes to the Boot.ini file if you are unfamiliar with how it works. Improper editing can result in your computer not booting at all.

Use options in the System Failure section to specify actions to perform if the computer suddenly stops. Items include writing an event to the system log, sending an administrative alert, or automatically rebooting the computer.

You can also specify whether to write debugging information to a file (this process is called a *dump*) and how much information you want to record. Under Write Debugging Information, you can select from None (Do Not Write Debugging Information), Small Memory Dump (64 KB), or Kernel Memory Dump. You can specify a path for the dump file and choose whether to overwrite the file if it already exists.

Environment Variables

Environment Variables Windows XP and its programs use environment variables to behave in a certain way under certain conditions. An *environment variable* is a symbolic name that is associated with a value (string). Environment variables might include items such as paths for saving certain file types (such as temp files), paths to certain files (such as files needed by an application to run), the number of processors, and the processor architecture.

Click the Environment Variables button to open the Environment Variables dialog box. The upper portion of the dialog box displays variables that are defined for the current user. Use the New, Edit, and Delete buttons in this section to create new user variables.

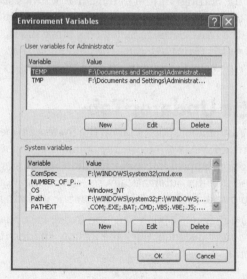

The lower portion of the dialog box displays system variables. Variables in this list are created by the computer administrator, by users of the computer, or by Windows applications. You must be logged on as a Computer Administrator to make changes to these variables. Use the buttons in the lower section of the dialog box to make changes to system variables.

TIP

You can also use the SET command at the command prompt to create environment variables.

Error Reporting

Error Reporting   Click the Error Reporting button in the System Properties dialog box to specify how you want to report Windows errors to Microsoft. This button opens the Error Reporting dialog box.

System Restore Tab

The System Restore tab in the System Properties dialog box allows you to track and reverse changes that are made to your computer. To disable the System Restore features, check the Turn Off System Restore on All Drives option that appears in the upper portion of the dialog box.

Click the Settings button in the Drive Settings section to change the amount of disk space used on each drive for System Restore files. This displays the Drive Settings dialog box. Move the Disk Space Usage slider toward the left (Min) to reduce the amount of space or toward the right (Max) to increase the amount of space. Click OK to apply your settings.

Automatic Updates Tab

Use the Automatic Updates tab in the System Properties dialog box to configure how you want to handle automatic updates for your software. Three options appear in the Notification Settings area. They allow you to download updates automatically, receive notification before you download and install files, or turn off automatic updating completely.

Use the Previous Updates section to display update notifications that you previously declined. Click the Restore Hidden Items button to redisplay them.

Remote Tab

Use the Remote tab to choose how remote users (such as those on your network or on the Internet) can connect to your computer. Check the "Allow remote assistance invitations to be sent from this computer" option to allow others to connect to your computer. Uncheck this option to turn this feature off.

Click the Advanced button to open the Remote Assistance Settings dialog box. You can enable or disable remote control of the computer and set the maximum amount of times that invitations remain open.

The Remote Desktop section of the Remote tab allows you to enable or disable remote desktop connections to this computer. Click the Select Remote Users button to add or remove user names that can connect to the computer.

See also   Add New Hardware, Device Manager, Safely Remove Hardware, User Accounts

SYSTEM CONFIGURATION UTILITY

Allows you to view and make changes to your system configuration files. To run the System Configuration Utility, choose Start ➤ Run, and enter **msconfig** in the Run dialog box.

The System Configuration Utility displays six tabs: General, SYSTEM .INI, WIN.INI, BOOT.INI, Services, and Startup.

General Tab

The General tab allows you to choose which files Windows XP processes when your system starts up. Choose Normal Startup to load all device drivers and services. Choose Diagnostic Startup to load basic device drivers and services so that you can diagnose and troubleshoot system-related problems. To customize your startup files, choose Selective Startup. Then check or uncheck the startup options you want to perform.

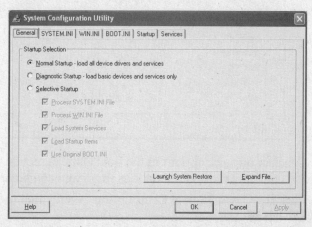

Click the Launch System Restore button to open the System Restore window (which is described in the main topic "System Restore"). Click the Expand File button to open the Expand One File from Installation Source dialog box. This dialog box allows you to extract compressed files from Windows XP installation disks and copy them to a specified folder on your hard drive.

SYSTEM.INI and WIN.INI Tabs

The SYSTEM.INI and WIN.INI tabs display lists of items that these files load upon startup. Check or uncheck any item in the list to enable or disable these resources, or click the Enable All or Disable All buttons. Use the buttons in the right side of the dialog box to move items up or down in the list or to enable or disable individual items. Click the Find button to locate a specific item. Click the New button to create a new item at the current cursor location. Click the Edit button to change an existing item.

BOOT.INI Tab

The BOOT.INI tab displays your BOOT.INI file in the upper section of the dialog box.

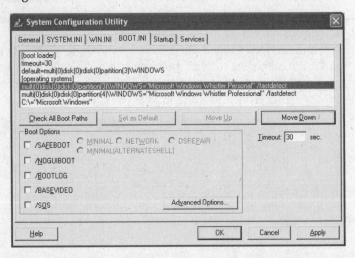

Check or uncheck options in the Boot Options section of the dialog box to configure the boot-up options when your computer starts.

Click the Check All Boot Paths button to verify that the entries in your BOOT.INI file are valid.

When you have multiple operating systems on your computer, you can change the order in which they appear in the list. Highlight the line that starts one of the operating systems, and use the Move Up or Move Down buttons to move it up or down in the list.

Use the Set as Default button to select the operating system that you want the BOOT.INI file to use for the default operating system.

Services Tab

The Services tab in the System Configuration Utility dialog box displays a list of services that start when your system starts. It also displays whether or not the service is essential to operation, the manufacturer of the service, and the status of the service. Check the Hide All Microsoft Services button to hide all services that were written by Microsoft. Check or uncheck items that you want to include or exclude from your startup options, or click the Enable All or Disable All buttons to include or exclude all items.

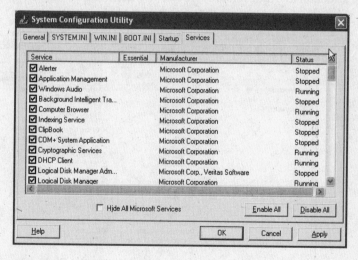

Startup Tab

The Startup tab in the System Configuration Utility dialog box displays applications that Windows XP runs when your system starts. Check or uncheck items that you want to include or exclude, or click the Enable All or Disable All buttons to enable or disable all items in the list.

See also   Help and Support Center

System Information

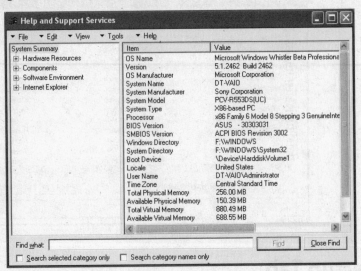 System Information MMC snap-in that collects and displays information about your Windows XP computer. To access System Information, choose Start ➤ All Programs (or Start ➤ Programs in the Classic Start menu) ➤ Accessories ➤ System Tools ➤ System Information.

System Information includes a system summary, along with many different items that are grouped into four categories: hardware resources, components, software environment, and Internet Explorer. You can see details about your configuration or provide the information collected by System Information to service technicians who are troubleshooting your computer.

System Summary

Displays a summary of essential system information, such as operating system name and version, processor type, Windows directory, regional settings, and memory information, just to name a few.

Hardware Resources

Displays information about your hardware resources in several subfolders, including Conflicts/Sharing, DMA, Forced Hardware, I/O, IRQs, and Memory. Select each subfolder from the console tree to display detailed information in the Details pane. The type of information you see depends on the type of resource you selected. To see whether any hardware items share resources or whether resource conflicts exist, select the Conflicts/Sharing folder.

Components

Displays detailed information about the components of your Windows XP computer in several subfolders that may also contain other subfolders. Examples include Multimedia, Display, Infrared, Input, Modem, Network, Ports, Storage, Printing, Problem Devices, and USB. Select a subfolder from the console tree to display detailed information about a component. Information displayed in the Details pane includes the item (such as Resolution and Bits/Pixel for display) and the item's value (such as $640 \times 480 \times 60$ hertz and 32).

Software Environment

Displays detailed information about the software that is currently loaded in memory. This information appears in several subfolders that may also contain other subfolders. Examples include System Drivers, Environment Variables, Print Jobs, and Windows Error Reporting. Select a subfolder to display detailed information in the Details pane. The type of information that appears in the Details pane depends on your selection in the console tree.

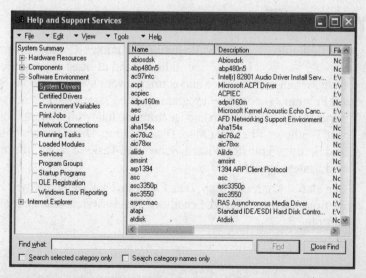

Internet Settings

Displays detailed information about Internet Explorer in several subfolders that can contain other subfolders. Examples include Summary, File Versions, Connectivity, Cache, Content, and Security. The type of information that appears in the Details pane depends on your selection in the console tree.

See also   Add New Hardware, Device Manager, Disk Cleanup, File Signature Verification Utility, Network and Internet Connections

SYSTEM MONITOR

Allows you to monitor the performance of your system. To open the System Monitor, choose Start ➢ Control Panel (or Start ➢ Settings ➢ Control Panel in the Classic Start menu), and select Performance and Maintenance. Click Administrative Tools, and double-click Performance to open the System Monitor in the console root.

SYSTEM RESTORE

See   Chapter 13

See also   Help and Support Center

SYSTEM TOOLS

System Tools   ▸ Predefined Windows XP program group that contains several utilities you can use to perform system maintenance and configure your system. Choose Start ➢ All Programs (or Start ➢ Programs in the Classic Start menu) ➢ Accessories ➢ System Tools to choose from the following system tools: Activate Windows, Character Map, Disk Cleanup, Disk Defragmenter, File and Settings Transfer Wizard, Scheduled Tasks, System Information, and System Restore.

See also   Character Map, Disk Cleanup, Disk Defragmenter, File and Settings Transfer Wizard, Scheduled Tasks, System Information, System Restore

TASKBAR

Interface panel that appears at the bottom of your screen by default.

TIP

To move the taskbar to the top, left, or right side of the screen, click an empty area of the taskbar and drag it to a new location.

The taskbar allows you to quickly launch and switch between applications. It contains three primary areas:

Start button On the left end of the taskbar. Click the Start button to display shortcuts that launch your Windows XP operating system and additional software.

Taskbar button area The main area of the taskbar. When a program is running, a button for that program appears in the main area of the taskbar. To switch to another opened application, simply click its button.

Notification area At the right end of the taskbar. This area contains your system clock. It may also contain additional icons that allow you to adjust sound or Desktop properties, monitor anti-virus software, or enable and disable hardware and software control panels. Icons also appear here when you are printing a document or when you have received e-mail. Finally, some applications flash or display icons and message balloons in the notification area to alert you to problems or other actions that you need to perform.

TIP

Hover the cursor over the system clock to display the current date. Double-click the system clock to adjust the date and time.

Toolbars

You can also display or hide additional toolbars in the taskbar. To add a new toolbar, right-click an empty area of the taskbar. Choose Toolbars from the shortcut menu, then drag your mouse to select a menu option.

NOTE

The Toolbars option will not be available if the taskbar is locked.

The five additional toolbars that you can display in the taskbar are:

Address   Allows you to enter a URL and click Go to automatically open Internet Explorer and navigate to the URL.

Links   Provides you with quick links to Hotmail and to the Microsoft Windows and Windows Media home pages. It also allows you to add your own custom links.

Desktop   Places shortcuts for the items found on your Desktop (such as My Computer and My Network Places) in the taskbar.

Quick Launch   Lets you quickly launch applications, such as Internet Explorer and Outlook Express, by clicking the corresponding button. Also contains the Show Desktop button, which you can use to bring the Desktop to the front.

TIP

To create a Taskbar shortcut that points to an application, simply drag an application from My Computer or Windows Explorer to the Quick Launch toolbar. To remove the shortcut, right-click it and choose Delete.

New Toolbar   Allows you to create a shortcut to a folder or a URL.

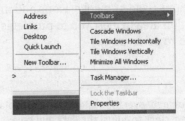

To remove a toolbar from the taskbar, right-click the toolbar and click Close Toolbar. If the Confirm Toolbar Close dialog box appears (you can optionally disable it), choose OK to close the toolbar.

NOTE

You may need to resize toolbars that are already in the taskbar to create enough space for your new toolbars. To resize or move toolbars, move the cursor over the vertical bar at the left of the toolbar. Then click and drag the toolbar left or right. You can also drag and drop the toolbar to the Desktop to create a floating toolbar.

Switching between Applications

Windows XP allows you to multitask your applications, so you can run more than one application at the same time. There are two ways to switch between open applications: You can use the taskbar or a keystroke shortcut.

Using the Taskbar

When you open an application, the taskbar displays a button with the icon and name of the application. To switch to any other open application, click the appropriate button on the taskbar. A taskbar button may at first show the entire name of the application and any open documents or folders.

Windows XP also groups similar buttons into a single button. For example, if you have multiple documents open in Word, or if you have several Explorer windows open, the taskbar displays a common button that displays the number of open documents. Click the application button to display a submenu of open documents, and select the document you want to bring to the front.

TIP

Drag the top of the taskbar upward, and you'll have two bars available on which to place buttons. However, keep in mind that this reduces the size available to the Desktop.

Using the Alt+Tab Key Combination

As you open more applications, the taskbar buttons become smaller and the names truncate to fit all the buttons into the taskbar. When several applications are open at the same time, it can become difficult to determine which buttons are associated with which applications. In these cases, you can use the Alt+Tab key combination to switch between applications. To do so, follow these steps:

1. Hold down the Alt key and keep it held down while you complete the next steps.

2. Press and release the Tab key. A dialog box displays a selection border around the icon for the application you last used. The name of the selected icon appears in the bottom of the dialog box. Additional icons appear for each window that is open.

3. Press and release the Tab key to move through the list one icon at a time until the border surrounds the application you want to open.

4. Release the Alt key to bring the selected application to the foreground.

See also   Start Menu, Taskbar and Start Menu

TASKBAR AND START MENU

See   Chapter 10

See also   Start Menu, Taskbar

TASK MANAGER

Lets you view the status of and control programs and processes that are running on the Windows XP computer. You can also view performance indicators for processes. Using Task Manager, you can see which programs (tasks) are running, end them if they're no longer responding, see which processes are running, and view system resource information about these processes as well as overall system usage information.

To access Task Manager, press Ctrl+Alt+Delete. The Windows Task Manager dialog box opens, with menus at the top of the window. Four tabs also appear in the main Task Manager dialog box: Applications, Processes, Performance, and Networking. A status bar appears at the bottom of the dialog box.

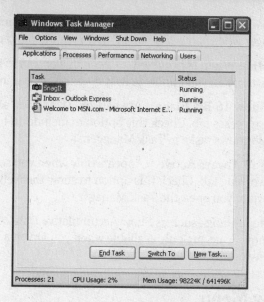

The status bar at the bottom of the Task Manager window displays information about the number of processes that are currently running, the current CPU usage, and the current memory usage.

Menus

Task Manager has several menus: File, Options, View, Windows, Shut Down, and Help. The options available on the View menu change depending on the Task Manager tab you have selected.

File Menu

New Task (Run...)   Opens the Create New Task dialog box. Enter the path to a new task and click OK to run it.

Exit Task Manager   Ends Task Manager.

Options Menu

Always on Top   Check this option to run Task Manager on top of other programs.

Minimize on Use   Check this option to minimize Task Manager when you switch to another running program.

Hide When Minimized   Check this option to hide Task Manager when you minimize it. It does not appear in the taskbar.

Show 16-Bit Tasks   Appears only when you select the Processes tab. Check this option to include 16-bit Windows tasks in Task Manager.

Tab Always Active   Appears only when you select the Networking tab. Check this option to show the Networking tab when you open the Task Manager.

Other options, such as Show Accumulative Data, Auto Scale, Reset, and Show Scale, are only available when you are on a network and select the Networking tab.

View Menu

Refresh Now   Refreshes the Task Manager screen immediately.

Update Speed   Configures how often the Task Manager screen refreshes automatically. From the submenu, choose High (twice per second), Normal (every two seconds), Low (every four seconds), or Paused (no automatic refresh).

Large Icons, Small Icons, Details   Appear only when you select the Applications tab. Display tasks as large or small icons, or as a list of tasks and their status (the default setting).

Select Columns   Appears when you select the Processes, or Networking tab. Choose this option to open the Select Columns dialog box, which allows you to configure columns that appear for each view.

CPU History   Appears only when you select the Performance tab. Displays one graph per CPU if your computer has more than one processor.

Show Kernel Times   Appears only when you select the Performance tab. Displays kernel time in the CPU and Memory Usage and Usage History graphs.

Network Adapter History   Appears only when you select the Networking tab. Displays kernel time in the CPU and Memory Usage and Usage History graphs.

Shut Down Menu

Stand By, Hibernate   Places your computer in the appropriate mode.

Turn Off, Restart   Turns your computer off, or shuts down and restarts it.

Log Off (Username)   Logs the current user off.

Lock Computer   Appears only when one user is configured on the computer. Click to lock the computer. You will need to enter your password to unlock the computer.

Tabs

Task Manager contains the Application, Processes, Performance, Networking, and Users tabs, which you can use to view and control tasks and processes as well as view performance information.

Applications   Displays all applications (tasks) that are currently running. To terminate a task, select it and click End Task. To switch to another task, select that task and click Switch To. To create a new task, click New Task.

Processes   Displays a list of processes that are currently running. Default columns display details about the image name of the application that is running, the username, and the CPU and memory being used by the task. To add additional columns, choose View ➢ Select Columns. To terminate a process, select one from the list and click End Process.

You can also assign priorities to processes. Right-click a process and choose Set Priority. Choices in the submenu include Realtime, High, Above Normal, Normal (default), Below Normal, and Low.

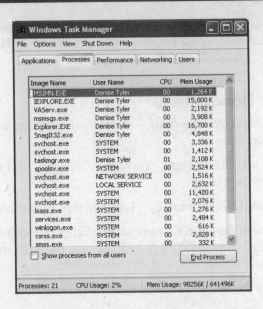

Performance   Graphically displays system performance information such as usage and history for CPU and memory.

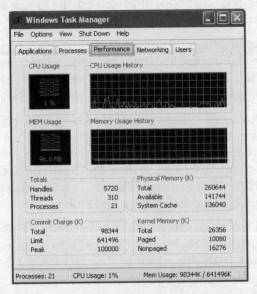

Networking   Displays a graph of network connection usage for each network adapter installed on your computer.

TURN OFF COMPUTER

To turn off your computer, click the Start button to display the Start menu. Then click Turn off Computer, located in the bottom-right corner. The Turn Off Computer dialog box appears.

Stand By   Click Stand By to put your computer in a low-power state. In Stand By mode, you can quickly resume your Windows session when you press and release the on/off button on your computer.

Shift-click Stand By to put your computer in hibernation. This mode saves your Desktop state to your hard drive so that you can resume Windows where you left off. Then it shuts your computer down.

Turn Off   Powers down your computer. Windows XP prompts you to save any unsaved changes in programs that are currently opened before your computer shuts down.

Restart   Reboots your computer. Windows XP prompts you to save any unsaved changes in programs that are currently opened before it reboots your computer.

UPDATES

See   Windows Update

USER ACCOUNTS

See   Chapter 11

See also   Fast User Switching, Forgotten Password Wizard, Help and Support Center, .NET Passport Wizard, Network Passwords

UTILITY MANAGER

 Utility Manager   Program used by Computer Administrators to manage the Windows XP Magnifier, Narrator, and On-Screen Keyboard Accessibility options.

The preferred way to start Utility Manager is to press the Windows Logo Key + U at the Windows XP Welcome screen. Starting Utility Manager using this method enables you to manage your programs when you lock or unlock your computer.

Alternatively, choose Start ➤ All Programs ➤ Accessories ➤ Accessibility➤ Utility Manager. When you use this method, Utility Manager cannot manage your programs when you lock or unlock your computer, and some options will be disabled.

TIP

You must have administrative privileges to run Utility Manager and to configure utility options.

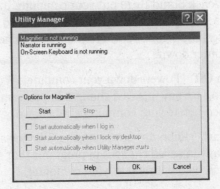

The Utility Manager displays the Accessibility utilities currently installed in Utility Manager: Magnifier, Narrator, and On-Screen Keyboard are installed automatically during Windows XP setup. The status of each device appears as Running, Not Running, or Not Responding. The Narrator utility runs automatically when you open Utility Manager.

To start or stop a utility, select it from the list and click Start or Stop.

Three additional options appear in the lower portion of the Utility Manager. These options are disabled if you start Utility Manager through the Start menu. They allow you to start the selected utility automatically when you log in, when you lock your Desktop, or when Utility Manager starts. Check or uncheck each of these options as desired for each utility.

See also   Accessibility, Magnifier, Narrator, On-Screen Keyboard

VIRTUAL MEMORY

See   System

VOLUME CONTROL

Lets you control the volume, balance, and other audio settings for speakers and other audio devices used for sound recording and playback. To open the Volume Control dialog box, choose Start ➢ All Programs ➢ Accessories ➢ Entertainment ➢ Volume Control.

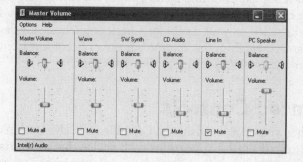

TIP

There are other ways to open the Volume Control dialog box. One way is to double-click the Sound icon in the notification area of the taskbar. Or, in Sound Recorder's Audio Properties dialog box, click Volume under any device on the Audio Devices tab. Or, from Sounds and Audio Devices (in Control Panel), click Volume for any audio device that appears in the Audio tab.

By default, the Volume Control dialog box displays controls used for audio playback. The Volume Control portion of the dialog box displays a master set of Balance and Volume sliders and a Mute All check box. These controls affect all of the audio devices that are shown in the Volume Control dialog box. In addition, each audio device has its own controls that you can set independently.

The Volume Control Options menu has three choices: Properties, Advanced Controls, and Exit.

Properties

Click Options ➤ Properties to open the Properties dialog box. If you have more than one mixer device installed on your computer, use the Mixer Device drop-down list to choose between them. The Adjust Volume For section allows you to choose devices that are displayed during Playback, Recording, or Other (depending on the capabilities of your mixer device). By default, the Volume Control dialog box displays settings for Playback mode. (To configure recording settings, click the Recording radio button and your dialog box and menu options will change accordingly.) The bottom of the Properties dialog box contains a list of the audio devices that are installed on your computer. Check or uncheck any device to add or remove them from the Volume Control or Recording Control dialog box, then choose OK to return to that dialog box.

Advanced Controls

When you choose Advanced Controls from the Options menu, an Advanced button appears for each device that supports additional settings. Click it to open the Advanced Controls for *Device Name* dialog box. Use the Bass and Treble sliders in the Tone Controls section to adjust between Low and High settings. Other control options may appear in the dialog box, depending on your audio hardware. Consult your hardware documentation for further information on using these settings.

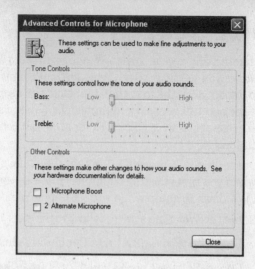

See also   Sound Recorder, Sounds and Audio Devices

WEB PUBLISHING WIZARD

Publish this file to the Web Allows you to publish your files to MSN or XDrive (each of which requires a user account). You can also publish your files to shared folders or shared webs on your network, or to an FTP site.

To open the Web Publishing Wizard, use one of the following methods:

▶ Choose Start ➤ My Documents. Select one or more files or folders. From the File and Folder Tasks section in the left pane of the My Documents window, click Publish This File (or Folder) to the Web.

▶ Choose Start ➤ My Computer. Double-click a drive on your computer. Select the files or folders you want to publish. From the File and Folder Tasks section in the left pane, click Publish This File (or Folder) to the Web.

After the Web Publishing Wizard screen opens, click Next to continue. Follow the prompts in the wizard to publish your selected files and folders to the location you specify in the wizard.

WELCOME SCREEN

Screen that initially appears when Windows first starts. The Welcome screen allows you to log on to any user account that is set up on the computer. To log on, click the icon that applies to the user account you want to use. If the account is password-protected, Windows XP prompts you to enter the account password. Press Enter after you complete these steps to open Windows XP.

You can configure Windows XP so that the Welcome screen does not appear when you first start the computer. Instead, your computer will display the Windows Desktop when you first open Windows.

To disable the Welcome screen, follow these steps:

1.   Log on to Windows XP as a Computer Administrator.

2.   Choose Start ➤ Control Panel (or Start ➤ Settings ➤ Control Panel in the Classic Start menu) and click User Accounts to open the User Accounts window.

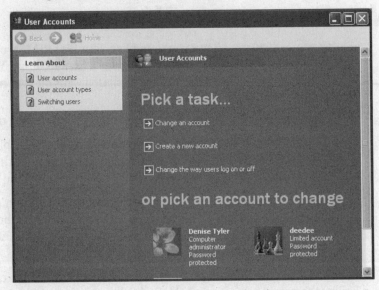

3.   In the Pick a Task section, select Change The Way Users Log On Or Off. The Select Logon And Logoff Options window appears.

4. Deselect the Use the Welcome Screen option.

5. Choose Apply Options to apply the new settings.

NOTE

When you disable the Use the Welcome Screen option, the Welcome screen no longer appears when you start the computer. Instead, the standard Log On to Windows dialog box appears. Enter your username, and password if you use one, in the dialog box to log on to the computer.

NOTE

To re-enable the Welcome screen, repeat these steps and, at Step 4, check the Use The Welcome Screen option.

What's This

 Dialog box feature that allows you to access context-sensitive help. To access What's This, right-click an item in a dialog box. If available, the What's This selection pops up. Click it to read help information about the item.

Some dialog boxes display a question mark in the top right corner. Click the icon to attach a What's This question mark to the cursor. Then place the cursor over the item in the dialog box for which you want help. Click the item to read help information.

See also Help and Support Center

Windows Components

 Windows XP Home installs many Windows components on your computer, and also provides many other components to suit your specific needs.

Examples of Windows components installed by default include WordPad, Calculator, Phone Dialer, Media Player, and Volume Control.

To add additional components that Windows XP does not install by default, choose Start ➢ Control Panel (or Start ➢ Settings ➢ Control Panel in the Classic Start menu) ➢ Add or Remove Programs. Select Add/Remove Windows Components from the left pane. For information about each of the available components, look under the specific main topic elsewhere in this book or use Windows XP Help and Support Center.

See also   Add or Remove Programs, Control Panel, Help and Support Center

WINDOWS EXPLORER

See   Explorer

WINDOWS MEDIA PLAYER

See   Chapter 22

WINDOWS MESSENGER

Windows Messenger   A communications utility that allows you to communicate in real time with other Windows Messenger users. To start Windows Messenger, choose Start ➢ All Programs ➢ Windows Messenger.

When you first open the Windows Messenger, you are prompted to sign in. Use the Click Here to Sign In link in the middle of the window (or choose File ➢ Sign In) to sign in to Windows Messenger. If you have not yet established a .NET Passport account, a wizard steps you through the process of configuring a new account; see ".NET Passport Wizard" elsewhere in this book for further information.

After you establish and connect through your .NET Passport account, the Windows Messenger dialog box appears. This dialog box displays the names of your contacts and shows whether they are online.

The main window displays three icons:

▶ Click the Add button to open the Add a Contact Wizard. This wizard helps you add contacts to your Windows Messenger contact list. Follow the steps in the wizard to search by e-mail address or by contact name.

▶ Click the Send button to send a message to the selected contact.

▶ Click the Call button to call the selected contact.

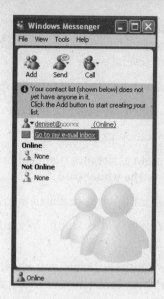

Windows Messenger Menus

The Windows Messenger contains four menus: File, View, Tools, and Help. Menu commands are briefly described in the following sections.

File Menu

Commands in the File menu allow you to perform the following:

- ▶ Sign into or out from the Windows Messenger.

- ▶ Display your status as online, busy, be right back, away, on the phone, out to lunch, or appear offline.

- ▶ Add, delete, or display properties of a contact.

- ▶ Send a file to someone, or open received files.

- ▶ Close Windows Messenger.

View Menu

Commands in the View menu allow you to display or hide the toolbar or the status bar, and to always display the Windows Messenger window on top of other windows.

Tools Menu

Commands in the Tools menu allow you to establish contact with your online contacts in several ways:

- ▶ Send an instant message to a selected contact.

- ▶ Call a contact to participate in an audio or video conference.

- ▶ Send an invitation to a contact.

- ▶ Ask for remote assistance, using shared applications, remote assistance, or the whiteboard.

- ▶ Send e-mail or display your e-mail inbox.

- ▶ Open the Audio/Video Tuning Wizard to configure audio and video settings.

- ▶ Display the Options dialog box, which allows you to configure Personal, Phone, Preferences, Privacy, and Connection information settings.

Windows Messenger Options

Choose Tools ➤ Options to display the Options dialog box, which consists of five tabs: Personal, Phone, Preferences, Privacy, and Connection.

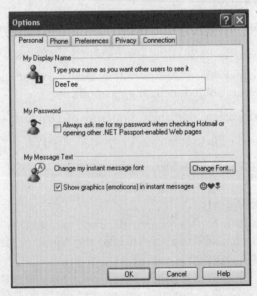

Personal tab　Use to enter your display name as you would like others to see it. You can also enable or disable the password prompt, and change the font that you use in instant messages. Check or uncheck the option to show graphics (emoticons) in your messages.

Phone tab　Use to choose a country/region code, and to enter your home, work, and mobile phone numbers. If you do not want others to view this information, leave these fields blank.

Preferences tab　Use to configure Windows Messenger preferences. You can run Windows Messenger whenever Windows starts, run it in the background, and automatically show you as "away" when the computer is inactive for longer than a specified time. You can also configure visual or audio alerts when contacts come online, when you receive an instant message, or when contacts sign in or send messages to you. Use the File Transfer drop-down list to enter or choose a folder in which to store files that you receive from other contacts.

Privacy tab　Use to select users that are allowed to see your online status and who can send you messages. You can also add contacts to a block list, to prevent users from seeing your online status or sending you messages. Use the Allow or Block buttons to switch users from one list to the other.

To view the names of users that have added you to their contact list, click the View button. Check or uncheck the option to receive an alert when others add you to their contact list.

Connection tab　Windows Messenger automatically detects your Internet connection for you. If you have trouble with the Internet connection, you can use the Connection tab to configure a proxy server. Check the option to use a proxy server, then choose the proxy server type. Enter the server name and port and your user ID and password.

WINDOWS MOVIE MAKER

See　Chapter 23

WINDOWS UPDATE

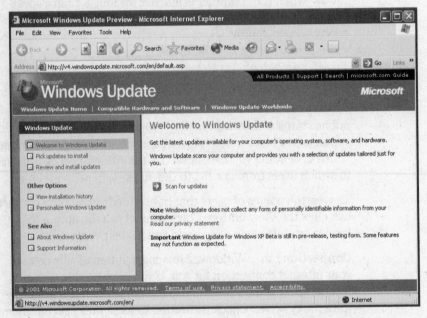 Windows Update   Choose Start ➢ All Programs (or Start ➢ Programs in the Classic Start menu) ➢ Windows Update to connect to the Microsoft Windows Update home page. Windows Update scans your computer and provides you with a list of the latest updates that help keep your Windows XP operating system, hardware, and software running at peak performance. Windows Update also tracks the updates you have already installed so that you do not have to download them again. Click the appropriate links to find the information you're looking for, such as critical updates, recommended updates, top picks, device drivers, additional Windows features, and help on using the site.

You can also configure Windows XP to automatically notify you when updates are available. To configure update notification, follow these steps:

1. Choose Start ➢ Control Panel (or Start ➢ Settings ➢ Control Panel in the Classic Start menu) ➢ Performance and Maintenance.

2. Click the System control panel icon to open the System Properties dialog box.

3. Select the Automatic Updates tab.

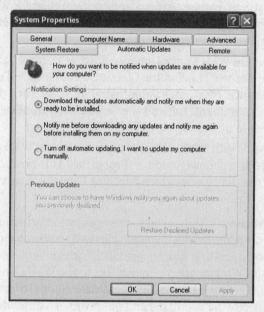

4. Choose one of the following self-explanatory options from the Notification Settings section of the dialog box:

    ▶ Download the updates automatically and notify me when they are ready to be installed.

    ▶ Notify me before downloading any updates and notify me again before installing them on my computer.

    ▶ Turn off automatic updating. I want to update my computer manually.

5. By default, Windows Update hides update notification items that you previously declined. To make these updates available again, click the Restore Declined Updates button.

6. Choose OK to apply your settings and exit the System Properties dialog box.

See also   Add or Remove Programs

WMI CONTROL

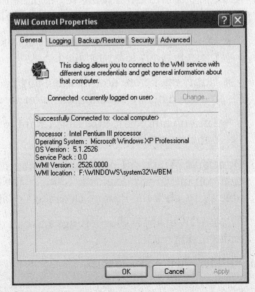 WMI Control   MMC console snap-in for Windows XP Home Edition that allows you to manage settings and configuration for Windows Management Instrumentation (WMI), which is designed to let you manage your enterprise over the Internet or an intranet.

To access WMI Control, choose Start ➢ Control Panel (or Start ➢ Settings ➢ Control Panel in the Classic Start menu) ➢ Performance and Maintenance. Next, click Administrative Tools, then double-click Computer Management. Expand the Services and Applications category in the console tree to view the WMI Control snap-in.

To work with WMI Control properties, select WMI Control in the console tree and choose Action ➢ Properties. This opens the WMI Control Properties dialog box, which contains five tabs: General, Logging, Backup/Restore, Security, and Advanced.

General   Allows you to view general information about the computer to which you are currently connected (such as processor, operating system, operating system version, WMI version, and WMI location). To connect to the WMI Control service as a different user, click Change, deselect Log On as Current User, specify the username and password of a different user, and click OK.

WMI Control Properties

General | Logging | Backup/Restore | Security | Advanced

This dialog allows you to connect to the WMI service with different user credentials and get general information about that computer.

Connected <currently logged on user>   Change...

Successfully Connected to: <local computer>

Processor : Intel Pentium III processor
Operating System : Microsoft Windows XP Professional
OS Version : 5.1.2526
Service Pack : 0.0
WMI Version : 2526.0000
WMI location : F:\WINDOWS\system32\WBEM

OK   Cancel   Apply

Logging   Allows you to specify the logging level (Disabled, Errors Only, or Verbose with extra information for Microsoft troubleshooting), and the maximum size and location of log files.

Backup/Restore   Allows you to back up the WMI repository to a file, if a change to the repository has occurred since the last time you performed a backup. Also allows you to restore from a backup and specify the automatic backup interval. To manually backup or restore the WMI repository, click the Back Up Now or Restore Now buttons, respectively, and follow the prompts.

Security   Allows you to configure permissions for any name space (directory) in the WMI directory structure.

Advanced   Allows you to specify advanced settings, such as the name space WMI Scripting should use by default.

TIP

For more information about WMI services, see the WMI software development kit (SDK), which is available on the Microsoft Developer Network (MSDN).

See also   Computer Management

WordPad

See   Chapter 7

See also   Notepad

INDEX

Note to the reader: Throughout this index **boldfaced** page numbers indicate primary discussions of a topic. *Italicized* page numbers indicate illustrations.

ABOUT THE CONTRIBUTORS

Some of the best—and best-selling—Sybex authors have contributed chapters from their current books to *Windows XP Home Edition Complete*.

Robert Cowart has written over 30 books on computer programming and applications, with 12 books on Windows, including the best-selling *Mastering Windows 95* and *Mastering Windows 98, Mastering Windows 98 Premium Edition, Windows 95 Quick and Easy, Windows NT Server 4: No Experience Required*, and *Windows 3.1 Quick and Easy*. His articles have appeared in *PC Week, PC World, PC Magazine*, and *Microsoft Systems Journal*.

Guy Hart-Davis is the author of several popular Sybex titles including *Internet Piracy Exposed, Word 2000 Developer's Handbook*, and *Mastering VBA 6*.

Mark Henricks wrote *Business Plans Made Easy* (Entrepreneur Media, 4/99), and has co-authored or ghostwritten five others including *Guerrilla Marketing for the Home-Based Business* and *AOL's Student's Guide to the Internet*. He has written on business and technology for publications like *Entrepreneur, American Way, Popular Science, The New York Times, Sports Illustrated for Kids, Southwest Airlines Spirit*, and *Men's Health*. He was also a contributing editor of *PC World* and a technology columnist for *Kiplinger's*.

John Ross has been writing about computers and data communication for more than 20 years. He's been lead author on a dozen computer books and has co-authored or contributed to many more, including *The ABCs of Internet Explorer* from Sybex.

Denise Tyler is a technical writer with more than eight years of experience writing books on Windows applications and Internet-related topics. She has served as a consulting and training specialist for a software company that develops Windows multimedia applications.

Faithe Wempen has written over 20 computer books on topics including Microsoft Windows Me, Windows 98, Office, Access, and PowerPoint. Her Indianapolis-based training operation teaches beginners how to use PCs. Not only is Wempen A+ certified, but she also earned her master's degree in English from Purdue University and has taught writing and composition.

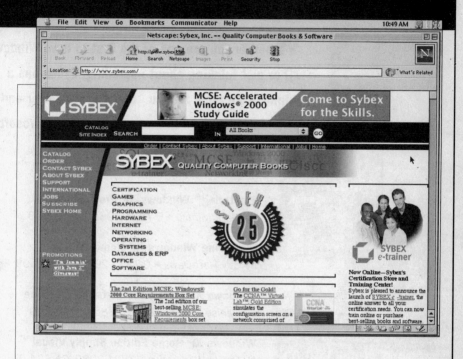